965672

Mathematics for Business and Economics

Mathematics for Business and Economics

Robert H. Nicholson
University of Richmond

McGraw-Hill Book Company
New York St. Louis San Francisco Auckland Bogotá Hamburg
Johannesburg London Madrid Mexico Montreal New Delhi
Panama Paris São Paulo Singapore Sydney Tokyo Toronto

MATHEMATICS FOR BUSINESS AND ECONOMICS
INTERNATIONAL EDITION

Copyright © 1986
Exclusive rights by McGraw-Hill Book Co. — Singapore
for manufacture and export. This book cannot be re-exported
from the country to which it is consigned by McGraw-Hill.

1st Printing 1986.

Copyright © 1986 by McGraw-Hill, Inc.
All rights reserved. No part of this publication may be reproduced or distributed
in any form or by any means, or stored in a data base or retrieval system,
without the prior written permission of the publisher.

This book was set in Times Romany by General Graphic Services.
The editors were Sam Costanzo and Linda A. Mittiga.
The design was done by Caliber Design Planning.
The production supervisor was Leroy A. Young.
The drawings were done by J & R Services, Inc.

Library of Congress Cataloging-in-Publication Data

Nicholson, Robert H.
  Mathematics for business and economics.

  Includes indexes.
  1. Business mathematics.   2. Economics, Mathematical.
  I. Title.
  HF5691.N45   1986   510'.2465   85-15190
  ISBN 0-07-046491-X

When ordering this title use ISBN 0-07-100587-0

Printed and Bound in Singapore by Fong & Sons Printers Pte Ltd

*To my wife June
and my daughter Bryn,
for their help and perseverance.*

Contents

Preface   xvii

1 An Introduction to Mathematical Analysis   1

1.1 Introduction   1
1.2 Mathematical Analysis in Organizations   2
1.3 Mathematical Modeling   2

Mathematical Models   2
The Modeling Process   3

1.4 Modeling Business Problems—Three Examples   6
1.5 Mathematical Modeling and This Textbook   9
1.6 Chapter Summary   9
1.7 Problem Set   10

Review Questions   10

2 A Review of Basic Concepts   11

2.1 Introduction   11
2.2 Sets and Set Theory (optional)   12

The Algebra of Sets   14
Exercises   16

2.3   Real Numbers   18

Rational and Irrational Numbers   18
Variables and Constants   18

2.4   Equations and Inequalities   19
2.5   Properties of Real Numbers   20

Closure   20
Commutativity   20
Associativity   20
Distributivity   21

2.6   The Priority of Mathematical Operations   21
2.7   Exponents   22

Definition of an Exponent   23
The Radical Sign   23
Computational Rules   24
Exercises   25

2.8   Factoring: A Brief Summary   26

Exercises   29

2.9   Chapter Summary   30
2.10   Problem Set   30

Review Questions   30
Review Problems   30

3   Mathematical Functions: An Introduction   35

3.1   Introduction   35
3.2   Relations and Functions   36
3.3   Dependent and Independent Variables   37
3.4   Drawing Functional Relationships   38
3.5   Functions with One Independent Variable   40

Polynomials with One Independent Variable   40
Nonalgebraic Functions   41

3.6   Functions with More than One Independent Variable   42

The Degree of a Polynomial with More than One Independent Variable   42

3.7   Chapter Summary   43
3.8   Problem Set   44

Review Questions 44
Review Problems 45

4 Linear Functions 47

- 4.1 Introduction 47
- 4.2 Linear Models in Business 48
- 4.3 The Slope and the Intercept 49

  Values for the Slope and Intercept 50
  Exercises 54

- 4.4 The Standard Form of a Linear Equation 55
- 4.5 Determining the Equation of a Line 58

  The Two-Point Method 58
  The Point-Slope Method 61
  Exercises 62

- 4.6 Multivariate Functions: An Interpretation 63
- 4.7 Chapter Summary 64
- 4.8 Problem Set 65

  Review Questions 65
  Review Problems 66

5 Systems of Linear Equations and Inequalities 71

- 5.1 Introduction 71
- 5.2 Systems and Solutions 72
- 5.3 Linear Demand-and-Supply Analysis 74
- 5.4 Break-Even Analysis 76

  Exercises 78

- 5.5 The Elimination Method 80

  Two Applications 84

- 5.6 Inconsistent and Dependent Equations 87

  Exercises 89

- 5.7 Overconstrained and Underconstrained Systems of Equations 91
- 5.8 Inequalities: Properties and Operations 92
- 5.9 Solving Inequalities and Systems of Inequalities 94

  Introduction 94
  Single Inequalities 94

   Systems of Inequalities 97
   Looking Ahead: Linear Programming 101
   Exercises 101

5.10 Chapter Summary 103
5.11 Problem Set 104

   Review Questions 104
   Review Problems 105

6 Matrix Algebra 109

6.1 Introduction 109
6.2 Basic Concepts 110
6.3 Addition and Subtraction of Matrices 112
6.4 Matrix Multiplication 113

   Exercises 117

6.5 The Matrix Form of a System of Linear Equations 120

6.6 Solution of Systems of Linear Equations by Matrices 123

   Exercises 129

6.7 Solution of Systems of Linear Equations by the Inverse Matrix 129

   The Gauss-Jordan Method of Inversion 131
   Exercises 135

6.8 The Inverse Matrix: Additional Considerations 138
6.9 Input-Output Analysis 140
6.10 Chapter Summary 144
6.11 Problem Set 145

   Review Questions 145
   Review Problems 146

7 Linear Programming 151

7.1 Introduction 151
7.2 Three Linear Programming Problems 152
7.3 Linear Programming Problems in Algebraic Form 153
7.4 Linear Programming Problems in Matrix Form 154
7.5 Maximization and Minimization: A Geometrical Interpretation 156

   Graphing the Constraints 157

7.6   Other Solution Possibilities   165

  Exercises   *166*

7.7   The Simplex Method: Principles   168
7.8   The Simplex Method: Solution   170
7.9   Interpretation of the Optimal Tableau   174

  Shadow Price Ranges   *175*
  Exercises   *178*

7.10   The Dual in Linear Programming   180
7.11   Minimization By Maximizing the Dual   182

  Formation of the Dual   *183*

7.12   Interpretation of the Optimal Dual Tableau   188

  Computing Primal-Shadow-Price Ranges from the Dual   *189*
  Concluding Remarks   *191*
  Exercises   *192*

7.13   Additional Considerations   194
7.14   Computers and Linear Programming   195
7.15   Chapter Summary   195
7.16   Problem Set   197

  Review Questions   *197*
  Review Problems   *198*

8   Nonlinear Functions   203

8.1   Introduction   203
8.2   Quadratic Functions and the Quadratic Formula   204

  The Quadratic Formula   *207*
  Exercises   *208*

8.3   Cubic Functions   209
8.4   Exponential Functions   211

  Properties of Exponential Functions   *211*
  Exponential Functions When b *Is Greater than 1*   *212*
  Exponential Functions When b *Is between 0 and 1*   *213*
  The Base e   *213*
  Exponential Growth and Exponential Decay   *214*
  A Modified Exponential Function   *216*
  Exercises   *218*

8.5   Logarithmic Functions   220

  Introduction   *220*

Logarithmic Functions and Exponential Functions   *221*
Logarithmic Functions in Business   *222*

8.6   Chapter Summary   223
8.7   Problem Set   224

Review Questions   *224*
Review Problems   *225*

Appendix: Using the Table of Natural Logarithms   227

Exercises   *230*

9   The Mathematics of Finance   231

9.1   Introduction   231
9.2   Sequences and Series   232

Finite and Infinite Series   *232*
Geometric Series   *233*
A Geometric Series: The Multiplier   *233*
Exercises   *235*

9.3   Simple Interest and Simple Discount   235
9.4   Compound Interest   237
9.5   Present Value with Compounding   239

Exercises   *240*

9.6   The Future Value of an Annuity   241

Sinking Funds   *244*
Exercises   *245*

9.7   The Present Value of an Annuity   246

Loan Amortization   *249*
Exercises   *251*

9.8   A Perpetuity as an Infinite Geometric Series   252

Exercises   *254*

9.9   Continuous Compounding   254

The Base e *and Continuous Compounding*   *254*
Exercises   *257*

9.10   Nominal Interest Rates and Effective Interest Rates   258
9.11   Chapter Summary   258
9.12   Problem Set   261

Review Questions   *261*
Review Problems   *261*

10   Differential Calculus: Principles   265

10.1   Introduction   265
10.2   Business Analysis and Calculus   266
10.3   Limits and Continuity   267

Limits   *267*
Limit Theorems   *270*
Continuity   *272*
Exercises   *275*

10.4   The Secant Slope and the Tangent Slope   275
10.5   The Derivative   278

Continuity and the Derivative   *278*
Computing the Derivative by the Simple Power Rule   *280*
The Derivative and the Slope   *282*

10.6   Additional Rules of Differentiation   283

Exercises   *287*

10.7   The Differentiation of Exponential Functions   288
10.8   The Differentiation of Logarithmic Functions   290

Exercises   *291*

10.9   Higher-Order Derivatives   292

Exercises   *293*

10.10   Implicit Differentiation   294
10.11   Partial Differentiation   298

Higher Partial Derivatives   *300*
Exercises   *302*

10.12   Chapter Summary   303

A Summary of the Rules of Differentiation   *304*

10.13   Problem Set   305

Review Questions   *305*
Review Problems   *306*

11   Differential Calculus: Applications   309

11.1   Introduction   309

Marginal Measurements and Mathematical Models   *310*

11.2 Identification of Stationary Points on Functions with One Independent Variable   310

Finding Stationary Points   312
The Second-Derivative Test   314
When the Second-Derivative Test Fails   315
Exercises   318

11.3 Differential Calculus and Profit Maximization   319

Optimizing a Profit Function   319
Principles of Marginal Analysis   320
Marginal Analysis and Profit Maximization   324
Exercises   327

11.4 Differential Calculus and Cost Analysis   329

Finding a Firm's Shut-Down Price   329
Diminishing Marginal Returns of Inputs   331

11.5 Marginal Productivity Analysis   333

Exercises   336

11.6 Elasticity of Demand   337

Other Elasticity Measurements   342
Exercises   344

11.7 Identification of Stationary Points on Functions with Two Independent Variables   345

11.8 Constrained Optimization Models and Lagrangian Multipliers   348

The Method of Lagrangian Multipliers: A Restatement   351
Exercises   352

11.9 A Note on Functional Form   354
11.10 Chapter Summary   354
11.11 Problem Set   355

Review Questions   355
Review Problems   356

12 Integral Calculus with Applications   361

12.1 Introduction   361
12.2 Integral Calculus and Mathematical Models   362
12.3 Indefinite Integrals and the Antiderivative   363
12.4 The Definite Integral   365
12.5 The Rules of Integration   368

Integrals of Exponential and Logarithmic Functions   370

12.6	Definite Integrals and the Rules of Integration	373
	Exercises 374	
12.7	Integration By Parts 375	
	Exercises 378	
12.8	Using Tables of Integrals 378	
	Exercises 380	
12.9	Applications: Indefinite Integrals 380	
	Marginal Relationships and Total Relationships 380	
12.10	Applications: Definite Integrals 384	
	Exercises 390	
12.11	Improper Integrals 393	
	Exercises 397	
12.12	Chapter Summary 398	
12.13	Problem Set 399	
	Review Questions 399	
	Review Problems 399	

13 Probability: Principles and Applications   403

13.1	Introduction 403	
13.2	Business Analysis and Probability 403	
13.3	Counting Techniques 404	
	Tree Diagrams 405	
	Subsets 406	
	Permutations and Combinations 407	
	Exercises 410	
13.4	Basic Definitions of Probability 411	
	Sample Spaces and Events 411	
	Venn Diagrams 411	
	Mutually Exclusive Events 412	
	Joint Events and Conditional Events 412	
	Dependent and Independent Events 415	
	The Union of Events 417	
13.5	The General Rules of Multiplication and Addition 419	
	Exercises 420	
13.6	Bayes' Rule 421	

	Exercises 425	
13.7	Discrete Probability Distributions	427
	The Binomial Probability Distribution	427
13.8	Continuous Probability Distributions	429
	The Mean and the Variance 430	
13.9	The Normal Distribution 432	
	Applications of the Normal Distribution 434 *Exercises* 438	
13.10	Chapter Summary 439	
13.11	Problem Set 440	
	Review Questions 440 *Review Problems* 441	

14 Mathematical Models and Business Analysis: A Final Word 445

14.1	Introduction 445	
14.2	Linear Models 446	
14.3	Nonlinear Models 447	
14.4	Probabilistic (Stochastic) Models 448	
14.5	Mathematical Analysis in Business: The Future 449	

Appendix: The Summation Operator 451

Exercises 454

Tables 456

Glossary 477

Answers to Even-Numbered Exercises 485

Index 521

Preface

The ever-increasing complexity of our modern economic structure and the impact on business of the computer as a computational tool have produced quantum leaps in quantitative training in business and economics and in other professional fields. This new focus has come primarily from the changing demands of employment within traditional industry, the emerging high-technology fields, the service sector, and government. As a result, many college and university courses in applied mathematics now stress business applications.

This text is designed specifically to meet the current demand for a compact and relevant text; that is, one that stresses brief theoretical explanations, easily understood applications, and the interpretation of quantitatively structured problems. The author's intent is to provide the methodology and techniques applicable to quantitative problems faced by a range of individuals with diverse interests. An attempt is made to keep applications as universal as possible so that each person can adapt them more easily to his or her specific field. Unnecessary mathematical jargon is eliminated without a loss in precision.

Several specific features of this book deserve elaboration. First, all concepts are presented by means of brief theoretical explanations relying on a minimum of proofs. Examples are introduced at the early stages of each topic. However, readers are offered explanations which are adequate for understanding a wide range of related applications. Applications are kept numerically simple and easy to comprehend so that principles are reinforced.

Second, the relation between problem formulation, mathematical computation, and the interpretation of results is emphasized throughout the book. The author believes that the ability to formulate quantitative problems from unstructured real-world situations and to translate the results of the analysis back to the real world is a skill equal in importance to computational ability. Thus, the issues of model formulation and construction are addressed in the text.

Finally, the book provides discussions of how aids such as the computer and hand calculator are used in specific analyses and of computational methods which have been modified because of computerized analyses. However, reliance on the computer has not been used as a justification for omitting computational methods which may be helpful in explaining particular analytical techniques. The relation between mathematical analysis and the computer is incorporated into the overall problem-solving process where appropriate.

The sequence to the chapters and the emphases given to topics within chapters are designed to make mathematics a relevant field of study. A basic theme of this book is that mathematics need not be, nor appear to be, abstract, but that it should provide a set of techniques which can be used to better understand the various business-related disciplines.

Little previous exposure to college-level mathematics is necessary to use this text. A familiarity with the basic terminology of management science and economics may be helpful in understanding some of the applications but is not a prerequisite for an overall comprehension of the material.

The textbook is adaptable to either one- or two-semester courses, and only the depth to which each topic is covered must be adjusted. Thus, if it is used for a one-semester course, instructors will not have to omit chapters and topics in a way which might reduce the book's usefulness. Alternatively, sufficient material and examples are included for a two-semester course which presents each topic in more detail. The book also may be used for courses in mathematical analysis either at the undergraduate level or for "refresher" courses at the introductory graduate level.

Thus, this book offers several distinct advantages to the student of mathematical analysis. The following chapter-by-chapter description further explains some of its techniques and learning aids.

The book contains 14 chapters. The first chapter is an overview of mathematical terms and problem-solving methodology which serves as an introduction to applied mathematics. In this chapter, readers will immediately encounter business use of the fundamentals of mathematics. Particular emphasis is on developing, understanding, and interpreting mathematical models. As this chapter makes clear, mathematical models provide a framework for applying mathematics to real-world problems.

Chapter 2 includes a review of basic mathematical concepts. Topics included are set theory, the real number system and its properties, exponents, and factoring. This chapter will be a helpful review for readers and will serve as a foundation for the study of applied mathematics.

Chapter 3 gives a summary of many of the mathematical functions used in business-oriented models. This material serves as the conceptual framework for many of the applications and models found in the text. Of special significance in this chapter are the definitions of a relation and a function.

Overall, the first three chapters provide an introduction to applied mathematics. That is, mathematical models provide the analytical structure within which basic mathematical concepts and functions are employed. These first three chapters will prepare and stimulate readers for the more specialized topics of later chapters.

Chapters 4 to 7 include topics in linear mathematics. Chapter 4 discusses linear functions and their characteristics. Here, the emphasis is on understanding the slope and intercept of a linear function. Chapter 5 extends this introduction to examine the solution of systems of linear equations and systems of linear inequalities. Matrix algebra, an additional set of techniques for working with groups of numbers and particularly for solving systems of linear equations, is the topic of Chapter 6.

The fundamentals of linear programming are covered in Chapter 7. This topic combines some of the earlier material on equations and inequalities with matrix algebra in describing a technique applied to many business problems. In general, linear programming is a method for addressing problems of optimization (e.g., minimizing cost or maximizing profit) given a set of constraints (e.g., maintaining product-quality standards or producing with a limited pool of resources). The placement of this chapter within the book and the particular focus of its presentation offer two advantages. First, following the chapter on matrix algebra, linear programming can be discussed using the concept of a matrix and the techniques of matrix algebra where applicable. Second, the chapter emphasizes computer-generated solutions to linear programming problems and the interpretation of such solutions. Thus, the "by-hand" computations of linear programming are discussed for completeness, but the focus is on the interpretation of results. These two aspects of Chapter 7 will enrich the reader's understanding of this topic and increase his or her ability to apply linear programming to problems in related courses or in business.

Chapter 8 broadens the scope of the book by introducing four of the nonlinear functions used in business analysis: quadratic, cubic, exponential, and logarithmic functions. Particular emphasis is placed on the uses of the constant e ($e = 2.71828 \ldots$) in analytical models.

The mathematics of finance is the topic of Chapter 9. This technique-oriented discussion uses many of the functional forms of Chapter 8 and applies them to problems involving various time and interest-rate considerations. The use of financial tables to solve problems is stressed in this chapter.

Differential and integral calculus are discussed in the next three chapters (Chapters 10, 11, and 12). These topics will include reference to both linear and nonlinear relations. Consequently, readers will find helpful at this point the material on functions found in Chapters 3 and 8.

Some of the specific topics included in these chapters are optimization techniques, evaluation of rates of change, area estimation, and the analysis of constrained functions. Chapter 11 is particularly important as it covers many of the business applications of differential calculus. The more theoretical discussions of Chapters 10 and 12 include very few proofs and are linked with applications as an essential part of the presentation. Thus, the entire presentation of calculus is at an applied level.

The principles of probability are included in Chapter 13. This material builds on the discussion of sets in Chapter 2 and that of integral calculus in Chapter 12. This chapter is not intended to be a course in business statistics, but rather is offered as an additional component of a complete overview of applied mathematics. For some, Chapter 13 also will provide introductory material for subsequent courses in sampling and statistical inference.

The final chapter (Chapter 14) is a restatement of the relation between problem formulation, mathematical models, and quantitative techniques. These three topics are the components of modern quantitative business analysis. In this summary chapter, the techniques of Chapters 3 to 13 are presented in a condensed way that reinforces their connection to the process of mathematical modeling. Many textbooks in applied mathematics do not stress this linkage adequately and in the proper perspective. The textbook theme of mathematical modeling is thus stressed in Chapter 14.

Problem sets including conceptual, computational, and application questions are presented within each chapter and at the end of each. The noncomputational review questions at the end of each chapter provide readers with a means of summarizing the definitions and concepts presented in the chapter. These questions may be particularly helpful in clarifying concepts before application problems are attempted. Answers to selected problems are included at the end of the book. The objectives of the problem sets are (1) to test an understanding of important concepts, (2) to extend this knowledge to business applications, and (3) to relate each topic to ideas presented earlier in the text.

In all, the book presents a unified approach to many different aspects of applied mathematics. Topics continually are related so that students will become more flexible in using a particular technique or combinations of techniques in solving problems.

It is anticipated that, after study of this text, readers will have acquired an appreciation of the business uses of applied mathematics. It is hoped that this book will be beneficial to both their education and their professional development.

I would like to express my thanks for the many useful comments and suggestions provided by colleagues who reviewed this text during the course of its development, especially to Allen Ashley, Adelphi University; Paul Baum, California State University, Northridge; Carl Cowen, Purdue University; Robert Limburg, St. Louis Community College; and Charles Margenthaler, Loyola College.

Robert H. Nicholson

An Introduction to Mathematical Analysis

1.1 Introduction

The objective of this chapter is to provide a conceptual foundation for the study of applied mathematical analysis. Specifically, this chapter introduces mathematical modeling, a technique applicable to the topics presented in later chapters.

This textbook promotes the belief that mathematical techniques assume added relevance when used to analyze actual situations in business and economics. This relationship imposes on business professionals the need to be able to formulate real-world problems in an understandable, quantitative context. Today, that skill is an important factor in successful business management.

Often, developing the quantitative context for a particular problem involves formation of a *mathematical model*. These models of reality constitute an important part of mathematical analysis. Thus, the development and application of mathematical models which reflect real business situations is the topic which connects the various quantitative techniques of this book.

An Introduction to Mathematical Analysis 2

Mathematical modeling builds on a firm understanding of the basic terminology, notation, and methodology of mathematics. Thus, this and the next chapter include (1) a discussion of mathematical modeling and (2) a review of basic mathematics. Together, these topics give a foundation for understanding mathematics as applied to problems in business and economics.

1.2 Mathematical Analysis in Organizations

Businesses, research firms, and public agencies often have large amounts of economic and business data which must be transformed into information which can be used for decision making. Several examples will demonstrate the information problem faced by public and private organizations.

1. Based on company history, a tire manufacturer knows the relation between its output and manufacturing cost per unit. The firm wants to use these historical data to determine that level of output which will result in the lowest per unit cost of manufacturing.
2. A consulting firm wants to advise a large poultry-processing firm as to how its various feed ingredients may be mixed to lower the cost of the feed formula and, at the same time, maintain an acceptable level of product quality.
3. A government agency wants to assess the impact on the level of national economic activity (Gross National Product) of a strike by automobile workers.

Analysis of problems such as these often requires application of the relevant data to a mathematical model. Quantitative techniques are employed to analyze the data in accordance with the specific model. Thus, the mathematical model both formally defines the problem in quantitative terms and specifies the required computational steps. With this combination, mathematical models are able to furnish an abstract analytical structure for a real-world problem. Increasingly, organizations find this method of analysis helpful to the process of transforming data into information.

1.3 Mathematical Modeling

Mathematical Models

There are two kinds of mathematical models, probabilistic and deterministic.

A *probabilistic model* (also called a *stochastic model*) yields an outcome subject to an element of uncertainty. In other words, the outcome of a problem analyzed according to a probabilistic model may or may not occur, with the likelihood of occurrence specified by the particular model. For example, each month the U.S. government collects unemployment data from a relatively small group of American households. Based on these results, the government assesses the unemployment rate for the entire nation. Because of the possible error caused by using a small group of people, it may be correct to state only that there is a 95 percent chance that the national unemployment rate is as specified. Thus, the outcome is expressed as a statement of uncertainty.

In a *deterministic model,* the outcome is not subject to chance. For example, deterministic models may be used to establish the equilibrium price and quantity in the market for a product (the intersection of the demand and supply of the product) or to specify the point of lowest per unit production cost for a product. In these and similar problems, the results are stated without a probabilistic qualification. Both probabilistic and deterministic models will be used in the discussion, examples, and problems of this text. Next, the development of mathematical models is considered.

The Modeling Process

The following is a brief statement of an unstructured quantitative business problem where data are available and the organization wants to obtain information from the data. This example will serve as the basis for presentation of the modeling process.

Example 1.1

An appliance manufacturer knows the production cost per refrigerator for various levels of production. The firm wants to use these data to develop a relation between cost per refrigerator and the number of refrigerators produced. These data will be helpful in future production planning decisions.

In this case, the firm wants to specify a relation between output level and per unit refrigerator cost. These results will provide a means (1) to assess the per unit cost at any current or proposed output level and (2) to determine the level of production corresponding to the lowest per unit cost. This latter point is the desirable level of production for the firm.

A mathematical model provides an effective means to understand this cost-output relationship. A mathematical model uses symbols and numbers to develop an abstraction of a real-world situation (e.g., the production level–unit cost relationship). This abstraction furnishes an analytical structure of the specific situation and a means to generalize to a broader range of problems.

Through generalization, the mathematical model should provide organizational decision makers (e.g., the vice president in charge of production for the appliance manufacturer) with alternative courses of action from which to choose. Thus, by expanding from the isolated case to the larger problem, mathematical models permit the evaluation of options. For example, a mathematical model for this situation may be used to evaluate per unit production costs for output levels which have never been attempted by the firm. This will assist planning decisions.

Steps in the mathematical modeling process are listed below, followed by a discussion of each.

1. Problem specification
2. Data collection
3. Model development
4. Data analysis
5. Interpretation of results
6. Model verification
7. Model implementation
8. Model auditing and updating

First, the problem or objective of the study must be stated in a way that reflects accurately the needs of the organization. In other words, what does the firm want to determine from the analysis?

In the refrigerator manufacturing case, it may be that the firm wants to have a model to assess per unit costs for output levels which may occur over the next 10 years. In addition, the firm may want flexibility in the model to permit the evaluation of options under changing cost conditions. In general, before the model is constructed, the needs of the organization must be *assessed* and *understood* by the model builders. This requires a substantial degree of mutual understanding between decision makers and quantitative analysts. Often, an impractical or inadequate model results from a misunderstanding at this point in the modeling process.

The second step in mathematical modeling includes finding data relevant to the problem which can be applied to the model. For example, data relating output and cost per unit for the past 5 years (referred to as time-series data) may be adequate for model development. Or, data on output and refrigerator cost per unit (referred to as cross-sectional data) may be collected from a group of factories for the same week.

A second part of the data collection process often includes "scaling" of the measurements to be employed in the model. For example, it may be that per unit production costs are measured in dollars ($421.67 per refrigerator) and output in production units (1, 2, 3 refrigerators). But, for modeling, it may be more useful to measure costs in hundreds of dollars ($4.2167 per refrigerator) and output in hundreds of refrigerators (3 represents 300 refrigerators). This scaling process often yields a more realistic model, the results of which are comprehended more easily.

Appropriate measurement units are essential to the efficient application of computational techniques and the interpretation of results. The measurement scales used in the applications of this book are considered important to the comprehension of the problems. In general, each measurement scale is used to improve the interpretative value of the mathematical model.

The third step in the modeling process is development of a mathematical model which addresses the concerns of the organization. In developing the mathematical model, the primary goal is to provide a quantitative structure for analyzing a large group of possible situations.

Model formulation frequently includes selection of the appropriate mathematical functions to explain the phenomenon. For example, it may be that the relation between refrigerator production and per unit cost is specified most closely by a function with production quantity amounts raised to the second power (squared).

Often, techniques of experimental statistics (not a topic of this book) are used to determine the mathematical function which best describes a relationship. Mathematical functions are introduced and defined in later chapters (particularly Chapters 3, 4, and 8).

In the fourth step, the data collected at step 2 are applied to the mathematical model to obtain quantitative results. The data are analyzed to determine per units costs for the output levels included in the sample data. Also, for this study the model may be used to help determine the output level corresponding to minimum per unit cost.

Step 5 includes interpretation of the analysis completed in step 4. For the refrigerator production cost example, this means that the mathematical results are explained with respect to their impact on the firm's operation. It is very important that results be interpreted in a clear and comprehensible way for those decision makers in the organization who may not have participated in the development of the model. For example, the cost analysis division of the firm may develop the model but the results are to be used by production line managers. The interpretation process is fundamental to the model's successful use by the firm.

Next, the results of the analysis are verified as to their applicability to a wide range of possibilities for the firm. The ability of a model to predict accurately is fundamental to verification. For example, the model relating per unit cost and output may have included only a limited range of observations on refrigerator production. Verification requires accurate prediction of per unit costs corresponding to output levels not included in the initial analysis. Thus, the model must predict accurately the per unit costs for facilities and time periods not studied when building the model.

If the model is verified as useful to the organization, it should be implemented and become part of the decision-making process of the firm. Thus, the mathematical model relating per unit production cost and output should be employed by those responsible for deciding refrigerator output at the various production facilities. A model which is easily interpreted at all levels of decision making will have a much higher probability of successful implementation and *day-to-day use* by the organization.

After implementation, use of the model may lead to (1) additional applications for it and similar models, (2) adjustments and refinements of the model, or (3) eventual rejection of the mathematical model if it is found inapplicable to the decision-making process. This process of auditing and updating the model should be carried out continually as changing conditions may alter both the model and its place in the organization's decision making.

This section has presented a brief outline of the modeling process and its applicability to one hypothetical situation. Readers should appreciate the role of model development in applied mathematics and how models give added significance to quantitative techniques. Many of the quantitative techniques in this book are presented by introducing mathematical models which utilize them. This format reinforces the view that mathematical techniques in business are relevant only when directed toward the solution of practical problems.

1.4 Modeling Business Problems—Three Examples

In this section, the modeling process is applied to three cases in business. Each of the models introduced here will be discussed again with accompanying quantitative data in later chapters. At this point, the examples are used to illustrate further the modeling process. When reading these cases, the reader should relate the steps in the modeling process to specific points in the description.

Case 1: Farm-Pure Dairy Incorporated

Production planning managers at Farm-Pure Dairy want to determine the milk output (measured in gallons) which will permit the firm to cover its production costs exactly. Thus, the firm wants to understand the relation between revenues and costs so that the output level corresponding to zero profit (*break-even point*) can be determined.

Farm-Pure wants to develop a mathematical model which can be used to specify the break-even point under various revenue and cost situations. Output in excess of the break-even point will result in a profit, and lower production will result in a loss.

Building a model to assess the break-even point under a variety of possible cost and price conditions requires collection of previous price and cost data. Thus, data describing past price–total revenue and output quantity–total cost relationships are compiled. These data yield revenue and cost functions which can be applied to a break-even analysis model.

Application of these data to the model results in an evaluation of the current break-even point for Farm-Pure. Thus, analysis of the data will enable the firm to know the minimum level of milk production required to earn a profit. These results and their implications for production planning must be interpreted for the relevant decision makers.

The ability of the model to predict correctly break-even points under a variety of price and cost conditions must be assessed before the model is considered reliable. Additional data to allow such prediction may be available if conditions change frequently in the industry. Otherwise, data may have to be tested experimentally. Because milk prices and costs change infrequently, this latter case may be the feasible option for Farm-Pure.

After model validation, plans should proceed to implement break-even analysis in the firm's decision-making process. This implies that production decisions will be made, in part, on the basis of the model's evaluation of the relationship between revenue and cost at a particular proposed output level.

Auditing of the model includes continual updating of the relations among output, total revenue, and total cost. Although the concept of break-even analysis has been adopted by Farm-Pure, the specific form of the model may have to be changed as cost-price situations change.

Case 2: Chemcor Incorporated

Chemcor Incorporated, a producer of specialty chemicals, is faced with a problem in the optimum allocation of its labor and machinery resources.

The firm produces three chemicals which use all the available labor and machinery time. Chemcor executives want to know how much of each chemical to make so that revenues are maximized, given the available quantities of resources. In other words, the company's planners want to determine the optimum allocation of its resources to the production of the three chemicals.

After specifying the problem in this way, researchers must collect data to solve it. The data needed include

1. The market price of each chemical
2. The resources required to produce each chemical

In this case, the measurements of output (pounds, tons, tank cars, etc.) must be the same for both the market price (e.g., *dollars per ton*) and production requirements (e.g., *hours of labor per ton*).

As may be apparent to readers, this example is typical of the problems faced by many firms. Consequently, a technique known as linear programming (described in Chapter 7) has been developed to analyze many problems of this kind. This technique as applied to Chemcor, therefore, may constitute the analytical model used.

Subsequently, data on prices and resource demands are analyzed by the linear programming model. As will be pointed out again in Chapter 7, this model is often analyzed with the assistance of a computer program. The results will indicate for Chemcor executives how resources should be allocated to maximize revenue from the sale of these three chemicals.

The analysis of a linear programming model yields a large amount of data applicable to production planning. These results must be interpreted for executives in a practical and easily comprehended manner. The interpretation of the results of a linear programming problem is a major component of Chapter 7.

Verification of the model includes, in this case, not only an assessment of the accuracy of predicted results, but also an evaluation of the feasibility of adopting the changes in resource allocation suggested by the model. For example, the model may yield results which, if implemented, necessitate the layoff of workers or the idling of machinery. Considering the feasibility of these changes is a part of model verification.

For Chemcor, model implementation may require incorporation of a mathematically advanced system of resource allocation in place of a more subjective allocation method. This may require substantial changes in the operational techniques employed by the firm's management.

If the model is successfully implemented, it must be continually updated to incorporate market price changes and changes in the production methods used for each chemical. Changes in the data will alter the results and, consequently, have implications for resource allocation. Hopefully, the price and production changes will not be so frequent that the linear programming model causes instability in the firm's operation.

Case 3: Oceanic Electric Company

Oceanic Electric, a large West Coast public utility, is interested in understanding better the relation between electricity output and the per unit cost of electricity. Specifically, Oceanic wants to determine the output level corresponding to minimum per unit cost. The company wants to use a mathematical model to evaluate this cost-output situation.

Data collection for this problem requires, first, determination of the unit measurements to use. For example, are costs and output to be measured in kilowatthours, in thousands of kilowatthours, or on some other easily interpreted scale? After this decision is made, costs representing past time periods (e.g., months) or various locations served by the utility may be selected as data for the analysis.

As this problem requires cost minimization, a model appropriate to this task must be selected. Differential calculus (Chapters 10 and 11) provides techniques for determining the minimum value of a function. Thus, in this case, model development includes determination of a cost function and analysis of that function by means of differential calculus.

Data analysis includes evaluation of the function as specified by the model and determination of the output level corresponding to minimum per unit cost of electricity generation.

Next, these results and the model employed must be interpreted for Oceanic's decision makers. When using a theoretically advanced model (such as one requiring differential calculus, in this situation), it is appropriate to discuss the model, in addition to the results, thoroughly.

The ability of the model to predict Oceanic's lowest cost production point may be assessed by considering hypothetical cost-output relationships and determining the accuracy of the resulting minimum cost point for each case. The model also will be verified by the evaluation of actual cost-output combinations as they arise.

Successful implementation of this model implies that Oceanic's management use the results in planning current and future production levels and for related tasks such as determining the optimum size of new generating facilities. In general, implementation involves incorporation of mathematical cost minimization into the utility's decision making.

Auditing and updating of the model necessitates periodic revision of the cost function to account for new and changing cost components. Less accurate prediction by the model indicates that either the model or the data applied to it need revision. This assessment and alteration should be a continuing part of the model's utilization.

1.5 Mathematical Modeling and This Textbook

The previous examples have demonstrated that mathematical models provide a quantitative framework in which business problems often are analyzed. Mathematical models help to define the problem in analytical terms, guide the data collection, and specify the evaluation procedure. Thus, mathematical models help to direct the analysis of business problems.

Because of the relation between mathematical models and business analysis, the quantitative techniques in this textbook are presented in combination with mathematical models of realistic business situations. Models of business problems provide the vehicle for a discussion of each quantitative technique.

In the first part of the book (Chapters 4 to 7), models using linear functions to explain business problems are emphasized. In later chapters (Chapters 8 to 12), models which employ nonlinear functions are discussed. The linear and nonlinear models in all these chapters are deterministic. Chapter 13 includes a discussion of probability; consequently, probabilistic models are applied to the examples.

Thus, mathematical modeling connects the seemingly separate topics of the text. Readers should understand that this theme both provides a flow to the total presentation and reflects the reality of applied quantitative methods. It is important to stress that the quantitative techniques presented in this book are used to analyze actual business problems and are not topics which can be dismissed as irrelevant to the real world.

1.6 Chapter Summary

This chapter has introduced mathematical analysis in business and presented a summary of mathematical modeling. Emphasis has been on the relationship of mathematical analysis to the evaluation of actual situations in business and economics. Mathematical models are effective mechanisms for relating quantitative techniques to real-world problems.

Mathematical modeling provides a structured method for problem analysis. The modeling process not only yields an analysis of data but also is a means for incorporating quantitative analysis into organizational decision making. The steps of mathematical modeling can be applied to most quantitative business problems.

Mathematical models and the modeling process also serve as learning aids by emphasizing the applied aspects of mathematical analysis. As this book stresses the use of mathematics to solve real-world problems, this introduction to mathematical modeling has furnished a background for consideration of a diversity of quantitative techniques.

1.7 Problem Set*

Review Questions

1. Distinguish between data and information. Describe a business example which demonstrates this difference.
2. In what way do probabilistic and deterministic mathematical models differ?
3. Why is selection of the appropriate measurement scale important to the successful development of a mathematical model?
4. Mathematical models allow decision makers to evaluate alternative courses of action. Explain.
5. What is included in the auditing and updating step of mathematical model development? Describe an example of this procedure.
6. Why must both the mathematical model and the results be easily comprehended by individuals other than the ones who develop the model?
7. What is meant by "model implementation"?
8. Why is correct problem specification important to successful model development?
9. Mathematical models provide a link between quantitative techniques and real-world problems. Explain.
10. In your opinion, why have mathematical models become, in recent years, an increasingly important part of organizational decision making?

---

*For this chapter, the problem set includes only narrative review questions. In Chapters 2 to 13, problem sets include both review questions and review problems.

A Review of Basic Concepts

2.1 Introduction

The objective of this chapter is to introduce the fundamental terminology and procedures of applied mathematics. The chapter topics will be applied to various quantitative techniques and mathematical models presented in the following chapters.

Specifically, sets, real numbers, exponents, and factoring are introduced in this chapter. These topics are presented at an introductory level, primarily including basic definitions and computational rules. Consequently, applications of these topics are limited. However, the concepts will be particularly important to an understanding of applications in subsequent chapters. This material will provide a mathematical foundation for all readers.

After careful study of this chapter, each reader should have an increased understanding of the principles of mathematical analysis and be prepared to examine the more specialized techniques and models which follow.

2.2 Sets and Set Theory

As may be apparent from the examples of Chapter 1, one characteristic of mathematical models is that they use groups of data observations. Often, such a data group makes up what is referred to as a *set*. Because of the importance of sets to mathematical analysis, the following section is concerned with the definitions, concepts, and applications of set theory.

In mathematics, a set is a collection of items. For a particular application, a set may be the incomes for the top executives from a group of 50 corporations. The items in a set are referred to as its *elements*.

For purposes of notation, the elements of a set are listed within braces and the set is referred to by a single capital letter. For example, the set of integers from 1 to 5 may be referred to as the set S. Thus, the elements of set S can be expressed

$$S = \{1, 2, 3, 4, 5\}$$

If a set has a definite number of elements, it is a *finite set,* whereas an *infinite set* includes an unlimited number of elements.

To indicate that a particular element x is a member of a set S, the notation used is

$$x \in S$$

And if an item y is not an element of a set S, the applicable notation is

$$y \notin S$$

Two sets are equal if every element of the two sets is the same.

Frequently, *subsets* of a given set exist: Set B is a subset of set A if and only if every element of B also is an element of A. For example, given the set of integers

$$A = \{1, 2, 3, 4, 5\}$$

the set

$$B = \{2, 3, 4\}$$

is a subset of A. The notation used to show that B is a subset of A is

$$B \subset A$$

Several special sets are of importance to mathematical analysis. The *universal set* (often denoted U) is the set containing all elements relevant to a particular problem. In addition, a set with no elements is referred to as the *empty set* or *null set*. The empty set is denoted $\emptyset$. The empty set is a subset of every set.

The *complement* of a set is the set of all elements in the universal set that are *not* members of a particular defined set. The complement of the set S is denoted S'. For example, if the universal set includes all the residents of a given city and S represents all male residents, then the set of all female residents may be designated S'.

Often, it is useful to form new sets by combining elements from two or more existing sets. Two types of set combination particularly useful in mathematical analysis are intersections and unions.

The *intersection* of two sets is the set including all elements in the universal set which are members of both sets. This definition is applicable to the intersection of any number of sets, if the principle of membership in all sets is maintained. The intersection of two sets S and T is denoted $S \cap T$. If two or more sets have no common elements ($S \cap T = \emptyset$), the sets are referred to as *disjoint sets*.

Example 2.1
The set A includes all people who have seen a recent television advertisement for a product. The set B includes all the people who have heard a recent radio advertisement for the same product. The intersection of these two sets forms a set C, where $C = A \cap B$. The set C includes all the people who have been exposed to both advertisements.

Example 2.2
If set S includes all the women in a city's work force and set T includes all unemployed members of the city's work force, then set R, where $R = S \cap T$ includes all the unemployed women in the city.

The *union* of two sets is the set consisting of all the elements belonging to *either* set—or to *both* sets. This definition also can be extended to include the union of more than two sets. The designation for the union of two sets, S and T, is $S \cup T$. Two examples will demonstrate the formation of a union between sets.

Example 2.3
A restaurant chain operates two types of restaurants. Set S includes all the people who have been customers at the chain's cafeteria-style restaurants and set T includes all the customers at the table-service restaurants. The union of S and T, designated as set R where $R = S \cup T$, includes all the people who have been to either type of restaurant—or to both. Each element of S and T (in this case, each customer) appears only once in set R.

Example 2.4
A hospital wants to enumerate certain patient categories to determine patterns of room usage. Set A includes all patients remaining in semiprivate rooms for longer than 7 days, and set B includes all patients staying in private rooms for 1 night or more. Thus, set C, representing the union of A and B and designated $C = A \cup B$, includes all patients who are either in private rooms for at least 1 night or in semiprivate rooms for more than 7 days.

Often, *Venn diagrams* are used to provide pictorial descriptions of sets, subsets, intersections, and unions. In a Venn diagram, the universal set U is represented by a rectangle and subsets are represented by circles or parts of circles within the rectangle. Figure 2.1(*a*), (*b*), and (*c*) shows a universal set containing, respectively, the subset A, the intersection of A and B, and the union of A and B. The intersection and union are designated by the shaded areas of 2.1(*b*) and (*c*), respectively.

These definitions permit a more detailed examination of sets, referred to as the *algebra of sets*.

The Algebra of Sets

Several characteristics of sets and how they combine can be expressed in a group of axioms or postulates. These postulates form the algebra of sets. Some of these postulates will be defined and applied to problems in this section.

THE COMMUTATIVE LAW OF SETS:

$S \cap T = T \cap S$

$S \cup T = T \cup S$

This law permits the interchange of sets when expressing the components of an intersection or union of sets. For example, the intersection of S and T is the same as the intersection of T and S.

THE ASSOCIATIVE LAW OF SETS:

$(S \cap T) \cap R = S \cap (T \cap R)$

$(S \cup T) \cup R = S \cup (T \cup R)$

This law permits alternatives in the pairing of sets when forming intersections and unions. For example, the intersection of set R with the intersection of S and T is the same as the intersection of set S with the intersection of T and R.

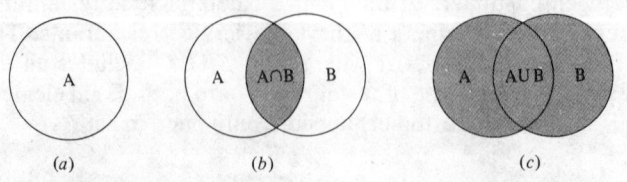

FIGURE 2.1 Venn diagrams showing (*a*) the subset A, (*b*) the intersection of A and B, and (*c*) the union of A and B.

THE DISTRIBUTIVE LAW OF SETS:

$S \cap (T \cup R) = (S \cap T) \cup (S \cap R)$

$S \cup (T \cap R) = (S \cup T) \cap (S \cup R)$

The distributive law will be demonstrated by means of two examples.

Example 2.5
Set S includes all people who have purchased a household cleaning product at a supermarket. Set T includes those who have bought the product at a hardware store, and set R includes those who have purchased it at a drug store. In order to understand its customers and develop a marketing strategy, the product's manufacturer wants to know the set of all people who have *both* bought the product in a supermarket and at either one or both of the other two types of outlets.

This relationship is shown in the Venn diagram of Figure 2.2.

The set $T \cup R$ includes all of circles T and R including their intersection. What the firm needs to know is the set including the intersection of set S with this union of T and R. This set is shown in the shaded area of Figure 2.2. Observe that it includes the union between the intersection of sets S and T and the intersection of sets S and R. This shaded area demonstrates the distributive law

$$S \cap (T \cup R) = (S \cap T) \cup (S \cap R)$$

In the context of this problem, the shaded area of Figure 2.2 includes those people who have purchased the product at (1) both a supermarket and a hardware store, (2) both a supermarket and a drug store, or (3) a supermarket, hardware store, and drug store. As stated above, in the final computed set, each element (person) is counted only once.

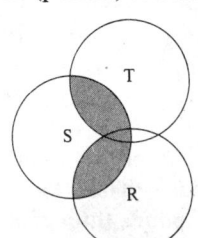

FIGURE 2.2 The distributive law of sets as applied to the household cleaning product of Example 2.5. The shaded area represents
$S \cap (T \cup R) = (S \cap T) \cup (S \cap R)$

Example 2.6
A state social service agency, when determining eligibility for a particular assistance program, considers people in three categories: over 65 (set S), blind (set T), and annual income under $7500 (set R). Anyone is eligible for the program who is over 65 or, regardless of age, who is blind and has an annual income under $7500.

The state agency knows from previous program records the two separate sets (1) over 65, blind, or both and (2) over 65, annual income under $7500, or both. The agency wants to determine the set of people eligible for the new program based on these previous records.

The distributive law of sets states that

$$S \cup (T \cap R) = (S \cup T) \cap (S \cup R)$$

The sets $S \cup T$ and $S \cup R$ are known; thus, the shaded area of the Venn diagram in Figure 2.3 shows the set of those eligible for the new program.

The shaded area in Figure 2.3 is $(S \cup T) \cap (S \cup R)$, or the intersection of (1) the union of the sets of those over 65 and blind and (2) the union of the sets of those over 65 and those with annual incomes under $7500. This area also can be expressed as $S \cup (T \cap R)$. In either form this group includes all people over 65 and those people that are 65 and under who are blind and have annual incomes under $7500. This group is eligible for the new program.

Examples 2.5 and 2.6 have helped to define the distributive law of sets and apply this law to two problems. The commutative, associative, and distributive laws will be referred to again in Section 2.5 when they are applied to the set of real numbers.

Four other rules of sets considered here relate to the universal set, the null set, and the complement of a set. If S is any set, the following four rules apply:

$S \cap U = S$

$S \cup \emptyset = S$

$S \cap S' = \emptyset$

$S \cup S' = U$

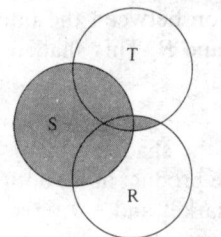

FIGURE 2.3 The distributive law of sets as applied to the program eligibility criteria of Example 2.6. The shaded area represents $S \cup (T \cap R) = (S \cup T) \cap (S \cup R)$

Each of these utilizes previous definitions and should be confirmed by each reader. Although this discussion has not been an exhaustive description of the algebra of sets, it has provided an introduction to this fundamental topic of mathematical analysis.

The principles of manipulating data groups are useful at various points in the model development process. The concepts of set theory particularly are applicable to problem specification, data collection, and data analysis for both deterministic and probabilistic models. Thus, these rules and procedures will be referred to again at various points throughout the text. The following problem set will provide practice in applying the principles of set theory.

EXERCISES

1. If $U = \{1, 2, 3, 4, 5, 6, 7, 8, 9, 10\}$, set $A = \{1, 2, 3, 4, 5, 6\}$, and set $B = \{2, 4, 6, 8, 10\}$, find
   a. $A \cup B$
   b. $A \cap B$
   c. $A \cup \emptyset$
   d. $A \cap U$
   e. $A \cup A'$

2. If U includes all people between 16 and 64 years of age in a city, S includes all males in the city between 25 and 44 years of age, and T includes all unemployed people between 16 and 64 years of age, give a written description of each of the following:
   a. $S \cup T$
   b. $S \cap T$
   c. S'
   d. T'
   e. $S' \cup T$
   f. $S' \cap T'$

3. If set $A = \{2, 4, 6, 8, 10, 12, 14, 16\}$, which of the following is not a subset of A? Why?
   a. $\{2, 4, 6\}$ c. $\emptyset$
   b. $\{2, 3, 4, 5, 6\}$ d. $\{2, 4, 6, 8, 10, 12, 14, 16\}$
4. Assume that the universal set includes the entire population of the United States. In addition, let set A include all family heads, set B include all individuals with incomes under \$25,000 per year, and set C include all females. Show by written description and Venn diagram the associative law of the intersection of sets as applied to this grouping.
5. A food manufacturer conducts a survey of consumer usage of three similar breakfast cereals (A, B, and C) which it produces. A total of 5000 consumers is sampled and the following results are obtained:
   a. 1500 have used cereal A.
   b. 600 have used cereal B.
   c. 700 have used cereal C.
   d. 300 have used A and B.
   e. 200 have used A and C.
   f. 50 have used B and C.
   g. None have used all three.
      (1) Draw a Venn diagram showing these survey results.
      (2) With these results, demonstrate the distributive law of sets of the form, $A \cap (B \cup C) = (A \cap B) \cup (A \cap C)$.
6. Using the survey results from Problem 5, find
   a. A'
   b. $(A \cap B)'$—that is, the complement of $A \cap B$.
   c. $(B \cup C)'$—that is, the complement of $B \cup C$.
   d. The number of survey respondents who have not tried any of the three cereal brands.
   e. Express your answer to part (d) using set notation.
7. Democratic and Republican candidates are the only individuals running for U.S. Representative and U.S. Senator in a district. A preelection survey of 2000 voters establishes the following voter intentions:
   a. 400 plan to vote for the Republican in both races.
   b. 900 plan to vote Republican for U.S. Senator.
   c. 1200 plan to vote Republican for U.S. Representative.
      (1) Assuming that all survey respondents stated their intentions as definite, construct a Venn diagram describing the survey results.
      (2) How many people do not intend to vote Republican in any of the races?
8. A group of 1000 elderly citizens in a city have received the following vaccinations in the past year. Only these data are available.
   a. 300 have received no vaccinations.
   b. 200 have received a Type A flu vaccination.
   c. 700 have received a Type B flu vaccination.
   d. 400 have received a pneumonia vaccination.
   e. 150 have received all three vaccinations.

(1) Construct a Venn diagram showing these results.
(2) How many have received both Type A flu and pneumonia vaccinations?
(3) Demonstrate the validity of the associative law of the union of sets by using these data.

2.3   Real Numbers

Although there are other number systems (such as imaginary numbers), the numbers of relevance to most of mathematical analysis are referred to as *real numbers*. This book will use only real numbers in all discussions and problems. The following introduces the set of real numbers.

Rational and Irrational Numbers

The set of real numbers includes two types of numbers, rational and irrational. *Rational numbers* can be stated as the ratio of two integers. (The integers include the whole numbers, positive and negative, and 0.) Examples of rational numbers are $\frac{6}{2}$ (the real number 3) and $\frac{5}{4}$ (the real number 1.25). Excluded from real numbers are those ratios with 0 in the denominator. *Irrational numbers* cannot be expressed as the ratio of two numbers. Examples of irrational numbers are the square root of 2 and the square root of 3.

The distinction between rational and irrational numbers may be clarified further by considering the decimal representation of each. Real numbers include those with three decimal representations: (1) terminating, as in $\frac{6}{1} = 6.00$; (2) repeating, as in $\frac{1}{3} = 0.333\ldots$; and (3) not repeating, as in $\sqrt{2} = 1.414213\ldots$. Rational numbers are those with terminating or repeating decimal representations; irrational numbers have decimal representations which are not repeating or terminating. Thus, the real number system includes all possible decimal representations.

Variables and Constants

Mathematical models often are expressed as groups of symbols, each comprising some combination of variables and constants. These symbols represent single real numbers or groups of real numbers. A *variable* is a symbol designating a group of real numbers within a given problem, and a *constant* is a symbol expressing a single real number in a given problem.

For example, the letter X may be used to represent incomes for a number of individuals in a city (a variable), and K (a constant) may represent a fixed sales tax percentage (such as 4 percent) to be multiplied by sales data from a group of stores. Thus, for a particular problem, X will take on various values but K will be fixed at a given real number value.

2.4 Equations and Inequalities

Mathematical models often include one statement or a group of statements involving various symbols for variables and constants. The statements in mathematical form are referred to as *expressions*. If an expression has parts separated by positive and/or negative signs, the individual parts (including their respective signs) are called *terms*. Factors often are present within each term. A *factor* is one of the separate multipliers in a product. An example will explain these definitions.

Example 2.7
Consider the following mathematical statement:

$2XYZ + XZ - 4XY$

This statement is an expression involving the integers 2 and 4 and the variables X, Y, and Z. The terms in the expression are
1. $+2XYZ$
2. $+XZ$
3. $-4XY$

The first term has four factors: $+2$, X, Y, and Z. There are two factors in the second term ($+X$ and Z) and three factors in the third term (-4, X, and Y).

Although variables and corresponding expressions may exist by themselves, they are most important to model development when used in equations or inequalities. An *equation* is a statement that two expressions are equal, and an *inequality* is a statement that two expressions are not equal.

An example of an equation is

$Y = 4.62X$

In this equation X and Y are variables. For example, X may represent the number of bushels of wheat sold by a farmer and Y may represent total income from wheat sales. In this case 4.62 represents the price per bushel of wheat ($4.62). This equation may be part of a model analyzing wheat prices or some other aspect of the agricultural industry.

An example of an inequality is

$5X < 270$

This is read "$5X$ is less than 270." In this case, assume X is a variable representing the number of machine parts manufactured by a firm. In addition, 5 represents the worker-hours required to manufacture one machine part and 270 represents the number of worker-hours available for producing these parts. Thus, the inequality expression states that the firm must use 5 worker-hours to produce one machine part and that no more than 270 worker-hours may be used by the firm in producing machine parts. This inequality may be part of a mathematical model explaining the firm's production process.

As equations and inequalities are a basic component of mathematical models, these topics will be described in more detail in Chapters 3 and 4.

2.5 Properties of Real Numbers

Operations (such as addition, subtraction, multiplication, and division) carried out on real numbers exhibit certain properties similar to the properties encountered in the algebra of sets. A particular property may apply to some operations and not to others, e.g., to addition but not to division. This section is a brief description of these properties and their relation to individual operations.

A convenient notation to indicate the general case of a mathematical operation is the symbol o. This symbol will be used to define each property and at other points in the discussion where the more familiar notations for addition ($+$), subtraction ($-$), multiplication ($\cdot$), and division ($\div$) are not appropriate. All properties discussed below refer to the real number system.

Closure

Any operation is said to demonstrate the *closure* property if, for all real numbers a and b, the result of $a \circ b$ also is a real number. When an operation exhibits the closure property, the operation is said to be *closed*.

For the real numbers a and b, addition, subtraction, and multiplication are closed. Division also is closed for all real numbers a and b except when the divisor is 0. Thus, the operations $a + b$, $a - b$, $a \cdot b$, and $a \div b$ are closed for all real numbers except that $a \div b$ is not defined if $b = 0$.

Commutativity

An operation is *commutative* if, for all real numbers a and b, $a \circ b = b \circ a$.

This property applies to addition ($a + b = b + a$) and multiplication ($ab = ba$). By the closure property, the commutative property also applies to the addition and multiplication of any series of numbers. For example, $a + b + c = c + b + a$ and $a \cdot b \cdot c \cdot d = d \cdot c \cdot b \cdot a$.

The commutative property does not apply to subtraction and division, as is demonstrated by the following examples:

$8 - 6 \neq 6 - 8$

$20 \div 5 \neq 5 \div 20$

Associativity

An operation has the *associative* property if, for all real numbers a, b, c, $(a \circ b) \circ c = a \circ (b \circ c)$

This property also applies only to addition and multiplication. Therefore,

$(a + b) + c = a + (b + c)$

$(a \cdot b) \cdot c = a \cdot (b \cdot c)$

As for subtraction and division, note the examples:

$(7 - 3) - 5 \neq 7 - (3 - 5)$

and

$(12 \div 3) \div 2 \neq 12 \div (3 \div 2)$

Distributivity

The *distributive* property relates to a combination of two operations on real numbers. The distributive law states that multiplication may be distributed over addition or subtraction. If a, b, and c are any real numbers, the distributive law can be expressed as follows:

$a(b + c) = ab + ac$

$a(b - c) = ab - ac$

The use of parentheses around the expressions $b + c$ and $b - c$ instructs one to multiply a by the sum or difference of the terms and not by only one of the terms (such as b).

Examples of the distributive law are

$5(4 + 8) = (5)(4) + (5)(8) = 5(12) = 60$

$8(6 - 3) = (8)(6) - (8)(3) = 8(3) = 24$

Although these properties may seem abstract, they often are helpful in manipulating the terms and equations found in mathematical models. For example, grouping terms in different ways on each side of an equation may violate the commutative property, serving to negate the equation. Thus, the properties of real numbers should serve as a guide to correct data manipulation and analysis.

2.6 The Priority of Mathematical Operations

The previous section's properties and computations may be clarified further by the following discussion of the accepted order of mathematical operations.

In general, these rules help to eliminate any ambiguity in a series of computations within one solution process. Also, as computerized solutions of problems in mathematical analysis use this same order, knowledge of these principles is necessary for the preparation and interpretation of computer programs.

To give correct meaning to an expression with multiple operations, operations within parentheses are carried out first. If there are nested parentheses (one set of parentheses inside another), operations on the innermost one are completed first. Within parentheses, the first operation is to raise all variables and constants to the powers specified by their respective exponents (operations on exponents are described in more detail in the next section).

After exponential operations are completed, accepted procedure is that multiplication and division take precedence over addition and subtraction. In addition to this stated order, operations with the same priority are carried out from left to right within the expression. Thus, the order of mathematical operations is

1. Those within parentheses (innermost first)
2. Raising all terms to powers
3. Multiplication and division
4. Addition and subtraction
5. Among operations with the same priority through step 4, proceed from left to right

Example 2.8
The following computation, showing each step in proper order, demonstrates the rules of order.
Solve:

$[(8)^2 \cdot 4] \cdot 12 + 14$

Steps:

$(8)^2 = 64$

$(64 \cdot 4) = 256$

$256 \cdot 12 = 3072$

$3072 + 14 = 3086$

Therefore:

$[(8)^2 \cdot 4] \cdot 12 + 14 = 3086$

2.7 Exponents

Often the terms or factors in an expression are raised to a power other than one. Thus, exponents are required. The following is a short description of the principles of exponents and computations involving exponents.

Definition of an Exponent

Exponents are used to indicate the power to which a variable or a constant is to be raised. If X is any real number and n is a positive integer, it is defined that

$$X^n = \underbrace{X_1 \cdot X_2 \cdot X_3 \cdots X_n}_{n \text{ terms}}$$

Thus, $Y^3 = Y \cdot Y \cdot Y$ and $6^4 = 6 \cdot 6 \cdot 6 \cdot 6$.

Further, if X is any real number and n is a positive integer, the following result applies to negative exponents:

$$X^{-n} = \frac{1}{X^n} = \frac{1}{X_1 \cdot X_2 \cdots X_n}$$

If $n = 0$, it is defined that

$$X^0 = 1$$

Principles for fractional exponents ($X^{1/2}$, $X^{3/8}$, etc.) are discussed under the next heading.

The Radical Sign

The symbol $\sqrt{}$ is called a *radical sign*. This symbol is used to express fractional exponents of the form

$$X^{m/n}$$

where X is any real number and m and n are positive integers.

For the above fractional exponents, when $m = 1$ and n is an integer greater than 1, the radical sign denotes the nth root of X. Thus $X^{1/3}$ is the third root of X ($\sqrt[3]{X}$) and $X^{1/6}$ is the sixth root of X ($\sqrt[6]{X}$). The number n is the *index* on the radical sign, and X is called the *radicand*. The expression $X^{1/2} = \sqrt[2]{X}$ notates the square root of X. For square roots, the index 2 is omitted. Thus $X^{1/2} = \sqrt{X}$.

When m is a positive integer other than 1, the following relationship applies:

$$X^{m/n} = (\sqrt[n]{X})^m = \sqrt[n]{X^m}$$

Either form is acceptable for fractional exponents.[1]

For $X^{-m/n}$ where m and n are positive integers, the following rule applies:

---

[1]Throughout this discussion, only positive roots will be considered. For example, the square root of 4 is equal to $+2$ or -2. However, only $+2$ will be a relevant root for this discussion.

Mathematics for Business and Economics 24

$$X^{-m/n} = \frac{1}{X^{m/n}} = \frac{1}{\sqrt[n]{X^m}} = \frac{1}{(\sqrt[n]{X})^m}$$

Example 2.9

$64^{1/4} = \sqrt[4]{64} = 2$

$16^{1/2} = \sqrt{16} = 4$

$81^{3/2} = (\sqrt{81})^3 = 9^3 = 729$

$8^{4/3} = (\sqrt[3]{8})^4 = 2^4 = 16$

$16^{-1/4} = \dfrac{1}{\sqrt[4]{16}} = \dfrac{1}{2}$

The previous discussion and additional points are summarized in the following group of computational rules for exponents.

Computational Rules

A group of computational rules for exponents are helpful for carrying out operations on mathematical expressions. For the following rules, assume that m and n are positive integers and X and Y are any positive real numbers.

Rule 1: $X^m \cdot X^n = X^{m+n}$
   Example: $2^3 \cdot 2^5 = 2^{3+5} = 2^8 = 256$

Rule 2: $(X^m)^n = X^{mn}$
   Example: $(3^2)^3 = 3^6 = 729$

Rule 3: $(XY)^n = X^n Y^n$
   Example: $[(5)(4)]^2 = 5^2 \cdot 4^2 = 400$

Rule 4: $\left(\dfrac{X}{Y}\right)^n = \dfrac{X^n}{Y^n}$
   Example: $\left(\dfrac{3}{7}\right)^3 = \dfrac{3^3}{7^3} = \dfrac{27}{343} = 0.0787$

Rule 5: $\dfrac{X^m}{X^n} = X^{m-n}$
   Example: $\dfrac{4^4}{4^2} = 4^{4-2} = 4^2 = 16$

Rule 6: $X^{1/n} = \sqrt[n]{X}$ (the nth root of X)
   Example: $27^{1/3} = \sqrt[3]{27} = 3$

Rule 7: $X^{m/n} = \sqrt[n]{X^m}$
   Example: $8^{2/3} = \sqrt[3]{8^2} = 4$

Rule 8: $X^{-m} = \dfrac{1}{X^m}$

Example: $5^{-3} = \dfrac{1}{5^3} = \dfrac{1}{125} = 0.008$

Rule 9: $X^1 = X$
Example: $9^1 = 9$

Rule 10: $X^0 = 1$
Example: $14^0 = 1$

Rule 11: $1^m = 1$, one raised to any power equals 1
Example: $1^5 = 1$

Exponents will be used in expressions throughout this book and computations on exponents will be required at various points. The following problems will provide practice in the application of these rules.

EXERCISES

1. Simplify the following expressions:
   a. $(X^4)(X^{1/2})(X^{-3})$
   b. $(X^2)^{1/3}$
   c. $\dfrac{X^4}{3X^3}$
   d. $\left(\dfrac{1}{X^3}\right)\left(\dfrac{X^2}{Y^{1/3}}\right)$
   e. $X^3 + X^2$
   f. $\dfrac{\dfrac{X^6}{Y^2}}{\dfrac{6}{Y}}$
   g. $\dfrac{X^4 + 3 + 5X^2}{Y^2}$
   h. $(X^2Y)^4(Y^2)$
   i. $\left(\dfrac{X^5}{Y^2}\right)\left(\dfrac{Y^3}{X^8}\right)$
   j. $X^4 + (X^6)(X^{-1/2})$
   k. $(\tfrac{2}{3}X^{-1/2})(\tfrac{3}{4}X^{1/2})$
   l. $(XY)(X^3Y^3)$
   m. $\left(\dfrac{X^4}{Y^2}\right)(Y^{1/2})$
   n. $(X^2Y^2)^3(Y^{1/4})$
   o. $(XYW)^2(W^2X^3)^{1/2}$
   p. $(X^{3/2})(X^{-5})$
   q. $\dfrac{1}{X} + \dfrac{X^5}{3}$
   r. $\dfrac{X^3}{6} + \dfrac{X^2}{3X^4}$
   s. $\dfrac{1}{W^2}(3XYW)^4$
   t. $\tfrac{2}{3}XYW^{-2}(XW)^5$

2. Evaluate each of the following expressions.
   a. $(27)^{-1/3}$
   b. $(8^2)^{1/3}$
   c. $\dfrac{4^{1/2}}{6^2}$
   d. $6(25)^{3/2}$
   e. $9^{1/2}\,3^{-1}$
   f. $\dfrac{(125)^{1/3}}{5^2}$
   g. $(6)^{-1}(4)^{-1/2}$
   h. $[(7)^0(8)^{1/3}]^{-5}$
   i. $(8^2)(6^{-2})$
   j. $(9^{3/2})(3^{-2})$
   k. $(\tfrac{1}{5})^{-3}$
   l. $(\tfrac{1}{8})^{-2/3}$
   m. $(27^{1/3})(27^{2/3})$
   n. $(5)^0(9^{-1/2})$
   o. $(\tfrac{1}{2})^3(2^3)$
   p. $(3^2)^2$
   q. $(\tfrac{1}{4})^3$
   r. $(100^{1/2})^4$
   s. $(10^5)^{2/5}$
   t. $(16^{1/2})^{3/2}$

3. Solve for Y at each designated X value.
   a. $Y = X^2 + 3X + 16$ at $X = 4$
   b. $Y = X^3 + X^{-1/2} - 4$ at $X = 9$
   c. $Y = 4X^{1/2} + 3X^{3/2} - 2X$ at $X = 16$
   d. $Y = X^4 - 3X^{1/3} + 16$ at $X = 0$
   e. $Y = X^{2/5} + 4X - 17$ at $X = 32$
   f. $Y = \left(\dfrac{1}{X}\right)^{-2/3}$ at $X = 27$
   g. $Y = \left(\dfrac{1}{X}\right)^{-1/3}\left(\dfrac{3X}{4}\right)^2$ at $X = 8$
   h. $Y = \left(\dfrac{X}{3}\right)^4$ at $X = 5$
   i. $Y = X^4 - X^{-3} + 3$ at $X = 1$
   j. $Y = \dfrac{X^2 + 3}{(X + 4)^2}$ at $X = -2$

2.8 Factoring: A Brief Summary

The distributive property of real numbers permits removal of parentheses in a product of factors to form the sum or difference of two terms. This was shown above as

$a(b + c) = ab + ac$

The process of factoring starts with the expression to the right of the above equality and finds the factors on the left. In other words, factoring is a process by which an expression ($ab + ac$) is written as a product of its factors [a and ($b + c$)]. As factoring is a useful technique for simplifying expressions and solving problems, the following is a short description of some of the principles of factoring.

When a group of terms has one factor in common (as shown by a above, which is in both ab and ac), the process of combining terms into factors is referred to as *monomial factoring*. As an example of monomial factoring, consider the expression below.

Example 2.10
Factor completely:

$4Y^3 - 5XY^2 + 6Y$

The common factor Y is in each term. Monomial factoring of this expression is completed by writing the product of the common factor and an expression including all remaining terms. Thus, the factors are

$4Y^3 - 5XY^2 + 6Y = Y(4Y^2 - 5XY + 6)$

The mathematical justification for this operation is the distributive law of real numbers.

When an expression has two common factors, the procedure used to find these factors is called *binomial factoring*. Finding binomial factors is a useful technique of mathematical analysis. As an example, consider the expression below.

Example 2.11
Factor completely

$Y = X^2 - 7X + 12$

To find the factors for this expression, two unknowns a and b can be used to construct the two factors as follows.

$Y = (X + a)(X + b)$

Expansion of these two new factors yields

$Y = X^2 + (a + b)X + ab$

As applied to the example, it is assumed that $(a + b)$ is the coefficient of X—that is, -7—and ab is the value of the constant term 12. Thus,

$a + b = -7$

$ab = 12$

This procedure helps guide the solution process as it establishes a pattern for the components of each factor. However, specific numerical values for a and b are found by trial and error. In this case

$a = -4$

$b = -3$

yields proper values for $X^2 - 7X + 12$. The assignment of the numerical values -4 and -3 to either a or b does not change the final result of the factoring.

Therefore, the factors for this expression are

$Y = X^2 - 7X + 12 = (X - 4)(X - 3)$

or

$Y = X^2 - 7X + 12 = (X - 3)(X - 4)$

The product $(X - 4)(X - 3)$ or $(X - 3)(X - 4)$ is computed as a check to determine that the original expression results. As values for a and b often must be found through trial and error, it should be apparent that the factors are not always easily identified.

A second example will describe a somewhat more complicated type of binomial factoring.

Example 2.12
Factor completely

$$Y = 8X^2 + 26X + 15$$

In this case, the expression can be restated using the following factors:

$$Y = (aX + c)(bX + d)$$

Expansion of these two factors yields

$$Y = abX^2 + (ad + cb)X + cd$$

Consequently, the problem requires finding values for a, b, c, and d. Again, trial and error must be used. In this case,

$$a = 4 \quad b = 2 \quad c = 3 \quad \text{and} \quad d = 5$$

Thus, the factors are as follows.

$$Y = (4X + 3)(2X + 5)$$

This result is verified by multiplication of the factors as follows:

$$Y = 8X^2 + 26X + 15$$

An expression of the general form $X^2 - b$, where b is the square of a real number, is referred to as the *difference of two squares*. Example 2.13 demonstrates and explains factoring of the difference of two squares.

Example 2.13
Factor completely

$$Y = X^2 - 25$$

The factors of this expression, found by trial and error, are

$$(X + 5)(X - 5)$$

Observe that X^2 is the square of X and 25 is the square of 5. If X and 5 are considered as two real numbers, it can be said that the difference between the squares of two numbers is the product of the sum of the numbers and the difference of the numbers.

These ideas can be extended to the sum and difference of two cubes.

Example 2.14
Factor completely

$$X^3 + 27$$

In this case, the following rule for factoring the sum of two cubes is applied:

$$X^3 + a^3 = (X + a)(X^2 - aX + a^2)$$

For this example, $a = 3$ and the following factors result.

$X^3 + 27 = (X + 3)(X^2 - 3X + 9)$

Again, multiplication of the factors will yield $X^3 + 27$.

Example 2.15
Factor completely

$X^3 - 125$

In this case, the rule for factoring the difference of two cubes is used.

$X^3 - a^3 = (X - a)(X^2 + aX + a^2)$

Here, $a = 5$, and the following factors result:

$X^3 - 125 = (X - 5)(X^2 + 5X + 25)$

Multiplication of these factors will yield $X^3 - 125$.

As this section has been a very limited presentation of some of the principles of factoring, stressing the frequent trial-and-error nature of the solution process, the following problems will allow readers to practice some of these techniques.

EXERCISES

1. For each of the following, find the product for each group of factors:
   a. $(XY)(Y + 4ZY - 3Y^3W + 0.5Y^2)$ d. $(X + 5)(X - 2)$
   b. $(2ab^2)(b - 4cd + 6ab^2c)$ e. $(X + 6)(X - 6)$
   c. $(X - 1)(X + 8)$ f. $(X + 11)(X - 11)$
2. Completely factor each of the following expressions. Check each answer by multiplication of the factors.
   a. $6X^3 - 4X^2 + 12XY$ d. $3ab - 6a^2b^2 + 9a^3b^3$
   b. $4X^3Y^2 - 2X^2Y + 16X^4Y^3 - 2X^4Y$ e. $6X^2 + 12X^4$
   c. $3WXY - 2WZ + 7W^2Z^2Y$ f. $Y^2 - 4Y^3 + 8Y^4 - Y^5$
3. Completely factor each of the following expressions. Check each answer by multiplication of the factors.
   a. $Y^2 + 6Y - 16$ d. $2X^2 - 6X - 8$
   b. $X^2 - 13X + 40$ e. $5Y^2 - 17Y + 14$
   c. $Y^2 + 4XY + 3X^2$ f. $6Y^2 - 16XY + 10X$
4. Find the factors for each of the following differences. Check each answer by multiplication of the factors.
   a. $X^2 - 36$ d. $X^4 - 25$
   b. $X^2 - 225$ e. $25X^2 - 169$
   c. $4X^2 - 16$ f. $16X^4 - 49$
5. Find the factors for each sum or difference of two cubes.
   a. $X^3 + 64$ e. $X^3 + 1000$
   b. $X^3 - 27$ f. $X^3 + 8000$
   c. $X^3 + 8$ g. $X^3 - 64$
   d. $X^3 - 216$ h. $X^3 - 729$

2.9 Chapter Summary

This chapter has been a discussion of many of the mathematical terms and concepts encountered in business and economics. The topics have included brief summaries of set theory, real numbers, equations, exponents, and factoring, all of which pertain to the development of mathematical models.

Only the basic principles of each topic have been presented as the book's applications will build on these in combination with techniques more directly related to business analysis. However, these principles should be thoroughly understood in order to prevent conceptual and computational problems in the study of the more advanced topics.

The problem set which follows reviews the terminology and methods presented above. These questions and problems should be thoroughly understood before moving on to subsequent chapters.

2.10 Problem Set

Review Questions

1. Distinguish between the empty set and the universal set.
2. Show by a Venn diagram that the complement of the universal set is the empty set.
3. Describe the union of the set of all coffee drinkers and the set of all females.
4. Describe a situation where the intersection and the union of two sets include the same elements.
5. Give an example demonstrating the associative law of sets.
6. The real number system includes all decimal representations. Explain.
7. Distinguish between a variable and a constant.
8. Give a practical business example of an inequality.
9. List all factors in the term $-4a^2b^2c$. List all terms in the expression:

   $Y = 3a^2 - 2ab^2 - 4a^2b^2c + 7c$

10. Show, by example, why the associative property does not apply to the division operation.
11. Give a real number example of the commutative law of multiplication.
12. State the accepted order for carrying out operations within a given mathematical equation.
13. What is represented by the index of the radical sign?
14. What conditions must an expression satisfy for the possibility of monomial factoring to exist?
15. What rule is used to facilitate factoring of the difference of two squares? Give an example which demonstrates this rule.

Review Problems

1. Use the accepted priority of mathematical operations to evaluate each of the following.

a. $(6)(3)^2 + 17$
b. $8 \div 5 + 6^2$
c. $5 \cdot 4 + 11 - 6 \div 2$
d. $16^2 \div 4 + (6 \cdot 8)$
e. $7 \cdot 5 + 12 - 4^3$
f. $(4 + 7)^2 \div -(5 \div 2)$
g. $(18^2 \div 4^3)(6 \cdot 4)$
h. $(4 \cdot 6)2^2 - 14$

2. For the following sets of real numbers:

$A = \{1,4,7,11,13\}$

$B = \{2,3,4,11,15\}$

$C = \{1,7,15,16,18\}$

Find:
a. $A \cap B$
b. $A \cup B$
c. $A \cup B \cup C$
d. $B \cup C$
e. $A \cap B \cap C$
f. $A \cup (B \cap C)$

3. For the following sets of real numbers:

Universal set $= U = \{1,2,3,4,5,6,7,8,9,10\}$

$X = \{3,4,5,6\}$

$Y = \{5,6,7,8\}$

Find:
a. $X \cup Y$
b. $X' \cup X$
c. $Y' \cap X$
d. $X' \cap Y'$
e. $(X \cup Y)'$
f. $(X \cap Y)'$

4. For the following sets of real numbers:

$X = \{2,4,6,8,10\}$

$Y = \{3,5,7,9,11\}$

$Z = \{2,3,4,5,6,7,8,9,10,11\}$

Find:
a. $(X \cup Y) \cup Z$
b. $(X \cap Y) \cap Z$

Show that:
c. $X \cup (Y \cap Z) = (X \cup Y) \cap (X \cup Z)$
d. $X \cap (Y \cup Z) = (X \cap Y) \cup (X \cap Z)$

5. Simplify each of the following expressions:
a. $\left(\dfrac{X^2}{Y^2}\right)^2 \left(\dfrac{1}{X^4}\right)$
b. $(X^{-3})(X^0)$
c. $(Y^3)(Y^{1/4})(Y^{2/5})$
d. $(X^{6/5})(X^{5/3})$
e. $(X^{3/2})^3$
f. $(WYZ)^2(X^2 Y^2)^3$
g. $(4X)^2(X^{-1})$
h. $(3YZ)(XZ)^2$
i. $(Y^{-4})^{-3}(Y^0)$
j. $(XYZ)^{-2}(XY)^{-3}(Z^4)$

6. Evaluate each of the following expressions:
a. $(3)^{-2} 4^2$
b. $(3^2)^{-3}$
c. $(\tfrac{1}{4})^{-2}$
d. $(\tfrac{1}{3})^2(4)^{-1}(16)$
e. $(\tfrac{1}{8})^{-2}(4)(3)^0$
f. $(6)^0(6)^{-2}(6)^4$
g. $-^7(16)^{1/4}$
h. $(16)^{-3/4}(8)$
i. $(10)^2(10^2)^{-1}$
j. $(0)^4(16)^{3/4}$

7. Solve for Y at each stated X value:
   a. $Y = (X^{1/3})^{-2}$ at $X = 27$
   b. $Y = (4X)^2(X^{-3})(X^2)$ at $X = 2$
   c. $Y = \left(\dfrac{1}{X}\right)^{-1/2}(X)^3$ at $X = 4$
   d. $Y = 15X - X^{-2}$ at $X = 1$
   e. $Y = \left(\dfrac{X^4}{X^2}\right)^2 \left(\dfrac{1}{X}\right)$ at $X = 10$
   f. $Y = \left(\dfrac{X^{1/3}}{X^{2/3}}\right)^2$ at $X = 1000$
   g. $Y = (X^2)^{-3}(X)^{-1}$ at $X = 2$
   h. $Y = (X^{-1/4})(X)^{1/2}$ at $X = 16$
   i. $Y = \left(\dfrac{X^2}{X^{-1}}\right)^2 (X^{-3})$ at $X = 5$
   j. $Y = [(X^{-3/4})^2]^2$ at $X = 3$

8. For the real numbers 5 and 20, show that
   a. Multiplication is both commutative and associative.
   b. Subtraction is neither commutative nor associative.
   c. Division is not commutative.

9. Factor each of the following. Check your answers by multiplication to make sure that the original expression results.
   a. $3abX + 4a - 6aY$
   b. $-X^2Y^2 + 16Y^5 - 7XY^3 + 4Y^4$
   c. $ab^2c + 4bcd - 14bc + 7abcd$
   d. $3a^2X - 6a^3b^4 + 12a^4d^2 - 6a^5bc^4$
   e. $X^5 + X^4Y - X^3YZ + X^2Z^2$
   f. $X^3 + 1$
   g. $X^3 - 64$
   h. $X^3 + 8$
   i. $\dfrac{X^2}{3} + \dfrac{2XY^2}{3} - \dfrac{4X^2Y^3}{9}$
   j. $\dfrac{XY^2}{8} + \dfrac{3X^4}{4} + \dfrac{5X^2Y^3}{16}$

10. Factor each of the following and check your answers by multiplication.
    a. $X^2 - 9$
    b. $X^2 + 3X - 18$
    c. $4X^2 - 16$
    d. $a^2 - 6ab - 16b^2$
    e. $a^4 - 25$
    f. $X^4 - 7X^2 - 8$
    g. $4X^2 + 38X + 48$
    h. $-3X^2 + 5X + 2$

11. Factor each cube.
    a. $X^3 + 125$
    b. $X^3 + 64$
    c. $X^3 - 1000$
    d. $X^3 - 8$
    e. $X^3 + 1$
    f. $X^3 - 1$
    g. $X^3 + 216$
    h. $X^3 - 27$

12. State each of the following by using a radical sign:
    a. $14^{3/2}$
    b. $21^{-4/5}$
    c. $16^{1/4}$
    d. $20^{-1/3}$
    e. $52^{-3/5}$
    f. $60^{4/3}$
    g. $25^{5/2}$
    h. $36^{-7/2}$

13. Answer the following questions assuming that the universal set includes all residents of Chicago who are 18 years of age and over.
    a. If the set S represents all males 18 and over in Chicago, describe the complement of S.
    b. Describe three subsets of this universal set, excluding the universal set and the null set.
    c. Describe the subset including all 16-year-olds in Chicago.
    d. If the set X includes all Chicago residents between 25 and 65, describe the complement of X.
    e. If the set Y includes all males in Chicago between 18 and 65, is the set of all physicians in Chicago a subset of this set? Why or why not?

14. In a survey of 5000 unemployed people between 16 and 65, the following results are obtained:
    a. 3000 are male (set S).
    b. 2500 are between 16 and 25 years old (set X).
    c. 1000 are females between 16 and 25 years old (set Y).
    d. 500 are males between 40 and 45 years old (set Z).
    Find the number of survey elements (people) in each of the following sets:
    a. X'
    b. $X \cap Y'$
    c. Y'
    d. $S \cap Y'$
    e. $S \cap (Y \cup Z)$
    f. $S' \cup X'$
15. Draw a Venn diagram of the following advertising exposure survey results for a new toothpaste based on 10,000 survey respondents:
    a. 6000 have seen a television advertisement for the new toothpaste.
    b. 1500 have heard a radio advertisement for the product.
    c. 2000 have seen a magazine advertisement for the new toothpaste.
    d. 1000 have both seen a television advertisement and heard a radio advertisement.
    e. 800 have seen both a television advertisement and magazine advertisement.
    f. 300 have both heard a radio advertisement and seen a magazine advertisement.
    g. 200 have been exposed to television, radio, and magazine advertisements for the new toothpaste.
    Based on this diagram, determine how many people in the survey have not seen the advertisement in any of the three media.

3 Mathematical Functions: An Introduction

3.1 Introduction

In Chapters 1 and 2, the basic definitions, concepts, and notation of applied mathematics were presented. Some business applications were mentioned, but the emphasis was on mathematical modeling and mathematical operations.

This chapter expands these fundamentals by introducing mathematical functions. The chapter presents the concept of a function, the graphical representation of functions, and a brief introduction to the various functions encountered in applied mathematics.

As mentioned in Chapter 1, in many cases functions are an important part of the mathematical model. When functions are considered appropriate for a particular model, selection of their type and form is essential to the model's development. Also, as functions guide the subsequent analysis and data interpretation, it should be stressed that proper function selection is vital to the successful implementation of the model.

A mathematical function expresses a formal correspondence between two sets of data. For example, the annual income of American families and annual refrigerator sales for a firm may be related by means of a mathematical function.

However, a function represents a specific type of correspondence between two data sets. The requirements which must be met before a correspondence in data is considered a function are discussed in the next section.

3.2 Relations and Functions

If the variables and constants making up the data sets are related in a specific way, a function is formed. To comprehend the precise definition of a function, first one must understand mathematical relations.

Consider a certain type of set referred to as a set of "ordered pairs" of elements. Each member of the set is itself a set having two elements. One element of each pair represents an observation of a particular variable or constant (referred to here as X), and the other element of the pair is an observation of a second variable or constant (referred to as Y). For example, a pair may represent family income (X) and refrigerator sales (Y) for a specific year.

Each element in pair i (e.g., a particular year) can be identified as X_i (if from the X category) or Y_i (if from the Y category). If the order of the elements in any given pair i, such as X_iY_i rather than Y_iX_i, has significance for the use of the elements, the two elements comprise an *ordered pair*. Consequently, in an ordered pair, Y values are associated with X values. This correspondence means that there is a relation between the variables X and Y.

The existence of a relation between X and Y means that, given an X_i value, one or more Y values will be specified by the relation. However, if for each X_i value there corresponds *one and only one* Y_i value, then Y is said to be a *function* of X. This functional relationship is symbolized as $Y = f(X)$ and read, "Y is equal to a function of X."

Thus, in a function, a value of X uniquely determines a value of Y. For example, a particular family income uniquely determines a value of refrigerator sales. The reverse of this statement does not have to be true as it is possible for more than one X value to be associated with the same Y value (e.g., more than one family income can be associated with the same value of refrigerator sales).

Figure 3.1(*a*) illustrates a functional relation between X and Y as one and only one Y value corresponds to each X value shown on the horizontal axis. In contrast, Figure 3.1(*b*) describes a relation between X and Y which is not a functional relation. Observe that three different Y values (Y_1, Y_2, Y_3) correspond to the X value shown (X_1).

Two brief examples of relations may further clarify this discussion. If $Y < X$ (where the symbol $<$ means "less than") and X is equal to 12, then

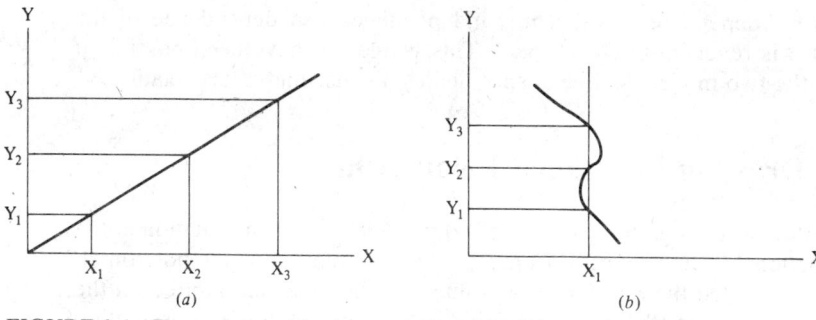

FIGURE 3.1 Two relationships between X and Y; (a) one that is a functional relationship and (b) one that is not a functional relationship.

Y can be equal to any value less than 12. Thus, the relation $Y < X$ is not a function as the stated X value corresponds to more than one Y value.

Second, consider the relation $Y = 5X^2 - 25X + 20$. In this relation, if $X = 1$ then $Y = 0$, and if $X = 4$ then $Y = 0$. Although more than one X value corresponds to the same Y value, the relation is a function as one and only one Y value corresponds to a given value for X.

When used in the form $Y = f(X)$, the values of X constitute the *domain* of the function and the set of corresponding Y values comprise the *range* of the function. Therefore, for a given function, each element of the domain corresponds to exactly one particular element of the range.

The previous discussion leads to the formal definition of a function:

A FUNCTION IS A RELATION IN WHICH EACH ELEMENT OF THE DOMAIN CORRESPONDS TO ONE AND ONLY ONE ELEMENT OF THE RANGE

3.3 Dependent and Independent Variables

In much of applied mathematics, the variable representing the domain values (X in the example above) is referred to as the *independent variable* and the variable specifying the range values (Y) is the *dependent variable*. Thus, within a problem, X values may be selected at the discretion of the analyst, and each Y value depends on the particular value of X. For example, it may be hypothesized that refrigerator sales Y depend on particular selected values of family income X.

This notion of independence and dependence should not be interpreted as identical, in all cases, to cause and effect. Often, mathematical models in business can be structured to include the possibility of interchanging dependent and independent variables. For example, a model may specify either that sales depend on advertising expenditures or that advertising expenditures depend on sales. Thus, independence and dependence of the variables is reversed in each model. This would not have been possible if one of the two models had been specified as a cause-and-effect relation.

3.4 Drawing Functional Relationships

A two-dimensional graph can be used to provide further information about the functional form $Y = f(X)$. Domain values are plotted on the horizontal, or X, axis (called the *abscissa*) and values for the range are plotted on the vertical, or Y, axis (the *ordinate*). This is the conventional representation for functions with one independent and one dependent variable. The coordinate axis used for this two-variable relationship is divided into four quadrants as shown in Figure 3.2. This is referred to as the *Cartesian coordinate system*.

On this graph, quadrant I includes the set of ordered pairs with positive values for both the domain and range. Both values are negative in quadrant III. In quadrant II, values for the range are positive and domain values are negative. Finally, range values are negative and domain values are positive in quadrant IV.

Each point on the abscissa (X axis) has a 0 value for the range, and each point on the ordinate (Y axis) has a 0 value for the domain. At the intersection of the two axes, referred to as the *origin*, values for both X and Y are 0. It should be noted that, for a substantial number of mathematical analyses in business and economics, functions are relevant only within the first quadrant (including the X and Y axes which border quadrant I) because measurements such as prices, quantities of goods, and personal income usually are nonnegative.

Points in the Cartesian coordinate system are identified by the notation (X_i, Y_i) where X_i refers to the X coordinate and Y_i refers to the Y coordinate

```
                    Y
                    |
       quadrant     |    quadrant
          II        |       I
                    |     (5,10)
                    |
                    |— (0,6)
                    |
                    |0
  -X ───────────────┼─────────────── X
                    |
                    |
       quadrant     |    quadrant
         III        |       IV
                    |
                    |
                   -Y
```

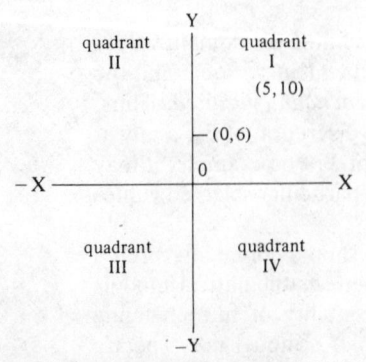

FIGURE 3.2 The coordinate axes and the four quadrants.

of the point. For example, (5, 10) specifies the point on the coordinate axis having an X value of 5 and a Y value of 10. Similarly, (0, 6) specifies a point on the Y axis ($X = 0$) where $Y = 6$.

This notation facilitates the graphical description of functions encountered in quantitative business applications.

The points (5, 10) and (0, 6) are shown in Figure 3.2.

Example 3.1

The data in Table 3.1 represent family income (X, measured in thousands of dollars) and refrigerator sales (Y, measured in thousands) for a major appliance manufacturer.

In analyzing the correspondence between these two data sets, it is beneficial first to graph the data. The five X, Y combinations of Table 3.1 are represented by the five coordinate points in Figure 3.3. These five points constitute a "scatter diagram" of the data. Finally, note the use of scaling in both Table 3.1 and Figure 3.3 as income and refrigerator sales are measured in thousands.

The graphical representation of the function results from connecting the five coordinate points. The characteristics of this graph help analysts determine the particular form of the relation between family income and refrigerator sales.

The decision regarding the form of relation has special relevance to two steps in the mathematical modeling process. First, graphical representation of the data will assist model development. Visual interpretation of the data may help indicate the particular function to use in the analysis. For example, is the relation between family income and refrigerator sales linear (straight line) or nonlinear? The answer to this question will guide selection of the functions to include in the model. Thus, graphical representation is an influencing factor in the choice of functions for the model.

Second, graphical representation is an important component in the interpretation of results. For example, the relation between family income and refrigerator sales may be understood more easily if graphs are used to associate the two data sets. Without graphs, decision makers who are not mathematically inclined may not fully comprehend and, consequently, not apply models in the decision process.

It should be noted that developments in computerized graphing (i.e.,

TABLE 3.1 Family Income and Refrigerator Sales for 5 Years

Year	X, Family income, $1000s	Y, Refrigerator sales, 1000s
1	16	30
2	17	35
3	18	40
4	19	45
5	20	50

```
                    Y
                 50 ┤                            (20,50)
                    │
                 45 ┤                     (19,45)
                    │
                 40 ┤              (18,40)
                    │
                 35 ┤       (17,35)
                    │
                 30 ┤ (16,30)
                    │
                    └─┼────┼────┼────┼────┼──── X
                      16   17   18   19   20
                         Family income (thousands)
```
FIGURE 3.3   Family income and refrigerator sales for five years.

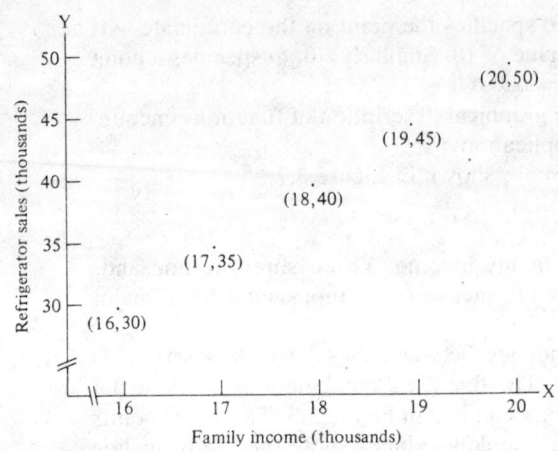

using the computer to relate data sets graphically) will give impetus to the practical business application of mathematical modeling. As graphical representation of large data sets is facilitated by the computer, selection of the functions to use in models and interpretation of model results will be both more accurate and less time-consuming. The graphical description of relations will be important to the discussion of many subsequent text topics.

3.5 Functions with One Independent Variable

To this point in the chapter, the expression $Y = f(X)$ has been used as a general statement of the existence of a functional relationship between one independent and one dependent variable. This section broadens this concept to describe three types of functions used in business and economics: (1) polynomials with one independent variable; (2) exponential functions; and (3) logarithmic functions. In this section, each of these functions will be discussed for the case of one independent variable (X). In Section 3.6, functions having more than one independent variable are described.

Each of the three types of function is defined in this section. In later chapters, specific business applications of each are presented in greater detail.

Polynomials with One Independent Variable

Polynomial functions have the general form:

$$Y = b_0 + b_1 X + b_2 X^2 + \cdots + b_k X^k$$

Mathematical Functions: An Introduction

re Y and X are the dependent and independent variables, respectively, $b_0, b_1, b_2, \ldots, b_k$ are constants. The constant b_k is not equal to 0 and nnegative. The integer k specifies the degree of the polynomial; e.g., if 2, the polynomial is a "second-degree" polynomial.

If $k = 0$, then as $X^0 = 1$, the function has the form $Y = b_0$. This is red to as a constant function. An example of a constant function, $b_0 = 4$ is shown in Figure 3.4. Observe that the value of Y does not ge regardless of the corresponding X value.

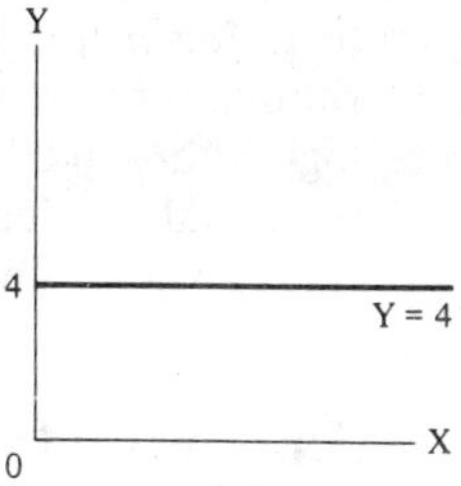

A *linear function* has a k value of one, or $Y = b_0 + b_1X^1 = b_0 + b_1X$. xample of a linear function is

$$12 + 1.6X$$

FIGURE 3.4 The constant function, $Y = 4$.

graphical description, interpretation, and computation of linear functions are the primary topics of the next four chapters of this book (Chapters 7).

Two other polynomials frequently used in applications are *quadratic* tions ($k = 2$, or $Y = b_0 + b_1X + b_2X^2$) and *cubic functions* ($k = 3$, or $b_0 + b_1X + b_2X^2 + b_3X^3$). Whenever k is greater than 1, the polyial is referred to as being *nonlinear*. Nonlinear functions will be described ore detail and applied to business and economics in Chapter 8 and the ters on calculus (Chapters 10 to 12).

algebraic Functions

function that can be expressed in terms of a polynomial of any degree ferred to as an *algebraic function*. There are also many types of nonoraic functions in mathematics, of which two of particular interest in ness and economics are exponential and logarithmic functions.

Functions in which the independent variable is expressed as an exnt are called *exponential functions*. For example, the expression $Y = a^X$, re a is any constant and X is the independent variable, specifies an nential function. Other exponential functions are $Y = 19^X$, $Y = 8^{X-4}$, $Y = 6^{X^2+X-3}$.

An exponential function often applied to the mathematics of finance is formula for compounding annually a stated amount of money P, the cipal of an account, for a specified number of years n at an interest rate percent per year. The value of the account A at the end of n years can xpressed as:

$$P(1 + i)^n$$

(years) is the independent variable and A (value of the account) is the ndent variable, this is an exponential function.

Functions of the form $Y = \text{logarithm}_a X$, are called *logarithmic func*. In this expression, $\text{logarithm}_a X$ is read "the base a logarithm of X" independent variable). Specifically, this means that Y is the power to which a (the base) must be raised to equal X, or $a^Y = X$. In the logarithmic form, a and X are given and Y must be found. For example, if $Y = $ logarithm$_{10}$ 1000, then $Y = 3$, since $10^3 = 1000$. As may be apparent, exponential and logarithmic functions are closely related. Both types of functions are examined further in Chapter 8.

3.6 Functions with More than One Independent Variable

The previous paragraphs have been concerned with polynomial, exponential, and logarithmic functions with one independent variable. Functions with more than one independent variable occur frequently in business and economics and can be expressed in algebraic or nonalgebraic form. These functions are referred to as *multivariate functions*.

The general form of this type of function is

$$Y = f(X_1, X_2, \ldots, X_n)$$

where each X_i represents a different independent variable and n is greater than one. Numerous examples of multivariate functions are found in business and economics.

The range of a function with more than one independent variable is much the same as in the case with functions of one independent variable. However, the domain includes sets of ordered numbers for all the independent variables. For example, for a function with three independent variables, the domain consists of sets of ordered triples. Consequently, in this case the range is a set of values including *one and only one* observation for each ordered triple of observations on the independent variables.

An example of a multivariate function is the relationship between refrigerator sales (the dependent variable) and (1) the price of refrigerators, (2) family income, and (3) the price of electricity. In this case, the domain consists of sets of ordered triples representing one value for each of (1), (2), and (3). Each ordered triple corresponds to a single value of the range, or Y, the dependent variable.

Polynomial functions with more than one independent variable can be linear or nonlinear with respect to each independent variable. In addition, algebraic (polynomial) functions with more than one independent variable may be of any degree. The next section includes a discussion of the determination of the degree of a polynomial with more than one independent variable.

The Degree of a Polynomial with More than One Independent Variable

The following rules are applied to determine the degree of a polynomial with more than one independent variable:

1. The degree of a term is equal to the sum of the exponents on the variables in that term.
2. The degree of a polynomial is equal to the degree of the term of highest degree in the polynomial.

Several examples will clarify these rules.

Example 3.2
In the function
$$Y = b_0 + b_1X_1 + b_2X_2 + b_3X_3 + b_4X_4$$
each b_i is a constant and each X_i is a separate independent variable. As each term has a degree of one, the function is linear in the four independent variables X_1, X_2, X_3, and X_4.

Example 3.3
In the function
$$Y = b_0 + b_1X_1 + b_2X_2^2 + b_3X_3 + b_4X_4^3$$
there are various degrees for the individual terms. The degrees of b_1X_1 and b_3X_3 are 1, the degree of $b_2X_2^2$ is 2, and the degree of $b_4X_4^3$ is 3. Therefore, according to the second rule above, the degree of the polynomial is 3.

Using functions with more than one independent variable is an effective way of describing the various influences affecting a given measurement. Although there are advantages to the simplification of the model with a single independent variable, greater explanatory power often is provided by the inclusion of more variables.

Selection of the variables to include in a model is a task requiring both practical knowledge of the relationships and the ability to apply proper quantitative techniques. This selection process is discussed briefly in later sections of this book and in advanced textbooks in mathematics and statistics.

Chapter 4 continues this discussion of functions by examining the development and interpretation of linear functions.

3.7 Chapter Summary

This chapter has been a brief introduction to mathematical functions and their place in applied mathematical analysis.

The concept of a function was presented by showing that a function is a specific type of relation between sets of data. Frequently, functions are constructed in a framework with independent and dependent variables, indicating that one variable (independent) is selected at the discretion of the analyst and the other (dependent) takes on values in accordance with this selection.

The graphing of functions also was described in the chapter. Graphical analysis is particularly useful in model development and the interpretation of a model's results. The use of graphs in applied mathematics is becoming increasingly important because of advances in computer graphics.

The chapter included definitions and brief descriptions of the algebraic and nonalgebraic functions that will be encountered in the remainder of this book. These functions are applied to the representation of linear and nonlinear relationships between sets of data.

Finally, the chapter concluded by introducing algebraic functions with more than one independent variable. This type of function was described for the general case and rules were stated for determining the degree of this type of polynomial.

Thus, this chapter has provided a very important background for the remainder of the book. As functions are employed in many mathematical descriptions of real-world problems, their correct development and interpretation is essential to the application of quantitative techniques of business problems. The functions introduced in this chapter will be discussed in greater detail in succeeding chapters.

3.8 Problem Set

Review Questions

1. Distinguish between a relation and a function. State a relation between the variables X and Y which is not a function.
2. Distinguish between an independent and a dependent variable.
3. State three relations from business that are expressed in a dependent variable–independent variable form.
4. What is the value of each variable at the origin (meeting point of the two axes) of the Cartesian coordinate system?
5. In which quadrant of the Cartesian coordinate system is each of the following points?
   a. $(6, -4)$
   b. $(1, 10)$
   c. $(-3, 7)$
6. Briefly discuss how graphical analysis assists the process of mathematical modeling.
7. Distinguish between algebraic and nonalgebraic functions.
8. Describe the constant function $y = b_0$ by giving a business-oriented example.
9. State an exponential function with one independent variable.
10. How does an exponential function differ from a logarithmic function for the case of one independent variable?
11. What is included in the domain and range for a function with one dependent variable and two independent variables?
12. State the rules for determining the degree of a polynomial with more than one independent variable. Apply these rules in finding the degree of the following function:

    $Y = b_0 + b_1 X_1^3 + b_2 X_1 X_2 X_3 + b_3 X_2 X_3 + b_4 X_2 X_3^3$

Review Problems

1. For each group of domain and range values below, state whether or not a function can be formed between the two sets. If so, why? If not, why not?

a.
Domain	Range
3	14
6	16
8	20
10	24

c.
Domain	Range
7	12
7	12
8	15
9	18
9	19

b.
Domain	Range
3	7
4	11
4	15
4	22

d.
Domain	Range
18	14
19	14
20	14
21	15

2. State whether each of the following meets the criteria for a mathematical function. If the relation is not a mathematical function, explain why?
   a. $Y = 6X - 14$
   b. $Y > X$
   c. $Y = 3^x$
   d. $Y < X^2 + 4$
   e. $Y = 4X^3 - 20$
   f. $Y = X^{1/2}$

3. On graph paper, plot each of the following points and name the quadrant where each is located:
   a. (3, 4)
   b. (−2, −2)
   c. (6, −5)
   d. (−1, 4)
   e. (7, −8)
   f. (−21, 10)

4. On graph paper, draw each of the following functions:
   a. $Y = -2$
   b. $Y = X$
   c. $X = 7$
   d. $Y = 3X$

5. Plot the points on each function below corresponding to $X = 2$, $X = 4$, and $X = 6$. Connect the three points for each function.
   a. $Y = 4X - 8$
   b. $Y = X^2 - 2X - 8$
   c. $Y = 5X$
   d. $Y = -X$

6. For the following exponential function

   $$Y = 2^X$$

   find the coordinate when $X = 2$, $X = 4$, $X = 6$ and connect the three points. Characterize the shape of the line formed by the three points.

7. For each function below, find the largest value possible for X and for Y if the function must be confined to the first quadrant. (Maximum points will be on the X axis and Y axis, respectively.)
   a. $Y = 14 - 2X$
   b. $Y = 28 - 7X$
   c. $Y = 2 - 6X$
   d. $Y = 12 - 12X$
   e. $Y = 200 - X$

8. Find the degree of each of the following polynomial functions:
   a. $Y = 14 + 7X_1^2 + 16X_1^2 X_2 + 13X_2^2$
   b. $Y = 15X_1 + 14X_1 X_2 + 21X_2^2$
   c. $Y = 54 - 6X_1^2 X_2^2 + 7X_2^4$

d. $Y = 22 + 6X_1 + 7X_2 - 14X_3$
e. $Y = 3X_1 - 7X_2 - X_2^2 + X_2^3 - 4X_4^6$

9. It is assumed by a lending institution that the home mortgage interest rate is always 2.5 percent higher than the prime interest rate.
   a. Is the home mortgage rate a function of the prime rate? Why, or why not?
   b. If your answer to (a) is yes, state the function relating these two variables.
10. For a shoe manufacturer, fixed costs of production are $850,000 and variable costs are $16.75 per unit (pair of shoes) produced.
    a. Set up a function relating total cost of production to units of production.
    b. Why is this a functional relationship?
    c. What is the degree of the polynomial in (a)? Why?
11. A computer manufacturer utilizes labor-hours and machine-hours to produce small parts. For each labor-hour used, 2.1 small parts can be produced, and for each hour of machinery time used, 3.5 parts can be made.
    a. Set up a function relating parts production to the number of labor-hours and machine-hours used.
    b. Why is this relationship a multivariate function?
    c. What is the degree of the polynomial relating these variables? Why?

Linear Functions

4.1 Introduction

In Chapter 3, a polynomial with one independent variable was defined as having the form

$$Y = b_0 + b_1X + b_2X^2 + \cdots + b_kX^k$$

In this equation, Y is the dependent variable, X signifies the independent variable, and the nonnegative integer k is the degree of the polynomial.

This chapter focuses on polynomials where $k = 0$ and $k = 1$. In other words, functions with the following forms are discussed:

$Y = b_0$ constant function

and

$Y = b_0 + b_1X$ linear function

where b_1 is not equal to zero. For simplification purposes, these two functions *together* will be referred to as "linear" at many points in the chapter.

Constant and linear polynomials are used to explain many business and economic relations. In addition, these functions often are employed to approximate more complicated relationships because they are considered the easiest functions to understand and to manipulate mathematically. A thorough understanding of these two types of function provides a background for the study of other functional forms in later chapters.

This chapter presents several topics related to linear functions. These include interpretation of linear functions for the cases of one independent variable and multiple independent variables, the "standard form" of a linear equation, and two methods for determining the linear function relating two variables. Several applications of linear relations are included to assist the presentation of each of these topics.

4.2 Linear Models in Business

The following three examples are indicative of the types of linear model employed in business analysis.

Example 4.1
Researchers for a trade association of beef producers have determined that each time the price of pork increases by $0.01 per pound, the per capita annual beef consumption of the United States increases by 0.5 pound per year. The trade association wants to include these data as part of a larger mathematical model used to predict per capita beef consumption for future years.

Example 4.2
A television manufacturer has established that the total operating cost at a factory includes a fixed cost of $600,000 per year and other costs of $185 per television produced. The firm wants to develop a function relating the quantity of television output to the total cost of operation at the factory. This function will be used to assess current and future cost and profit levels.

Example 4.3
A distributor of home heating oil uses two models of delivery truck. One truck model has an operating cost (gas, oil, licenses, insurance, and depreciation) of $1.14 per mile and the other model has an operating cost of $1.27 per mile. The distributor wants to use these cost figures to develop a function relating total transportation expenditures to the mileage traveled by both kinds of truck.

This function may be applied to allocation problems such as finding the mileage for each truck which will meet exactly or be less than some maximum transportation budget. Thus, this function may be part of an overall resource allocation model for the oil distributor.

Each of these examples describes linear relations between two or more sets of data. This means that the independent variable in each case (price of pork, quantity of televisions produced, and mileage for each truck, respectively) is enumerated at the first power, or the actual measurement units of the variable. Thus, for example, pork prices are measured as price per pound, as opposed to price per pound squared. Similarly, televisions and truck mileage are enumerated at the first power. Therefore, each function is shown graphically as a straight line. The next section examines some of the characteristics of this straight line.

4.3 The Slope and the Intercept

A linear function is shown graphically as a straight line with a nonzero slope. The slope is the same at every point on the function and is expressed by the coefficient b_1 in $Y = b_0 + b_1 X$. This coefficient measures the change in the value of the dependent variable Y in response to a one-unit change in the value of the independent variable X.

For the function $Y = 16 - 3X$, the slope is -3. This slope value indicates that for each one-unit increase in X (as measured in X units), Y decreases by 3 units (as measured in Y units). Similarly, for a one-unit decrease in X, Y will increase by three units. This relation is valid between any two (X, Y) coordinate points.

THE SLOPE OF A LINEAR FUNCTION WITH ONE INDEPENDENT VARIABLE IS EQUAL TO THE CHANGE IN THE DEPENDENT VARIABLE DIVIDED BY THE CHANGE IN THE INDEPENDENT VARIABLE

The other coefficient in a linear function, b_0, is called the Y intercept. The Y intercept measures the value of Y when X equals 0. For example, in $Y = 16 - 3X$, the Y intercept is 16, indicating that Y equals 16 when X equals zero.

THE Y INTERCEPT OF A LINEAR FUNCTION WITH ONE INDEPENDENT VARIABLE IS EQUAL TO THE VALUE OF THE DEPENDENT VARIABLE WHEN THE VALUE OF THE INDEPENDENT VARIABLE IS ZERO

Example 4.4
As an example of a linear function, assume that transportation costs for a small delivery truck (Y = transportation cost) are dependent on the mileage traveled by the truck (X = mileage). The specific function is $Y = 54 + 1.29X$, where Y is measured in dollars and X is measured in miles.

This function is shown in Figure 4.1.

In this function, $b_0 = \$54$, indicating that transportation costs are $54 whether or not the delivery truck is in operation. In applications, the Y intercept should be evaluated in the context of the problem. For example, $54 is a dollar amount representing those elements of transportation cost not explained by mileage, such as license fees and a part of depreciation.

The slope of the line, b_1, measures the change in transportation cost (in dollars) in response to a 1-mile change in miles traveled. Since $b_1 = \$1.29$, transportation costs increase $1.29 for each additional mile traveled. Similarly, for each 1-mile reduction, transportation costs decrease by $1.29. This same relationship applies regardless of the miles traveled by the truck.

Values for the Slope and Intercept

Direct linear relations (as described above and shown in Figure 4.1) have positive slope coefficients. This means that the dependent variable changes in the same direction as the change in the independent variable.

A negative value (i.e., $Y = b_0 - b_1 X$) for the slope coefficient indicates a linear relation in which the dependent variable changes in a direction opposite to the change in the independent variable.

For a constant function, where $b_1 = 0$ and therefore $Y = b_0$, the dependent variable does not change in response to a change in the independent variable. This function is represented by a horizontal line extending from the Y intercept on the Y axis.

Figure 4.2 shows a horizontal line extending into quadrant I from a Y intercept value of 6. Thus, the expression for the function is $Y = 6$. The value of the slope for a constant function is zero. It should be noted that a vertical line extending from the X axis has an undefined slope as Y values change but X values remain constant.

Values for the Y intercept, or b_0, can be positive, negative, or zero depending on the problem. Existence of a negative Y intercept value means that at least part of the linear function will lie outside of the first quadrant. At times, this situation can cause interpretive problems in cases where Y is

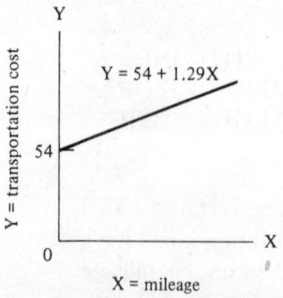

FIGURE 4.1 The linear transportation cost function $Y = 54 + 1.29 X$

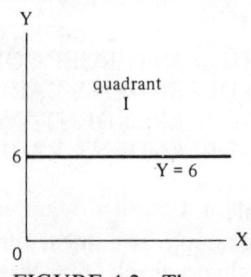

FIGURE 4.2 The constant function $Y = 6$.

a variable with practical meaning only for positive values (such as prices or incomes). However, nonsensical interpretations can be avoided if it is kept in mind that the Y intercept measures influences on the dependent variable not accounted for by the independent variable used in the function. These influences may act on the dependent variable in such a way as to cause an "unrealistic" negative value for Y in the absence of the independent variable.

The following examples will demonstrate some applications of linear and constant functions.

Example 4.5

State government revenue analysts know that annual tax revenues for the state are dependent to a large extent on the unemployment rate in the state. They have determined that this relationship is explained by the following linear function:

$$Y = 11.7 - 0.4X$$

where Y = annual state tax revenues in billions of dollars (e.g., $Y = 11$ indicates $11 billion in state tax revenues)
X = unemployment as a percentage of the state work force (e.g., $X = 8$ means that 8 percent of the state work force is unemployed)

This function has a Y intercept of 11.7 and a slope of -0.4, denoting that tax revenues and the unemployment rate vary in opposite directions.

The value of the Y intercept indicates that if unemployment is at 0 percent of the work force, annual tax revenues to the state will equal $11.7 billion.

The slope value of -0.4 means that each 1 percent increase in unemployment (for example, from 7 to 8 percent of the work force) will cause tax revenues to decrease by $0.4 billion (or $400 million). Similarly, a 1 percent decrease in unemployment will cause a $400 million increase in tax revenues.

As an example of determining annual tax revenues by this function, consider the amount of tax revenues associated with a state unemployment rate of 8 percent.

$$Y = 11.7 - (0.4)(8)$$
$$= 11.7 - 3.2$$
$$= 8.5$$

Thus, at an 8 percent unemployment rate, annual tax revenues will be $8.5 billion.

Example 4.6

Many times, the total cost of manufacturing a product can be expressed as a linear function of the quantity produced. As total costs include fixed costs (such as rent, property taxes, and interest payments) and variable costs (such as wages, utilities, and raw materials), the following notation can be used for this linear function:

$$TC = F + VQ$$

where TC = total cost for a given number of units produced
F = fixed cost
V = variable cost per unit
Q = number of units produced

Fixed costs are incurred regardless of output level. However, variable costs change as output changes. Thus, total cost is a linear function of output Q where fixed costs represent the Y intercept b_0 and the variable cost corresponding to a unit change in output is b_1, or the slope.

As an example of a total cost function, assume that the total cost of producing light bulbs can be expressed as the linear function

$$TC = \$5500 + 0.14Q$$

Observe that fixed costs of $5500 must be paid by the firm at all levels of output including the point of zero production. Each additional light bulb adds $0.14 to total cost, representing the variable cost per light bulb produced. Therefore, the total cost of producing 10,000 light bulbs for this firm is $6900, as shown below.

$$TC = \$5500 + (0.14)(10{,}000)$$
$$= \$5500 + 1400$$
$$= \$6900$$

This function shows a direct relation between the quantity produced and total cost; i.e., as quantity increases, total cost increases, and as quantity decreases, total cost of output decreases. This last part of the statement means that an output reduction of one light bulb will decrease total costs by $0.14.

Example 4.7

"Pure competition," in the jargon of economics, refers to a market structure where the price received for a good by an individual seller is unaffected by the quantity of that good demanded from the individual seller. The demand function expressing this relationship states that price P is a function of quantity demanded Q. However, the function has a zero slope since price is constant regardless of the quantity demanded.

Thus, in pure competition, the demand function for a single seller is

$$P = b_0 + b_1 Q$$

with

$b_1 = 0$

$P = b_0$

where P = price received per unit
  $b_0 = Y$, or price, intercept
  b_1 = slope coefficient = 0
  Q = quantity demanded

Thus, the constant price under conditions of pure competition is equal to the Y intercept of the demand function. This demand situation is typical of few sellers. However, some agricultural markets exhibit this characteristic.

For example, if the price of wheat is $3.50 per bushel, various levels of quantity consumed will have no effect on this price. Consequently, the demand function for a single farmer's wheat is a horizontal line at $3.50 on the price, or Y, axis. This constant function is shown in Figure 4.3.

Example 4.8
By using the previous example of a wheat farmer, a linear function for total revenue can be developed. This demonstrates the use of another typical linear function. Total revenue is equal to the price per unit received for a good multiplied by the number of units, or quantity, consumed. Therefore,

$TR = PQ$

where TR = total revenue
  P = price per unit
  Q = quantity consumed

If the wheat farmer sells 1 bushel, total revenue is $3.50; 2 bushels yield $7 in total revenue, and 3 bushels result in a total revenue of $10.50.

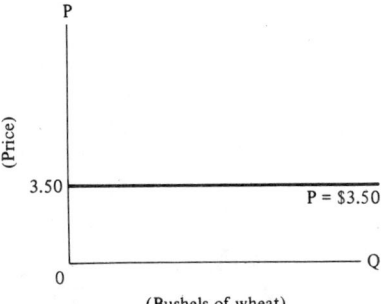

FIGURE 4.3 The constant demand function P = $3.50.

As can be seen, total revenue to the wheat farmer increases at the constant rate of $3.50 per bushel sold. In graphical form, total revenue as a function of the quantity sold is shown in Figure 4.4.

The function $Y = 3.50X$, or in this case TR $= 3.50Q$, is a straight line starting at the origin with a slope of $+3.50$. The Y intercept is equal to 0, indicating that total revenue is 0 when no bushels of wheat are sold. This type of function is referred to as a *linear function through the origin*.

EXERCISES

1. For the following linear functions, X and Y are measured in dollars. Interpret the values for the Y intercept and slope of each function.
   a. $Y = 16 - 1.20X$
   b. $Y = 25$
   c. $Y = 48.75 + 0.45X$
   d. $Y = 6.82X$
   e. $Y = 14.35 - 0.005X$
2. For the function $Y = 62 + 3X$, compute the change in the value of the function Y in response to each of the following:
   a. X increases from 10 to 34.
   b. X decreases from 15 to 6.
   c. The Y intercept increases from 62 to 70 and X remains at $X = 5$.
   d. X decreases from 14 to 12 and, simultaneously, the Y intercept increases from 62 to 75.
   e. X increases from 20 to 30 and, simultaneously, the Y intercept decreases from 62 to 50.
3. For the function $Y = 40 + 3X$, find Y at $X = 7$, $X = 10$, and $X = 15$. Increase the Y intercept to 60 and find Y at the same X values (7, 10, and 15). Relate the two sets of Y values. Based on these results, what general conclusion can be made about the effect of increasing the Y intercept on values of the function at particular points?
4. For each of the following functions, find the value of X when Y is 0. Interpret each such point.

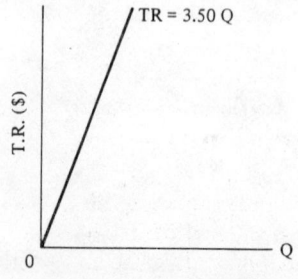

FIGURE 4.4   The total revenue function T.R. $= 3.50$ Q.

a. $Y = 16 - 0.6X$ d. $Y = 2 + 0.8X$
b. $Y = 36 - 4X$ e. $Y = 5.7X$
c. $Y = -12 + 8X$

5. A firm assumes that its new shaving cream will be sold at the constant retail price of $1.89 per unit. Find the function expressing total revenue from the sale of this new shaving cream. Draw this total revenue function in quadrant I of the coordinate axis.

6. A city newspaper has a fixed cost per daily printing of $7000 and a variable cost per copy printed of $0.12. State the total cost function for a daily printing of this newspaper. What is the total cost of a daily printing of 25,000 copies?

7. A metal stamping machine makes an increasing number of production errors per day as the number of days since the last machine maintenance increases. A function relating production errors per day Y to the days since the last machine maintenance X is the following:

$Y = 4 + 0.2X$

   a. How many errors per day will be made if there have been 8 days since the last machine maintenance?
   b. Interpret the value of the Y intercept in the context of this problem.
   c. If the machine makes six errors per day, what is the number of days since the last maintenance?
   d. In which quadrant is the coordinate point with $Y = 2$ for this function? Give a reason for its position.

8. A function relating annual family income X to annual purchases in dollars of new clothing by a family Y is the following. All measurements are in dollars.

$Y = -60 + 0.06X$

   a. Give a *realistic* interpretation of the value of the Y intercept for this function.
   b. Interpret the slope coefficient for this function.
   c. What are expected new clothing purchases for a family with an annual income of $15,000?
   d. What is the X intercept for this function? Interpret this point in the context of this problem.

4.4 The Standard Form of a Linear Equation

The previous discussion and examples have employed linear equations in the form $Y = b_0 + b_1X$. This is called the *slope-intercept form* of linear equation. When Y is the dependent variable and X the independent variable, this equation is referred to as being in *explicit form*.

Linear equations also can be stated in the *implicit form* $Y - b_1X = b_0$

where the dependence-independence relationship between the variables is not obvious from a reading of the function. In addition, this form is used where the question of the dependence or independence of X and Y may not be relevant to the particular problem.

By using the new constants c, d, and e for the coefficients of X and Y and the Y intercept in the implicit form, the *standard form* of a linear equation can be expressed as $cX + dY = e$.

The standard form of a linear equation is

$$cX + dY = e$$

The standard form is adaptable to various types of relationships between the variables and is not associated with a dependence and independence framework as is the explicit form.

It should be observed, however, that the standard form is an alternative to the slope-intercept form and does not express a different linear relationship between the two variables. That is, to express the standard form in slope-intercept form requires the following steps:

1. $cX + dY = e$
2. $dY = e - cX$
3. $Y = \dfrac{e}{d} - \dfrac{c}{d}X$

Consequently, the constant $-c/d$ is the slope coefficient and the constant e/d is the Y intercept.

One use of the standard form is to write constraints in equation form. In other words, when the equation or equations of a problem are used to describe limitations on the variables, the standard form of equation frequently is used.

Constraints on the amount of available resources may be important to the operation of a business. Thus, when using the standard form $cX + dY = e$, e often represents the total available amount of the resource. Other examples of constraints which may be put in equation form are product quality standards, weight restrictions on a product, and government regulations on a product or operation. Example 4.9 will demonstrate use of the standard form of linear equation in stating a constraint on the variables.

Example 4.9

A convenience-food manufacturer must have exactly 20 grams of carbohydrate in a serving of bread included as part of a packaged meal. The variables X and Y represent, respectively, wheat flour and rye flour, two of the primary ingredients used in the bread. It is known that an ounce of wheat flour has 12 grams of carbohydrate and an ounce of rye flour has 8 grams of carbohydrate. The manufacturer wants to determine the various combinations of ingredients which satisfy exactly the 20-gram carbohydrate constraint.

This constraint can be stated in the standard form as

$$12X + 8Y = 20$$

Thus, the 20-gram carbohydrate constraint can be met by various combinations of wheat flour and rye flour containing, respectively, 12 grams per ounce of carbohydrate and 8 grams per ounce of carbohydrate.

The slope-intercept form of this equation is established by solving for Y in terms of X as shown in the following steps. The function is shown in Figure 4.5.

1. $12X + 8Y = 20$
2. $8Y = 20 - 12X$
3. $Y = 2.5 - 1.5X$

The slope-intercept form permits additional description of the relationship between these two variables. The Y intercept is interpreted to mean that the 20-gram constraint can be met with 2.5 ounces of Y and no X. Similarly, as the X intercept is $\frac{5}{3}$, or 1.67, then the constraint also can be met by using $\frac{5}{3}$ ounces of X and no Y.

Combinations of X and Y between the two intercept values which satisfy the constraint are determined with the help of the slope coefficient. Therefore, to meet exactly the 20-gram constraint, each additional ounce of X (wheat flour) used requires a reduction in Y (rye flour) of 1.5 ounces. For example, if X usage is increased from 0 to 1 ounce, usage of Y must be decreased from 2.5 to 1 ounce.

This constraint may be one of many constraints on the production of the packaged meal. The standard form has provided a means of stating this constraint in a form consistent with the objective of the problem.

Further discussion of constraints will be included in later sections of the book (particularly Chapter 7 on linear programming). The standard form has been introduced at this point to stress both its relationship to the slope-intercept form and its use in applied problems.

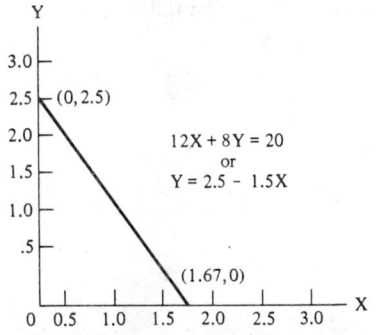

FIGURE 4.5 A graph of the equation $12X + 8Y = 20$

4.5 Determining the Equation of a Line

In many situations, it is desirable to find the value of the constants b_0 and b_1 for the slope-intercept form, $Y = b_0 + b_1X$. Determination of these values allows a general specification of the function as the slope and intercept are the same for all (X, Y) coordinate points. Finding the equation for the line allows one to extend the line for hypothesized values of the variables, assess the rate of change between the variables, and interpret the Y intercept as applied to this relation.

Before using available data to establish a linear function, one must have a basis for assuming the presence of linearity between the variables. In other words, *why* should this particular mathematical model be used to explain a situation? Often, confirmation of a linear function between two variables is based on a "scatter diagram" of the known values. Table 4.1 and Figure 4.6 show the data and corresponding scatter diagram for a group of four observations.

Visual inspection of the scatter diagram implies the presence of a positively sloped linear relation between the variables. The data confirm this as between each two points shown in Table 4.1, an increase of 4 in X is associated with an increase in Y of 8. Thus, the function apparently is linear. Other methods for confirming linearity include (1) reference to accepted theory, (2) previous research, and (3) statistical analysis.

If prior analysis points to the existence of a linear relation, two techniques frequently used to establish the specific function are the "two-point" and "point-slope" methods. Each provides a means of finding the value of the slope and Y intercept for a particular function. The available data for a relation often dictate which method is used in a situation. These procedures are discussed below.

The Two-Point Method

In some instances, two (X, Y) coordinate points are known and the relation between the variables is assumed to be linear. If two points are known, for example (X_1, Y_1) and (X_2, Y_2), the slope of a line segment between them can be computed by dividing the change in Y by the change in X, or

TABLE 4.1 Four Observations on the Variables X and Y

X	Y
10	12
14	20
18	28
22	36

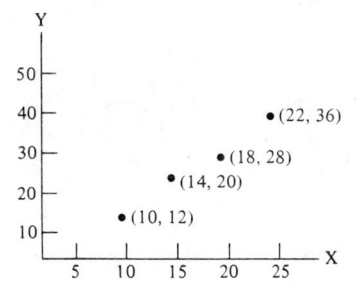

```
Y
50 ─
40 ─           • (22, 36)
30 ─       • (18, 28)
         • (14, 20)
20 ─
10 ─  • (10, 12)
    └──┼───┼───┼───┼──── X
       5  10  15  20  25
```
FIGURE 4.6 The scatter diagram of the data in Table 4.1.

Slope of line $= b_1 = \dfrac{Y_1 - Y_2}{X_1 - X_2}$

As the slope of a linear function is constant, the value of b_1 represents the slope between *any* two (X, Y) coordinate points on the linear function.

By using any other coordinate point (X_0, Y_0) and establishing the slope ratio between it and one of the two known points—e.g., (X_1, Y_1)—a second expression for the slope ratio is formed:

Slope of line $= b_1 = \dfrac{Y_0 - Y_1}{X_0 - X_1}$

As the slope is the same between any two points of a linear function, an expression equating the two slope ratios above can be formed:

Slope of line $= \dfrac{Y_0 - Y_1}{X_0 - X_1} = \dfrac{Y_1 - Y_2}{X_1 - X_2}$

This represents the general expression for the two-point method of finding the equation of a linear function. Substituting known values for X_1, X_2, Y_1, and Y_2, and solving for Y_0 in terms of X_0, yields values for b_0 and b_1 and, therefore, the equation for the line. Two examples will demonstrate the two-point method.

Example 4.10

Based on recently compiled data, Air Force analysts know that there is a linear relation between the monthly salary paid new recruits and the number of Air Force enlistments in a month. However, the analysts have data for only two current months; one with salaries of $600 and enlistments of 1000 and another month with a salary level of $725 and enlistments of 1200. The analysts want to use these two points to develop a linear function relating salary level (X, the independent variable) to enlistments (Y, the dependent variable).

Based on these two points, the slope of the linear function can be computed as follows,

$$b_1 = \frac{Y_1 - Y_2}{X_1 - X_2} = \frac{1200 - 1000}{725 - 600} = \frac{200}{125} = 1.6$$

This positive slope coefficient means that, over the range of this linear function, a $1 increase (decrease) in monthly salary leads to an increase (decrease) of 1.6 enlistments. This slope is the same between any two points of the function.

The function is found by establishing a ratio of Y coordinates to X coordinates using an unspecified point of the function and either of the points (X_1, Y_1) or (X_2, Y_2). This ratio then is set equal to the slope. Using (X_2, Y_2) or (600, 1000) as the known point, the ratio is

$$\frac{Y_0 - Y_2}{X_0 - X_2} = \frac{Y_0 - 1000}{X_0 - 600} = 1.6$$

The following algebraic steps yield the expression for the linear function.

1. $\dfrac{Y_0 - 1000}{X_0 - 600} = 1.6$
2. $Y_0 - 1000 = 1.6(X_0 - 600)$
3. $Y_0 - 1000 = 1.6 X_0 - 960$
4. $Y_0 \quad\quad\;\; = 40 + 1.6 X_0$

This function expresses the direct linear relation between monthly salary and monthly enlistments in the Air Force. It has a Y intercept of 40 and a constant positive slope of 1.6.

Example 4.11

A school district wants to determine the linear relationship between school population (X, the independent variable) and the per student cost of providing lunch at the school (Y, the dependent variable).

Lunch costs per student are known for only two schools in the district. In one school, with 900 students, lunch cost is $1.75 per student, and for a second school, with 1300 students, per student lunch cost is $1.25.

The function is determined by setting up the following equation between two slope ratios:

1. $\dfrac{Y_0 - Y_1}{X_0 - X_1} = \dfrac{Y_1 - Y_2}{X_1 - X_2}$

As $Y_1 = \$1.75$, $Y_2 = \$1.25$, $X_1 = 900$, and $X_2 = 1300$, the slope of the function is found as follows:

2. $\dfrac{Y_0 - 1.75}{X_0 - 900} = \dfrac{1.75 - 1.25}{900 - 1300} = \dfrac{0.50}{-400} = -0.00125$

With knowledge of the slope coefficient, the function relating number of students to per student cost of lunch can be computed as shown in steps 3 to 6:

3. $\dfrac{Y_0 - 1.75}{X_0 - 900} = -0.00125$
4. $Y_0 - 1.75 = -0.00125(X_0 - 900)$
5. $Y_0 - 1.75 = 1.125 - 0.00125 X_0$
6. $Y_0 = 2.875 - 0.00125 X_0$

The last expression (step 6) states the relation between the per student cost of providing lunch and the population of the school. It indicates that a graph of the function originates at the point (0, 2.875) and extends downward to the right with a slope of -0.00125. The value of the slope means that for each additional student in a school, the per student cost of providing lunch is decreased by $0.00125, or a little more than $\tfrac{1}{10}$ of 1 cent. Also, for each reduction in school population of one student, per student lunch costs increase by $0.00125.

Observe that both the slope and the intercept of a linear function are stated in the measurement scale of the dependent variable. Thus, in step 6 above, 0.00125 is a dollar measurement as is 2.875, the Y intercept.

The Point-Slope Method

Although two points of a relation frequently are known, at times the available data include a single (X, Y) coordinate point and a constant rate of change between the variables. Often, in these cases, the slope coefficient is based on theory or some historical knowledge of the relationship. This situation enables one to use the "point-slope" method of finding the equation for the line.

To use the point-slope method, the known slope coefficient is set equal to a ratio of the differences between an unspecified Y point Y_0 and the established Y point Y_1 on the one hand and an unspecified X point X_0 and the known X point X_1 on the other. This can be expressed as

$$\dfrac{Y_0 - Y_1}{X_0 - X_1} = b_1$$

where b_1 is the slope coefficient. Solving for Y_0 in terms of X_0 yields the equation for the linear function. An example will demonstrate computation of a linear function by the point-slope method.

Example 4.12
A steel-products manufacturer currently is producing 3000 pounds of output per month and has a monthly heating-oil bill of $400 at one small factory. Based on the experience of several years, the firm knows that output poundage affects oil bills in a constant proportion such that each increase (decrease) in production of 1 pound per month increases (decreases) the firm's oil bill by $0.04 per month. What is the linear function relating monthly production to monthly heating-oil expenses?

Computation of the function proceeds according to the following steps using X_0 and Y_0 to denote the coordinates of any point.

1. $\dfrac{Y_0 - 400}{X_0 - 3000} = 0.04$
2. $Y_0 - 400 = 0.04(X_0 - 3000)$
3. $Y_0 - 400 = 0.04 X_0 - 120$
4. $Y_0 = 280 + 0.04 X_0$

The coefficients b_0 and b_1 are measured in dollars and indicate that when no output is produced, oil costs at the factory (e.g., the cost of maintaining a heated facility) are $280 per month. Oil costs rise $0.04 above $280 for each additional pound of output. Thus, with this equation, the monthly heating-oil bill corresponding to any monthly output level can be established.

Examples 4.10, 4.11, and 4.12 have shown that the two-point and point-slope methods provide a means to establish functional relations given a limited amount of information. Each method uses the principle that a linear function has a constant slope throughout its range, reflecting the change in the dependent variable in response to a given change in the independent variable. The following problems will allow further practice with the techniques presented in this section.

EXERCISES

1. For each set of three coordinate points below, determine whether or not the function is linear between the three points.
   a. (3, 5), (1, 3), (−1, 1)   c. (8, 12), (6, 9), (4, 6)
   b. (−2, 4), (0, 0), (2, 4)   d. (6, 10), (8, 14), (10, 16)
2. For each pair of (X, Y) coordinate points, find the linear function $Y = b_0 + b_1 X$.
   a. (0, 0), (6, 3)   d. (4, −2), (0, 6)
   b. (3, 5), (10, 2)   e. (2, 2), (10, 12)
   c. (−6, −4), (10, 8)   f. (12, 0), (6, 9)
3. For each (X, Y) coordinate point and corresponding slope coefficient b_1, find the linear function $Y = b_0 + b_1 X$.
   a. (2, 6), $b_1 = 0.4$ d. (−4, −2), $b_1 = 6.2$
   b. (5, 8), $b_1 = -1.6$ e. (1, 8), $b_1 = -2.8$
   c. (5, 4), $b_1 = 0$ f. (2, 8), $b_1 = 4.8$
4. A firm knows the per unit cost of output for a particular product at two of its manufacturing facilities. Daily output at factory I is 3500 units and the cost per unit is $228. At factory II, daily output is 5400 units and the cost per unit is $190. A linear function is assumed to exist between output and cost per unit of output. Determine this function.
5. An insurance company assumes that the number of policies written per month by its new employees is a linear function of the number of months that an individual has been employed. Based on the company's past

records, it is believed that for each additional month of employment, a new employee writes, on the average, 3.6 new policies. One group of employees has been employed for 3 months, and the group is writing 14 new policies per person a month. Based on these data, establish the linear function between months of employment and number of new policies written per month.

6. A frozen-food-products manufacturer knows that sales of frozen food are higher in census tracts with higher average family incomes. The relation between income and sales is assumed to be linear.

    In a test market city, family income and sales of frozen foods are known for only two census tracts. In tract I, average family income is $16,000 and frozen-food sales per year are $6500. In census tract II, average family income is $22,000 and frozen-food sales are $9200 per year. Find the linear function relating the average family income of a census tract to annual frozen-food sales in that tract.

7. Recent nationwide findings have shown a negative relationship between parents' years of education and the number of children in a family. Preliminary estimates are that this relationship can be expressed as a linear function with number of children per family decreasing 0.06 children for each additional year of combined education of the parents.

    Accurate data are available only for those with 24 years of combined education (e.g., wife and husband both having 12 years of education). This group has an average number of children per family of 2.48. Based on these data, find the linear function relating years of parental education to number of children in a family. Interpret the Y intercept for this function.

8. The total cost of producing aspirin is assumed to be a positive linear function of the number of bottles produced. The variable cost of producing a 100-tablet bottle of aspirin is $0.60. The total cost of producing 5000 bottles of this size is $4500.

    Find the linear total cost function for the production of aspirin bottles of this size. What is the fixed cost of this production process? What is the total cost of producing 10,000 bottles of this size?

4.6 Multivariate Functions: An Interpretation

Multivariate functions with degrees higher than one are nonlinear in the specified variables. Since the next three chapters stress linear functions, while functions of higher degree are discussed in later chapters, a function with several independent variables, all of degree one, is described briefly in Example 4.13.

Example 4.13: The Demand for Household Furniture

In order to better understand the forces affecting nationwide furniture sales, industry analysts have formulated the following function having four independent variables:

$$Y = b_0 + b_1X_1 + b_2X_2 + b_3X_3 + b_4X_4$$

where Y = annual furniture sales in millions of dollars
b_0 = Y intercept
X_1 = price of furniture
X_2 = personal income
X_3 = sales of new homes
X_4 = number of marriages in the past year
b_1, b_2, b_3, b_4 = coefficients for each corresponding independent variable

This function is of degree 1 and therefore is a linear polynomial in four independent variables.

In the model, the Y intercept b_0 represents furniture sales not explained by the four variables and is equal to the value of Y when $X_1 = X_2 = X_3 = X_4 = 0$. The coefficient for each independent variable measures the change in furniture sales given a one-unit change in that independent variable, *holding all other independent variables constant* at some given value for each. The emphasized part of this sentence deserves elaboration.

Assume that the coefficient on the variable for new home sales, b_3, is $+0.2$. This means that if new home sales increase by 1 million it can be expected that furniture sales will increase by $(0.2)(1,000,000) = \$200,000$ (or $0.2 million), if all of the other independent variables are held constant. This means, for example, that the number of marriages in the past year is to be held constant at some value such as 1.8 million as sales of new homes change.

A similar interpretation can be given to the value of each coefficient for an independent variable. Holding all other independent variables constant permits isolation of the effect on the dependent variable of the single independent variable. Each coefficient may have a positive, negative, or zero value indicating a positive relationship, a negative relationship, or the absence of a relationship, respectively, with the dependent variable. This interpretation of the values of coefficients can be applied with some small difference to functions of any degree having more than one independent variable.

4.7 Chapter Summary

This chapter has emphasized the interpretation and computation of linear functions. Linear functions with two variables and those with more than two variables have been discussed.

Linear functions with two variables X and Y can be expressed in the slope-intercept form,

$$Y = b_0 + b_1X$$

If Y is the dependent variable and X is the independent variable, this form is referred to as the explicit form of the linear equation. Alternatively, a linear function in two variables can be expressed in standard form as

$$cX + dY = e$$

The independent variable–dependent variable relation between X and Y is not assumed when using the standard form. However, slope and Y intercept values have similar meaning in both explicit and standard forms.

The slope and Y intercept are two important measurements for a linear function. The slope, which measures the change in the Y variable in response to a one-unit change in the X variable, is constant between any two points of a linear function. The Y intercept measures the value of Y at a value of 0 for X.

Slope and Y intercept values, in addition to being interpretative measurements, can be used to determine the linear function relating two variables. The two-point method provides a means to specify a function knowing only two (X, Y) coordinate points. The point-slope method is a technique for finding a linear function when one (X, Y) coordinate point and the value of the constant slope are known. Both methods are dependent on the existence of a linear relation between the variables under consideration.

Knowledge of the specific linear relation between variables permits additional analyses such as determination of the value of one variable based on a hypothesized value for the other, interpretation of the slope and Y intercept, and modification of the function to allow for only positive values for the domain and the range.

The chapter also included a short discussion of polynomial functions of degree 1 which have more than one independent variable. Presented were an example and interpretation of the slope and the coefficient values for the independent variables.

Linear functions frequently are used in mathematical analysis both to quantify an existing relation and to yield an easily understood and manipulated approximation of reality for any relation.

Because of their primary position in mathematical analysis, linear functions are the focus of Chapter 5 (Systems of Linear Equations and Inequalities), Chapter 6 (Matrix Algebra), and Chapter 7 (Linear Programming). Thus, the importance of Chapter 4 to mathematical analysis and, in particular, to an understanding of this book must be emphasized.

4.8 Problem Set

Review Questions

1. Distinguish between a positively sloped and a negatively sloped linear relation for a function with one independent variable.

2. What is measured by the slope coefficient in a linear function with one independent variable?
3. What interpretation should be given to a negative Y intercept for a linear function relating two variables, such as prices and quantities, which do not have practical meaning if negative?
4. What is the slope of a line extending horizontally from the Y axis in quadrant I? Why?
5. For a linear total cost function with fixed and variable costs, why is fixed cost represented by the value of the Y intercept?
6. Distinguish between the explicit and standard forms of linear equation.
7. How is a scatter diagram used in the development of a linear function relating two variables?
8. What information is required before computing a linear function between two variables by means of the point-slope method?
9. For the function

$$Y = 0.6X$$

what is the Y intercept?
10. Why is it possible to develop a linear function between two variables based on knowledge of only two (X, Y) coordinate points?
11. Relate constraints on a linear relation to the constant term in the standard form of linear equation. Give an example.
12. What are the coordinates of the X intercept in the function

$$Y = 20 - 0.3X?$$

Using the coefficients b_0 and b_1 for the Y intercept and slope, respectively, state a general formula for computing the X coordinate of the X intercept.
13. State a numerical example of a linear function through the origin. Give a practical example of such a function.
14. State the correct interpretation of the value of the coefficient for any one independent variable in an equation of degree 1 with more than one independent variable.
15. What is represented by the value of the Y intercept in a function with four independent variables and one dependent variable?

Review Problems

1. For the function

$$Y = 350 - 0.05X$$

Find:
a. Y for $X = 150$
b. Y for $X = 1000$
c. Y for $X = -46$
d. Y for $X = 0$
e. X for $Y = 0$
f. X for $Y = -3$
g. X for $Y = 100$
h. X for $Y = 200$

2. For the function

$$Y = 5.8 + 0.1X$$

Find:
a. The change in Y when X increases from 20 to 30.
b. The change in Y when X decreases from 55 to 40.
c. The change in X when Y increases from 10 to 12.
d. The change in X when Y decreases from 16 to 9.
e. The change in Y when $X = 25$ and the Y intercept increases from 5.8 to 8.2.
f. The change in Y when $X = 48$ and the Y intercept decreases from 5.8 to 1.16.
3. For each coordinate point and slope below, find the Y intercept for the linear function.
 a. $(4, 8)$, $b_1 = 2.0$ d. $(6, 0)$, $b_1 = -1.5$
 b. $(-2, -4)$, $b_1 = 8.4$ e. $(-2, 7)$, $b_1 = -2.5$
 c. $(5, 4)$, $b_1 = -3.0$
4. Find the Y intercept for each function with slope b_1 and coordinate point as indicated below. Also, find the X intercept for each function.
 a. $b_1 = 3.0$, $(6, 2)$ d. $b_1 = -0.6$, $(8, 0)$
 b. $b_1 = -2.5$, $(4, 1)$ e. $b_1 = 7.0$, $(1, 5)$
 c. $b_1 = 0.1$, $(5, 5)$
5. For each standard form of linear equation below, determine the slope-intercept form $Y = b_0 + b_1 X$.
 a. $3X + 4Y = 12$ c. $0.5X + 0.5Y = 20$
 b. $2X - Y = 8$ d. $7X + 0.2Y = 30$
6. For each pair of coordinate points, find the linear function $Y = b_0 + b_1 X$.
 a. $(5, 5)$, $(8, 6)$ d. $(-1, -4)$, $(7, 7)$
 b. $(2, 8)$, $(12, 4)$ e. $(0, 0)$, $(8, 2)$
 c. $(10, 14)$, $(4, 2)$ f. $(0, 3)$, $(8, 3)$
7. For each slope b_1 and coordinate point, find the linear function $Y = b_0 + b_1 X$.
 a. $b_1 = -0.5$, $(4, 3)$ d. $b_1 = -2.0$, $(-4, 16)$
 b. $b_1 = 0$, $(4, 7)$ e. $b_1 = 4.0$, $(0, 0)$
 c. $b_1 = 3.2$, $(8, 1)$ f. $b_1 = -2.2$, $(0, 20)$
8. Values for the variables X and Y used in a particular linear function do not have practical meaning if negative. Two known points on the function are $(4, 15)$ and $(10, 12)$. Find the maximum possible values for X and Y given this restriction to nonnegative values.
9. Products X and Y are made of both plastic and glass. Product X uses 6 pounds of glass and 2.5 pounds of plastic per production unit. Product Y uses 5 pounds of glass and 3.5 pounds of plastic per unit.
    For a given week, 2500 pounds of plastic and 4600 pounds of glass are available to the firm. Write the equations in standard form expressing the production possibilities which will utilize all available amounts of each ingredient exactly.
10. For the next quarter, a firm assumes that it can produce as many steel fasteners as desired at a unit variable cost of $1.50. Fixed costs of fastener production are $450.
    a. Write the total cost function for fasteners.
    b. Graph the total cost function.
11. A firm has no fixed cost associated with the use of a rented computer system. System costs are $40 per minute of time used.
    a. Write the total cost function for this computer system.
    b. What is the Y intercept for this function?

c. If a firm uses 30 minutes of computer time per week, is the above rental fee better or not as good as a fee including a weekly charge of $400 plus $20 per minute? Why?

12. For the total cost function

$$TC = F + VQ$$

where $F = \$15,000$ and $V = \$2.50$ per unit, find
   a. The total cost of an output of 3000 units.
   b. The effect on the total cost of 10,000 units of an increase in the variable cost per unit from $2.50 to $3.00.
   c. The output corresponding to a total cost of $60,000 using the original total cost function.
   d. The effect on the total cost of 2200 units of an increase in fixed costs from $15,000 to $18,000 and a decrease in variable costs per unit from $2.50 to $2.25.

13. A regional planning commission wants to establish a linear relation between the monthly unemployment rate in a county and monthly sales tax revenues in that county. Data for 1 month in two different counties are to be used to derive this linear function.

   In county A, for a recent month the unemployment rate was 7.6 percent and monthly sales tax revenues were 6.4 million dollars. In county B, for the same month, the unemployment rate was 8.4 percent and sales tax revenues were $5.8 million. Based on these data, find the linear function relating sales tax revenues Y to the monthly unemployment rate X. Interpret the slope coefficient and Y intercept for this function.

14. Industry analysts have developed the following function relating monthly new car sales in a city Y to the monthly consumer loan interest rate in the city X_1 and average family income in the city for the current year X_2. The function is as follows:

$$Y = 850 - 30X_1 + 0.05(X_2 - 15,000)$$

where Y = number of new cars sold during the month
   X_1 = current month's consumer loan interest rate in percent
   (e.g., 13 percent is $X_1 = 13$)
   X_2 = average family income in the city for the current year in dollars

   a. Interpret the coefficient for X_1 in this function.
   b. Interpret the term $0.05(X_2 - 15,000)$ in the context of the problem.
   c. If the consumer loan interest rate is 10.8 percent and family income is $17,200, what is the expected number of new car sales for the month?
   d. If the consumer loan interest rate increases from 9 percent to 12.4 percent, what will be the effect on new car sales if annual family income does not change from a level of $19,000?

15. Recent medical data have established that there is a linear relation between the age of first-time heart attack victims who are over 60 years of age and the fatality rate for the first heart attack. Research has confirmed that the fatality rate per 100 heart attack victims increases by 2.8 people for each 1-year increase over 60 in the victim's age.

   Data exist only for first-time heart attack victims at age 65 ($X = 5$). For this group, the fatality rate per 100 victims is 20.4. Based on these data, find the linear function relating age over 60 to the fatality rate per 100 victims. Find the expected fatality rate for first-time victims at age 72 ($X = 12$).

16. The realtors' association in an urban area has determined that a linear function can be used to relate monthly residential housing sales (the dependent variable) and the average monthly mortgage interest rate (the independent variable). The function has the form

$$Y = 4500 - 90X$$

where Y = number of houses sold
X = mortgage interest rate as a percent (e.g., $X = 12$ means 12 percent)

   a. Interpret the Y intercept and slope coefficient for this function.
   b. If the monthly mortgage interest rate is 14 percent, what are expected housing sales for the month?
   c. If the mortgage interest rate declines from 15 percent to 12.5 percent, what is the expected change in housing sales?

5
Systems of Linear Equations and Inequalities

5.1 Introduction

The discussion in Chapter 4 was limited to the analysis of a single linear equation. In explicit form, this type of equation has the form $Y = b_0 + b_1 X$, where b_1 is the slope coefficient and b_0 is the Y intercept. If equations are considered conditions or constraints on a set of variables, Chapter 4 analyzed only those situations where one constraint is imposed on the variables.

Frequently, a mathematical model may involve more than one constraint on a set of variables. If each constraint is expressed as a linear equation, the constraints form a *system* of linear equations. Examples of sets of constraints are limitations on the amount of resources used in a production process, the requirements of a delivery schedule, or a group of product-quality standards. Thus, the analysis of systems of linear equations is extended easily to models associated with coping with scarcity and choice in the business and economic environment.

This chapter discusses the interpretation and analysis of systems of linear equations. Included in the presentation are conceptual explanations of types of systems of equations, solution methods for each, and several business applications.

A description of linear inequalities also is included in the chapter. These are expressions used to state a condition, or conditions, where quantities in the expression are not equal. Within this topic, the chapter includes definitions of different types of inequalities, descriptions of mathematical operations on single inequalities, and techniques for solving systems of inequalities.

In all, this chapter provides the conceptual framework and techniques for analyzing linear constraints as a group. This material will be developed further in the next two chapters on matrix algebra and linear programming. These are two mathematical methods often applied to the analysis of systems of linear equations and inequalities. These three chapters and Chapter 4 provide an introduction to linear mathematics and its application to business.

5.2 Systems and Solutions

The first part of this chapter examines systems of linear equations. Linear inequalities are discussed beginning in Section 5.8.

The solution to a system of linear equations is a set of values which simultaneously satisfy all the equations (or conditions) of the system. For any system of linear equations, three possibilities exist: There may be no solutions, a single (or *unique*) solution, or an unlimited number of solutions.

These three possibilities can be described most easily by considering a system of two equations and two variables. The solution of a system of two linear equations in two variables is represented graphically by the point of intersection of the two lines (equations). This is shown in Figure 5.1(a).

The no-solution case for a system of two equations and two variables is represented by two lines which are parallel (i.e., they do not intersect). This is shown in Figure 5.1(b). Figure 5.1(c) describes a situation in which there are an unlimited number of solutions for a system of equations. For this situation, the lines are the same. Unlimited solutions apply when the

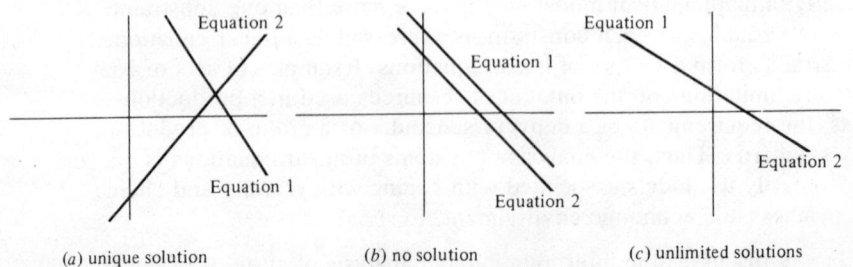

FIGURE 5.1   Three solution possibilities for a system of two equations and two variables.

terms of one equation are a constant multiple of the terms of the other equation.

The three descriptions of Figure 5.1 apply to systems of equations with two variables regardless of the number of equations. For three variables, graphical description of the three solution possibilities requires the use of planes. And, for a system of equations with more than three variables, graphical description cannot be employed.

Thus, for any system of linear equations, three solution possibilities exist:

1. A system of linear equations having a unique solution is a *consistent* system of equations.
2. A system of linear equations not having a solution is an *inconsistent* system of equations.
3. A system of linear equations having an unlimited number of solutions is a *dependent* system of equations, as any solution of one equation also is a solution of the others.

These possible solutions will be referred to again as the chapter continues.

The concept of constraints as applied to equations provides an additional classification method for systems of linear equations. Systems which have an equal number of equations and unknowns (variables) are referred to as *exactly constrained systems*. For example, if a system of linear equations has two equations and two unknowns, the system is said to be exactly constrained. An *overconstrained system* has a number of equations which exceeds the number of variables. And *underconstrained systems* of equations have more variables than equations. Equations in all three classification groups can be stated in explicit or standard form (see Chapter 4).

Because systems of equations may have any number of equations and variables, there exists an abbreviated way for describing the number of equations and variables in a system. A system with three equations and three variables is referred to as being 3×3 (read "three by three"), and a system with four equations and two variables is called a 4×2 system of equations (read "four by two"). Thus, the abbreviation condenses the expression "number of equations" by "number of variables."

The next four sections (5.3 through 5.6) examine different types of exactly constrained systems of equations and the solution and interpretation of each. Sections 5.3 and 5.4 introduce two examples of systems of equations having two equations and two unknowns, linear demand-and-supply analysis and break-even analysis. Section 5.5 presents the elimination method which can be used to solve exactly constrained systems with any number of equations and variables. Exactly constrained systems which do not have a single (or unique) solution are discussed in Section 5.6. Overconstrained and underconstrained systems of equations are introduced in Section 5.7.

In Chapter 6, the Gauss-Jordan method of elimination is introduced. This method can be used to determine the solution for any system of equations, whether or not the number of equations and number of variables are equal. The Gauss-Jordan elimination procedure is understood most easily within the study of matrix algebra; thus, it is deferred until the next chapter.

5.3 Linear Demand-and-Supply Analysis

At times, both the demand and supply functions for a product are linear with one independent variable. In these instances, the demand function can be stated

$$P_D = f(Q_D)$$

where Q_D is of degree 1. In this equation, P_D represents price (often in dollars) and Q_D represents the quantity of a good demanded by consumers. A linear supply function with one independent variable can be expressed similarly as

$$P_S = f(Q_S)$$

where Q_S is of degree 1. Here, P_S represents price and Q_S indicates the quantity of a good supplied by producers.

Often, the objective of a market analysis is to find the "equilibrium" price and quantity, or that price-quantity combination representing equality between the demand function and the supply function. Thus, if the unknown price and quantity are designated P_E and Q_E, respectively, the demand and supply functions form a system with two equations and two unknowns. Figure 5.2 is a graphical description of equilibrium price and quantity (P_E and Q_E). As can be seen, the intersection of the demand and supply curves indicates equilibrium price and quantity.

An example will demonstrate determination of equilibrium price and

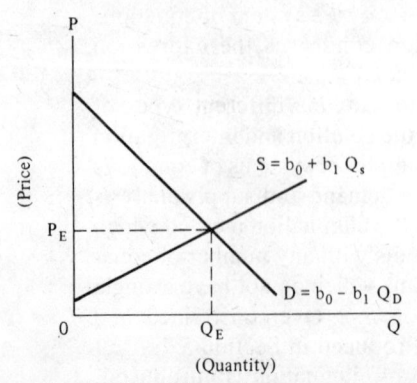

FIGURE 5.2 Linear demand-and-supply curves and their intersection—representing equilibrium price and quantity.

quantity for linear demand and supply functions. The solution process is concerned with finding values for two unknowns in a system of two equations.

Example 5.1

The demand for automobile tires can be expressed as a linear function where price P_D is dependent on the quantity consumed in the following way:

$$P_D = 132 - 0.005Q_D$$

In this demand function, P_D is measured in dollars and Q_D designates the number of tires desired by consumers.

Similarly, a linear function also describes the supply relationship between price P_S and the quantity supplied Q_S as

$$P_S = 38 + 0.003Q_S$$

In this function also, P_S is measured in dollars and Q_S represents the number of tires offered for sale.

The objective of a market equilibrium analysis is to determine the price and quantity coordinates representing the intersection of the demand and supply functions (designated P_E and Q_E). The solution is obtained by setting the demand and supply functions equal to each other and solving for Q_E as follows:

$$P_D = P_S$$
$$132 - 0.005Q_D = 38 + 0.003Q_S$$
$$Q_D = Q_S = Q_E$$
$$0.008Q_E = 94$$
$$Q_E = 11,750$$

Thus, at the quantity of 11,750 tires, demand will equal supply. The equilibrium price P_E corresponding to Q_E is found by substituting $Q_E = 11,750$ into *either* the demand function *or* the supply function. Both substitutions will be shown below.

$$P_D = 132 - 0.005(11,750)$$
$$P_D = 132 - 58.75$$
$$P_D = 73.25 = P_E$$

and

$$P_S = 38 + 0.003(11,750)$$
$$P_S = 38 + 35.25$$
$$P_S = 73.25 = P_E$$

Therefore, the intersection of demand and supply functions is the point $Q_E = 11{,}750$ and $P_E = \$73.25$. In equilibrium, 11,750 tires will be sold at a price of \$73.25 per tire. This is the unique solution to the system of two equations and two unknowns.

5.4 Break-Even Analysis

A second business application of a system of two linear equations and two unknowns is break-even analysis. Break-even analysis is concerned with determining the quantity of sales corresponding to the equality between total revenue and total cost. Below this sales level, cost exceeds revenue and above it, revenue exceeds cost.

To apply the break-even technique described here, it is assumed that both the total revenue function and the total cost function are linear with positive slopes. The assumption of linearity may not be accurate at all sales levels. However, over a selected sales range, perhaps the range relevant to a short period of time, the use of linear total cost and total revenue functions often may be realistic.

Linear total cost and total revenue functions were presented in Chapter 4. At that point, it was shown that a linear total cost function has the form

$$TC = F + VQ$$

where TC = total cost
 F = fixed cost
 V = variable cost per unit of output
 Q = quantity of output

Linear total revenue functions are represented by straight lines through the origin (0, 0) and have the following form:

$$TR = PQ$$

where TR = total revenue
 P = price per unit
 Q = quantity of sales

For a linear total revenue function it is assumed that price P is a constant.

Thus, two limitations are associated with the use of linear total cost and total revenue functions. First, linearity in the total revenue function implies that price does not change as the quantity demanded by consumers changes. Secondly, a linear total cost function is associated with a constant variable cost per unit of output. A constant price and a constant per unit variable cost over a *relatively small* quantity range are two assumptions which are not unrealistic.

Linear break-even analysis requires setting the total revenue and total cost functions equal to each other and solving for the quantity coordinate of the intersection point Q_E. This intersection is shown in Figure 5.3. This point Q_E can be derived in the following way:

Total cost = total revenue

$$TC = TR$$
$$F + VQ = PQ$$
$$F = PQ - VQ$$
$$F = Q(P - V)$$
$$Q_E = Q = \frac{F}{P - V}$$

It is shown that the break-even quantity is found by dividing fixed costs F by the difference between market price P and per unit variable cost of output V. The dollar figure corresponding to the quantity Q_E can be found by substituting Q_E into either the total revenue or total cost function. This step yields the two solution values for this system of linear equations.

One consequence of this formula is that, for a given fixed cost, as the difference between P and V increases, break-even quantity will occur at a relatively lower quantity point. A low break-even quantity, in most cases, is a favorable situation for a firm.

The difference between P (price per unit) and V (per unit variable cost) is often referred to as *profit contribution* or *profit margin*. This difference must be applied first to covering fixed costs and, when fixed costs are met, the remainder will contribute to profit.

The following example demonstrates linear break-even analysis.

Example 5.2

A consumer products firm wants to determine the break-even quantity for a new dishwashing detergent to be marketed in the next quarter. It is assumed that both the total revenue and total cost functions are linear over the relevant sales quantity range.

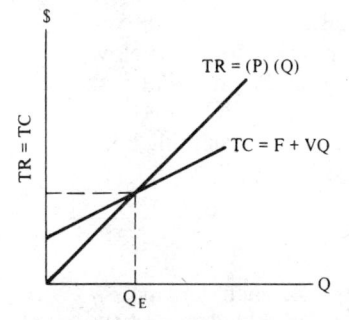

FIGURE 5.3 Linear total revenue and total cost curves and their intersection—representing the break-even quantity of sales.

The firm plans to sell the standard family-size box for $2.40. Production estimates have shown that the variable cost of producing one unit of the product is $2.16. Fixed costs of production are $3600.

What is the break-even volume of sales?

The total revenue function TR is linear and of the form

$$TR = (P)(Q) = 2.40Q$$

The total cost function TC is

$$TC = F + VQ = 3600 + 2.16Q$$

Break-even quantity Q_E is established by equating total revenue and total cost functions and solving for Q_E. Thus,

$$TR = TC$$
$$2.40Q = 3600 + 2.16Q$$
$$2.40Q - 2.16Q = 3600$$
$$Q_E = \frac{3600}{2.40 - 2.16} = \frac{3600}{0.24}$$
$$Q_E = 15{,}000$$

All intermediate steps are shown to demonstrate the relation between fixed cost, product price, and variable cost per unit of output. Revenue and cost corresponding to this quantity can be found by substituting Q_E into either the total revenue or the total cost function as the dollar figures are equal. This is computed below using the total revenue function.

Total cost = total revenue = (price)(quantity)

$$TC = TR = 2.40 Q_E$$
$$TC = TR = (2.40)(15{,}000)$$
$$TC = TR = \$36{,}000$$

This analysis has determined that the firm will earn a profit after the sale of the first 15,000 boxes. Total revenue and total cost at 15,000 boxes will each be equal to $36,000 and losses will be incurred at quantities below 15,000 boxes. These results apply unless changes occur in the price and cost data.

The following exercises will give additional practice in computing both demand and supply equilibrium and break-even points.

EXERCISES

1. Interpret the Y intercept (price intercept) and slope for each demand P_D and supply P_S function below. P_D and P_S are measured in dollars and Q_D and Q_S are physical quantities measured in units.

a. $P_D = 14.25 - 0.53Q_D$ c. $P_S = 19 + 0.22Q_S$
b. $P_D = 289 - 0.03Q_D$ d. $P_S = 687 + 1.23Q_S$
2. Find equilibrium price and quantity for each demand function P_D and supply P_S function below.
   a. $P_D = 24 - 0.16Q_D$; $P_S = 4 + 0.48Q_S$
   b. $P_D = 260 - 2Q_D$; $P_S = 82 + 1.2Q_S$
   c. $P_D = 42$; $P_S = 17 + 0.04Q_S$
3. a. If the demand for a brand of shoes is linear and of the form $P_D = 84 - 0.14Q_D$ and the linear supply function has the form $P_S = 18 + 0.02Q_S$, find the equilibrium price and quantity for the firm's shoes. P_D and P_S are measured in dollars and Q_D and Q_S designate number of pairs of shoes.
   b. If the demand function shifts to $P_D = 96 - 0.14Q_D$ find the new equilibrium price and quantity. Describe the change in demand by comparing the two demand functions.
4. The demand for a candy bar is expressed by the function $P_D = 0.70 - 0.003Q_D$ and the supply function is $P_S = 0.18 + 0.001Q_S$. P_D and P_S are measured in dollars and Q_D and Q_S represent the number of candy bars. Find the equilibrium price and quantity sold for this candy bar. Suppose that demand changes because of consumer preference, and supply changes because of cost factors. The new relationships are

$P_D = 0.82 - 0.004Q_D$

$P_S = 0.28 + 0.002Q_S$

Find the new equilibrium price and quantity sold. Compare the new equilibrium points with the old and explain the changes in the market for the candy bar.
5. For each total revenue (TR) and total cost (TC) function below, find the break-even quantity. Find total revenue and total cost corresponding to each break-even quantity.
   a. TR $= 4.5Q$; TC $= 1025 + 4.00Q$
   b. TR $= 0.6Q$; TC $= 650 + 0.35Q$
   c. TR $= 2.50Q$; TC $= 810 + 2.3Q$
   d. TR $= 5.00Q$; TC $= 15 + 3.00Q$
6. Two firms, A and B, have identical total revenue and total cost functions as shown below.
   Firm A: $TR_A = 6.00Q$; $TC_A = 3000 + 5.25Q$
   Firm B: $TR_B = 6.00Q$; $TC_B = 3000 + 5.25Q$
   a. Find the break-even quantity for each firm.
   b. If fixed costs to firm A increase to $4500, what is the effect on break-even quantity for this firm? Interpret this answer in relation to your answer to part a.
   c. If, in addition to the change mentioned in part b, variable cost per unit to firm B increases to $5.50, compare the new break-even points for both firms resulting from the changes described in parts b and c.

7. A dairy cooperative sells its members' butter at the constant price of $1.50 per pound. For a typical member, fixed costs are $6000 and production costs are $1.35 per pound. Find the break-even quantity in pounds for a typical member. Interpret the answer.
8. The constant price of newspapers in a city is $0.25 per copy. Fixed costs of newspaper printing and distributing are $20,000 per daily printing, and variable costs are $0.09 per copy. What is the break-even daily circulation for this newspaper? What is the effect on break-even circulation if variable costs increase to $0.17 per copy?

5.5 The Elimination Method

The elimination method is one technique used to find the solution to exactly constrained systems of equations with any number of equations and variables. In addition, the elimination method also provides a means to detect systems of equations which have no solution or an unlimited number of solutions. These two cases are discussed in Section 5.6. When a unique solution for the system of equations does exist, the elimination method provides the values for each variable at that solution point.

The elimination method is based on the mathematical principle that, when carrying out computations on equations, equals may be added to, subtracted from, or multiplied by equals. Thus, for the equation $4X - 5Y = 16$, multiplication of both sides by 3 leads to the equivalent result $12X - 15Y = 48$.

This principle also permits the formation of *linear combinations* of equations. Example 5.3 demonstrates development of a linear combination of two equations.

Example 5.3
The following is a system of two equations (Eq. 1 and Eq. 2) in two unknowns X and Y.

Eq. 1: $2X + Y = 12$

Eq. 2: $3X - 2Y = 5$.

A linear combination of Eq. 1 and Eq. 2 can be formed by multiplying Eq. 1 by 2 and then adding the product to Eq. 2. This results in the following:

2(Eq. 1): $4X + 2Y = 24$

\+ Eq. 2: $3X - 2Y = 5$

Eq. 3: $7X = 29$

This new equation, Eq. 3 ($7X = 29$), is a linear combination of the original two equations. Therefore, mathematical operations can be carried out on the entire system of equations or on linear combinations of equations in the system. The objective of these mathematical operations is to eliminate variables from the system until a solution for one variable is determined.

For a system of two equations and two unknown variables, mathematical operations are conducted to eliminate one variable and solve for the remaining variable. For systems of equations which are $n \times n$ (where n is greater than 2), $n - 1$ linear combinations of pairs of equations are formed while eliminating the same variable. Every equation in the system should be used in at least one of the linear combinations. This combination procedure is continued until the value of one unknown is determined.

After this step, "backward substitution" of known values into successively larger equations will provide a solution for the entire system. The complete solution includes a group of values which simultaneously satisfy all equations in the system.

In Example 5.3, the linear combination leads to the result $7X = 29$. Therefore, X is equal to $\frac{29}{7}$. Substitution of $X = \frac{29}{7}$ into Eq. 1 leads to the following value for Y:

$$2X + Y = 12$$

$$2\left(\frac{29}{7}\right) + Y = 12$$

$$\frac{58}{7} + Y = \frac{84}{7}$$

$$Y = \frac{26}{7}$$

As may be apparent, for larger systems of equations more elimination and backward substitution steps are required.

Examples of the elimination method applied to systems with two equations and two variables and those with three equations and three variables are presented below.

Example 5.4
For the following equations (Eqs. 1 and 2) with the variables X and Y in standard form, solve for X and Y.

Eq. 1: $3X + 2Y = 8$

Eq. 2: $X + 4Y = 10$

The Y variable can be eliminated from the system by multiplying both sides of Eq. 1 by $+2$ and subtracting Eq. 2 from this modified Eq. 1 as follows:

(2)(Eq. 1): $6X + 4Y = 16$

− Eq. 2: $\underline{X + 4Y = 10}$

$5X = 6$

$X = 1.2$

For this 2 × 2 system of equations, the value of the second variable is determined by substituting $X = 1.2$ into either of the original equations. Using Eq. 1, Y is equal to

$3X + 2Y = 8$

$3(1.2) + 2Y = 8$

$3.6 + 2Y = 8$

$2Y = 4.4$

$Y = 2.2$

Therefore, $X = 1.2$ and $Y = 2.2$ are the solution values for this system of equations. Alternatively, X could have been eliminated first, thus solving for Y, without causing any change in basic procedure, and giving an identical solution.

Example 5.5
Solve the following system of three equations in the three variables X, Y, and Z.

Eq. 1: $2X + 3Y + Z = 6$

Eq. 2: $X + 4Y + 3Z = 12$

Eq. 3: $3X + Y + 2Z = 10$

For a 3 × 3 system of equations, the elimination method requires selecting two *different* pairs of equations and eliminating the same variable from each pair. This process results in a 2 × 2 system which is then solved as demonstrated in Example 5.4.

In the above system, Z is eliminated by combining Eqs. 1 and 2 into one equation and Eqs. 1 and 3 into another. The variable Z is eliminated from the Eq. 1, Eq. 2 pair by multiplying Eq. 1 by 3 and subtracting Eq. 2. This forms a new Eq. 4 as follows,

(3)(Eq. 1): $6X + 9Y + 3Z = 18$

− Eq. 2: $\underline{X + 4Y + 3Z = 12}$

Eq. 4: $5X + 5Y = 6$

To eliminate Z from the Eq. 1, Eq. 3 pair, Eq. 1 is multiplied by 2 and Eq. 3 is subtracted from the result. This forms a new Eq. 5 as follows:

(2)(Eq. 1): $4X + 6Y + 2Z = 12$
− Eq. 3: $3X + Y + 2Z = 10$
Eq. 5: $X + 5Y = 2$

Thus, Eqs. 4 and 5 constitute a new 2 × 2 system. These are solved for X by subtracting Eq. 5 from Eq. 4 as follows:

Eq. 4: $5X + 5Y = 6$
− Eq. 5: $X + 5Y = 2$
         $4X = 4$
         $X = 1$

As the value of one unknown (X) is now established, substitution into the appropriate equations will yield values for Y and Z.

Substitution of $X = 1$ into Eq. 4 or Eq. 5 leads to a value for Y. Thus,

Eq. 4: $5X + 5Y = 6$
if $X = 1$: $5(1) + 5Y = 6$
             $5 + 5Y = 6$
             $5Y = 1$
             $Y = 0.2$

Substitution of $X = 1$ and $Y = 0.2$ into any one of the three original equations (Eq. 1 is used here) will specify a value for Z.

Eq. 1: $2X + 3Y + Z = 6$
if $X = 1$ and $Y = 0.2$: $2(1) + 3(0.2) + Z = 6$
                          $2 + 0.6 + Z = 6$
                          $Z = 6 - 2.6$
                          $Z = 3.4$

Therefore, the solution for this system of equations is $X = 1$, $Y = 0.2$, and $Z = 3.4$. Verification of this solution can be carried out by substituting these three values into one of the other original equations. For example, substituting into Eq. 3 verifies the solution.

Eq. 3: $3X + Y + 2Z = 10$
if $X = 1, Y = 0.2, Z = 3.4$: $3(1) + 0.2 + (2)(3.4) = 10$
                                 $3 + 0.2 + 6.8 = 10$
                                 $10 = 10$

Finally, observe that the elimination method is a two-phase procedure. First, one should successively reduce the size of the system until the value of one variable is determined. Then, beginning with the established value, substitute this value and others, as they are determined, into successively larger subsystems until the solution is complete.

Two Applications

As mentioned previously, variable names such as X, Y, and Z often are used to denote quantities in the business world. Thus, X may represent sales figures for a group of stores, or Y may be used to specify production levels at a number of factories.

The following two examples apply the elimination method to business situations. Readers should note particularly how a system of equations using variable names is developed from a problem stated in narrative form.

Example 5.6
An office-furniture manufacturer has exactly 260 pounds of plastic and 240 pounds of wood available each week for the production of two products, X and Y.

Each X produced requires 20 pounds of plastic and 15 pounds of wood. Each Y requires 10 pounds of plastic and 12 pounds of wood. How many X's and Y's should be made each week to utilize exactly the available amounts of plastic and wood?

To answer this problem, a system of equations must be developed from the facts of the situation.

The constraint due to the amount of plastic is stated as

$20X + 10Y = 260$

This indicates that 20 pounds of plastic are used in each X, 10 pounds in each Y, and that 260 pounds per week should be used.

The constraint due to the amount of wood is expressed similarly as

$15X + 12Y = 240$

Thus, a unit of product X requires 15 pounds of wood, a unit of Y uses 12 pounds of wood, and exactly 240 pounds of wood should be used each week.

These two equations (constraints) form the following system:

$20X + 10Y = 260$

$15X + 12Y = 240$

Simultaneous solution of these equations will give the quantity of each product (X and Y) to be produced each week to utilize exactly the available plastic and wood. The solution is as follows:

Eq. 1: $20X + 10Y = 260$
Eq. 2: $15X + 12Y = 240$

4(Eq. 2): $60X + 48Y = 960$
− 3(Eq. 1): $60X + 30Y = 780$

$$18Y = 180$$
$$Y = 10$$

Substituting $Y = 10$ into Eq. 1 yields the value of X.

$$20X + 10(10) = 260$$
$$20X + 100 = 260$$
$$20X = 160$$
$$X = 8$$

Thus, the firm should produce 8 units of product X and 10 units of product Y each week to utilize the available amounts of plastic and wood.

Example 5.7

An aircraft manufacturer uses three machines (X, Y, and Z) to manufacture three different parts, referred to as A, B, and C. The machines are used to make other parts, but no other machines are required for the production of A, B, and C. The manufacturer wants to determine the number of hours per month to use each machine for A, B, and C production under the following constraints.

To produce one part A requires the use of 3 hours of X, 4 hours of Y, and 1 hour of Z. Each month, 380 A's must be produced. If X, Y, and Z are used to represent hours of use for the respective machines (X, Y, and Z), this production constraint for part A can be expressed as follows:

$$3X + 4Y + Z = 380$$

In this form X, Y, and Z represent the hours that each machine is operated per month to make the 380 A parts.

One part B requires 2 hours of use by machine X, 4 hours of Y use, and 2 hours' use of machine Z. Each month, 400 B's must be produced. Thus, this constraint is as follows:

$$2X + 4Y + 2Z = 400$$

Finally, each part C requires 6 hours of X, and 2 hours of Y, and 2 hours of Z. There must be 520 C's produced each month. This constraint is the following:

$$6X + 2Y + 2Z = 520$$

To determine how many hours per month each machine should be operated for the three products, the system of equations must be solved simultaneously. A solution is shown below.

$$\text{Eq. 1:} \quad 3X + 4Y + Z = 380$$
$$\text{Eq. 2:} \quad 2X + 4Y + 2Z = 400$$
$$\text{Eq. 3:} \quad 6X + 2Y + 2Z = 520$$
$$\text{Eq. 1} - \text{Eq. 2:} \quad X \quad - Z = -20$$
$$\text{Eq. 4:} \quad X - Z = -20$$
$$2(\text{Eq. 3}): \quad 12X + 4Y + 4Z = 1040$$
$$-\quad \text{Eq. 2:} \quad 2X + 4Y + 2Z = 400$$
$$\text{Eq. 5:} \quad 10X + 2Z = 640$$

Thus, the system of two equations and two unknowns with Y eliminated is as follows:

Eq. 4: $X - Z = -20$

Eq. 5: $10X + 2Z = 640$

The following steps yield a value of X, or the number of hours machine X should be used:

$2(\text{Eq. 4}) + \text{Eq. 5:} \quad 12X = 600$

$$X = 50$$

Substituting $X = 50$ into Eq. 4 yields a Z value of 70 as follows:

Eq. 4: $\quad X - Z = -20$

$\quad \quad \quad 50 - Z = -20$

$\quad \quad \quad \quad \quad Z = 70$

Substituting $X = 50$ and $Z = 70$ into Eq. 1 yields a Y value of 40:

Eq. 1: $\quad 3X + 4Y + Z = 380$

$\quad \quad \quad 3(50) + 4Y + 70 = 380$

$\quad \quad \quad 150 + 4Y + 70 = 380$

$\quad \quad \quad \quad \quad 4Y = 160$

$\quad \quad \quad \quad \quad Y = 40$

Thus, the simultaneous solution has determined that the required production of parts A, B, and C can be satisfied exactly by using machine X for 50 hours per month, machine Y for 40 hours per month, and machine Z for 70 hours per month.

Systems of Linear Equations and Inequalities

The problem set after Section 5.6 will provide additional practice in setting up and solving systems of equations based on problems in narrative form.

These descriptions and examples have discussed using the elimination method to determine the unique solution to a set of linear equations. However, the elimination method also can be helpful in detecting situations where a system of equations has either no solutions or an unlimited number of solutions. This topic is included in the next section. The exercises after the next section will provide practice in applying the elimination method to exactly constrained systems of equations with all solution possibilities.

5.6 Inconsistent and Dependent Equations

When the coefficients of the variables in a system of equations are proportional between equations, a unique solution does not exist. Proportionality will be demonstrated below by numerical example. At this point, note that proportionality between the coefficients in the two-variable case means that the slopes of the lines are equal. This indicates that the functions do not have a *unique* point in common.

With equal slopes, it is possible either that (1) the lines are parallel and have *no* points in common (no solution) or (2) the lines are the same and have *infinitely many* points in common (infinite solutions).

Proportionality between the coefficients of a group of equations is demonstrated in Examples 5.8 and 5.9.

Example 5.8
Find the solution to the following 2 × 2 system of equations.

Eq. 1: $2X + 3Y = 7$

Eq. 2: $4X + 6Y = 12$

Prior to applying the elimination method, observe the result of transforming each equation to explicit form, or $Y = f(X)$.

Eq. 1: $2X + 3Y = 7$

$$3Y = 7 - 2X$$

$$Y = \frac{7}{3} - \frac{2}{3}X$$

Eq. 2: $4X + 6Y = 12$

$$6Y = 12 - 4X$$

$$Y = 2 - \frac{2}{3}X$$

Although each equation has a different Y intercept, the slopes are both $-\frac{2}{3}$. Consequently, the lines are parallel and never intersect. Proportionality occurs because each coefficient in Eq. 2 is twice as large as the corresponding coefficient in Eq. 1. Proportionality also is shown by establishing a ratio between the X and Y coefficients for each equation. This ratio is $Y:X = 3:2 = 6:4$. The existence of proportionality between the coefficients means that a unique solution to the system of equations does not exist. In this case, there is no solution to the system of equations.

Often, proportionality can be detected while carrying out the elimination method. Assume that one wants to multiply 2 times Eq. 1 and subtract Eq. 2 to eliminate Y. The result is as follows:

$$(2)(\text{Eq. 1}): \quad 4X + 6Y = 14$$
$$-\quad \text{Eq. 2}: \quad \underline{4X + 6Y = 12}$$
$$0 = 2$$

A contradiction has occurred, since $0 \neq 2$. Finding a contradiction during the elimination method is an indication that the equations in the system are inconsistent and that no solution exists for the system.

Example 5.9
Solve for X and Y in the following system:

Eq. 1: $\quad 5X + 2Y = 10$

Eq. 2: $\quad 20X + 8Y = 40$

In this system, also, the coefficients for X and Y in each equation are proportional, as $Y:X = 2:5 = 8:20$.

Solving for the explicit form of each equation leads to the following results:

Eq. 1: $\quad 5X + 2Y = 10$
$$2Y = 10 - 5X$$
$$Y = 5 - \frac{5}{2}X$$

Eq. 2: $\quad 20X + 8Y = 40$
$$8Y = 40 - 20X$$
$$Y = 5 - \frac{5}{2}X$$

Not only are the slopes equal for each equation, as in Example 5.8, but so also are the Y intercepts. Therefore, the two equations generate the same line and there are an infinite number of solutions to the system.

Applying the method of elimination to this system demonstrates a means of identifying the infinite solution case. For this system, Eq. 2 is exactly 4 times Eq. 1. Thus, the elimination method leads to the result $0 = 0$ as follows:

(4)(Eq. 1): $4(5X + 2Y = 10)$

Eq. 2: $\underline{20X + 8Y = 40}$

(4)(Eq. 1): $20X + 8Y = 40$

− Eq. 2: $\underline{20X + 8Y = 40}$

$\qquad\qquad 0 = 0$

The result $0 = 0$ (or any other identity such as $7 = 7$ or $2 = 2$) indicates that the equations of the system are the same and, therefore, that there are an infinite number of solutions to the system.

Notice that these equations are linear combinations, as Eq. 2 is exactly 4 times Eq. 1. This means that the equations are linearly dependent on each other. Linear dependence and its implications will be discussed in greater detail in Chapter 6 (Matrix Algebra). At this point, it should be remembered that a unique solution does not exist for a system of equations having linearly dependent equations.

These two sections have examined systems of equations which are exactly constrained. A common method used to solve such systems is the elimination method. The elimination method will (1) find a unique solution if one exists and (2) detect systems of equations which have no solution or have an infinite number of solutions.

The elimination method can be tedious when applied to large systems of equations. Chapter 6 will discuss some techniques of matrix algebra which can be used to find solutions (or the absence of solutions) for large systems of linear equations.

The following exercises are concerned with various applications of the elimination method.

EXERCISES

1. Solve each of the following systems of equations by the elimination method (round all answers to two decimal places).

   a. $2X + Y = 24$
      $5X - 3Y = 20$

   b. $4X + 3Y = 16$
      $X - 2Y = 4$

   c. $2X + Y = 2$
      $3X + 3Y = 4$

   d. $X - Y = 16$
      $4X + 2Y = 28$

2. For each 2 × 2 system of equations below, find the explicit form, $Y = b_0 + b_1 X$, of each equation. Compare the equations of each pair and draw a conclusion about the relationship between them. (That is, do they intersect at a point, form the same line, or never intersect?)

a. $3X + 2Y = 8$ c. $3X + Y = 18$
   $X + 3Y = 4$ $12X + 4Y = 52$
b. $X - 2Y = 6$ d. $4X + Y = 10$
   $4X - 8Y = 24$ $8X - 2Y = 20$

3. State whether each of the following 2 × 2 systems of equations has either no solutions or an infinite number of solutions. Defend your choice in each case.

   a. $2X - Y = 10$ c. $Y = 15 - 3X$
      $8X - 4Y = 40$ $6X + 2Y = 20$
   b. $12X + 3Y = 18$ d. $X = 3Y$
      $8X + 2Y = 16$ $4X - 12Y = 28$

4. Solve each 3 × 3 system of equations below, if a solution exists. If a solution does not exist, explain why.

   a. $3X - Y + Z = 12$ c. $5X + 3Y - Z = 10$
      $X + Y = 10$ $-3X + 4Y + Z = 14$
      $4X - 2Y + 3Z = 18$ $X + 4Y - 3Z = 8$
   b. $X - Y + 2Z = 16$ d. $X - Y + 4Z = 16$
      $3X + 6Y + 6Z = 21$ $2X - 2Y + 8Z = 28$
      $X + 2Y + 2Z = 7$ $8X + Y - 6Z = 10$

5. A firm manufactures two products, dishwashers (X) and air conditioners (Y). Each requires for its production a mix of worker-hours and machine-hours. The firm has 2200 worker-hours and 1600 machine-hours available each week for production of the two products.

   Hour requirements for the manufacture of one unit of each product are as follows:

	Required Hours	
	Worker-Hours	Machine-Hours
Dishwashers	6	2
Air conditioners	4	6

How many dishwashers and air conditioners should be made each week in order to utilize exactly all available resources? Round answers to two decimal places.

6. Two ingredients (X and Y, each measured in pounds) are used by a drug manufacturer to make batches of two different high-potency vitamin C tablets. For tablet I, X and Y must be mixed in the weight ratio of $5X$ to $3Y$. For tablet II, the weight ratio is $6X$ to $2Y$.

   Production requirements are 4000 pounds of tablet I and 3000 pounds of tablet II. How much of each ingredient should be purchased to satisfy production requirements?

7. An investor has $200,000 to invest between a low income–low risk investment X and a high income–high risk investment Y. Annual returns

are 7 percent on investment X (0.07) and 13 percent on investment Y (0.13).

The investor wants to determine how much of the $200,000 to put into each investment in order to have an annual rate of return of 9 percent on the total investment of $200,000. What are these amounts? Round answers to two decimal places.

8. A food manufacturer uses three ingredients (X, Y, and Z) to make a fortified fruit product. The ingredients are mixed in small production batches. Each batch must contain exactly 48 grams of vitamin A, 60 grams of vitamin C, and 36 grams of vitamin E.

An ounce of each ingredient supplies a number of grams of each vitamin as shown in the following table:

Ingredient	Vitamin Grams per Ounce of Ingredient		
	Vitamin A	Vitamin C	Vitamin E
X	3	4	1
Y	2	2	3
Z	1	2	3

Find the number of ounces of each ingredient needed to meet exactly the vitamin requirements of a production batch.

5.7 Overconstrained and Underconstrained Systems of Equations

Although exactly constrained systems occur frequently, there are instances where the number of equations and the number of variables are not equal. Thus, the number of constraints may be greater than or less than the number of variables.

When the number of equations exceeds the number of variables, a system of equations is overconstrained. In this case, the system may have a unique solution, no solution, or an infinite number of solutions. Although these three possibilities exist, it is often the case that an overconstrained system of equations does not have a solution. Furthermore, as the number of constraints on a given group of variables increases, it becomes less likely that a solution exists for the system. Consequently, overconstrained systems of equations are used infrequently in mathematical analysis as they often lead to no conclusion.

If the number of variables exceeds the number of equations, the system of equations is underconstrained. In this case, there are either no solutions or an unlimited number of solutions to the system. Techniques exist for limiting the infinite solution situation, but they are omitted here for brevity of presentation.

The method of elimination discussed above is limited as it is applicable only to the solution of exactly constrained systems of equations. In Chapter 6, the Gauss-Jordan elimination method of solving a system of equations is introduced. This technique can be used to find the solution (or absence of a solution) to systems of equations with any number of variables and equations (not necessarily equal numbers of each).

5.8 Inequalities: Properties and Operations

The analogy between equations and constraints can be extended to the topic of inequalities. In many applications, constraints are expressed not as equations but as inequalities. Examples of constraints in the form of inequalities are: A food product must have *at least* 10 grams of protein per serving or a television must be manufactured with the use of *no more than* 30 worker-hours of labor. This section and the next examine the topic of linear inequalities including their basic properties, mathematical operations using inequalities, and solving single inequalities and systems of inequalities.

First, consider the concept of an inequality. A property of real numbers is that they are ordered. Thus, along a line of increasing real numbers, one real number may be to the right (larger), to the left (smaller), or at the same point as (equal to) a second number. Therefore, if a and b are two real numbers, three possibilities exist for their relationship to each other: (1) a is greater than b (expressed $a > b$); (2) a is less than b (expressed $a < b$); (3) a is equal to b ($a = b$). Items (1) and (2) are *inequality statements*. The relationship associated with the symbols $<$ and $>$ is referred to as the *sense* of the inequality.

Statements such as $a > b$ and $a < b$ are called *strong* inequalities, whereas expressions which combine an inequality statement with an equality, such as "a is greater than or equal to b" ($a \geq b$) are *weak* inequalities.

Some mathematical operations on inequalities cause a change in the sense of the inequality. This means that a particular operation may cause, for example, $a > b$ to become $a' < b'$ where a' and b' are the new values of a and b after the mathematical operation. This concept is relevant to some of the following operational principles.

First, the addition of a constant to or subtraction of a constant from both sides of an inequality does not change the sense of the inequality. Thus, If a, b, and c are real number constants and $a > b$, then

$a + c > b + c$

and

$a - c > b - c$

Systems of Linear Equations and Inequalities   93

The effect on the sense of an inequality of multiplying or dividing both sides of an inequality by a real number constant is dependent on the value of the constant.

If a constant c is greater than 0, the multiplication or division of both sides of an inequality between a and b by the constant does not change the sense of the inequality. However, if c is less than 0, multiplication or division of both sides of an inequality by c changes the sense of the inequality. These rules are valid regardless of the values of a and b.

Example 5.10
For the inequality $a > b$ and the constant c, where $a = 6, b = 3$, and $c = +2$, the following are valid operations:

1. $a + c > b + c$ or $(6 + 2) > (3 + 2)$
2. $a - c > b - c$ or $(6 - 2) > (3 - 2)$
3. $(a)(c) > (b)(c)$ or $(6)(2) > (3)(2)$
4. $(a \div c) > (b \div c)$ or $(6 \div 2) > (3 \div 2)$

Example 5.11
For the inequality $a > b$ and the constant c where $a = 6, b = 3$, and $c = -2$, the following are valid operations:

1. $a + c > b + c$ or $(6 - 2) > (3 - 2)$
2. $a - c > b - c$ or $(6 + 2) > (3 + 2)$
3. $(a)(c) < (b)(c)$ or $(6)(-2) < (3)(-2)$
4. $(a \div c) < (b \div c)$ or $(6 \div -2) < (3 \div -2)$

Two other operational principles of inequalities concern double inequalities and nonnegativity constraints.

A *double inequality* is used to express the bounded range of values for a variable. A condition on both the right-hand side and the left-hand side of this range is stated in a single expression. For example, the inequality statement

$$3 < X < 15$$

means that the variable X can have any value between 3 and 15 *excluding* the points $X = 3$ and $X = 15$.

Alternatively, the weak inequality

$$3 \leq X \leq 15$$

means that X can have any value between 3 and 15 *including* the points $X = 3$ and $X = 15$.

The notational efficiency of double inequalities is not appropriate when one intends to exclude a range of values by use of the inequality. For example, if one wants to state that X can have any value greater than $+17$ or smaller than 4, two inequalities must be used:

$X > 17$ and $X < 4$

Writing these as a single expression $4 > X > 17$ leads to an *inconsistent* statement as the condition $X > 17$ conflicts with the condition $X < 4$. Thus, a double inequality is inconsistent if both statements cannot be true, or in other words, if no value can satisfy both conditions.

Nonnegativity constraints are used to restrict the values of a variable or variables. This restriction is particularly useful in business applications as many measurements (e.g., prices, incomes, and production levels) do not have practical meaning if negative. To limit the variable X to nonnegative values, the following inequality expression is used:

$X \geq 0$

5.9   Solving Inequalities and Systems of Inequalities

Introduction

The solution of a single inequality or a system of inequalities often is not a line or an intersection point between lines but rather a *solution space*. A solution space is an area of the coordinate plane including all points which satisfy the inequality or simultaneously satisfy all the inequalities.

When finding a solution space, the inequality statements are treated as equations for purposes of finding boundary lines for the solution space and intersections between boundary lines. For example, the inequality $3X + Y \geq 8$ is treated as $3X + Y = 8$ when establishing the boundary line of the solution space. However, the sense of the inequality must be used to give a correct interpretation to the solution space. In the following discussion, single inequalities and systems of inequalities are analyzed separately and examples of each are offered.

Single Inequalities

For a single inequality such as $2X + 3Y > 8$ or $4X - 5Y \geq 12$, the solution space includes all the points on one side of the line established by the corresponding equality, e.g., $2X + 3Y = 8$. The solution space excludes the points on the line in the case of a strong inequality ($2X + 3Y > 8$) and includes the points on the line for a weak inequality ($4X - 5Y \geq 12$). The remainder of the solution space is specified by the sense of the inequality.

Example 5.12
Find the solution space for the inequality

$2X + 5Y \leq 30$

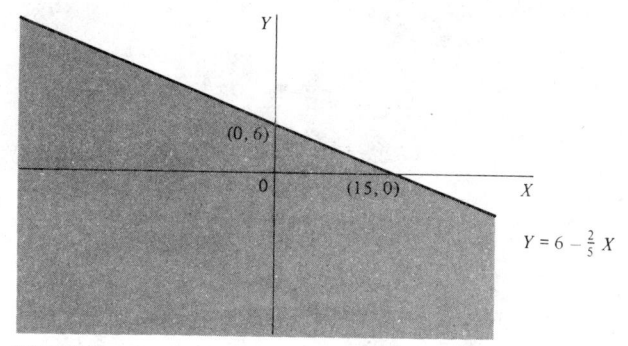

FIGURE 5.4 The solution space for the inequality

$$2X + 5Y \leq 30$$

To find the solution space for this inequality, the equality $2X + 5Y = 30$ is used to find the slope-intercept form, or Y in terms of X. This will yield a line on the coordinate plane:

$$2X + 5Y = 30$$
$$5Y = 30 - 2X$$
$$Y = 6 - 0.4X$$

This is the equation for the boundary line of the solution space.[1]

The weak inequality ($\leq$) in the final form $Y \leq 6 - 0.4X$ indicates that all points on the coordinate plane *on* or *below* the line $Y = 6 - 0.4X$ constitute the solution space. Figure 5.4 shows this solution space as the shaded area.

The Y intercept is at the point (0, 6) and the slope is -0.4 for the boundary. The solution space extends into all four quadrants including both positive and negative values for the X and Y variables.

Imposing nonnegativity constraints on both X and Y in this case reduces the solution space to the shaded area of Figure 5.5. In this new solution

---

[1]This boundary line also can be established by the following three-step procedure:
1. Set $Y = 0$ in $2X + 5Y = 30$ and solve for X.
2. Set $X = 0$ in $2X + 5Y = 30$ and solve for Y.
3. Construct a line joining the points found in steps 1 and 2.

This procedure yields the X intercept and the Y intercept. A line joining the two intercept points is the boundary line of the solution space. The points (0, 6) and (15, 0) and the line joining them are indicated in both Figure 5.4 and Figure 5.5.

Either of these techniques can be used to establish the boundary line (or lines) for an inequality (system of inequalities). However, the slope-intercept method of finding the boundary line will be applied in the remainder of the chapter as its use may serve to reinforce the fundamentals of linear relationships.

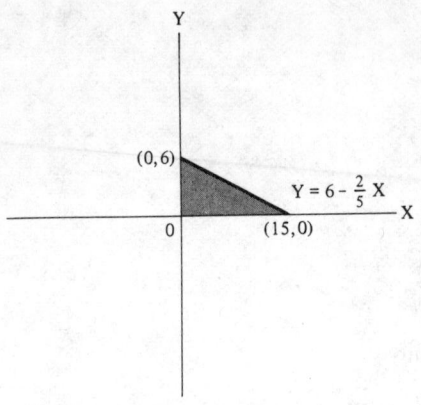

FIGURE 5.5 The solution space for the inequality $2X + 5Y \leq 30$ where both X and Y are restricted to nonnegative values.

space all points are in quadrant I including points *on* the Y axis from 0 to $+6$ ($X = 0$) and *on* the X axis from 0 to $+15$ ($Y = 0$).

After finding the boundary line, the sense of the inequality dictates whether the solution space extends above or below the boundary. Care must be exercised when manipulating inequalities so that the correct sense is maintained.

Example 5.13 demonstrates a solution process where the sense of the inequality is altered by manipulation of the constraint.

Example 5.13
Find the solution space for

$$3X - 4Y \leq 36$$

This solution space is determined by, first, solving for Y in terms of X then, constructing a graph and interpreting the correct sense of the inequality.

Solving for Y in terms of X yields

$$3X - 4Y = 36$$

1. $-4Y = 36 - 3X$
2. $Y = -9 + \frac{3}{4}X$

The equation $Y = -9 + \frac{3}{4}X$ is the boundary of the solution space. However, step 2 above involved multiplication of both sides of the equation by $-\frac{1}{4}$. This operation changes the sense of the inequality from

$$3X - 4Y \leq 36$$

to

$$Y \geq -9 + \frac{3}{4}X$$

The solution space for this inequality is the shaded area of Figure 5.6.

The solution space includes all points above (increasing values on the Y axis) the line $Y = -9 + \frac{3}{4}X$. The Y intercept of the boundary line is -9 and the slope is $+\frac{3}{4}$. Thus, the rules for operations on inequalities are used to provide a correct interpretation to this solution space.

Systems of Inequalities

The previous examples have described methods for finding the solution space for a single inequality statement. Systems of inequalities are employed frequently in business to express a group of constraints as, for example, on time, resource availability, or product quality control. Thus, a firm may produce a product with restricted amounts of labor and machine time. In this case, each resource constraint produces an inequality statement.

To determine the solution space for a system of inequalities, the boundary line for each inequality and the intersection points between the boundaries, if they exist, must be found. Boundary lines are established as for single inequalities. Intersection points are found by the method of elimination as applied to systems of equations. After finding boundaries and intersections, a solution space is specified in accordance with the sense of all the inequalities. A graph of the system is helpful in understanding the solution space. In the following examples, the notation i followed by a number refers to a particular inequality in the system.

Example 5.14

Find the solution space for the following two inequalities in two variables X and Y.

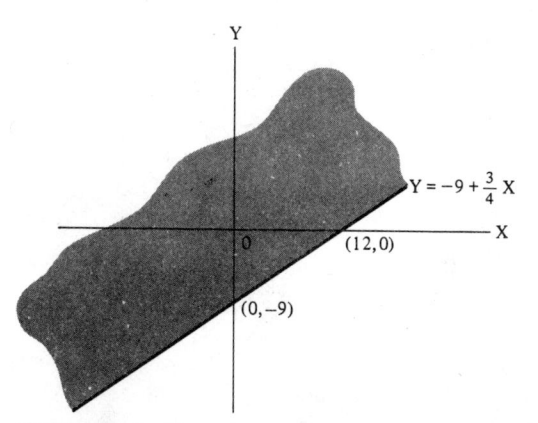

FIGURE 5.6 The solution space for the inequality
$$3X - 4Y \leq 36.$$

i1: $3Y + 2X \leq 30$

i2: $5Y - 4X \geq 10$

First, find two equations of the slope-intercept form $Y = b_0 + b_1 X$

i1: $3Y + 2X = 30$
$\ 3Y = 30 - 2X$
$\ Y = 10 - \frac{2}{3}X$

i2: $5Y - 4X = 10$
$\ 5Y = 10 + 4X$
$\ Y = 2 + \frac{4}{5}X$

These two equations representing the boundary lines for the system are graphed in Figure 5.7.

The solution space for this system consists of all points on or above $Y = 2 + \frac{4}{5}X$ which are also below $Y = 10 - \frac{2}{3}X$.

Complete specification of the solution space requires finding the intersection point of the lines (shown as c in Figure 5.7). To find this point, the two inequalities are treated as a system of two equations in two unknowns and the method of elimination is applied as follows.

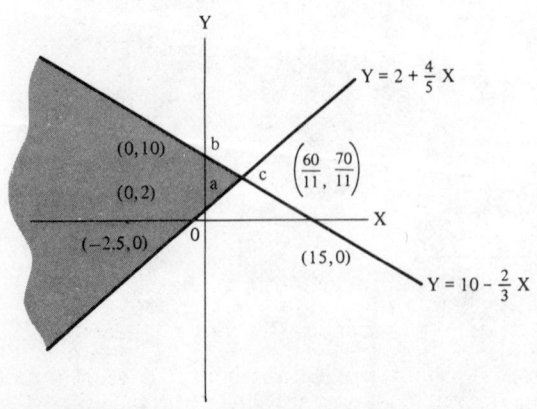

$$
\begin{array}{rl}
\text{i1:} & 3Y + 2X = 30 \\
\text{i2:} & \underline{5Y - 4X = 10} \\
(2)(\text{i1}): & 6Y + 4X = 60 \\
+\quad \text{i2:} & \underline{5Y - 4X = 10} \\
& 11Y = 70 \\
& Y = \dfrac{70}{11}
\end{array}
$$

FIGURE 5.7 The solution space for the system of inequalities:

$$3Y + 2X \leq 30$$

$$5Y - 4X \geq 10$$

Substitution of $Y = \frac{70}{11}$ into i1 yields the X coordinate of the intersection point as

i1: $3\left(\dfrac{70}{11}\right) + 2X = 30$

$\dfrac{210}{11} + 2X = 30$

$2X = \dfrac{120}{11}$

$X = \dfrac{60}{11}$

The intersection point c is at $(\frac{60}{11}, \frac{70}{11})$. It is now possible to state the solution space as all points which are

1. On or above the line $5Y - 4X = 10$
2. On or below the line $3Y + 2X = 30$
3. To the left of the point $(\frac{60}{11}, \frac{70}{11})$

This solution space includes the shaded area of quadrants I, II, and III in Figure 5.7. Imposing nonnegativity constraints on both X and Y reduces the solution space to the triangle abc in Figure 5.7. These points are exclusively in quadrant I.

Example 5.15

A firm manufactures two products, movie cameras (X) and tape recorders (Y) under resource-availability constraints of 50 worker-hours and 80 machine-hours, in each case per day. Production of each movie camera requires 2 worker-hours and 5 machine-hours. A tape recorder requires 4 worker-hours and 1 machine-hour. The firm wants to know the various daily production alternatives for these two products within the resource constraints.

The constraints are expressed by the following system of inequalities:

i1: $2X + 4Y \leq 50$ (worker-hour constraint)

i2: $5X + Y \leq 80$ (machine-hour constraint)

i3: $X \geq 0$ (nonnegativity constraint on the production of movie cameras)

i4: $Y \geq 0$ (nonnegativity constraint on the production of tape recorders)

Solving for the slope-intercept form of the worker-hour (i1) and machine-hour (i2) constraints yields the following:

i1: $2X + 4Y = 50$
$\quad\quad 4Y = 50 - 2X$
$\quad\quad Y = 12.5 - 0.5X$

i2: $5X + Y = 80$
$\quad\quad Y = 80 - 5X$

These boundary lines are shown in Figure 5.8. Because of the non-negativity constraints (i3 and i4), Figure 5.8 is restricted to the first quadrant.

As the sense of both inequalities is less than or equal to ($\leq$), the solution space includes all points within both lines, or the area $0abc$ including the line segments $0a$, ab, bc, and $0c$.

Point a specifies maximum possible production of tape recorders if no movie cameras are produced (12.5). Similarly, point c indicates that 16 movie cameras can be produced within the resource constraints if no tape recorders are produced.

The intersection point of the two constraints (point b) is found by simultaneous solution of the two boundary-line equations. Thus,

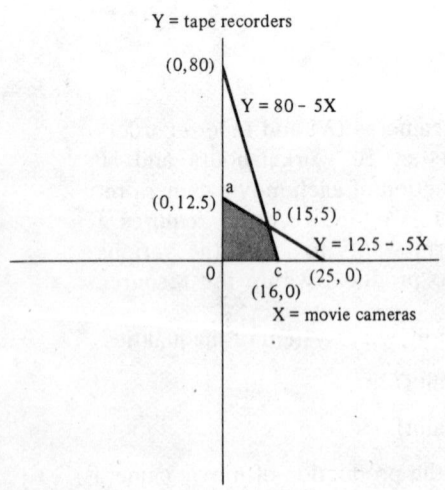

$$
\begin{aligned}
\text{i1:} \quad & 2X + 4Y = 50 \\
\text{i2:} \quad & \underline{5X + Y = 80} \\
(4)(\text{i2}): \quad & 20X + 4Y = 320 \\
\text{i1:} \quad & \underline{2X + 4Y = 50} \\
& 18X = 270 \\
& X = 15
\end{aligned}
$$

FIGURE 5.8 The solution space for the system of inequalities

$$2X + 4Y \leq 50$$
$$5X + Y \leq 80$$
$$X \geq 0$$
$$Y \geq 0$$

Substitution of $X = 15$ into i1 yields $Y = 5$ as follows:

i1: $2X + 4Y = 50$
  $2(15) + 4Y = 50$
  $30 + 4Y = 50$
  $4Y = 20$
  $Y = 5$

Consequently, point b represents the production of 15 movie cameras and 5 tape recorders.

This analysis provides information about the firm's daily production possibilities and the impact of the resource constraints. For example, if 12.5 tape recorders are produced, no movie cameras can be manufactured as no more worker-hours are available. Similarly, if 16 movie cameras are produced, no tape recorders can be made as machine-hours are completely utilized. At point b, all worker-hours and machine-hours are utilized in the production of 15 movie cameras and 5 tape recorders.

Between points a and b, production is limited by worker-hours and there are excess machine hours. However, between b and c, machine time is the limiting resource and there are excess worker-hours.

This last example has shown the application of a system of inequalities to a production process operating within a limited set of resources. Both examples have stressed that the solution of systems of inequalities requires a combination of graphical analysis, the method of elimination, and interpretation of the sense of inequalities.

Looking Ahead: Linear Programming

Linear programming is the subject of Chapter 7. Inequalities, systems of inequalities, and the analysis of solution spaces provide the background for an understanding of linear programming. Specifically, linear programming is a technique for optimizing an objective (such as maximum profit or minimum cost) given a set of contraints. Often, the constraints form a system of inequalities.

Linear programming identifies the point within the solution space which optimizes the value of the objective while satisfying all the constraints. Although this topic is deferred until after the presentation of the Gauss-Jordan method and an introduction to matrix algebra in Chapter 6, readers should remember that this material on inequalities will be fundamental to an understanding of linear programming.

EXERCISES

1. For the following, find the inequality expression for Y in terms of X. In each case, on which side of the line does the solution space lie (above or below the line)? Also, does the solution space include the line?

a. $4X + 3Y \leq 36$ e. $2X \geq Y + 14$
b. $3X - 2Y \geq 20$ f. $-X + 5.5Y \leq 44$
c. $-2X + 6Y \geq 48$ g. $3X - 6Y > 12$
d. $1.5X - 7.5Y < 60$ h. $X - Y \geq 8$

2. Find the solution space for each inequality at the stated value for X.
   a. $5X - Y \geq 40$ at $X = 16$ d. $6X + 4Y \leq 48$ at $X = 30$
   b. $-3X + 2Y \leq 24$ at $X = 4$ e. $-X + 4Y \geq 76$ at $X = 21$
   c. $X - 4Y \geq 60$ at $X = 150$

3. Find the solution space for each of the following systems of inequalities. Use techniques of linear algebra to find boundary lines and intersections. Graphically describe the solution space.
   a. $3X - Y \leq 10$
      $5X + 2Y \geq 30$
      $X \geq 0, Y \geq 0$
   b. $4X + 3Y \geq 12$
      $X \leq 2$
      $X \geq 0, Y \geq 0$
   c. $2X + Y \leq 16$
      $X + Y \geq 11$
      $X \geq 0, Y \geq 0$
   d. $3X + 5Y \geq 15$
      $X + 5Y \leq 30$
      $X + 6Y \geq 9$
      $X \geq 0, Y \geq 0$

4. A firm uses two resources (labor and machinery) to produce two products, X and Y. Total worker-hours used per week cannot exceed 640, and machine-hour use cannot exceed 400 hours per week. A unit of X requires 4 worker-hours and 5 machine-hours for its production and a unit of Y requires 4 worker-hours and 1 machine-hour. Find all the boundaries and intersection points between boundaries for this system of inequalities. Graph the solution space.

5. For Problem 4, add to the constraints a management time constraint of no more than 60 hours per week. It is estimated that X requires 0.6 management hour per unit and Y requires 0.3 management hour per unit. Describe boundaries, intersections, and the graph of the solution space for the system of three constraints.

6. In addition to the three constraints described in Problems 4 and 5, include the additional constraint that at least 50 units of X must be made each week. Define and present a graph of the solution space incorporating the four constraints. Include all boundary lines and intersection points in the description.

7. A food manufacturer produces a breakfast cereal which uses two main ingredients: wheat (X) and rye (Y). Each production unit must satisfy a protein, a carbohydrate, and a fat constraint. In a unit, there must be at

least 80 grams of protein, at least 200 grams of carbohydrate, and no more than 40 grams of fat.

An ounce of each ingredient has the following components, in grams per ounce:

	Protein	Carbohydrate	Fat
Wheat (X)	20	25	4
Rye (Y)	5	20	2

Graphically describe the solution space showing all possible combinations of wheat and rye which satisfy the three constraints. Include all boundary lines and intersection points in the description.

8. A firm uses two mainframe computers for production analysis. Computer X is owned by the firm and computer Y is shared with several other firms. Management has set a limitation of no more than 75 hours per week for computer use related to production analysis. Production control managers have decided that at least 48 hours of computer time, divided between the two mainframes, is required each week. Time sharing restricts the use of computer Y by this firm to no more than 36 hours per week. Graphically describe the solution space showing all feasible usage patterns for these two computers. Find boundary lines and intersection points.

5.10 Chapter Summary

This chapter has presented several of the analytical fundamentals of linear algebra. Included have been descriptions of systems of linear equations and methods of expressing inequalities and solving systems of equations and systems of inequalities.

The method of elimination as used to solve systems of equations has been stressed in the chapter. This technique is employed to find values for the unknown variables in a system of equations by successively reducing the number of variables in the system until one value is established. Subsequent substitution of known values into progressively larger subsystems of the system leads to all other values.

At times a system of equations may have no solutions (parallel lines in graphical form for the two-variable case) or an unlimited number of solutions (the same line for the two-variable case). In addition, a system of equations may be classified as exactly constrained (the number of equations and variables are the same), overconstrained (number of equations exceeds the number of variables), or underconstrained (number of equations is less than the number of variables). Overconstrained and underconstrained systems of equations cause computational problems when one uses the method of elimination. This limitation may be overcome by using the Gauss-Jordan elimination method presented in the next chapter.

A second topic in the chapter has been inequalities. A discussion of the concepts and operational rules of inequalities was expanded to include the solution of systems of inequalities. Solution of this type of system often results in a solution space rather than an intersection point. Graphical description, correct interpretation of the sense of an inequality, and the method of elimination are some of the techniques applied to finding the solution space for a system of inequalities. This topic is particularly relevant to the principles of linear programming found in Chapter 7.

The next two chapters on matrix algebra and linear programming extend the topics of this chapter to two fields of linear mathematics frequently utilized in business. Both chapters will refer frequently to particular points in the present chapter.

5.11 Problem Set

Review Questions

1. If two linear equations in a system with two variables have an unlimited number of points in common, what can be said about these two lines?
2. Define:
   a. Overconstrained system of equations
   b. Underconstrained system of equations
   c. Exactly constrained system of equations
3. Describe a 4 × 3 system of linear equations with respect to number of equations and number of variables. Is this system overconstrained or underconstrained?
4. What is meant by the "equilibrium" price and quantity in a system of equations having a linear demand function and a linear supply function?
5. What is the relation between fixed cost, variable cost per unit, and product price in a break-even analysis using a linear revenue function and a linear cost function?
6. What is the correct interpretation of the slope coefficient on a linear demand function where $P(D) = f(Q_D)$?
7. If a contradiction is found during solution of a system of equations by the elimination method, what can be concluded about the solution to this system?
8. Give a mathematical example of two inequality constraints which cannot be satisfied simultaneously.
9. Briefly explain how the infinite-solution case for a system of equations can be detected by use of the elimination method.
10. What is the graphical representation of the values in a unique solution to a system of equations with two variables?
11. Why is the single inequality statement

    $4 > X \geq 12$

    an incorrect statement of these constraints on X?
12. Distinguish between a strong and a weak inequality statement.

13. Does multiplication of both sides of an inequality by the same negative number change the sense of the inequality? Why or why not? Give a numerical example.
14. What is described by the solution space for a system of inequalities?
15. Why are nonnegativity constraints especially relevant to many mathematical analyses in business and economics?

Review Problems

1. For each system of equations below, state whether the system is overconstrained, underconstrained, or exactly constrained.
   a. $3X + 2Y - Z = 20$
      $4X + Y = 5$
      $X - 4Z = 16$
   b. $2X = 40$
      $X - Y = 17$
   c. $2X + 4Y = 28$
      $8Y - 2Z = 20$
   d. $4X + 6Y = 12$
      $X - Y = 2$
      $5X + 0.5Y = 10$

2. For each demand function P_D and supply function P_S below, find equilibrium price and quantity.
   a. $P_D = 400 - 1.40Q_D$
      $P_S = 150 + 1.1Q_S$
   b. $P_D = 180$
      $P_S = 6 + 3.2Q_S$
   c. $P_D = 325 - 0.025Q_D$
      $P_S = 255 + 0.015Q_S$
   d. $P_D = 18$
      $P_S = 4 + 0.08Q_S$

3. For the demand P_D and supply P_S functions
   $$P_D = 30 - 0.5Q_D$$
   $$P_S = 8 + 0.6Q_S$$
   a. Find equilibrium price and quantity.
   b. Find equilibrium price and quantity if demand changes from the original function to $P_D = 30 - 0.8Q_D$ and supply does not change.
   c. Find equilibrium price and quantity if demand changes from the original function to $P_D = 40 - 0.5Q_D$ and supply changes from the original function to $P_S = 7 + 0.6Q_S$.

4. For each linear function for total revenue (TR) and total cost (TC) below, find the break-even quantity of sales. In each case, show that a lower quantity than break-even will result in a loss. Round all answers to two decimal places.
   a. $TR = 16Q$
      $TC = 2800 + 6Q$
   b. $TR = 2.50Q$
      $TC = 1800 + 0.10Q$
   c. $TR = 24Q$
      $TC = 9800 + 20Q$
   d. $TR = 1.38Q$
      $TC = 7800 + 0.18Q$

5. Find the solution values for each of the following systems of two equations with two unknowns.
   a. $2X + 3Y = 18$
      $X - Y = 2$
   b. $-X + 5Y = 40$
      $0.5X + 0.5Y = 10$
   c. $4X - 8Y = 20$
      $3X - 5Y = 8$
   d. $2X + 6Y = 36$
      $X + Y = 6$

6. For each system of equations below, there does not exist a unique solution. In each case, explain whether there exists an infinite number of solutions or no solution, and the reason for either situation.

a. $2X + 4Y = 8$
   $X + 2Y = 4$
b. $3X - Y = 6$
   $10.5X - 3.5Y = 30$
c. $4X - 8Y = 14$
   $3X - 6Y = 8$
d. $8X + 2Y = 12$
   $28X + 7Y = 42$

7. For each 3 × 3 system, find a unique solution if one exists. If there is not a unique solution, demonstrate why.
   a. $4X - Y + Z = 10.5$
      $X + 4Y - 2Z = 9$
      $6X - 2Y + 4Z = 15$
   b. $3X - Y + 5Z = 16$
      $X + 4Y - 3Z = 10$
      $9X - 3Y + 15Z = 48$
   c. $X - 2Y + 2Z = 20$
      $2X + Y + Z = 7$
      $4X - 3Y + 2Z = 29$
   d. $X + 2Y - 3Z = 8$
      $X - Y + 4Z = 6$
      $5X + Y + 6Z = 34$
   e. $4X + 2Y - 2Z = 8$
      $X + 3Y + Z = 12$
      $6X - Y - 3Z = 8$

8. Express each of the following in slope-intercept form with Y in terms of X and the constant. On which side of the line for each inequality does the solution space lie?
   a. $4X - 3Y \geq 16$
   b. $X + 6Y \leq 34$
   c. $4X - Y \leq 4$
   d. $-3X + 5Y \geq 12$
   e. $3X + 2Y \geq -4$
   f. $2X - Y \geq 0$

9. For each part of Problem 8, impose nonnegativity constraints on both X and Y and graphically describe each resulting solution space.

10. Find and show graphically the solution space for each system of inequalities. Find equations for all boundary lines and establish all intersection points.
   a. $3X + Y \leq 12$
      $2X - 3Y \geq 3$
      $X \geq 0$
      $Y \geq 0$
   b. $2X + 6Y \leq 24$
      $4X + Y \geq 10$
      $X \geq 0$
      $Y \geq 0$
   c. $X + Y \geq 6$
      $2X + 10Y \leq 30$
      $X \geq 0$
      $Y \geq 0$
   d. $3Y \leq 18$
      $2Y + 4X \leq 30$
      $X \geq 0$
      $Y \geq 0$
   e. $3X + 1.5Y \leq 60$
      $X + 2Y \geq 24$
      $X \geq 12$
      $Y \geq 0$
   f. $3Y - X \geq 0$
      $2Y + 5X \geq 20$
      $X \geq 0$
      $Y \geq 0$

11. The linear demand function for home heating oil in a city is found to be

$$P_D = 2.70 - 0.0002 Q_D$$

where P_D is dollars per gallon of oil and Q_D is the quantity of oil consumed measured in gallons.

The supply function for home heating oil in this city is

$$P_S = 0.60 + 0.0001 Q_S$$

Interpret the slope and intercept of both the demand and supply functions. Find the equilibrium price and quantity of home heating oil sold in this city.

12. Assume that the demand for home heating oil described in Problem 11 changes to

$$P_D = 2.85 - 0.0002Q_D$$

and the supply function does not change. Describe this change in demand. Find the new equilibrium price and quantity.

13. Many agricultural markets are "purely competitive," indicating that one seller can sell as much or as little as desired at the existing market price. For this problem, assume that the market for wheat is purely competitive to a single seller and that the price of wheat is $4.60 per bushel.

The supply function for a typical wheat farmer is

$$P_S = 1.80 + 0.002Q_S$$

where P_S is the price per bushel and Q_S represents the number of bushels sold by the farmer. Find equilibrium price and quantity for a typical wheat farmer. If the supply function changes to

$$P_S = 1.80 + 0.0016Q_S$$

find the new equilibrium price and quantity. Describe the change in the supply function.

14. For the wheat price of Problem 13 ($4.60), what is the total revenue function for a farmer? If the total cost function is

Total cost = $54,000 + 3.80Q$

where

Total cost = fixed cost + (variable cost per unit)(quantity)

find the break-even number of bushels for a wheat farmer.

15. A firm plans to put a new programmable calculator on the market during the next month. The price will be $165. Fixed costs are projected at $23,000 and the variable cost per calculator is $125.

Find the break-even quantity of calculators for this firm. What will be the total profit if 800 calculators are sold during the initial sales period?

16. Two machines X and Y can be used to manufacture a specialized automobile part. The machines are to be used, in total, exactly 90 hours per week for the production of this part. Machine X can manufacture 40 parts per hour and machine Y can turn out 32 parts per hour. Exactly 3000 parts per week are required. How many hours per week should each machine be used to satisfy *exactly* these two restrictions?

17. A specialty steel manufacturer produces three home-gardening products. The firm has decided that only a specific amount of labor time, machine time, and management time can be used to produce these three items. These amounts are 890 worker-hours, 610 machine-hours, and 220 management-hours.

Hour requirements for each unit of product X, Y, and Z are as follows:

Product	Worker-hours per unit	Machine-hours per unit	Management-hours per unit
X	2	3	0.2
Y	1.5	1	0.5
Z	2	0.5	0.1

How many units of each product should be manufactured to utilize *exactly* all available resource time?

18. A food manufacturer uses two refrigerated trucks to deliver products. Truck X has a per mile operating cost of $2.40 and truck Y has a per mile operating cost of $1.20. Total mileage requirements are *at least* 4000 miles per month. The firm wants to spend *no more than* $7200 per month for the operation of these two trucks.

    Find the graphical solution space for this system of inequalities including all boundary lines and intersection points between the boundary lines.

19. In addition to the restrictions of Problem 18, the firm must use truck X for at least 800 miles per month for specialized shipments. Present graphically the solution space which includes this limitation as well as the restrictions of Problem 18. Include all boundary lines and intersection points.

20. A pharmaceutical firm is developing a new vitamin supplement which uses two ingredients, X and Y. Each production batch of the supplement is to be made up of a combination of ounces of X and Y which satisfies three criteria. There must be *no more than* 1200 grams of vitamin A, *at least* 300 grams of vitamin E, and *at least* 400 grams of vitamin C in a batch. Grams of vitamins A, E, and C in an ounce of X and of Y are shown below:

Ingredient	Vitamin A	Vitamin E	Vitamin C
X	5	5	8
Y	5	5	4

Describe the solution space specified by these three constraints. Include all boundary lines and intersection points and an appropriate graph in your description.

Matrix Algebra 6

6.1 Introduction

In mathematics, it is often helpful to use groups of values rather than individual values for the variables and constants in a problem. For example, a firm may consider prices for 20 different products as a single term in computing total dollar sales (price times the number of units sold). In other cases, combining observations may be useful because some of the techniques of linear algebra discussed in Chapter 5, such as the elimination method, become difficult to employ as the number of variables and equations in the system increases.

Matrix algebra includes a set of techniques that can be used to manipulate grouped data. Specifically, matrix algebra is beneficial when groups of values are treated as single terms and when working with large systems of linear equations. In addition, computer analyses of problems involving systems of equations often apply matrix-algebra solution techniques. Consequently, an understanding of the basics of matrix algebra is required to develop input, interpret errors, and comprehend the output of many computer-based analyses. Thus, matrix algebra is a basic component of a thorough knowledge of quantitative techniques.

The term used for a particular group of data is a *matrix*. More exactly, a matrix is any rectangular (or square) array of numbers. If an array has only one row or one column of numbers, it is called a *vector* (row vector or column vector, respectively). A single real number is referred to as a *scalar* in the terminology of matrix algebra. The interest rates charged by a bank for various types of loans, sales figures for various automobile models, and steel output for each of the 10 largest manufacturers are examples of data that can be put in the form of arrays.

Consider briefly three problems where data may be expressed as matrices and vectors and which may be solved by the techniques of matrix algebra.

1. A ball-point-pen manufacturer sells pens at four prices: $0.79, $1.09, $1.39, and $1.79. The firm has a record of the number of pens sold at each price in each of five regions (e.g., 4 million $1.09 pens have been sold in the southeast region). The firm wants to determine total national sales for each price line.
2. A chemical firm uses three chemicals (nitrogen, phosphorous, and potassium) in varying weight proportions to produce a unit (tank car) of each of three different products. The weight proportions for each ingredient for each product are known, as is the required number of carlots to be produced for each product. How many pounds of each ingredient must be used to satisfy the total output requirements for each product?
3. A government agency wants to determine the output level for each industry (steel, automobiles, etc.) necessary for that industry to meet all the demands for the goods of that industry both from industries (including itself) and the final consumer. Solution of this problem will yield the output level for each industry sufficient to prevent any bottlenecks in the nation's economic system.

As this chapter continues, methods of using matrix algebra to solve problems similar to these are presented. Techniques for adding, subtracting, and multiplying arrays of numbers will be presented. Also, emphasis will be placed on explaining, conceptually and by example, how matrix algebra can be used to solve systems of linear equations. Although large systems of equations usually are solved by computer, readers should understand the fundamentals of matrix algebra in order to develop and comprehend these computer analyses. Thus, the "by-hand" calculations shown below are important to an understanding of many computer applications.

6.2 Basic Concepts

The individual numbers in a matrix or vector are referred to as its *elements*. The number of elements in a row or column vector is its *dimension*. Arrays

$$A = \begin{pmatrix} a_{11} & 0 & 0 & 0 \\ 0 & a_{22} & 0 & 0 \\ 0 & 0 & a_{32} & 0 \\ 0 & 0 & 0 & a_{44} \end{pmatrix} \qquad B = \begin{pmatrix} 1 & 0 & 0 & 0 \\ 0 & 1 & 0 & 0 \\ 0 & 0 & 1 & 0 \\ 0 & 0 & 0 & 1 \end{pmatrix}$$

(a)   (b)

FIGURE 6.1 A diagonal matrix of order four (a) and a unit, or identity, matrix of order four (b).

other than vectors have multiple rows and/or columns. The dimension of such a matrix is expressed as $m \times n$ (read "m by n"), indicating a matrix with m rows and n columns. Consequently, a matrix with four rows and five columns has the dimension 4×5. Finally, a square matrix has the dimension $m \times n$ where $m = n$. For a square matrix, the number of rows *or* columns represents the *order* of the matrix. For example, a 5×5 matrix has an order of 5.

Three other types of matrices should be mentioned. First, a matrix or vector containing all 0s is called the *null matrix* or *null vector,* respectively. A square matrix with 0s everywhere *except* on the main diagonal positions (i.e., first row–first column, second row–second column, etc.) is referred to as a *diagonal matrix.* One particular diagonal matrix has ones in all main-diagonal positions and zeroes in all other positions. This matrix is called the *unit* or *identity matrix* and is important to several other aspects of matrix algebra. The notation for the identity matrix is **I**. Figure 6.1(a) and (b) shows a diagonal and identity matrix of order four, respectively.

The elements of a matrix are enclosed by parentheses (as in Figure 6.1), but the name of the matrix (**A** and **B** in Figure 6.1) is not enclosed. Individual elements within a matrix often must be referred to during the computation or interpretation of problems. The position of an element within a matrix is identified by two subscripts on the lowercase letter corresponding to the name of the matrix, such as a for **A**. Thus, for the matrix **A**, a_{42} refers to the element in the fourth row and second column. In general, the notation a_{ij} refers to the element of matrix **A** which is in the ith row and jth column.

At times, the elements of a matrix are manipulated when carrying out a computation. One manipulation results in forming the *transpose* of a matrix. The transpose of a matrix is developed by interchanging its rows and columns. Therefore, the first row of the original matrix becomes the first column of the transpose, the second row becomes the second column, and the process continues until all rows and columns are interchanged. Thus, the element a_{ij} in the original matrix is a_{ji} in the transposed matrix, and a matrix of dimension $m \times n$ has the dimension $n \times m$ when transposed. The transpose of a matrix **A** is notated $\mathbf{A}^T$ or $\mathbf{A}'$. Figure 6.2 shows a 3×4 matrix **A** and its transpose $\mathbf{A}^T$, which has a dimension of 4×3.

These concepts of notation and dimension will be utilized in the following sections on matrix computations.

$$A = \begin{pmatrix} a_{11} & a_{12} & a_{13} & a_{14} \\ a_{21} & a_{22} & a_{23} & a_{24} \\ a_{31} & a_{32} & a_{33} & a_{34} \end{pmatrix} \qquad A^T = \begin{pmatrix} a_{11} & a_{21} & a_{31} \\ a_{12} & a_{22} & a_{32} \\ a_{13} & a_{23} & a_{33} \\ a_{14} & a_{24} & a_{34} \end{pmatrix}$$

FIGURE 6.2 A 3×4 matrix and its transpose.

6.3 Addition and Subtraction of Matrices

In matrix algebra there are operations analogous to the addition, subtraction, and multiplication of real numbers. However, all techniques are not identical. The fact that matrices are groups of numbers treated somewhat like a single term causes many of these variations. This and the following sections explain many of the properties and computational techniques applicable to matrices and vectors.

First, a brief statement concerning the equality of two or more matrices is appropriate. Two or more matrices are equal only if each and every element of one matrix is equal to the corresponding element of the other matrix.

Only matrices having *the same dimension* can be added or subtracted. A matrix of dimension 4×3, therefore, cannot be added to or subtracted from a matrix of dimension 5×4. When matrices have the same dimension, addition or subtraction is carried out element by element with the resulting sums or differences constituting the elements of a matrix with the dimension of the original matrices. Two examples will demonstrate matrix addition and subtraction.

Example 6.1
A firm maintains sales records for four products over the past 3 months in two matrices with dimension 4×3. One matrix is for the eastern region's stores and the other is for stores in the western region. The sales department wants to compile a combined matrix. The following demonstrates addition of the two matrices:

Sales in Thousands

	East				West				Total		
	Month				Month				Month		
Product	1	2	3	Product	1	2	3	Product	1	2	3
A	8	4	7	A	6	8	9	A	14	12	16
B	5	4	10	B	7	12	5	B	12	16	15
C	3	10	13	C	14	10	9	C	17	20	22
D	6	11	16	D	3	2	5	D	9	13	21

Example 6.2
As a numerical example of matrix subtraction, consider the matrices **A** and **B** and their difference, matrix **C**.

$$\begin{matrix} A & - & B & = & C \end{matrix}$$

$$\begin{pmatrix} 3 & 2 & 8 \\ 14 & 11 & 7 \\ 6 & 5 & 9 \end{pmatrix} - \begin{pmatrix} 7 & 5 & 0 \\ 7 & 5 & 0 \\ 4 & 3 & 2 \end{pmatrix} = \begin{pmatrix} -4 & -3 & 8 \\ 7 & 6 & 7 \\ 2 & 2 & 7 \end{pmatrix}$$

The principles applicable to both matrix addition and matrix subtraction are (1) the matrices must be of the same dimension, (2) addition or subtraction is carried out element by element, and (3) the resulting matrix has the same dimension as each of the original matrices. Finally, observe that the presence of negative numbers or zeroes has no effect on these principles.

6.4 Matrix Multiplication

As shown above, addition and subtraction of matrices is restricted to matrices of the same dimension. Other considerations of matrix size restrict the application of matrix multiplication. These factors and other principles of matrix multiplication are discussed below.

When a matrix is multiplied by a scalar (real number), each element in the matrix is multiplied by the scalar and the dimension of the resulting product matrix is the same as that of the original matrix. If the scalar is 1, the product is the original matrix, and if the scalar is 0, the null matrix results.

Example 6.3
Perform the following multiplication:

(0.05)**A**

where

$$A = \begin{pmatrix} 20 & 30 & 20 & 10 & 7 \\ 30 & 0 & 10 & 12 & 8 \\ 40 & 3 & 16 & 15 & 25 \end{pmatrix}$$

$$(0.05)A = \begin{pmatrix} 1 & 1.5 & 1 & 0.5 & 0.35 \\ 1.5 & 0 & 0.5 & 0.6 & 0.4 \\ 2 & 0.15 & 0.8 & 0.75 & 1.25 \end{pmatrix}$$

The other principles of matrix multiplication are presented by means of three examples including discussion of the solution method for each. Numerical results are provided only for the third example.

Example 6.4

A newly created bank holding company knows the rate of return earned on investments and the total amount invested by each of its six banks. The firm wants to determine the total dollar return for the combined six banks (one number).

If matrix multiplication is used to find this answer, rates of return are listed in a row vector **A** with six elements and the investment value for each bank is listed in a column vector **B**.[1] The elements for each are shown as

$$\mathbf{A} = (a_1\ a_2\ a_3\ a_4\ a_5\ a_6)$$

$$\mathbf{B} = \begin{pmatrix} b_1 \\ b_2 \\ b_3 \\ b_4 \\ b_5 \\ b_6 \end{pmatrix}$$

The total amount earned on investments for the six banks (a single dollar amount) is determined by multiplying matrix **A** and matrix **B** according to the following procedure.

To obtain the product of a row vector and a column vector, a group of products is computed. Each member of the group is the product of two factors: an element from the row vector and the corresponding subscripted element from the column vector. The number of products formed in this way is equal to the number of elements in either the row vector or the column vector. (This is why a requirement for this multiplication process is that the number of elements in the row vector must equal the number of elements in the column vector.)

Therefore, the product is a scalar, the sum of the following terms:

$$\mathbf{AB} = a_1b_1 + a_2b_2 + a_3b_3 + a_4b_4 + a_5b_5 + a_6b_6$$

The product **AB** is a dollar figure representing bank earnings.

Example 6.5

An automobile-parts manufacturer knows the replacement cost of each of the 20 products that it manufactures. At the end of each month, the firm receives reports on the inventory quantity of each product at each of its 10 warehouses. Using these data, the company wants to determine the total replacement cost of the inventory at each warehouse.

To find this answer, a row vector of the 20 replacement costs is first

---

[1] Often, vectors are notated by "boldface" lowercase letters (**a** and **b** in the above case). However, this text will use capital letters to identify both matrices and vectors in order to avoid any confusion between array names and the names of individual elements in the array.

established. This is called **A**. Second, an array **B** consisting of the inventory figures for the 20 products at each warehouse is constructed. Matrix **B** is a 20 × 10 matrix each row of which represents a particular automobile part. Multiplication of **A** by **B** yields a row vector **C** consisting of 10 elements, one element for the replacement cost of the inventory at each of the 10 warehouses. In notation form this product is

$$(\mathbf{A}_{1 \times 20})(\mathbf{B}_{20 \times 10}) = \mathbf{C}_{1 \times 10}$$

Each element in matrix **C** is the sum of 20 products, each formed through row-by-column multiplication in the following way. If,

$$\mathbf{A} = (a_1, a_2, \ldots, a_{20}) \quad \text{and} \quad \mathbf{B} = \begin{pmatrix} b_{1,1} & b_{1,2} & \cdots & b_{1,10} \\ b_{2,1} & b_{2,2} & \cdots & b_{2,10} \\ \cdots & \cdots & \cdots & \cdots \\ b_{20,1} & b_{20,2} & \cdots & b_{20,10} \end{pmatrix}$$

then

$$c_1 = (a_1)(b_{1,1}) + (a_2)(b_{2,1}) + \cdots + (a_{20})(b_{20,1})$$
$$c_2 = (a_1)(b_{1,2}) + (a_2)(b_{2,2}) + \cdots + (a_{20})(b_{20,2})$$
$$\cdot$$
$$\cdot$$
$$\cdot$$
$$c_{10} = (a_1)(b_{1,10}) + (a_2)(b_{2,10}) + \cdots + (a_{20})(b_{20,10})$$

Example 6.6 presents another problem which will enable a general statement to be made about the rules for matrix multiplication.

Example 6.6
Find the product of **A** and **B**, where

$$\mathbf{A} = \begin{pmatrix} 3 & 1 & 4 \\ 2 & 5 & 1 \end{pmatrix} \quad \mathbf{B} = \begin{pmatrix} 8 & 0 & -2 & 4 \\ 6 & 3 & 2 & -4 \\ 2 & -1 & 3 & 1 \end{pmatrix}$$

To determine this product, row-by-column multiplication is applied to the elements of each *column* of **B** and each *row* of **A**. This forms the product matrix **C** with the following elements:

$$\begin{matrix} \mathbf{A} & \times & \mathbf{B} & = & \mathbf{C} \end{matrix}$$

$$\begin{pmatrix} 3 & 1 & 4 \\ 2 & 5 & 1 \end{pmatrix} \begin{pmatrix} 8 & 0 & -2 & 4 \\ 6 & 3 & 2 & -4 \\ 2 & -1 & 3 & 1 \end{pmatrix} = \begin{pmatrix} 38 & -1 & 8 & 12 \\ 48 & 14 & 9 & -11 \end{pmatrix}$$

Each element of **C** is determined in the following way by using appropriate subscript notation as,

$c_{11} = (a_{11})(b_{11}) + (a_{12})(b_{21}) + (a_{13})(b_{31}) = 24 + 6 + 8 = 38$
$c_{12} = (a_{11})(b_{12}) + (a_{12})(b_{22}) + (a_{13})(b_{32}) = 0 + 3 - 4 = -1$
$c_{13} = (a_{11})(b_{13}) + (a_{12})(b_{23}) + (a_{13})(b_{33}) = -6 + 2 + 12 = 8$
$c_{14} = (a_{11})(b_{14}) + (a_{12})(b_{24}) + (a_{13})(b_{34}) = 12 - 4 + 4 = 12$
$c_{21} = (a_{21})(b_{11}) + (a_{22})(b_{21}) + (a_{23})(b_{31}) = 16 + 30 + 2 = 48$
$c_{22} = (a_{21})(b_{12}) + (a_{22})(b_{22}) + (a_{23})(b_{32}) = 0 + 15 - 1 = 14$
$c_{23} = (a_{21})(b_{13}) + (a_{22})(b_{23}) + (a_{23})(b_{33}) = -4 + 10 + 3 = 9$
$c_{24} = (a_{21})(b_{14}) + (a_{22})(b_{24}) + (a_{23})(b_{34}) = 8 - 20 + 1 = -11$

Thus, the matrix **A** with dimension 2×3 is multiplied by the matrix **B** with dimension 3×4, resulting in a product matrix **C** with dimension 2×4.

Several principles of matrix multiplication can be derived from these three examples. First, row-by-column multiplication means that the element in a specific position of a product matrix (such as the second row, third column) comprises the sum of the products of corresponding elements in the row (second) and column (third) of the respective matrices. Each element in the product matrix found by this row-by-column multiplication is referred to as an *inner product*.

A second principle is that, in order to multiply two matrices, the number of columns in the first matrix must equal the number of rows in the second matrix. Matrices which satisfy this condition are considered *conformable* for multiplication. The resulting product matrix has a number of rows equal to the number of rows of the first matrix and a number of columns equal to the number of columns in the second matrix.

This principle demonstrates that the commutative law of multiplication (Chapter 2) does not apply to matrix multiplication as it does to multiplying real numbers. In Example 6.6, it was found that $\mathbf{A} \times \mathbf{B} = \mathbf{C}$. However, the product $\mathbf{B} \times \mathbf{A}$ cannot be formed and, therefore, it cannot be equal to the matrix **C**. Because of the importance of sequence in matrix multiplication, the terminology used to express the product of two matrices $\mathbf{A} \times \mathbf{B}$ is that **A** is *postmultiplied* by **B** or, alternatively, **B** is *premultiplied* by **A**. Thus, in Example 6.6, **B** can be premultiplied by **A**, but **A** may not be premultiplied by **B** as the dimensions of each, *in this order,* are not conformable for multiplication.

As a final technique of matrix multiplication, note that if a square matrix of order n is postmultiplied or premultiplied by an identity matrix of the same order, the product is the original matrix. In notation form, this is shown as

$$(\mathbf{X}_{n \times n})(\mathbf{I}_{n \times n}) = \mathbf{X}_{n \times n} = (\mathbf{I}_{n \times n})(\mathbf{X}_{n \times n})$$

This principle helps to point out that the identity matrix has characteristics similar to those of the number 1 in the multiplication of real numbers.

The following exercises will provide an opportunity to apply the principles of matrix addition, subtraction, and multiplication.

EXERCISES

1. Perform the following operations as indicated:

   a. $\begin{pmatrix} 3 & 4 & 1 \\ 4 & 6 & 2 \end{pmatrix} + \begin{pmatrix} 0 & -3 & 0 \\ 0 & 1 & 7 \end{pmatrix}$

   b. $\begin{pmatrix} -2 & -1 & 0 \\ -3 & -4 & 5 \end{pmatrix} - \begin{pmatrix} -3 & -1 & 0 \\ 2 & 4 & -3 \end{pmatrix}$

   c. $3 \begin{pmatrix} 2 & -1 \\ 0 & 6 \end{pmatrix} + \begin{pmatrix} 7 & 0 \\ 8 & -4 \end{pmatrix}$

   d. $0.5 \begin{pmatrix} 6 & -4 \\ 10 & 12 \end{pmatrix} - 3 \begin{pmatrix} 2 & 4 \\ -2 & 3 \end{pmatrix}$

   e. $(6 \quad 7 \quad 2 \quad 0 \quad -4) + (-3 \quad 12 \quad 8 \quad 4 \quad -5)$

   f. $3(2 \quad -4 \quad 12 \quad 14)$

   g. $\begin{pmatrix} 6 & 2 & 1 \\ 3 & 1 & 2 \end{pmatrix} + \begin{pmatrix} 5 & 0 & 0 \\ 1 & -2 & 3 \end{pmatrix} - \begin{pmatrix} -6 & -2 & 3 \\ -4 & 5 & 4 \end{pmatrix}$

   h. $\begin{pmatrix} 0.5 & -0.4 \\ 0.8 & 0.2 \end{pmatrix} - \begin{pmatrix} 1 & -3 \\ 2 & -0.5 \end{pmatrix} + \begin{pmatrix} 1 & 0 \\ 0 & 1 \end{pmatrix}$

2. Multiply the following matrices:

   a. $(4 \quad 10 \quad 2) \begin{pmatrix} 6 \\ 3 \\ -4 \end{pmatrix}$

   b. $\begin{pmatrix} 4 \\ -2 \\ 3 \end{pmatrix} (6 \quad 0 \quad 7)$

   c. $\begin{pmatrix} 6 & 4 & 2 \\ 7 & 0 & -3 \end{pmatrix} \begin{pmatrix} 4 & 0 \\ 3 & 6 \\ -2 & -7 \end{pmatrix}$

   d. $\begin{pmatrix} 1 & 0 & 0 \\ 0 & 1 & 0 \\ 0 & 0 & 1 \end{pmatrix} \begin{pmatrix} 16 & 10 & -4 \\ 8 & 8 & -3 \\ -5 & 0 & 15 \end{pmatrix}$

   e. $\begin{pmatrix} 3 & 1 \\ 6 & 4 \end{pmatrix} \begin{pmatrix} 8 & 0 & -2 \\ -4 & 2 & 3 \end{pmatrix}$

   f. $(4 \quad 2 \quad 9 \quad 3) \begin{pmatrix} 6 & 1 & 5 & 6 \\ 2 & 3 & 2 & -3 \\ 0 & 4 & 2 & -3 \\ 1 & 1 & 1 & 0 \end{pmatrix}$

   g. $\begin{pmatrix} 1 & 0 & 0 \\ 0 & 1 & 0 \\ 0 & 0 & 1 \end{pmatrix} \begin{pmatrix} -5 & 0.5 & 4 \\ -7 & 2.5 & 8 \\ 6 & 2 & -0.5 \end{pmatrix}$

   h. $\begin{pmatrix} 5 & 0 & 0 \\ 0 & 5 & 0 \\ 0 & 0 & 5 \end{pmatrix} \begin{pmatrix} 1 & 3 & 4 & -1 \\ -2 & 0 & 6 & 1 \\ -3 & -4 & 5 & 9 \end{pmatrix}$

3. Show that the commutative law of multiplication does not apply to each of the following products.

a. $\begin{pmatrix} 2 & 6 \\ 3 & 1 \end{pmatrix} \begin{pmatrix} 7 & -1 \\ 0 & 4 \end{pmatrix}$ d. $\begin{pmatrix} 4 & -2 \\ 6 & 8 \end{pmatrix} \begin{pmatrix} 0 & 1 \\ 1 & 0 \end{pmatrix}$

b. $\begin{pmatrix} 0 & 1 \\ 1 & 0 \end{pmatrix} \begin{pmatrix} 5 & 6 \\ 7 & 8 \end{pmatrix}$ e. $(-6 \quad 3 \quad 8) \begin{pmatrix} 5 \\ 4 \\ 2 \end{pmatrix}$

c. $(4 \quad 2 \quad 1) \begin{pmatrix} 6 \\ -3 \\ 4 \end{pmatrix}$

4. For the following vector **X** and matrix **A**

$$\mathbf{X} = (4 \quad 2 \quad 1 \quad 5) \qquad \mathbf{A} = \begin{pmatrix} 2 & 0 & 2 & -5 \\ 3 & 6 & 4 & 2 \\ 1 & 3 & 0 & 2 \\ 1 & -1 & -3 & 6 \end{pmatrix}$$

Find:
a. $\mathbf{A}^T$ b. $\mathbf{XA}$ c. $\mathbf{AX}^T$ d. $\mathbf{XA}^T$ e. $\mathbf{XX}^T$ f. $\mathbf{AA}^T$

5. A consumer products firm sells its popular detergent at four prices corresponding to different sizes: $1.20, $1.50, $1.80, and $2.00. Sales of boxes (in thousands) per week for each size for each of four national regions are listed below.

		Region		
Size	I	II	III	IV
$1.20	2	0.5	2	0.6
1.50	1.5	1	2.2	1.1
1.80	3	2	1	3
2.00	1	1.2	1.5	1.2

Use matrix multiplication to find the total weekly dollar sales for each region.

6. A chemical firm uses five ingredients to manufacture three products. The price per pound (in dollars) of each ingredient is shown in the following vector **X**:

$$\mathbf{X} = (0.50 \quad 1.25 \quad 1.50 \quad 2.00 \quad 2.20)$$

The following 5 × 3 matrix lists the pounds of each ingredient required to produce a carlot of each product:

	Product, Pounds per Carlot		
Ingredient	A	B	C
1	30	10	8
2	10	5	30
3	20	20	8
4	30	10	5
5	40	15	20

  a. Find the cost of a carlot of each product.
  b. If the firm receives an order for 6 carlots of product A, 9 carlots of B, and 20 carlots of C, how many pounds of each ingredient will be required to satisfy the order?
7. An insurance firm maintains claims data in two arrays. One includes historical or "rule of thumb" costs for processing a claim in each of four claim categories for each of four customer classifications. These data, representing processing cost per claim, are in the following matrix:

Customer Classification	Processing Cost per Claim			
	Claim Category			
	1	2	3	4
1	2.00	4.00	4.50	5.00
2	2.00	2.00	4.50	5.00
3	3.00	3.50	6.00	6.00
4	3.50	3.50	6.50	7.00

The firm also includes in a matrix the number of claims processed each month for the same customer and claim categories. A recent month's data are

Customer Classification	Claims per Month			
	Claim Category			
	1	2	3	4
1	50	40	60	10
2	10	30	40	20
3	10	20	30	30
4	20	20	20	50

Use matrix multiplication to find:
  a. Total processing cost for each claim category for this month.
  b. Total processing cost for each customer category this month. In both a and b, construct a product matrix including only those elements

relevant to the answer requested. Leave blank all other matrix positions.

8. A firm has employment records in two arrays. One includes the number of worker-hours used during the past month in each of five job classifications at three production facilities. These data are

Job Classification	Number of Worker-Hours at Production Facility		
	1	2	3
1	4000	3000	2000
2	3000	3000	4000
3	2000	4500	5000
4	2000	2500	1000
5	3000	1000	2500

Another array includes the average hourly wage for each job classification at each production facility as follows:

Job Classification	Average Hourly Wage at Production Facility		
	1	2	3
1	$6.00	$5.00	$5.50
2	5.00	5.00	6.00
3	7.00	8.00	9.00
4	8.00	9.00	8.50
5	8.00	10.00	9.00

Use matrix multiplication to find:
a. Total wages paid during the month at each production facility.
b. Total wages paid during the month for each job classification. Include in each answer matrix only those elements relevant to answering the problem and leave blank all other matrix positions.

6.5 The Matrix Form of a System of Linear Equations

The primary topic of the remainder of this chapter is the use of matrix algebra in solving systems of linear equations. Example 6.7 will be the basis of this discussion. Although the scope of this example and the data used are intentionally simple, the principles derived from its analysis are relevant to larger and more complex systems of equations. Thus, Example 6.7 will be referred to at various points in this and the next three sections.

Example 6.7

A manufacturer of machine motors produces three motor types: type R, type S, and type T. Each motor requires for its production a specific amount of labor time, machine time, and support-service time (management and staff time). The firm has available each week for production of these three kinds of motor 3000 worker-hours, 2400 machine-hours, and 3600 support-service-hours.

The firm's management wants to determine how many motors of each type to produce to utilize exactly the available amounts of these resources. Techniques of matrix algebra can be used to answer this question.

First, the resource requirements for the production of each motor must be known. These requirements are shown in Table 6.1.

The data in Table 6.1 allow formation of a system of equations where each equation represents a resource constraint. These constraints are the following:

Worker-hour constraint:

$3R + 4S + T = 3000$

Machine-hour constraint:

$2R + 3S + 5T = 2400$

Support-service-hour constraint:

$4R + 3S + T = 3600$

In these equations, R, S, and T represent the number of each machine type produced (type R, type S, and type T, respectively). The objective of the analysis is to determine the production levels for R, S, and T which will satisfy exactly the three resource constraints. Matrix algebra provides techniques for finding these values. Before describing these techniques, we shall consider some useful notation.

This system of equations can be expressed in matrix notation. The system has three data sets which can be put into arrays: (1) coefficients, (2) unknowns, and (3) constants.

The coefficient matrix, by convention, is notated **A**. Thus, for this example,

TABLE 6.1 Hour Requirements for One Unit of Each Machine

Machine	Worker-Hours	Machine-Hours	Support-Service-Hours
R	3	2	4
S	4	3	3
T	1	5	1

$$\mathbf{A} = \begin{pmatrix} 3 & 4 & 1 \\ 2 & 3 & 5 \\ 4 & 3 & 1 \end{pmatrix}$$

The variables representing the unknown production levels for each motor are listed in a column vector **X**

$$\mathbf{X} = \begin{pmatrix} R \\ S \\ T \end{pmatrix}$$

The constants, or the total available resource hours in this problem, are put in a column vector **B**:

$$\mathbf{B} = \begin{pmatrix} 3000 \\ 2400 \\ 3600 \end{pmatrix}$$

Thus, this system, like any $m \times n$ system of linear equations, can be stated in matrix form by setting the product of the coefficient matrix and the vector of unknowns equal to the vector of constants. Consequently,

$$\mathbf{AX} = \mathbf{B}$$

or

$$\begin{pmatrix} 3 & 4 & 1 \\ 2 & 3 & 5 \\ 4 & 3 & 1 \end{pmatrix} \begin{pmatrix} R \\ S \\ T \end{pmatrix} = \begin{pmatrix} 3000 \\ 2400 \\ 3600 \end{pmatrix}$$

Readers should confirm by matrix multiplication (row by column) that $\mathbf{AX} = \mathbf{B}$ results in the system of equations shown above.

Therefore, for any system with m equations and n variables, the matrix form of the system of equations can be expressed as

$$\mathbf{A} \cdot \mathbf{X} = \mathbf{B}$$

$$\begin{pmatrix} a_{11} & a_{12} & \cdots & a_{1n} \\ a_{21} & a_{22} & \cdots & a_{2n} \\ \vdots & \vdots & & \vdots \\ a_{m1} & a_{m2} & \cdots & a_{mn} \end{pmatrix} \begin{pmatrix} x_1 \\ x_2 \\ \vdots \\ x_n \end{pmatrix} = \begin{pmatrix} b_1 \\ b_2 \\ \vdots \\ b_m \end{pmatrix}$$

where **A** designates the matrix of coefficients, **X** designates the vector of unknowns, and **B** designates the vector of constants.

This section has described the matrix notation for any system of equations and introduced a specific example of a system with three equations and three unknowns. These principles and the example will be referred to in the following sections.

6.6 Solution of Systems of Linear Equations by Matrices

As may be apparent after the study of Chapter 5, solving large systems of equations by the method of elimination often is tedious. This section describes the solution of systems of equations by using matrices. Matrices are used by computers to solve large systems of equations; thus, this technique is applicable to current computerized business analysis. The specific technique presented in this section is the Gauss-Jordan method of elimination.

The Gauss-Jordan method of elimination is a matrix-algebra procedure which transforms a system of equations into a form where the solution can be read by inspection. Components of the matrix form of a system of equations are used to carry out this transformation.

The first step in the Gauss-Jordan method is to place the coefficient matrix **A** to the left of the vector of constants **B** to form an *augmented matrix* of the following type:

$(A \mid B)$

As can be seen, a dashed line is used to separate the two matrices.

The Gauss-Jordan method requires that algebraic operations be performed on the augmented matrix until that part representing the coefficient matrix **A** has become an identity matrix of the same order as **A**. At this point, the part which originally represented the vector of constants **B** has become the solution set for the system of equations. An example using matrix notation will explain this concept.

Example 6.8
The following is a 3 × 3 system of equations in polynomial form:

$a_{11}x_1 + a_{12}x_2 + a_{13}x_3 = b_1$
$a_{21}x_1 + a_{22}x_2 + a_{23}x_3 = b_2$
$a_{31}x_1 + a_{32}x_2 + a_{33}x_3 = b_3$

Thus, the matrix of coefficients, vector of unknowns, and vector of constants are the following:

$$\mathbf{A} \cdot \mathbf{X} = \mathbf{B}$$
$$\begin{pmatrix} a_{11} & a_{12} & a_{13} \\ a_{21} & a_{22} & a_{23} \\ a_{31} & a_{32} & a_{33} \end{pmatrix} \cdot \begin{pmatrix} x_1 \\ x_2 \\ x_3 \end{pmatrix} = \begin{pmatrix} b_1 \\ b_2 \\ b_3 \end{pmatrix}$$

and the augmented matrix includes **A** and **B** separated by a dashed line:

$$\begin{pmatrix} a_{11} & a_{12} & a_{13} & \vdots & b_1 \\ a_{21} & a_{22} & a_{23} & \vdots & b_2 \\ a_{31} & a_{32} & a_{33} & \vdots & b_3 \end{pmatrix}$$

Finally, arithmetic operations on this matrix will continue until the following augmented matrix results.

$(I \mid S)$

$$\begin{pmatrix} 1 & 0 & 0 & | & s_1 \\ 0 & 1 & 0 & | & s_2 \\ 0 & 0 & 1 & | & s_3 \end{pmatrix}$$

In this final form, the vector S in the augmented matrix represents the solution set. The identity matrix is used to read the answers by inspection as shown by the coefficients and variable notation below:

$1x_1 = s_1$ or $x_1 = s_1$
$1x_2 = s_2$ or $x_2 = s_2$
$1x_3 = s_3$ or $x_3 = s_3$

The particular operations carried out on the augmented matrix to achieve this result are referred to as *row operations*. Row operations include the following:

1. The interchange of two rows
2. Multiplication or division of a row by a nonzero constant
3. Addition of the multiple of one row to another row

These row operations are carried out on the rows of the augmented matrix until the coefficient matrix **A** is an identity matrix **I** and the vector of constants **B** is the solution set vector **S**.

One common procedure for carrying out row operations, though not the only one, is called the *zeroes-first method*. This means that the row operations are directed toward first obtaining 0s in all the off-diagonal positions of the coefficient matrix. Then, additional row operations are conducted to obtain 1s in the main diagonal positions of the coefficient matrix.

Example 6.9 uses the zeroes-first method to solve a 2×2 system of equations.

Example 6.9

Use the Gauss-Jordan method of elimination to solve the following system of equations:

$2X_1 + 5X_2 = 18$
$X_1 + 3X_2 = 10$

First, the coefficient matrix and vector of constants are used to develop the augmented matrix.

$$(A \mid B) = \begin{pmatrix} 2 & 5 & | & 18 \\ 1 & 3 & | & 10 \end{pmatrix}$$

The row operations are

Operation	Result
1. Replace row 2 by $\frac{1}{2}$ (row 1) − row 2:	$\begin{pmatrix} 2 & 5 & \vert & 18 \\ 0 & -\frac{1}{2} & \vert & -1 \end{pmatrix}$
2. Replace row 1 by 10(row 2) + row 1:	$\begin{pmatrix} 2 & 0 & \vert & 8 \\ 0 & -\frac{1}{2} & \vert & -1 \end{pmatrix}$
3. Replace row 1 by $\frac{1}{2}$ (row 1):	$\begin{pmatrix} 1 & 0 & \vert & 4 \\ 0 & -\frac{1}{2} & \vert & -1 \end{pmatrix}$
4. Replace row 2 by −2(row 2):	$\begin{pmatrix} 1 & 0 & \vert & 4 \\ 0 & 1 & \vert & 2 \end{pmatrix}$

Thus, the solution of the system of equations is

$X_1 = 4$
$X_2 = 2$

Substitution of these values into the original system of equations will verify the solution.

In most cases, the number of row operations required for solution increases with increasing size of the system of equations. The following solution of the motor-production problem described in the previous section demonstrates this point.

Example 6.10
The system of equations for the motor-production problem is as follows:

$3R + 4S + T = 3000$
$2R + 3S + 5T = 2400$
$4R + 3S + T = 3600$

where R, S, and T represent the number of the three types of motors and the equations represent, respectively, the worker-hour, machine-hour, and support-service-hour constraints.

First, the augmented matrix is formed as follows:

$$(A \vert B) = \begin{pmatrix} 3 & 4 & 1 & \vert & 3000 \\ 2 & 3 & 5 & \vert & 2400 \\ 4 & 3 & 1 & \vert & 3600 \end{pmatrix}$$

The following row operations are carried out by using the zeroes-first method:

Operation | Result

1. Replace row 2 by
   $\frac{2}{3}$ (row 1) − row 2:
   $$\begin{pmatrix} 3 & 4 & 1 & | & 3000 \\ 0 & -\frac{1}{3} & -\frac{13}{3} & | & -400 \\ 4 & 3 & 1 & | & 3600 \end{pmatrix}$$

2. Replace row 3 by
   $\frac{4}{3}$ (row 1) − row 3:
   $$\begin{pmatrix} 3 & 4 & 1 & | & 3000 \\ 0 & -\frac{1}{3} & -\frac{13}{3} & | & -400 \\ 0 & \frac{7}{3} & \frac{1}{3} & | & 400 \end{pmatrix}$$

3. Replace row 3 by
   7(row 2) + row 3:
   $$\begin{pmatrix} 3 & 4 & 1 & | & 3000 \\ 0 & -\frac{1}{3} & -\frac{13}{3} & | & -400 \\ 0 & 0 & -30 & | & -2400 \end{pmatrix}$$

4. Replace row 1 by
   12(row 2) + row 1:
   $$\begin{pmatrix} 3 & 0 & -51 & | & -1800 \\ 0 & -\frac{1}{3} & -\frac{13}{3} & | & -400 \\ 0 & 0 & -30 & | & -2400 \end{pmatrix}$$

5. Replace row 1 by
   $-\frac{17}{10}$ (row 3) + row 1:
   $$\begin{pmatrix} 3 & 0 & 0 & | & 2280 \\ 0 & -\frac{1}{3} & -\frac{13}{3} & | & -400 \\ 0 & 0 & -30 & | & -2400 \end{pmatrix}$$

6. Replace row 2 by
   $-\frac{13}{90}$ (row 3) + row 2:
   $$\begin{pmatrix} 3 & 0 & 0 & | & 2280 \\ 0 & -\frac{1}{3} & 0 & | & -\frac{160}{3} \\ 0 & 0 & -30 & | & -2400 \end{pmatrix}$$

7. Replace row 1 by
   row 1 ÷ 3:
   $$\begin{pmatrix} 1 & 0 & 0 & | & 760 \\ 0 & -\frac{1}{3} & 0 & | & -\frac{160}{3} \\ 0 & 0 & -30 & | & -2400 \end{pmatrix}$$

8. Replace row 2 by $-3(\text{row } 2)$:
$$\begin{pmatrix} 1 & 0 & 0 & | & 760 \\ 0 & 1 & 0 & | & 160 \\ 0 & 0 & -30 & | & -2400 \end{pmatrix}$$

9. Replace row 3 by row $3 \div -30$:
$$\begin{pmatrix} 1 & 0 & 0 & | & 760 \\ 0 & 1 & 0 & | & 160 \\ 0 & 0 & 1 & | & 80 \end{pmatrix}$$

The final step (step 9) indicates the solution as follows:

$R = 760$
$S = 160$
$T = 80$

Thus, these values indicate the number of each type of machine that should be produced by the firm to utilize exactly the available resources.

As this example demonstrates, the required row operations may be burdensome when carried out by hand calculation. Many computer programs exist which use the Gauss-Jordan method of elimination. The previous two examples will assist readers in understanding the technique utilized in these programs.

If row operations lead to a row of zeroes in the coefficient matrix (left-hand side of the dashed line), a unique solution to the system of linear equations does not exist. At this point, further row operations will not lead to a solution.

The next two examples demonstrate, respectively, the case of no solution and that of an infinite number of solutions to a system of linear equations. Readers should note the parallels to the same solution possibilities resulting from the method of elimination (Chapter 5).

Example 6.11
Solve the following system of equations by the Gauss-Jordan method of elimination:

$4X_1 - 7X_2 + X_3 = 15$
$2X_1 - X_2 + 2X_3 = 10$
$12X_1 - 21X_2 + 3X_3 = 24$

The augmented matrix is as follows:

$$(\mathbf{A} \,|\, \mathbf{B}) = \begin{pmatrix} 4 & -7 & 1 & | & 15 \\ 2 & -1 & 2 & | & 10 \\ 12 & -21 & 3 & | & 24 \end{pmatrix}$$

Row operations lead to the following:

Operation	Result
1. Replace row 2 by $-\frac{1}{2}$ (row 1) + row 2:	$\begin{pmatrix} 4 & -7 & 1 & \vert & 15 \\ 0 & \frac{5}{2} & \frac{3}{2} & \vert & \frac{5}{2} \\ 12 & -21 & 3 & \vert & 24 \end{pmatrix}$
2. Replace row 3 by -3(row 1) + row 3:	$\begin{pmatrix} 4 & -7 & 1 & \vert & 15 \\ 0 & \frac{5}{2} & \frac{3}{2} & \vert & \frac{5}{2} \\ 0 & 0 & 0 & \vert & -21 \end{pmatrix}$

At this point, it is observed that the third implicit equation ($0X_1 + 0X_2 + 0X_3 = -21$) can never be true. Thus, the system has no solution, since a contradiction has been established.

Example 6.12
Solve the following system of equations by the Gauss-Jordan method of elimination:

$2X_1 + X_2 - 5X_3 = 8$
$4X_1 - 3X_2 + X_3 = 19$
$8X_1 + 4X_2 - 20X_3 = 32$

First, the augmented matrix is formed:

$$(\mathbf{A} \vert \mathbf{B}) = \begin{pmatrix} 2 & 1 & -5 & \vert & 8 \\ 4 & -3 & 1 & \vert & 19 \\ 8 & 4 & -20 & \vert & 32 \end{pmatrix}$$

Row operations lead to the following results:

Operation	Result
1. Replace row 2 by -2(row 1) + row 2:	$\begin{pmatrix} 2 & 1 & -5 & \vert & 8 \\ 0 & -5 & 11 & \vert & 3 \\ 8 & 4 & -20 & \vert & 32 \end{pmatrix}$
2. Replace row 3 by 4(row 1) − row 3:	$\begin{pmatrix} 2 & 1 & -5 & \vert & 8 \\ 0 & -5 & 11 & \vert & 3 \\ 0 & 0 & 0 & \vert & 0 \end{pmatrix}$

As step 2 yields the result $0 = 0$ for the third equation, it is concluded that any number for X_1, X_2, and X_3 satisfies the equation. Consequently, there are an infinite number of solutions to the system.

The following exercise set and the exercises after the next section will provide practice in solving systems of equations by the Gauss-Jordan procedure.

EXERCISES

1. For each system of equations, set up the augmented matrix required for solution by the Gauss-Jordan method of elimination.
   a. $3X - 2Y = 10$
      $6X + Y = 16$
   b. $3X + 6Y + 4Z = 14$
      $3X + 10Y = 22$
      $X + 4Y + 5Z = 12$
   c. $2X - Y = 15$
      $3X - 2Y = 0$
   d. $X + 4Y + Z = 32$
      $2X + 2Z = 21$
      $3X - Y + 4Z = 40$

2. Solve each 2×2 system of equations by the Gauss-Jordan method of elimination.
   a. $3X - Y = 8$
      $2X + 2Y = 16$
   b. $2X + 5Y = 21$
      $3X + 3Y = 7$
   c. $3X + 7Y = 18$
      $10X + 2Y = 60$
   d. $2X + 8Y = 22$
      $X + 3Y = 10$

3. Solve each 3×3 system of equations by the Gauss-Jordan method of elimination. Check your answers by substitution into the original system.
   a. $2X + 2Y + Z = 13$
      $4X - Y + 2Z = 21$
      $X + 4Y - 2Z = -3$
   b. $4X + 2Y + 3Z = 15$
      $X - Y + 4Z = 9$
      $2X + 2Y + Z = 9$
   c. $X + Y + 2Z = 12$
      $3X + Y = 12$
      $3X + 2Y + Z = 20$
   d. $X + 2Y + Z = 30$
      $2X + 3Y + 2Z = 53$
      $5X + Y + 3Z = 63$

4. For each system of equations below, use the Gauss-Jordan method of elimination to determine whether there are either no solutions or an unlimited number of solutions.
   a. $2X - 3Y = 10$
      $8X - 12Y = 6$
   b. $6X - Y + Z = 9$
      $4X + 2Y + 2Z = 18$
      $24X - 4Y + 4Z = 36$
   c. $4X - 2Y + 12Z = 22$
      $2X + Y - 5Z = 12$
      $10X - 5Y + 30Z = 50$
   d. $X + Y - 2Z = 12$
      $5X + 6Y - 5Z = 42$
      $2X + 3Y + Z = 6$
   e. $X + 4Y = 8$
      $8X + 32Y = 64$
   f. $4X - 2Y + 6Z = 36$
      $X - Y + 5Z = 10$
      $-2X + Y - 3Z = 2$
   g. $2X + 2Y + Z = 10$
      $4X - 2Y + 10Z = 50$
      $2X - Y + 5Z = 25$
   h. $3X + 2Y + 6Z = 36$
      $4X + 8Y + 2Z = 28$
      $5X + 6Y + 7Z = 40$

6.7 Solution of Systems of Linear Equations by the Inverse Matrix

Row operations also can be used to find the inverse of a matrix. The inverse of a matrix is utilized in an alternative technique for finding the solution to a system of linear equations. Before discussing this technique, the concept of an inverse must be introduced.

If the product of two matrices is the identity matrix, the matrices are *inverses* of each other. Thus, for the two square matrices **A** and **B** and the identity matrix **I**, if **AB** = **I** = **BA** then **A** and **B** are inverses of each other. This equality must be true whether **A** is premultiplied or postmultiplied by **B**. If one considers **B** the inverse of **A**, then **B** can be designated $\mathbf{A}^{-1}$, where the superscript -1 notes an inverse and *does not mean* that **A** is to be raised to the power of negative one. Consequently, two matrices are inverses if

$$\mathbf{AA}^{-1} = \mathbf{A}^{-1}\mathbf{A} = \mathbf{I}$$

The relationships $\mathbf{AA}^{-1} = \mathbf{I}$ and $\mathbf{IX} = \mathbf{X}$ (mentioned in Section 6.4) can be used to demonstrate the solution to a system of linear equations by use of the inverse matrix.

Consider the system of linear equations in matrix form,

$$\mathbf{AX} = \mathbf{B}$$

Multiplication of both sides of the equation by the inverse of **A** (that is to say, $\mathbf{A}^{-1}$) yields the solution for **X**, the vector of unknowns, as follows:

$$\mathbf{A}^{-1}\mathbf{AX} = \mathbf{A}^{-1}\mathbf{B}$$
$$\mathbf{IX} = \mathbf{A}^{-1}\mathbf{B}$$
$$\mathbf{X} = \mathbf{A}^{-1}\mathbf{B}$$

Therefore, if the inverse of **A**, the coefficient matrix, can be determined, the solution to the system of linear equations can be established. In the case of the motor-production problem of Example 6.7, this method of solution requires finding $\mathbf{A}^{-1}$ where

$$\mathbf{A} = \begin{pmatrix} 3 & 4 & 1 \\ 2 & 3 & 5 \\ 4 & 3 & 1 \end{pmatrix}$$

The solution is stated as

$$\mathbf{X} = \mathbf{A}^{-1}\mathbf{B}$$

or

$$\begin{pmatrix} R \\ S \\ T \end{pmatrix} = \begin{pmatrix} 3 & 4 & 1 \\ 2 & 3 & 5 \\ 4 & 3 & 1 \end{pmatrix}^{-1} \begin{pmatrix} 3000 \\ 2400 \\ 3600 \end{pmatrix}$$

Before discussing ways to find the inverse of a matrix, several points should be emphasized. First, only a square matrix has an inverse. With respect to systems of linear equations, this restriction means that only systems with equal numbers of unknowns and equations have coefficient matrices with inverses. Second, there are square matrices which do not have inverses. They are referred to as *singular matrices*. Some ways to identify singular matrices are explained in a subsequent section. Therefore, only a *square, nonsingular* matrix has an inverse. The coefficient matrix must meet these criteria before the inversion technique can be used to solve a system of linear equations.

Next, the Gauss-Jordan method of matrix inversion is described and applied to the coefficient matrix for the motor-production example. Other methods for finding an inverse exist. However, the Gauss-Jordan technique is preferred for large systems of equations and frequently is used in the computer-assisted inversion process.

The Gauss-Jordan Method of Inversion

The first step in the Gauss-Jordan method of inversion is to place the matrix to be inverted to the left of an identity matrix of the same order. Together, the two matrices comprise an augmented matrix. For the matrix **A** of order n this means that the augmented matrix is developed as

$(\mathbf{A}_{n \times n} \mid \mathbf{I}_{n \times n})$

The Gauss-Jordan method requires that row operations be performed on the augmented matrix until the part representing the coefficient matrix **A** becomes an identity matrix of the same order. At this point, the part originally representing the identity matrix **I** is the inverse of the coefficient matrix. In notation form,

$(\mathbf{A}_{n \times n} \mid \mathbf{I}_{n \times n})$

becomes

$(\mathbf{I}_{n \times n} \mid \mathbf{A}_{n \times n}^{-1})$

Example 6.13 demonstrates inversion of the coefficient matrix and solution of the motor-production problem using the inverse matrix. It should be emphasized that the row operations for inversion are identical to the row operations performed in Example 6.10. The difference is that the right-hand part of the augmented matrix is an identity matrix and not the vector of constants as in Example 6.10.

Example 6.13
Solve the motor-production problem of this chapter by means of the inverse matrix.

First, the equations are stated.

$3R + 4S + T = 3000$ worker-hour constraint
$2R + 3S + 5T = 2400$ machine-hour constraint
$4R + 3S + T = 3600$ support-service-hour constraint

Next, the augmented matrix $(\mathbf{A} \mid \mathbf{I})$ is developed as follows:

$$(\mathbf{A} \mid \mathbf{I}) = \begin{pmatrix} 3 & 4 & 1 & \mid & 1 & 0 & 0 \\ 2 & 3 & 5 & \mid & 0 & 1 & 0 \\ 4 & 3 & 1 & \mid & 0 & 0 & 1 \end{pmatrix}$$

Thus, the following row operations are applied to transform $\mathbf{A}$ into an identity matrix of dimension 3×3:

Operation   Result

1. Replace row 2 by $\frac{2}{3}$(row 1) − row 2:

$$\begin{pmatrix} 3 & 4 & 1 & \mid & 1 & 0 & 0 \\ 0 & -\frac{1}{3} & -\frac{13}{3} & \mid & \frac{2}{3} & -1 & 0 \\ 4 & 3 & 1 & \mid & 0 & 0 & 1 \end{pmatrix}$$

2. Replace row 3 by $\frac{4}{3}$(row 1) − row 3:

$$\begin{pmatrix} 3 & 4 & 1 & \mid & 1 & 0 & 0 \\ 0 & -\frac{1}{3} & -\frac{13}{3} & \mid & \frac{2}{3} & -1 & 0 \\ 0 & \frac{7}{3} & \frac{1}{3} & \mid & \frac{4}{3} & 0 & -1 \end{pmatrix}$$

3. Replace row 3 by 7(row 2) + row 3:

$$\begin{pmatrix} 3 & 4 & 1 & \mid & 1 & 0 & 0 \\ 0 & -\frac{1}{3} & -\frac{13}{3} & \mid & \frac{2}{3} & -1 & 0 \\ 0 & 0 & -30 & \mid & 6 & -7 & -1 \end{pmatrix}$$

4. Replace row 1 by 12(row 2) + row 1:

$$\begin{pmatrix} 3 & 0 & -51 & \mid & 9 & -12 & 0 \\ 0 & -\frac{1}{3} & -\frac{13}{3} & \mid & \frac{2}{3} & -1 & 0 \\ 0 & 0 & -30 & \mid & 6 & -7 & -1 \end{pmatrix}$$

5. Replace row 1 by $-\frac{17}{10}$(row 3) + row 1:

$$\begin{pmatrix} 3 & 0 & 0 & \mid & -\frac{12}{10} & -\frac{1}{10} & \frac{17}{10} \\ 0 & -\frac{1}{3} & -\frac{13}{3} & \mid & \frac{2}{3} & -1 & 0 \\ 0 & 0 & -30 & \mid & 6 & -7 & -1 \end{pmatrix}$$

Matrix Algebra

6. Replace row 2 by
   $-\frac{13}{90}$(row 3) + row 2:
$$\begin{pmatrix} 3 & 0 & 0 & | & -\frac{12}{10} & -\frac{1}{10} & \frac{17}{10} \\ 0 & -\frac{1}{3} & 0 & | & -\frac{18}{90} & \frac{1}{90} & \frac{13}{90} \\ 0 & 0 & -30 & | & 6 & -7 & -1 \end{pmatrix}$$

7. Replace row 1 by
   row 1 $\div$ 3:
$$\begin{pmatrix} 1 & 0 & 0 & | & -\frac{12}{30} & -\frac{1}{30} & \frac{17}{30} \\ 0 & -\frac{1}{3} & 0 & | & -\frac{18}{90} & \frac{1}{90} & \frac{13}{90} \\ 0 & 0 & -30 & | & 6 & -7 & -1 \end{pmatrix}$$

8. Replace row 2 by
   -3(row 2):
$$\begin{pmatrix} 1 & 0 & 0 & | & -\frac{12}{30} & -\frac{1}{30} & \frac{17}{30} \\ 0 & 1 & 0 & | & \frac{18}{30} & -\frac{1}{30} & -\frac{13}{30} \\ 0 & 0 & -30 & | & 6 & -7 & -1 \end{pmatrix}$$

9. Replace row 3 by
   row 3 $\div$ -30:
$$\begin{pmatrix} 1 & 0 & 0 & | & -\frac{12}{30} & -\frac{1}{30} & \frac{17}{30} \\ 0 & 1 & 0 & | & \frac{18}{30} & -\frac{1}{30} & -\frac{13}{30} \\ 0 & 0 & 1 & | & -\frac{6}{30} & \frac{7}{30} & \frac{1}{30} \end{pmatrix}$$

10. Therefore, the inverse is the following:
$$\mathbf{A}^{-1} = \begin{pmatrix} -\frac{12}{30} & -\frac{1}{30} & \frac{17}{30} \\ \frac{18}{30} & -\frac{1}{30} & -\frac{13}{30} \\ -\frac{6}{30} & \frac{7}{30} & \frac{1}{30} \end{pmatrix}$$

The resulting matrix is the inverse of the coefficient matrix for the motor-production problem. Readers should confirm this inverse by finding the products $\mathbf{AA}^{-1}$ and $\mathbf{A}^{-1}\mathbf{A}$ and showing that each yields a 3 × 3 identity matrix.

The elements of the **X** vector or the production of each motor type required for full resource usage are found by multiplying $\mathbf{A}^{-1}$ by **B** as follows:

$$\mathbf{A^{-1}AX = A^{-1}B}$$
$$\mathbf{IX = A^{-1}B}$$
$$\mathbf{X = A^{-1}B}$$

Thus, the product $\mathbf{A^{-1}B}$ yields the vector of unknowns as follows:

$$\begin{pmatrix} R \\ S \\ T \end{pmatrix} = \begin{pmatrix} -\dfrac{12}{30} & -\dfrac{1}{30} & \dfrac{17}{30} \\ \dfrac{18}{30} & -\dfrac{1}{30} & -\dfrac{13}{30} \\ -\dfrac{6}{30} & \dfrac{7}{30} & \dfrac{1}{30} \end{pmatrix} \begin{pmatrix} 3000 \\ 2400 \\ 3600 \end{pmatrix}$$

$$= \begin{pmatrix} \dfrac{22{,}800}{30} \\ \dfrac{4800}{30} \\ \dfrac{2400}{30} \end{pmatrix}$$

$$= \begin{pmatrix} 760 \\ 160 \\ 80 \end{pmatrix}$$

Principles of matrix multiplication and the concept of the inverse have provided a solution to this system of equations. As was shown in the previous section by means of the Gauss-Jordan method of elimination, the firm should produce each week 760 type R motors, 160 type S motors, and 80 type T motors.

Although the method of elimination and the inverse method of solving a system of equations lead to the same result, the inverse method has an additional benefit. Once the inverse has been computed, it can be used to find a solution to the system of equations for a different set of constants. The practical significance of this will be explained by reference to the motor-production problem.

The answers to the motor-production problem concern the number of each motor type which should be made to utilize exactly the worker-, machine-, and support-service-hours available in a week. Because the inverse of the coefficient matrix is known, however, new motor-production levels can be computed rapidly if the available hours of resources should change. A brief example will demonstrate this technique.

Example 6.14

How many motors of each type should be made if the firm has available to it 3000 worker-hours, 2500 machine-hours, and 3500 support-service-hours? In other words, the former constraints of 3000 worker-hours, 2400 machine-hours, and 3600 support-service-hours have been adjusted to these new amounts, and new production levels must be computed.

Since the coefficient matrix has not changed, the new production levels (the vector **X**) can be computed by multiplying the new constants by the inverse of the coefficient matrix. This leads to the following result:

$$\begin{pmatrix} R \\ S \\ T \end{pmatrix} = (X) = (A^{-1}B)$$

$$= X = \begin{pmatrix} -\dfrac{12}{30} & -\dfrac{1}{30} & \dfrac{17}{30} \\ \dfrac{18}{30} & -\dfrac{1}{30} & -\dfrac{13}{30} \\ -\dfrac{6}{30} & \dfrac{7}{30} & \dfrac{1}{30} \end{pmatrix} \begin{pmatrix} 3000 \\ 2500 \\ 3500 \end{pmatrix}$$

$$= X = \begin{pmatrix} \dfrac{21{,}000}{30} \\ \dfrac{6{,}000}{30} \\ \dfrac{3{,}000}{30} \end{pmatrix} = \begin{pmatrix} 700 \\ 200 \\ 100 \end{pmatrix} = \begin{pmatrix} R \\ S \\ T \end{pmatrix}$$

This example demonstrates an important advantage to using the inverse method of solution. If the constants represent constraints, as they often do in applied problems, new solutions under an altered set of constraints can be computed easily if the inverse of the coefficient matrix is known. This advantage will be referred to again in the discussion of input-output analysis (Section 6.9).

The following exercises will allow readers to practice finding inverses and using inverses to solve systems of linear equations.

EXERCISES

1. Find the inverse A^{-1} of each of the following matrices. Confirm each inverse by showing that $A^{-1}A = I = AA^{-1}$.

   a. $\begin{pmatrix} 3 & 4 \\ -1 & 2 \end{pmatrix}$ d. $\begin{pmatrix} 3 & -8 \\ 2 & 10 \end{pmatrix}$

b. $\begin{pmatrix} 5 & 4 \\ 0 & 4 \end{pmatrix}$ e. $\begin{pmatrix} 0 & 6 \\ 5 & 2 \end{pmatrix}$

c. $\begin{pmatrix} 3 & 6 \\ 8 & -4 \end{pmatrix}$ f. $\begin{pmatrix} -2 & -3 \\ -5 & -9 \end{pmatrix}$

2. Find the inverse A^{-1} for each 3×3 matrix below. Confirm each inverse by showing that $A^{-1}A = I = AA^{-1}$.

a. $\begin{pmatrix} 2 & -3 & -1 \\ 0 & 4 & -5 \\ -2 & 3 & 2 \end{pmatrix}$ b. $\begin{pmatrix} 3 & 4 & -1 \\ 2 & 6 & 5 \\ 1 & 2 & 1 \end{pmatrix}$ c. $\begin{pmatrix} 5 & 3 & 2 \\ 4 & 1 & 1 \\ 0 & 0 & 2 \end{pmatrix}$

3. Set up each of the following systems of equations in matrix form, $AX = B$.
   a. $3X - Y + Z = 12$ c. $3X - Y = 8$
      $ - Y + 4Z = 8$ $2X + 7Y = 14$
      $4X + 4Y + 4Z = 10$ $-3X - 24Y = -34$
   b. $2X - 4Y = 16$ d. $2X - 4Y - Z = 56$
      $0.5X + Y = 4$ $X - 2Y + 6Z = 32$

4. Find the system of equations corresponding to each group of matrices representing coefficients, unknowns, and constants, respectively.

a. $\begin{pmatrix} 4 & 2 & 5 \\ 0 & 1 & 3 \\ -4 & 6 & -1 \end{pmatrix} \begin{pmatrix} X \\ Y \\ Z \end{pmatrix} = \begin{pmatrix} 17 \\ 38 \\ 20 \end{pmatrix}$

b. $(4 \quad 6 \quad -2 \quad 4) \begin{pmatrix} x_1 \\ x_2 \\ x_3 \\ x_4 \end{pmatrix} = (78)$

c. $\begin{pmatrix} 2 & 1 & 4 \\ 6 & -2 & 3 \end{pmatrix} \begin{pmatrix} x_1 \\ x_2 \\ x_3 \end{pmatrix} = \begin{pmatrix} 44 \\ 29 \end{pmatrix}$

d. $\begin{pmatrix} 11 & 8 & 6 \\ 4 & -6 & 10 \end{pmatrix} \begin{pmatrix} x_1 \\ x_2 \\ x_3 \end{pmatrix} + \begin{pmatrix} 14 & -6 \\ 2 & 12 \end{pmatrix} \begin{pmatrix} y_1 \\ y_2 \end{pmatrix} = \begin{pmatrix} 121 \\ 87 \end{pmatrix}$

5. Solve each of the following systems of equations by the method of matrix inversion.
   a. $3X + 4Y = 29$ c. $X + 6Y = 22$
      $X + 2Y = 13$ $8X - 5Y = -36$
   b. $6X + Y = 28$ d. $5X + Y = 8$
      $4X - 2Y = 8$ $2X + 2Y = 16$

6. Solve each 3×3 system of equations by means of matrix inversion.
   a. $2X - Y + 3Z = 19$ c. $X + 6Y = 35$
      $X + 4Y + Z = 16$ $4X - 2Y + 3Z = 22$
      $5X + 2Z = 25$ $4Y + Z = 24$

b. $X + 4Y + Z = 16$
        $-3X + Y + 4Z = -9$
        $4X - Y + 2Z = 13$

7. For the following system of equations,

$$4X + 2Y + 8Z = 40$$
$$6X + 2Z = 24$$
$$3X + Y + Z = 32$$

the inverse of the coefficient matrix is

$$\mathbf{A}^{-1} = \begin{pmatrix} -0.05 & 0.15 & 0.10 \\ 0 & -0.5 & 1 \\ 0.15 & 0.05 & -0.3 \end{pmatrix}$$

a. Find solution values for X, Y, and Z. Confirm your results by substitution of X, Y, and Z into the original equations.
b. Change the vector of constants from

$$\mathbf{B} = \begin{pmatrix} 40 \\ 24 \\ 32 \end{pmatrix} \quad \text{to} \quad \mathbf{B} = \begin{pmatrix} 50 \\ 20 \\ 10 \end{pmatrix}$$

and solve for the new values of X, Y, and Z.

8. A drug manufacturer uses two ingredients X and Y in a product. Ingredient X contains 2 milligrams of folic acid per ounce and ingredient Y contains 6 milligrams of folic acid per ounce. The product must contain 48 milligrams of folic acid per production unit. Also, because of other constraints on the product, a production unit must have 12 more ounces of X than of Y.

    Set up the system of equations representing the two constraints on this product. Use the method of matrix inversion to find the quantity of ounces of X and Y in a production unit which will satisfy exactly the two constraints.

    If there must be only 8 more ounces of X than Y and the folic acid constraint remains at 48 milligrams, find the new weights of X and Y which satisfy exactly the constraints. Confirm your answers to both questions by use of the Gauss-Jordan method of elimination.

9. A chemical firm uses three ingredients (X, Y, and Z) to make a compound. The firm wants to produce exactly 10,000 pounds of the compound. In addition, X costs $2 per pound, Y costs $4 per pound, and Z costs $6 per pound. The firm wants to spend exactly $30,000 on the production of this compound. Finally, the compound formula requires that there be 2 pounds of ingredient X for each pound of Y used.

    Set up the system of linear equations used to determine the pounds of each ingredient necessary to satisfy exactly the constraints. Solve by both the Gauss-Jordan method of elimination and the method of matrix inversion.

10. A tire manufacturer uses three primary materials (X, Y, and Z) to make three types of tires. The following table shows the pounds of each material required for the manufacture of one tire of each type:

	Material		
Tire Type	X	Y	Z
1	4	1	1
2	2	2	4
3	2	4	3

The firm must produce monthly exactly 4300 type 1 tires, 4800 type 2 tires, and 5500 type 3 tires.

Use the Gauss-Jordan method of elimination and the method of matrix inversion to determine the number of pounds of each material required to meet exactly the output constraints for the three tires.

6.8 The Inverse Matrix: Additional Considerations

As pointed out above, only a square matrix can have an inverse, and some square matrices do not have inverses. A matrix that does not have an inverse is referred to as a *singular matrix*. This section concerns identification of square matrices which do not have inverses and the relation of this type of matrix to the solution of a system of linear equations.

If during the row operations a row of zeroes occurs in the left-hand side of an augmented matrix, the matrix does not have an inverse. This means that further row operations will not be productive in changing the left-hand side of the augmented matrix into the identity matrix.

Example 6.15

$$\mathbf{A} = \begin{pmatrix} 6 & -4 & 2 \\ 6 & 5 & 4 \\ -3 & 2 & -1 \end{pmatrix}$$

The following steps are applied to finding the inverse:

$$(\mathbf{A} \mid \mathbf{I}) = \begin{pmatrix} 6 & -4 & 2 & \mid & 1 & 0 & 0 \\ 6 & 5 & 4 & \mid & 0 & 1 & 0 \\ -3 & 2 & -1 & \mid & 0 & 0 & 1 \end{pmatrix}$$

Operation

1. Replace row 2 by row 1 − row 2:

Result

$$\begin{pmatrix} 6 & -4 & 2 & \mid & 1 & 0 & 0 \\ 0 & -9 & -2 & \mid & 1 & -1 & 0 \\ -3 & 2 & -1 & \mid & 0 & 0 & 1 \end{pmatrix}$$

2. Replace row 3 by
2(row 3) + row 1:
$$\begin{pmatrix} 6 & -4 & 2 & | & 1 & 0 & 0 \\ 0 & -9 & -2 & | & 1 & -1 & 0 \\ 0 & 0 & 0 & | & 1 & 0 & 2 \end{pmatrix}$$

After step 2, there is a row of 0s in the left-hand side of the augmented matrix; thus, the inverse of **A** does not exist and **A** is shown to be a singular matrix.

If the matrix **A** in this case represents coefficients for a system of equations, the absence of the inverse of **A** implies that there is no unique solution to the system of equations. Thus, it may have either no solution or an infinite number of solutions.

The primary reason for a square matrix to be singular is that the rows and/or the columns of the matrix are *linearly dependent*. Thus, the rows and columns of a square matrix must be linearly independent if the matrix is to have an inverse.

To understand linear dependence and linear independence as applied to matrices, note that a matrix is a set of row vectors and a set of column vectors. Assume that one set of vectors (either rows or columns) for an $n \times n$ matrix is referred to as $a_1, a_2, a_3, \ldots, a_n$. If there is a set of real numbers $\lambda_1, \lambda_2, \lambda_3, \ldots, \lambda_n$, *not all zero,* such that

$$\lambda_1 a_1 + \lambda_2 a_2 + \lambda_3 a_3 + \cdots + \lambda_n a_n = 0$$

then the set of vectors is linearly dependent. If there is no such set of λ's (except all 0s), then the set of vectors is linearly independent. If a matrix is a linearly dependent set of vectors, the inverse of the matrix does not exist. This means that if any row (or column) of a matrix is linearly dependent on the other rows (or columns), then the matrix does not have an inverse. Linear dependence also means that a row (or column) of the matrix is a linear combination of the other rows (or columns) in the matrix.

Example 6.16
The concept of linear dependence may be clarified by considering the 2×2 matrix **A**:

$$\mathbf{A} = \begin{pmatrix} 6 & -4 \\ 3 & -2 \end{pmatrix}$$

Observe that each element in the first row is twice as large as the corresponding element in the second row; i.e., $(3)(2) = 6$ and $(-2)(2) = -4$. The linear relation between row one (a_1) and row two (a_2) is expressed $a_1 - 2a_2 = 0$. The λ values are nonzero (1 and -2) and the rows have been shown to be linearly dependent. Thus, an inverse does not exist for this 2×2 matrix.

Example 6.16 illustrates a simple form of linear dependence where one row is a multiple of the other row in a 2×2 matrix. However, linear de-

Matrix Algebra   **140**

pendence between the rows or columns of a matrix is not always detected easily. Row operations may be required in order to demonstrate linear dependence by finding a row of zeroes at some point.

Finally, it must be stressed again that a system of linear equations does not have a unique solution unless the equations of that system are linearly independent.

6.9   Input-Output Analysis

The identity matrix, matrix multiplication, and matrix inversion are some of the topics that can be applied to *input-output analysis*. Input-output analysis is a mathematical technique used to study relationships between industries in an international, national, or regional economy. More specifically, as developed by Wassily W. Leontief, input-output analysis is a method for estimating the necessary levels of output for the industries in an economy which will meet exactly the demand for their products.[2]

The words "input-output" imply an interdependency between an economy's industries (also called *sectors*) such that the output of one industry is a necessary input to one or more industries, often including itself. Consequently, the output of one industry depends in part on the input requirements of other industries, and the input requirements of each industry partially affect output levels in other industries. One goal of an input-output analysis is to determine output levels for all industries consistent with the input requirements of all industries. This means that no production shortages or surpluses will occur and that the economy will function in a coordinated way.

Other factors must be included before an input-output analysis reflects an economy accurately. There are final demands for goods (primarily from consumers) which must be satisfied. And the sector which creates these final demands also supplies a "primary" input not produced by industry (labor services).

Interindustry requirements and final demands constitute the data sets necessary for completing an input-output analysis. The objective of the analysis is to determine the output level for each industry which is exactly sufficient to meet all interindustry requirements (including that industry's own requirements) and final demand. Interindustry data are presented in a "technological matrix" (to be explained below) and final demands are listed by industry in a vector.

Although input-output analyses usually include large amounts of data, an abbreviated example will be used here to explain both the relevant matrices and the solution process.

[2]Wassily W. Leontief, *Structure of the American Economy 1919–1939*, 2d ed., Oxford University Press, Fair Lawn, N.J., 1951.

Example 6.17

An economy has three sectors: agriculture, manufacturing, and households. The agricultural and manufacturing sectors are interdependent as some of the output of each is a necessary input for the other. Final demands and primary inputs originate in the household sector.

The input-output relations between agriculture and manufacturing are expressed in the following technological matrix:

Technological Matrix

Input (Producer)	Output (User)	
	Agriculture	Manufacturing
Agriculture	0.1	0.2
Manufacturing	0.3	0.6

The components of this interindustry, or technological, matrix (referred to as matrix **A**) should be explained. The first column of this 2 × 2 matrix states that for every dollar of agricultural output, this sector requires $0.10 worth of input from agriculture and $0.30 of input from the manufacturing sector. The remaining $0.60 of input per dollar of output is supplied by the primary (household) sector. (The household sector is not included in the technological matrix.) Similarly, every dollar of output by manufacturing requires $0.20 of input from agriculture, $0.60 of input from manufacturing, and $0.20 from the primary, or household, sector.

The *final demand vector* **D** representing final household sector demands for output from agriculture and manufacturing is the following:

$$\mathbf{D} = \begin{pmatrix} d_1 \\ d_2 \end{pmatrix} = \begin{pmatrix} 75 \\ 180 \end{pmatrix}$$

The amount d_1, or 75, is the final demand for agricultural goods (in billions of dollars for this example). The final demand for manufacturing goods, d_2, is $180 billion.

The object of the input-output analysis for this simple economy is to determine the production level for each industry which will be exactly sufficient to meet all interindustry and final demands. Let x_1 represent output for the agricultural sector and x_2 represent the output for the manufacturing sector. Values for x_1 and x_2 are expressed in billions of dollars.

Each dollar of agricultural output requires $0.10 of input from the agricultural sector and each dollar of manufacturing output requires $0.20 of input from agriculture. Combining these data with a final demand for agricultural goods of $75 billion, the required output for agriculture, x_1, can be expressed as the following equation:

$$x_1 = 0.1x_1 + 0.2x_2 + 75$$

Following similar reasoning, the expression for total output from manufacturing is

$x_2 = 0.3x_1 + 0.6x_2 + 180$

Therefore, the system of output equations in the two-industry economy is

$x_1 = 0.1x_1 + 0.2x_2 + 75$
$x_2 = 0.3x_1 + 0.6x_2 + 180$

These equations help to point out that the coefficients in the output equation for each industry, or sector, are taken from the appropriate row of the technological matrix. The constant in the output equation for each industry is the final demand for that industry.

For solution purposes, these equations should be rearranged so that all x_1 terms are on one side of the equality and the constant is on the other:

$x_1 - 0.1x_1 - 0.2x_2 = 75$
$x_2 - 0.3x_1 - 0.6x_2 = 180$

Combining terms leads to the following:

$0.9x_1 - 0.2x_2 = 75$
$-0.3x_1 + 0.4x_2 = 180$

The revised coefficient matrix

$$\begin{pmatrix} 0.9 & -0.2 \\ -0.3 & 0.4 \end{pmatrix}$$

also can be found by subtracting **A** (the technological matrix) from the identity matrix, as:

$$\mathbf{I} - \mathbf{A} = \begin{pmatrix} 1 & 0 \\ 0 & 1 \end{pmatrix} - \begin{pmatrix} 0.1 & 0.2 \\ 0.3 & 0.6 \end{pmatrix} = \begin{pmatrix} 0.9 & -0.2 \\ -0.3 & 0.4 \end{pmatrix}$$

Therefore, the 2×2 system of equations can be expressed in matrix notation as:

$(\mathbf{I} - \mathbf{A})\mathbf{X} = \mathbf{D}$

where **D** is the vector of final demands. To solve for the vector of unknowns $\begin{pmatrix} x_1 \\ x_2 \end{pmatrix}$, the matrix $(\mathbf{I} - \mathbf{A})$ will be inverted as opposed to using the Gauss-Jordan method of elimination. Solving by inversion leads to the following steps:

$$((\mathbf{I} - \mathbf{A}) \mid \mathbf{I}) = \begin{pmatrix} 0.9 & -0.2 & \mid & 1 & 0 \\ -0.3 & 0.4 & \mid & 0 & 1 \end{pmatrix}$$

or, in fractional form,

$$\begin{pmatrix} \frac{9}{10} & -\frac{2}{10} & \mid & 1 & 0 \\ -\frac{3}{10} & \frac{4}{10} & \mid & 0 & 1 \end{pmatrix}$$

Row operations are used to find $(I - A)^{-1}$ by the zeroes-first technique, as follows:

Operation	Result

1. Replace row 2 by $\tfrac{1}{3}$(row 1) + row 2:

$$\begin{pmatrix} \dfrac{9}{10} & -\dfrac{2}{10} & 1 & 0 \\ 0 & \dfrac{1}{3} & \dfrac{1}{3} & 1 \end{pmatrix}$$

2. Replace row 1 by $\tfrac{3}{5}$(row 2) + row 1:

$$\begin{pmatrix} \dfrac{9}{10} & 0 & \dfrac{6}{5} & \dfrac{3}{5} \\ 0 & \dfrac{1}{3} & \dfrac{1}{3} & 1 \end{pmatrix}$$

3. Replace row 1 by $\tfrac{10}{9}$(row 1):

$$\begin{pmatrix} 1 & 0 & \dfrac{4}{3} & \dfrac{2}{3} \\ 0 & \dfrac{1}{3} & \dfrac{1}{3} & 1 \end{pmatrix}$$

4. Replace row 2 by 3(row 2):

$$\begin{pmatrix} 1 & 0 & \dfrac{4}{3} & \dfrac{2}{3} \\ 0 & 1 & 1 & 3 \end{pmatrix}$$

Thus, the inverse, $(I - A)^{-1}$, is equal to

$$(I - A)^{-1} = \begin{pmatrix} \dfrac{4}{3} & \dfrac{2}{3} \\ 1 & 3 \end{pmatrix}$$

Values for x_1 and x_2 can be determined by the following

$$X = (I - A)^{-1} D$$

$$\begin{pmatrix} x_1 \\ x_2 \end{pmatrix} = \begin{pmatrix} \dfrac{4}{3} & \dfrac{2}{3} \\ 1 & 3 \end{pmatrix} \begin{pmatrix} 75 \\ 180 \end{pmatrix}$$

$$x_1 = \left(\dfrac{4}{3}\right)(75) + \left(\dfrac{2}{3}\right)(180) = 220$$

$$x_2 = (1)(75) + (3)(180) = 615$$

Therefore, the agricultural sector should have an output of $220 billion and the manufacturing sector's output should be $615 billion. These outputs will satisfy exactly all demands, both interindustry and final.

A useful feature of input-output analysis is that when the values of $(I - A)^{-1}$ are known, the effect on the final output of all industries from a change in the final demand for any industry can be determined. For example, assume that the final demand for agricultural goods increases from $75 billion to $90 billion. This causes the following changes in the required outputs of all industries:

$$\begin{pmatrix} x_1 \\ x_2 \end{pmatrix} = \begin{pmatrix} \frac{4}{3} & \frac{2}{3} \\ 1 & 3 \end{pmatrix} \begin{pmatrix} 90 \\ 180 \end{pmatrix}$$

$x_1 = 120 + 120 = 240$
$x_2 = 90 + 540 = 630$

Although demand has increased for only one sector, output requirements have increased for both sectors. This demonstrates the interdependency which is characteristic of the economy.

The effect on final outputs of changes in input in one or more industries also can be assessed. Changes of this type require alteration of the technological matrix and computation of a new inverse. This process permits assessment of the output effects of variations in production techniques and the adoption of new technology.

As input-output analyses normally include large numbers of sectors or industries, many computer programs have been developed to invert $(I - A)$ and compute final outputs. However, the reliance on computers for computational assistance does not diminish the need to understand the principles underlying this technique.

As a concluding point, readers should understand that the data required for the technological matrix often are difficult to acquire or derive. Therefore, not only is the computation of an input-output analysis a formidable task, but basic data collection often can be a barrier to its application.

6.10 Chapter Summary

Matrix algebra includes a group of techniques for organizing and carrying out mathematical operations on arrays of numbers grouped as scalars, vectors, and matrices.

Two or more vectors or matrices can be added or subtracted element by element if they have the same dimension. Multiplication of vectors or matrices is carried out through row-by-column multiplication if the arrays have conformable dimensions (that is, the number of columns in the first array is equal to the number of rows in the second array). The division operation does not exist in matrix algebra.

There are two matrix-algebra techniques frequently employed to solve systems of linear equations. One is the Gauss-Jordan method of elimination. This technique requires forming an augmented matrix consisting of the coefficient matrix and the vector of constants. After developing this augmented matrix, row operations are carried out to transform the coefficient matrix into an identity matrix so that solution values can be read by inspection.

The Gauss-Jordan method of elimination also can be used to detect systems of equations which have either no solutions or an infinite number of solutions.

A second solution technique utilizes the concept of the inverse of a matrix. When solving a system of equations by matrix inversion, the Gauss-Jordan method of inversion usually is employed. This procedure utilizes a series of mathematical operations to find the inverse of the coefficient matrix. This inverse, when computed, is multiplied by the vector of constants to yield solution values for the system of equations. The Gauss-Jordan method of matrix inversion is included in many computer applications; consequently, it has been applied to problems such as ingredient mixes, resource usage, and input-output analysis.

There is a unique solution to a system of linear equations only if the inverse of the coefficient matrix exists (i.e., the matrix is square and nonsingular). In addition, if the equations in the system are linearly dependent, the inverse of the coefficient matrix does not exist.

It is hoped that this chapter has been an informative and interesting introduction to the topic of matrix algebra and its uses in business and economics. Some of the concepts and techniques discussed in this chapter will be used to explain linear programming, the topic of Chapter 7.

6.11 Problem Set

Review Questions

1. Specify the location of element a_{52} in a 6 × 6 matrix **A**.
2. Distinguish between the null matrix and the identity matrix.
3. For a 3 × 5 matrix, what is the dimension of its transpose? Describe the location of element a_{24} of the original 3 × 5 matrix in the transposed matrix.
4. What are the rules for two matrices to be comfortable for multiplication? How is the dimension of the product matrix determined?
5. What is the result of multiplying a square matrix by the identity matrix of the same order?
6. How is the Gauss-Jordan method of elimination used to identify systems of linear equations which have (*a*) no solutions and (*b*) an infinite number of solutions?
7. State the conditions required for two matrices to be inverses of each other.
8. What is the final objective of inversion by the zeroes-first method? Describe this method.
9. What can be concluded about a system of equations which does not have an inverse for the matrix of coefficients?
10. Briefly state the primary cause of a singular square matrix.

11. The Gauss-Jordan method of inversion requires that two matrices be altered. Describe this alteration.
12. What conclusion can be reached if a row of zeroes occurs during the row operations of the Gauss-Jordan method of inversion?
13. Solution of an input-output problem gives the "correct" output level for each industry. Explain.
14. Describe the matrix that must be inverted in solving an input-output analysis by means of matrix inversion.
15. What is the correct interpretation of the numbers in the second row of the following technological matrix?

Technological Matrix

	Steel	Automobiles
Steel	0.1	0.3
Automobiles	0.2	0.3

16. What numbers form the vector of constants in an input-output analysis?

Review Problems

1. Carry out the specified operations on the following matrices:

   a. $(3 \quad 2 \quad 4 \quad 0 \quad -6) + (6 \quad 5 \quad 1 \quad -7 \quad 3)$

   b. $\begin{pmatrix} 6 & 1 & 7 \\ 2 & 3 & -4 \\ 0 & 2 & 2 \end{pmatrix} + \begin{pmatrix} 3 & 4 & -2 \\ 0 & 0 & 5 \\ 3 & 7 & 1 \end{pmatrix}$

   c. $\begin{pmatrix} 3 & 1 \\ 4 & 4 \end{pmatrix} - \begin{pmatrix} 2 & 6 \\ 1 & -4 \end{pmatrix}$

   d. $\begin{pmatrix} 4 \\ 1 \\ 3 \\ 5 \end{pmatrix} - \begin{pmatrix} -3 \\ 0 \\ 4 \\ 4 \end{pmatrix}$

   e. $\begin{pmatrix} 6 & -4 \\ 2 & -2 \end{pmatrix} + \begin{pmatrix} 3 & 0 \\ 0 & 8 \end{pmatrix} - \begin{pmatrix} 4 & -1 \\ -2 & 3 \end{pmatrix}$

   f. $\begin{pmatrix} 4 & 5 \\ 7 & -3 \end{pmatrix} - \begin{pmatrix} 0 & 4 \\ 0 & 6 \end{pmatrix} - \begin{pmatrix} -2 & -3 \\ 0 & 2 \end{pmatrix}$

2. Multiply each of the following matrices, or state the reason why the noted multiplication is not possible.

   a. $4 \begin{pmatrix} 6 & 2 & 1 \\ 7 & 7 & 8 \\ -2 & 3 & 1 \end{pmatrix}$

   b. $\begin{pmatrix} 6 \\ 2 \\ 7 \\ 1 \end{pmatrix} (2 \quad 3 \quad 0 \quad -6 \quad 7)$

c. $\begin{pmatrix} 4 & 3 & 1 \\ 2 & -1 & 6 \end{pmatrix} \begin{pmatrix} 2 & 4 \\ 6 & 3 \\ 17 & 6 \\ 8 & -4 \end{pmatrix}$
e. $\begin{pmatrix} 4 & 0 & 0 \\ 0 & 6 & 0 \\ 0 & 0 & 3 \end{pmatrix} \begin{pmatrix} 9 & 7 & 8 \\ 14 & 6 & 2 \\ 3 & 3 & -3 \end{pmatrix}$

d. $\begin{pmatrix} 2 & 4 \\ 6 & 3 \\ 18 & -2 \\ 3 & -1 \end{pmatrix} \begin{pmatrix} 4 & 4 & 1 \\ 2 & -5 & 9 \end{pmatrix}$
f. $\begin{pmatrix} 6 & 0 & 0 \\ 0 & 6 & 0 \\ 0 & 0 & 6 \end{pmatrix} \begin{pmatrix} -2 & 3 & 0 \\ 0 & 1 & 5 \\ 4 & 2 & -3 \end{pmatrix}$

3. Multiply each of the following:

   a. $(11 \quad 8 \quad -7 \quad 4) \begin{pmatrix} 3 \\ -1 \\ 4 \\ 5 \end{pmatrix}$

   b. $\begin{pmatrix} 3 & 2 & 12 \\ 10 & 8 & 7 \\ 6 & 13 & 3 \\ 2 & 3 & 5 \end{pmatrix} \begin{pmatrix} 3 & 2 & 1 & 4 \\ 11 & -2 & 1 & -1 \\ 8 & 6 & 7 & 3 \end{pmatrix}$

   c. $\begin{pmatrix} 1 & 0 & 0 \\ 0 & 1 & 0 \\ 0 & 0 & 1 \end{pmatrix} \begin{pmatrix} 3 & 16 & 14 \\ 0 & -5 & 24 \\ 37 & 13 & 18 \end{pmatrix}$

4. Given the 3 × 3 matrix:

   $$X = \begin{pmatrix} 3 & 2 & 7 \\ 0 & 3 & 0 \\ 4 & 8 & 2 \end{pmatrix}$$

   Find the transpose of **X** and multiply **X** by its transpose.

5. An office supply company sells five different pens, with prices of $0.39, $0.59, $0.79, $0.99, and $1.39. Sales of each by price line are 4793, 3822, 4111, 6032, and 4890, respectively. Set up matrices in the proper form, and use matrix multiplication to find total pen sales for the firm.

6. A jewelry firm must pay excise taxes on items in three classes. The tax on class I items is 4 percent of gross receipts, on class II the tax is 5 percent of gross receipts, and on class III goods, the tax is 6 percent of gross receipts. The following table represents gross receipts for each class for each of three stores.

	Gross Receipts		
	Store 1	Store 2	Store 3
Class I	$10,200	$7,450	$6,827
Class II	11,020	8,225	7,400
Class III	9,574	4,711	5,112

By using matrix multiplication, find the total excise taxes owed for each store.

7. For each system of equations, construct the matrix of coefficients, the vector of constants, and the vector of unknowns.

a. $3X + 6Y + 4W + 5Z = 84$
$X + Y + 3Z = 25$
$2X + 7Y + 6W - 6Z = 28$
$6Y + 10W = 36$

b. $4a + 7b - c = 24$
$-2a - 6c + 3d = 18$
$6a + 5b + 2c - 8d = 40$

8. Solve each system of equations by the Gauss-Jordan method of elimination.
   a. $2X + 4Y = 14$
   $4X + 5Y = 16$
   b. $4X + 2Y + Z = 14$
   $3X + Y + Z = 9$
   $7X - Y + 3Z = 9$
   c. $3X + 3Y + Z = 13$
   $X + 2Y + 4Z = 12$
   $X - Y + 4Z = 0$
   d. $3X + 4Y = 15$
   $X - 3Y = 5$
   e. $4X - 2Y + Z = 20$
   $5X + Y - 2Z = 5$
   $X + Y + 3Z = 13$
   f. $2X + Y - Z = 16$
   $X + Y + Z = 32$
   $4X + 2Y - 4Z = 8$

9. Which of the following pairs of matrices are inverses? Justify your answer.

   a. $\begin{pmatrix} 3 & 1 \\ 2 & 4 \end{pmatrix} \cdot \begin{pmatrix} \frac{4}{10} & -\frac{1}{10} \\ -\frac{2}{10} & \frac{3}{10} \end{pmatrix}$

   c. $\begin{pmatrix} -1 & 0 \\ 0 & -1 \end{pmatrix} \begin{pmatrix} 1 & 0 \\ 0 & 1 \end{pmatrix}$

   b. $\begin{pmatrix} -6 & 0 \\ 8 & -3 \end{pmatrix} \begin{pmatrix} -\frac{1}{6} & 0 \\ -\frac{4}{6} & -\frac{2}{6} \end{pmatrix}$

   d. $\begin{pmatrix} 6 & 7 \\ -1 & 3 \end{pmatrix} \begin{pmatrix} \frac{3}{25} & -\frac{7}{25} \\ \frac{1}{25} & \frac{6}{25} \end{pmatrix}$

10. Find the inverse for each 2×2 matrix below. Confirm each inverse.
    a. $\begin{pmatrix} 2 & 0 \\ -3 & 4 \end{pmatrix}$
    c. $\begin{pmatrix} 10 & 12 \\ 8 & 10 \end{pmatrix}$
    b. $\begin{pmatrix} -4 & -2 \\ -1 & -3 \end{pmatrix}$
    d. $\begin{pmatrix} 4 & 5 \\ 2 & 2 \end{pmatrix}$

11. Use row operations to find the inverse of each 3×3 matrix below. Confirm each inverse.

    a. $\begin{pmatrix} 2 & 0 & 3 \\ 1 & 1 & 3 \\ -2 & 4 & 2 \end{pmatrix}$
    c. $\begin{pmatrix} 4 & 1 & -1 \\ 2 & 0 & 3 \\ 1 & 2 & 5 \end{pmatrix}$
    b. $\begin{pmatrix} 3 & 3 & 3 \\ 0 & 4 & 4 \\ 1 & 5 & 3 \end{pmatrix}$
    d. $\begin{pmatrix} -3 & 4 & 0 \\ 1 & -3 & 1 \\ -2 & 4 & 1 \end{pmatrix}$

12. For the following system of equations,

    $3X + Y + 2Z = 5$
    $X + 4Y + 2Z = 9$
    $4X + 2Y + 3Z = 8$

    the inverse of the coefficient matrix, or $\mathbf{A}^{-1}$, is

$$\mathbf{A}^{-1} = \begin{pmatrix} 8 & 1 & -6 \\ 5 & 1 & -4 \\ -14 & -2 & 11 \end{pmatrix}$$

   a. Confirm that $\mathbf{A}^{-1}$ is the inverse of the coefficient matrix.
   b. Solve for X, Y, and Z.
   c. Substitute the constants 10, 18, and 16 for 5, 9, and 8, respectively, and solve for X, Y, and Z.
   d. Compare your answers to parts b and c and interpret.
13. Solve the following system of two equations in two unknowns by the Gauss-Jordan method of inversion. Check your answer by the Gauss-Jordan elimination method.

    $3X + 7Y = 18$
    $4X + Y = 10$

14. Solve by matrix inversion and check by the Gauss-Jordan method of elimination:

    $12X + 3Y = 48$
    $10X + Y = 32$

15. Given the system of equations:

    $3X + 2Y + 4Z = 30$
    $2X + Y + 2Z = 16$
    $5X + Y + Z = 20$

    a. Solve by the Gauss-Jordan method of elimination.
    b. Solve by the method of matrix inversion.
16. For the coefficient matrix of Problem 15, find
    a. $\mathbf{A}^T$
    b. $\mathbf{AA}^T$
    c. $(\mathbf{I} - \mathbf{A})$
17. For each system of equations below, use the Gauss-Jordan method of elimination to determine whether there are no solutions or an infinite number of solutions.

    a. $2X + 3Y = 14$ e. $X - 2Y + 5Z = 12$
       $12X + 18Y = 84$ $2X + 2Y + 3Z = 22$
    b. $X - Y = 12$ $4X - 2Y + 13Z = 46$
       $-3X + 3Y = 4$ f. $6X + 2Y - 8Z = 10$
    c. $5X + 30Y = 72$ $2X \qquad - 6Z = 2$
       $2X + 12Y = 54$ $X + Y + 2Z = 6$
    d. $2X + Y - Z = 14$
       $4X + 3Y + Z = 12$
       $8X + 4Y - 4Z = 56$

18. For each matrix below, the inverse does not exist. Explain why.

    a. $\begin{pmatrix} 4 & 6 & -2 \\ 5 & 4 & 3 \\ 2 & 3 & -1 \end{pmatrix}$ c. $\begin{pmatrix} 2 & 5 & 1 \\ -6 & -15 & 1 \\ -8 & -20 & 1 \end{pmatrix}$

    b. $\begin{pmatrix} 4 & 2 & 1 \\ 2 & -2 & 1 \\ 12 & 6 & 3 \end{pmatrix}$ d. $\begin{pmatrix} 3 & 18 & -24 \\ 4 & 2 & 11 \\ -2 & -12 & 16 \end{pmatrix}$

19. A retail chain knows the profit per dollar of sales for each of four product lines. These profit amounts (dollars per dollar of sales) are shown in the vector **P**.

    P = (0.08 0.03 0.07 0.02)

    The firm also has estimates for dollar sales of each product line by store for the next quarter. These are shown in the matrix **S** in thousands of dollars.

	Product Line			
Store	1	2	3	4
1	14	22	17	16
2	31	36	29	27
3	21	27	17	30
4	20	32	12	24

    Use matrix multiplication to find expected profit per store for the next quarter.

20. An electronics firm produces three products: stereos, home computers, and televisions. Three materials used in each are aluminum (X), steel (Y), and plastic (Z). Requirements to produce one stereo are 5 pounds of aluminum, 6 pounds of steel, and 2 pounds of plastic. For a home computer, requirements are 4 pounds of aluminum, 3 pounds of steel, and 4 pounds of plastic. A television requires 6 pounds of aluminum, 4 pounds of steel, and 5 pounds of plastic. In planning production for the next 3 months, the firm must know how much of each of the three materials to order. It is anticipated that 20,000 stereos, 22,000 home computers, and 30,000 televisions will be manufactured during this period. Set up the system of equations necessary to estimate basic material needs. Solve the system by use of the inverse matrix and state purchase requirements for each material. Check your answers by solving by means of the Gauss-Jordan method of elimination.

21. The matrix **A** below is the technological matrix for an input-output table.

	User		
Producer	Oil	Chemicals	Coal
Oil	0.25	0.32	0.27
Chemicals	0.20	0.23	0.36
Coal	0.10	0.15	0.22

    a. Interpret each number in the third column of the matrix **A**.
    b. How much primary input per dollar of output is used by the oil industry?
    c. Set up the matrix (**I** − **A**).
    d. For the final demands of oil = 400, chemicals = 750, coal = 297, set up a system of equations for the equilibrium production of each.

22. For the study of a regional economy, it is assumed that there are only two industries, steel and chemicals. Each dollar of output for the steel industry needs $0.30 worth of input from itself and $0.60 worth of input from the chemical industry. The chemical industry requires, for each dollar of output, $0.10 worth of steel input and $0.20 of input from the chemical industry. The steel industry also must satisfy $400 (million) of final demand, and the chemical industry has a final demand of $900 million. Find the output level for each industry necessary for the satisfaction of all interindustry and final demands.

Linear Programming

7.1 Introduction

At times, the objectives of an organization are stated in an unqualified way such as maximization of profits or minimization of costs. In many more cases, however, organizations attempt to pursue objectives within a set of limitations or constraints. For example, a firm may attempt to maximize profits within a given available pool of resources (labor and machinery). Similarly, organizations may attempt to minimize costs while meeting various internally and externally imposed quality specifications. Thus, organizational objectives often are pursued within a constrained environment. This reflects the reality of resource scarcity and societal demands.

The particular objective of an organization can be expressed in terms of a mathematical model in equation form. Constraints on this objective also may be stated mathematically. Often, the most realistic description of constraints is through the use of inequality statements. Examples of constraints stated as inequalities are that a firm must use no more than 100 labor-hours per week for production of a particular good or that the government has stated that a particular drug must contain at least 5 milligrams of folic acid per tablet.

Mathematical programming includes techniques for evaluating problems of optimization under constraints. When the objective and constraints are expressed in linear form, a type of mathematical programming called linear programming is applied to the problem. This chapter discusses linear programming and its application to situations of constrained optimization. Several examples of linear programming problems may help introduce this topic.

7.2 Three Linear Programming Problems

1. A firm uses labor, machinery, and management resources in manufacturing two small household appliances. For appliance X_1, the profit per unit is $6, and the profit per unit for X_2 is $5.

    A unit of X_1 requires 2.5 labor-hours, 4 machine-hours, and 1.5 management-hours for its production. A unit of X_2 requires 2 labor-hours, 3 machine-hours, and 2 management-hours. Total weekly availability of labor, machinery, and management time for these two products is not to exceed 200 hours, 260 hours, and 180 hours, respectively.

    How many units of each appliance should be manufactured each week in order to maximize profits for this firm while operating within the stated resource constraints?

2. A food products company uses two primary ingredients in its best-selling brand of breakfast cereal. Ingredient X_1 costs $0.25 per ounce and ingredient X_2 costs $0.30 per ounce.

    Each box of cereal must meet three production criteria. First, the total weight of X_1 and X_2 in a box must be at least 16 ounces. A box also must contain at least 260 grams of carbohydrate and 70 grams of protein. An ounce of X_1 contains 25 grams of carbohydrate and 5 grams of protein. An ounce of X_2 contains 30 grams of carbohydrate and 6 grams of protein.

    How many ounces of each ingredient should be used in a box in order to minimize costs and satisfy all the requirements?

3. This example is included in a category of linear programming problems referred to as "transportation problems."

    A hardware products manufacturer ships products from four production facilities to central retail distribution points for nine large chain stores. The cost of transporting a carlot shipment from each production point to each retail distribution point is known, as are the total production capabilities (in carlots) for each manufacturing facility and the total demand (in carlots) at each chain's distribution point.

    The objective of the analysis is to determine the number of carlots that should go from each origin (production point) to each destination (distribution point) which will lead to minimum total transportation costs while meeting all distribution center demands and not exceeding production capacity at any facility.

These three examples indicate some of the applications of linear programming problems. The examples point out that linear programming problems primarily concern questions of optimum resource allocation within an organization. The following sections describe methods for finding and interpreting the solutions to similar problems.

7.3 Linear Programming Problems in Algebraic Form

Three groups of linear relations are included in the statement of a linear programming problem. First, a single objective function in equation form expresses the goal of the organization (maximize profit, minimize cost, etc.). Second, a set of inequality expressions is used to state the constraints on the objective function. Equations can be used to express particular constraints; however, all examples in this chapter will state constraints as inequalities. The third group of relations is nonnegativity restrictions (≥ 0) on the variables of the problem. As most linear programming problems concern the production, sale, or purchase of tangible goods and services, it is only logical to restrict any solution to zero or positive amounts. The variables of the problem (i.e., ounces of each ingredient or number of appliances) are referred to as *activity,* or *choice, variables.*

In notational form, a linear programming problem with n activity variables subject to m constraints is written as follows for the maximization and minimization cases, respectively:

Maximize: $Z = c_1 X_1 + c_2 X_2 + \cdots + c_n X_n$

Subject to:
$a_{11} X_1 + a_{12} X_2 + \cdots + a_{1n} X_n \leq b_1$
$a_{21} X_2 + a_{22} X_2 + \cdots + a_{2n} X_n \leq b_2$
$\vdots$
$a_{m1} X_1 + a_{m2} X_2 + \cdots + a_{mn} X_n \leq b_m$

and $X_1 \geq 0\ X_2 \geq 0 \ldots; X_n \geq 0$

Minimize: $Z = c_1 X_1 + c_2 X_2 + \cdots + c_n X_n$

Subject to:
$a_{11} X_1 + a_{12} X_2 + \cdots + a_{1n} X_n \geq b_1$
$a_{21} X_2 + a_{22} X_2 + \cdots + a_{2n} X_n \geq b_2$
$\vdots$
$a_{m1} X_1 + a_{m2} X_2 + \cdots + a_{mn} X_n \geq b_m$

and $X_1 \geq 0\ X_2 \geq 0 \ldots; X_n \geq 0$

Some of the characteristics of these expressions should be mentioned. The value of the objective function is noted by the letter Z, and Z is a linear function of each activity variable X_i with coefficient c_i.

Each of the m constraints on the objective function is associated with a particular constant b_i. For example, no more than 200 labor-hours per week are available ($b_1 = 200$). For the maximization problems described in this chapter, all constraints on the objective function are of the form less than or equal to ($\leq$), and for minimization problems constraints are expressed as greater than or equal to ($\geq$) inequalities. This convention is not a mandatory feature of linear programming problems but is a useful simplifying technique for an introductory discussion.

The less than or equal to statements in a maximization problem are similar to *restrictions* on the objective (e.g., resource scarcity, time restrictions, or a monetary constraint). The greater than or equal to statements of a minimization problem are similar to *requirements* which must be met while achieving an objective (e.g., requirements such as quality controls, safety rules, or government standards). Thus, an organization may attempt to maximize profit subject to a set of restrictions or minimize costs subject to a set of requirements. Thus, restrictions generally set maximum amounts and requirements establish minimum amounts (e.g., minimum product standards).

Nonnegativity restrictions on the activity variable (e.g., $X_i \geq 0$) are the last set of statements. Thus, the objective function, constraints on the objective, and nonnegativity restrictions on the activity variables, all in linear form, comprise the system of relations for a linear programming problem.

7.4 Linear Programming Problems in Matrix Form

In many analyses and interpretations, it is useful to express linear programming problems in matrix form. Using the same notation for coefficients, constraints, and variables as in the previous section, four arrays can be developed. If the problem includes n activity variables and m constraints, the coefficients of the activity variables in the objective function can be listed in an $n \times 1$ vector **C** as follows:

$$\mathbf{C} = \begin{pmatrix} c_1 \\ c_2 \\ \cdot \\ \cdot \\ \cdot \\ c_n \end{pmatrix}$$

Similarly, the activity variables are shown in an $n \times 1$ vector **X** as

$$X = \begin{pmatrix} x_1 \\ x_2 \\ \cdot \\ \cdot \\ \cdot \\ x_n \end{pmatrix}$$

The coefficients for the constraints are placed in an $m \times n$ matrix **A**, and the constants of the constraint equations are included in an $m \times 1$ vector **B** as follows:

$$A = \begin{pmatrix} a_{11} & a_{12} & \cdots & a_{1n} \\ a_{21} & a_{22} & \cdots & a_{2n} \\ \cdots & \cdots & \cdots & \cdots \\ a_{m1} & a_{m2} & \cdots & a_{mn} \end{pmatrix}$$

$$B = \begin{pmatrix} b_1 \\ b_2 \\ \cdot \\ \cdot \\ \cdot \\ b_m \end{pmatrix}$$

These arrays lead to the statement of the objective function as

$$Z = C^T X$$

The system of constraints on the objective function can be expressed

1. $AX \leq B$ or
2. $AX \geq B$

depending on whether the problem is a maximization (1) or a minimization (2). The nonnegativity restrictions in matrix form are

$$X \geq 0$$

where **0** represents a null vector with dimension $n \times 1$.

In summary, then, a maximization linear programming problem in matrix notation is

Maximize: $Z = C^T X$

Subject to: $AX \leq B$

and $X \geq 0$

Minimization problems can be stated similarly as

Minimize: $Z = C^T X$

Subject to: $AX \geq B$

and $X \geq 0$

Both the algebraic and matrix representations of a linear programming problem will be used and referred to in the following discussion.

7.5 Maximization and Minimization: A Geometrical Interpretation

When examining a linear programming problem in geometrical form, the object is to determine the point that optimizes the value of the objective function. However, it is possible that a particular problem may not have a unique solution. Situations where a unique solution does not exist are analyzed in Section 7.6. The present section explains the geometrical solution to a maximization problem and a minimization problem, each having a unique solution. These two problems also will serve as a basis for much of the remainder of the chapter's presentation. It should be kept in mind that the principles presented in discussing these problems are applicable to all linear programming problems having a unique solution.

Example 7.1: Profit Maximization Within a Set of Resource Constraints

A diversified appliance manufacturer is analyzing its production of two products, electric space heaters X_1 and toaster ovens X_2. Resources available for the production of these two goods are restricted to the following maximum weekly amounts: 200 management-and-support-staff-hours, 320 machine-hours, and 280 labor-hours.

An electric space heater requires for its production 1 management-and-support-staff-hour, 1 machine-hour, and 2 labor-hours. A toaster oven requires 1 management-and-support-staff-hour, 2 machine-hours, and 0.8 labor-hour. Finally, the firm knows that an electric space heater yields $6 gross profit per unit and a toaster oven yields $8 gross profit per unit. The manufacturer wants to determine the profit-maximizing weekly output of each product while operating within the set of resource limitations.

In this case, the unknowns or activity variables are the number of electric heaters X_1 and number of toaster ovens X_2 that should be manufactured each week. As the objective is to maximize profit with profit per unit equal to $6 for X_1 and $8 for X_2, the objective function is the following:

Maximize: $Z = 6X_1 + 8X_2$

There are three less than or equal to inequality constraints and two nonnegativity restrictions on this production process.

First, management-and-support-staff-hours cannot exceed 200, and a unit of output for either product requires 1 management-and-support-staff-hour. This is expressed as

1. $X_1 + X_2 \leq 200$

The machine-hour constraint is 320 hours, with an electric heater requiring 1 hour and a toaster oven requiring 2 hours. Therefore, the machine-hour constraint is

2. $X_1 + 2X_2 \leq 320$

Labor-hours are restricted to 280, and requirements are 2 labor-hours per heater and 0.8 labor-hour per toaster oven. This inequality constraint is represented by

3. $2X_1 + 0.8X_2 \leq 280$

The nonnegativity restrictions on output are

4. $X_1 \geq 0$
5. $X_2 \geq 0$

In summary, this profit maximization problem is stated in algebraic form as follows:

Maximize: $Z = 6X_1 + 8X_2$

Subject to:
$$X_1 + X_2 \leq 200$$
$$X_1 + 2X_2 \leq 320$$
$$2X_1 + 0.8X_2 \leq 280$$

and $X_1 \geq 0$
$X_2 \geq 0$

Graphing the Constraints

Each less than or equal to resource constraint and each nonnegativity restriction establishes a boundary for the objective. When all boundaries are considered together, the resulting area consisting of points corresponding to possible solution values for the problem is referred to as the *region of feasible solutions*.

Some generalizations can be made about the region of feasible solutions in linear programming problems. First, nonnegativity restrictions confine the region to the first quadrant. Secondly, feasible solution points lie on or *inside* (toward the origin from) lines representing less than or equal to constraints and on or *outside* (further from the origin than) lines representing greater than or equal to constraints. Thus, less than or equal to constraints impose outer boundaries and greater than or equal to constraints impose inner boundaries. Finally, the region of feasible solutions includes all points which satisfy simultaneously all the constraints.

The region of feasible solutions for the appliance production problem will be constructed using these three principles. First, the problem is restated in expression form:

Maximize: $Z = 6X_1 + 8X_2$

Subject to: $X_1 + X_2 \leq 200$
$X_1 + 2X_2 \leq 320$
$2X_1 + 0.8X_2 \leq 280$

and $X_1 \geq 0, X_2 \geq 0$

Because of the nonnegativity restrictions, the region of feasible solutions is in quadrant I. The boundary line for each constraint can be established by drawing the equation form of each constraint (i.e., $X_1 + X_2 = 200$). These three lines are shown on the quadrant I graph of Figure 7.1.

As each equation represents a less than or equal to constraint, the firm cannot exceed any of them. Consequently, the firm must operate at production levels on or within (toward the origin from) *all* the constraints. This area, the region of feasible solutions, is shown as $abcd0$ in Figure 7.1.

The construction of this region is described further by examining the X_1 and X_2 intercepts. If no toaster ovens are produced ($X_2 = 0$), maximum space heater production is 140 ($X_1 = 140$). At this point, point d in Figure 7.1, the 280 available labor-hours is the constraint which prevents further production. Thus, available labor time is a "binding constraint" at this point. Similarly, if no electric heaters are produced, a maximum of 160 toaster ovens may be produced. This is point a in Figure 7.1. At this point, available machine-hours (320) restrict further production and machine time is a binding constraint.

At various other combinations of heater and toaster production, one or the other or both of the constraints is binding. Therefore, the region of

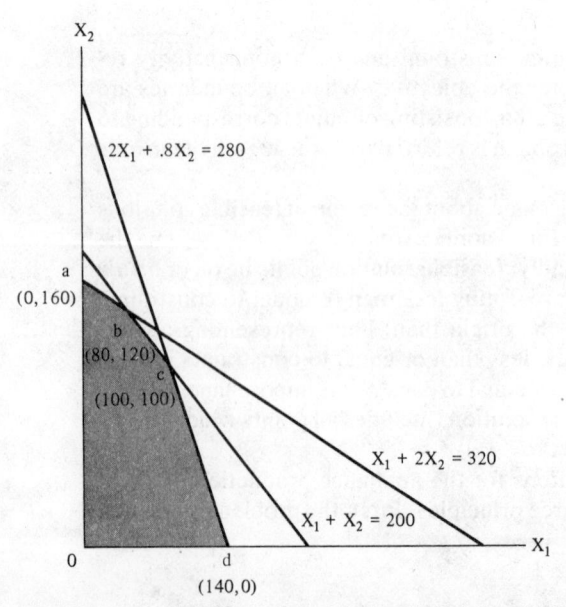

FIGURE 7.1 The region of feasible solutions for a maximization problem.

feasible solutions includes all production combinations in quadrant I which are on or within all three constraints.

The object of the problem is to find the level of production of each product which will maximize profit for the firm within the resource constraints, given the per unit profit of $6 for an electric heater and $8 for a toaster oven. To determine this point graphically, the line $Z = 6X_1 + 8X_2$ must be added to Figure 7.1. This is shown by the *dashed lines* in Figure 7.2.

In slope-intercept form, the objective function is

$$X_2 = Z - 0.75X_1$$

To find the maximum profit point, this line must be moved out from the origin to that point in the region of feasible solutions which is a maximum distance from the origin. Examples of this movement away from the origin are shown by the dashed lines I, II, and III in Figure 7.2. Lines such as I, II, and III are referred to as *isoprofit lines* as each yields a different value for the objective function. The word "isoprofit" means that profit is the same at all points on a given line (i.e., profit is equal at all points on line I). Thus, maximum profit is represented by that isoprofit line which is a maximum distance from the origin but on or within the resource constraints.

An important relationship in determining the solution point is that if a unique solution exists, the particular output point corresponding to maximum profit is

1. On the boundary of the region of feasible solutions.
2. At an intersection of two or more constraints (including the nonnegativity restrictions). These intersection points are referred to as *corner points*.

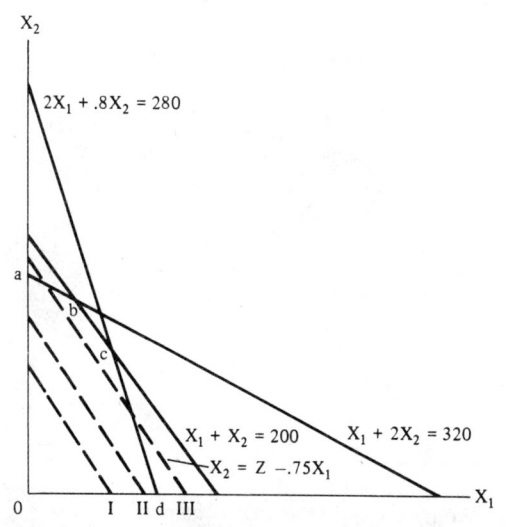

FIGURE 7.2 The region of feasible solutions and the objective function.

These two statements can be understood by referring to Figures 7.1 and 7.2.

First, observe that for a given X_1 (or X_2), the maximum value of Z is obtained by making X_2 (or X_1) as large as possible. Thus, maximum profit Z must occur on the boundary of the region of feasible solutions.

To explain why the optimum point must be at a corner of the region of feasible solutions, the concept of a convex set must be introduced. A *convex set* is a set of points such that if any two arbitrarily selected points within the set are connected by a straight line, all elements on the line segment are also members of the set. Figure 7.3 shows two sets; one (*a*) is not a convex set and the other (*b*) is a convex set in accordance with the previous statement. In addition, it can be demonstrated (although not proven here) that (1) a linear objective function is a convex set and (2) any region of feasible solutions also is a convex set.

Finally, it is a mathematical principle that for any convex set moved through a second convex set, the last point touched before the first set moves completely outside the second must include at least one corner point of the second set. Therefore, as the line representing the profit maximization objective function is moved through the region of feasible solutions, the last point (the optimal profit point) before leaving the region includes at least one corner of the region of feasible solutions.

The previous discussion leads to the conclusion that, if a maximum profit point exists, it will be on the boundary of the region of feasible solutions and it will be at an intersection of two or more constraints, including the nonnegativity restrictions.

Applying these two principles to the problem shown in Figures 7.1 and 7.2, the maximum profit must occur at one of the following corner points:

1. The origin (0)
2. Point *a*
3. Point *b*
4. Point *c*
5. Point *d*

This "by-hand" calculation procedure requires finding X_1 and X_2 at each of the above points and computing the corresponding profit at each by substitution into $Z = 6X_1 + 8X_2$. The first corner point is the origin, with coordinates (0, 0). Corner points *a* and *d* represent, respectively, the X_2 intercept (0, 160) and X_1 intercept (140, 0).

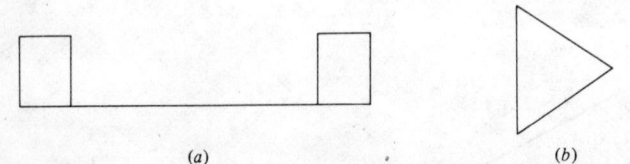

(*a*) (*b*)

FIGURE 7.3 Two sets; (*a*) one that is not convex and (*b*) one that is convex.

Corner points b and c are found by solving the system of equations for each of the two intersecting lines. Thus, for point b,

$$\text{Eq. 1: } X_1 + X_2 = 200$$
$$\text{Eq. 2: } X_1 + 2X_2 = 320$$
$$\text{Eq. 2} - \text{Eq. 1:} \quad X_2 = 120$$
$$\text{By substitution: } X_1 + 120 = 200$$
$$X_1 = 80$$
Point b: (80, 120)

And for point c, the system of equations yields

$$\text{Eq. 1: } X_1 + X_2 = 200$$
$$\text{Eq. 3: } 2X_1 + 0.8X_2 = 280$$
$$2(\text{Eq. 1}) - \text{Eq. 3:} \quad 1.2X_2 = 120$$
$$X_2 = 100$$
$$\text{By substitution: } X_1 + 100 = 200$$
$$X_1 = 100$$
Point c: (100, 100)

These five points and their coordinates yield the profit figures shown in Table 7.1.

The data in Table 7.1 indicate that profit is maximized at corner point b, which is associated with the production of 80 electric heaters and 120 toaster ovens. Thus, the firm will achieve a maximum profit of $1440 per week by operating within the constraints at these production levels.

At this point, it is useful to summarize the steps followed in determining the maximum profit point:

1. Draw on the coordinate axis all constraints expressed as equations.
2. Find the region of feasible solutions, including the nonnegativity restrictions.
3. Identify all feasible corner points by their coordinates.
4. Substitute each set of corner-point coordinates into the objective function and compute the value of the objective function at that point.

TABLE 7.1 Appliance Firm's Profit at Each Corner Point of the Region of Feasible Solutions

Corner Point	Coordinate (X_1, X_2)	Value of the Objective Function $(Z = 6X_1 + 8X_2)$
Origin	(0, 0)	$Z = 6(0) + 8(0) = 0$
a	(0, 160)	$Z = 6(0) + 8(160) = 1280$
b	(80, 120)	$Z = 6(80) + 8(120) = 1440$
c	(100, 100)	$Z = 6(100) + 8(100) = 1400$
d	(140, 0)	$Z = 6(140) + 8(0) = 840$

5. Select the coordinate point yielding the optimum value for the objective function.

Further practice in these steps will be provided by the following example of a problem of cost minimization under a set of linear requirements.

Example 7.2: Cost Minimization under a Set of Product Quality Requirements

A food manufacturer is planning production of a fortified convenience food to be used primarily by hospitals. The product uses two ingredients, X_1 and X_2. An ounce of X_1 costs $0.15 and an ounce of X_2 costs $0.20. The firm wants to produce each serving of this food using a least-cost combination of ounces of X_1 and ounces of X_2 while satisfying the product specification requirements.

The first requirement is that a serving must have at least 30 grams of carbohydrate. An ounce of X_1 contains 5 grams of carbohydrate and an ounce of X_2 also has 5 grams of carbohydrate. Thus, the first requirement is expressed as

1. $5X_1 + 5X_2 \geq 30$

Second, a serving of the product must contain at least 25 grams of protein. An ounce of X_1 has 5 grams of protein and an ounce of X_2 has 4 grams of protein. The second requirement, therefore, is

2. $5X_1 + 4X_2 \geq 25$

The third requirement is that a serving must contain at least 4 grams of fat. As an ounce of X_1 has 0.5 gram of fat and an ounce of X_2 has 1 gram of fat, the third requirement is

3. $0.5X_1 + X_2 \geq 4$

Finally, nonnegativity restrictions apply to both X_1 and X_2 as

4. $X_1 \geq 0$
5. $X_2 \geq 0$

Combining requirements 1 through 5 with the ingredient-cost data yields the following statement of the problem:

Minimize: $Z = 0.15X_1 + 0.20X_2$

Subject to: $5X_1 + 5X_2 \geq 30$
$5X_1 + 4X_2 \geq 25$
$0.5X_1 + X_2 \geq 4$

and $X_1 \geq 0, X_2 \geq 0$

Requirements 1 through 5 establish boundaries for the objective function. Points in quadrant I which are outside of 1, 2, and 3, *considered together*, constitute the region of feasible solutions. Points *on* this inner boundary also are included in the region of feasible solutions. The region is shown in Figure 7.4.

As each constraint is a greater than or equal to requirement, the region of feasible solutions can be defined as all points on Figure 7.4 in quadrant I which are

1. Further from the origin than the line segments ab, bc, and cd
2. On the line segments ab, bc, and cd
3. On the X_2 axis and equal to or greater than a
4. On the X_1 axis and equal to or greater than d

Between points a and b, the protein requirement is binding, as it prevents costs from being reduced. However, between b and c the carbohydrate requirement is binding on further cost reductions. And between c and d the fat requirement is binding.

The X_2 intercept of 6.25 ounces indicates that, if no X_1 is used in the product, at least 6.25 ounces of X_2 are required to satisfy all the requirements. Similarly, the X_1 intercept shows that if no X_2 is used, at least 8 ounces of X_1 are necessary to meet all requirements.

To determine the combination of ingredients which yields minimum cost, the line representing the objective function must be moved as close as possible to the origin while satisfying all the requirements. Figure 7.4 shows three levels of the objective function in slope-intercept form,

$$X_2 = Z - 0.75X_1$$

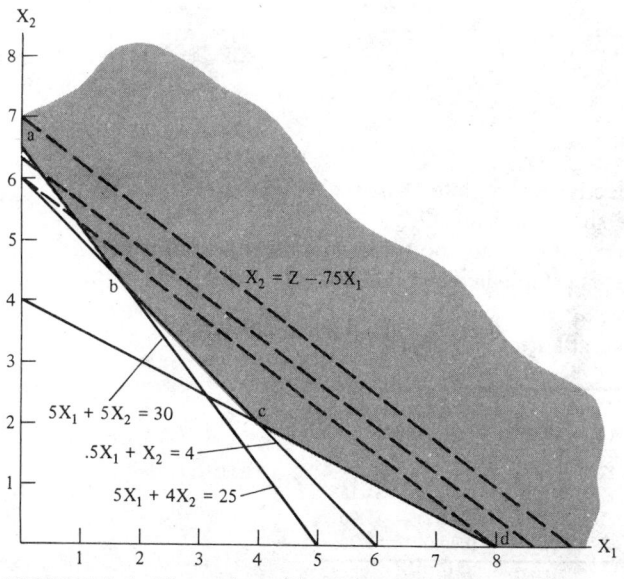

FIGURE 7.4 The region of feasible solutions for a minimization problem.

As each dashed line represents various ingredient combinations which result in the same cost, the lines are referred to as *isocost lines*.

As the region of feasible solutions is a convex set and the objective function is linear, the minimum cost point must occur at a corner of the region of feasible solutions, i.e., at an intersection of two or more requirements (including the nonnegativity restrictions). The least-cost corner represents the point closest to the origin within which the objective function line may not be moved if all requirements are satisfied.

On Figure 7.4, point a is the X_2 intercept (0, 6.25) and point d is the X_1 intercept (8, 0). Point b is the intersection of the protein and carbohydrate requirements, which is determined as follows:

$$\text{Eq. 1:} \quad 5X_1 + 5X_2 = 30$$
$$\text{Eq. 2:} \quad 5X_1 + 4X_2 = 25$$
$$\text{Eq. 1} - \text{Eq. 2:} \quad X_2 = 5$$
$$\text{By substitution:} \quad 5X_1 + 5(5) = 30$$
$$5X_1 = 5$$
$$X_1 = 1$$

Point b: (1, 5)

Point c is the intersection of the carbohydrate and fat requirements as follows:

$$\text{Eq. 1:} \quad 5X_1 + 5X_2 = 30$$
$$\text{Eq. 3:} \quad 0.5X_1 + X_2 = 4$$
$$\text{Eq. 1} - 5(\text{Eq. 3}): \quad 2.5X_1 = 10$$
$$X_1 = 4$$
$$\text{By substitution:} \quad 5(4) + 5X_2 = 30$$
$$5X_2 = 10$$
$$X_2 = 2$$

Point c: (4, 2)

All corners, their respective coordinates, and the value of the objective function at each corner are shown in Table 7.2.

This "by-hand" corner solution method demonstrates that minimum cost within the requirements is established by combining 4 ounces of X_1 with

TABLE 7.2 Food Product Cost at Each Corner Point of the Region of Feasible Solutions

Corner Point	Coordinate (X_1, X_2)	Value of Objective Function $(Z = \$0.15X_1 + \$0.20X_2)$
a	(0, 6.25)	$Z = 0.15(0) + 0.20(6.25) = \$1.25$
b	(1, 5)	$Z = 0.15(1) + 0.20(5) = \$1.15$
c	(4, 2)	$Z = 0.15(4) + 0.20(2) = \$1.00$
d	(8, 0)	$Z = 0.15(8) + 0.20(0) = \$1.20$

2 ounces of X_2 in each serving. This leads to a per serving cost of $1.00. At this production level, the carbohydrate and fat requirements are satisfied exactly but the protein requirement is exceeded as there will be 28 grams of protein in each serving [$5X_1 + 4X_2 = (5)(4) + (4)(2) = 28$] compared with the 25-gram requirement.

Both examples in this section have shown that an optimum point, if it exists, will be at a corner of the region of feasible solutions. The process used to find the exact optimum point has involved computation of the value of the objective function at each feasible corner. As will be described below, there is an efficient alternative to this by-hand calculation procedure. Prior to this discussion, the following is a short description of situations where other than a unique optimum solution exists.

7.6 Other Solution Possibilities

Three alternatives to the unique solution case for a linear programming problem are briefly considered in this section. First, it is possible that the objective function is parallel to one of the constraints or requirements forming the boundary of the region of feasible solutions. Figure 7.5 illustrates this situation.

In this case, the constraint $20X_1 + 25X_2 = 60$ and the objective function $Z = 4X_1 + 5X_2$ are parallel lines. When this occurs, there exist an unlimited number of optimum solutions, each corresponding to the same value for the objective function.

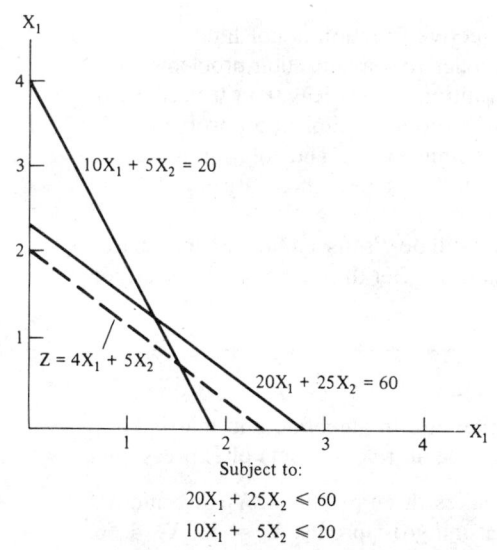

Subject to:
$20X_1 + 25X_2 \leq 60$
$10X_1 + 5X_2 \leq 20$

FIGURE 7.5 An objective function parallel to one of the constraints.

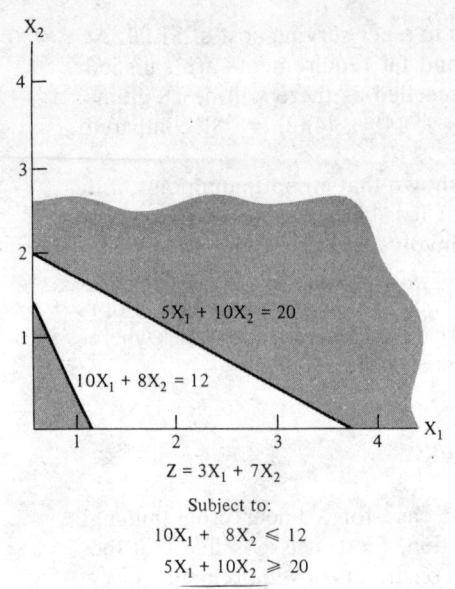

FIGURE 7.6 A group of constraints that mutually cannot be satisfied.

$$Z = 3X_1 + 7X_2$$
Subject to:
$$10X_1 + 8X_2 \leq 12$$
$$5X_1 + 10X_2 \geq 20$$

A second possibility is that no points may satisfy all the constraints or requirements. Figure 7.6, which combines a less than or equal to constraint with a greater than or equal to constraint, demonstrates this situation. For a problem of this type, no optimal solution exists and the problem cannot be solved as stated.

Finally, it is possible that the objective function is not limited by the constraints. Realistically, this usually applies to maximization problems since minimization problems cannot have solution values less than 0 because of the nonnegativity restrictions. Thus, in a profit maximization problem, this situation occurs when resources do not limit profit. The solution to such a problem is referred to as being "unbounded"; i.e., there are no relevant limits to the value of the objective function.

Each of these solution possibilities will be discussed further and related to particular outcomes of the simplex method after this technique is described in the following sections.

EXERCISES

For Problems 1 and 2 below, set up the data in algebraic and matrix form acceptable for linear programming. Include all relevant sets of expressions.

1. A home hardware manufacturer makes three products, X_1, X_2, and X_3. The products have the following per unit gross profits: $X_1 = \$3$, $X_2 = \$6$, and $X_3 = \$10$.

Two resources, labor and machinery, are used to manufacture each product. A unit of X_1 requires 2 labor-hours and 2 machine-hours for its production. A unit of X_2 requires 3 labor-hours and 1 machine-hour. A unit of X_3 uses 4 labor-hours and 2 machine-hours. Labor- and machine-hours used to make these three products cannot exceed 400 and 350 hours per week, respectively.

The goal of this firm is to maximize gross profit from these three products without exceeding any of the resource constraints.

2. A firm manufactures two small automobile parts (A and B) using three machines, X_1, X_2, and X_3. Machine X_1 costs \$20 per hour to operate, X_2 costs \$15 per hour, and X_3 costs \$24 per hour of operation. Machine X_1 can produce 3 units of A and 1 unit of B per hour, X_2 can turn out 2 units of A and 2 units of B per hour, and X_3 can manufacture 3 units of A and 4 units of B per hour.

The firm must produce at least 200 units of part A and 300 units of part B per week.

The question the firm wants to answer is, how many hours per week should each machine be operated to achieve these production levels at the least possible total cost of machinery operation?

For each of the following, find the optimum point by evaluating the objective function at every *feasible* corner.

3. Maximize: $Z = X_1 + 2.5X_2$
   Subject to: $2X_1 + 4X_2 \leq 60$
   $3X_1 + 4X_2 \leq 70$
   and $X_1 \geq 0, X_2 \geq 0$

4. Minimize: $Z = 3X_1 + 3X_2$
   Subject to: $3X_1 + X_2 \geq 24$
   $X_1 + X_2 \geq 16$
   and $X_1 \geq 0, X_2 \geq 0$

5. Maximize: $Z = 4X_1 + 4X_2$
   Subject to: $2X_1 + 4X_2 \leq 60$
   $5X_1 + 2X_2 \leq 50$
   and $X_1 \geq 0, X_2 \geq 0$

6. Minimize: $Z = 4X_1 + 2X_2$
   Subject to: $X_1 + 3X_2 \geq 15$
   $2X_1 + 2X_2 \geq 20$
   and $X_1 \geq 0, X_2 \geq 0$

7. Maximize: $Z = 3X_1 + 2X_2$
   Subject to: $X_1 + X_2 \leq 8$
   $3X_1 + 5X_2 \leq 30$
   $2X_1 + 8X_2 \leq 40$
   and $X_1 \geq 0, X_2 \geq 0$

8. Minimize: $Z = 2X_1 + 3X_2$
   Subject to: $X_1 + X_2 \geq 10$
   $6X_1 + X_2 \geq 24$

$$4X_1 + 2X_2 \geq 30$$
$$\text{and } X_1 \geq 0, X_2 \geq 0$$

9. Maximize: $Z = 3X_1 + 5X_2$
   Subject to: $4X_1 + 5X_2 \leq 60$
   $$2X_1 + X_2 \leq 24$$
   $$X_1 + 5X_2 \leq 48$$
   $$\text{and } X_1 \geq 0, X_2 \geq 0$$

10. Minimize: $Z = 2X_1 + 2X_2$
    Subject to: $2X_1 + 4X_2 \geq 40$
    $$X_1 + 8X_2 \geq 24$$
    $$4X_1 + 2X_2 \geq 32$$
    $$\text{and } X_1 \geq 0, X_2 \geq 0$$

7.7 The Simplex Method: Principles

The method used to solve Examples 7.1 and 7.2, including in each case a graphical description and by-hand calculation for each feasible corner, is limited to relatively simple linear programming problems. As the number of constraints and variables increase, both the geometrical description and the computation of the optimal value become complex and time consuming.

The simplex method is a nongraphical procedure for finding the optimum value of the objective function in constrained optimization problems. This technique has been incorporated in many computer programs, thus providing a rapid solution to many complex linear programming problems.

To find the optimum point by means of the simplex method, an iterative process is applied until the optimum value of the objective function is determined. Each iteration involves solution of a system of linear equations.

The simplex method provides for evaluation of the objective function at feasible corners in such a way that the value of the objective function at each successive corner is at least as good as the result at the previous corner. When no further improvements are possible, the objective function has been maximized (as in Example 7.1) or minimized (as in Example 7.2). The evaluation at each feasible corner is one iteration in the eventual solution.

The specifics of the iterative procedure used in the simplex method can be explained most easily by using Gauss-Jordan row operations as presented in Chapter 6. Because several additional factors must be considered in minimization problems, this and the following section describe the simplex method as applied to the maximization problem of Example 7.1. As a final introductory comment, it should be emphasized that much of the computation shown below usually is carried out by computer. The reasons for including the steps in this presentation are to (1) describe how computers carry out the simplex method and (2) assist in the explanation of the results obtained in the simplex procedure.

As a basis for this discussion, consider again the maximization problem of Example 7.1.

Example 7.3
Solve by the simplex method:

Maximize: $Z = 6X_1 + 8X_2$

Subject to:
$$X_1 + X_2 \leq 200$$
$$X_1 + 2X_2 \leq 320$$
$$2X_1 + 0.8X_2 \leq 280$$

and $X_1 \geq 0, X_2 \geq 0$

Before using the simplex solution procedure, the algebraic formulation of the simplex method must be explained.

As all solution possibilities occur on the boundary of the region of feasible solutions, the inequalities must be converted to equations. This is carried out by introducing a *slack variable* (S_1, S_2, and S_3) for each of the less than or equal to constraints. In addition, the objective function is set equal to 0. Thus the constraints and the objective function can be expressed in the following system of equations:

$$Z - 6X_1 - 8X_2 = 0$$
$$X_1 + X_2 + S_1 = 200$$
$$X_1 + 2X_2 + S_2 = 320$$
$$2X_1 + 0.8X_2 + S_3 = 280$$

For the constraints, the slack variables represent unused resources. For example, if there are 280 labor-hours available and 80 units of X_1 are produced with 100 units of X_2, there will be 40 unused labor-hours or $S_3 = 40$. This is computed as

$$2X_1 + 0.8X_2 + S_3 = 280$$
$$2(80) + 0.8(100) + S_3 = 280$$
$$160 + 80 + S_3 = 280$$
$$S_3 = 40$$

As Z is a variable which does not affect the solution, but rather its value at any point is a result of the decision process, it is not considered part of the determining set of variables. Thus, the system of equations above has five variables of interest: X_1, X_2, S_1, S_2, and S_3. Two of these, X_1 and X_2, are the focus of the production decision and are the activity variables. Therefore, excluding the objective function, the system of equations relevant to the simplex method has five variables and three equations. In general, a linear programming problem will have m equations, representing the number of constraints, and $m + n$ variables, where m is the number of slack variables and n is the number of activity variables.

As stated previously, the points of interest in a linear programming problem are the corners of the region of feasible solutions. Any corner will have *at most m* variables with nonzero values. This is because each corner represents the solution of an $m \times m$ system of equations (one equation for each constraint). As a result of this relation, every corner also must have *at least n* variables with 0 values. For example, if in a problem there are four activity variables and seven slack variables (i.e., seven constraints), any corner in the region of feasible solutions will have at most seven variables with nonzero values and at least four variables with zero values.

Additional terminology is used to describe the variables at each corner. First, each solution (set of values for the variables) at a feasible corner is referred to as a *basic feasible solution*. The m variables with nonzero values at this point are referred to as *basic variables* and they constitute the *basis* at this point.[1] The remaining n variables with zero values are called *nonbasic* variables. Thus, at any feasible solution point the number of basic variables must be equal to the number of constraints in the problem.

The simplex method is a mathematical procedure used to solve for the value of the objective function at various corners. The process used to accomplish this is to solve various systems of m equations in $m + n$ variables by setting n variables equal to zero and solving for the remaining m variables. The iterations stop when the particular basic feasible solution which yields an optimal value for the objective function has been found. The process is such that once the optimal value is found, no additional corners have to be evaluated. Consequently, in many cases, this reduces substantially the required number of steps when compared with a geometrical solution.

The simplex solution process as applied to the appliance firm's profit maximization problem is the topic of the next section.

7.8 The Simplex Method: Solution

As this iterative process has been written into many computer programs, it should be emphasized again that the following presentation is intended to

1. Describe the process used in many of these programs
2. Serve as an instructive means to discuss the interpretation of the final results of a linear programming problem

Although the specific steps in the simplex method and the calculation required for each are shown, students should concentrate on the *pattern* of solution and the *interpretation* of results and should understand that the iterations usually are not computed by hand.

The simplex method, in solving the various sets of m equations in

---

[1] All m variables do not necessarily have to have nonzero values, but this group represents those variables considered a part of the solution at this point.

$m + n$ variables, uses the coefficients for each of the $m + n$ variables in setting up a *tableau* (similar to an augmented matrix). These coefficients are used to derive various basic feasible solutions by altering the mix of basic and nonbasic variables according to the set of rules described below (the rules comprise the simplex method).

The first solution point, expressed in the *initial tableau,* includes the slack variables as the basis (rows), and the activity variables are nonbasic (columns). An additional row is included in the tableau for the objective function. Thus, beginning with the system of equations listed previously,

$$Z - 6X_1 - 8X_2 = 0$$
$$X_1 + X_2 + S_1 = 200$$
$$X_1 + 2X_2 + S_2 = 320$$
$$2X_1 + 0.8X_2 + S_3 = 280$$

the initial tableau of coefficients is developed, as shown in Table 7.3. This initial tableau includes a row for each slack variable and a column for each of the $m + n$ variables. A column for the Z variable is omitted in all tableaus as it would always have a one in the first row followed by a string of zeroes. The Z row, on the other hand, includes in the initial tableau all the coefficients for the objective function.

The column titled RHS (meaning right-hand side) includes values for the objective function at this particular corner (zero above) and for each basic variable. Thus, the initial tableau describes a basic feasible solution (corner point) where $Z = 0$, $S_1 = 200$, $S_2 = 320$, and $S_3 = 280$. Profit is zero at this point as nothing is produced ($X_1 = 0$, $X_2 = 0$). Therefore, the initial tableau describes the origin, where all resources are unused and profit is zero.

At this stage of the analysis the question asked is, "Is this basic feasible solution optimal?" The following rule is applied when answering this question at this point and after every iteration.

A PARTICULAR BASIC FEASIBLE SOLUTION IS NOT
OPTIMAL IF A NEGATIVE NUMBER OCCURS FOR ANY
NONBASIC VARIABLE IN THE Z ROW OF THE TABLEAU.

Specifically, a negative coefficient in the Z row for any nonbasic variable indicates that profit (as measured by Z in the objective function) can be

TABLE 7.3 The Initial Tableau

		Nonbasic Variables					
		X_1	X_2	S_1	S_2	S_3	RHS
	Z	−6	−8	0	0	0	0
Basic Variables	S_1	1	1	1	0	0	200
	S_2	1	2*	0	1	0	320
	S_3	−2	0.8	0	0	1	280

increased if the variable having a negative coefficient is given a positive one instead.

As there are negative coefficients for each nonbasic variable in this initial tableau, the solution is not optimal at this point. Thus, the mix of basic and nonbasic variables should be changed. The nonbasic variable to replace is the one with the largest negative number in the Z row, as increasing that variable will have the greatest impact on the value of Z. (In the case of ties, either of the nonbasic variables may be selected arbitrarily.) In this example, therefore, X_2 is replaced as a nonbasic variable, and the X_2 column is referred to as the *pivot column*.

To compensate for this change of X_2 from nonbasic to basic, one of the basic variables must be made nonbasic. To determine this, each value in the RHS column is divided by the respective row coefficient in the X_2 column for those basic variables having positive coefficients. In this case all have positive coefficients in the X_2 column. The row corresponding to the *smallest positive quotient* is the basic variable that is removed and made nonbasic.

For the initial tableau, the quotients are as follows:

$$\text{Quotient for } S_1 = \frac{200}{1} = 200$$

$$\text{Quotient for } S_2 = \frac{320}{2} = 160$$

$$\text{Quotient for } S_3 = \frac{280}{0.8} = 350$$

Therefore, S_2 should be made nonbasic. By selecting the row with the smallest quotient, it is assured that the added output (of X_2 in this case) will be small enough to ensure that none of the resource constraints will be exceeded.

The analysis has shown that the intersection of the S_2 row and the X_2 column, the coefficient 2, is the *pivot element*. It is identified by an asterisk in Table 7.3.

The next step is to incorporate X_2 into the basis. To do this, the X_2 column must be transformed into a vector with a one in the pivot position and zeroes elsewhere. In other words, the X_2 column must be altered from

$$\begin{pmatrix} -8 \\ 1 \\ 2 \\ 0.8 \end{pmatrix} \text{ to } \begin{pmatrix} 0 \\ 0 \\ 1 \\ 0 \end{pmatrix}$$

This is accomplished by Gauss-Jordan row operations using the zeroes-first technique, as described in Chapter 6. Table 7.4 is a restatement of Table 7.3 and a summary of the necessary row operations. Table 7.5 is the new, or second, tableau.

TABLE 7.4 The Initial Tableau and Row Operations

Initial Tableau	X_1	X_2	S_1	S_2	S_3	RHS
(Row 1) Z	−6	−8	0	0	0	0
(Row 2) S_1	1	1	1	0	0	200
(Row 3) S_2	1	2*	0	1	0	320
(Row 4) S_3	2	0.8	0	0	1	280

Row Operations

1. Replace row 1 by 4(row 3) + row 1
2. Replace row 3 by: row 3 − row 2
3. Replace row 4 by −0.4(row 3) + row 4
4. Divide row 3 by 2

Observe that the value of the objective function in Table 7.5 is $Z = 1280$ and that 160 units of X_2 and no X_1 are produced at this point [(8)(160) = 1280].

Although this second tableau is an improvement over the initial situation, the solution is not optimal because the negative coefficient −2 in the X_1 column of the Z row indicates that production of X_1 would increase total profit. Therefore, X_1 also should be a basic variable. To determine which current basic variable should now be removed from the basis, the quotient of each positive value in the X_1 column and its corresponding RHS value is found. These quotients, from the second tableau, are

Quotient for $S_1 = \dfrac{40}{0.5} = 80$

Quotient for $X_2 = \dfrac{160}{0.5} = 320$

Quotient for $S_3 = \dfrac{152}{1.6} = 95$

Thus, in accordance with the previous rule, S_1 is moved from the basis and replaced by X_1. The new pivot element is +0.5 at the intersection of the X_1 column and S_1 row. This is indicated by an asterisk (*) in the second tableau (Table 7.5). The object is to form a third tableau in which the X_1 column is altered by row operations from

$$\begin{pmatrix} -2 \\ 0.5 \\ 0.5 \\ 1.6 \end{pmatrix} \text{ to } \begin{pmatrix} 0 \\ 1 \\ 0 \\ 0 \end{pmatrix}$$

TABLE 7.5 The New (Second) Tableau

	X_1	X_2	S_1	S_2	S_3	RHS
Z	−2	0	0	4	0	1280
S_1	0.5*	0	1	−0.5	0	40
X_2	0.5	1	0	0.5	0	160
S_3	1.6	0	0	−0.4	1	152

TABLE 7.6 The Second Tableau and Required Row Operations

	X_1	X_2	S_1	S_2	S_3	RHS
(Row 1) Z	-2.0	0	0	4	0	1280
(Row 2) S_1	0.5*	0	1	-0.5	0	40
(Row 3) X_2	0.5	1	0	0.5	0	160
(Row 4) S_3	1.6	0	0	-0.4	1	152

Row Operations

1. Replace row 1 by: 4(row 2) + row 1
2. Replace row 3 by: row 3 − row 2
3. Replace row 4 by: −3.2(row 2) + row 4
4. Multiply row 2 by 2

TABLE 7.7 The Third Tableau

	X_1	X_2	S_1	S_2	S_3	RHS
Z	0	0	4	2	0	1440
X_1	1	0	2	-1	0	80
X_2	0	1	-1	1	0	120
S_3	0	0	-3.2	1.2	1	24

Table 7.6 shows the second tableau and a list of the required row operations. The new (third) tableau is included in Table 7.7.

The Z row (objective function row) in the third tableau has no negative elements. Thus, no further movements of variables into or out of the basis will increase total profit. This tableau represents an optimal basic feasible solution.

Before an interpretation of this optimal tableau is presented, observe that the simplex procedure found this optimum after only two steps. Also, after each iteration the value of Z was increased. Thus, it was not necessary to evaluate profit at every feasible corner as was required with the geometrical solution.

7.9 Interpretation of the Optimal Tableau

Several important aspects of the optimal tableau deserve mention. First, the right-hand-side (RHS) column gives the value of the objective function and each basic variable at the optimum point. Therefore, in this example (Table 7.7) it is concluded that the firm should manufacture 80 electric heaters (X_1) and 120 toaster ovens (X_2). This will lead to a profit of $1440 per week as

$Z = \$6(80) + \$8(120) = \$480 + \$960 = \$1440$

This result is consistent with the corner point values shown in Table 7.1.

At this optimal point, the RHS column also indicates that there will be 24 slack hours (unused hours) of the labor resource. This can be seen by referring to Figure 7.1, since the intersection point for (80, 120) is inside (toward the origin) the labor-hour constraint line. Also, note that the slack can be determined by substituting 80 and 120 into the labor-hour constraint equation as follows:

$$2X_1 + 0.8X_2 + S_3 = 280$$
$$2(80) + 0.8(120) + S_3 = 280$$
$$160 + 96 + S_3 = 280$$
$$S_3 = 280 - 256$$
$$S_3 = 24$$

The values for the nonbasic variables in the optimal solution also yield analytically useful information. First, any activity variable which is nonbasic in the optimal tableau (there are none in this category in the present example) has an optimal value of zero. This means, for example, that it is optimal for none of that particular product to be produced.

Second, any slack variable that is nonbasic in the optimal tableau (S_1 and S_2 above) has a value of zero indicating that this resource is fully utilized at the optimum point. Thus, these resources are "binding" on the objective function in that they restrict, in this problem, profit from being increased beyond the optimum level ($1440). Their importance can be assessed more directly by looking at any positive number which occurs for a nonbasic slack variable in the objective function (Z row). Such positive numbers represent *shadow prices*[2] of the fully utilized resources. Examples from the current problem will demonstrate the concept of a shadow price.

In the optimal (third) tableau of Table 7.7, the number under the S_1 column in the Z row is 4. This is the shadow price of management and staff time which is fully utilized at the level of 200 hours in the optimal solution. The number 4 represents (1) the additional profit possible if one more hour of this resource were made available and (2) the decrease in profit if one hour less of this resource were used. Similarly, the +2 under the S_2 column in the Z row is the shadow price of machine time. Consequently, one more hour of available machine time will increase total profit by $2 and one hour of slack in machine time will decrease profit by $2. Thus, shadow prices are similar to values which can be imputed to the fully utilized resources in an optimal solution.

Shadow Price Ranges

The previous interpretations given to shadow prices are not applicable if the change in the use of a resource is of such a magnitude as to change the basis

[2]Shadow prices also are referred to frequently as *marginal values*. The use of this term will be apparent after reading the following discussion.

of the optimal solution. Thus, there are limitations to the effect on profit of changes in the use of each completely utilized resource. For example, the $4 per hour shadow price for management and staff time may not continue to be valid as use of this resource expands in excess of 200 hours per week, such as to 250 or 260 hours per week. A technique exists for determining the range of resource use over which specific shadow prices are applicable. Evaluation of these ranges requires a discussion of some of the numbers in the optimal tableau which have not been discussed.

The numbers in the nonbasic slack variable columns, excluding the Z-row entries, represent substitution rates between each nonbasic variable and the respective basic variable. To explain these substitution rates, consider the $+2$ in Table 7.7 at the intersection of the X_1 row and S_1 column. This $+2$ indicates that a 1-hour increase (decrease) in management time used (e.g., from 200 to 201) will be associated with a two-unit increase (decrease) in the production of X_1. In other words, changes in management time have a direct relationship to changes in the production of X_1.

Alternatively, the -1 element at the intersection of the X_2 row and S_1 column means that a 1-hour increase (decrease) in management time used will be associated with a one-unit decrease (increase) in the production of X_2. Therefore, changes in management time are negatively related to changes in the production of X_2. Both relationships taken together show that an additional hour of management time should be used, for optimal profit, to produce two more X_1 units and one less X_2 unit.

It should be noted that each change described in the previous paragraph results in a change in the optimal value of the basic variables X_1 and X_2 (as measured by their right-hand values). As changes in resource use are continued, eventually the right-hand-side value of some basic variable may be less than 0. At this point, the basis as stated in the optimal solution is no longer optimal. Consequently, the shadow prices for the nonbasic slack variables also are no longer valid.

To determine the range of resource use within which shadow prices remain applicable, the following question must be answered: How much can the use of each nonbasic resource be increased or decreased without altering the basis of the optimal tableau?

Answering this question requires using (1) the substitution rates between a *given* nonbasic variable and *all* basic variables and (2) the right-hand-side values for all basic variables. In general, each nonbasic variable may be changed by, at most, an amount that will make the respective right-hand-side value equal to 0.

As there is interest only in reducing the right-hand-side value, one only need consider the following two resource-use changes:

1. Increases in resource use as affecting a basic variable for which there is a negative substitution rate
2. Decreases in resource use as affecting a basic variable for which there is a positive substitution rate

To determine the exact range over which the shadow price for a given nonbasic variable is applicable, a ratio is formed between the right-hand-side value and substitution rate for each basic variable. Then the following two rules are applied:

Rule 1: For all positive substitution rates, the *minimum* ratio represents the *largest allowable decrease* in the range of resource use.

Rule 2: For all negative substitution rates, the *minimum* ratio *in absolute value* represents the *largest allowable increase* in the range of resource use.

The data in Table 7.7, reprinted below as Table 7.8, will demonstrate application of these rules.

For S_1 (management time with a current availability of 200 hours), there is only one positive substitution rate (+2 when related to X_1). Thus, ratio one (designated R_1) is equal to the following:

$$R_1 = \frac{80}{2} = 40$$

Therefore, 40 hours per week is the maximum possible reduction in management time while maintaining the applicability of the $4 per hour shadow price.

There are two negative substitution rates in the S_1 column (in the X_2 and S_3 rows). These lead to the following ratios for R_2 and R_3:

$$R_2 = \frac{120}{-1} = -120 \quad |-120| = 120$$

$$R_3 = \frac{24}{-3.2} = -7.5 \quad |-7.5| = 7.5$$

Following the previous rule, it is determined that the largest allowable increase in management time without changing the basis is 7.5 hours per week.

The analysis demonstrates that the shadow price of management time is applicable within a range of 160 (200 − 40) hours per week to 207.5 (200 + 7.5) hours per week. Changes in management time usage exceeding these limits change the basis and, consequently, change the current optimal solution and related resource shadow prices.

Students should be able to show by a similar analysis that the shadow

TABLE 7.8 The Optimal Tableau for Example 7.1

	X_1	X_2	S_1	S_2	S_3	RHS
Z	0	0	4	2	0	1440
X_1	1	0	2	−1	0	80
X_2	0	1	−1	1	0	120
S_3	0	0	−3.2	1.2	1	24

price for machine-hours S_2, \$2 per hour, is valid over the range 300 hours per week (320 − 20) to 400 hours per week (320 + 80). Again, changes in resource usage outside of this range will change the basis of the optimal solution.

This section has discussed several interpretative aspects of the optimal tableau. These are summarized in the following five points:

1. The value in the right-hand-side column of the Z row of the objective function represents the optimal value of the objective function.
2. The other right-hand-side numbers represent optimal values for the basic variables.
3. Nonbasic variables have an optimal value of 0 in the final tableau. In the case of activity variables, this means they do not enter into the optimal solution. For a slack variable, a 0 value means that the particular resource is fully utilized at the optimal solution point.
4. Positive numbers in the objective function row under the slack variables represent the shadow price of that resource, or the value (in terms of the objective function) of additional or smaller amounts of that resource.
5. Numbers in the optimal tableau under the column for each nonbasic slack variable (excluding the value in the objective function row) represent substitution rates between the slack variable and corresponding basic variable. These substitution rates can be used to derive the range of resource use over which a particular shadow price is applicable.

EXERCISES

1. A firm is attempting to maximize profit Z from the production of two products, X_1 and X_2. The production process is constrained by the availability of three resources associated with the slack variables, S_1, S_2, and S_3. The following is the initial tableau for a linear programming solution to this problem:

	X_1	X_2	S_1	S_2	S_3	RHS
Z	−4	−8	0	0	0	0
S_1	4	2	1	0	0	200
S_2	3	6	0	1	0	240
S_3	5	1	0	0	1	400

a. What point in the solution space is described by the initial tableau? How can you determine this point from an examination of the initial tableau?
b. Which is the pivot column in this tableau? Why?
c. Which is the pivot element in the pivot column? Why?

2. A firm is attempting to maximize profit Z from the production of three products, X_1, X_2, and X_3. Profits are constrained by two resources with associated slack variables S_1 and S_2. The following is a tableau developed during the simplex solution method:

	X_1	X_2	X_3	S_1	S_2	RHS
Z	-3	-1	0	0	3	200
S_1	2	-3	0	1	4	40
X_3	-4	2	1	0	-3	150

a. In this problem, how many variables are basic? Why?
b. Is the solution associated with this tableau optimal? Why, or why not?
c. If the solution is not optimal, what should be the new pivot element? Defend your selection.
d. Which slack variable represents a resource which has at least part of its availability unused at this point? Why?

3. A firm produces two products, X_1 and X_2, which contribute to profit Z at the rate of $5 per unit and $4 per unit respectively. Profit is constrained by three resources with slack variables, S_1, S_2, and S_3. In using linear programming to solve this problem of constrained optimization, the following optimum tableau is obtained:

	X_1	X_2	S_1	S_2	S_3	RHS
Z	0	0	6	3	0	220
X_1	1	0	2	3	0	20
X_2	0	1	-1	-3	0	30
S_3	0	0	4	2	1	16

a. Why is this tableau optimal?
b. Which resources are used to capacity at this production level? What are their shadow prices? If $Z = \$220$ and all resources are measured in hours, give a correct interpretation of each shadow price.
c. Which resources are not used to capacity? How much excess capacity exists for these resources?
d. Show how total profit can be determined using the right-hand-side values for X_1 and X_2.

4. For the following optimal tableau, X_1, X_2, and X_3 are activity variables and S_1 and S_2 are slack variables associated with two limited resources. The objective function for profit is $4X_1 + 2X_2 + 5X_3 = Z$ where 4, 2, and 5 represent the gross profit contribution, in dollars, for X_1, X_2, and X_3, respectively.

	X_1	X_2	X_3	S_1	S_2	RHS
Z	3	0	0	10	3	1450
X_2	4	1	0	−5	4	400
X_3	−1	0	1	4	−1	130

  a. In order to maximize profits, should all three products be produced? Why or why not?
  b. State the amount and interpret the value of any resource shadow prices.
  c. How many nonbasic variables are in this solution? Why?
5. The following optimal tableau concerns profit maximization Z for the production of two goods, X_1 and X_2, subject to three resource constraints associated with the slack variables, S_1, S_2, and S_3. In the initial tableau, the right-hand-side values of S_1, S_2, and S_3 were 300, 200, and 220, respectively, with each number representing hours available per week.

	X_1	X_2	S_1	S_2	S_3	RHS
Z	0	0	4	3	0	440
X_1	1	0	−3	−2	0	40
X_2	0	1	2	4	0	50
S_3	0	0	−4	5	1	20

  a. State the shadow price for each slack variable if any exist.
  b. What interpretation should be given to the −3 element at the intersection of the X_1 row and S_1 column?
  c. Find the range of resource use over which each price stated in part a is valid. Why do these limits on shadow prices exist?

7.10 The Dual in Linear Programming

For every linear programming problem, there exists a counterpart problem called the *dual*. This means that for every maximization problem with ≤ constraints (called the *primal problem*), there exists a comparable minimization problem with ≥ constraints (the dual). Similarly, for every primal minimization problem with ≥ constraints, there exists a dual maximization problem with ≤ constraints.

Optimal solution values of the objective function for both the primal and the dual problem are equal. Other interpretations of the solution values for each problem also can be compared, as will be described below. Thus, for any particular linear programming problem, one can solve either the primal or the dual problem, depending on which is easier to compute. Results are directly comparable between the two.

Examples 7.3 and 7.4 are primal and dual problems expressed in both algebraic and matrix forms for a maximization primal problem and minimization primal problem, respectively.

Example 7.3

Algebraic Form

Primal

Maximize: $6X_1 + 7X_2 = Z$

Subject to: $4X_1 + 5X_2 \leq 17$
$9X_1 - 3X_2 \leq 22$
$X_1 + 2X_2 \leq 14$

and $X_1 \geq 0, X_2 \geq 0$

Dual

Minimize: $17Y_1 + 22Y_2 + 14Y_3 = Z^*$

Subject to: $4Y_1 + 9Y_2 + Y_3 \geq 6$
$5Y_1 - 3Y_2 + 2Y_3 \geq 7$

and $Y_1 \geq 0, Y_2 \geq 0, Y_3 \geq 0$

Matrix Form

Primal

Maximize: $\begin{pmatrix} 6 & 7 \end{pmatrix} \begin{pmatrix} X_1 \\ X_2 \end{pmatrix} = (Z)$

Subject to: $\begin{pmatrix} 4 & 5 \\ 9 & -3 \\ 1 & 2 \end{pmatrix} \begin{pmatrix} X_1 \\ X_2 \end{pmatrix} \leq \begin{pmatrix} 17 \\ 22 \\ 14 \end{pmatrix}$

and $X_1 \geq 0, X_2 \geq 0$

Dual

Minimize: $\begin{pmatrix} 17 & 22 & 14 \end{pmatrix} \begin{pmatrix} Y_1 \\ Y_2 \\ Y_3 \end{pmatrix} = (Z^*)$

Subject to: $\begin{pmatrix} 4 & 9 & 1 \\ 5 & -3 & 2 \end{pmatrix} \begin{pmatrix} Y_1 \\ Y_2 \\ Y_3 \end{pmatrix} \geq \begin{pmatrix} 6 \\ 7 \end{pmatrix}$

and $Y_1 \geq 0, Y_2 \geq 0, Y_3 \geq 0$

Example 7.4

Algebraic Form

Primal

Minimize: $2X_1 + 3X_2 = Z$

Subject to: $4X_1 - 5X_2 \geq 16$
$X_1 + 6X_2 \geq 21$
$-2X_1 + 7X_2 \geq 30$

and $X_1 \geq 0, X_2 \geq 0$

Dual

Maximize: $16Y_1 + 21Y_2 + 30Y_3 = Z^*$

Subject to: $4Y_1 + Y_2 - 2Y_3 \leq 2$
$-5Y_1 + 6Y_2 + 7Y_3 \leq 3$

and $Y_1 \geq 0, Y_2 \geq 0, Y_3 \geq 0$

Matrix Form

Primal

Minimize: $\begin{pmatrix} 2 & 3 \end{pmatrix} \begin{pmatrix} X_1 \\ X_2 \end{pmatrix} = (Z)$

Subject to: $\begin{pmatrix} 4 & -5 \\ 1 & 6 \\ -2 & 7 \end{pmatrix} \begin{pmatrix} X_1 \\ X_2 \end{pmatrix} \geq \begin{pmatrix} 16 \\ 21 \\ 30 \end{pmatrix}$

and $X_1 \geq 0, X_2 \geq 0$

Dual

Maximize: $\begin{pmatrix} 16 & 21 & 30 \end{pmatrix} \begin{pmatrix} Y_1 \\ Y_2 \\ Y_3 \end{pmatrix} = (Z^*)$

Subject to: $\begin{pmatrix} 4 & 1 & -2 \\ -5 & 6 & 7 \end{pmatrix} \begin{pmatrix} Y_1 \\ Y_2 \\ Y_3 \end{pmatrix} \leq \begin{pmatrix} 2 \\ 3 \end{pmatrix}$

and $Y_1 \geq 0, Y_2 \geq 0, Y_3 \geq 0$

Several aspects of these two examples deserve elaboration. First, the value of each primal objective function Z and each dual objective function Z^* will be the same for a given problem. Of course, one will represent a maximum and the other will represent a minimum value in the context of the problem.

Second, for this presentation, X_i are used to designate primal activity variables and Y_i are used to denote dual activity variables.

Third, the sense of the constraints is reversed for each primal and dual problem. For example, greater than or equal to constraints in a primal problem are associated with less than or equal to constraints in its dual problem. As a fourth point, observe that the coefficients on the activity variables in the primal problem are the constraint constants in the dual and vice versa.

Finally, with respect to the matrix form of Examples 7.3 and 7.4, note that the matrix of constraint coefficients for the primal and dual problems are transposed matrices.

Each of these relationships will be given a more detailed interpretation in the following presentation of a problem and its solution using the dual.

7.11 Minimization by Maximizing the Dual

Although dual solutions exist for primal problems involving both maximization and minimization, this and the following sections concern using the dual to solve a primal minimization problem with greater than or equal to constraints. This is emphasized because the solution of a primal minimization problem includes some computational complexities not found in a primal maximization problem. Also, several methods exist for solving primal minimization problems; therefore, the procedure is not generalized as easily as the solution of a maximization problem.

As the dual maximization problem yields all the information of the primal minimization problem, the dual will be used to solve the food production problem of Example 7.2. Thus, the problem will be set up in dual format and solved as a maximization problem.

The food production cost minimization problem is restated as Example 7.5.

Example 7.5

Primal

Minimize: $Z = 0.15X_1 + 0.20X_2$

Subject to: $5X_1 + 5X_2 \geq 30$ (carbohydrate requirement)
$5X_1 + 4X_2 \geq 25$ (protein requirement)
$0.5X_1 + X_2 \geq 4$ (fat requirement)

and $X_1 \geq 0, X_2 \geq 0$

where X_1 and X_2 are two ingredients costing \$0.15 and \$0.20 per ounce, respectively. The requirement coefficients represent nutrient grams per ounce in each ingredient, and the requirement constants represent the minimum number of grams of each nutrient in a serving.

As each requirement is stated in terms of greater than or equal to, an amount must be subtracted from the left-hand side of each inequality to form an equation. A variable must be created to represent this amount for each requirement. These new variables are referred to as surplus variables to indicate that the requirements must be met or exceeded (an excess results in a surplus of that factor). For this problem, the surplus variable for carbohydrate grams is designated P_1, for protein grams it is P_2, and for fat grams the surplus variable is P_3.

The primal problem, therefore, can be expressed in the following system of equations.

Primal

Minimize: $Z = 0.15X_1 + 0.20X_2$

Subject to: $5X_1 + 5X_2 - P_1 = 30$
$5X_1 + 4X_2 - P_2 = 25$
$0.5X_1 + X_2 - P_3 = 4$

In matrix form, this system can be expressed as follows:

Primal

Minimize: $(0.15 \quad 0.20) \begin{pmatrix} X_1 \\ X_2 \end{pmatrix} = (Z)$

Subject to: $\begin{pmatrix} 5 & 5 \\ 5 & 4 \\ 0.5 & 1 \end{pmatrix} \begin{pmatrix} X_1 \\ X_2 \end{pmatrix} - \begin{pmatrix} P_1 \\ P_2 \\ P_3 \end{pmatrix} = \begin{pmatrix} 30 \\ 25 \\ 4 \end{pmatrix}$

and $X_1 \geq 0, X_2 \geq 0$

Formation of the Dual

The following is the dual problem corresponding to the previous primal problem of cost minimization:

Dual

Maximize: $Z^* = 30Y_1 + 25Y_2 + 4Y_3$

Subject to: $5Y_1 + 5Y_2 + 0.5Y_3 \leq 0.15$
$5Y_1 + 4Y_2 + \quad\quad Y_3 \leq 0.20$

and $Y_1 \geq 0, Y_2 \geq 0, Y_3 \geq 0$

By using the slack variables D_1 and D_2, the dual can be expressed in the following system of equations:

Dual

Maximize: $Z^* = 30Y_1 + 25Y_2 + 4Y_3$

Subject to: $5Y_1 + 5Y_2 + 0.5Y_3 + D_1 = 0.15$
$\qquad\quad\; 5Y_1 + 4Y_2 + Y_3 + D_2 = 0.20$

and $Y_1 \geq 0, Y_2 \geq 0, Y_3 \geq 0$

This dual maximization problem is also stated in the following matrix notation:

Dual

Maximize: $(30 \quad 25 \quad 4) \begin{pmatrix} Y_1 \\ Y_2 \\ Y_3 \end{pmatrix} = (Z^*)$

Subject to: $\begin{pmatrix} 5 & 5 & 0.5 \\ 5 & 4 & 1 \end{pmatrix} \begin{pmatrix} Y_1 \\ Y_2 \\ Y_3 \end{pmatrix} + \begin{pmatrix} D_1 \\ D_2 \end{pmatrix} = \begin{pmatrix} 0.15 \\ 0.20 \end{pmatrix}$

and $Y_1 \geq 0, Y_2 \geq 0, Y_3 \geq 0$

Observe that there are five changes in altering the primal problem matrix notation to form the dual problem:

1. Use the vector of Y_1, Y_2, and Y_3 in the dual in place of the two vectors of primal activity variables X_1 and X_2.
2. Transpose the requirement constants vector in the primal problem,

$\begin{pmatrix} 30 \\ 25 \\ 4 \end{pmatrix}$

and use this as the vector of objective function coefficients in the dual.
3. Transpose the objective function coefficients vector in the primal problem (0.15 0.20) and use this as the vector of requirement constants in the dual.
4. Transpose the primal matrix of requirement coefficients and use this as the matrix of requirements in the dual.
5. Add a vector of dual slack variables D_1 and D_2 in place of the vector of primal surplus variables P_1, P_2, and P_3.

This dual structure requires some interpretation so that the changes do not appear to be purely mechanical.

First, P_1, P_2, and P_3 are surplus variables in the primal problem and are measured as grams of the respective nutrients (carbohydrate, protein, and fat). Alternatively, D_1 and D_2 are slack variables in the dual and are measured in dollar units.

In addition, X_1 and X_2, the primal activity variables, are measured in ounces of each ingredient. The dual activity variables, Y_1, Y_2, and Y_3, are dollar amounts representing the imputed value of each nutrient (carbohydrates, protein, and fat, respectively). In other words, the nutrients found in X_1 and X_2 impute a value to the food product that the food product would not have without these nutrients. Consequently, the objective of the dual problem is to maximize the imputed value (measured in dollars) of the nutrients. Finally, as Y_1, Y_2, and Y_3 are dollar values, they may not be negative.

The dual problem constraints imply that the total value imputed to an ingredient (e.g., $5Y_1 + 5Y_2 + 0.5Y_3$ in an ounce of X_1) cannot exceed the price of that ingredient (X_1 costs $0.15 per ounce). This fact gives rise to the less than or equal to constraints in the dual as this is a limitation on the producing firm.

Readers should observe a second relation implied by the dual constraints. That is, rational firms will not buy an ingredient if its price ($X_1 = \$0.15$) exceeds the imputed value of the nutrients in the ingredient. Therefore, only those ingredients with prices exactly equal to the imputed values of their nutrients will be purchased. This means that X_1 and X_2 will be in the primal optimal basis only if they meet these criteria. The ingredients and related amounts will be inferred from the solution of the dual problem.

It can be seen that there is an interesting parallel between the primal and dual problems in a typical cost minimization primal problem. That is, it has been shown that to minimize cost within a set of greater than or equal to constraints is the same as to maximize the value imputed to the food by primal constraints given a set of less than or equal to constraints. This relation allows one to transpose the matrix of constraint coefficients in deriving the dual from the primal problem statement.

Table 7.9 summarizes the notation, measurement units, and correspondence between the sets of variables used in the primal and dual problems.

TABLE 7.9 The Relation between the Primal and Dual Problems

Primal		Dual	
Activity Variables (Ounces of Each Ingredient)	Surplus Variables (Grams of Each Nutrient)	Activity Variables (Imputed Values in Dollars of Each Corresponding Nutrient Requirement)	Slack Variables (Opportunity Cost of Each Corresponding Subscripted Ingredient)
X_1	P_1 (carbohydrates)	Y_1 (carbohydrates)	D_1
X_2	P_2 (protein)	Y_2 (protein)	D_2
	P_3 (fat)	Y_3 (fat)	

With this conceptual background, Example 7.6 describes the solution of the primal minimization problem by solving the dual. The solution process is followed by an interpretation of the dual results and their relation to the primal problem.

Example 7.6
Minimize the following by solving the dual problem.

Primal

Minimize: $Z = 0.15X_1 + 0.20X_2$

Subject to: $5X_1 + 5X_2 \geq 30$
$5X_1 + 4X_2 \geq 25$
$0.5X_1 + X_2 \geq 4$

and $X_1 \geq 0, X_2 \geq 0$

Dual

Maximize: $Z^* = 30Y_1 + 25Y_2 + 4Y_3$

Subject to: $5Y_1 + 5Y_2 + 0.5Y_3 \leq 0.15$
$5Y_1 + 4Y_2 + Y_3 \leq 0.20$

and $Y_1 \geq 0, Y_2 \geq 0, Y_3 \geq 0$

The dual maximization problem will be solved by the simplex method demonstrated in Section 7.8. First, the dual objective function is listed, and the two constraints are set up as a system of two equations and five variables (three activity variables, Y_1, Y_2, and Y_3, and two slack variables, D_1 and D_2).

$Z^* - 30Y_1 - 25Y_2 - 4Y_3 = 0$
$5Y_1 + 5Y_2 + 0.5Y_3 + D_1 = 0.15$
$5Y_1 + 4Y_2 + Y_3 + D_2 = 0.20$

Thus, Y_1, Y_2, and Y_3 represent, respectively, the imputed values of the carbohydrate, protein, and fat requirements. This system of equations is used to set up the initial tableau as shown in Table 7.10.

This solution represents a 0 level for the imputed values as none of the nutrients are used. The pivot column is Y_1 (the largest negative number in the Z^* row) and the pivot row is D_1 (0.15/5 < 0.20/5).

TABLE 7.10 The Initial Tableau for the Dual Problem

		Nonbasic Variables					
		Y_1	Y_2	Y_3	D_1	D_2	RHS
	Z^*	−30	−25	−4	0	0	0
Basic	D_1	5**	5	0.5	1	0	0.15
Variables	D_2	5	4	1	0	1	0.20

TABLE 7.11 The Second Basic Feasible Solution

	Y_1	Y_2	Y_3	D_1	D_2	RHS
Z^*	0	5	−1	6	0	0.9
Y_1	1	1	0.1	0.2	0	0.03
D_2	0	−1	0.5**	−1	1	0.05

The pivot element, 5, is notated by a double asterisk. Consequently, Y_1 and D_2 constitute the basis for the next iteration. The following row operations are used to find the second basic feasible solution as shown in Table 7.11.

Row Operations to Determine the Second Tableau

1. Replace row 1 by: 6(row 2) + row 1
2. Replace row 3 by: row 3 − row 2
3. Divide row 2 by 5

This solution is not optimal because the −1 in the Z^* row under Y_3 indicates that the objective function can be increased by entering Y_3 in the basis. Thus, the new pivot column is Y_3 and pivot row is D_2 (0.05/0.5 < 0.03/0.1). The pivot element is indicated by the double asterisk. In the third tableau (Table 7.12), Y_1 and Y_3 are basic.

The following row operations lead to the third (and optimal) tableau of Table 7.12.

Row Operations to Determine the Third Tableau:

1. Replace row 1 by: 2(row 3) + row 1
2. Replace row 2 by: −0.2(row 3) + row 2
3. Multiply row 3 by 2

The optimum value of the objective function is found at this point as all nonbasic variables in the Z^* row have nonnegative coefficients. Thus, the dual problem is solved after two steps. A complete interpretation of the optimal dual tableau and its relationship to the solution of the primal problem is included in the next section.

TABLE 7.12 The Third Basic Feasible Solution

	Y_1	Y_2	Y_3	D_1	D_2	RHS
Z^*	0	3	0	4	2	1.00
Y_1	1	1.2	0	0.4	−0.2	0.02
Y_3	0	−2	1	−2	2	0.10

7.12 Interpretation of the Optimal Dual Tableau

The tableau of Table 7.12 yields all the information necessary to interpret the solution to the primal cost minimization problem.

First, the optimum value of the objective function in the dual ($Z^* = 1.00$) represents the minimum cost of manufacturing one serving of the food product ($Z = \$1.00$ in the primal problem). The specific interpretation of Z^* is that $1.00 is the maximum value imputed to the product by the nutrient constraints. That is, $1.00 is the maximum value that can be imputed to the products by the nutrients found in X_1 and X_2.

The dual basic variables, Y_1 and Y_3, representing the imputed value of the carbohydrates and the imputed value of the fat, respectively, indicate that these two nutrients are the factors which give the food product an imputed value. In contrast, Y_2, or the protein requirement, which is nonbasic in the dual solution, does not contribute to the imputed value of the product. This information can be used to assess the values of the three surplus variables, P_1, P_2, and P_3, in the primal problem.

As Y_1 and Y_3 contribute to the imputed value of the food product, it is concluded that the related nutrient requirements (carbohydrate and fat) are binding in the primal problem. This means that these two requirements prevent cost reductions below $1.00 per serving.

The imputed values Y_1 and Y_3 as related to the primal problem are found in the RHS column of the dual solution. Therefore, the imputed value Y_1 is $0.02, indicating that the per serving cost can be reduced by $0.02 if the carbohydrate constraint of 30 grams is reduced by 1 gram. Similarly, the per serving cost will be reduced by $0.10 in response to a 1-gram reduction in the fat requirement.

The dual variable Y_2, corresponding to the primal surplus variable P_2 (the protein requirement), is nonbasic in the dual solution. Two meanings can be attached to this result. First, this indicates that no marginal value is imputed to the product by this requirement. And second, with respect to the primal problem, this dual result demonstrates that the protein requirement is not binding on further cost reductions. Thus, the protein requirement of 25 grams per serving is exceeded in the final product. Its value of 3 applied to the primal solution indicates that there is a surplus of 3 grams of protein in the food. In other words, there are 28 grams of protein per serving in the final product.

Therefore, the surplus variables in the primal problem are associated with:

1. Binding requirements if the corresponding dual activity variable is basic
2. Nonbinding requirements (surpluses) if the corresponding dual activity variable is nonbasic

As D_1 and D_2 are not in the dual basis, they have optimum values of zero. This means that there is a zero opportunity cost for each ingredient.

Linear Programming 189

TABLE 7.13 The Relation between Results of the Dual Problem and Solution of the Primal Problem

Dual $Z^* = \$1.00$		Primal $Z = \$1.00$	
Activity Variables (Imputed Value of the Nutrients)	Slack Variables (Opportunity Cost of Ingredients)	Activity Variables (Number of Ounces of Each Ingredient to Use in the Food)	Surplus Variables (Amount of Nutrients in Excess of Minimum Amount Required by the Constraints)
Y_1 = RHS of Y_1 row = 0.02	$D_1 = 0$	$X_1 = Z^*$ row coefficient of D_1 = 4	$P_1 = Z^*$ row coefficient of Y_1 = 0
$Y_2 = 0$	$D_2 = 0$	$X_2 = Z^*$ row coefficient of D_2 = 2	$P_2 = Z^*$ row coefficient of Y_2 = 3
Y_3 = RHS of Y_3 row = 0.10			$P_3 = Z^*$ row coefficient of Y_3 = 0

This result indicates that the prices of $X_1 = \$0.15$ and $X_2 = 0.20$ are not exceeded by the imputed values of the nutrients. This is optimal for the firm as it shows that the ingredients X_1 and X_2 do not have a positive opportunity cost or alternative use value. Thus, it is concluded that ingredients X_1 and X_2 should be used in the amount of 4 ounces and 2 ounces, respectively, to minimize food cost per serving.

Table 7.13 summarizes the dual solution and the relation of these results to solution of the primal problem.

The following points summarize the relation between primal and dual solutions discussed thus far:

The optimal value of the objective function is the same for both dual and primal problems ($Z = Z^* = 1.00$).
Basic activity variables in the dual solution Y_1 and Y_3 correspond to binding requirements in the primal problem (constraints 1 and 3 associated with the surplus variables P_1 and P_3).
The values for nonbasic activity variables in the dual solution ($Y_2 = 3$) correspond to values for primal surplus variables associated with non-binding requirements ($P_2 = 3$).
Z^* row coefficients of nonbasic slack variables in the dual solution ($D_1 = 4$ and $D_2 = 2$) correspond to optimal values for the primal activity variables ($X_1 = 4, X_2 = 2$).
Slack variables which are basic in the dual solution correspond to activity variables which are nonbasic in the primal solution. Thus, these primal activity variables do not enter into the primal solution. This does not occur in the example presented above.

Computing Primal Shadow-Price Ranges from the Dual

As stated above, the dual activity variables with positive right-hand-side column values ($Y_1 = 0.02$ and $Y_3 = 0.10$) correspond to requirements which are binding in the primal problem (carbohydrate and fat constraints). Furthermore, $Y_1 = 0.02$ and $Y_3 = 0.10$ are imputed values, or shadow prices, associated with the corresponding nutrient constraints (carbohydrate and fat, respectively).

In Section 7.9, it was pointed out that shadow prices are valid only over a range of resource use which does not change the basis. Data in the dual solution can be used to find the applicable range for these shadow prices (imputed values). To demonstrate this, the optimal dual tableau of Table 7.12 is repeated as Table 7.14.

The imputed values of \$0.02 for Y_1 and \$0.10 for Y_3 are applicable only if the basis of the dual problem is not changed. Thus, the values in the Z^* row, $Y_2 = 3$, $D_1 = 4$, and $D_2 = 2$, cannot be negative if the basis is to remain unchanged. The computation of the range for the shadow price proceeds as shown in Section 7.9; the evaluated shadow prices correspond to the dual activity variables $Y_1 = 0.02$ and $Y_3 = 0.10$.

The dual basic variable Y_1 has positive substitution rates with Y_2 and D_1; thus, decreases in Y_1 will decrease Y_2 and D_1. The maximum allowable decrease in Y_1 (before Y_2 and D_1 become negative and change the basis) is the smaller of

1. $\dfrac{3}{1.2} = 2.5$ and

2. $\dfrac{4}{0.4} = 10$

The amount 2.5 represents the maximum possible decrease in the carbohydrate binding constraint if the imputed value of Y_1 is to be valid at \$0.02. As the carbohydrate constraint is 30 grams, it is demonstrated that the imputed value $Y_1 = \$0.02$ is valid if the carbohydrate constraint is reduced no lower than 27.5 grams.

The maximum possible increase in the carbohydrate constraint is found by dividing the negative substitution rate between Y_1 and D_2 (-0.2) into the optimal D_2 value (2). That the result is 10 means that the carbohydrate constraint can increase by as much as 10 grams without affecting the imputed value of \$0.02 for Y_1.

Thus, the imputed value Y_1 (\$0.02) has been shown to be valid in the carbohydrate range of 27.5 grams ($30 - 2.5 = 27.5$) to 40 grams ($30 + 10 = 40$).

TABLE 7.14 The Optimal Dual Tableau for the Cost Minimization Problem

	Y_1	Y_2	Y_3	D_1	D_2	RHS
Z^*	0	3	0	4	2	1.00
Y_1	1	1.2	0	0.4	-0.2	0.02
Y_3	0	-2	1	-2	2	0.10

The applicable range for the $Y_3 = \$0.10$ imputed value (the imputed value associated with the fat requirement) is found similarly. The negative substitution rates between Y_3 and Y_2 and between Y_3 and D_1 provide data to determine the maximum allowable increase in the fat constraint. This increase is represented by the smaller absolute value of

1. $\left|\dfrac{3}{-2}\right| = |-1.5| = 1.5$

2. $\left|\dfrac{4}{-2}\right| = |-2.0| = 2.0$

The imputed value Y_3 is valid, therefore, to 5.5 grams ($4 + 1.5 = 5.5$). The largest reduction in the fat constraint is found by dividing the positive substitution rate between Y_3 and D_2 (2.0) into the optimal value for D_2 (2). Consequently, the fat constraint may decrease by as much as 1 gram without affecting the imputed value. This demonstrates that the Y_3 imputed value of $0.10 per gram is valid between 3 fat grams per serving and 5.5 fat grams per serving. Larger changes will affect the basis of the dual solution.

Concluding Remarks

The previous discussion has emphasized the many parallels between information contained in the optimal dual tableau and the solution of the primal problem. These relations exist for both primal maximization problems with less than or equal to constraints and primal minimization problems with greater than or equal to requirements. However, as primal minimization problems often involve several computational complexities not found in maximization problems, the dual method of solution is particularly advantageous in the primal minimization case.

In addition to the computational advantages often associated with the dual solution, there are several important interpretative aspects of the dual. In the case of primal minimization problems, the dual solution provides information about the imputed value of the requirements. These interpretations have been discussed. For primal maximization problems, the dual provides information about the opportunity cost of the resources used in the problem. This means that the dual furnishes information about the value of the resources in their present use (e.g., labor used to manufacture appliances) compared to alternative uses of these resources. In general, maximizing a profit objective subject to resource constraints (the primal problem) is identical to minimizing the opportunity cost, or alternative use value, of the resources (the dual problem).

Thus, the dual provides important information for both profit maximization and cost minimization primal problems. It is an aspect of linear programming found beneficial to many management and economic analyses.

EXERCISES

For each of the following primal cost minimization problems in algebraic form (1, 2, and 3), set up the initial tableau for the dual maximization problem. Use Y_i for dual activity variables and D_i for dual slack variables.

1. Minimize: $Z = 4X_1 + 7X_2$
   Subject to: $X_1 + 3X_2 \geq 210$ (surplus variable P_1)
   $\phantom{\text{Subject to: }}2X_1 + 2X_2 \geq 350$ (surplus variable P_2)
   $\phantom{\text{Subject to: }}4X_1 + X_2 \geq 320$ (surplus variable P_3)
   and $X_1 \geq 0, X_2 \geq 0$

2. Minimize: $Z = 10X_1 + 7X_2 + 4X_3$
   Subject to: $2X_1 + 4X_2 + 5X_3 \geq 300$ (surplus variable P_1)
   $\phantom{\text{Subject to: }}X_1 + 5X_2 + 3X_3 \geq 200$ (surplus variable P_2)
   and $X_1 \geq 0, X_2 \geq 0, X_3 \geq 0$

3. Minimize: $Z = 0.3X_1 + 0.9X_2$
   Subject to: $4X_1 + 5X_2 \geq 50$ (surplus variable P_1)
   $\phantom{\text{Subject to: }}X_1 + 0.5X_2 \geq 10$ (surplus variable P_2)
   $\phantom{\text{Subject to: }}2X_1 + 7X_2 \geq 42$ (surplus variable P_3)
   $\phantom{\text{Subject to: }}3X_1 + 3X_2 \geq 28$ (surplus variable P_4)
   and $X_1 \geq 0, X_2 \geq 0$

4. A firm uses two machines, X_1 and X_2, to manufacture three complementary items of office furniture, P_1, P_2, and P_3. Each hour of operation for machine X_1 costs \$45 and an hour of operation for machine X_2 costs \$60. In 1 hour, machine X_1 can produce two units of item P_1, one of P_2, and five of P_3. In an hour of operation, machine X_2 can turn out four units of item P_1, three of P_2, and two of P_3. In a week, at least 450 units of item P_1, 520 units of P_2, and 610 units of P_3 must be manufactured to meet demand. The firm wants to minimize total operational costs for X_1 and X_2 while meeting all product demands.

   a. Set up the initial dual tableau for this primal cost minimization problem. Use Y_i for dual activity variables and D_i to notate dual slack variables.
   b. Interpret the constraints in the dual problem.
   c. What is maximized in the dual objective function?
   d. Compare the number of basic and nonbasic variables in the primal problem with the corresponding numbers in the dual problem and explain the differences.

5. The following optimal dual tableau includes the activity variables Y_1, Y_2, and Y_3 and the dual slack variables D_1 and D_2. The primal objective as

measured by the function Z is cost minimization. The primal activity variables are measured in hours of machine operation (X_1 and X_2) and the surplus variables represent units of production (P_1, P_2, and P_3).

	Y_1	Y_2	D_1	D_2	Y_3	RHS
Z^*	0	0	14	24	20	700
Y_1	1	0	2	1	−0.5	9
Y_2	0	1	−0.5	−3	0.8	7.5

a. Why is this solution optimal?
b. Does a surplus exist for any of the constraints in the optimal primal solution? If so, for which ones, and how much is the surplus? If not, how is this fact determined?
c. How many hours should each machine be operated to minimize cost?
d. What is the minimum cost of operation?
e. State and interpret all dual shadow prices.

6. The following is the algebraic form of a cost minimization problem.

Minimize: $Z = 0.5X_1 + 0.2X_2 + 0.25X_3$

Subject to: $X_1 + 3X_2 + 5X_3 \geq 50$ (surplus variable P_1)
 $2X_1 + X_2 + 5X_3 \geq 60$ (surplus variable P_2)
 $6X_1 + 4X_2 + 4X_3 \geq 90$ (surplus variable P_3)

and $X_1 \geq 0, X_2 \geq 0, X_3 \geq 0$

The activity variables X_1, X_2, and X_3 represent three ingredients used in a multivitamin. The objective function is measured in dollars as are the individual coefficients of the objective function. Constants (50, 60, and 90) in the constraint inequalities represent the minimum required units of the three vitamins in each bottle of the final product. Constraint coefficients represent the units of each vitamin in an ounce of each ingredient.
a. Construct the initial dual tableau and interpret the RHS value of each basic variable in the initial dual tableau. Use Y_i for dual activity variables and D_i for dual slack variables.

The following optimal dual tableau is found for this problem.

	Y_1	Y_2	Y_3	D_1	D_2	D_3	RHS
Z	36.25	0	0	0	13.125	9.375	4.969
D_1	−3.75	0	0	1	−1.375	−0.125	0.194
Y_2	0.625	1	0	0	0.313	−0.063	0.047
Y_3	0.500	0	1	0	−0.25	0.250	0.012

b. What is the minimum cost of a bottle of the multivitamins?
c. Which variables are basic in the primal solution?

d. Are there any ingredients that should not be used in the final product? If so, name the ingredient(s).
e. Which vitamin(s) is in surplus in the final primal solution? State the amount(s).
f. Interpret the imputed value obtained from the dual solution associated with any primal binding constraint.

7.13 Additional Considerations

This brief section expands the discussion of Section 7.6 to include ways of detecting situations in which there is no unique optimum solution. Degeneracy, a complexity which was encountered in the solution of some linear programming problems but not discussed in Section 7.6, is also explained below.

Unbounded solutions occur when the constraints do not restrict the value of the objective function. For example, the resource availability faced by a firm may not restrict its profits. In the simplex procedure, unbounded solutions are identified whenever quotients do not exist between the right-hand-side values and the elements of the pivot column. This means that the pivot row and therefore the pivot element cannot be identified. Thus, the simplex procedure must stop at this point.

Also, it is possible that a particular linear programming problem has multiple optimum solutions. Graphically, this case is demonstrated by two constraints which are represented by the same line along at least part of the boundary of the region of feasible solutions. There is no universally established way to detect this possibility using the simplex method. However, it is *likely* that a problem has multiple solutions when a zero value is found in the objective function row for a nonbasic variable in the optimum solution. For example, assume that a particular slack variable in a maximization problem is nonbasic and has a value of zero in the optimum solution. This means both that there is full utilization of the resource and that it has a zero shadow price. This combination leads to the possibility that there are multiple optimal solutions to the problem.

A third problem often discovered during the simplex solution process is degeneracy. In graphical form, degeneracy is identified when more than two constraint-equation lines intersect at a feasible corner in a problem with two activity variables. In the simplex method, degeneracy is detected when two or more quotients are tied in the determination of the pivot row. This tie may cause the simplex procedure to continue to yield the same optimal value for several iterations. Procedures exist for preventing degeneracy and shortening this iteration repetition. However, these procedures are not discussed in this introductory examination of linear programming.

Thus, the simplex procedure will determine the single optimum solution if it exists. Also, during the simplex solution process, the presence of possible alternatives to a unique optimum solution may be detected.

7.14 Computers and Linear Programming

As may be apparent to many readers, hand computation using the simplex procedure can be a difficult and time-consuming task. In most real-world applications, computer programs are used to generate solutions to linear programming problems. Many of these programs are easy to use and require little in the way of required input steps.

In general, these programs request from a user the data sets associated with any linear programming problem in a form acceptable to the particular program. These data sets include an objective function, including specification of the activities; a set of restrictions (for maximization problems) or requirements (for minimization problems); the initial right-hand-side values; and a set of nonnegativity expressions.

With these data, computer programs rapidly can find an optimum solution if one exists. With some programs, a user may be able to request and obtain the iterations of the simplex process.

Although computer solutions reduce much of the work of a linear programming analysis, the primary job for one using such programs remains that of presenting an accurate and meaningful understanding and interpretation of the results. This chapter has provided both a description of the primary technique used in computer programs (the simplex method) and the background necessary to interpret computer-generated results.

7.15 Chapter Summary

Linear programming includes a set of techniques for evaluating and interpreting constrained optimization problems where the objective function and all the constraints are linear. These techniques often are applied to problems of constrained profit maximization and constrained cost minimization in organizations.

The following three data sets are included in a linear programming problem:

1. The objective function, including all activity variables
2. A group of inequality constraints
3. A set of nonnegativity restrictions on the activity variables

In general, the inequality constraints represent restrictions in a profit maximization problem and minimum requirements in the case of cost minimization. The sense of the inequalities usually is less than or equal to for maximization problems and greater than or equal to for minimization problems. However, the sense of the inequalities may be mixed for any particular problem. The inequality constraints are changed into equations by means of slack variables (for less than or equal to constraints) and surplus variables (for greater than or equal to constraints) when solving the problem.

Two approaches to solving linear programming problems include geometrical solution and an iterative process referred to as the simplex method. Both utilize the principle that a unique optimum value, if it exists, occurs (1) on the boundary of the region of feasible solutions and (2) at an intersection (corner point) of two constraints (including the nonnegativity restrictions).

A geometrical solution includes evaluation of the objective function at each feasible corner and selection of the maximum or minimum value depending on the problem. This solution technique is limited, as computational and geometrical complexities are encountered with increasing numbers of activity variables and constraints.

The simplex method is an iterative procedure for identifying feasible corners and determining the optimum value of the objective function. The procedure assures that the resulting objective function value after each iteration is at least as good as the result of the previous iteration. Also, iterations stop as soon as an optimum is established although all feasible corners may not have been evaluated. Each iteration analyzes a group of basic variables (equal to the number of constraints) and a group of nonbasic variables (equal to the number of activity variables).

The final, or optimal, iteration yields a tableau of data useful for planning within an organization. Values for the basic variables in the optimal tableau indicate (1) optimal use of the activity variables, (2) the amount of each resource which is unused in the case of slack variables, and (3) a requirement which is exceeded in the case of surplus variables. Nonbasic variables in the final tableau indicate (1) activity variables which do not enter into the solution and (2) slack or surplus variables for which the associated constraint is satisfied exactly.

Final tableau values for nonbasic slack variables in the maximization case represent shadow prices or marginal values. Thus, the value (for example, in terms of increased profit) of more of a binding resource can be determined from these numbers. The shadow prices are valid only over a range of resource use which does not change the basis of the optimal solution.

For every linear programming problem there exists a dual problem; i.e., for a maximization problem there exists a comparable minimization problem and vice versa. Dual problems are useful both to provide an easier solution method in some cases and as a means to provide interpretative results complementary to the primal solution.

Optimal values for the objective function in both primal and dual solutions are identical. Thus, to maximize profit within a set of resource constraints is the same as minimizing the opportunity cost (alternative use value) of the resources. And minimizing cost subject to a set of requirements is the same as maximizing the imputed value of the requirements. In general, the dual problem is a way to quantify relations between the efficiency of resource use and the attainment of an objective.

By introducing linear programming, this chapter has provided readers with the ability to apply these techniques to optimization problems in organizations. Although the computational aspects of linear programming problems usually are carried out by computers, the ability to correctly formulate and interpret the results of such computer analyses is a quantitative skill important in many business fields.

7.16 Problem Set

Review Questions

1. Name the three data sets which comprise a typical linear programming problem.
2. Define unbounded solution. Give an example of conditions leading to an unbounded solution.
3. Why will the optimum value for the objective function always occur on the boundary of the region of feasible solutions?
4. Define convex set. Explain the relation between convex sets and the corner-point-solution principle of linear programming.
5. Distinguish between slack variables and surplus variables. How is each used in setting up the initial tableau for a linear programming problem?
6. For a problem with four activity variables and nine constraints, how many variables form the basis for the simplex method? Why?
7. Why are activity variables nonbasic in the initial tableau of a maximization problem?
8. When using the simplex method to solve a profit maximization problem, how is the pivot column determined for a particular iteration? Why is this procedure used?
9. In determining the pivot row for a particular simplex iteration, why is the smallest quotient between each element in the pivot column and the corresponding right-hand-side value selected?
10. What is indicated by the right-hand-side value for a basic activity variable in the optimal tableau?
11. Why are shadow prices useful to a firm attempting to maximize profits subject to a set of resource constraints?
12. What is measured by the dual objective function for a primal cost minimization problem with a set of product quality requirements?
13. Why are shadow prices in a profit maximization problem valid only over a range for the particular resource?
14. What is indicated about a resource if its corresponding slack variable is nonbasic in the optimal tableau?
15. When using the simplex method to solve a maximization problem, how is the optimum value of the objective function identified? Why is this rule used?
16. What is the relationship between the matrix of constraint coefficients in a particular primal problem and the corresponding matrix for the dual?
17. The Z^* value for the dual of a primal profit maximization problem indicates the minimum value of the resource opportunity costs. Explain.

Review Problems

1. For each problem below. stated in matrix form, give the algebraic form:

   a. Minimize: $(4 \quad 2 \quad 2) \begin{pmatrix} X_1 \\ X_2 \\ X_3 \end{pmatrix} = (Z)$

   Subject to: $\begin{pmatrix} 4 & 1 & 3 \\ 0.5 & 2 & 1 \\ 3 & 0.8 & 5 \end{pmatrix} \begin{pmatrix} X_1 \\ X_2 \\ X_3 \end{pmatrix} \geq \begin{pmatrix} 200 \\ 275 \\ 310 \end{pmatrix}$

   and $X_1 \geq 0, X_2 \geq 0, X_3 \geq 0$

   b. Maximize: $(1 \quad 3 \quad 4) \begin{pmatrix} X_1 \\ X_2 \\ X_3 \end{pmatrix} = Z$

   Subject to: $\begin{pmatrix} 6 & 2 & 1 \\ 4 & 3 & 3 \\ 5 & 1 & 7 \end{pmatrix} \begin{pmatrix} X_1 \\ X_2 \\ X_3 \end{pmatrix} \leq \begin{pmatrix} 600 \\ 708 \\ 770 \end{pmatrix}$

   and $X_1 \geq 0, X_2 \geq 0, X_3 \geq 0$

2. For the following problems, solve each geometrically by evaluating the objective function at all feasible corner points.

   a. Maximize: $Z = 2X_1 + 4X_2$
   Subject to: $2X_1 + X_2 \leq 60$
   $3X_1 + 4X_2 \leq 190$
   and $X_1 \geq 0, X_2 \geq 0$

   b. Minimize: $Z = 2X_1 + 3X_2$
   Subject to: $X_1 + 3X_2 \geq 160$
   $3X_1 + 3X_2 \geq 240$
   and $X_1 \geq 0, X_2 \geq 0$

   c. Minimize: $Z = 3X_1 + 1.5X_2$
   Subject to: $X_1 + X_2 \geq 60$
   $2X_1 + 6X_2 \geq 150$
   $3X_1 + 4X_2 \geq 210$
   and $X_1 \geq 0, X_2 \geq 0$

   d. Maximize: $Z = 3X_1 + 2X_2$
   Subject to: $4X_1 + 2X_2 \leq 200$
   $X_1 + 3X_2 \leq 300$
   $2X_1 + 5X_2 \leq 400$
   and $X_1 \geq 0, X_2 \geq 0$

3. Set up the initial tableau necessary for using the simplex procedure to solve each of the following problems. In each case, identify the pivot element for the first iteration.

   a. Maximize: $Z = 6X_1 + 10X_2 + 12X_3$
   Subject to: $2X_1 + 2X_2 + X_3 \leq 200$
   $3X_1 + X_2 + 3X_3 \leq 300$
   and $X_1 \geq 0, X_2 \geq 0, X_3 \geq 0$

   b. Maximize: $Z = 0.5X_1 + 0.6X_2$
   Subject to: $3X_1 + 4X_2 \leq 500$
   $X_1 + 8X_2 \leq 650$

$$5X_1 + X_2 \leq 700$$
$$2X_1 + 2X_2 \leq 200$$
$$\text{and } X_1 \geq 0, X_2 \geq 0$$

4. For each tableau below, X_1, X_2, and X_3 are activity variables and S_1, S_2, and S_3 are slack variables in a primal maximization problem. State whether or not each solution is optimal at the point described and defend your decision. If the solution is not optimal, identify the pivot element for the next iteration.

a.

	X_1	X_2	X_3	S_1	S_2	S_3	RHS
Z	2	0	3	0	0	4	120
X_2	-2	1	-1	0	0	2	30
S_1	3	0	1	1	0	4	12
S_2	1	0	4	0	1	1	6

b.

	X_1	X_2	X_3	S_1	S_2	S_3	RHS
Z	-6	-4	0	0	3	0	40
S_1	4	2	0	1	-2	0	30
X_3	-2	1	1	0	4	0	18
S_3	3	6	0	0	4	1	42

c.

	X_1	X_2	X_3	S_1	S_2	S_3	RHS
Z	-3	0	0	4	0	16	80
X_2	1	1	0	-2	0	2	16
S_2	4	0	0	-1	1	-2	22
X_3	2	0	1	3	0	-4	12

5. A firm manufactures two brands of office lighting fixtures, X_1 and X_2. Fixture X_1 contributes $10 profit per unit and X_2 contributes $12 profit per unit. Production of the fixtures is constrained by the availability of labor (slack S_1), machinery (slack S_2), and packaging hours (slack S_3). They are restricted to 200 hours per week for S_1, 240 hours per week for S_2, and 180 hours per week for S_3. In attempting to determine the profit-maximizing level of weekly production for these two products, the following optimal tableau is developed:

	X_1	X_2	S_1	S_2	S_3	RHS
Z	0	0	40	0	28	7840
X_1	1	0	-2	0	4	400
S_2	0	0	1	1	-⌣	30
X_2	0	1	5	0	-1	320

a. By using the objective function, show the computation of total profit as attributable to sales of X_1 and sales of X_2.
b. Are any resources not used completely in the solution? If so, name them and state the amount of slack for each.

6. a. In the optimal tableau of Problem 5, interpret the -2 and the $+5$ in the S_1 column.
   b. Find the applicable range for each resource shadow price shown in the tableau of Problem 5.
7. For each constrained cost minimization problem below, set up the initial dual tableau. Use Y_i for dual activity variables and D_i for dual slack variables.
   a. Minimize: $Z = 6X_1 + 5X_2$
      Subject to: $3X_1 + X_2 \geq 25$ (surplus variable P_1)
                  $2X_1 + 4X_2 \geq 40$ (surplus variable P_2)
                  $6X_1 + 2X_2 \geq 50$ (surplus variable P_3)
      and $X_1 \geq 0, X_2 \geq 0$
   b. Minimize: $Z = 0.5X_1 + 0.4X_2 + 0.7X_3$
      Subject to: $4X_1 + 2X_2 + 4X_3 \geq 17$ (surplus variable P_1)
                  $X_1 + 4X_2 + X_3 \geq 26$ (surplus variable P_2)
      and $X_1 \geq 0, X_2 \geq 0, X_3 \geq 0$
   c. Minimize: $Z = 2X_1 + 8X_2$
      Subject to: $4X_1 \geq 30$ (surplus variable P_1)
                  $2X_1 + 5X_2 \geq 70$ (surplus variable P_2)
                  $3X_1 + 7X_2 \geq 100$ (surplus variable P_3)
      and $X_1 \geq 0, X_2 \geq 0$
8. A firm uses two machines, X_1 and X_2, to manufacture three grades of plastic. Machine X_1 costs $25 per hour to operate and X_2 costs $31 per hour of operation. Each week, production must be at least 800 pounds of grade P_1 plastic, 900 pounds of grade P_2 plastic, and 950 pounds of grade P_3 plastic (grade names can be used to identify the surplus variables).
   In 1 hour of operation, machine X_1 can produce 6 pounds of P_1, 5 pounds of P_2, and 6 pounds of P_3. Machine X_2 can produce 3 pounds of P_1, 7 pounds of P_2, and 8 pounds of P_3 per hour. The firm wants to determine the number of hours per week to operate each machine in order to minimize cost subject to the production constraints.
   a. Set up the initial dual tableau for this primal cost minimization problem. Use Y_i for dual activity variables and D_i for dual slack variables.
   b. How many basic variables are in the dual solution? Why?
   c. State and interpret the objective of the dual problem.
   d. Interpret each constraint in the dual problem.
9. A firm uses two materials, copper (X_1) and aluminum (X_2) to make three electrical products, P_1, P_2, and P_3, in an integrated production process.
   The process is such that each pound of copper is used to make six units of P_1, five units of P_2, and two units of P_3. Each pound of aluminum is used to manufacture four units of P_1, six units of P_2, and eight units of P_3. Minimum required production is 600 units of P_1, 450 units of P_2, and 500 units of P_3. The cost per pound of copper to the firm is $1.00, and aluminum costs $0.75 per pound.
   The firm wants to determine the least-cost combination of copper and aluminum which will meet all the requirements of the process. In determining this answer by linear programming, the following optimal dual tableau results where Y_1, Y_2, and Y_3 are dual activity variables and D_1 and D_2 are dual slack variables.

	Y_1	Y_2	Y_3	D_1	D_2	RHS
Z^*	0	170	0	70	45	103.75
Y_1	1	0.7	0	0.2	-0.05	0.162
Y_3	0	0.4	1	-0.1	0.15	0.013

Answer the following questions based on the results of this optimal dual tableau:
   a. How many pounds of each material should be used to minimize production costs?
   b. What is the minimum cost of meeting all requirements?
   c. Are any primal requirements exceeded in the optimal solution? If so, which ones?
   d. Find any shadow prices in the dual tableau and interpret the meaning of each with respect to the primal solution.
   e. Find the applicable resource use range for any shadow price found in d and interpret this range as applied to the primal problem.

10. A firm uses three ingredients, X_1, X_2, and X_3, to make a chemical compound. The per pound price of each ingredient is $X_1 = \$9$, $X_2 = \$10$, and $X_3 = \$12$. The compound must meet three requirements P_1, P_2, and P_3. In a batch of the compound there must be at least 400 ounces of P_1, 600 ounces of P_2, and 750 ounces of P_3.

     Each pound of X_1 has 2 ounces of P_1, 3 ounces of P_2, and 3 ounces of P_3. A pound of X_2 has 1 ounce of P_1, 3 ounces of P_2, and 4 ounces of P_3. Ingredient X_3 contains 2 ounces of P_1, 1 ounce of P_2, and 4 ounces of P_3 per pound. In determining the amount of each ingredient necessary to meet all three requirements at a minimum cost, the following optimal dual tableau is developed. In this dual tableau, Y_1, Y_2, and Y_3 represent dual activity variables, and D_1, D_2, and D_3 notate dual slack variables.

	Y_1	Y_2	Y_3	D_1	D_2	D_3	RHS
Z^*	0	90	0	170	60	0	2130
Y_1	1	0.6	0	0.8	-0.6	0	1.2
Y_3	0	0.6	1	-0.2	0.4	0	2.2
D_3	0	-2.6	0	-0.8	-0.4	1	0.8

   a. How many pounds of each ingredient should be used to minimize cost?
   b. State the minimum cost of a batch and how this amount is computed.
   c. Are any requirements exceeded in the primal solution? If so, state each requirement and interpret the amount of the surplus of each.
   d. For all binding constraints in the primal problem, show that the requirement is met exactly.
   e. Find the applicable range of all positive shadow prices in the dual solution and interpret this result with respect to the primal problem.

Nonlinear Functions

8.1 Introduction

The next several chapters (Chapters 8 to 12) extend mathematical analysis to both linear and nonlinear functions. This chapter includes an introductory examination of polynomial functions of degrees higher than 1, exponential functions, and logarithmic functions. Topics presented in this chapter will be helpful in understanding the applications of the following four chapters.

These three types of function were defined in Chapter 3. In this chapter, additional concepts, computational techniques, and applications associated with each are discussed. Readers should note particularly the interpretation of each function when used in a mathematical model. In most cases, the functions are presented with two variables, one independent and one dependent. However, each functional form can be applied to situations with any number of variables.

Many times, quantitative business relations are described most accurately by nonlinear functions. In these cases, the dependent variable does not change by a constant amount when changes take place in the independent variable.

Three examples of nonlinear business relationships will provide an introduction to these functions. Each example will be examined in greater detail as the chapter continues. Further computations and applications associated with each also will be found in later chapters.

1. In most cases the average or per unit production cost of a particular product does not change at a constant rate as the quantity of production expands. Thus, as automobile production increases, the cost of producing a single automobile does not remain the same.

   The variation in average cost relates to production efficiency. For example, at low levels of production the cost of producing an automobile is high because labor and machinery are underutilized. At very high levels of production, inefficiencies in management (quality control problems, errors on the production line, etc.) may cause high average costs. Between these two extremes, labor and machinery are operating more efficiently and, consequently, average costs are low.

   Thus, it can be seen that the average cost of producing an automobile does not change by a constant amount as output expands. This means that a nonlinear function should be applied to this relationship.

2. A second nonlinear relationship in business is reflected in the total revenue (product price times quantity sold) received by a firm as the quantity sold increases.

   In order to stimulate additional sales, most firms must gradually decrease the product price. These price adjustments cause total revenue to change at a variable rate as the quantity sold increases. Thus, total revenue as a function of quantity sold is described most accurately by a nonlinear function.

3. Measuring rates of growth is important to business and economic analysis. Population, additions to the capital stock of a nation or region, and sales of a new product are some of the variables which frequently are measured as a function of time (weeks, months, years, etc.).

   As will be pointed out later in the chapter, rates of growth usually are measured by nonlinear functions (in most cases, exponential functions). This is because as time progresses, additions to these variables (e.g., additional population of a country each year) are made to a continually changing base (population of the country at the beginning of each year). This relationship causes the rate of growth in these variables to vary over time and leads to the application of nonlinear functions.

8.2 Quadratic Functions and the Quadratic Formula

If k is greater than 1 in the polynomial with one independent variable,

$$Y = b_0 + b_1X + b_2X^2 + \cdots + b_kX^k$$

the function is nonlinear. This section discusses quadratic functions where $k = 2$ and the next section focuses on cubic functions where $k = 3$. Although polynomials of higher degree are used in business, quadratic and cubic functions are encountered frequently and can be used to derive some generalizations for all nonlinear polynomials. Therefore, for purposes of brevity, the discussion of nonlinear polynomials is limited to these two functions.

Quadratic functions have the form $Y = b_0 + b_1X + b_2X^2$ where b_0, b_1, and b_2 are constants and b_2 is not equal to zero. When graphed on the coordinate axis, a quadratic function is a vertical parabola. Two vertical parabolas are shown in Figure 8.1(*a*) and (*b*).

A vertical parabola is characterized by one turning point where the function changes direction either from increasing to decreasing or from decreasing to increasing. This turning point is called the *vertex*. The vertex is either a maximum as in Figure 8.1(*a*) or a minimum as in Figure 8.1(*b*).

Without a graph, maximum and minimum points can be determined by the sign of the coefficient b_2. If b_2 is less than zero, the vertical parabola will appear as in Figure 8.1(*a*). It is referred to as being *concave downward*. This means that Y, the value of the function, is at its maximum point at the vertex. In Figure 8.1(*b*), b_2 is greater than zero; thus, the function is characterized as being *concave upward*. In this case, Y is at its minimum point at the vertex.

The X coordinate point of the vertex is found by setting X equal to $-b_1/2b_2$. Substitution of the resulting X value into the quadratic function yields the value of Y and, therefore, the coordinates of the vertex. An example will demonstrate these computations.

Example 8.1
The demand for televisions sold by a chain of retail outlets is expressed by the following linear equation where price is a function of the quantity sold.

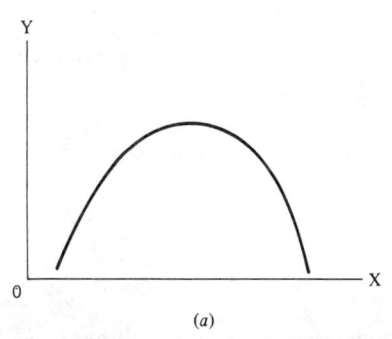

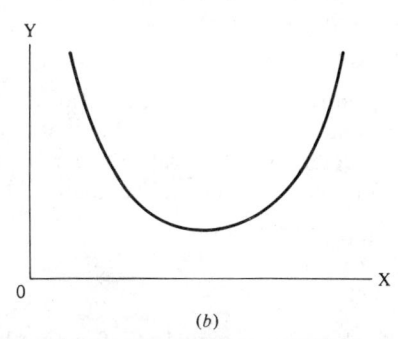

FIGURE 8.1 Two vertical parabolas showing (*a*) a maximum vertex and (*b*) a minimum vertex.

$P = 710 - 0.09Q$

with P = price in dollars and Q = quantity of televisions demanded.

The total revenue derived from television sales is equal to price times the quantity sold. Thus,

Total revenue (TR) = price (P) · quantity (Q)

By substituting the demand function for price in the total revenue equation, a function relating total revenue and quantity sold can be formed as follows:

$$\begin{aligned} TR &= P \cdot Q \\ &= (720 - 0.09Q)Q \\ &= 720Q - 0.09Q^2 \end{aligned}$$

Therefore, a quadratic total revenue function with $b_0 = 0$ is formed.

In this expression, b_2 is negative, indicating that the function is concave downward. The X coordinate (or quantity consumed) at the vertex can be found by solving for X in

$$X = \frac{-b_1}{2b_2}$$

where $b_1 = 720$ and $b_2 = -0.09$. Therefore, X, or the quantity of televisions corresponding to maximum total revenue, is equal to

$$Q = X = \frac{-720}{2(-0.09)} = \frac{-720}{-0.18} = 4000$$

Thus, this firm will achieve maximum total revenue by selling 4000 televisions.

The total revenue corresponding to this quantity is found by substituting $Q = 4000$ into the total revenue function as follows:

$$\begin{aligned} TR &= 720Q - 0.09Q^2 \\ &= 720(4000) - (0.09)(4000)^2 \\ &= 2{,}880{,}000 - (0.09)(16{,}000{,}000) \\ &= 2{,}880{,}000 - 1{,}440{,}000 \\ &= \$1{,}440{,}000 \end{aligned}$$

Consequently, the maximum point of the total revenue function specifies a total revenue of $1,440,000 and a quantity of 4000 televisions.

To determine the price corresponding to this quantity, $Q = 4000$ is substituted into the demand equation as follows:

$$\begin{aligned} P &= 720 - 0.09(4000) \\ &= 720 - 360 \\ &= \$360 \end{aligned}$$

Analysis of this quadratic function has shown that the retailer will be able to achieve a maximum total revenue of $1,440,000 by selling 4000 televisions at a price of $360 per television.

Alternative methods for finding maximum and minimum points of quadratic functions and polynomials of other degrees are included in the chapters on calculus. This analysis has been considered in some detail to demonstrate one business application and related computations for a quadratic function.

The Quadratic Formula

By using the coefficients a, b, and c in place of b_2, b_1, and b_0, respectively, a quadratic equation can be stated as

$$aX^2 + bX + c = Y$$

And, if $Y = 0$, the equation can be expressed,

$$aX^2 + bX + c = 0$$

In this second form, solution values for X (also called the *roots* of the equation) can be determined either by factoring or by the quadratic formula. As factoring has been discussed in Chapter 1, this section introduces the quadratic formula. The quadratic formula states that

$$X = \frac{-b \pm \sqrt{b^2 - 4ac}}{2a}$$

The resulting solution represents the X value (or values), if any, which satisfies the equation $aX^2 + bX + c = 0$. In graphical form, any X value represents an X coordinate of the X intercept ($Y = 0$).

The term under the radical sign ($b^2 - 4ac$) is termed the *discriminant*. The discriminant determines whether there are zero, one, or two X intercepts for the vertical parabola.

If $b^2 - 4ac$ is negative, there are no X intercepts since the vertical parabola is either completely above or completely below the X axis. If $b^2 - 4ac$ is equal to 0, there is one intercept. Consequently, the vertical parabola touches the X axis at a single point, the vertex. In this case, the X intercept is equal to $-b/2a$, which is equivalent to the formula shown above for the X coordinate of the vertex, $-b_1/2b_2$. Finally, if $b^2 - 4ac$ is positive, there are two different X intercepts for the vertical parabola. An example will demonstrate application of the quadratic formula.

Example 8.2
For the quadratic equation,

$$5X^2 - 6X + 1 = 0$$

find all X intercepts.

Using the quadratic formula with $a = +5$, $b = -6$, and $c = +1$, the following solution is found:

$$X = \frac{-b \pm \sqrt{b^2 - 4ac}}{2a}$$

$$= \frac{6 \pm \sqrt{36 - 4(5)(1)}}{5(2)}$$

$$= \frac{6 \pm \sqrt{16}}{10}$$

$$= \frac{6 \pm 4}{10}$$

$X = 1$ and $X = 0.2$

Thus, the vertical parabola intersects the X axis at two points, $X = 1$ and $X = 0.2$.

Example 8.3 applies the quadratic formula to the total revenue function of Example 8.1.

Example 8.3

For the total revenue (TR) function,

$$TR = 720Q - 0.09Q^2$$

Find the Q intercepts of the function. In this case,

$a = -0.09 \qquad b = 720 \qquad c = 0$

Thus, the Q coordinate points where total revenue equals zero are

$$Q = \frac{-b \pm \sqrt{b^2 - 4ac}}{2a}$$

$$= \frac{-720 \pm \sqrt{(720)^2 - 4(0.09)(0)}}{2(-0.09)}$$

$$= \frac{-720 \pm 720}{-0.18}$$

$Q = 0 \qquad Q = \dfrac{-1440}{-0.18} = 8000$

The vertical parabola representing total revenue intersects the quantity axis at $Q = 0$ and $Q = 8000$. Thus, total revenue is zero when no quantity is sold and it is also zero when 8000 televisions are sold, as the price would have to be zero to sell this amount (a hypothetical case).

Several problems in the following group will provide practice in solving quadratic equations and applying the quadratic formula.

EXERCISES

1. For each quadratic function below, find the coordinate point (X, Y) of the vertex. In each case, is the vertical parabola concave upward or concave downward? Why?

a. $Y = 4X^2 - 8X + 12$ c. $Y = 5X^2 - 40X + 120$
b. $Y = -0.03X^2 + 9X - 100$ d. $Y = -X^2 + 24X + 100$

2. For each quadratic equation below of the form $aX^2 + bX + c = 0$, find the value of the discriminant. Based on the value of the discriminant, will there be zero, one, or two solutions to the quadratic equation? Why?
   a. $5X^2 - 6X + 4 = 0$ d. $12X^2 - 16 = 0$
   b. $2X^2 - 8X + 8 = 0$ e. $5X^2 + 0.08X = 0$
   c. $0.1X^2 + 10X - 20 = 0$ f. $4X^2 + 2X + 6 = 0$

3. Solve each quadratic function of the form $aX^2 + bX + c = 0$ using the quadratic formula. Describe each point or points found by this method.
   a. $0.01X^2 + 4X = 0$ d. $3X^2 - 30X + 72 = 0$
   b. $X^2 - 6X + 5 = 0$ e. $2X^2 - 8 = 0$
   c. $X^2 + 4X - 12 = 0$ f. $2X^2 - 16X - 18 = 0$

4. For the following demand function for shirts where price (in dollars) is a function of the quantity demanded:

   $P = 36 - 0.06Q$

   a. Find the total revenue function for shirts.
   b. Find the vertex of the total revenue function.
   c. Show that this point represents maximum total revenue.
   d. What is the price charged for shirts at the vertex of the total revenue function?

5. Given the following average cost (per unit cost) function for the production of programmable calculators:

   Average cost per unit $= 0.06Q^2 - 84Q + 30,000$

   a. Find the quantity at the vertex of the average-cost-per-unit function.
   b. Find the average cost per unit at the vertex.
   c. Is this vertex a maximum point or a minimum point? Why?

8.3 Cubic Functions

Polynomials of degree 3 with one independent variable, referred to as cubic functions, have the form

$$Y = b_0 + b_1X + b_2X^2 + b_3X^3$$

where b_3 is not equal to zero.

    A definitive statement about the shape of all cubic functions is not possible. Often, however, a cubic function has two turning points. In other words, many cubic functions include a segment which is concave downward and a segment which is concave upward.

    This discussion of cubic functions will be concerned with only some of the applications of cubic functions in business and economics. Two particular applications are associated with production: the law of diminishing returns and the related total cost function.

The law of diminishing returns states that when units of a variable factor (e.g., labor) are added to a fixed factor (e.g., land), the output resulting from additional units of labor first increases at an increasing rate, then increases at a decreasing rate, and finally decreases. The function used to express this law is referred to as a *production function*. The production function in this case specifies a relation between output and the use of the variable factor.

Operation of the law of diminishing returns causes the typical production function to be cubic as there is (1) a concave upward segment where returns to the variable factor are increasing at an increasing rate and (2) a concave downward segment where returns to the variable factor are first increasing at a decreasing rate and then decreasing. Figure 8.2(*a*) is a typical production function reflecting the law of diminishing returns.

The total cost of production is related to returns from the use of variable factors. In general, if returns from a factor are increasing at an increasing rate, total costs of production are increasing at a decreasing rate. And if factor returns are increasing at a decreasing rate or decreasing, total costs of production are increasing at an increasing rate.

Thus, the total cost function, expressing total cost as a function of a firm's output, also frequently is cubic. However, in this case, there is a concave downward segment followed by a concave upward segment. Figure 8.2(*b*) shows a typical total cost function.

A cubic total cost function has the functional form

$$Y = b_0 + b_1 X + b_2 X^2 + b_3 X^3$$

where Y = total cost
X = quantity of output
$b_3 \neq 0$

A typical graph of this function shows that as output increases, costs increase at a decreasing rate and, subsequently, increase at an increasing

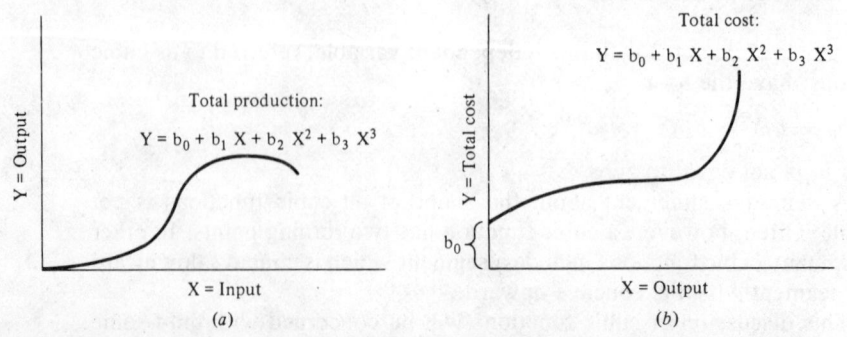

FIGURE 8.2 Two cubic functions describing (*a*) a typical production function and (*b*) a typical total cost function.

rate as diminishing returns to the variable factor occur. Thus, a concave upward segment follows a concave downward segment of the curve as output increases.

As a final point, note that in the equation for total cost, b_0 represents fixed cost or those costs which do not vary with output. This fixed cost component also is shown as b_0 in Figure 8.2(b).

In contrast to the total cost function, b_0 often equals 0 in a production function as output is not possible without the application of at least some of the variable input.

In the chapters on calculus, methods for determining various points on the total cost function and developing other cost functions based on total cost will be discussed in more detail.

Cubic functions have many more uses and applications. However, this short description has been included to demonstrate some of the characteristics of these functions and how they may be employed to describe real-world relationships.

8.4 Exponential Functions

In Chapter 3, an exponential function was defined as a nonalgebraic function where the independent variable is an exponent or part of an exponent for a constant. Examples of exponential functions with one independent variable are

$Y = 10^X$

$Y = 6^{X-3}$

$Y = e^X$

where e is the nonrepeating decimal constant 2.71828 . . . , Y is the dependent variable, and X is the independent variable.

The following is a discussion of some principles and applications of exponential functions.

Properties of Exponential Functions

For the following properties of exponential functions, consider the general expression $Y = b^X$ where Y is the dependent variable, X is the independent variable, and b is any constant base.

1. The base b for an exponential function can be any positive real number except 1, as 1 raised to any power is equal to 1.
2. The domain (X values) for exponential functions includes all re mbers. However, for simplification purposes, when the function is $Y - b^{-X}$, the form $Y = 1/b^X$ is used.

3. The range (Y values) for exponential functions includes all positive real numbers.
4. The Y intercept for all exponential functions of the form $Y = b^x$ is at the coordinate point $(0, 1)$. This property demonstrates the rule of exponents that $b^0 = 1$ for all b.

As property 1 above states, the limits for the base b are the positive real numbers excluding 1. Several additional properties of exponential functions are better explained by considering the separate situations where (1) b is greater than 1 and (2) b is between 0 and 1 (excluding the points 0 and 1).

Exponential Functions When b Is Greater than 1

Two properties applicable to exponential functions with b greater than 1 can be explained by the functions shown in Figure 8.3.

Observe that for each of the functions, the value of the function Y approaches the X axis as X approaches $-\infty$. In other words, Y approaches 0, but never equals it, as X decreases. In more formal terms, this means that the exponential function $Y = b^x$ when b is greater than 1 is *asymptotic* to the X axis as X approaches $-\infty$.

A second property is that Y is continually increasing for increasing values of X. The terminology describing this property is that $Y = b^x$ when b is greater than 1 is a *monotonically increasing* function of X.

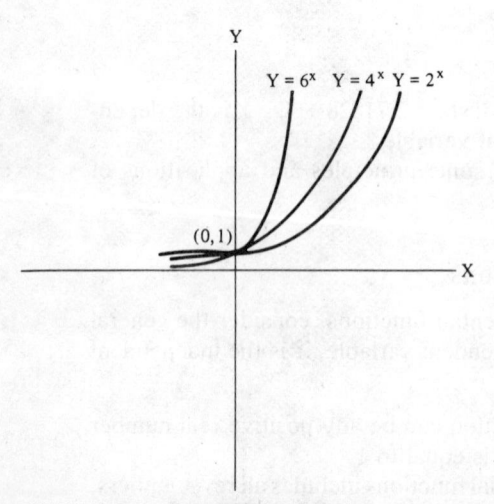

FIGURE 8.3 Exponential functions where the value of b is greater than one.

Exponential Functions When b Is between 0 and 1

To help visualize the properties of exponential functions with a base b between 0 and 1, Figure 8.4 shows three exponential functions.

In this case, all the functions $Y = b^X$ are asymptotic to the X axis as X approaches $+\infty$.

In addition, the value of the function $Y = b^X$ when b is between 0 and 1 becomes less with increasing values of X. Thus, the function $Y = b^X$ is a *monotonically decreasing* function of X when b is between 0 and 1.

The terms "monotonically increasing function" and "monotonically decreasing function" introduced here are descriptive of many situations in business and economics. For example, automobile sales may rise continually as national employment increases. Thus, automobile sales are a monotonically increasing function of national employment.

The Base e

Although all positive real numbers except 1 can be used as a base in exponential functions, the base e, where $e = 2.71828\ldots$, has special significance for a wide range of applications in business and economics.

Readers should understand the importance of this constant. The value of e is found by evaluating the expression $(1 + 1/n)^n$ as n approaches infinity. Although this constant is used in many fields, the most easily understood

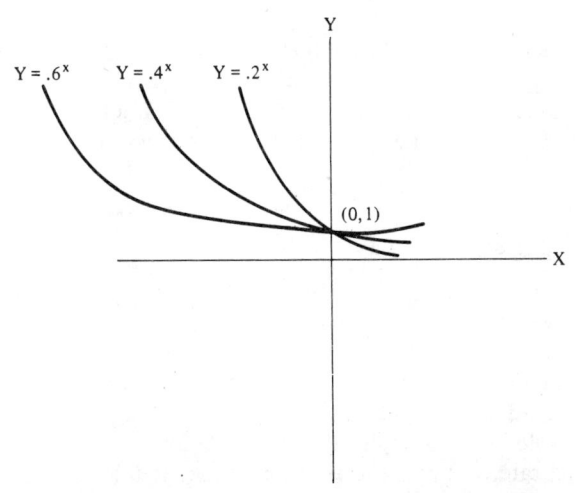

FIGURE 8.4 Exponential functions where the value of b is between zero and one.

explanation of e is based on the continuous compounding of money as practiced by financial institutions. The complete derivation, as applicable to finance, is included in Chapter 9. The final result of the derivation is presented here without proof so that some nonfinancial applications can be discussed in the present chapter.

The constant e measures the value of $1 compounded continuously for 1 year at the annual rate of 100 percent. In other words, $1 invested for 1 year in a bank at 100 percent per year, continuously compounded, will be worth $2.71828 . . . at the end of the year. As 100 percent is an unrealistic rate, e can be raised to an exponent i representing the annual interest rate (such as 0.08 for 8 percent). Thus,

1. e^i

represents the value of $1 invested for 1 year at the continuously compounded annual rate of i percent.

To determine the value of this $1 after some time other than 1 year, the exponent is multiplied by the time in years. This second factor in the exponent is given the abbreviation t. Therefore, the value of $1 invested at the continuously compounded annual rate of i percent per year for t years is

2. e^{it}

Finally, this entire expression can be multiplied by an amount representing the initial deposit P (for principal) in the account. The value of the account A at the end of t years is

3. $A = Pe^{it}$

As the mathematics of finance is the topic of Chapter 9, this description of e has been presented as a means to introduce the nonfinancial uses of e in measuring processes of continuous (or exponential) growth and continuous (or exponential) decay. This generalization of the application of e is discussed below.

Exponential Growth and Exponential Decay

The principles underlying processes of exponential growth and exponential decay are similar to those involved with the continuous compounding of money.

Exponential growth refers to a pattern where equal absolute increases in the independent variable are related to constant and continuous percentage increases in the dependent variable. For example, if the population of a country grows at the exponential rate of 2 percent per year, it means that population is growing at the rate of 2 percent per year continuously compounded.

Nonlinear Functions **215**

An exponential decay process refers to a situation where equal absolute increases in the independent variable are related to constant and continuous percentage decreases in the dependent variable. For example, canned goods in a food storage warehouse may spoil at the continuously compounded (exponential) annual rate of 4 percent. For both the growth and decay process, the dependent variable changes by ever larger absolute amounts, but by a constant percentage, as the independent variable changes by equal absolute amounts (year to year in these examples).

Example 8.4

With several notational changes, the compound interest expression above can be used to describe exponential population growth. This is shown as

$P = Se^{rt}$

where r = exponential rate of growth per time period
t = time periods
P = population after t time periods
S = population at $t = 0$

For example, this new expression can be used to find population at some future time knowing that a region has a population of 8 million people on January 1, 1985, and that population is growing at the exponential rate of 2 percent per year. What will the population be on January 1, 1990 (after 5 years)?

To solve this problem, the following values are substituted into the expression for exponential population growth:

$P = Se^{rt}$

where S and P are measured in millions

$S = 8$
$e = 2.71828 \ldots$
$r = 0.02$
$t = 5$

(Thus, $rt = 0.10$.)

The exponent of e, rt, can be treated as a single variable X. Values for e^X and e^{-X} are found in Table III at the end of the book. Thus, as $rt = X = 0.1$, Table III yields the value $e^{0.1} = 1.1052$. The population on January 1, 1990, therefore, will be:

$P = 8e^{0.1} = 8(1.1052) = 8.8416$

This process has demonstrated that, at a continuously compounded growth rate of 2 percent per year, the region will have a population of 8,841,600 at the beginning of 1990.

Example 8.5

A procedure similar to 1 through 3 above can be used to derive a general expression for exponential decay. However, as this process is based on the principles of discounting discussed in Chapter 9, it will be stated here without proof. An exponential decay process can be explained by

4. $W = Ve^{-rt}$

where $e = 2.71828\ldots$
r = rate of exponential decay per time period
t = time periods
V = beginning value for the measured variable
W = ending value for the measured variable

Assume an institutional food distributor has a canned goods inventory worth $22 million on January 1, 1986. Goods are spoiling at the exponential rate of 3 percent per year, indicating that inventory deteriorates at this rate continuously compounded.

What will be the value of this inventory on December 31, 1987, assuming no additions are made to the initial amount?

In this case, $r = 0.03$, $t = 2.0$ (2 years), and $e^{-rt} = e^{-X} = e^{-0.06}$ is found in Table III to be 0.9417. Therefore, the value of the inventory at the end of 2 years is found by applying the appropriate data to expression 4 as follows:

$W = Ve^{-rt}$

where W and V are measured in millions of dollars. The following steps yield the value for W:

1. $W = 22e^{-(0.03)(2)}$
2. $ = 22e^{-0.06}$
3. $ = 22(0.9417)$
4. $ = \$20{,}717{,}400$

The value of the original $22 million inventory will be $20,717,400 after deteriorating at the exponential rate of 3 percent per year for 2 years.

A Modified Exponential Function

The function having the general form $Y = 1 - e^{-X}$ has many business applications. Figure 8.5 will help to explain some of the characteristics of this function.

Table III shows that the value of e^{-X} decreases and approaches zero as X increases. Consequently, as X increases, the expression $1 - e^{-X}$ approaches 1, and the function $Y = 1 - e^{-X}$ is asymptotic to the line $Y = 1$. Also, the function increases rapidly at low X values and increases more slowly as $Y = 1$ is approached.

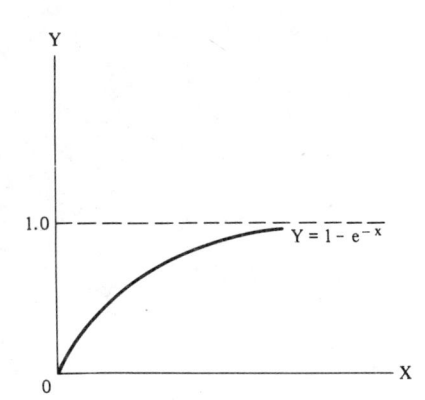

FIGURE 8.5 An exponential function, $Y = 1 - e^{-x}$.

This function is particularly useful in describing consumer or producer response patterns. For example, the attitudes of consumers may create an upper limit to market expansion, or available resources may impose a limit on production possibilities.

The general form $Y = 1 - e^{-X}$ can be altered by, for example, multiplying the entire expression by a constant and multiplying X by a coefficient in the exponent of e. Applying both of these changes leads to the function

$$Y = K(1 - e^{-mX})$$

In this form, the function is asymptotic to K because $1 - e^{-mX}$ approaches 1 as X increases. The term mX often is used to denote time and is given the notation t. This form is used in the following example.

Example 8.6
A large household products manufacturer has decided to print coupons for its popular detergent in a group of Sunday newspapers. Company history indicates that the percentage of coupons redeemed at any point in time is an exponential function of the form $Y = 1 - e^{-t}$ where t is an independent variable representing weeks since publication of the coupon. Past records also indicate that the firm can expect a maximum redemption rate of 40 percent.

The function expressing this consumer response pattern is

$$R = 0.40(1 - e^{-t})$$

where R = redemption rate as a percentage of coupons dispersed
$\quad\quad\; t$ = weeks elapsed since publication
$\quad\quad\; e$ = 2.71828 . . .

The graph of this function is shown in Figure 8.6.

Using Table III, values for $e^{-mX} = e^{-t}$ can be found for various weeks.

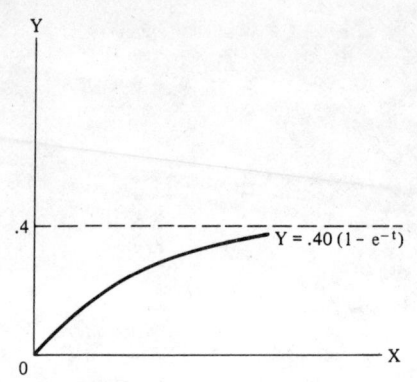

FIGURE 8.6 An exponential function $Y = .40(1 - e^{-t})$.

After 1 week, the percentage of all coupons redeemed is the following:

$R = 0.40(1 - e^{-1})$
$ = 0.40(1 - 0.3679)$
$ = 0.40(0.6321)$
$ = 0.2528$

Thus, about 25 percent of all coupons will have been redeemed after 1 week. The analysis can be extended to 3 weeks with the following results:

$R = 0.40(1 - e^{-3})$
$ = 0.40(1 - 0.0498)$
$ = 0.40(0.9502)$
$ = 0.3801$

This indicates that few additional coupons will be redeemed after 3 weeks if historical patterns apply to this situation. Thus, this exponential function has provided a means to describe this response pattern.

This section has explained some of the nonfinancial business uses of exponential functions with the base e. Functions of this type will be referred to again within the mathematics of finance (Chapter 9) and the chapters on calculus (Chapters 10, 11, and 12).

EXERCISES

1. Find the value of Y at each designated point on the exponential function (use Table III).
    a. $Y = e^j$ at $j = 2.00$
    b. $Y = e^X$ at $X = -1.5$
    c. $Y = e^{ij}$ at $i = 0.5$ and $j = 0.2$
    d. $Y = e^{-t}$ at $t = 0.42$
    e. $Y = e^{-mX}$ at $m = 0.4$ and $X = 4$

2. For each exponential function below find the value of Y at $X = 2$ and at $X = 4$.
   a. $Y = 3^{X-2}$
   b. $Y = 5^{X+1}$
   c. $Y = 0.1^{X+1}$
   d. $Y = 0.5^{X-3}$
   e. $Y = 3^{X^2-3X}$
   f. $Y = 0.1^{-X+2}$
3. For each exponential function below, state whether the function is
   a. A monotonically increasing or monotonically decreasing function of X.
   b. Asymptotic to the X axis as X approaches $+\infty$ or asymptotic to the X axis as X approaches $-\infty$.
   (1) $Y = 3^{X-5}$
   (2) $Y = 0.7^{3X}$
   (3) $Y = e^{5X+4}$
   (4) $Y = 0.06^{X+2}$
   (5) $Y = 2^{-X+3}$
   (6) $Y = e^{-X}$
4. Given the exponential growth function as applied to population
   $$P = Se^{rt}$$
   find P for the following values of S, r, and t. Interpret each if S and P are measured as millions of people, r is the annual percentage growth rate, and t is the number of years.
   a. $S = 15$, $r = 0.03$, $t = 4$
   b. $S = 180$, $r = 0.01$, $t = 12$
   c. $S = 45$, $r = 0.05$, $t = 5$
   d. $S = 20$, $r = 1.0$, $t = 1$
   e. $S = 56$, $r = 3.2$, $t = 0.5$
5. The number of reported cases of a rare disease over time can be explained by the exponential decay function
   $$W = Ve^{-rt}$$
   In this function, W and V represent the number of reported cases of the disease, r is the annual percentage rate of decay, and t designates number of years since a given starting date ($t = 0$). Find W for each given set of V, r, and t and interpret each answer.
   a. $V = 120$, $r = 0.25$, $t = 2$
   b. $V = 200$, $r = 0.10$, $t = 7$
   c. $V = 250$, $r = 0.08$, $t = 12$
   d. $V = 30$, $r = 0.4$, $t = 1$
   e. $V = 325$, $r = 0.06$, $t = 0.5$
6. An exponential response function in which the percentage of restaurant customers purchasing a new menu item Y is dependent on t, the number of weeks after introduction, has the following form:
   $$Y = 0.3(1 - e^{-t})$$
   a. What percentage of customers have tried the new menu item after 2 weeks?
   b. What percentage of customers have tried the new menu item after 3 weeks?
   c. Characterize the value of the function Y as the number of weeks increases indefinitely.

8.5 Logarithmic Functions

Introduction

In Chapter 3, a logarithm was defined as the power to which a base must be raised to yield a given number. This is expressed $Y = \text{logarithm } _b X$, indicating that Y equals the logarithm of X to the base b, or $b^Y = X$.

The base of a logarithmic scale can be any positive number except 1. However, the two most utilized bases are 10 (for *common* logarithms) and $e = 2.71828\ldots$ (for *natural* logarithms). The abbreviation *log* is used to denote a common logarithm; *ln* designates a natural logarithm. Consequently, the log of 100 is the number to which 10 must be raised to equal 100, and the ln of 100 is the number to which $2.71828\ldots$ must be raised to equal 100.

Values for common logarithms are found in Table I at the end of the book, and Table II includes values for natural logarithms. Hand calculators and computers have eliminated much of the need to use these tables. However, the tables will be referred to at various points throughout the book and readers should be familiar with them.

Listed below are some of the basic computational rules for logarithms. These rules are applicable to both common and natural logarithms. Before stating these rules, it should be noted that as a logarithm is a form of exponent, there is a close similarity in the computations using each. (See Chapter 2 for a review of operations on exponents.)

For the following rules, assume that x, y, and z are any positive real numbers.

1. Logarithms of sums and differences cannot be taken term by term; i.e., it is *invalid* to state:

    logarithm $(x + y)$ = logarithm x + logarithm y

    or   logarithm $(x - y)$ = logarithm x - logarithm y

2. Products: logarithm (xy) = logarithm x + logarithm y
3. Quotients: logarithm (x/y) = logarithm x - logarithm y
4. Powers of a variable: logarithm (x^y) = y logarithm x
5. Roots of a variable: logarithm $(\sqrt[y]{x})$ = $1/y$ (logarithm x)
6. Fractional roots of a variable: logarithm $\sqrt[y]{x^z}$ = z/y (logarithm x)
7. Logarithm of 1: logarithm 1 = 0

The significance of the constant e to business and economics has been stressed previously. Therefore, this discussion of logarithmic functions will emphasize functions which use the base e, or natural logarithms. For interested readers, the Appendix to this chapter describes how to use the table of natural logarithms.

Logarithmic Functions and Exponential Functions

For every logarithmic function, there is a corresponding exponential function. For example, using natural logarithms and the variables X and Y,

If $X = \ln Y$, then $e^X = Y$

If $Y = \ln X$, then $e^Y = X$

Figure 8.7 shows the functions $Y = \ln X$ and $e^Y = X$.

Points on Figure 8.7 can be found by either of two methods:

1. Select values of X and, using the table of natural logarithms (Table II), find the corresponding values of Y ($\ln X$).
2. Select values of Y and, using the table of e values (Table III), find the corresponding values of X (e^Y).

Method 1 is similar to the dependent variable–independent variable framework used thus far in the book. However, either method will lead to the function shown in Figure 8.7.

Figure 8.7 demonstrates that the function $Y = \ln X$ is monotonically increasing as X increases and is asymptotic to the Y axis as X approaches 0. The X intercept is at the point (1, 0), indicating that Y is positive for X values greater than 1 and negative for X values between 0 and 1.

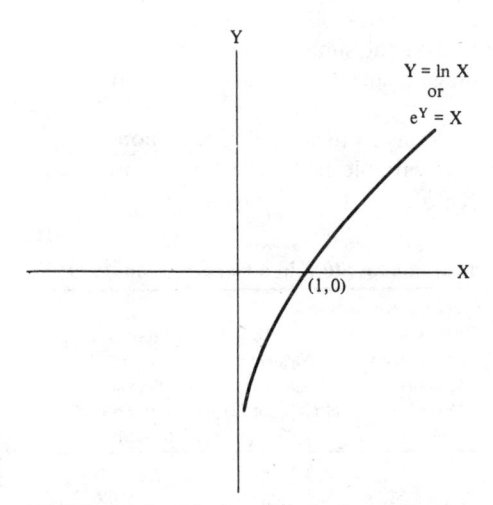

FIGURE 8.7 The logarithmic function $Y = \ln X$ or, in exponential form, $e^y = X$.

Logarithmic Functions in Business

At times, the use of logarithmic values rather than real number values for observations of a variable provides a more precise analysis of a relationship. An example comparing these two measurements will help to explain this increased precision.

Example 8.7

A researcher wants to establish a mathematical model expressing the growth of nonagricultural capital stock (dependent variable) in a county as a function of time measured in years (independent variable). Table 8.1 includes hypothetical data for the value of capital stock in nonagricultural industries in the county at 5-year intervals during a recent 20-year period.

The first two columns of Table 8.1 describe the value of capital stock for each of the specified years. Column (3) shows the absolute change in the value of capital stock between time periods. These data indicate that capital stock has grown over time by ever-increasing amounts. However these absolute amounts may be a deceptive measure of growth, as pointed out by column (4). This column, measuring percentage change in the value of capital stock over time, shows a stable growth pattern. The percentage differences that do exist are small and, in fact, indicate a smaller percentage increase through time. Consequently, this relationship may not be described accurately by using actual observations for the values of the dependent variable. The problem associated with numerical measurements in this case is that each year's absolute change reflects growth from an ever-larger base.

An alternative model may be formed by examining columns (5) and (6). By using natural logarithms for the capital stock observations, rate of change is incorporated into the analysis. Observe the similarity in the pattern of growth as shown by column (4), percentage change in actual values, and column (6), change in natural logarithms.

Figure 8.8 includes the graph for each analysis using Y (value of nonagricultural capital stock) as the dependent variable in Figure 8.8(a) and ln Y as the dependent variable in Figure 8.8(b).

TABLE 8.1
Hypothetical Data for the Value of Nonagricultural Capital Stock in a County, 1960–1980

Year (1)	Value of Nonagricultural Capital Stock, $ million (2)	Change in Column (2) from Previous Period (3)	Percentage Change in Column (2) from Previous Period (4)	Natural Logarithm of Column (2) (5)	Change in Column (5) from Previous Period (6)
1960	75			4.31749	
1965	95	20	26.67	4.55388	0.23639
1970	120	25	26.32	4.78749	0.23361
1975	150	30	25.00	5.01064	0.22315
1980	185	35	23.33	5.22036	0.20972

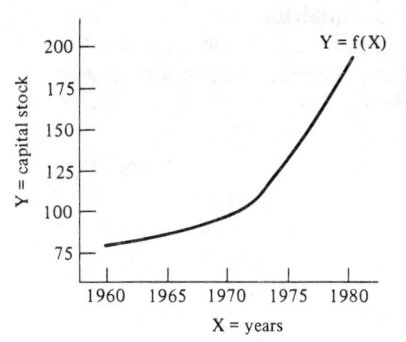

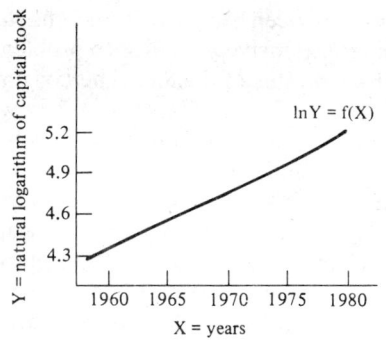

FIGURE 8.8 Growth in (a) capital stock as a function of time and the logarithm of capital stock as a function of time.

Figure 8.8(a) shows rapidly increasing growth through time, whereas Figure 8.8(b) demonstrates more stability in growth. Thus, measuring the dependent variable by means of natural logarithms more accurately demonstrates the growth in nonagricultural capital stock. This same principle applies to many business problems concerned with analyzing rates of growth.

The past two sections have emphasized the use of the constant e in both exponential and logarithmic functions. The need to evaluate growth patterns accurately makes this constant and functions related to it an essential component of applied mathematical analysis. The constant e will be particularly important in Chapter 9 (The Mathematics of Finance).

8.6 Chapter Summary

Functions other than linear polynomials frequently are used to describe mathematical relationships. This chapter has discussed a number of these, including polynomials of degree 2 and degree 3 and two nonalgebraic functions. Each function has been associated with at least one application. The chapter's Appendix presents a short discussion of how to use tables of natural logarithms.

A quadratic polynomial is characterized by one turning point (the vertex), and a cubic polynomial often has two turning points. These contrast with linear functions which have a constant slope and no turning points. Frequently, the quadratic formula must be used to find the X intercept values for a quadratic equation. Thus, this formula yields the value(s) of X (if any) when $Y = 0$. Techniques also were presented for finding the vertex of a quadratic function and to establish whether the quadratic function is concave downward or concave upward. Other methods for identifying particular points on nonlinear polynomials will be presented in the chapters on calculus.

The use of the constant e ($e = 2.71828\ldots$) in explaining many phenomena has been stressed in the chapter. Exponential functions with the base e are extensively applied to problems of compounding money, rates of growth, and rates of decline. The constant e also is encountered in a group of functions called *response functions* which express growth patterns constrained by some upper boundary (such as consumer acceptability).

Logarithmic functions, at times, explain particular phenomena more accurately than polynomials. When a variable increases or decreases at a relatively constant percentage rate, logarithmic rather than numerical measurement of the variable may be preferred. Because of the importance of the base e and the connection between exponential and logarithmic functions, logarithmic functions often employ logarithms to the base e (natural logarithms).

Overall, this chapter has introduced a number of nonlinear functions and some of the applications of each. In the following chapters, the functions discussed in this chapter, as well as linear functions, will be applied to various analytical situations. Consequently, an understanding of this chapter complements the previous chapters and provides a background for the prudent and accurate use of many kinds of functions.

8.7 Problem Set

Review Questions

1. Distinguish between a concave upward and a concave downward vertical parabola. How can each be identified by inspection of the equation for the vertical parabola?
2. In the quadratic equation $aX^2 + bX + c = 0$, what points on the coordinate axis are found when the equation is solved?
3. In the total cost equation, where cost is a function of the quantity produced $C(Q)$:

    $C(Q) = -0.2Q^3 + 0.03Q^2 + 2Q + 1500$

    What cost component is represented by the constant 1500?
4. Why are there both concave upward and concave downward segments on a typical total cost curve?
5. What are the coordinate points of the Y intercept for all exponential functions with one independent variable and one dependent variable? Why?
6. If Y is a monotonically increasing function of X, what can be concluded about values of the function as the independent variable increases in value?
7. What characteristic of the constant e makes it applicable to many functions measuring business relationships?
8. The function $Y = e^{-X}$ is asymptotic to the X axis as X approaches positive infinity. Explain.
9. Briefly describe the relevance of the function $Y = 1 - e^{-X}$ to response functions (such as the measurement of consumer response or producer response).
10. Why is it not feasible to use the base 1 for a logarithmic scale?

11. Why is a logarithmic scale sometimes preferable to a real-number scale when explaining growth rates of financial and economic variables?
12. What are the coordinate points of the X intercept for the function $Y = \ln X$? Why?

Review Problems

1. For the following demand function where price $P(Q)$ is a function of the quantity Q demanded,

   $P(Q) = 600 - 0.02Q$

   a. Find the total revenue function.
   b. Find the vertex of the total revenue function and state whether it is a maximum or a minimum point.
   c. Find the price at the vertex of the total revenue function.
   d. Solve the total revenue function for Q where total revenue equals zero.
   e. Briefly describe the points found in part d.

2. Given the following average cost function where cost $C(Q)$ is a function of quantity produced Q,

   $C(Q) = 0.04Q^2 - 6Q + 400$

   a. Is the vertex of this function a minimum or a maximum point? Why?
   b. What is the average cost at the vertex?
   c. Solve this equation for Q in the form $aQ^2 + bQ + c = 0$. What can you conclude from your answer?

3. For each of the following exponential functions, find Y when X is equal to -3, to 0, and to $+3$:

   a. $Y = 3^X$ e. $Y = 0.2^X$
   b. $Y = 8^X$ f. $Y = e^X$
   c. $Y = 0.4^X$ g. $Y = e^{-X}$
   d. $Y = 5^{-X}$ h. $Y = 3^{-X+4}$

4. Based on the pattern of answers to 3a through 3h above, what can be concluded about the characteristics of exponential functions?

5. The following function describes the percent of consumers buying a new toothpaste over time. If Y represents the percent of consumers buying the product and X represents weeks since introduction of the new toothpaste, then

   $Y = 0.3(1 - e^{-0.2X})$

   a. Find Y when X is equal to 0, 0.8, 3, 6, and 12.
   b. Describe the importance of the term 0.3 in the function.

6. The resale value of a particular mainframe computer is believed to decrease at the exponential rate of 8 percent per year. The original value of the computer is $1.6 million.
   a. Write the function showing the value (in millions of dollars) of this computer at any point in time (use the variable t to represent years).
   b. What is the resale value of this computer 4 years after purchase? What is the value 6 years after purchase?

7. Average daily attendance at a new theme amusement park has been growing at

the exponential rate of 4 percent per year. Average daily attendance in 1983 was 11,400. What is the average daily attendance expected to be in 1988 (after 5 years), if current patterns continue?

8. During the 1970s, annual reported cases of poliomyelitis in a state declined at an exponential rate of 4 percent per year. Reported cases in 1969 were 42.
   a. Estimate the number of reported cases at the end of the 1970s (after 10 years) if this rate of decay applies to the full period. ·
   b. Find the decline between the end of 1972 (year 3) and the end of 1975 (year 6).

9. In an agricultural region of an underdeveloped country, swamp areas are being converted to arable (agriculturally productive) land over time according to the function

   $$Y = 1 - e^{-mX}$$

   where Y = percentage of land in region converted to agricultural use
   m = the annual exponential rate of conversion
   X = number of years since the beginning of the conversion program

   Agricultural experts believe that no more than 50 percent of the swamp area can be converted to agricultural use. Successful conversion is occurring at the exponential rate of 8 percent per year.
   a. Restate the function to incorporate the 50 percent conversion limitation and the other data given.
   b. Using the function specified in a, find the percent of land converted to agricultural use at the end of the following time periods:
   (1) 1 year
   (2) 3 years
   (3) 5 years
   (4) 10 years

10. For the function $Y = \ln X$, find Y when X is equal to
    a. 2   d. 8
    b. 4   e. 10
    c. 6   f. 12
    What can you conclude about the pattern of the answers to a through f in order?

11. For the function $Y = X^2 + 3$, find Y and $\ln Y$ for each of the following values of X: 2, 3, 4, 5, and 6. Then, find the difference between each two successive Y values and that between each two successive $\ln Y$ values. What can be concluded from the pattern of the differences?

12. The following function, developed in Chapter 9, is used to determine the amount S_n in a savings account n years after an initial deposit of P dollars, with interest compounded annually at i percent per year:

    $$S_n = P(1 + i)^n$$

    In this function, the decimal representation for i is used; e.g., 11 percent interest is designated as $i = 0.11$.

    Methods for a tabular solution to this problem are discussed in Chapter 9. At this point, use natural logarithms and associated computational rules to solve the following problems:
    a. If $P = \$500$ and $i = 0.09$, what is the value of the account after 5 years?
    b. If $P = \$800$ and $i = 0.07$, what is the value of the account after 2 years?

c. If $P = \$100$ and $i = 0.12$, what is the value of the account after 10 years?
d. If $S_n = \$1,000$, $i = 0.08$, and $n = 5$, find P.
e. If $S_n = \$750$, $i = 0.10$, and $n = 8$, find P.

13. The following data show annual sales in millions over a 6-year period for a video game manufacturer. Find the natural logarithm for each sales figure. Compare actual with logarithmic sales data. Which set of data more accurately demonstrates the growth rate of sales over time for this manufacturer? Why?

Year	Sales, in millions
1977	12
1978	54
1979	110
1980	160
1981	200
1982	240

APPENDIX: Using the Table of Natural Logarithms

Values for logarithms to the base e are found in Table II. In Table II, N designates a number and the corresponding natural logarithm is read from the body of the table. Necessary instructional notes concerning decimal places and negative values are included with the table. Several examples from Table II are listed below. Each answer is the power to which e must be raised to equal N.

Example 8.8

1. $N = 21$; $\ln 21 = 3.04452$
2. $N = 0.6$; $\ln 0.6 = -0.51083$
3. $N = 4.6$; $\ln 4.6 = 1.52606$
4. $N = 523$; $\ln 523 = 6.25958$

For any N not in Table II, the value of the natural logarithm must be found by interpolation. Interpolation involves setting up a proportion that includes the unlisted N, the closest listed entry less than N and the closest listed entry greater than N, and the logarithms of the two entries. Example 8.9 will demonstrate formation of this proportion and the use of interpolation to find a logarithm.

Example 8.9

Find the natural logarithm of $N = 3.465$, which is not listed in Table II. Table II does include

$N = 3.46$; $\ln 3.46 = 1.24127$

$N = 3.47$; $\ln 3.47 = 1.24415$

Using these data, the following ratio is established, where x represents the unknown logarithm of 3.465:

$$\frac{3.470 - 3.465}{3.470 - 3.460} = \frac{1.24415 - x}{1.24415 - 1.24127}$$

As 3.465 is exactly halfway between the closest listed N values, x represents a natural logarithm value exactly halfway between the corresponding listed logarithms. Solving for x yields

$$\frac{3.470 - 3.465}{3.470 - 3.460} = \frac{1.24415 - x}{1.24415 - 1.24127}$$

$$\frac{0.005}{0.010} = \frac{1.24415 - x}{0.00288}$$

$$0.5 = \frac{1.24415 - x}{0.00288}$$

$$0.00144 = 1.24415 - x$$
$$x = 1.24415 - 0.00144 = 1.24271$$

Thus, the solution of this equation indicates that the natural logarithm of 3.465 is 1.24271. A similar procedure can be used for any number not included in Table II.

When logarithms are used to perform a numerical computation, the answer often must be converted back to numerical form. To accomplish this, it is necessary to find the antilogarithm of the logarithmic result. This result is in numerical form.

The *antilogarithm* of the logarithm x for any base a is equal to a^x. Thus, for the base e and the logarithmic value x,

antilogarithm $x = e^x$

The abbreviation for the antilogarithm of the natural logarithm x is

antiln $x = e^x$

To find antilogarithms, the body of Table II must be searched. If the antilogarithm in question is present, then interpolation is not required and there will be a corresponding number N in the margins representing the antilogarithm. Example 8.10 demonstrates this case.

Example 8.10

antiln $1.41342 = e^{1.41342} = 4.11$

or

ln $4.11 = 1.41342$

In this case, the body of Table II is searched for 1.41342 and the corresponding number N is 4.11.

If the natural logarithm is not in the body of Table II, interpolation is required to find N. A ratio similar to that used to find the unlisted logarithm for N is constructed. This ratio, however, is solved for the unknown antilogarithm. An example will demonstrate this technique.

Example 8.11
Find antiln 1.42600.

The solution to this problem requires finding the closest logarithms less than and greater than 1.42600 and corresponding antilogarithms. These values are

antiln $1.42552 = 4.16$

antiln $1.42792 = 4.17$

A ratio is formed where x represents the antilogarithm of 1.42600:

$$\frac{1.42600 - 1.42552}{1.42792 - 1.42552} = \frac{x - 4.16}{4.17 - 4.16}$$

Solving for x yields the following:

$$\frac{0.00048}{0.00240} = \frac{x - 4.16}{0.01}$$

$$0.2 = \frac{x - 4.16}{0.01}$$

$$0.002 = x - 4.16$$

$$x = 4.162$$

Thus, interpolation has shown that the antilogarithm of 1.42600 is 4.162.

To conclude this discussion, a problem using natural logarithms for its solution is presented.

Example 8.12
Find $(2.07)^8$ using natural logarithms. The answer is designated x.

$$(2.07)^8 = x$$
$$\ln [(2.07)^8] = \ln x$$
$$8(\ln 2.07) = \ln x$$
$$8(0.72755) = \ln x$$
$$5.8204 = \ln x$$

Using interpolation where antiln $5.8204 = x$,

$$\frac{5.82040 - 5.82008}{5.82305 - 5.82008} = \frac{x - 337}{338 - 337}$$

$$\frac{0.00032}{0.00297} = \frac{x - 337}{1}$$

$$0.1077 = x - 377$$
$$x = 337.1077 = 337.11$$
$$(2.07)^8 = 337.11$$

Although computers and calculators have eliminated the necessity for many of the calculations shown above, knowing how to use logarithmic tables remains an important part of one's quantitative skills.

EXERCISES

1. Use Table II to find the natural logarithm of each number below. Use interpolation where necessary.
    a. 16.3
    b. 0.556
    c. 3.855
    d. 194.4
    e. 58.3
    f. 172.45
    g. 0.0475
    h. 11.45
    i. 0.026
    j. 84.23
    k. 125.3
    l. 1.00
2. Find the value of X for each of the following. Use interpolation where necessary. The abbreviation ln refers to natural logarithms.
    a. $\ln X = 2.62$
    b. $\ln X = 1.483$
    c. $\ln X = -0.45$
    d. $\ln X = 1.0867$
    e. $\ln X = 0.00$
    f. $\ln X = 4.000$
3. Find answers to each problem below in natural logarithmic form. Then convert to numbers, using antilogarithms and interpolation where necessary.
    a. $Y = \sqrt[3]{24^2}$
    b. $Y = 15^{5/2}$
    c. $Y = (3.2)(54)$
    d. $Y = 6^{4/3}$
    e. $Y = 0.1^{-2.1}$
    f. $Y = 16^{-1/3}$
    g. $Y = 1^9$
    h. $Y = (16)(14)^{-2}$
4. For each value of X, find Y where $Y = \ln X$ and show the relationship between e^Y and X by using Table III. Round values of Y to two decimal places before using Table III.
    a. $X = 1.90$
    b. $X = 2.51$
    c. $X = 0.63$
    d. $X = 8.17$
    e. $X = 3.67$
    f. $X = 0.71$

9 The Mathematics of Finance

9.1 Introduction

Many business applications of nonlinear functions are found in the mathematics of finance. This broad topic includes procedures for combining interest rate and time considerations in addressing questions of loan payments, the value of various types of financial assets, and investment strategy.

In this chapter, a limited group of mathematical techniques used in the field of finance is presented. In many of the topics discussed, the independent variable is the number of time periods the analysis covers. The corresponding dependent variable often is a dollar measure representing the value of an account, a required periodic payment into an account, or the per period payment of a loan. The similarity of each technique to a functional relationship explained in Chapters 3, 4, and 8 is stressed where applicable.

For many of the following examples, "hand" calculation is shown so that the technique may be thoroughly understood. However, for many topics in the mathematics of finance, tables have been constructed to facilitate rapid computation. Tables applicable to some of the most common financial procedures are included at the end of the book. Each table is described and applied to examples in this chapter.

Prior to the discussion of specific financial topics, a short introduction to sequences and series in mathematics is presented in the next section. These ideas frequently are applied to financial computations and a general description will be useful to many readers.

Also, in the next section a nonfinancial application of a series is included to assist understanding of this concept.

9.2 Sequences and Series

A *sequence* is a succession of numbers formed according to some order, and a *series* is the sum of the numbers of a sequence. Because of this characteristic of series, the summation notation discussed in the appendix at the back of the book will be employed in the following discussion. Those unfamiliar with the summation notation may want to read the appendix at this point.

For a sequence, the domain of the function can be put in a one-to-one correspondence with a set of positive integers in order. Specific numbers in the domain are based on a predetermined order or "rule" for the sequence.

Example 9.1

Consider the sequence of numbers $1, \frac{1}{2}, \frac{1}{4}, \frac{1}{8}, \frac{1}{16}$. These numbers result from following the rule that each number in the sequence is equal to $\frac{1}{2}$ times the previous term, starting with the integer 1. If S_i represents any number in this sequence as specified by the rule, then the series for this five-member sequence can be expressed as

$$\sum_{i=1}^{5} S_i \quad \text{or} \quad \sum_{i=1}^{5} S_i = \frac{31}{16}$$

Finite and Infinite Series

A series is considered to be *finite* if the corresponding sequence includes a specific group of numbers and *infinite* if the sequence includes an unlimited group of numbers.

An infinite series can be either convergent or divergent. If there is a real number value for the sum of an unlimited sequence, it is referred to as a *convergent infinite series*. A *divergent infinite series* does not yield a real number value for the sum of an unlimited sequence. This difference also can be based on the existence or absence of a limit to the sum. However, as the definition of limit is not discussed until Chapter 10, the real number value criterion is more appropriate at this point.

The difference between convergent and divergent infinite series can be noted in summation notation. If S_i represents any number in the sequence and b is a real number, then a convergent series is expressed

$$\sum_{i=1}^{\infty} S_i = b$$

and a divergent series is

$$\sum_{i=1}^{\infty} S_i = \text{undefined}$$

Geometric Series

One series particularly useful in business and economics is the *geometric series*. A geometric series is the sum of a geometric progression. If a sequence starts with any number a and each successive term is multiplied by a constant r (referred to as the common ratio), the resulting set of numbers $a, ar, ar^2, \ldots, ar^n$ is a geometric progression. The sum of this geometric progression is the geometric series

$$\sum_{i=0}^{n} ar^i = a + ar + ar^2 + \cdots + ar^n$$

In the above expression, as n approaches infinity, the series is infinite. For the infinite case, when the common ratio r has an absolute value less than 1, the series is convergent. The infinite geometric series is divergent for all other values of r. The term of convergence for an infinite geometric series when r has an absolute value less than 1 is $a/(1 - r)$.

Summation notation can be used to express this convergent geometric series as follows:

$$\sum_{n=0}^{\infty} ar^n = a + ar + ar^2 + \cdots + ar^{\infty} = \frac{a}{1 - r}$$

where r has an absolute value of less than 1. If $a = 1$, the series is referred to as a *unit geometric series* and the term of convergence is $1/(1 - r)$.

These basic ideas of finite, infinite, convergent, and divergent series will be applied to financial computations as the chapter continues. At this point, however, consider a nonfinancial application of a series.

A Geometric Series: The Multiplier

The unit geometric series is used to represent the *multiplier*, a measurement encountered in economic analysis.

The multiplier measures the impact on national income of a $1 change in some component of expenditure (such as capital investment spending or government spending). Although much of the following discussion concerns increases in spending, the multiplier is applicable to both increases and decreases in spending.

In other words, the multiplier is a measure of the monetary impact of a $1 change in spending as it circulates through the economy. This $1 never stops circulating although the proportion of the original dollar becomes progressively smaller as it goes from one spending unit (household, business, etc.) to another. Consequently, the spending pattern for all units combined can be expressed as an infinite geometric progression. The sum of this progression is a convergent infinite geometric series with a term of convergence equal to $1/(1-r)$. This expression can be used to measure the total economic impact of a $1 change in spending.

What does r, the common ratio, represent in the geometric series for the multiplier? In the case of an increase in spending, as each individual receives part of the increase in income, he or she, in turn, spends only part of the amount received. When considering the entire economy, this portion spent is a constant called the *marginal propensity to consume*.

The marginal propensity to consume is the portion of an additional dollar of income which is spent by the recipient (the remainder is saved). For example, if the marginal propensity to consume is 0.9, each spending unit spends 90 percent of any increase in income and saves 10 percent. Each spending unit in the circulation chain receives 90 percent of the previous recipient's increase in income. Therefore, the common ratio r in the geometric series for the multiplier is the marginal propensity to consume. Finally, as it is assumed that the marginal propensity to consume is less than 1 (or 100 percent), the multiplier can be described by a convergent infinite geometric series with a convergence term of $1/(1-r)$.

Example 9.2

Researchers have determined that the national marginal propensity to consume is 0.8. This means that the typical spending unit spends $0.80 of any additional $1 of income. In this case, the full impact of $1 in new spending is expressed by the geometric series

$$\sum_{n=0}^{\infty} ar^n = 1 + (1)(0.8) + (1)(0.8)^2 + \cdots + (1)(0.8)^{\infty}$$

$$= \frac{1}{1-0.8} = \frac{1}{1-r} = 5$$

Since this series converges to $1/(1-r)$, the full economic impact of this additional $1 of spending is $1/(1-0.8) = 1/0.2 = \$5$. Thus, it is determined that $1 of additional spending results in $5 of additional national income at the end of its infinitely long circulation process.

The multiplier can be applied to dollar amounts other than $1, as only the numerator, or the value of a, must be changed. With a marginal propensity to consume r of 0.8, the total economic impact of a $3 billion government public works project will be $15 billion, as $3/(1-0.8) = 3/0.2 = 15$.

Finally, note that the only change in the convergence term for a reduction in spending is that the numerator a will be a negative number. For example, a $3 billion reduction in government spending with $r = 0.8$ will cause a $15 billion reduction in national income, as $-3/(1 - 0.8) = -3/0.2 = -15$.

The multiplier is only one of many applications using series and sequences. Applications of this concept to the mathematics of finance will be presented as the chapter continues.

EXERCISES

1. List the first five numbers for the geometric progression specified by each value of a and r given below.
   a. $a = 2, r = \frac{1}{2}$ d. $a = 6, r = -\frac{1}{2}$
   b. $a = 12, r = \frac{1}{3}$ e. $a = 4, r = 2$
   c. $a = 10, r = \frac{1}{4}$

2. Find the value of the geometric series for the first four numbers of each geometric progression with a and r as designated below.
   a. $a = 4, r = \frac{1}{4}$ d. $a = 10, r = -2$
   b. $a = 4, r = -\frac{1}{4}$ e. $a = 15, r = \frac{1}{3}$
   c. $a = 8, r = \frac{3}{2}$

3. Find the value of the convergence term for the infinite geometric series associated with the following values for a and r:
   a. $a = 1, r = \frac{5}{6}$ e. $a = 14, r = \frac{1}{3}$
   b. $a = 1, r = \frac{9}{10}$ f. $a = 260, r = \frac{1}{10}$
   c. $a = 1, r = \frac{2}{3}$ g. $a = -64, r = \frac{1}{5}$
   d. $a = 1, r = \frac{7}{9}$ h. $a = -20, r = \frac{14}{15}$

4. For each marginal propensity to consume (MPC) below, find the value of the multiplier. From these results, what can you conclude about the relationship between the value of the multiplier and the MPC?
   a. MPC $= 0.75$ d. MPC $= 0.5$
   b. MPC $= 0.9$ e. MPC $= 0.3$
   c. MPC $= 0.95$

5. Given an MPC of 0.75, determine the impact on national income of each of the following changes in spending:
   a. Private investment increases by $4 billion.
   b. Government spending decreases by $2 billion.
   c. Government spending increases by $1.5 billion.
   d. Private investment increases by $10 billion at the same time that government spending decreases by $7.5 billion.

9.3 Simple Interest and Simple Discount

Usually, interest rates are quoted as yearly rates in percentage terms, such as 11 percent per year. However, for financial computations, the decimal representation, 0.11 per year, is used.

"Simple" interest, or interest that is not compounded, is equal to the *principal* (the initial amount) of the account times the product of the yearly interest rate and the number of years (or fraction of a year) over which the money is invested. This can be expressed by the following equation:

$$I = Prt$$

where I = amount of interest earned
P = principal of the account
r = annual interest rate
t = number of years or fractions of a year

The value of an account, including the principal plus all interest earned over a period of time, can be specified by S in the following expression which uses the interest formula and related abbreviations:

$$S = P + I \qquad S = P + Prt \quad \text{or} \quad S = P(1 + rt)$$

The last form above, $S = P(1 + rt)$, is useful for many extensions in the mathematics of finance.

Example 9.3

To demonstrate the computation of simple interest and the future value of an account, consider the total value of a $4000 principal after 2 years in a savings account which pays 7 percent per year without compounding. The third form of S yields this amount:

$$S = P(1 + rt)$$

where P = 4000
r = 0.07
t = 2

Therefore,

$$\begin{aligned} S &= \$4000[1 + 0.07(2)] \\ &= 4000(1.14) \\ &= \$4560 \end{aligned}$$

This analysis shows that after 2 years the account is worth $4560, of which $4000 is principal and $560 is interest earned.

In many financial transactions, it is important to estimate the *present value* of a stated or given future amount of money. In the above example, an individual will have an account of $4560 after 2 years, with an original principal of $4000. Thus, $4560 after 2 years at an annual interest rate of 7 percent has a present value of $4000. The process used to describe computation of the $4000 figure from the future value ($4560) is referred to as "simple discounting."

Using notation from the formula above, the computation of present value necessitates solving for P given S, an annual interest rate r, and the number of years or fractions of years t. Therefore, the formula for computing the simple present value of a future amount is the following:

$$P = \frac{S}{1 + rt}$$

Example 9.4
An individual wants to know how much to invest now in an account earning 8 percent per year (not compounded) so that there will be $2000 in the account at the end of 2 years. Thus,

$$P = \frac{S}{1 + rt}$$

where $S = 2000$
$r = 0.08$
$t = 2$

By substitution,

$$P = \frac{2000}{1 + (0.08)(2)}$$

$$= \frac{2000}{1.16}$$

$$= 1724.14$$

Therefore, $1724.14 must be put in an account earning 8 percent per year to assure that the depositor has $2000 at the end of 2 years.

The estimation of the future and present values of an account is applied more widely in situations where interest is compounded. Thus, formulas and applications of compound interest and compound discounting are discussed in the following sections.

9.4 Compound Interest

Extension of interest computations to applications with compounding requires the definition of several terms. For the following discussion, i represents the *per period* interest rate and n designates the number of time periods.

The per period interest rate i is determined by dividing the annual nominal interest rate (r above) by the number of compounding periods in the year. The number of compounding periods in the year times the number of years yields n. For example, an 8 percent annual interest rate compounded quarterly yields a per period interest rate of 2 percent ($i = 0.02$). Similarly, if the 2 percent quarterly rate is paid on a 5-year savings certificate, the value of n is 20 (4 periods per year × 5 years).

Example 9.5
Determine the future value of a savings account with a $1500 principal at the end of 3 years with interest compounded annually at 6 percent.

Notice that the future amount S in the account after the first year is equal to

$$S_1 = P(1 + 0.06)$$

Similarly, after the second year the value of the account is S_2:

$$S_2 = S_1(1 + 0.06)$$

or
$$S_2 = P(1 + 0.06)(1 + 0.06)$$
$$= P(1.06)^2$$

Finally, after the third year, the amount S_3 is

$$S_3 = S_2(1 + 0.06)$$

or
$$S_3 = P(1 + 0.06)(1 + 0.06)(1 + 0.06)$$
$$= P(1.06)^3$$

The generalization that can be derived from this example is that the future value S_n of a principal P in an account at the end of n time periods with interest compounded at the rate of i percent per period is

$$S_n = P(1 + i)^n$$

Therefore, $1500 in principal at the end of 3 years at 6 percent per year compounded annually will be worth $1786.53, as the following demonstrates:

$$S_3 = 1500(1 + 0.06)^3$$
$$= 1500(1.19102)$$
$$= 1786.53$$

As may be apparent to readers, hand calculation of compound interest problems becomes difficult as n increases. Table IV at the end of the book is a compound interest table listing the value of the term $(1 + i)^n$ for various combinations of i and n. These tabular values are the future value of $1 after n periods with a compounded interest rate of i per period. Multiplying appropriate tabular values by the amount of the principal yields the value S_n. An example will demonstrate the use of Table IV.

Example 9.6
An investor wants to compute the value of an account at the end of 5 years with a $2000 principal and interest compounded quarterly at an 8 percent annual rate. For this problem, $i = 0.08 \div 4 = 0.02$; therefore, the per period interest rate is 2 percent. The value of n is 20 as there are 5 years with four compounding periods in each.

The value from Table IV for $i = 0.02$ and $n = 20$ is 1.48595. This represents the future value of $1 at the end of the 20 time periods with an interest rate of 2 percent compounded per period. Therefore, the account will be worth $2971.90 as shown below:

$$S_{20} = P(1 + i)^n$$
$$= 2000(1.48595)$$
$$= \$2971.90$$

9.5 Present Value with Compounding

Determination of the present value corresponding to a stated future amount is similar to the interest compounding process shown above. However, for this type of problem, the factor $(1 + i)^n$ represents the denominator, and is divided into the future amount. This yields the principal P required to accumulate a future amount S_n:

$$P = \frac{S_n}{(1 + i)^n}$$

In this case, also, i is the per period interest rate and n is the number of time periods.

Example 9.7
An individual wants to determine the present value of an account which will be worth $3000 at the end of 4 years with interest compounded annually at 5 percent per year. In other words, how much should the individual deposit now to yield $3000 at the end of 4 years?

From the previous discussion, the present value of S without compounding was stated as

$$P = \frac{S}{1 + rt}$$

Therefore, for this problem the present value of $3000 for 1 year in the future is P_1:

$$P_1 = \frac{3000}{1 + 0.05}$$

The present value needed to have $3000 two years in the future is stated as P_2:

$$P_2 = \frac{3000}{1 + 0.05} \frac{1}{1 + 0.05} = \frac{3000}{(1 + 0.05)^2}$$

This process can be extended to compute the present value P_n of any stated amount S at the end of n time periods with interest compounded at i percent per period. This formula is

$$P_n = \frac{S_n}{(1 + i)^n} = S_n(1 + i)^{-n}$$

Therefore, the present value required to accumulate $3000 four years from now at a 5 percent annual compounded interest rate is P_4:

$$P_4 = \frac{3000}{(1 + 0.05)^4} = 3000(1 + 0.05)^{-4}$$

Hand calculation shows that $(1.05)^4 = 1.215506$. Thus, the amount of money which must be deposited now is P_4:

$$P_4 = \frac{3000}{1.215506} = 3000 \left(\frac{1}{1.215506}\right) = (3000)(0.822702) = 2468.11$$

In the second expression for P_4, the second factor also is equal to the $1/1.215506 = 0.822702$. In other words, the present value of $1 in 4 years at a 5 percent interest rate annually compounded is $0.822702. This form, or $(1 + i)^{-n}$, is employed in Table V to give the present value of $1 for various time periods n and per period interest rate i combinations. An example will demonstrate the use of Table V.

Example 9.8
Find the present value of $7500 five years from now if interest is compounded quarterly at an 8 percent annual interest rate. Thus, $S_{20} = \$7500$, $i = 0.02$ and $n = 20$ (5 years with quarterly compounding).

To solve this problem, the present value P_{20} which $1 will have 20 time periods (quarters) from now, $(1 + i)^{-20}$, must be evaluated. As hand calculation is burdensome in this case, Table V yields this answer as $(1 + i)^{-20} = 0.672971$. Thus, it is determined that $P = (S_n)(1 + i)^{-n} = (7500)(0.672971) = \$5047.28$. This amount must be placed in the account today to have $7500 in 5 years.

EXERCISES

1. Use Table IV to find the future value of $1 deposited in an account for each stated interest rate and number of time periods.
    a. 16 percent annually, compounded quarterly for 3 years.
    b. 8 percent annually, compounded annually for 10 years.
    c. 6 percent annually, compounded semiannually for 20 years.
    d. 12 percent annually, compounded monthly for 6 months.
    e. 8 percent annually, compounded semiannually for 1 year.
2. Use Table V to find the present value of $1 at the end of the following number of time periods with interest paid at the stated rate:
    a. 12 percent annually, compounded quarterly for 8 years.
    b. 4 percent annually, compounded semiannually for 20 years.
    c. 8 percent annually, compounded annually for 1 year.
    d. 10 percent annually, compounded semiannually for 5 years.
    e. 12 percent annually, compounded quarterly for 6 months.

3. What is the value of a $2500 principal amount after 3 years if interest is compounded at the annual rate of 6 percent?
4. What is the value of a $10,000 principal amount after 6 years at an 8 percent annual interest rate compounded quarterly?
5. What is the difference in interest earned between a 10 percent and an 8 percent annual rate compounded semiannually for 5 years on an initial $3000 principal?
6. How much should an individual deposit today to have a $3000 balance in a savings account after 5 years if interest is compounded quarterly at a 12 percent annual rate?
7. How much must be deposited today to have $10,000 in an account after 15 years with interest compounded semiannually at an 8 percent annual rate?
8. If annual interest rates fall from 8 to 6 percent, how much more must be deposited in an account to have $5000 in 3 years, if both rates are compounded semiannually?
9. An account earning an 8 percent annual interest rate compounded quarterly was established 6 years ago. Today, the account is worth $7,500. What was the initial amount in the account?
10. What amount of money deposited today at a 12 percent annual rate compounded monthly will provide exactly enough to pay for $3,000 in college fees due 3 years from now?

9.6 The Future Value of an Annuity

To this point of the chapter, examples have been limited to the effects of compounding on the future value or the present value of a stated amount of money. Often, however, amounts are deposited into an account or paid periodically over time. Financial instruments exhibiting this characteristic of periodic payment are called *annuities*. Examples are monthly payments into a savings account, car payments, mortgages, and payments to a retirement fund. The following sections discuss procedures for computing the future value and the present value of annuities.

For this discussion, examples are limited to ordinary annuities. This means that payments or deposits are made at the end of the stated interest period. Thus, interest is earned at the end of each period on the previous balance. Example 9.9 clarifies the concept of the future value of an ordinary annuity.

Example 9.9
An individual wants to deposit $600 at the beginning of each year for 4 years into an ordinary annuity account which pays 7 percent interest per year compounded annually. The first payment will be made on January 1, 1986, and the last will be made on January 1, 1989. What is the value of this

account after the last deposit is made on January 1, 1989? Table 9.1 summarizes the increases in the value of the annuity.

The initial deposit of January 1, 1986, receives 7 percent interest on January 1, 1987 and interest on the compounded amount on January 1, 1988 and January 1, 1989. Using the formula for compound interest yields a value of this deposit on January 1, 1989 of $(600)(1.07)^3 = \$735.03$.

Similarly, the deposit made on January 1, 1987 earns two interest payments and the deposit on January 1, 1988, earns only 1 year of interest. The final deposit of $600 on January 1, 1989 earns no interest. These amounts also are shown in Table 9.1. The value of the annuity on January 1, 1989, is the sum of these compounded values of $2663.97. This example describes an ordinary annuity. It is impractical, in all cases, to find the sum of each year's compounded amount. Thus, a formula exists for determining the future value of an annuity. This formula uses the concept of a unit geometric series introduced in Section 9.2.

As described in Section 9.2, a unit geometric series is the sum of a geometric progression where the first term is 1 and each successive term is multiplied by a constant r. In contrast to the use of an infinite geometric series to determine the multiplier, for annuity problems r is greater than 1 as it represents the interest term $1 + i$ (where i is the per period interest rate). As r is greater than 1, the geometric series is not convergent.

The formula for n terms of a geometric series s_n where r is greater than 1 is

$$s_n = \frac{r^n - 1}{r - 1}$$

Substituting $1 + i$ for r in this equation gives the expression for the future value of a $1 per period payment over n periods at an interest rate of i percent per period. For R dollars per period, s_n is adjusted as follows:

$$S_n = R \left[\frac{(1 + i)^n - 1}{i} \right]$$

TABLE 9.1 Computation of the Future Value of an Annuity

Deposit Date	Value of Each Deposit on January 1, 1989
January 1, 1986	$(600)(1.07)^3 = \$\ 735.03$
January 1, 1987	$(600)(1.07)^2 =\ \ \ 686.94$
January 1, 1988	$(600)(1.07)^1 =\ \ \ 642.00$
January 1, 1989	$=\ \ \ 600.00$
Total value of annuity on January 1, 1989	$2663.97

The Mathematics of Finance   243

Table VI lists future values of a $1 per period payment for various numbers of time periods n and interest rates i, or s_n. Prior to an application of this table, consider the following hand calculation.

Example 9.10
If an individual deposits $500 at the end of each year for 5 years into a savings account paying 8 percent per year compounded annually, what is the total value of the account at the end of 5 years?

For this problem, $i = 0.08$, $n = 5$, and $R = 500$. Therefore, the value of the annuity is given as S_5:

$$S_5 = 500\left[\frac{(1 + 0.08)^5 - 1}{0.08}\right]$$

Hand calculation establishes that the term $(1.08)^5$ is equal to 1.469328. Therefore, the value of the account at the end of 5 years is 2933.30, as the following computation demonstrates:

$$S_5 = 500\left(\frac{1.469328 - 1}{0.08}\right)$$

$$= 500\left(\frac{0.469328}{0.08}\right)$$

$$= 500(5.86660)$$

$$= \$2933.30$$

The number in parentheses or $5.86660, represents the future value of a $1 payment per period for five periods with interest of 8 percent compounded at the end of each period.

Determination of the future value of a $1 payment per period for various interest rates and time periods is facilitated by Table VI. Example 9.11 describes the use of Table VI in solving a problem.

Example 9.11
If an individual deposits $200 at the end of every quarter into an account which yields 12 percent per year compounded quarterly, what is the value of the account in 3 years?

Table VI can be used to find this value. In this problem $i = 0.12/4 = 0.03$ and $n = 12 = $ (3 years)(four periods per year). The tabular value of a $1 annuity for $i = 0.03$ and $n = 12$ is $14.19203. Consequently, the value of the annuity account is $2,838.41 as shown below:

$$S_{12} = R(s_{12})$$

$$= 200(14.19203) = 2838.406$$

$$= \$2838.41 \quad \text{(rounding to the nearest \$0.01)}$$

Sinking Funds

Table VI also can be used to determine the periodic payment R required to accumulate a specified amount S_n at the end of a number of time periods n.

Many businesses must have an amount of money on hand at the end of a stated time period to pay off bonds or other types of debt. Accounts holding such committed amounts are referred to as *sinking funds*. A relevant question to businesses is determination of the periodic payment required to accumulate the total amount. This required payment can be derived by use of the formula for the future value of an ordinary annuity.

In the previous example, it was shown that the accumulated amount in an annuity S_n is equal to R, the periodic payment, times the value of a $1 per period payment over n periods, or

$$S_n = R\left[\frac{(1+i)^n - 1}{i}\right]$$

To determine the required periodic payment, this equation is solved for R as shown below:

$$R = \frac{S_n}{\frac{(1+i)^n - 1}{i}}$$

The expression in brackets also can be found in Table VI for various i and n.

Example 9.12

A firm wants to set aside an amount each quarter for 5 years which will result in an accumulated amount sufficient to pay off a $600,000 loan at the end of the period. Payments are to be paid into an account yielding a 16 percent annual rate of interest compounded quarterly.

The quarterly payments are equal to R in the following expression.

$$R = \frac{S_n}{\frac{(1+i)^n - 1}{i}}$$

where $S_n = 600,000$
$i = 0.04$
$n = 20$

The value of a $1 per period payment for 20 periods at 4 percent is found in Table VI to be $29.77808. Therefore, the necessary quarterly payment is computed below to be $20,149.05:

$$R = \frac{600,000}{29.77808} = \$20,149.05$$

Thus, the firm must deposit $20,149.05 each quarter into this account in order to have $600,000 at the end of 5 years.

Some sets of financial tables list the amount $1/\{[(1 + i)^n - 1]/i\}$, which can be multiplied by S_n to yield the periodic payment. The amount $1/\{[(1 + i)^n - 1]/i\}$ represents the per period equivalent of $1 in future value. Using the situation as described above, this amount is $0.03358175, as

$$\frac{1}{29.77808} = \$0.03358175$$

This means that $0.03358175 invested per period at 4 percent for 20 periods will yield $1. In addition, $(0.03358175)(600,000) = 20,149.05$, also represents the required payment into the sinking fund.

Students should be familiar with both methods of solving for a periodic payment although the exclusion of tabular values for $1/\{[(1 + i)^n - 1]/i\}$ makes only the first method applicable to this textbook.

EXERCISES

1. Find the value of an ordinary annuity with a $1 payment per period for the following interest rates and numbers of years:
   a. Quarterly payments for 3 years at an 8 percent annual interest rate compounded quarterly.
   b. Semiannual payments for 5 years at a 10 percent annual interest rate compounded semiannually.
   c. Annual payments for 30 years at an 8 percent interest rate compounded annually.
   d. Monthly payments for 6 months at a 24 percent annual interest rate compounded monthly.

2. Find the future amount of each ordinary annuity below:
   a. $100 per month for 2 years at a 12 percent annual rate compounded monthly.
   b. $500 every quarter for 5 years at an 8 percent annual rate compounded quarterly.
   c. $1000 every six months for 15 years at a 10 percent annual rate compounded semiannually.
   d. $300 per month for 30 months at a 12 percent annual rate compounded monthly.

3. Find the per period equivalent of $1 in future value for the following per period interest rates i and numbers of time periods n:
   a. $i = 0.04, n = 20$ d. $i = 0.01, n = 36$
   b. $i = 0.06, n = 10$ e. $i = 0.04, n = 24$
   c. $i = 0.08, n = 2$

4. An individual deposits $50 at the end of each month into an account which yields an annual interest rate of 12 percent compounded monthly. What is the value of the account at the end of 18 months?

Mathematics for Business and Economics   **246**

5. Mr. and Mrs. Brown want to deposit $500 at the end of every 6 months for 5 years into an annuity account to pay for their daughter's first year in college. It is expected that the first year will cost $5000. The annuity account yields an interest rate of 10 percent per year compounded semiannually. Will the Browns save enough in this account to pay for their daughter's first year in college?

6. A firm is establishing an interest-bearing contingency fund yielding 16 percent per year compounded quarterly. The firm believes that it will be able to deposit $10,000 into the fund at the end of each quarter. What will be the value of the contingency fund at the end of 2 years?

7. A recently married couple wants to establish a savings account to provide enough for them to make a $15,000 down payment on a home in 6 years. The account pays 12 percent per year compounded semiannually. How much should they deposit at the end of every 6 months to assure an exactly sufficient amount in this account?

8. A firm wants to set aside an amount each quarter during the next 2 years to have $325,000 on hand to buy a technologically superior computer expected on the market by that time. How much should the firm place in the account each quarter if the account yields an annual interest rate of 16 percent compounded quarterly?

9. An individual deposits $250 at the end of each 6-month period into a retirement account paying 8 percent annually compounded semiannually. What will be the amount in the account when the person retires in 15 years?

10. Bonds worth $2 million issued by a corporation must be redeemed in 3 years. Corporate officials want to determine how much to deposit each quarter into a sinking fund in order to have a sufficient amount to pay all bondholders on time. The firm will earn a 12 percent annual rate compounded quarterly on all deposits. What is the required quarterly deposit?

9.7   The Present Value of an Annuity

Often, an individual or business wants to invest an amount into an account in order to receive payments of a specified sum from the account at designated future times, for example yearly or monthly. Receipt of the first payment is one time period after the initial deposit. An assumption of this type of analysis is that the account will have a balance of zero after the last payment is received.

Finding the amount of the initial deposit requires determination of the present value of each payment. An example will demonstrate computation of the present value of an annuity.

Example 9.13

A retired person wants to know how much to deposit into a 7 percent annually compounded account to provide for four annual $1200 withdrawals from principal and accumulated interest. The first withdrawal will be 1 year after the initial deposit and the value of the account will be zero after the four withdrawals are made.

To determine the required deposit, the present value of each of the four $1200 withdrawals must be computed. Using the present value formula from Section 9.5, the four present value figures are shown in Table 9.2. For example, the present value of the withdrawal made at the end of year 3 is equal to $(\$1200)(1.07)^{-3}$. Each present value is found in the same way.

Thus, this individual must deposit $4064.65 in an account today to receive four yearly payments of $1200 each from the account. The value of the account will be zero after the last withdrawal.

Although Example 9.13 describes the process of finding the present value of an annuity, it may be apparent to readers that finding the sum of present values is a rather tedious process. Thus, a more efficient formula and corresponding table have been developed to find the present value of an annuity. The following discusses these aids.

Computation of the present value of an annuity entails finding the future value of the annuity and discounting it to the present. As described in Section 9.6, the future value of a $1 annuity payment s_n is equal to the expression

1. $s_n = \dfrac{(1 + i)^n - 1}{i}$

Similarly, the compound discount factor previously has been shown to be

2. $(1 + i)^{-n}$

Multiplication of these two expressions yields the equation for a $1 present value of an annuity paid over n periods at an interest rate of i percent per period. This is shown as a_n:

3. $a_n = \left[\dfrac{(1 + i)^n - 1}{i} \right](1 + i)^{-n}$

TABLE 9.2 Computation of the Present Value of an Annuity

Year	Present Value of Withdrawal at End of Year
1	$1200(1.07)^{-1}$ = $1121.49
2	$1200(1.07)^{-2}$ = 1048.13
3	$1200(1.07)^{-3}$ = 979.56
4	$1200(1.07)^{-4}$ = 915.47
Total required deposit	$4064.65

Multiplication yields expression 4, which equals a_n for application purposes:

4. $a_n = \dfrac{1 - (1 + i)^{-n}}{i}$

Expression 4 measures the present value of $1 placed in an annuity account for n periods at an interest rate of i percent per period. To receive R dollars per period with payments made at the end of each of n periods, R is multiplied by a_n:

5. $A_n = Ra_n = R\left[\dfrac{1 - (1 + i)^{-n}}{i}\right]$

The amount A_n represents a principal which, when added to accumulated interest, allows R dollars per period to be paid to the owner of the account. At the end of the last time period, A_n will be equal to zero.

Example 9.14

For the case of the retired person planning to receive $1200 per year for 4 years from an account paying 7 percent interest compounded annually, the required investment is found using expression 5 above and hand calculation.

$A_n = Ra_n$

$= 1200 \left[\dfrac{1 - (1 + 0.07)^{-4}}{0.07}\right]$

As $(1.07)^{-4} = \dfrac{1}{(1.07)^4} = \dfrac{1}{1.310796} = 0.7628952$, then

$A_n = 1200 \left(\dfrac{1 - 0.7628952}{0.07}\right)$

$= 1200 \left(\dfrac{0.2371048}{0.07}\right)$

$= 1200(3.38721)$

$= 4064.65$

These computations show that the individual must deposit $4064.65 today to receive four yearly payments of $1200, beginning 1 year from today. After the last payment 4 years from today, the value of the account will be zero. This confirms the result found by summation of the present values in Example 9.13.

In this example a_n is equal to $3.38721. This means that $3.38721 must be deposited today in a 7 percent annually compounded account to yield four consecutive annual payments of $1 each from the account.

Values for the expression $a_n = [1 - (1 + i)^{-n}]/i$, or the present value of $1 per time period for various interest rates and numbers of time periods are listed in Table VII. An example will explain the use of this table.

Example 9.15
An investor wants to receive $500 semiannually for 8 years from a savings certificate which yields 10 percent interest per year compounded semiannually. The investor wants to know how much to place in the certificate account to assure receipt of the $500 payments beginning 6 months from the day of deposit.

In this case, $R = 500$, $i = 0.10/2 = 0.05$ and $n = 16$. Table VII gives the present value of $1 per period for 16 time periods at 5 percent interest compounded per period a_{16} as $10.83777. Consequently, the required initial investment is equal to A_{16} as follows:

$$A_{16} = 500 \left[\frac{1 - (1 + 0.05)^{-16}}{0.05} \right]$$
$$= 500(10.83777)$$
$$= \$5418.88$$

This analysis shows that an investment of $5418.88 today at 10 percent compounded semiannually will enable an individual to receive $500 every 6 months for the next 8 years. The first payment will be received 6 months after initial deposit and the total, A_{16}, will be exhausted at the end of the 8-year period.

Loan Amortization

The expression for the present value of an annuity, $A_n = Ra_n$, can be employed in modified form to determine the periodic payment required on consumer, commercial, and home mortgage loans. For these situations A_n, or present value in the previous analysis, is equivalent to the principal of the loan. The principal is referred to by the symbol P.

The objective of a loan amortization analysis is to determine the periodic payment R given the principal P, an interest rate per compounding period i, and the number of compounding periods n.

If P is similar to A_n in expression 5 above, the periodic payment can be shown to be given by

$$R = \frac{P}{[1 - (1 + i)^{-n}]/i} = P \left[\frac{i}{1 - (1 + i)^{-n}} \right]$$

The last expression in brackets represents the per period equivalent of $1 present value. This is also called the *capital recovery factor*.

The bracketed expression measures the required payment per period on a loan of $1 at an interest rate of i percent per period for n periods. Values for the capital recovery factor for various per period interest rates and numbers of periods are listed in Table VIII. Two examples will explain further the process of loan amortization and the application of Table VIII.

Example 9.16

An accountant wants to borrow $5000 for 2 years to purchase a small computer. The interest rate charged is 12 percent compounded semiannually. Payments must be made on the loan every 6 months. Before discussing the loan with bank officials, the accountant would like to know the required payments on the computer.

In determining the required payments, it should be kept in mind that the sum of the present values for all periodic payments must equal the principal of the loan, or $5000. By adhering to this rule, the sum of the periodic payments will include the principal plus all interest in accordance with the stated interest rate and number of compounding periods.

The periodic payment R is equal to the principal multiplied by the per period equivalent of $1 present value. As $P = \$5000$, $i = 0.12/2 = 0.06$ per time period and $n = $ (2 years) (two payments per year) $= 4$, R can be found by the following expression:

$$R = P\left[\frac{i}{1 - (1 + i)^{-n}}\right]$$

$$= 5000\left[\frac{0.06}{1 - (1 + 0.06)^{-4}}\right]$$

The value of the expression in brackets is found in Table VIII for $i = 0.06$ and $n = 4$. Therefore, the per period equivalent of $1 present value for this problem is $0.288591. This means that four payments of $0.288591 will be required to amortize each $1 borrowed in order to compensate the bank for both principal and interest. The value for R, the required payment, is therefore

$$R = (5000)(0.288591) = \$1442.96$$

Thus, the accountant must pay $1442.96 every 6 months to pay back the loan and interest charges during the 2-year period.

Example 9.17

Estimate the monthly payments on a $2000 consumer loan for 3 years at an interest rate of 12 percent compounded monthly.

For this problem, $P = 2000$, $i = 0.01$, and $n = 36$. The expression for R is the following:

$$R = 2000\left[\frac{0.01}{1 - (1 + 0.01)^{-36}}\right]$$

The expression in brackets, or the per period equivalent of $1 present value for $n = 36$ and $i = 0.01$, is found in Table VIII. This value is 0.033214. Consequently, as shown below, monthly payments R are $66.43 (rounding to the nearest $0.01).

$R = 2000(0.033214)$
$= \$66.43$

This monthly payment leads to total payments of $2391.48 ($66.43 × 36) of which $391.48 represents total interest paid on the loan.

As a final point, note the similarity between the principal of a loan P and the present value of an annuity A_n. The only difference is in the application of the per period analysis. The term R in a loan amortization problem represents per period payments and, in an annuity, R represents payments received at stated time periods after an initial deposit.

EXERCISES

1. Find the present value of $1 per compounding period placed in an annuity for the following time periods and interest rates:
   a. 8 years at 12 percent per year compounded quarterly.
   b. 20 years at 8 percent per year compounded annually.
   c. 15 years at 8 percent per year compounded every 6 months.
   d. 3 years at 16 percent per year compounded quarterly.
2. Find the per period payment required to amortize a loan of $1 for each stated time period and interest rate.
   a. 20 years at 8 percent per year compounded annually.
   b. 8 years at 20 percent per year compounded quarterly.
   c. 10 years at 4 percent per year compounded semiannually.
   d. 2 years at 24 percent per year compounded monthly.
3. Find the present value of each of the following per period payments for the stated interest rate and time:
   a. $100 per month for 2 years with annual interest of 12 percent compounded monthly.
   b. $1000 yearly for 20 years with annual interest of 8 percent compounded annually.
   c. $2000 every 6 months for 6 years with annual interest of 10 percent compounded semiannually.
   d. $250 each quarter for 6 years with annual interest of 16 percent compounded quarterly.
4. Find the periodic payment required to amortize the following loans:
   a. Semiannual payments on a $30,000 loan for 20 years at a 10 percent annual interest rate compounded semiannually.
   b. Quarterly payments on a $275,000 loan for 5 years at a 16 percent per year quarterly compounded rate.
   c. Monthly payments on a $6000 loan for 3 years at a 24 percent per year interest rate compounded monthly.
   d. Semiannual payments on a loan of $800,000 for 10 years at an interest rate of 12 percent per year compounded semiannually.
5. George Smith is coordinating the construction of his new house. To meet

unexpected building expenses, he wants to deposit enough money in an account to be able to withdraw $300 each month for the next 6 months. The account pays 12 percent per year compounded monthly. How much should Mr. Smith deposit in the account today to have enough for these six withdrawals, assuming that the value of the account will be zero after 6 months?

6. A retired couple deposits $2200 in a savings account in anticipation of withdrawing $500 at the end of each year for the next 5 years to use for vacations. The account pays a yearly interest rate of 8 percent compounded annually. The couple wants the account balance to be zero at the end of 5 years. Has the correct amount been deposited into the account? If not, what is the correct amount?

7. A firm wants to establish a fund to use for computer time expenses over the next 3 years. The firm wants to withdraw $2000 each quarter over this 3-year period. Interest on the account is 16 percent per year compounded quarterly. How much should the firm initially place in the account to provide for these expenses?

8. An individual plans to borrow $4000 to buy a new car and would like to keep the monthly payments below $125 a month. The loan will be for 3 years at a 12 percent annual rate compounded monthly. Will the monthly payments exceed the $125 per month limit established by the borrower?

9. A medium-sized food distributor has borrowed $95,000 to buy a small warehouse. The loan is for 10 years at an annual interest rate of 16 percent compounded quarterly. What is the amount of the quarterly payments which the firm must make to amortize this loan?

10. A self-employed sales representative must borrow $2000 from his local bank to meet his federal income tax obligation. The money has been borrowed for 6 months at an annual interest rate of 12 percent compounded monthly. What are the monthly payments required to amortize this loan?

9.8 A Perpetuity as an Infinite Geometric Series

A *perpetuity* is a type of annuity with payments from a principal beginning on a given date and continuing forever. Examples of perpetuities are funds established for scholarships, awards, and the maintenance of parks and museums.

Computations for perpetuities involve the use of the infinite geometric series as related to the present value of an annuity. An example will help to explain determination of the value of a perpetuity.

Example 9.18
A philanthropist wants to establish a scholarship at his former university which will award $800 a year to a deserving student. The philanthropist wants to determine how much to place in an account yielding 7 percent

interest compounded annually to permit perpetual payment of the scholarship from interest earned each year. The scholarship is to be paid the first year prior to any interest being earned.

Given the previous information, it can be concluded that the present value required to carry out the scholarship program is equal to the geometric series with terms as follows:

$$800 + 800(1.07)^{-1} + 800(1.07)^{-2} + \cdots$$

The first term represents the $800 award made prior to any interest being earned. Each successive term represents the present value of $800 for the stated number of years into the future (as shown by the absolute value of the exponent of 1.07).

This series is similar to the convergent geometric series used in Section 9.2 to explain the multiplier. In this case, $a = 800$ and $r = (1 + i)^{-1}$, where i is the per period interest rate (7 percent). The series can be expressed by the following summation:

$$S_n = \sum_{n=0}^{\infty} 800(1.07)^{-n}$$

As the term $(1.07)^{-n}$ is less than 1, the series converges to the expression shown below (using notation for a and r from Section 9.2 and substituting P for the general term S_n).

$$P = \sum_{n=0}^{\infty} (800)(1.07)^{-n} = \frac{a}{1-r} = \frac{800}{1-(1.07)^{-1}}$$

This expression yields the required amount P for the perpetuity as follows:

$$P = \frac{800}{1-(1.07)^{-1}} = \frac{800}{1-1/1.07}$$

$$= \frac{800}{1-0.9345794}$$

$$= \$12{,}228.56$$

Therefore, $12,228.56 must be deposited in the account to provide $800 for the first year and $800 interest from the remaining balance each succeeding year. The accuracy of this analysis can be demonstrated by subtracting $800 from the initial deposit and computing 7 percent of the remainder as follows:

Balance after first payment = $12,228.56 − $800 = $11,428.56

Interest for each succeeding year = (0.07)($11,428.56) = $800

As (0.07)($11,428.56) = $800, the analysis shows that the amount P will be a sufficient sum to allow an $800 scholarship to be paid from interest each year after the first year.

EXERCISES

1. Find the value of the term $1 - (1 + i)^{-1}$ for the following interest rates (i values):
   a. $i = 0.10$ d. $i = 0.01$
   b. $i = 0.12$ e. $i = 0.08$
   c. $i = 0.05$ f. $i = 0.18$
2. Based on the answers to Question 1 above, what can you conclude about the relationship between the value of i and the value of the term $1 - (1 + i)^{-1}$?
3. What is the difference in the principal required to establish a $1500 annual perpetuity between (a) a 12 percent annual rate of interest and (b) a 7 percent annual rate of interest? Both perpetuities are compounded annually and each includes payment of the first $1500 prior to any interest being earned.
4. Find the initial deposit required to establish each of the following perpetuities. Each includes the first payment prior to any interest being earned.
   a. $1000 per year with a 10 percent annually compounded interest rate.
   b. $600 every 6 months with interest compounded semiannually at an 8 percent annual rate.
   c. $5000 each quarter with interest compounded quarterly at a 16 percent annual rate.
   d. $100 per month with interest compounded monthly at a 12 percent annual rate.
5. For parts a and b in Question 4 above, show that the computed amount provides sufficient principal for the first payment and interest on the remaining principal for all subsequent payments.
6. A benefactor of an art museum wants to establish a perpetual fund for the maintenance of the works in a special collection. Maintenance requirements are $2500 per year. How much should the individual place in a perpetual account paying 9 percent per year compounded annually to allow for the first year's maintenance payment from principal and each successive payment from interest?

9.9 Continuous Compounding

Increasingly in recent years, various financial instruments have provided for the continuous compounding of interest. Therefore, a short discussion of the mathematical principles of continuous compounding is an important part of a survey of the mathematics of finance.

The Base e and Continuous Compounding

In Chapter 8, the application of the constant e to processes of continuous compounding was described. Although the nonfinancial uses of this constant were emphasized, the relationship between e and the continuous compounding of money was introduced. This relationship is explained in more detail at this point.

As was stated in Chapter 8, e is found by evaluating the expression

1. $\left(1 + \dfrac{1}{n}\right)^n$

as n approaches infinity. The relationship of expression 1 to the continuous compounding of money can be derived by the following procedure.

Consider compounding a principal P at i percent per year for t years. The expression, presented earlier in this chapter is shown as

2. $S_t = P(1 + i)^t$

In expression 2, t is used to denote years. Expression 2 yields the amount in an account at the end years. However, if there are m compounding periods per year, expression 2 must be modified as follows:

3. $S_t = P\left(1 + \dfrac{i}{m}\right)^{mt}$

For example, 8 percent per year compounded quarterly for 5 years yields 2 percent interest per period ($i/m = 0.08/4 = 0.02$) for 20 time periods [$mt = (4)(5) = 20$].

In order to demonstrate the connection between e and continuous compounding, the expression $(1 + i/m)^{mt}$ in expression 3 must be shown to be equivalent to expression 1, or $(1 + 1/n)^n$.

As $i/m = 1/(m/i)$, expression 3 can be written as

4. $S_t = P\left(1 + \dfrac{1}{m/i}\right)^{mt}$

As $(m/i)(it) = mt$, the expression $[1 + 1/(m/i)]$ can be raised to the exponent $(m/i)(it)$ without altering expression 4. This is shown in expression 5 below with additional brackets added:

5. $S_t = P\left[\left(1 + \dfrac{1}{m/i}\right)^{(m/i)}\right]^{(it)}$

But $[1 + 1/(m/i)]^{m/i}$ is equivalent to expression 1 for the case where $n = m/i$. Thus, the expression in brackets approaches e as $m \to \infty$, or the number of compounding periods increases without bound.

These steps have shown that the value of an account paying i percent per year for t years, with continuous compounding, is shown by

6. $S_t = Pe^{it}$

Therefore, the constant e measures the value of $1 compounded continuously for 1 year at 100 percent. The exponent it allows for rates less than 100 percent i and various time periods t, in years or fractions of years.

Positive and negative powers of the constant e are listed in Table III. These values are used in the following examples.

Example 9.19
An individual wants to determine the future value of an account S_t with a principal P of \$2000 invested at an 8 percent continuously compounded rate for 18 months. This amount is determined by the following formula:

$$S_t = Pe^{it}$$

where $P = 2000$
$i = 0.08$
$t = 1.5$ (for 18 months)
$it = 0.12$
$e = 2.71828\ldots$

Substitution yields the following value for S_t:

$$S_{1.5} = 2000e^{0.12}$$
$$= 2000(1.1275)$$
$$= \$2255$$

The value for $e^{0.12} = 1.1275$ is found in Table III. Thus, the individual will earn \$255 in interest during the 18-month period and the initial deposit will be worth \$2255.

The constant e also can be applied to the computation of the present value of a stated future amount of money with continuous compounding. The present value P of a future amount S with continuous compounding is found by the following formula:

7. $P = Se^{-it}$

where i is the annual interest rate and t is the number of years or fractions of years.

Expression 7 can be derived by a process similar to that for expressions 1 through 6 above, but the derivation is omitted for purposes of brevity.

Example 9.20
An individual wants to deposit an amount in an account today sufficient to have \$5000 in 4 years. The account pays a 9 percent annual rate of interest compounded continuously. What amount should be deposited?

Using expression 7 this amount can be determined by use of e values from Table III as follows:

$$P = Se^{-it}$$

where $S = 5000$
$i = 0.09$
$t = 4$
$it = 0.36$
$e = 2.71828\ldots$

Therefore

$P = 5000e^{-(0.09)(4)}$
$= 5000e^{-0.36}$

Table III gives the value of $e^{-0.36} = 0.6976$. Therefore, the required deposit is $3488.50, as shown below:

$P = 5000(0.6976)$
$= \$3488$

The analysis has concluded that the individual must deposit $3488 today at a 9 percent annual rate with continuous compounding to have $5000 in 4 years.

EXERCISES

1. Find the value of $1 continuously compounded for the following annual interest rates and stated number of years:
   a. 8 percent for 6 months.
   b. 12 percent for 3 years.
   c. 4 percent for 3 months.
   d. 8 percent for 5 years.
   e. 14 percent for 1 year.
2. Find the present value of $1 after the stated number of years with continuous compounding at the given annual interest rate.
   a. 7 percent for 5 years.
   b. 12 percent for 3 months.
   c. 8 percent for 1 year.
   d. 10 percent for 6 months.
   e. 16 percent for 15 years.
3. Find the future value for each stated principal, continuously compounded annual interest rate i, and time.
   a. $2000 for 30 months at $i = 0.08$.
   b. $500 for 4 years at $i = 0.0525$.
   c. $7500 for 6 years at $i = 0.085$.
   d. $10,000 for 2 years at $i = 0.14$.
4. Find the present value of each of the following future amounts with continuously compounded annual interest rate and time as stated:
   a. $6000 at the end of 2 years with an interest rate of 7.5 percent.
   b. $10,000 at the end of 5 years with an interest rate of 9 percent.
   c. $2500 at the end of 1 year with an interest rate of 7 percent.
   d. $40,000 at the end of 20 years with an interest rate of 9.5 percent.
5. Find the value of $5000 continuously compounded at an annual interest rate of 7 percent at the end of (a) 3 years, (b) 6 years, (c) 10 years.
6. Find the present value of $8000 after each stated time period if interest is paid at the continuously compounded annual rate of 8 percent.

a. 6 months
b. 4 years
c. 20 years
7. An individual deposits a recently received inheritance of $3000 in an account which yields an 8 percent continuously compounded annual interest rate. The individual hopes to have $4800 in the account at the end of 5 years. Will the person's goal be achieved? If not, what is the difference between the actual amount and $4800?
8. How much must a firm invest today in an account which pays a 10 percent annual interest rate continuously compounded to assure that $500,000 will be on hand in 4 years?

9.10 Nominal Interest Rates and Effective Interest Rates

The final topic of this chapter concerns use of the constant e to determine the *effective* rate of interest knowing the *nominal* annual rate under continuous compounding.

To understand this relation, consider the case of continuous compounding of $1 ($P = 1$) for 1 year ($t = 1$) at an interest rate of i percent per year. The previous section derived this amount as

$$S = 1(e^{it})$$
$$= e^i$$

where $t = 1$ and i is the annual nominal interest rate.

The effective rate of interest I_E stated in decimal form is, therefore,

$$I_E = e^i - 1$$

For example, assume the annual nominal rate is 7 percent. The value of $1 compounded continuously for 1 year is equal to $e^{0.07}$, or $1.0725 (the value $e^{0.07} = 1.0725$ is taken from Table III). In other words, $1 is worth $1.0725 after 1 year, indicating that the effective interest rate is $I_E = 1.0725 - 1.0000 = 0.0725$, or 7.25 percent.

Similarly, a nominal rate of 11 percent per year with continuous compounding yields an effective rate of 11.63 percent as $I_E = e^{0.11} - 1 = 1.1163 - 1 = 0.1163 = 11.63$ percent.

In general, if X in Table III represents the nominal annual interest rate with continuous compounding, then $e^X - 1$ represents the decimal form of effective rate of interest. Each resulting decimal can be converted to percentage terms if desired.

9.11 Chapter Summary

In this chapter, some of the frequently used mathematical techniques of finance have been explained and applied to problems. These descriptions

The Mathematics of Finance 259

have necessitated the frequent use of abbreviations and notation. To summarize these techniques, the following is a brief restatement of each procedure including interpretation of symbols and identification of the appropriate table to assist with solving that class of problem.

1. SIMPLE INTEREST
   FORMULA: $S = P(1 + rt)$
   APPLICATION: To find the value of an account S at the end of t years with interest paid at r percent per year without compounding. The initial amount in the account is called the principal P.

2. SIMPLE DISCOUNT
   FORMULA: $P = \dfrac{S}{1 + rt}$
   APPLICATION: To determine the beginning balance P required to accumulate a stated amount S after t years at an interest rate of r percent per year without interest compounding.

3. COMPOUND INTEREST
   FORMULA: $S_n = P(1 + i)^n$
   APPLICATION: To determine the amount S_n in an account at the end of n time periods with interest compounded at the rate of i percent per time period. The value of i is equal to the annual interest rate r divided by the number of compounding periods per year. Values for the expression $(1 + i)^n$ for various interest rates and numbers of time periods are found in Table IV.

4. COMPOUND DISCOUNT
   FORMULA: $P = \dfrac{S_n}{(1 + i)^n} = S_n(1 + i)^{-n}$
   APPLICATION: To determine the principal P required to accumulate a stated amount S_n at the end of n time periods with interest compounded at the rate of i percent per time period. Values for $(1 + i)^{-n}$ for various interest rates and numbers of time periods are found in Table V.

5. FUTURE VALUE OF AN ANNUITY
   FORMULA: $S_n = Rs_n = R\left[\dfrac{(1 + i)^n - 1}{i}\right]$
   APPLICATION: To determine the future value of payments of R dollars per period for n periods with interest compounded at i percent per period. It is assumed that payments are made and interest computed at the end of each time period. Future values of $1 per period at various interest rates and number of time periods, $[(1 + i)^n - 1]/i = s_n$, are found in Table VI.

6. REQUIRED PERIODIC PAYMENT TO ACCUMULATE A SPECIFIED AMOUNT (SINKING FUND)
   FORMULA: $R = \dfrac{S_n}{[(1 + i)^n - 1]/i}$
   APPLICATION: To determine the required periodic payment R to accumulate S_n dollars within n time periods at a stated interest rate of i

percent per time period. Interest is compounded each period at the end of the period.

Values for $[(1 + i)^n - 1]/i$ also are found in Table VI. Some tables include values for $1/\{[(1 + i)^n - 1]/i\} = i/[(1 + i)^n - 1]$, thus eliminating division in the expression for R.

7. PRESENT VALUE OF AN ANNUITY

   FORMULA: $A_n = Ra_n = R\left[\dfrac{1 - (1 + i)^{-n}}{i}\right]$

   APPLICATION: To determine the total deposit into an annuity account A_n required to receive R dollars per time period for n time periods at an interest rate of i percent per time period with interest compounded at the end of each period. The expression $a_n = [1 - (1 + i)^{-n}]/i$ represents the present value of $1 per period over the stated number of time periods. Values for a_n for various interest rates and time periods are found in Table VII.

8. LOAN AMORTIZATION

   FORMULA: $R = \dfrac{P}{a_n} = P\left(\dfrac{1}{a_n}\right) = P\left[\dfrac{i}{1 - (1 - i)^{-n}}\right]$

   APPLICATION: To determine the periodic payment R required to amortize a loan of principal P dollars over n time periods at a compounded interest rate of i percent per period. Values for $1/a_n$, or the per period equivalent of $1 present value, are found in Table VIII for various interest rates and time periods. The expression $1/a_n$ is also referred to as the capital recovery factor.

9. PERPETUITIES

   FORMULA: $P = \dfrac{a}{1 - r}$, where $r = (1 + i)^{-1}$; therefore,

   $$P = \dfrac{a}{1 - 1/(1 + i)}$$

   APPLICATION: To determine the total amount required to establish an infinite series of periodic payments of a dollars each from an investment earning the compounded rate of i percent per period. The first payment is made before any interest is received on the investment and subsequent payments are made from interest.

10. FUTURE VALUE WITH CONTINUOUS COMPOUNDING

    FORMULA: $S_t = Pe^{it}$

    APPLICATION: To determine the value of an account S_t with principal P at the end of t years with a continuously compounded nominal interest rate of i percent per year. Values for $e^{it} = e^x$ are found in Table III.

11. PRESENT VALUE WITH CONTINUOUS COMPOUNDING

    FORMULA: $P = S_t e^{-it}$

    APPLICATION: To determine the amount P that must be deposited in an account to accumulate an amount S_t at the end of t years, with a continuously compounded nominal interest rate of i percent per year. Values for $e^{-it} = e^{-x}$ are found in Table III.

12. FINDING THE EFFECTIVE RATE OF INTEREST FROM THE NOMINAL RATE
    FORMULA: $I_E = e^i - 1$
    APPLICATION: To determine the decimal form of the effective rate of interest I_E given a nominal rate of i percent per year with continuous compounding. Values for $e^i = e^x$ are found in Table III. The answer I_E is converted to percentage terms to be interpreted (e.g., 0.0725 = 7.25 percent).

9.12 Problem Set

Review Questions

1. Distinguish between the nominal annual interest rate and the per period interest rate.
2. What is measured by the compound discount factor? What is the independent variable in a typical compound discount problem?
3. Describe an ordinary annuity. What does r, the common ratio in a geometric series, represent when used in computing the future value of an annuity?
4. Briefly describe one business application of a sinking fund payment analysis.
5. What is measured by the present value of an annuity?
6. Explain the computational similarity between the present value of an annuity and the principal of a loan.
7. What is the relation between the interest rate and the present value of an annuity, holding time constant? Why?
8. What is the relation between the interest rate and the required per period payment for loans of the same duration and amount? Why?
9. If a $1 deposit yields e dollars (where e = 2.71828 . . .) after investment for 1 year, what are the interest rate and compounding period characteristics of this investment?
10. State the exponential function relating nominal and effective interest rates of $1 with continuous compounding for 1 year. Give two examples of the use of this function.

Review Problems

1. Find the future dollar amount for each stated principal P, annual interest rate, and time.
    a. P = $2000 for 7 years at 8 percent per year compounded annually.
    b. P = $10,000 for 5 years at 6 percent per year compounded semiannually.
    c. P = $4800 for 6 years at 12 percent per year compounded quarterly.
    d. P = $25,000 for 3 years at 12 percent per year compounded monthly.
2. Find the present value for each future amount S, annual interest rate, and time.
    a. S = $8000 after 4 years at 8 percent per year compounded semiannually.
    b. S = $50,000 after 25 years at 8 percent per year compounded annually.

c. $S = \$28{,}000$ after 10 years at 12 percent per year compounded quarterly.
d. $S = \$2500$ after 1 year at 8 percent per year compounded quarterly.
3. A couple deposits $200 in a savings account on the day their first child is born. The account pays an annual interest rate of 6 percent compounded semiannually. What will be the value of the account on the child's 18th birthday if no further deposits are made to this account?
4. The owner of a small business wants to place an amount in a savings account sufficient to pay a $4800 office furniture bill due in exactly 18 months. The account pays 8 percent per year compounded quarterly. How much should the owner place in the account to be able to pay the bill in full in 18 months?
5. An individual withdraws $5000 after 3 years from a savings certificate originally purchased for $15,000. The certificate has earned interest at an 8 percent annual rate compounded semiannually. What is the remaining balance of the certificate after this withdrawal?
6. Find the future value of the annuity for each of the following per period payments, annual interest rates, and time periods:
   a. $250 every 6 months for 6 years at an annual interest rate of 10 percent compounded semiannually.
   b. $1000 every quarter for 8 years at an annual interest rate of 16 percent compounded quarterly.
   c. $650 monthly for 8 months at an annual interest rate of 12 percent compounded each month.
   d. $600 annually for 5 years at an annually compounded interest rate of 7 percent.
7. Determine the required periodic payment to accumulate the stated amount for each interest rate and time period below.
   a. Quarterly payments to accumulate $6000 with interest at 12 percent per year compounded quarterly over 6 years.
   b. Semiannual payments to accumulate $10,000 with interest at 14 percent per year compounded semiannually over 3 years.
   c. Annual payments to accumulate $5000 with interest at 6 percent per year compounded annually over 5 years.
   d. Monthly payments to accumulate $20,000 with interest at 24 percent per year compounded monthly over 3 years.
8. An individual deposits $300 every 6 months into a retirement account. The account pays an annual interest rate of 12 percent per year compounded semiannually. What will be the value of the account after 15 years?
9. A firm wants to make quarterly payments of $4500 each into an office expense account. The account will yield a 12 percent annual rate of interest compounded quarterly. What will be the value of the account after 4 years? How much less will the account be worth after 4 years if the annual interest rate is 8 percent compounded quarterly?
10. Mr. and Mrs. Johnson believe that they will need $20,000 to pay for the college education of their recently born son. An annuity account which yields a 10 percent annual rate of interest compounded semiannually is available to them. How much should the Johnson's deposit into the account every 6 months to have a balance of $20,000 in 18 years?
11. A construction company will need $30,000 in exactly 3 years to repay a construction loan. The company president decides to deposit $2000 each quarter during these 3 years into an account which yields 16 percent per year compounded

quarterly. Will the company accumulate enough in this account to pay the bill at the end of 3 years? What must the quarterly payments be to have $30,000 after 3 years at an annual interest rate of 12 percent compounded quarterly?

12. Find the present value of the following per period payments given each interest rate and time:
    a. $400 each quarter for 5 years at an interest rate of 8 percent per year compounded quarterly.
    b. $3500 every 6 months for 10 years at an interest rate of 12 percent compounded semiannually.
    c. $200 every month for 3 years at an interest rate of 12 percent per year compounded monthly.
    d. $1500 each year for 25 years at an interest rate of 6 percent per year compounded annually.

13. Determine the periodic payment per compounding period required to amortize each loan described below.
    a. A $10,000 loan for 3 years at a 12 percent annual interest rate compounded monthly.
    b. A $45,000 loan for 10 years at a 12 percent annual interest rate compounded quarterly.
    c. A $7,000 loan for 1 year at an 8 percent annual interest rate compounded quarterly.
    d. An $80,000 loan for 15 years at a 10 percent annual interest rate compounded semiannually.

14. The owner of an apartment complex wants to deposit enough in an account to provide for insurance payments on the apartments over the next 5 years. Payments of $2750 must be made each quarter. The account yields an 8 percent annual rate compounded quarterly. How much must be deposited to be able to pay exactly all insurance payments during the 5-year period?

15. A city police department plans to set aside $30,000 in an annuity to provide $500 every 6 months for the next 5 years to each of seven retired members of the force. The account pays 10 percent interest per year compounded semiannually. Has the police department set aside enough money to make all the payments?

16. A firm borrows $400,000 to build a new factory. The loan is for 10 years at a 14 percent annual rate of interest compounded semiannually. How much are the firm's semiannual payments?

17. An individual borrows $7000 to buy a new car. The loan must be paid back over the next 3 years at a 12 percent annual rate of interest compounded monthly. Compute the individual's monthly payments.

18. For a $5000 loan, will a consumer have higher semiannual payments with (1) a 6-year loan at an 8 percent annual interest rate compounded semiannually, or (2) a 5-year loan at a 10 percent annual interest rate compounded semiannually?

19. A charity wants to establish a perpetuity sufficient to enable a citizen to receive a $1000 award each year. It is planned to make the $1000 payment from interest each year after the first year's award, which will be made from the principal. The account to be used to hold the funds yields 8 percent, compounded annually. How much should the charity deposit initially to fund the award program?

20. A firm wants to establish a library maintenance fund for a university. The firm would like to provide $2500 every 6 months from the fund to the library. The fund yields a 10 percent annual rate of interest compounded semiannually. What

is the initial deposit required to establish a perpetual stream of payments from interest every 6 months after making the first payment from principal?
21. An individual deposits $4000 in a savings account which yields 8 percent per year continuously compounded. The person wants to have $5000 at the end of 3 years. Will this goal be realized?
22. Bank A offers depositors a 5-year savings certificate which pays 8 percent per year compounded quarterly. Bank B offers a 5-year certificate which pays a 6 percent annual interest rate continuously compounded. If an individual has $1600 to deposit for 5 years, which bank should be selected to maximize the value of the account after 5 years?

Differential Calculus: Principles

10.1 Introduction

Throughout this book, a recurrent theme has been that an understanding of functions is basic to quantitative ability. Calculus is an aspect of mathematics which concentrates on the analysis of rates of change in functions. Particularly, calculus is concerned with the *instantaneous rate of change* of a function, or the rate of change at a point of the function.

In contrast to the topics of the first seven chapters, calculus includes techniques applicable both to linear functions, with constant rates of change (the same at all points on the function), and to nonlinear functions, which exhibit different rates of change at various points. Thus, all the types of functions defined and discussed in Chapters 3 and 8 are included in this presentation.

Two areas of study within calculus are differential calculus and integral calculus. Each is associated with a specific primary operation: differentiation and integration, respectively. The two operations are inverses, just as addition and subtraction are inverses, and both operations concern the instantaneous rate of change of functions. Differentiation includes a set of techniques for determining the rate of change at points on an established function. Integration is used to determine areas or volumes bounded by a function knowing the form of the function and the boundaries of the area or volume.

In this and the next chapter, the principles and business applications of differential calculus are discussed. The focus of Chapter 12 is integral calculus. Together, the three chapters provide a basic knowledge of calculus and the means to apply this branch of mathematics to problems in business and economics.

To introduce calculus, several analytical situations where the principles of differential and integral calculus may be applied are described in the next section.

10.2 Business Analysis and Calculus

The basic calculus measurement, the rate of change of a function at a point, is useful in the quantitative analysis of business problems. Many analytical questions can be answered by using marginal, or incremental, analysis. For example, a firm may want to know whether to hire an additional worker or whether to manufacture an additional unit of output. Often, the marginal measurements required to answer such questions are associated with the instantaneous rate of change of a function.

For example, if one knows the relationship expressing total cost as a function of output, the rate of change in the function is the *incremental cost* (*marginal cost*) of an additional unit of output at a point on the total cost function. Further interpretation of marginal cost will be included in Chapter 11.

The remainder of this chapter will demonstrate how to determine this instantaneous rate of change. At this point, consider three questions and how each relates to the measurement of the instantaneous rate of change of a function:

1. A firm knows the functional relation between total revenue and units sold and the relation between total cost and units sold. The firm wants to use these data to determine that output level which will lead to maximum profit.
2. A firm is interested in determining the level of production at which the per unit cost of production is lowest. This will indicate the production point representing efficiency in the use of the firm's resources. Data available to the firm have specified the functional relation between quantity of production and per unit cost of production.
3. An automobile manufacturer wants to determine the total cost of producing between 1000 and 3000 cars per week at a particular facility. The company knows the total cost function relating any output level to cost.

Differential Calculus: Principles **267**

Calculus techniques can be used to answer each of these problems. Thus, as will be demonstrated in this and the next two chapters, calculus is a means to answer many questions of demand, cost, profitability, and operational efficiency. In addition, calculus provides a standardized method for analyzing complex functions which may be difficult, if not impossible, to describe graphically.

The following sections of this chapter include the theoretical and computational principles of differential calculus. Business applications such as described above are treated more extensively in the following two chapters.

10.3 Limits and Continuity

An understanding of the meaning of the instantaneous rate of change of a function is dependent on the concepts of *limit* and *continuity*. These two topics are introduced in this section.

Limits

To explain the concept of the limit of a function, four elements are introduced: (1) an independent variable X; (2) the function of X, $f(X)$; (3) the constant a; and (4) the constant L.

Assume that values for $f(X)$ can be made to differ by an arbitrarily small amount from L by taking values of X that are close to, but not equal to, a. Thus, as X gets closer in value to a, the value of $f(X)$ approaches L. If this is true for all values of X, then it is said that "$f(X)$ approaches the limit L as X approaches a."

To apply numbers to this concept assume the following:

$f(X) = 3X^2$

$L = 48$

$a = 4$

Thus, $f(X)$ approaches $f(4) = 3(16) = 48$ as X approaches, but does not equal, a value of 4. The following formal definition for the limit of a function is related to this description.

The statement that a variable X approaches a indicates that X approaches the constant a as a limit when X varies in such a way that the absolute difference between X and a ($|X - a|$) remains less than any preassigned positive number, regardless of how small this positive number may be.

The statement "X approaches a" is designated,

$X \to a$

Thus, if $f(X)$ approaches the value of L as X approaches but does not take on the value a, then L is the limit of $f(X)$ as X approaches a. This is written

$$\lim_{X \to a} f(X) = L$$

or

$$f(X) \to L \text{ as } X \to a$$

Therefore, proper notation for the example presented above is

$$\lim_{X \to 4} (3X^2) = 48$$

Thus, the function $3X^2$ approaches 48 as X approaches but does not take on the value of 4.

An extension of these concepts is demonstrated when either X or $f(X)$ becomes arbitrarily large or arbitrarily small (i.e., approaches positive or negative infinity). If the difference between the function $f(X)$ and a constant L is less in absolute value than some small positive number for all positive values of X that are sufficiently large, then $f(X)$ is said to approach L as X increases without limit. In notation, this is expressed as

$$\lim_{X \to \infty} f(X) = L$$

Similar notation can be applied to $f(X)$ when X decreases without limit as follows:

$$\lim_{X \to -\infty} f(X) = L$$

When referring to the function of X, the phrase "approaching infinity" implies that if $f(X)$ is greater than an arbitrarily large positive number for all values of X near a, then $f(X)$ becomes positively infinite as X approaches a. This is expressed

$$\lim_{X \to a} f(X) = \infty$$

And, if $f(X)$ becomes negatively infinite as X approaches a, the appropriate notation is

$$\lim_{X \to a} f(X) = -\infty$$

Finally, it is possible that both X and $f(X)$ approach infinity. Thus, when $f(X)$ becomes positively infinite as X increases without limit, the notation is

$$\lim_{X \to \infty} f(X) = \infty$$

Similar expressions are used when both X and $f(X)$ approach negative infinity or when there are opposite infinite movements for each.

All of these concepts and expressions are fundamental to an understanding of the instantaneous rate of change of a function.

An additional principle is that a particular limit L is independent of the direction from which X approaches a. Thus, the limit must be the same whether X approaches a from the left (lower values) or from the right (higher values). In the example

$$\lim_{X \to 4} (3X^2) = 48$$

the limit must be 48 whether X approaches 4 from the left (i.e., 2, 3, 3.5) or from the right (i.e., 6, 5, 4.5). One implication of this principle is that one must avoid determining the limit of $f(X)$ as X approaches a by simply evaluating $f(X)$ at $X = a$. An example will demonstrate this.

Example 10.1
Find

$$\lim_{X \to 2} \frac{X^2 - 4}{X - 2}$$

In this case, substitution of $X = 2$ into the expression yields an undefined value and one would conclude incorrectly that a limit as $X \to 2$ does not exist.

However, as X approaches 2 from the left (1, 1.5, 1.8, etc.) the value of 4 is approached, and as X approaches 2 from the right (3.2, 2.5, 2.1, etc.) the value of 4 is also approached. Therefore, although a value for the function does not exist at $X = 2$, a limit of 4 exists at this point. Figure 10.1 further describes this situation.

Consequently, one should not substitute a for X when evaluating the expression

$$\lim_{X \to a} f(X)$$

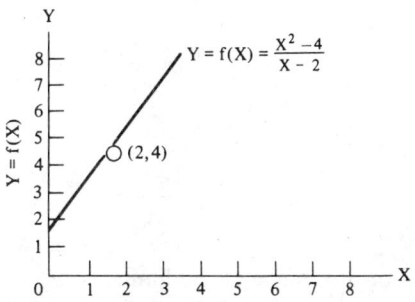

FIGURE 10.1 The limit as $X \to 2$ of $f(X) = \dfrac{X^2 - 4}{X - 2}$.

but should identify the behavior of the values of $f(X)$ as X approaches a. Often, this process is carried out by simplifying the expression. Solution of the example shows this process.

$$\lim_{X \to 2} \frac{X^2 - 4}{X - 2} = \lim_{X \to 2} \frac{(X - 2)(X + 2)}{X - 2}$$

$$\lim_{X \to 2} X + 2 = 4$$

Although many limits can be determined by evaluating the function at the limiting point, it is a better procedure to simplify an expression before finding the limit.

Limit Theorems

In determining limits, it is often helpful to use one or more of the following limit theorems. These theorems may simplify or avoid the necessity of specifying the behavior of the function as the variable approaches the limiting value.

Each limit theorem below is demonstrated by means of an example but the proof is not given here.

1. The limit of any real constant K is K itself:

$$\lim_{X \to a} K = K$$

Example 10.2

$$\lim_{X \to 3} 14 = 14$$

Observe that the constant does not involve the X term; therefore, finding the limit has no effect on the constant.

2. A constant term may be placed inside or outside the limit symbol:

$$\lim_{X \to a} K f(x) = K \lim_{X \to a} f(x)$$

Example 10.3

$$\lim_{X \to 4} 5X^2 = 5 \lim_{X \to 4} X^2$$

$$= 5(16) = 80$$

3. The limit of a sum or difference is the sum or difference of the limits:

$$\lim_{X \to a} [f(x) \pm g(x)] = \lim_{X \to a} f(x) + \lim_{X \to a} g(x)$$

Example 10.4

$$\lim_{X \to 5}(X^3 - 2X^2 + 4X + 6) = \lim_{X \to 5} X^3 - \lim_{X \to 5} 2X^2 + \lim_{X \to 5} 4X + \lim_{X \to 5} 6$$
$$= 125 - 50 + 20 + 6$$
$$= 101$$

4. The limit of a product is the product of the limits:

$$\lim_{X \to a}[f(x) \cdot g(x)] = \lim_{X \to a} f(x) \cdot \lim_{X \to a} g(x)$$

Example 10.5

$$\lim_{X \to 3}(X + 4)(X - 1) = \left[\lim_{X \to 3}(X + 4)\right]\left[\lim_{X \to 3}(X - 1)\right]$$
$$= (7)(2)$$
$$= 14$$

5. The limit of a quotient is the quotient of the limits if the denominator's limit is not zero:

$$\lim_{X \to a} \frac{f(x)}{g(x)} = \frac{\lim_{X \to a} f(x)}{\lim_{X \to a} g(x)} \quad \text{if } \lim_{X \to a} g(x) \neq 0$$

Example 10.6

$$\lim_{X \to 4} \frac{X^2 + 4}{X - 2} = \frac{\lim_{X \to 4}(X^2 + 4)}{\lim_{X \to 4}(X - 2)}$$
$$= \frac{20}{2}$$
$$= 10$$

Example 10.7 is a case where the denominator limit is zero.

Example 10.7

$$\lim_{X \to 4} \frac{X^2 + 4}{X - 4} = \frac{\lim_{X \to 4}(X^2 + 4)}{\lim_{X \to 4}(X - 4)} = \frac{20}{0} = \text{undefined}$$

6. The limit of a power of $f(X)$ is the power of the limit of $f(X)$:

$$\lim_{X \to a}[f(X)]^n = [\lim_{X \to a} f(X)]^n$$

Example 10.8

$$\lim_{X \to 4} (X - 2)^3 = \left[\lim_{X \to 4} (X - 2) \right]^3 = (2)^3 = 8$$

The function shown in each example can be evaluated at the limit by substitution of the value for *a* into the expression. As mentioned, however, there are other functions which should be simplified before evaluating the limit. This technique is especially applicable to quotient functions. Example 10.9 demonstrates this.

Example 10.9
Find

$$\lim_{X \to 6} \frac{X^2 - 36}{X - 6}$$

Factoring the numerator yields the following result.

$$\lim_{X \to 6} \frac{X^2 - 36}{X - 6} = \lim_{X \to 6} \frac{(X + 6)(X - 6)}{X - 6}$$
$$= \lim_{X \to 6} (X + 6) = 12$$

Contrast this result with Example 10.10, which cannot be factored.

Example 10.10
Find

$$\lim_{X \to 6} \frac{X^2 + 36}{X - 6} = \frac{\lim_{X \to 6} (X^2 + 36)}{\lim_{X \to 6} (X - 6)} = \frac{72}{0} = \text{undefined}$$

Continuity

A second concept necessary for an understanding of the instantaneous rate of change of a function is the *continuity* of a function. From a graphical perspective, a function is *continuous* if it can be sketched without lifting a pencil from the paper. If there are breaks in the function, the function is termed *discontinuous*. On a more formal level, limits and continuity are related concepts.

For a function $f(X)$ to be continuous at a point $X = a$, three conditions must be met.

1. $\lim_{X \to a} f(X)$ must exist.
2. $f(a)$ must be defined.
3. $\lim_{X \to a} f(X) = f(a)$.

Thus, for a function to be continuous at a point the limit of the function must exist at that point, the function must be defined at the point, and the limit at the point must equal the value of the function at that point.

If any one (or more) of these three conditions is not met, the function $f(X)$ is not continuous at $X = a$. Discontinuous functions are described in the next several examples.

First, consider that the limit of $f(X)$ when X approaches a may exist, but the function may not be defined at $f(a)$.

Example 10.11
Above, it was pointed out that

$$\lim_{X \to 2} \frac{X^2 - 4}{X - 2} = 4$$

However, $f(2)$ is not in the domain of the function as

$$f(2) = \frac{2^2 - 4}{2 - 2} = 0 = \text{undefined}$$

Therefore, although $\lim_{X \to 2} [(X^2 - 4)/(X - 2)]$ exists, the function is not continuous at $X = 2$.

Example 10.12
Consider the following function of X:

$$f(X) = \begin{cases} 4X + 1 & \text{for } X \leq 3 \\ 2X & \text{for } X > 3 \end{cases}$$

This function is graphed in Figure 10.2. At the point $X = 3$, the function is defined as $f(3) = 13$. However, the limit as X approaches 3 does not exist as there is a discontinuity at this point. This can be seen by the gap in Figure 10.2.

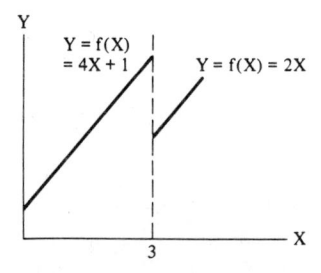

FIGURE 10.2 The function $f(X) = \begin{matrix} 4X + 1 \text{ for } X \leq 3 \\ 2X \text{ for } X \geq 3 \end{matrix}$

Example 10.13

As a third example of a discontinuous function, consider the function shown in Figure 10.3. This function is

$$f(X) = \begin{cases} X^2 - 2 & \text{for all } X \text{ except } 4 \\ 10 & \text{for } X = 4 \end{cases}$$

Observe that the limit as X approaches 4 exists as it is equal to

$$\lim_{X \to 4} X^2 - 2 = 14$$

and $f(X)$ is defined at $X = 4$ as $f(X) = 10$ at this point. However,

$$\lim_{X \to 4} X^2 - 2 \neq f(4)$$

Consequently, as shown in Figure 10.3, there is a discontinuity on the function at the point $X = 4$.

These examples have described various discontinuous functions. A function is continuous in an interval if it is continuous at every point in the interval. If this is not the case, the function has a discontinuity, or it is discrete over some range.

In business, discontinuous functions frequently are encountered. For example, the demand function for computers does not include a quantity point such as 478.2 computers. However, readers should be aware that many business relations expressed by discontinuous functions are assumed to be continuous for analytical convenience. Thus, although continuity is a necessary assumption for many applications in calculus, interpretation of such analyses should make note of the inherent discreteness of the relation.

With this conceptual background, the next section examines more specifically the question of the instantaneous rate of change of a function.

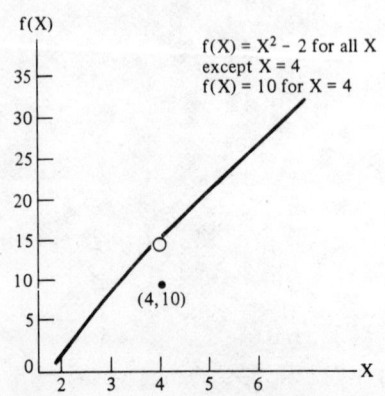

FIGURE 10.3 A function with a discontinuity at $X = 4$.

EXERCISES

1. Find the limit as specified for each of the following:
    a. $\lim\limits_{X \to 4} 6$
    b. $\lim\limits_{X \to 0} 8$
    c. $\lim\limits_{X \to 3} \dfrac{6X^2}{5}$
    d. $\lim\limits_{X \to -3} -2X^3$
    e. $\lim\limits_{X \to 0} (X^2 + 4X + 7)$
    f. $\lim\limits_{X \to 4} (X^3 - 3X^2 - 4X + 8)$
    g. $\lim\limits_{X \to 2} \dfrac{4X^2 + 8X}{X - 6}$
    h. $\lim\limits_{g \to 3} \dfrac{2g^2 - 6g + 15}{2g}$
    i. $\lim\limits_{y \to 3} \dfrac{y^2 - 3y}{-6y - 4}$
    j. $\lim\limits_{X \to 3} (X^2 - 4X + 10)^2$
    k. $\lim\limits_{X \to 8} \sqrt[3]{X^2}$
    l. $\lim\limits_{X \to 0} X^{3/4}$

2. Find the limit for each of the following expressions. If the limit does not exist, explain why.
    a. $\lim\limits_{X \to 3} \dfrac{X^2 - 9}{X - 3}$
    b. $\lim\limits_{X \to 4} \dfrac{X^2 + 16}{X - 4}$
    c. $\lim\limits_{X \to 2} \dfrac{X^2 - 4X + 4}{X - 2}$
    d. $\lim\limits_{X \to 0} \dfrac{X^2 + 6X + 12}{X - 3}$
    e. $\lim\limits_{X \to -5} \dfrac{X^2 - 3X + 2}{X + 5}$
    f. $\lim\limits_{X \to -4} \dfrac{X^2 + 8X + 16}{X + 4}$

3. Show either that each of the following functions is continuous or that it is not continuous at the specified point. Justify your decision in each case.
    a. $f(X) = \dfrac{X^2 - 25}{X - 5}$ at $X = 5$
    b. $f(X) = 3X^2 - 12X$ at $X = 4$
    c. $f(X) = 2X^2$ for all X except $X = 8$
    $f(X) = 100$ for $X = 8$
    Test for continuity at $X = 8$
    d. $f(X) = 2X^2$ for all X except $X = 3$
    $f(X) = 18$ for $X = 3$
    Test for continuity at $X = 3$
    e. $f(X) = X^2 + 5X - 150$ for all X except $X = 10$
    $f(X) = 10$ for $X = 10$
    Test for continuity at $X = 10$
    f. $f(X) = \dfrac{X^2 - 18X + 81}{X - 9}$ at $X = 9$

10.4 The Secant Slope and the Tangent Slope

In Chapter 5, the slope of a linear function, b_1 in $Y = b_0 + b_1 X$, is interpreted as the change in the dependent variable resulting from a single unit change in the independent variable. This value is the same between any two points of a linear function. In this section, concepts of change are extended to all kinds of functions.

In mathematics, an abbreviated notation used to describe change is the delta (Δ) symbol. In words, Δ is read "the change in." For example, ΔX means the change in the variable X and ΔY means the change in Y. If Y is a function of X, the change in the function of X is expressed as $\Delta f(X)$. As the function of X changes in response to a change in X, $\Delta f(X)$ is computed as

$$\Delta f(X) = f(X + \Delta X) - f(X)$$

Example 10.14
For $f(X) = X^2 + 4$, $X = 2$ and $\Delta X = 1$, find $\Delta f(X)$.

$$\begin{aligned}\Delta f(X) &= f(X + \Delta X) - f(X) \\ &= f(2 + 1) - f(2) \\ &= [(3)^2 + 4] - [(2)^2 + 4] \\ &= (9 + 4) - (4 + 4) \\ &= 13 - 8 = 5\end{aligned}$$

Thus, the change in the function $f(X) = X^2 + 4$ is equal to 5 when X changes from 2 to 3.

Following the delta notation, the value for the slope of a straight line can be expressed as $\Delta Y/\Delta X$. If Y is $f(X)$, then the slope of a straight line is expressed as

$$\frac{\Delta f(X)}{\Delta X} = \frac{f(X + \Delta X) - f(X)}{\Delta X}$$

This is the general form of the *difference quotient*. The difference quotient has the same value for any two coordinate points (X, Y) selected on a straight line.

For nonlinear functions, the difference quotient also can be used to estimate the slope of a curve over an interval between two points. The slope over the interval is determined by evaluating the slope of a straight line connecting the two points. This yields the slope of the *secant line*. Observe that for nonlinear curves, in contrast to straight lines, the slope of the secant line varies depending on the points selected.

This discussion of the difference quotient and secant line considers the slope for an interval of a function. The important concept for calculus, however, is the instantaneous rate of change *at a point*. As this rate of change is equivalent to the slope of the function at a point, one must apply the concept of the *tangent line*.

It is important to note that the slope of a line tangent to a point on a curve is by definition the slope of the curve at that point. Interestingly, there is a relation between the secant line and the tangent line which may be explained with the assistance of Figure 10.4.

To determine the slope of $f(X)$ over the interval AB, the slope of the straight line (or secant line) AB must be computed. In addition, the line CC' is the line of tangency to $f(X)$ at the point A because it touches $f(X)$ only at A and never intersects $f(X)$. The slope of this tangent line CC' is equivalent to the slope of $f(X)$ at point A.

Above, it was stated that the slope of the secant line AB is equal to the difference quotient, $\Delta f(X)/\Delta X$.

$$\text{Slope of } AB = \frac{\Delta f(X)}{\Delta X} = \text{slope of secant line } AB$$

Observe that as the point B or, in fact, any point on $f(X)$ except A, is moved closer to A, the secant line and tangent line become more and more the same and their slopes approach the same value.

More formally, as ΔX approaches 0 (i.e., approaches one point on the function), the slope of the secant line approaches the slope of the tangent line. This can be expressed by notation and terminology developed above as follows:

$$\text{Tangent slope} = \lim_{\Delta X \to 0} \text{ secant slope}$$

$$\text{Tangent slope} = \lim_{\Delta X \to 0} \frac{\Delta f(X)}{\Delta X}$$

$$\text{Tangent slope} = \lim_{\Delta X \to 0} \frac{f(X + \Delta X) - f(X)}{\Delta X}$$

This demonstrates that the limit, if it exists, of the difference quotient (or secant slope) as ΔX approaches 0 yields the slope of the tangent line at X. Consequently, this limit is the slope of the function at the single point X on the function.

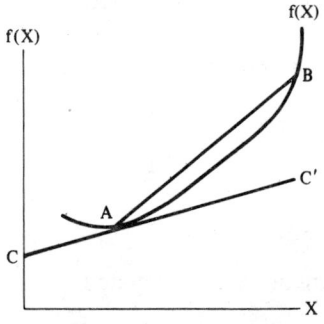

FIGURE 10.4 A secant line and a tangent line.

10.5 The Derivative

One aspect of the previous result is that the limit, if it exists, of the difference quotient as ΔX approaches 0 also yields the instantaneous rate of change of the function at that point. In calculus, this measurement is referred to as the *first derivative*, or simply the derivative. The derivative of $Y = f(X)$, notated dY/dX, is defined as

1. $\dfrac{dY}{dX} = \lim\limits_{\Delta X \to 0} \dfrac{f(X + \Delta X) - f(X)}{\Delta X}$

THE DERIVATIVE OF A FUNCTION MEASURES THE INSTANTANEOUS RATE OF CHANGE IN THE DEPENDENT VARIABLE IN RESPONSE TO AN INFINITESIMALLY SMALL CHANGE IN THE INDEPENDENT VARIABLE.

The notation dY/dX *does not indicate division* but is a mathematical instruction for finding the derivative of Y with respect to X. Alternative notations for the derivative of Y with respect to X are the following:

2. $\dfrac{df(X)}{dX}$

3. $f'(X)$

The three notations represent the same instruction; that is, to determine the limit of the secant slope on Y as the change in X approaches 0. The process of finding the derivative is referred to as *differentiation*.

Finally, it should be remembered that the derivative of a function, when determined, is a general expression for the slope of the tangent line at any point X in the domain of the function.

Continuity and the Derivative

If the derivative exists at a point on the function $f(X)$ such as $X = a$, then the function is said to be *differentiable* at $X = a$. For a function to be differentiable at a point, it is a *necessary but not sufficient condition* that the function be continuous at that point.

In Section 10.3, it was stated that a function is continuous at a point on $f(X)$ such as $X = a$ if

1. $\lim\limits_{X \to a} f(X)$ exists.
2. $f(a)$ is defined.
3. $\lim\limits_{X \to a} f(X) = f(a)$.

If any of these conditions is not met, the function cannot be differentiated at $X = a$.

TABLE 10.1 Values for X and $f(X)$ where $f(X) = |6X|$

X	$f(X) = |6X|$
−3	18
−2	12
−1	6
0	0
1	6
2	12
3	18

Satisfaction of these three conditions is only a *necessary* condition for differentiability. Even if the conditions are met, the function may not be able to be differentiated. To demonstrate this point, consider the following function of X:

$$f(X) = |6X|$$

A set of values for this function is listed in Table 10.1 and plotted in Figure 10.5.

This discussion particularly is concerned with the point (0, 0). Observe that at (0, 0) the function has a very sharp point where it stops decreasing and begins to increase. At the point (0, 0), the function is continuous since the following conditions are satisfied:

1. $\lim_{X \to 0} |6X|$ exists.
2. $f(0) = f(|(6)(0)|)$ is defined.
3. $\lim_{X \to 0} f(0) = 0$.

Although the conditions for continuity are satisfied, the limit of the difference quotient as X approaches 0 does not exist. The following steps computing the difference quotient demonstrate this situation:

1. $Y = |6X|$

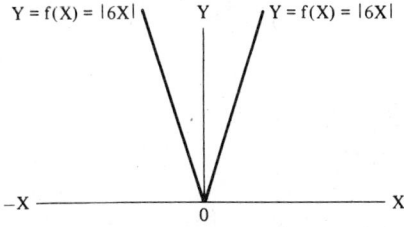

FIGURE 10.5 The function $f(X) = |6X|$.

2. $\dfrac{dY}{dX} = \lim\limits_{\Delta X \to 0} \dfrac{f(0 + \Delta X) - f(0)}{\Delta X}$

3. $\dfrac{dY}{dX} = \lim\limits_{\Delta X \to 0} \dfrac{|6(0 + \Delta X)| - |6(0)|}{\Delta X}$

4. $\dfrac{dY}{dX} = \lim\limits_{\Delta X \to 0} \dfrac{|6\Delta X|}{\Delta X}$

Using step 4, observe that as $f(X)$ approaches 0 from the left (i.e., $X = -1$, $X = -0.5$, $X = -0.3$, etc.) the slope approaches -6. However, as $f(X)$ approaches 0 from the right (i.e., $X = 1$, $X = 0.5$, $X = 0.3$, etc.) the slope of the function approaches $+6$. Therefore, the limit of the difference quotient as X approaches 0 does not exist and the function is not differentiable at $X = 0$.

This discussion has shown that for a function to be differentiable at a point, not only must the conditions of continuity be met, but the function also must not have any sharp changes of direction at that point. Although such exceptions to differentiability exist, continuity and smoothness of all functions will be assumed throughout this presentation.

Computing the Derivative by the Simple Power Rule

The simple power rule is a technique frequently used to compute the derivative of a function. An example will help to explain this technique while providing additional insight into the concept of the derivative.

Example 10.15
For $f(X) = X^2$, find the derivative.
   Solving this problem requires determination of the functional expression for the instantaneous rate of change at any point on the function. The general expression for the difference quotient is

$$\dfrac{f(X + \Delta X) - f(X)}{\Delta X}$$

Substituting $f(X) = X^2$ leads to the following derivation of the difference quotient:

$$Y = f(X) = X^2$$

$$\dfrac{f(X + \Delta X) - f(X)}{\Delta X} = \dfrac{(X + \Delta X)^2 - X^2}{\Delta X}$$

$$= \dfrac{X^2 + 2X\Delta X + (\Delta X)^2 - X^2}{\Delta X}$$

$$= \dfrac{2X\Delta X + (\Delta X)^2}{\Delta X}$$

Therefore,

$$\frac{f(X + \Delta X) - f(X)}{\Delta X} = 2X + \Delta X$$

As described above, the derivative, or $dY/dX = d(X^2)/dX$, is found by determining the limit of the difference quotient as ΔX approaches 0. This leads to the following conclusion:

$$\frac{df(X)}{dX} = \frac{d(X^2)}{dX} = \lim_{\Delta X \to 0} 2X + \Delta X = 2X$$

It is concluded that the derivative of X^2 is equal to $2X$. This means that any value for X can be substituted into $2X$ and the result represents the slope of the function $Y = X^2$ at that point. For example, if $X = 4$, then $f(X) = X^2 = 16$ and the slope at this point is equal to $2X = 2(4) = 8$. Consequently, the function has an instantaneous rate of change (slope) equal to $+8$ at the point $X = 4$, $Y = 16$.

Another example will provide a generalization of the simple power rule.

Example 10.16
For $f(X) = X^3$, find the derivative.

Again, the difference quotient is determined by using $f(X) = X^3$ as follows:

$$\text{Difference quotient} = \frac{f(X + \Delta X) - f(X)}{\Delta X}$$

$$Y = f(X) = X^3$$

$$\frac{f(X + \Delta X) - f(X)}{\Delta X} = \frac{(X + \Delta X)^3 - X^3}{\Delta X}$$

$$= \frac{(X + \Delta X)[X^2 + 2X\Delta X + (\Delta X)^2] - X^3}{\Delta X}$$

$$= \frac{X^3 + 2X^2\Delta X + X(\Delta X)^2 + X^2\Delta X + 2X(\Delta X)^2 + (\Delta X)^3 - X^3}{\Delta X}$$

Combining terms in the numerator yields:

$$\frac{f(X + \Delta X) - f(X)}{\Delta X} = \frac{3X^2\Delta X + 3X(\Delta X)^2 + (\Delta X)^3}{\Delta X}$$

Dividing each term in the numerator by ΔX gives the expression for the difference quotient.

$$\frac{f(X + \Delta X) - f(X)}{\Delta X} = 3X^2 + 3X\Delta X + (\Delta X)^2$$

The tangent slope is determined by finding the limit of the difference quotient (secant slope) as $\Delta X \to 0$. This yields the following result:

$$\lim_{\Delta X \to 0} [3X^2 + 3X \Delta X + (\Delta X)^2] = 3X^2$$

And it is shown that the derivative of $f(X) = X^3$ is $3X^2$:

$$\frac{df(X)}{dX} = f'(X) = 3X^2$$

Although these examples constitute a very brief demonstration, they permit a general statement of the simple power rule for determining the derivative of a function.

Rule 1: The Simple Power Rule:

If $f(X) = X^n$
then $f'(X) = nX^{n-1}$

Example 10.17

If $\quad f(X) = X^7$
then $\quad f'(X) = 7X^6$

Example 10.18

If $\quad f(X) = X^{2/3}$
then $\quad f'(X) = \frac{2}{3} X^{-1/3}$

Example 10.19

If $\quad f(X) = X^{-2/5}$
then $\quad f'(X) = \frac{-2}{5} X^{-7/5}$

The Derivative and the Slope

This discussion has pointed out that the derivative yields a function expressing the instantaneous rate of change of the original function at any point where the latter is continuous and smooth.

This relation permits use of the derivative to find the slope of a function at various points. A positive first derivative when substituting a given X value indicates that the function is increasing at that point. Similarly, a negative first derivative is an indication of a decreasing function at a point. If the first derivative is zero, the function is stationary (neither increasing nor decreasing) at that point. Observe that a given function may satisfy any or all of the three conditions over its range. These slope relations are useful for many business applications of calculus.

10.6 Additional Rules of Differentiation

The remainder of this chapter focuses on additional techniques of differentiation. Only a few applications are introduced at this point as the primary goal is to introduce the techniques. Chapter 11 concentrates on the business applications of differentiation.

Identification of rules by number includes a continuation from the simple power rule (Rule 1). Rules 2 to 6 employ the prime notation $f'(X)$ to designate the first derivative of a function.

Rule 2: The derivative of any constant is zero.

$$\text{If } f(X) = K, \text{ where } K \text{ is any constant,}$$
$$\text{then } f'(X) = 0$$

Example 10.20

If $\quad f(X) = 18$

then $\quad f'(X) = 0$

For $f(X) = 18$, the function does not change in response to a change in X. Therefore, the numerator of the difference quotient has a value of zero as $f(X + \Delta X) = 18$ and $f(X) = 18$. Thus, the limit of the difference quotient as ΔX approaches 0 is zero. The function $f(X) = 18$ is stationary throughout its range as it has a slope of zero.

Rule 3: A constant factor may be placed inside or outside the differentiation instruction without changing the result.

$$\text{If } f(X) = Kg(X)$$
$$\text{then } f'(X) = Kg'(X) = g'(KX)$$

Example 10.21

If $\quad f(X) = 3X^2$

then $\quad f'(X) = 6X$

or $\quad 3f'(X^2) = (3)(2X) = 6X$

Both formulations are equivalent. Note also the following example:

Example 10.22

If $\quad f(X) = 7X$

then $\quad f'(X) = 7$

or $\quad 7f'(X) = (7)(1)(X^0) = 7$

Rule 4: The derivative of a sum or difference is equal to the sum or difference of the derivatives.

If $f(X) = g(X) \pm h(X)$
then $f'(X) = g'(X) \pm h'(X)$

Example 10.23

If $\quad f(X) = 3X^3 - 4X^2 + 6X - 20$

then $\quad f'(X) = \dfrac{d(3X^3)}{dX} - \dfrac{d(4X^2)}{dX} + 6\dfrac{d(X)}{dX} - \dfrac{d(20)}{dX}$

$\qquad\qquad\quad = 9X^2 - 8X + 6 - 0$

$\qquad\qquad\quad = 9X^2 - 8X + 6$

Rule 4 is derived from the rule for taking the limit of a sum or difference.

Rule 5: The Product Rule:

The derivative of the product of two differentiable functions is equal to the first function times the derivative of the second function plus the second function times the derivative of the first function.

If $f(X) = g(X)h(X)$
then $f'(X) = g(X)h'(X) + h(X)g'(X)$

Example 10.24

If $\quad g(X) = 3X^2 \quad$ and $\quad h(X) = 6X^5$
and $\quad f(X) = g(X)h(X) = (3X^2)(6X^5)$
then $\quad f'(X) = g(X)h'(X) + h(X)g'(X)$
$\qquad\qquad\quad = 3X^2 h'(6X^5) + 6X^5 g'(3X^2)$
$\qquad\qquad\quad = 3X^2(30X^4) + 6X^5(6X)$
$\qquad\qquad\quad = 90X^6 + 36X^6 = 126X^6$

Rule 6: The Quotient Rule:

The derivative of the quotient of two functions is equal to the denominator times the derivative of the numerator minus the numerator times the derivative of the denominator, all divided by the square of the denominator.

If $f(X) = \dfrac{g(X)}{h(X)}$

then $f'(X) = \dfrac{h(X)g'(X) - g(X)h'(X)}{[h(X)]^2}$

Example 10.25

If $\quad g(X) = 3X^2 + 2 \quad$ and $\quad h(X) = 2X - 5$

and $\quad f(X) = \dfrac{g(X)}{h(X)} = \dfrac{3X^2 + 2}{2X - 5}$

then $\quad f'(X) = \dfrac{h(X)g'(X) - g(X)h'(X)}{[h(X)]^2}$

$= \dfrac{(2X - 5)(6X) - (3X^2 + 2)(2)}{(2X - 5)^2}$

$= \dfrac{12X^2 - 30X - 6X^2 - 4}{4X^2 - 20X + 25}$

$= \dfrac{6X^2 - 30X - 4}{4X^2 - 20X + 25}$

The next rule is the *chain rule of differentiation*. It is applicable to many of the other rules to follow. The chain rule is a technique for differentiating composite functions where, in general, Y is a function of U, U is a function of X, and the derivative of Y with respect to X is desired.

Rule 7: The Chain Rule of Differentiation:

If $Y = f(U)$ and $U = f(X)$

then $\dfrac{dY}{dX} = \dfrac{dY}{dU} \dfrac{dU}{dX}$

For example, the chain rule could be used if a cosmetics firm knows that profit is a function of sales and that sales are a function of advertising expenditures. The firm wants to determine the first derivative of profit with respect to advertising expenditures.

Example 10.26

For a cosmetics company,

$P = 0.002S^2 + 50$

$S = 4A^2 - 30$

where P = profit, S = sales, and A = advertising expenditures measured in thousands of dollars. Find dP/dA.

By the chain rule,

$\dfrac{dP}{dA} = \dfrac{dP}{dS} \dfrac{dS}{dA}$

$\dfrac{dP}{dS} = 0.004S$

$\dfrac{dS}{dA} = 8A$

Consequently,

$$\frac{dP}{dA} = (0.004S)(8A)$$

Substituting $S = 4A^2 - 30$ yields the derivative dP/dA as follows:

$$\frac{dP}{dA} = 0.004(4A^2 - 30)(8A)$$

$$= (0.016A^2 - 0.12)(8A)$$

$$= 0.128A^3 - 0.96A$$

This last expression represents the change in profit in response to a change in advertising expenditures at any point on the composite function relating profit and advertising.

The same result is obtained by the substitution of $S = 4A^2 - 30$ into the original profit function and differentiation of P with respect to A. However, the chain rule often is employed to simplify calculations requiring more detailed substitutions.

In using the chain rule, remember that notations such as dP/dS and dS/dA are differentiation instructions, not fractions. Thus, in this example, the dS notations are not simply divided in the expression for the first derivative.

Several techniques of differentiation which use the chain rule are discussed below as separate sections of the chapter. First, however, to conclude this section, the power function rule, one of the primary extensions of the chain rule, is presented.

Rule 8: The Power Function Rule:

> The derivative of the nth power of a differentiable function is the product of three terms: the power n, the function raised to the power $n - 1$, and the derivative of the function, shown below by the prime notation $f'(X)$.

This is shown in notational form as follows:

If $Y = [f(X)]^n$

then $\dfrac{dY}{dX} = n[f(X)]^{n-1} [f'(X)]$

Example 10.27

If $Y = (3X^2 - 14)^2$

then $\dfrac{dY}{dX} = 2(3X^2 - 14)(6X)$

$= 36X^3 - 168X$

Differential Calculus: Principles

These eight rules include many of the fundamental operations of calculus. The next two sections concern specific techniques, the differentiation of exponential functions and logarithmic functions, respectively.

EXERCISES

1. Find the derivative $f'(X)$ for each of the following functions:
   a. $f(X) = 4$
   b. $f(X) = 25$
   c. $f(X) = \dfrac{3}{X}$
   d. $f(X) = 4X^{-1/3}$
   e. $f(X) = 3X^{1/2}$
   f. $f(X) = 6X^{-2}$
   g. $f(X) = \dfrac{1}{(2X + 6)^2}$
   h. $f(X) = 3X^0$
   i. $f(X) = \dfrac{X^3 + 7}{4}$
   j. $f(X) = 3X^{-1/2} + 2X^3 - X^{-4}$
   k. $f(X) = 27X^{1/3}$
   l. $f(X) = \dfrac{1}{8X + 14}$
   m. $f(X) = \dfrac{X^{-2/3}}{4}$
   n. $f(X) = \dfrac{1}{X^{-3/4}}$
   o. $f(X) = \dfrac{4}{3X^{-3}}$
   p. $f(X) = X^{7/3}$
   q. $f(X) = 2X^{1/2} + 3X^{2/3}$
   r. $f(X) = 4X^3 - 2X + 17$
   s. $f(X) = \dfrac{X^{1/3} + 17}{20}$
   t. $f(X) = 6X^{-1/2} - 2X^3 + 15$

2. Find the first derivative with respect to X for each of the following products and quotients. Simplify as much as possible.
   a. $f(X) = (3X)(4X^2 + 2)$
   b. $f(X) = (6X^2 + 7)(2X^{1/2} - 3)$
   c. $f(X) = \dfrac{4X^2 - 2X + 5}{2X + 8}$
   d. $f(X) = \dfrac{3X^2 + 5X - 16}{X - 2}$
   e. $f(X) = (3X^{1/2})(2X^{-1/3})$
   f. $f(X) = \dfrac{X^2}{2}(X^{-3})$
   g. $f(X) = \dfrac{X^4 + 3X^2 + 14}{X - 2}$
   h. $f(X) = (2X + 5)(2X - 5)$
   i. $f(X) = \dfrac{2X + 6}{3X^{1/3}}$
   j. $f(X) = (X)(3X^0 + 4)$

3. Find each derivative as instructed. Use the chain rule of differentiation where applicable.
   a. $Y = 6X^2$ and $X = 2Z + 1$. Find $\dfrac{dY}{dZ}$
   b. $Y = 2X^{1/2} + 14X$ and $X = Z$. Find $\dfrac{dY}{dZ}$
   c. $G = 3H$ and $H = 7L^2 - 10$. Find $\dfrac{dG}{dL}$
   d. $Y = 3X$ and $X = 4Z^{1/2} - Z^2$. Find $\dfrac{dY}{dZ}$
   e. $S = 3X + 6$ and $X = (2T^2 + 5)(3T - 2)$. Find $\dfrac{dS}{dT}$

f. $G = 2H^{-1/3}$ and $H = 8L^3 + 5$. Find $\dfrac{dG}{dL}$

4. Find dY/dX for each of the following. Simplify as much as possible.
   a. $Y = (3X + 6)^2$
   b. $Y = (4X - 2)^{1/2}(2X)$
   c. $Y = (4X^2 + X - 14)^3$
   d. $Y = (2X^{-1} + 3X^{-3})^2$
   e. $Y = (14X - 21X^{1/3})^2$
   f. $Y = (6X^3 - 3X^2 + 17X - 20)^5$

5. For each function below, find the value of the first derivative with respect to X at the specified point. Is the function increasing, decreasing, or constant at the specified point?
   a. $f(X) = 3X^3 - 7$ at $X = 1$
   b. $f(X) = 4X + 15$ at $X = 7$
   c. $f(X) = X^2 - 6X + 30$ at $X = 4$
   d. $f(X) = (2X + 3)(X^2 + 5X)$ at $X = 3$
   e. $f(X) = 4X^3 - 3X^2 + 5$ at $X = 2$
   f. $f(X) = 2X^2 - 20X + 15$ at $X = 5$
   g. $f(X) = -3X^3 + X^2 - 10X + 18$ at $X = 3$
   h. $f(X) = 20$ at $X = 15$

10.7 The Differentiation of Exponential Functions

As Rules 9, 10, and 11 concern exponential functions, a brief review of them may be useful. In the earlier discussion of functions (especially Chapter 8), exponential functions were described as those functions where the independent variable or variables are exponents. Also, it was pointed out that the constant e ($= 2.71818\ldots$) is applied frequently as a base for exponential functions used in business and economic analysis. In addition to the reasons offered in Chapter 8, the constant e also is used because the function $Y = e^X$ is its own derivative, thus facilitating measurement of rates of change.

Rules 9 and 10 relate to differentiation of exponential functions using the base e, and Rule 11 generalizes these principles to all bases:

Rule 9: The Exponential Rule for Base e:

If $Y = e^X$

then $\dfrac{dY}{dX} = \dfrac{d(e^X)}{dX} = e^X$

Example 10.28

$Y = e^X$ at $X = 2.9$

$\dfrac{dY}{dX} = e^{2.9} = 18.174$ (Table III)

Rule 10: The Exponential Function Rule for Base e:

If $Y = e^{f(X)}$

then $\dfrac{dY}{dX} = \dfrac{d}{dX}(e^{f(X)}) = e^{f(X)} f'(X)$

Example 10.29

$Y = f(X) = e^{3X^2 + 5X - 4}$

$\dfrac{dY}{dX} = \dfrac{d}{dX} e^{3X^2 + 5X - 4}$

$= (e^{3X^2 + 5X - 4})(6X + 5)$

As with the power function rule, Rules 9 and 10 are special cases of the chain rule. In Rule 9 observe that the derivative dY/dX of X is equal to 1. Rule 10 also employs the chain rule as the exponent of the e term is differentiated.

Rule 11 extends these rules to include all positive bases except 1 (1 raised to any power is equal to 1).

Rule 11: The Exponential Function Rule:

If $Y = a^{f(X)}$

then $\dfrac{dY}{dX} = \dfrac{d}{dX} a^{f(X)} = a^{f(X)} (\ln a) f'(X)$

where a is any positive number except 1 and $\ln a$ indicates the natural logarithm of a.

Notice that as $\ln e = 1$ and $d/dX(X) = 1$, Rules 9 and 10 are special cases of Rule 11 where $a = e = 2.71828$. ...

Example 10.30

If $Y = 4^{X^3 - 2X^2 + 14}$

then $\dfrac{dY}{dX} = 4^{X^3 - 2X^2 + 14}(\ln 4)(3X^2 - 4X)$

As $\ln 4 = 1.38629$ (Table II),

$\dfrac{dY}{dX} = 4^{X^3 - 2X^2 + 14}(1.38629)(3X^2 - 4X)$

$= 4^{X^3 - 2X^2 + 14}(4.15887X^2 - 5.54516X)$

Therefore, Rules 9, 10, and 11 include the methods necessary for the differentiation of functions where the independent variable or a function of the independent variable is an exponent.

10.8 The Differentiation of Logarithmic Functions

In Chapter 8 it was pointed out that there is a close association between logarithms and exponents since the logarithm of a number is the power to which a stated base must be raised to yield that number (e.g., log 100 = 2 with base 10 common logarithms means $10^2 = 100$). This relation can be used to explain the differentiation of functions where the independent variable is in logarithmic form, for example, $Y = \ln X$ or $Y = \ln [f(X)]$. The following discussion will concentrate on natural, or base e, logarithms.

If $Y = \ln X$, then $e^Y = X$ according to the relation between exponents and logarithms. Rule 12 can be derived by taking the first derivative with respect to X for each side of $e^Y = X$ as follows:

$$e^Y = X$$

$$\frac{d}{dX} e^Y = \frac{d}{dX} X$$

As $d/dX(X) = 1$, then

$$\frac{d}{dX} e^Y = 1$$

$$e^Y \frac{dY}{dX} = 1 \qquad \text{by Rule 10}$$

Therefore,

$$\frac{dY}{dX} = \frac{1}{e^Y}$$

As $e^Y = X$, then

$$\frac{dY}{dX} = \frac{1}{X}$$

Therefore, if $Y = \ln X$, then $dY/dX = 1/X$. This is Rule 12 for the differentiation of logarithmic functions.

Rule 12: The Logarithmic Rule for Differentiation:

If $Y = \ln X$

then $\dfrac{dY}{dX} = \dfrac{1}{X}$

Example 10.31

If $\qquad Y = \ln X \qquad$ at $X = 6$

then $\qquad \dfrac{d}{dX} = \dfrac{1}{6} = 0.167$

To determine the derivative with respect to X when $Y = \ln f(X)$, the chain rule and Rule 12 are combined.

Rule 13: The Logarithmic Function Rule:

If $Y = \ln f(X)$

then $\dfrac{dY}{dX} = \dfrac{1}{f(X)} f'(X) = \dfrac{f'(X)}{f(X)}$

Thus, Rule 13 states that the derivative of a logarithmic function ln $f(X)$ is equal to the reciprocal of the function multiplied by the derivative of the function.

Example 10.32

If $Y = \ln (3X^2 + 2X - 6)$

then $\dfrac{dY}{dX} = \dfrac{1}{3X^2 + 2X - 6}(6X + 2) = \dfrac{6X + 2}{3X^2 + 2X - 6}$

This expression can be used to find the instantaneous rate of change of the function $Y = \ln (3X^2 + 2X - 6)$ at any X value.

As mentioned in Chapter 8, the logarithmic form of a variable often is used to incorporate percentage changes into a functional relation. The frequency with which this measurement is used in business gives added importance to the differentiation of logarithmic functions. The following exercises will give practice in differentiating both exponential and logarithmic functions.

EXERCISES

1. For each function, find the first derivative with respect to X.
   a. $f(X) = e^3$
   b. $f(X) = e^{6X^2+4}$
   c. $f(X) = 5^{3X}$
   d. $f(X) = e^{-2X^2}$
   e. $f(X) = 12^{5X+6} + 16^{-2X^2}$
   f. $f(X) = (0.5)^{2X^2-3X}$

2. Find dY/dX for each function.
   a. $Y = \ln X^2$
   b. $Y = \ln (2X^2 - 5X + 16)$
   c. $Y = \ln (X^{-3})$
   d. $Y = \ln X$
   e. $Y = \ln (3X^{-2} + X^{-1})$
   f. $Y = \ln \dfrac{1}{X^3}$

3. Using Table II (natural logarithms) and Table III (e values), find the value of the first derivative at each specified point.
   a. $f(X) = e^{2X-7}$ at $X = 4$
   b. $f(X) = e^{X-2}$ at $X = 2$
   c. $f(X) = e^{X^2-4X-3}$ at $X = 5$
   d. $f(X) = \ln (3X^2 + 2X - 7)$ at $X = 5$
   e. $f(X) = \ln (X^{-2} - X + 16)$ at $X = 2$
   f. $f(X) = \ln X^3$ at $X = 4$

10.9 Higher-Order Derivatives

The concept of the derivative can be extended to higher derivatives, i.e., the second derivative, the third derivative, etc. As the first derivative measures the slope of a function at a point, the second derivative measures the instantaneous rate of change *of the slope*. The second derivative is the derivative of the first derivative and so on.

The second derivative of the function of X with respect to X is designated in any of the following ways:

$$\frac{d^2 f(X)}{dX^2}$$

$$\frac{d^2 Y}{dX^2}$$

$$f''(X)$$

Each of these gives an instruction to compute the second derivative of the function.

The rate of change concept can be applied similarly to third, fourth, or higher derivatives. However, in business applications importance is attached to the second derivative. An example stressing the computation and interpretation of the second derivative follows.

Example 10.33
Find the second derivative of $f(X) = 4X^2$. If $f(X) = 4X^2$, then $f'(X) = 8X$ by the simple power rule and Rule 3.

To find the second derivative, the simple power rule and Rule 3 must be applied to $f'(X) = 8X$. Thus

$$f'(X) = 8X$$

$$\frac{d^2 f(X)}{dX^2} = f''(X) = 8$$

An interpretation of the second derivative is provided by the three parts of Figure 10.6.

In part *a*, the function $f(X) = 4X^2$ is shown as a vertical parabola. The slope of this function at any point, the first derivative, is shown in part *b* as the linear function $f'(X) = 8X$. This indicates that the value of the slope is changing continually along the curve $f(X) = 4X^2$ and has both negative and positive values.

The second derivative graphed in part *c* is a straight line, $f''(X) = 8$. This indicates that the rate of change of the slope is $+8$ at all values of X. Although the function $f(X) = 4X^2$ is changing at varying rates throughout its range, the slope of the function has a constant rate of change throughout the range of the function. This means that at any point the slope is increasing

Differential Calculus: Principles

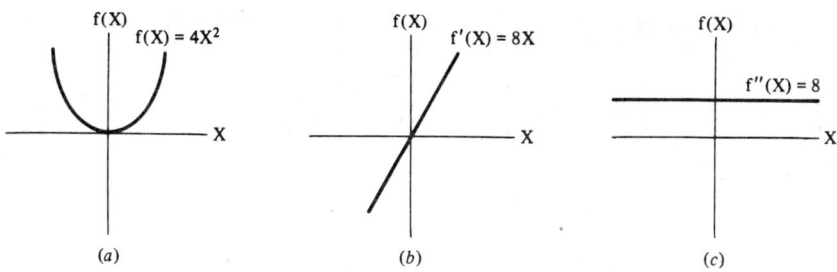

FIGURE 10.6 Graphical interpretation of the second derivative.

(a) $f(X) = 4X^2$
(b) $f'(X) = 8X$
(c) $f''(X) = 8$

by 8 *in absolute value*. In other words, negative slopes are becoming *less negative* by 8 units and positive slopes are increasing by 8 as X changes. This is explained further by the data in Table 10.2.

Thus, the slope is increasing at a constant rate of 8 units over the range of data selected.

Further interpretations and several important uses of the second derivative will be included in Chapter 11. A detailed discussion of derivatives higher than the second is not provided in this text as their application in business is limited.

EXERCISES

1. Find the second derivative with respect to X of each of the following functions:
    a. $f(X) = 5X$
    b. $f(X) = X^2 + 3X - 2$
    c. $f(X) = X^2 - 2X^{-3} + 5$
    d. $f(X) = X^{-1/3}$
    e. $f(X) = \dfrac{X^3}{4} - X^{3/2} + 5X$
    f. $f(X) = -3X^2 + X^{-2}$
    g. $f(X) = (X^2 + 1)(3X - 4)$
    h. $f(X) = (X^3 + 4X)^2$
    i. $f(X) = (2X^2)^3$
    j. $f(X) = (X^3)(2X - 14)$

TABLE 10.2 Values for X, $f(X) = 4X^2$, $f'(X) = 8X$, and $f''(X) = 8$

X	$f(X)$	$f'(X)$	$f''(X)$
-3	36	-24	8
-2	16	-16	8
-1	4	-8	8
0	0	0	8
1	4	8	8
2	16	16	8
3	36	24	8

2. For each function listed below, find the value of the second derivative with respect to X at the specified point. Interpret each value.
   a. $f(X) = 3X^3 - 2X^2 + X - 12$ at $X = 2$
   b. $f(X) = 10X^2 - 20X + 1$ at $X = 3$
   c. $f(X) = X^{1/3}$ at $X = 27$
   d. $f(X) = X^{-1/2}$ at $X = 4$
   e. $f(X) = 16X - 40$ at $X = 7$
   f. $f(X) = X^{5/2} + 6X$ at $X = 9$
3. For the following quadratic function,

   $$f(X) = 5X^2 - 6X + 8$$

   find the first and second derivative at $X = 3$ and $X = 5$. What can you conclude about the slope and rate of change of the slope at these two points? What can you conclude by comparing the difference in the rate of change of the slope at the two points?
4. a. Given the following linear function,

   $$f(X) = 6X - 10$$

   find the first and second derivatives with respect to X. Interpret each answer.

   b. For the following vertical parabola,

   $$f(X) = 3X^2 + 4X + 10$$

   find the first derivative and second derivative with respect to X at $X = -3$ and $X = +3$. What is indicated about the function at these two points?

   c. For the following cubic function,

   $$f(X) = -X^3 + 12X^2 + 7X - 4$$

   find the value of the first and second derivatives with respect to X at $X = 3$ and $X = 6$. Compare and interpret the slope and the rate of change of the slope at the two points.

10.10 Implicit Differentiation

This chapter concludes with a presentation of two additional techniques of differentiation, *implicit differentiation* and *partial differentiation*. First, implicit differentiation is considered.

In presenting the previous rules and techniques, the dependent variable Y has been stated as a function of the independent variable. For example, consider the following equation and related functional statement

1. $Y = \dfrac{X^2}{3X + 6}$ or $f(X) = \dfrac{X^2}{3X + 6}$

Differential Calculus: Principles

In this form, the function represents an explicit rule for determining Y based on the value of X. Thus, the equation is in explicit form.

If equation 1 is in the form,

2, $3XY + 6Y - X^2 = 0 \quad$ or $\quad f(X, Y) = 3XY + 6Y - X^2$

it is referred to as being in *implicit form* because Y is defined implicitly as a function of X based on some knowledge of the relation between Y, the dependent variable, and X, the independent variable. That is, there is an implied understanding of the functional relationship between the variables.

Implicit differentiation is a technique for determining the first derivative of the dependent variable with respect to the independent variable by using an equation in implicit form, as equation 2 above. The first derivative may be an expression having terms with both variables, but one variable is the implied dependent variable. Thus, differentiation is carried out with respect to the implied independent variable.

When using the implicit form of an equation, differentiation is carried out term by term with the objective of solving for dY/dX. For example, in the expression

$$3XY + 6Y - X^2 = 0$$

it must be implied that Y (the dependent variable) is a function of X (the independent variable) in order to find dY/dX.

A description of the process of implicit differentiation and an example using the expression $3XY + 6Y - X^2 = 0$ follows. When reading this material, keep in mind that the chain rule is important in implicit differentiation.

To carry out implicit differentiation, the expression is differentiated term by term. When differentiating terms which include Y but not X, the chain rule must be used. For these terms, the procedure is to find

$$\frac{dY(X)}{dY} \frac{dY}{dX}$$

where $dY(X)/dY$ indicates differentiation with respect to Y of the particular term. The notation $dY(X)/dY$ indicates that Y is a function of X but is not explicitly stated. For example, the derivative of the term $4Y^5$ with respect to X is found by using the chain rule as follows:

$$\frac{d(4Y^5)}{dX} = \frac{d}{dY}(4Y^5)\frac{dY}{dX}$$

$$= 20Y^4 \frac{dY}{dX}$$

The differentiation notation dY/dX is the unknown to be solved for in the implicit differentiation.

For terms which combine X and Y factors, the product rule and the chain rule are used to find dY/dX. For example, consider the term X^2Y and its differentiation with respect to X:

$$\frac{d}{dX}(X^2Y) = X^2 \frac{dY}{dY}\frac{dY}{dX} + Y\frac{d}{dX}(X^2)$$

$$= X^2 (1) \frac{dY}{dX} + Y(2X)$$

$$= X^2 \frac{dY}{dX} + 2XY$$

The process followed was to first use the product rule on the expression X^2Y and then use the chain rule for the differentiation of any Y terms in the formation of the product.

Finally, it should be remembered that the goal of implicit differentiation is to find an expression for dY/dX. The following example demonstrates solution by implicit differentiation.

Example 10.34

For $3XY + 6Y - X^2 = 0$ or $f(X, Y) = 3XY + 6Y - X^2$, find dY/dX. The derivative is determined through term-by-term differentiation as follows:

1. $\dfrac{d}{dX}(3XY + 6Y - X^2) = 3X\left[\dfrac{d}{dY}(Y)\dfrac{dY}{dX}\right] + Y\dfrac{dX}{dX} + \dfrac{d}{dY}(6Y)\dfrac{dY}{dX} - \dfrac{d}{dX}(X^2)$

2. $3X\dfrac{dY}{dX} + 3Y + 6\dfrac{dY}{dX} - 2X$

3. $3X\dfrac{dY}{dX} + 6\dfrac{dY}{dX} = 2X - 3Y$

4. $\dfrac{dY}{dX}(3X + 6) = 2X - 3Y$

5. $\dfrac{dY}{dX} = \dfrac{2X - 3Y}{3X + 6}$

Step 1 describes the operations required for the differentiation, including use of the product rule and the chain rule. As $d/dY\,(Y) = 1$, $d(6Y)/dY = 6$, and $d(X^2)/dX = 2X$, operations in step 1 yield the expression in step 2.

After step 2, the expression must be solved for dY/dX to complete the implicit differentiation. This is carried out in steps 3 through 5. Step 5 yields the derivative dY/dX. Thus, the expression in step 5 represents the instantaneous rate of change of Y with respect to X at any point on the implicit function $3XY + 6Y - X^2 = 0$.

An additional example will further demonstrate this technique.

Example 10.35

For $X^3Y^2 + 5X - 3Y^3 = 0$, find dY/dX.

Differential Calculus: Principles   297

$$\frac{d}{dX}(X^3Y^2 + 5X - 3Y^3) = X^3 \frac{d}{dY}(Y^2)\frac{dY}{dX} + Y^2 \frac{d}{dX}(X^3) + \frac{d(5X)}{dX} - \frac{d}{dY}(3Y^3)\frac{dY}{dX}$$

$$= X^3 2Y \frac{dY}{dX} + Y^2(3X^2) + 5 - 9Y^2 \frac{dY}{dX}$$

$$9Y^2 \frac{dY}{dX} - 2X^3Y \frac{dY}{dX} = 5 + 3X^2Y^2$$

$$\frac{dY}{dX}(9Y^2 - 2X^3Y) = 5 + 3X^2Y^2$$

$$\frac{dY}{dX} = \frac{5 + 3X^2Y^2}{9Y^2 - 2X^3Y}$$

Again, this example applies the product rule and chain rule in determining the derivative dY/dX. Readers should confirm the results of each step.

It should be remembered that implicit differentiation is used when the underlying relationship between dependent and independent variables is understood but the equation and related functional statement have combined both variables in a group of terms [e.g., $f(X, Y) = 0$]. Establishing the instantaneous rate of change of the function requires differentiation of the equation with respect to the implied independent variable. The final result dY/dX may include both variables but this derivative is equivalent to the first derivative of the explicitly stated equation.

Example 10.36
To demonstrate this last point, consider the equation from Example 10.34,
$$3XY + 6Y - X^2 = 0$$
In *explicit* form, with Y in terms of X, this equation is stated as
$$Y = \frac{X^2}{3X + 6}$$
Using the quotient rule, the derivative with respect to X of the explicit equation is established as follows:

1. $Y = \dfrac{X^2}{3X + 6}$

2. $\dfrac{dY}{dX} = \dfrac{(3X + 6)(2X) - (X^2)(3)}{(3X + 6)^2}$

3. $= \dfrac{6X^2 + 12X - 3X^2}{(3X + 6)^2}$

4. $= \dfrac{3X^2 + 12X}{(3X + 6)^2}$

At this point, observe that the derivative of the implicit form found in Example 10.34 was

5. $\dfrac{dY}{dX} = \dfrac{2X - 3Y}{3X + 6}$

Substitution of $Y = X^2/(3X + 6)$ into expression 5 yields the following result, shown in steps 6 through 10.

6. $\dfrac{dY}{dX} = \dfrac{2X - 3[X^2/(3X + 6)]}{3X + 6}$

7. $= \dfrac{2X - 3X^2/(3X + 6)}{3X + 6}$

8. $= \dfrac{2X(3X + 6) - 3X^2}{(3X + 6)^2}$

9. $= \dfrac{6X^2 + 12X - 3X^2}{(3X + 6)^2}$

10. $= \dfrac{3X^2 + 12X}{(3X + 6)^2}$

The identical results in steps 4 and 10 indicate the similarity of differentiating both the implicit and explicit forms of the equation.

10.11 Partial Differentiation

Thus far, the discussion has focused on functions with one dependent variable and one independent variable. This section concerns differentiation of functions with one dependent variable and more than one independent variable.

Functions with two or more independent variables are encountered frequently in business. For example, the sales of color televisions may be a function of (1) household income, (2) family size, and (3) the age of children in the family.

If the independent variables do not influence each other, then one (e.g., X_1) can vary without causing any change in the other independent variables. Consequently, the dependent variable will change in response to a change in this one independent variable.

In general, partial differentiation is a technique for isolating the effect on the dependent variable of one independent variable in a multiple-variable relationship. For example, partial differentiation is a means to evaluate the impact of increased household income on color television sales assuming no change in family size or age of children in the family.

The difference quotient expressing such a change can be taken to the limit of zero for a change in the independent variable. The result of this process yields the *partial derivative* of the dependent variable with respect to the specified independent variable. The partial derivative is defined as follows:

THE PARTIAL DERIVATIVE REPRESENTS THE INSTANTANEOUS RATE OF CHANGE IN THE DEPENDENT VARIABLE IN RESPONSE TO A CHANGE IN ONE INDEPENDENT VARIABLE HOLDING EACH OTHER INDEPENDENT VARIABLE CONSTANT AT SOME STATED VALUE

The symbol notating the partial differentiation operation uses the lowercase delta ∂. Thus, the partial derivative of Y with respect to X_1 is stated

$$\frac{\partial Y}{\partial X_1}$$

In comparison to the notation $f'(X)$ used for the derivative of functions with one independent variable, the notations f_1, f_2, f_3, etc. are used to express the partial derivative of Y with respect to X_1, X_2, X_3, etc., respectively.

Determination of partial derivatives often requires the application of rules concerning the value of zero for the derivative of a constant (Rule 2) and the placement of a constant within or outside the derivative symbol (Rule 3). As all independent variables other than the one being analyzed are considered constant terms, each of these is differentiated as a constant.

Example 10.37
For $Y = f(X_1, X_2, X_3) = 2X_1 + 4X_2 + X_3^2$, find $\partial Y / \partial X_2$:

$$\frac{\partial Y}{\partial X_2} = \frac{\partial(2X_1)}{\partial X_2} + \frac{\partial(4X_2)}{\partial X_2} + \frac{\partial(X_3)^2}{\partial X_2}$$

$$= 0 + 4 + 0 = 4$$

Observe that $2X_1$ and X_3^2 are treated as constants and the derivative of each is equal to zero.

Consider a second example where several terms include more than one independent variable.

Example 10.38
For $Y = f(X_1, X_2, X_3) = 3X_1 + 6X_1X_2 + 4X_2 + X_3^2$, find $\partial Y / \partial X_2$:

$$\frac{\partial Y}{\partial X_2} = 3\frac{\partial(X_1)}{\partial X_2} + 6\frac{\partial(X_1X_2)}{\partial X_2} + 4\frac{\partial(X_2)}{\partial X_2} + \frac{\partial X_3^2}{\partial X_2}$$

$$= 0 + 6X_1 + 4 + 0$$

$$= 6X_1 + 4$$

Thus, each X_1 and X_3 is treated as a constant for the differentiation process resulting in a zero value for the $3X_1$ and X_3^2 terms and a derivative of $6X_1$ for the $6X_1X_2$ term.

A third example will demonstrate computation of all partial derivatives for a function with three independent variables. Each result applies the previous techniques.

Example 10.39
For $Y = 3X_1^2 + 4X_2 - 2X_3^3 + X_1X_3 + 7X_1X_2^2$, find $\partial Y/\partial X_1$, $\partial Y/\partial X_2$, and $\partial Y/\partial X_3$:

$$\frac{\partial Y}{\partial X_1} = 6X_1 + X_3 + 7X_2^2$$

$$\frac{\partial Y}{\partial X_2} = 4 + 14X_1X_2$$

$$\frac{\partial Y}{\partial X_3} = X_1 - 6X_3^2$$

Each of these results is interpreted as the instantaneous rate of change in the function given a change in the particular independent variable holding all other independent variables constant at a stated value for each.

The final example will demonstrate partial differentiation of a function by use of the product rule.

Example 10.40
For $Y = f(X_1X_2) = (3X_1 - 7)(4X_1^2 - 3X_2^3)$, find $\partial Y/\partial X_1$ and $\partial Y/\partial X_2$:

$$\frac{\partial Y}{\partial X_1} = (3X_1 - 7)(8X_1) + (4X_1^2 - 3X_2^3)(3)$$

$$= 24X_1^2 - 56X_1 + 12X_1^2 - 9X_2^3$$

$$= 36X_1^2 - 56X_1 - 9X_2^3$$

$$\frac{\partial Y}{\partial X_2} = (3X_1 - 7)(-9X_2^2) + (4X_1^2 - 3X_2^3)(0)$$

$$= 63X_2^2 - 27X_1X_2^2 = 9(7X_2^2 - 3X_1X_2^2)$$

For each partial differentiation, the product rule is applied and each variable not included in the differentiation is treated as a constant. Readers should confirm each of these results.

Higher Partial Derivatives

As with derivatives, it is possible to compute partial derivatives of higher order. Thus, one can determine the second, third, or higher partial derivative

Differential Calculus: Principles

with respect to a certain independent variable. The notation used for the second partial derivative with respect to X_i is as follows:

$$\frac{\partial^2 Y}{\partial X_i^2}$$

For the third partial derivative with respect to X_i, the notation is

$$\frac{\partial^3 Y}{\partial X_i^3}$$

Of particular importance to the applications in this textbook will be second partial derivatives. To find the second partial derivative with respect to X_i, one must determine the partial derivative $\partial Y/\partial X_i$ and find the partial with respect to X_i of this result. This process is demonstrated in Example 10.41.

Example 10.41
For $Y = 3X_1^2 + 4X_1X_2 + 2X_2^3$, find $\partial^2 Y/\partial X_1^2$. First, $\partial Y/\partial X_1$ is determined as follows:

$$\frac{\partial Y}{\partial X_1} = 6X_1 + 4X_2$$

The partial derivative with respect to X_1 of this partial derivative is the second partial derivative. Thus,

$$\frac{\partial^2 Y}{\partial X_1^2} = \frac{\partial Y}{\partial X_1}(6X_1 + 4X_2) = 6$$

An extension of this concept concerns determination of *cross partial derivatives*. Cross partial derivatives are computed by first differentiating a function with respect to one independent variable and, subsequently, differentiating that result with respect to a second independent variable. The notation

$$\frac{\partial^2 Y}{\partial X_i \, \partial X_j}$$

indicates a cross partial derivative where the function is first differentiated with respect to X_i and the result is then differentiated with respect to X_j. An example will describe this technique.

Example 10.42
For $Y = 3X_1 - 6X_2^2 + 2X_1X_2 + 15$, find $\partial^2 Y/\partial X_2 \partial X_1$.

To obtain this result, Y first must be differentiated with respect to X_2.

The result of this operation then is differentiated with respect to X_1. These steps follow:

$$\frac{\partial^2 Y}{\partial X_2} = 2X_1 - 12X_2$$

$$\frac{\partial^2 Y}{\partial X_2 \, \partial X_1} = 2$$

Interpretation of the second partial derivative and the cross partial derivative follow from previous interpretations. That is, the second partial derivative of Y with respect to X_i measures the rate of change of the $\partial Y/\partial X_i$ with respect to X_i holding all other independent variables constant. The cross partial derivative

$$\frac{\partial^2 Y}{\partial X_i \, \partial X_j}$$

measures the rate of change of $\partial Y/\partial X_i$ with respect to X_j holding all other independent variables constant.

The second partial derivative and cross partial derivative are particularly useful in determining maximum and minimum points of functions with more than one independent variable. This technique and related applications are found in Chapter 11.

The following exercises will provide practice in both implicit differentiation and determination of partial derivatives.

EXERCISES

1. Find the partial derivative as instructed for each of the following functions:

   a. $Y = 6X_1^2 X_2 - 3X_2 + 5X_1 X_2^2$. Find $\dfrac{\partial Y}{\partial X_1}$.

   b. $Y = X_1 X_2^2 - X_2 X_3^{1/2} + 7X_3^2 - 2X_2^{1/2} X_3$. Find $\dfrac{\partial Y}{\partial X_3}$.

   c. $Y = -3X_1 + 2X_2^2 + 4X_2 X_3^2 - 2X_2^{1/2} X_3$. Find $\dfrac{\partial Y}{\partial X_2}$.

   d. $Y = 3X_1 + 4X_2 - 6X_1 X_2^2 + 4X_1^2 X_2^3$. Find $\dfrac{\partial^2 Y}{\partial X_1^2}$.

   e. $Y = 2X_1^2 X_2 + 5X_1^3 X_2^{1/5} + 6X_2$. Find $\dfrac{\partial^2 Y}{\partial X_2 \, \partial X_1}$.

   f. $Y = 3X_2 - 4X_1 + 5X_1 X_2$. Find $\dfrac{\partial^2 Y}{\partial X_1 \, \partial X_2}$ and $\dfrac{\partial^2 Y}{\partial X_2 \, \partial X_1}$.

2. For each equation below, find the expression for dY/dX assuming that Y is the dependent variable and X is the independent variable.

a. $2X^5 - 3X^3 + 4Y^2 - Y^4 = 0$ c. $3X^3 - 4XY + 2X^2Y^2 = 0$
b. $2X^2 + 3Y^2 - 7XY = 0$ d. $2X^{1/2} + Y^2 - 2X^3Y^2 = 0$

3. For each equation, where Y is implicitly a function of X, find dY/dX by implicit differentiation. Then, solve for Y and find dY/dX. Show the similarity in your answers.

   a. $3Y - 7X + 4XY = 0$ b. $Y - 5XY + 2X = 0$

4. For each function, find and interpret the specified partial derivative and evaluate the partial derivative at the selected point.

   a. $Y = 3X_1X_2 - X_2^2 + X_1^3 + 6X_2 - 3X_1$. Find $\dfrac{\partial Y}{\partial X_1}$ and evaluate at $X_1 = 2, X_2 = 3$.

   b. $Y = 4X_1^{1/2}X_2^{1/2} + X_1^2 + X_1^2X_2^2$. Find $\dfrac{\partial Y}{\partial X_2}$ and evaluate at $X_1 = 4, X_2 = 16$.

   c. $Y = X_2^{2/3}X_1X_3^2 + 6X_1X_3 - 4X_2X_3^2$. Find $\dfrac{\partial Y}{\partial X_3}$ and evaluate at $X_1 = 4, X_2 = 8$, and $X_3 = -3$.

   d. $Y = 2X_1^2X_2 - X_1 + 3X_2$. Find $\dfrac{\partial^2 Y}{\partial X_2 \, \partial X_1}$ and evaluate at $X_1 = 8, X_2 = 4$.

   e. $Y = 6X_1X_2^2 - 4X_2^3 + 3X_1^2 - X_1^2X_2$. Find $\dfrac{\partial^2 Y}{\partial X_1 \, \partial X_2}$ and evaluate at $X_1 = 8, X_2 = 5$.

10.12 Chapter Summary

This chapter has emphasized the fundamental definitions and techniques of differential calculus. Business applications have been limited as these are stressed in Chapter 11.

The concept of the derivative and its relation to the rate of change of a function have been explored and extended to other rate-of-change measurements referred to as higher derivatives. If a function can be differentiated, it is possible to identify the rate of change at any point on a function. Limitations on the differentiation process restrict this technique to functions which are continuous and smooth. The linkage between the limit of a function, continuity, and smoothness has been emphasized in defining the concept of the derivative and describing the techniques of differentiation.

Methods of differentiation have been specified in a series of rules found throughout the chapter. These rules include ways to differentiate product functions, quotient functions, composite functions, exponential functions, and logarithmic functions. In addition, implicit differentiation and partial differentiation have been described conceptually and by example. These two techniques allow, respectively, differentiation of functions where the independent-dependent variable relationship is not stated explicitly and differentiation of functions having more than one independent variable.

With an understanding of the concepts and techniques in this chapter, readers should be prepared to analyze the business applications of differential calculus found in Chapter 11. The last part of this section is a summary of the rules of differentiation found in the chapter. This summary will be a useful reference when studying Chapter 11.

A Summary of the Rules of Differentiation

Rule 1: The Simple Power Rule:
If $f(X) = X^n$,
then $f'(X) = nX^{n-1}$

Rule 2: The derivative of any constant is zero.
If $f(X) = K$ where $K =$ any constant,
then $f'(X) = 0$

Rule 3: A constant factor may be placed inside or outside the differentiation instruction without changing the result.
If $f(X) = Kg(X)$ where $K =$ any constant,
then $f'(X) = Kg'(X) = g'(KX)$

Rule 4: The derivative of a sum or difference is equal to the sum or difference of the derivatives.
If $f(X) = g(X) \pm h(X)$,
then $f'(X) = g'(X) \pm h'(X)$

Rule 5: The Product Rule:
If $f'(X) = g(X)h(X)$,
then $f'(X) = g(X)h'(X) + h(X)g'(X)$

Rule 6: The Quotient Rule:
If $f(X) = \dfrac{g(X)}{h(X)}$,
then $f'(X) = \dfrac{h(X)g'(X) - g(X)h'(X)}{[h(X)]^2}$

Rule 7: The Chain Rule of Differentiation:
If $Y = f(U)$ and $U = f(X)$,
then $\dfrac{dY}{dX} = \dfrac{dY}{dU} \dfrac{dU}{dX}$

Rule 8: The Power Function Rule:
If $Y = f(X)^n$,
then $\dfrac{dY}{dX} = n[f(X)]^{n-1} f'(X)$

Rule 9: The Exponential Rule for Base e:
If $Y = e^X$,
then $\dfrac{dY}{dX} = \dfrac{d(e^X)}{dX} = e^X$

Rule 10: The Exponential Function Rule for Base e:
If $Y = e^{f(X)}$,
then $\dfrac{dY}{dX} = \dfrac{d}{dX}[e^{f(X)}] = e^{f(X)} f'(X)$

Rule 11: The Exponential Function Rule:
If $Y = a^{f(X)}$,
then $\dfrac{dY}{dX} = \dfrac{d}{dX} a^{f(X)} = a^{f(X)} (\ln a) f'(X)$ for $a \neq 1$

Rule 12: The Logarithmic Rule of Differentiation:
If $Y = \ln X$,
then $\dfrac{dY}{dX} = \dfrac{1}{X}$

Rule 13: The Logarithmic Function Rule:
If $Y = \ln f(X)$,
then $\dfrac{dY}{dX} = \dfrac{1}{f(X)} f'(X) = \dfrac{f'(X)}{f(X)}$

10.13 Problem Set

Review Questions

1. State the correct interpretation of the expression for the limit of X as X approaches a or $\lim X = a$.
2. Why is it not always accurate to compute a limit by simple substitution of the limiting value into the expression?
3. Name the three conditions that must be satisfied for a function to be continuous at a point.
4. Distinguish between what is measured by the slope of the secant line and by the slope of the tangent line.
5. Describe the first derivative of a function by using the concept of the limit applied to the difference quotient.
6. What are the two conditions that must be satisfied for a function to be differentiable at a point?
7. What can be concluded about a function that has a negative value for the first derivative throughout its range?
8. Why is the first derivative of a constant always equal to zero?
9. Why is the exponential function rule for base e a special case of the exponential function rule?

10. Briefly describe a business problem requiring use of the chain rule of differentiation.
11. What is measured by the second derivative of a function? Interpret a constant value of -5 for the second derivative of a function.
12. What is the value of the second derivative of any linear function with one independent variable? What does this result imply about a linear function?
13. Explain why the power function rule of differentiation is a special case of the chain rule of differentiation.
14. What assumption about a function must be made before applying the technique of implicit differentiation?
15. What is measured by the first partial derivative with respect to one independent variable in a function with three independent variables?
16. What is measured by the cross partial derivative $\partial^2 Y/\partial X_1 \, \partial X_2$ in a function with two independent variables X_1 and X_2?

Review Problems

1. Find each limit as specified.
   a. $\lim\limits_{X \to 0} (3X^2 + 6X + 7)$
   b. $\lim\limits_{Z \to 3} (Z^2 + 2Z - 15)$
   c. $\lim\limits_{X \to 4} \dfrac{X^2 + 4}{X - 4}$
   d. $\lim\limits_{X \to 6} \dfrac{X^2 - 36}{X - 6}$
   e. $\lim\limits_{Y \to 5} (Y + 2)(Y - 3)$
   f. $\lim\limits_{X \to 3} (X - 4)^4$
   g. $\lim\limits_{X \to 8} X^{2/3}$
   h. $\lim\limits_{X \to 5} \dfrac{X - 5}{X + 3}$
   i. $\lim\limits_{X \to 4} \dfrac{X^2 - 4}{X - 6}$
   j. $\lim\limits_{X \to 0} (8X)$

2. For each set of $f(X)$, X, and ΔX, find $\Delta f(X)$.
   a. $f(X) = 2X^2 - 5;\ X = 3;\ \Delta X = 2$
   b. $f(X) = 3X^2 + 10;\ X = 5;\ \Delta X = 1$
   c. $f(X) = 2X^2 + X - 4;\ X = 4;\ \Delta X = -1$
   d. $f(X) = 40 - 0.5X;\ X = 12;\ \Delta X = 3$

3. Find the first derivative dY/dX for each of the following functions $Y = f(X)$:
   a. $Y = X^{1/3}$
   b. $Y = X^2 + 6X - 14$
   c. $Y = -X^3 + 3X^2 - 12X + 18$
   d. $Y = (X^2 + 7)(X^3 - 14X + 10)$
   e. $Y = (X^{-2} + 20)(X^{1/2} - 4)$
   f. $Y = \dfrac{X^2 + 3X + 8}{X^2 + 7}$
   g. $Y = \dfrac{X^{1/4}}{X^2 - 12}$
   h. $Y = 13$
   i. $Y = 7X$
   j. $Y = -7X^{-1/2} + 6X^{-4}$

4. a. For $Y = 2X^2 - 10X - 3$, find dY/dX; evaluate at $X = 4$ and $X = 6$; and interpret the results.
   b. For $Y = -X^2 + 25X + 4$, find dY/dX; evaluate at $X = 8$ and $X = 16$; and interpret the results.
   c. For $Y = X^2 - 14X + 49$, find dY/dX; evaluate at $X = 5$, $X = 7$, and $X = 9$; and interpret the results.
   d. For $Y = X^2 - 36$, find dY/dX; evaluate at $X = -3$, $X = 0$, and $X = 3$; and interpret the result.

5. For each composite function, find dY/dZ by means of the chain rule of differentiation.
   a. $Y = 3X^2 - 4X + 10$, $X = 2Z + 8$
   b. $Y = 0.03X^2 + 80$, $X = Z^2 - 10$
   c. $Y = 2X^2 - 14$, $X = Z^{1/2} + 5$
   d. $Y = 6X - 4$, $X = \dfrac{Z^4}{3} - Z^2 + 6$
   e. $Y = 4X^3 + 3X^2 - 12X$, $X = Z + 4$
   f. $Y = -3X^2$, $X = 16 - Z^2$
6. For each power function, find dY/dX and evaluate at the specified point:
   a. $Y = (6X - 3)^3$ at $X = 2$ c. $Y = (X^3 - 2X^2 + 6X)^3$ at $X = 2$
   b. $Y = (2X^2 - 5X + 5)^{4/3}$ at $X = 3$ d. $Y = (X^{1/4})^{1/2}$ at $X = 1$
7. For each function, find dY/dX and evaluate at the specified point. Use Table II and Table III at the end of the book where appropriate.
   a. $Y = e^X$ at $X = 1.5$ f. $Y = \ln(4X - 13)$ at $X = 5$
   b. $Y = e^{3X}$ at $X = 0.5$
   c. $Y = 5^{3X^2 - 6X + 2}$ at $X = 2$ g. $Y = \ln \dfrac{1}{X^2}$ at $X = 2$
   d. $Y = \ln X$ at $X = 0.4$ h. $Y = \ln(6X^2 - 24)$ at $X = 4$
   e. $Y = \ln(2X^2 - 4X + 5)$ at $X = 3$
8. For each function, find d^2Y/dX^2. Evaluate and interpret the value of the second derivative at the specified point.
   a. $Y = 3X^2 - 4X + 7$ at $X = 10$
   b. $Y = X^3 - 2X^2 + 20$ at $X = 5$ f. $Y = \dfrac{1}{3}(2X^4)$ at $X = 6$
   c. $Y = (X + 7)(2X^2 + 3X - 5)$ at $X = 4$ g. $Y = (3X^2 - 7)^2$ at $X = 2$
   d. $Y = e^X$ at $X = 1.2$ h. $Y = 7X - 30$ at $X = 8$
   e. $Y = X^{-2}$ at $X = 2$
9. For each implicit function of the form $f(X, Y) = 0$, find dY/dX.
   a. $2XY + X^2 + X^2Y = 0$ d. $X^2Y - 3Y^2 + X^4 = 0$
   b. $3X^2 - 4Y^3 + 7XY = 0$ e. $8XY + X^{-4} - Y^3 = 0$
   c. $X^2 + XY - Y^3 + X^2Y^3 = 0$ f. $X^2Y^2 + 4XY - Y^2 = 0$
10. For each function, find all specified partial derivatives.
    a. $Y = 6X_1^2 - 4X_2^3 + X_1X_2 - X_1^2X_2$. Find $\dfrac{\partial Y}{\partial X_1}$ and $\dfrac{\partial Y}{\partial X_2}$.
    b. $Y = X_1X_3 - X_2^2 + 4X_2X_3 - 3X_1^2X_3^3$. Find $\dfrac{\partial Y}{\partial X_3}$ and $\dfrac{\partial^2 Y}{\partial X_3^2}$.
    c. $Y = 3X_1 + 4X_2^2 - 3X_1^2X_2^2 - X_2^3$. Find $\dfrac{\partial^2 Y}{\partial X_1 \partial X_2}$.
    d. $Y = (X_1X_2 - 3)(X_2^2 - X_1^2X_2)$. Find $\dfrac{\partial Y}{\partial X_2}$.
    e. $Y = (X_1 - 3X_1X_2 + X_2^3)^2$. Find $\dfrac{\partial Y}{\partial X_1}$ and $\dfrac{\partial Y}{\partial X_2}$.
    f. $Y = 3X_2X_3 + 3X_1X_2X_3^2 - 6X_1 + 7X_2X_3 - 4X_1X_2X_3$. Find $\dfrac{\partial Y}{\partial X_2}$ and $\dfrac{\partial^2 Y}{\partial X_2 \partial X_3}$.
11. A firm has the following total revenue function explaining total revenue TR as a function of the quantity sold Q:
    $$TR = -0.04Q^2 + 40Q + 200$$

a. At the quantity point $Q = 400$, is total revenue increasing, decreasing, or remaining constant? Why?

b. At the quantity point $Q = 800$, is total revenue increasing, decreasing, or remaining constant? Why?

12. Average production cost per unit for a firm is the following, where average cost per unit AC is a function of the quantity produced Q:

$$AC = 0.02Q^2 - 60Q$$

a. Find the rate of change of AC at the following production points: $Q = 1200$, $Q = 1500$, and $Q = 1800$.

b. What conclusions can you reach about the pattern of costs per unit of production? What are some implications of this result that may be of interest to the firm?

13. Total production cost for a firm is the following, where total cost TC is a function of quantity produced Q:

$$TC = 0.01Q^3 + 10Q^2 - 20Q + 1800$$

a. Find the second derivative $\dfrac{d^2(TC)}{dQ^2}$.

b. What can you conclude from examination of the second derivative about the direction of the rate of change of total cost?

c. Interpret the value of the second derivative at $Q = 500$.

14. Sales of a new diet soft drink in a metropolitan area are dependent on the income and population of the area. The following function specifies this relationship:

$$Y = 0.03X_1^2 + X_1 X_2 + 0.04 X_1 X_2^3$$

where Y = hundreds of cases of the soft drink sold per week.
X_1 = average family income in thousands (e.g., $X_1 = 15$ means that average family income in the area is $15,000 per year).
X_2 = area population in hundreds of thousands (e.g., $X_2 = 6$ means that the population of the area is 600,000).

a. Find the partial derivative $\dfrac{\partial Y}{\partial X_1}$. What is measured by this relationship?

b. Find the partial derivative $\dfrac{\partial Y}{\partial X_2}$.

c. Substitute $X_1 = 18$ and $X_2 = 4$ into the result of (b) and interpret the answer.

15. A manufacturer of men's suits knows the function relating sales S to the price of suits P. Also, suit price is a function of the cost of suits C. These functions are shown below.

$$S = 500 - 0.08P^2$$

$$P = 0.07C^2$$

Find the first derivative of sales with respect to the cost of suits, dS/dC, by means of the chain rule of differentiation. What is expressed by this relationship?

11 Differential Calculus: Applications

11.1 Introduction

The topics introduced in Chapter 10 provide the foundation for business applications of differential calculus. Differential calculus is particularly important to business in providing a method for determining marginal measurements and in evaluating the rate of change at various points on functions. Many applications in this chapter are related to one or both of these issues.

The principles of marginal analysis are fundamental to the behavioral premises of contemporary business management. Questions such as whether or not to hire an additional worker or produce one more unit of output often are answered with the assistance of marginal analysis. As marginal measurements are represented by the instantaneous rate of change of a function, differentiation frequently is used in determining these measurements.

A second broad business application of differential calculus is the identification of significant points of functions. For example, firms may want to know the quantity of output representing the lowest per unit cost or may want to specify the number of workers to hire to achieve maximum output per worker.

There is a close relationship between marginal analysis and methods for determining specified points of functions. The two components of this relationship are introduced in this and the next section (11.2). The linkage will be demonstrated in the chapter's applications.

Marginal Measurements and Mathematical Models

Before introducing the specific applications of this chapter, it may be useful to describe a few of the marginal measurements used by businesses in analytical models. This discussion may help to clarify the terminology used in the chapter's applications and relate each to the presentation of Chapter 10.

The change in total production cost resulting from the production of one additional unit of a good is the *marginal cost* of that unit of production. If a firm knows the functional relationship for total production cost and the output level, the marginal cost of a particular unit is equal to the value of the first derivative at that quantity point. Thus, the marginal cost function is found by differentiation of the corresponding total cost function with respect to the quantity produced.

Similarly, the change in total revenue from the sale of one additional unit of a good is the *marginal revenue* of that unit. Differentiation of the total revenue function with respect to quantity sold yields the marginal revenue function.

Other marginal concepts are found through an analogous derivation process. Thus, the physical output of an additional unit of a resource (e.g., one more hour of labor) is called the *marginal product* of that resource and is equal to the first derivative of the total production function with respect to that resource. These three marginal measurements will be described further among the applications of this chapter.

The next section includes a second introductory component of applied calculus by discussing a technique for identifying significant points on functions.

11.2 Identification of Stationary Points of Functions with One Independent Variable

Quantitative business analysis often is directed toward finding the extreme point on a given function—for example, maximum profit or minimum cost. A third type of extreme point, the point where a function's rate of change shifts from increasing to decreasing or decreasing to increasing, also is important to several analytical questions. In general, these three types of extreme points—maximum, minimum, and changing rate of change—are associated with stationary points.

In calculus, a procedure exists for identifying the stationary points of functions. In order to understand this procedure, observe first that stationary points occur at points where a line tangent to the curve at that point is horizontal. Consequently, the first derivative of the function is equal to zero at this point.

More specifically, the first derivative of a function is equal to zero at one or more of the following points on a function: a *relative maximum,* a *relative minimum,* or a *stationary inflection point.* Each of these italicized terms deserves further elaboration. Figure 11.1(a), (b), and (c) show an example of each type of point.

The terms "relative maximum" and "relative minimum" [Figure 11.1(a) and (b), respectively] indicate that the point is higher or lower, respectively, than any point on a stated interval of the function. There may be a higher or lower value elsewhere on the function outside of the stated interval. The highest point and lowest point for the entire domain of a function is the *absolute maximum* or *absolute minimum,* respectively. Relative maximum and relative minimum points will be the concepts applicable to the discussion of this chapter.

It is possible that the first derivative is equal to zero at other than a relative maximum or relative minimum. Points in this category are called stationary inflection points, as in Figure 11.1(c). Stationary inflection points comprise a subset of all inflection points, i.e., points where the function changes from concave downward to concave upward or vice versa. If the point of changing concavity also is a point with a first derivative value of zero, the point is a stationary inflection point.

As the terms concave upward and concave downward were introduced in Chapter 8, a brief restatement may be helpful. These terms can be explained by means of geometry (as in Chapter 8) or calculus. A geometrical definition of a concave downward curve is the following:

IF ANY PAIR OF POINTS *A* AND *B* ON A CURVE ARE
SELECTED AND JOINED BY A STRAIGHT LINE, AND ALL

X_0 = Relative maximum of $Y = f(X)$

(a)

X_0 — Relative minimum of $Y = f(X)$

(b)

X_0 = Stationary inflection point on $Y = f(X)$

(c)

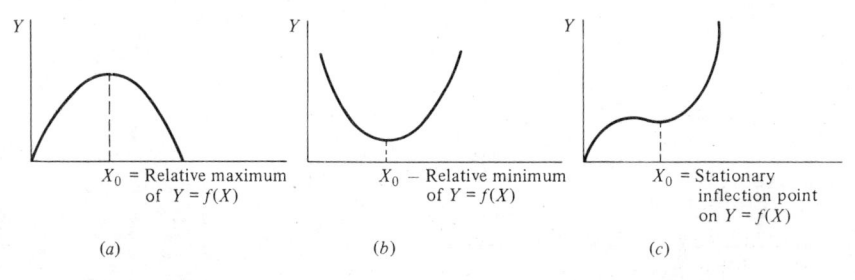

FIGURE 11.1 Stationary points on functions.

POINTS ON THE LINE EXCEPT *A* AND *B* LIE INSIDE THE CURVE, THE CURVE IS CONCAVE DOWNWARD BETWEEN *A* AND *B*.

If a similar construction of a line between two points leads to a line with points above the curve, the curve is concave upward between the two points. In Figure 11.2, (*a*) is a concave downward curve and (*b*) is concave upward.

Defining concave upward and concave downward by means of calculus will provide concepts relevant to several of the following applications. The definitions are as follow:

IF THE SECOND DERIVATIVE OF THE FUNCTION IS NEGATIVE FOR ALL *X* OVER AN INTERVAL OF THE FUNCTION, THE FUNCTION IS CONCAVE DOWNWARD OVER THIS INTERVAL. IF THE SECOND DERIVATIVE OF THE FUNCTION IS POSITIVE FOR ALL *X* OVER AN INTERVAL OF THE FUNCTION, THE FUNCTION IS CONCAVE UPWARD OVER THIS INTERVAL.

With this conceptual framework, a procedure is developed below for identifying stationary points, both where they occur on the function and the nature of the point (i.e., relative maximum, relative minimum, or stationary inflection point). These three types of points may occur alone or in any combination for a given function. And, as the case of linear functions demonstrates, no stationary points may be present.

Finding Stationary Points

Stationary points on functions with one independent variable [e.g., $Y = f(X)$] are established by setting the first derivative of the function equal to zero and solving the resulting equation for X. The X value or values found are subsequently substituted into the original function to find the Y coordinate of each stationary point. As mentioned above, stationary points do not exist on linear functions since the first derivative is the same nonzero constant at all points. The following two examples demonstrate determination of stationary points on a quadratic function.

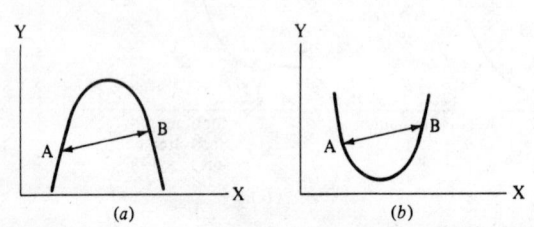

FIGURE 11.2 A concave downward curve (*a*) and a concave upward curve (*b*).

Example 11.1
For $Y = X^2 - 8X + 26$, find the coordinates of any stationary points.

$Y = X^2 - 8X + 26$

$\dfrac{dY}{dX} = 2X - 8$

$\phantom{\dfrac{dY}{dX}} = 2X - 8 = 0$

$2X = 8$

$X = 4$

Substituting $X = 4$ into $Y = f(X)$ gives the Y coordinate:

$Y = X^2 - 8X + 26$
$ = (4)^2 - (8)(4) + 26$
$ = 16 - 32 + 26 = 10$

A stationary point is established at
$X = 4, Y = 10$

Example 11.2
For $Y = -4X^2 + 40X + 20$, find the coordinates of any stationary points.

$Y = -4X^2 + 40X + 20$

$\dfrac{dY}{dX} = -8X + 40$

$\phantom{\dfrac{dY}{dX}} = -8X + 40 = 0$

$8X = 40$

$X = 5$

Substituting $X = 5$ into $Y = f(X)$ gives the Y coordinate:

$Y = -4X^2 + 40X + 20$
$ = (-4)(5)^2 + (40)(5) + 20$
$ = -100 + 200 + 20 = 120$

A stationary point is established at
$X = 5, Y = 120$

In each example the same procedure was followed including these steps.

1. Find the first derivative, dY/dX.
2. Set dY/dX equal to 0.
3. Solve for X.
4. Substitute the X value from (3) into $Y = f(X)$ to find Y.

Although the function in each of these examples has a single stationary point, it should be remembered that some functions have multiple stationary points. The procedure presented here is applicable to functions having any number of stationary points.

The Second-Derivative Test

After finding the stationary point or points each must be evaluated to determine whether it is a relative maximum, relative minimum, or stationary inflection point. There are several ways to reach this decision, but most common is the second-derivative test.

The second-derivative test uses the value of the second derivative of the function at the stationary point to specify the characteristic of the stationary point. The following rules make up the second-derivative test:

1. If substitution of the X coordinate value into the second derivative of the function results in a positive number, the point is a relative minimum.
2. If substitution of the X coordinate value into the second derivative of the function results in a negative number, the point is a relative maximum.
3. If substitution of the X coordinate value into the second derivative of the function results in a value of zero, the second-derivative test fails and no definitive statement can be made about the characteristics of the stationary point.

The rationale behind these rules is based on the concept of concavity. As the second derivative measures the rate of change of the slope, a positive value for the second derivative is an indication that the slope of the curve is increasing for any instantaneous change from the stationary point. In other words, the stationary point is at the extreme point of a concave upward curve, i.e., a relative minimum. Similarly, a negative value for the second derivative at a stationary point indicates that the slope of the curve is decreasing for any instantaneous change from the stationary point. Thus, the point is the maximum point of a concave downward curve or interval of a function.

The functions from Examples 11.1 and 11.2 are repeated below to show this identification process.

Example 11.3

For $Y = X^2 - 8X + 26$ and the stationary point $X = 4$, $Y = 10$, is the stationary point a relative maximum or a relative minimum or is no conclusion possible from the second-derivative test?

$$Y = X^2 - 8X + 26$$

$$\frac{dY}{dX} = 2X - 8$$

$$\frac{d^2Y}{dX^2} = 2$$

As the value of the second derivative is +2 at all points, substitution of $X = 4$ into the function for the second derivative is not required. Thus, the function $Y = X^2 - 8X + 26$ is concave upward at $X = 4$, $Y = 10$ and the stationary point is a relative minimum.

Example 11.4
For $Y = -4X^2 + 40X + 20$ and the stationary point $X = 5$, $Y = 120$, is the stationary point a relative maximum or a relative minimum or is no conclusion possible from the second-derivative test?

$$Y = -4X^2 + 40X + 20$$

$$\frac{dY}{dX} = -8X + 40$$

$$\frac{d^2Y}{dX^2} = -8$$

Again, as in the previous example, the value of the second derivative is -8 at all points; therefore, substitution of $X = 5$ is not required. The function $Y = -4X^2 + 40X + 20$ is concave downward at $X = 5$, $Y = 120$ and the point is a relative maximum.

When the Second-Derivative Test Fails

As rule 3 above indicates, a value of zero for the second derivative does not permit a statement to be made about the stationary point. In other words, the stationary point may be a relative maximum, a relative minimum, or a stationary inflection point. When this situation is encountered, two other tests often are used to investigate the stationary point. These are the original function test and the first-derivative test.

The original function test requires evaluation of the original function at values of the independent variable X close to and on either side of (values greater than and less than) the stationary point. If both resulting Y values are greater than the value of Y at the stationary point, the point is a relative minimum.

If both Y values are less than the Y value at the stationary point, the stationary point is a relative maximum. However, if one Y value is less than Y at the stationary point and one Y value is greater than Y at the stationary point, the stationary point is a stationary inflection point.

The original function test may be summarized by the following notation: Let

$f(X)$ = value of the function at the stationary point
$f(X_L)$ = value of the function at an X value less than X at the stationary point
$f(X_R)$ = value of the function at an X value greater than X at the stationary point

Then

1. If $f(X_L) > f(X)$ and $f(X_R) > f(X)$, the stationary point is a relative minimum.
2. If $f(X_L) < f(X)$ and $f(X_R) < f(X)$, the stationary point is a relative maximum.
3. If $f(X_L) > f(X) > f(X_R)$ or $f(X_L) < f(X) < f(X_R)$ the stationary point is a stationary inflection point.

This notation is used in Figure 11.3(a), (b), and (c) to describe each possibility.

Using similar notation where $f'(X)$ indicates the value of the first derivative, the rules for the first-derivative test also can be summarized in several statements:

Let

$f'(X_L)$ = the value of the first derivative at an X value close to and less than X at the stationary point

$f'(X_R)$ = the value of the first derivative at an X value close to and greater than X at the stationary point

Then

1. If $f'(X_L)$ is positive and $f'(X_R)$ is negative, the stationary point is a relative maximum.
2. If $f'(X_L)$ is negative and $f'(X_R)$ is positive, the stationary point is a relative minimum.
3. If $f'(X_L)$ and $f'(X_R)$ have the same sign, the stationary point is a stationary inflection point.

These three possibilities are shown in Figure 11.4(a), (b), and (c) using the notation employed here.

These rules can be clarified by considering that the slope of a curve is downward prior to a minimum point and upward after this point. The reverse is true of the slopes before and after a maximum point. At stationary inflection points, the slope of the function does not change at points less than and greater than the stationary point. Therefore, although the concavity

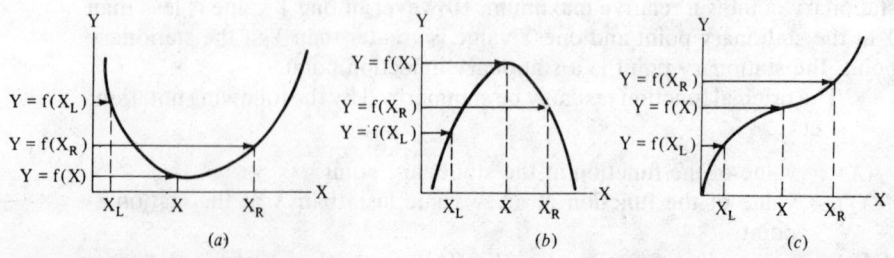

FIGURE 11.3 Graphical description of the original function test.

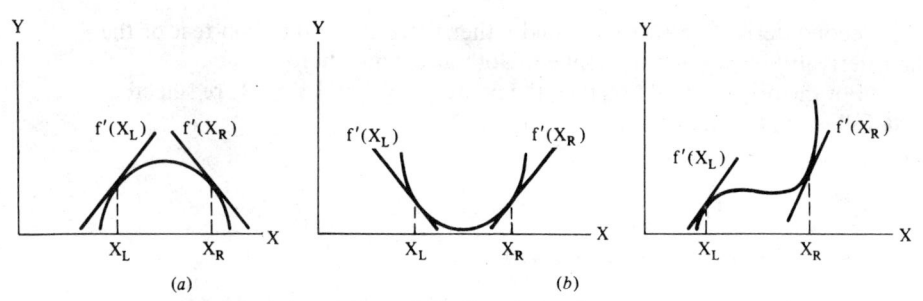

FIGURE 11.4 Graphical description of the first derivative test.

changes at this point, the function continues to move in the same direction on both sides of the stationary point.

Example 11.5 demonstrates the original function test and the first-derivative test.

Example 11.5
For the function

$$Y = f(X) = 2X^3 - 12X^2 + 24X$$

find and characterize all stationary points. First, the first derivative is found and set equal to zero.

$$Y = f(X) = 2X^3 - 12X^2 + 24X$$
$$\frac{dY}{dX} = f'(X) = 6X^2 - 24X + 24$$
$$= f'(X) = 0 = 6(X - 2)(X - 2) = 6(X - 2)^2$$

Solving for X in this case yields only one value, $X = 2$, as

$$6(X - 2)^2 = 0$$
$$X = 2$$

Substitution of $X = 2$ into the original function yields the Y coordinate of the stationary point as follows.

$$Y = f(X) = f(2) = (2)(2)^3 - (12)(2)^2 + (24)(2)$$
$$= f(2) = 16 - 48 + 48 = 16$$

The point $X = 2$, $Y = 16$ is a single stationary point on this function.
The second derivative is evaluated at $X = 2$, but a value of 0 results:

$$\frac{d^2Y}{dX^2} = f''(X) = 12X - 24$$

At $X = 2$

$$f''(2) = (12)(2) - 24 = 0$$

The second-derivative test fails, and either the original function test or the first-derivative test must be applied. Both are shown here.

For the original function test, the points $X = 1$ and $X = 3$ are selected. The following results are obtained:

$Y = f(X) = 2X^3 - 12X^2 + 24X$

$Y = f(2) = 16$

$Y = f(1) = (2)(1)^3 - (12)(1)^2 + (24)(1) = 2 - 12 + 24 = 14$

$Y = f(3) = (2)(3)^3 - (12)(3)^2 + (24)(3) = 54 - 108 + 72 = 18$

At a point to the left of $X = 2$, the value of the function is less than 16 and at a point to the right, the value of the function is greater than 16. Therefore, the original function test has established that the point (2, 16) is a stationary inflection point.

The first-derivative test using $X = 1$ and $X = 3$ confirms this finding:

$\dfrac{dY}{dX} = f'(X) = 6X^2 - 24X + 24$

$f'(1) = (6)(1)^2 - (24)(1) + 24 = +6$

$f'(3) = (6)(3)^2 - (24)(3) + 24 = +6$

As the sign on the first derivative does not change, the point $X = 2$, $Y = 16$ is shown to be a stationary inflection point. Thus, the slope of the function is increasing on both sides of the stationary point.

These rules and tests will be applied frequently in the specific applications starting in the next section. Section 11.7 extends these ideas about stationary points to functions with two independent variables.

EXERCISES

1. Describe the concavity at $X = -2$ and $X = 3$ for each of the functions below.
    a. $Y = X^3 + 2X^2 - 4X + 10$
    b. $Y = 4X^2 + 6X - 14$
    c. $Y = X^4 - 4X^3 - 4X^2 + 15$
    d. $Y = -3X^3 - 5X^2 + 14X - 50$
    e. $Y = 3X^2 - 14$
    f. $Y = X^5 - 4X^4 + 14$
2. For each function $f(X)$, determine any stationary points and characterize each by means of the second-derivative test, if possible. If the second-derivative test fails, show why. If the function does not have a stationary point, explain why.
    a. $f(X) = 0.5X^2 - 10X + 2$
    b. $f(X) = -3X^2 + 30X + 15$
    c. $f(X) = 2X^3 - 12X^2 + 40$
    d. $f(X) = 6X + 15$
    e. $f(X) = X^4 - 18X^2 + 81$
    f. $f(X) = 2X^3 - 96X$

g. $f(X) = 4X^3 + 21X^2 - 54X + 19$
h. $f(X) = \frac{1}{3} X^3 - 4X^2 + 12X + 15$
i. $f(X) = X^3 - 3X^2 - 24X + 5$
j. $f(X) = \frac{2}{3} X^3 - 10X^2 + 42X - 3$

3. For parts a through c below, find the stationary point and characterize it by application of the original function test. For parts d through f, find the stationary point and characterize it by application of the first-derivative test.
   a. $f(X) = 2X^2 + 14$
   b. $f(X) = 4X^2 - 40X + 100$
   c. $f(X) = -2X^2 + 8X - 8$
   d. $f(X) = 0.25X^2 - 3X + 16$
   e. $f(X) = -0.6X^2$
   f. $f(X) = 5X^2 - 20X + 30$

4. For each of the following, find the stationary point. Then
   a. Show that the second-derivative test fails.
   b. Characterize the stationary point by means of either the original function test or the first-derivative test.
   (1) $f(X) = 2X^3$
   (2) $f(X) = \frac{2}{3} X^3 - 12X^2 + 72X$
   (3) $f(X) = \frac{1}{3} X^3 - 4X^2 + 16X - 30$
   (4) $f(X) = 0.5X^4 + 50$
   (5) $f(X) = -\frac{1}{6} X^3 + 5X^2 - 50X + 41$
   (6) $f(X) = \frac{1}{4} X^5 - 20$

11.3 Differential Calculus and Profit Maximization

Optimizing a Profit Function

The most direct way to approach profit maximization occurs when the firm knows the functional relationship relating profit to the quantity of sales. In other words, the general functional statement is

$$PR = f(Q)$$

where PR represents profit in dollars and Q represents the quantity of goods sold.

When this function is known, determination of its maximum point will yield the output which should be sold by the firm to maximize profit. This computation is described in the next example.

Example 11.6

A firm knows that the relationship between its weekly sales Q and weekly profit PR is expressed by the following function:

$$PR = -0.002Q^2 + 10Q - 4000$$

The firm wants to determine the profit-maximizing level of weekly sales. This is established by the procedure for optimizing a function.

First, a possible optimum sales point is determined by setting the first derivative equal to 0 and solving for Q:

$$PR = -0.002Q^2 + 10Q - 4000$$

$$\frac{d(PR)}{dQ} = -0.004Q + 10$$

$$= 0 = -0.004Q + 10$$

$$0.004Q = 10$$

$$Q = 2500$$

The second-derivative test is then applied to confirm that $Q = 2500$ is a maximum point on the profit function:

$$PR = -0.002Q^2 + 10Q - 4000$$

$$\frac{d(PR)}{dQ} = -0.004Q + 10$$

$$\frac{d^2(PR)}{dQ^2} = -0.004$$

As the second derivative is equal to a negative constant, evaluation at $Q = 2500$ is not necessary. Thus, a sales level of 2500 units per week will maximize profit.

Finally, the profit corresponding to this sales level can be determined by substituting $Q = 2500$ into the profit function:

$$PR = -0.002Q^2 + 10Q - 4000$$

For $Q = 2500$

$$PR = (-0.002)(2500)^2 + (10)(2500) - 4000$$
$$= -12,500 + 25,000 - 4000$$
$$= \$8500$$

This example has demonstrated that maximum profit for this firm is $8500 per week, achieved by selling 2500 units per week.

The procedures described in Example 11.6 can be applied whenever the firm knows its profit function. Often, however, the firm knows only revenue and cost functions and wants to determine the profit-maximizing quantity of goods to sell. The next two subsections concern this case.

Principles of Marginal Analysis

As mentioned at the beginning of the chapter, business decisions often are based on marginal analysis; for example, should an additional worker be hired, or should an additional unit of output be produced? These concepts can be applied to finding the profit-maximizing level of output for a firm. To understand this relation, consider again the terms, marginal cost and marginal revenue, introduced in Section 11.1.

The change in total production cost resulting from production of an additional unit of output is the *marginal cost* of that unit. If a firm knows the functional relationship for total cost, where total cost = f(output), the marginal cost of a particular unit of output is computed by finding the value of the first derivative of the total cost function at that output point. A typical total cost function and corresponding marginal cost function are shown in Figure 11.5. In this case the total cost function is cubic and the marginal cost function is quadratic.

THE MARGINAL COST OF A UNIT OF OUTPUT IS THE VALUE OF THE FIRST DERIVATIVE OF THE TOTAL COST FUNCTION AT THAT POINT.

Example 11.7

A typewriter manufacturer has the following total cost function relating total cost TC to quantity sold Q:

$$TC = 0.05Q^3 - 0.2Q^2 + 17Q + 7000$$

Total cost is measured in dollars and quantity is measured in number of typewriters. This is a typical total cost function with fixed costs equal to $7000.

The marginal cost function is equal to the first derivative of the total cost function which is found as follows:

$$TC = 0.05Q^3 - 0.2Q^2 + 17Q + 7000$$

$$\frac{d(TC)}{dQ} = 0.15Q^2 - 0.4Q + 17$$

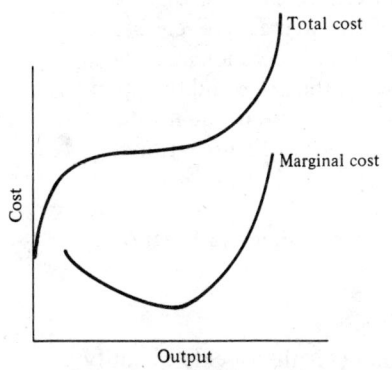

FIGURE 11.5 A total cost function and corresponding marginal cost function.

This step gives the marginal cost function for typewriters.

For example, at an output of 40 typewriters, marginal cost MC is the following:

$$\frac{d(TC)}{dQ} = MC = 0.15Q^2 - 0.4Q + 17$$

$$MC(40) = (0.15)(40)^2 - (0.4)(40) + 17$$
$$= 240 - 16 + 17 = \$241$$

This means that the additional cost of the 40th typewriter is $241. Similarly, at a quantity of 80 typewriters, marginal cost MC is:

$$MC = 0.15Q^2 - 0.4Q + 17$$
$$MC(80) = 960 - 32 + 17 = \$945$$

As marginal cost is the change in total cost from the production of one more unit of output, marginal revenue is the change in total revenue from selling one more unit. Total revenue TR is equal to the price of the product times the number of units sold $P \times Q$ and marginal revenue is the first derivative with respect to Q of this total revenue expression.

In some cases, firms do not have direct knowledge of their total revenue function but know only the expression for demand, stating price as a function of the quantity sold, $P = f(Q)$. A demand function of this form also can be considered a per unit or average revenue AR function. This is because

$$TR = P \times Q$$

$$P = \frac{TR}{Q} = \text{per unit or average revenue}$$

Therefore, knowing only the demand function of the form $P = f(Q)$, the total revenue function is found by multiplication of the demand function by Q.

A typical total revenue function and corresponding average revenue and marginal revenue functions are included in Figure 11.6. In this case, total revenue is a quadratic function and both the average revenue and marginal revenue functions are linear with negative slope coefficients. These slopes demonstrate the inverse relationship between the price and the quantity demanded of a good. Also, note that marginal revenue is equal to zero at the quantity where total revenue is maximized, Q_M on Figure 11.6.

Example 11.8

For the typewriter manufacturer of Example 11.7, the demand function is as follows:

$$P = 557 - 0.2Q$$

where P represents typewriter price in dollars and Q is the weekly quantity of typewriters sold.

$

|
| ╱‾‾╲   Total revenue
| ╱   ╲
|╱   ╲
|_____╲_____
         Quantity
           (a)

Price
|
|╲
| ╲
| ╲
| ╲ Average revenue
| ╲
|_____╲_____
  Q_M Quantity
           (b)
     Marginal revenue

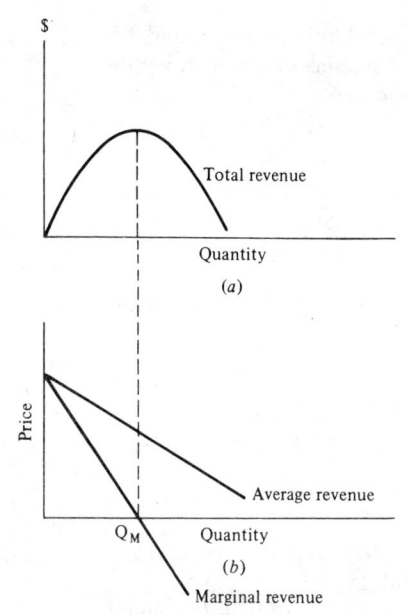

FIGURE 11.6 Total revenue, average revenue, and marginal revenue functions.

Find marginal revenue at $Q = 40$ and $Q = 80$.

To answer this problem, functions for total revenue TR and marginal revenue MR must be developed. These are shown below.

$$P = 557 - 0.2Q$$

$$\begin{aligned} TR &= P \times Q \\ &= (557 - 0.2Q)Q \\ &= 557Q - 0.2Q^2 \end{aligned}$$

$$MR = \frac{d(TR)}{dQ} = 557 - 0.4Q$$

This last expression above shows the marginal revenue function corresponding to the total revenue function of the previous expression. At a quantity of 40 typewriters, marginal revenue is equal to:

MR(40) = 557 − (0.4)(40) = $541

Marginal revenue at $Q = 80$ is:

MR(80) = 557 − (0.4)(80) = $525

These data indicate that the manufacturer will receive $541 in additional total revenue from the sale of the 40th typewriter and $525 in additional revenue from the sale of the 80th typewriter.

The quantity corresponding to maximum total revenue is found by setting the first derivative of total revenue (that is, the marginal revenue function) equal to zero and solving for Q_M as follows:

$MR = 557 - 0.4Q$
$0 = 557 - 0.4Q$
$0.4Q = 557$
$Q = Q_M$ at the point of maximum total revenue
$Q_M = 1392.5$

Total revenue corresponding to this quantity is equal to the following TR:

$TR = (557 - 0.2Q)Q$
$= [557 - 0.2(1392.5)](1392.5)$
$= (557 - 278.5)(1392.5)$
$= (278.5)(1392.5)$
$= \$387,811.25$

Thus, total revenue is maximized at the level of 1392.5 typewriters, and the resulting total revenue at this quantity is \$387,811.25.

Readers should understand thoroughly the technique for determining marginal revenue from the demand or average revenue function. First the demand function $P = f(Q)$ is multiplied by the quantity Q to yield the total revenue function. The first derivative with respect to quantity of the total revenue function yields the marginal revenue function. Specific quantity points can be substituted into this function to determine marginal revenue at each quantity level.

Marginal Analysis and Profit Maximization

The marginal cost and marginal revenue functions are used to determine the level of output for a firm which will either maximize profit or minimize losses. As the loss minimization case is discussed in the next section, only the principles of profit maximization are discussed here.

In attempting to obtain maximum profit, a firm wants to maximize total, not marginal or final unit profits. When deciding whether or not to sell a particular unit of a good, however, it is the marginal decision that is relevant. More specifically, if the revenue gained by selling the item (marginal revenue) exceeds the marginal cost of its production, sale of the good will increase total profit. If marginal cost exceeds marginal revenue for an item, its sale will reduce total profit and the item should not be offered for sale.

Over the relevant range of production options for the firm, marginal revenue is a decreasing or constant function of quantity sold and marginal cost is an increasing function of the quantity sold. Typical marginal revenue and marginal cost functions are shown in Figure 11.7.

On Figure 11.7, at points less than Q^*, total profit can be increased by

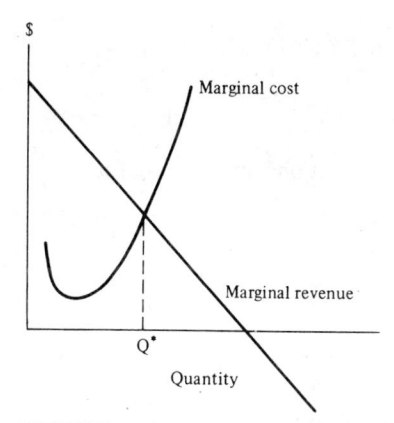

FIGURE 11.7 Marginal revenue and marginal cost functions.

the sale of additional units as the additional revenue obtained from each unit exceeds the additional cost of that unit. At quantity levels greater than Q^*, in contrast, profits are decreased for each additional unit sold. Therefore, total profit is maximized at the quantity point corresponding to the equality between marginal revenue and marginal cost.

Example 11.9 describes computation of the quantity point corresponding to maximum profit for the typewriter firm used in the previous two examples.

Example 11.9

For the following total cost function TC and demand function $P = f(Q)$, determine the quantity and price which will maximize profit. Also, determine this profit.

The total cost and demand functions, where Q represents quantity of typewriters in each function, are

$$\text{TC} = 0.05Q^3 - 0.2Q^2 + 17Q + 7000$$

$$P = 557 - 0.2Q$$

To solve the problem, the marginal revenue and marginal cost functions are found and set equal to each other. This will permit computation of the maximum profit quantity point. The marginal functions are determined as stated previously:

$$\begin{aligned}
\text{TR} &= P \times Q \\
&= (557 - 0.2Q)Q \\
&= 557Q - 0.2Q^2
\end{aligned}$$

$$\text{MR} = \frac{d(\text{TR})}{dQ} = 557 - 0.4Q$$

$$TC = 0.05Q^3 - 0.2Q^2 + 17Q + 7000$$

$$MC = \frac{d(TC)}{dQ} = 0.15Q^2 - 0.4Q + 17$$

The next step includes equating the two marginal functions and solving for the profit-maximizing quantity Q^*:

$$MR = MC$$
$$557 - 0.4Q = 0.15Q^2 - 0.4Q + 17$$
$$0.15Q^2 = 540$$
$$Q^2 = 3600$$
$$Q = Q^* \text{ at the point of maximum profit}$$
$$Q^* = 60$$

Therefore, to maximize total profit the firm should sell 60 typewriters per week. Selling less than 60 will lead to foregone profit and selling more than 60 will lead to a loss being incurred on each additional unit sold.

Price corresponding to the quantity point of 60 is found by substitution of $Q = 60$ into the demand function:

$$P = 557 - 0.2Q$$
$$= 557 - (0.2)(60)$$
$$= 557 - 12$$
$$= \$545$$

A price of $545 per typewriter will permit 60 typewriters to be sold and lead to maximization of profit.

Profit, representing the difference between total revenue and total cost at this combination of price and quantity, is computed. This number represents maximum profit.

$$\text{Total revenue } TR = 557Q - 0.2Q^2$$
$$TR = (557)(60) - (0.2)(60)^2$$
$$= 33{,}420 - 720$$
$$= \$32{,}700$$

$$\text{Total cost } TC = 0.05Q^3 - 0.2Q^2 + 17Q + 7000$$
$$TC = (0.05)(60)^3 - (0.2)(60)^2 + (17)(60) + 7000$$
$$= 10{,}800 - 720 + 1020 + 7000$$
$$TC = \$18{,}100$$

$$\text{Profit} = \text{total revenue} - \text{total cost}$$
$$= 32{,}700 - 18{,}100$$
$$= \$14{,}600$$

Therefore, it is determined that maximum profit per week at a price of $545 and a quantity of 60 typewriters is $14,600.

Readers should note that this same result can be obtained by computing a single profit function consisting of total revenue minus total cost and solving for price and quantity at the maximum point. As maximization of a profit function has been demonstrated above, this exercise is left for readers.

Overall, this section has introduced a calculus framework for computing maximum profit for a firm. Whether the profit function technique or marginal analysis is used often is dependent on the particular functions available to the researcher. The basic differentiation and maximization techniques are similar with the only differences being the functions.

EXERCISES

1. For each profit function PR, find the profit-maximizing quantity point. Show that each represents a maximum point. In each function, PR represents profit in dollars and Q represents quantity of output.
   a. PR $= -0.04Q^2 + 120Q - 9000$
   b. PR $= -1.2Q^2 + 150Q - 650$
   c. PR $= -0.03Q^3 + 324Q - 3000$
   d. PR $= -0.05Q^2 + 40Q - 300$
   e. PR $= -0.05Q^3 + 60Q - 400$
   f. PR $= -0.003Q^2 + 27Q - 7500$

2. For each total cost TC or total revenue TR function, find the corresponding marginal cost and marginal revenue function.
   a. TC $= 0.03Q^3 + 5Q^2 - 12Q + 400$ e. TC $= 3Q^2 + 783$
   b. TR $= -0.0016Q^2 + 0.04Q$ f. TR $= Q^3 + 0.2Q^2 + 6Q$
   c. TC $= 0.04Q^3 + 0.5Q^{1/2} + 1700$ g. TR $= -0.02Q^3 + 18Q$
   d. TC $= Q^{1/3} - 0.6Q^2 + 40Q + 2200$ h. TR $= 65Q$

3. a. For parts b and f of Question 2, find the demand function of the form $P = f(Q)$.
   b. What cost component is associated with the constant in each total cost function in Question 2?
   c. Why are there no constant terms in the total revenue functions in Question 2?

4. The total revenue TR and total cost TC functions for a certain brand of desk-top computer are as follows:

   TR $= -3Q^2 + 216Q$

   TC $= 0.08Q^3 - 3Q^2 + 120Q + 200$

   where Q represents the number of desk-top computers.
   a. Develop a profit function for the computer.
   b. Find the quantity of computers corresponding to the maximum profit point.

c. Show the computation of total profit by substitution of your answer to part b in both the profit function and the difference between total revenue and total cost.
5. A typical small farmer faces the following demand function for apples:

$P = \$4.20$

where P represents the price per bushel of apples.

Agricultural researchers have determined that the total cost TC function for apple production is the following, where TC is measured in dollars and Q represents bushels of apples.

$TC = 0.002Q^2 - 1.2Q + 2450$

a. Find the marginal cost and marginal revenue functions for this typical farmer and the profit-maximizing number of bushels the farmer should produce.
b. What is total profit at this output level?
c. Interpret the demand function for this typical farmer.

6. A home appliance retailer knows the total revenue TR and total cost TC functions for a brand of radio. These are as follows, where Q represents the quantity of radios.

$TR = -0.05Q^2 + 150Q$

$TC = 0.2Q^2 + 10Q + 800$

a. Find the corresponding marginal revenue and marginal cost functions.
b. Find the profit-maximizing quantity of radios.
c. What is profit at the quantity specified in part b?

7. A furniture company knows the total revenue TR and total cost TC functions for dining room tables.

$TR = -Q^2 + 550Q$

$TC = 0.03Q^3 - Q^2 - 26Q + 12{,}000$

where Q designates number of dining room tables.

The firm has decided to sell 75 dining room tables. Is this a profit-maximizing quantity to offer for sale? If so, why? If not, what is the profit-maximizing quantity?

8. The manufacturer has established the following total revenue TR and total cost TC functions for microwave ovens.

$TR = -1.5Q^2 + 250Q$

$TC = Q^2 - 10Q + 1400$

where Q represents the number of microwave ovens.

a. What is the profit-maximizing quantity of microwave ovens for the firm?
b. What is the price at this quantity?

c. What is total profit corresponding to this price and quantity combination?

11.4 Differential Calculus and Cost Analysis

At times, firms consider questions of efficiency from a cost perspective without revenue questions being of immediate concern. Many cost analyses involve finding stationary points on cost-related functions. Two specific subjects presented in this section are determination of a firm's shut-down price and computation of the point of diminishing returns of resource usage.

Finding a Firm's Shut-Down Price

In contrast to fixed costs such as facility rent, variable costs such as labor and utilities are those elements of production costs which change as output changes. Knowledge of the dollar value of minimum average (per unit) variable cost is useful to a firm.

If product price (average revenue) does not meet or exceed average variable cost, the firm should stop production. This does not imply that the firm goes out of business because the fixed costs (e.g., rent) must continue to be paid. However, if price does not meet or exceed the average variable cost and production continues, the firm loses not only its fixed costs but also a part of the variable cost on every unit produced.

Therefore, when product price falls below average variable cost, the firm will minimize its losses by ceasing production. The price corresponding to minimum average variable cost specifies the lowest possible price that the firm can face in the market and economically continue production. Frequently, this price is referred to as the firm's *shut-down price*.

Figure 11.8 shows a typical quadratic average variable cost curve. At

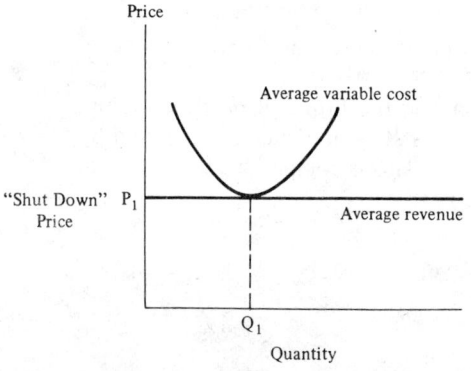

FIGURE 11.8 The "Shut-Down" price for a firm.

its minimum point (Q_1, P_1), a demand (average revenue) function touches the average variable cost curve. This price point P_1 corresponds to the lowest price a firm will accept for its product and continue production of the good.

An example will describe computation of a firm's shut-down price and the relevance of this price to production decisions.

Example 11.10

The following is the total cost function TC for voltage regulators used by various industries. Here, total cost is measured in dollars, and it is a function of the quantity of voltage regulators produced Q:

Total cost TC = $Q^3 - 24Q^2 + 230Q + 500$

The constant term 500 represents fixed cost and is not relevant to this particular analysis. Consequently, the remainder of the function expresses total variable cost TVC:

TVC = $Q^3 - 24Q^2 + 230Q$

Average variable cost AVC is a per unit measure of TVC:

$$\text{AVC} = \frac{\text{TVC}}{Q} = Q^2 - 24Q + 230$$

The object is to compute the price corresponding to minimum average variable cost. To minimize AVC, the first derivative is computed and set equal to zero:

$$\frac{d(\text{AVC})}{dQ} = 2Q - 24$$

$$= 0 = 2Q - 24$$

$$2Q = 24$$

$$Q = 12$$

The quantity point of 12 is a minimum point as the second derivative is equal to $+2$.

At a quantity of 12 voltage regulators, the firm will reach minimum average variable cost. The dollar value of AVC at this quantity is found by substituting $Q = 12$ into the AVC function. This is comparable to the lowest acceptable price to the firm. This price is $86:

$$\begin{aligned}
\text{AVC} &= Q^2 - 24Q + 230 \\
\text{AVC}(12) &= (12)^2 - (24)(12) + 230 \\
&= 144 - 288 + 230 \\
&= \$86
\end{aligned}$$

Shut-down price = $86

The firm should cease production if the price of voltage regulators is less than $86. If the price is less than $86, the firm will minimize its losses by stopping production and meeting only its fixed-cost obligations.

As this example demonstrates, techniques of calculus are adapted easily to answering managerial questions. A second type of analysis is described below.

Diminishing Marginal Returns of Inputs

The use of inputs (labor, machinery, management, etc.) often is associated with the principles of *diminishing marginal returns*. This means that the additional output because of the use of additional units of a resource increases up to a point and thereafter declines. The decline in marginal returns occurs because inefficiencies are encountered as resource use expands. At the point where the marginal returns of an input stop increasing and start to decrease, marginal returns are at their maximum point.

Input returns are reflected in the cost relationships of the firm. When marginal returns from inputs are increasing, the marginal cost of output is decreasing. Decreasing marginal returns from inputs are associated with an increasing marginal cost of output. Consequently, the point of change between increasing and decreasing marginal returns and decreasing and increasing marginal cost is of importance to the operation of a firm. The minimum point on a typical marginal cost function is shown in Figure 11.9.

This relationship also can be described by calculus notation. If total cost TC is a function of the quantity produced Q, and the quantity produced Q is a function of a resource input R, then:

TOTAL COST FUNCTION: $TC = f(Q)$
PRODUCTION FUNCTION: $Q = f(R)$

Thus, a production function is a quantitative relationship between an input factor or factors and the final output of a good or service.

Q_0 = minimum marginal cost

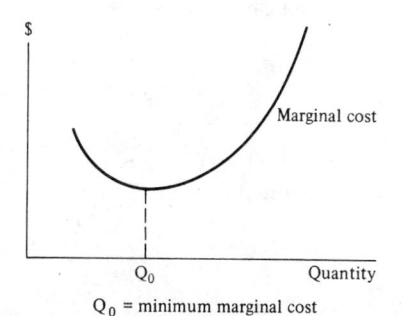

FIGURE 11.9 The minimum point on a typical marginal cost function.

It also follows that marginal cost MC is the first derivative with respect to quantity of the total cost function. Thus,

$MC = f'(Q)$

Using these functions, the following explains the relationship between decreasing and increasing marginal returns to inputs and increasing and decreasing marginal cost:

1. If $\dfrac{dQ}{dR} > 0$ then $\dfrac{d(MC)}{dQ} < 0$

   (increasing marginal returns to inputs)

2. If $\dfrac{dQ}{dR} < 0$ then $\dfrac{d(MC)}{dQ} > 0$

   (decreasing marginal returns to inputs)

3. If $\dfrac{dQ}{dR} = 0$ then $\dfrac{d(MC)}{dQ} = 0$

and the minimum quantity point of marginal cost has been established by the first-derivative test applied to (1) and (2) above.

The following example shows computation of the quantity point corresponding to minimum marginal cost. This point also represents the point of maximum marginal returns to input usage for a production process.

Example 11.11
A manufacturer of electric hot-water heaters knows the total cost function for the production process is

1. $TC = 0.1Q^3 - 12Q^2 + 800Q + 2100$

where TC represents total cost in dollars and Q represents the quantity of electric hot-water heaters.

Find the quantity of hot-water heaters corresponding to the point of minimum marginal cost.

To determine this quantity, the marginal cost function is derived as follows:

2. $MC = \dfrac{d(TC)}{dQ} = 0.3Q^2 - 24Q + 800$

To find a stationary point on this function, the first derivative is set equal to zero and the result is solved for Q. This is shown in steps 3, 4, and 5.

3. $\dfrac{d(MC)}{dQ} = 0.6Q - 24$

4. $\dfrac{d(MC)}{dQ} = 0 = 0.6Q - 24$

5. $0.6Q = 24$
   $Q = 40$

6. $\dfrac{d^2(MC)}{dQ^2} = 0.6$

Step 6 demonstrates that the point $Q = 40$ represents minimum marginal cost since the second derivative is positive at that point.
The marginal cost at $Q = 40$ is

7. $MC = 0.3Q^2 - 24Q + 800$
   $MC(40) = 0.3(40)^2 - 24(40) + 800$
   $= 480 - 960 + 800$
   $= 320$

The point $Q = 40$ with a marginal cost of $320 represents minimum marginal cost. Also, at this point, returns from use of input are at their highest level. At outputs higher than 40, diminishing marginal returns from use of input, and a corresponding increase in the marginal cost of output, take effect.

Thus, $Q = 40$ represents an output of maximum marginal returns from use of input and minimum marginal cost of producing electric hot-water heaters.

11.5 Marginal Productivity Analysis

Many of the concepts and terms of the previous section are related to the marginal productivity of a resource. The basic marginal productivity measurement is referred to as the *marginal physical product* of a resource.

Marginal physical product is measured in physical output, not dollars. Specifically, marginal physical product is an expression of the additional output resulting from the application of an additional unit of input, such as one more laborer or one more hour of machine time.

Marginal physical product is found by evaluating the instantaneous rate of change (first derivative) of the production function at a particular level of input use. Therefore, the first derivative of the production function with respect to this one input is the marginal physical product of the input. As the production of most goods and services requires use of more than one input, techniques of partial differentiation are important to the determination of marginal physical product.

The marginal physical product of a resource multiplied by the market value of the output produced by that resource yields a dollar figure representing the monetary value of the input to the firm. Consequently, the concept of marginal physical product is an important component of models concerned with wages, machinery usage, and other questions of resource allocation.

Two examples of the computation of marginal physical product are described below to explain this concept.

Example 11.12

Output Y per acre of wheat in bushels is a function of two inputs, labor-hours X_1 and pounds of herbicide applied to an acre X_2. The functional relationship is as follows:

$$Y = \tfrac{1}{4} X_1^4 - X_1 X_2 + X_2^2$$

The goal of this problem is to find the expressions for the marginal physical product of labor X_1 and the marginal physical product of herbicide application X_2. Consequently, the first partial derivatives with respect to X_1 and X_2 must be specified. In notation form, the expressions are as follows:

MARGINAL PHYSICAL PRODUCT OF LABOR:

1. $\mathrm{MPP}_{X_1} = \dfrac{\partial Y}{\partial X_1} = X_1^3 - X_2$

MARGINAL PHYSICAL PRODUCT OF HERBICIDE:

2. $\mathrm{MPP}_{X_2} = \dfrac{\partial Y}{\partial X_2} = -X_1 + 2X_2 = 2X_2 - X_1$

Expression 1 represents the additional output gained from one more hour of labor applied per acre, holding the amount of herbicide constant. Expression 2 represents the additional amount of output in response to one more pound of herbicide applied per acre, holding the amount of labor constant. For example, using 4 hours of labor and 10 pounds of herbicide per acre, the marginal physical product of each input is as follows:

For $X_1 = 4$ and $X_2 = 10$

$\mathrm{MPP}_{X_1} = X_1^3 - X_2 = (4)^3 - 10 = 54$

$\mathrm{MPP}_{X_2} = 2X_2 - X_1 = 2(10) - 4 = 16$

The marginal physical product of labor MPP_{X_1} is the change in total output (54 bushels) in response to a 1-hour change from the level of 4 labor-hours, holding herbicide treatment constant at 10 pounds per acre.

Similarly, a marginal physical product of 16 for herbicide is the output change (16 bushels) in response to a 1-pound change in herbicide application from its current level of 10 pounds per acre, holding labor constant at 4 hours per acre.

In this example, the marginal productivity amounts are relatively high due to the function selected to explain this technique. Often, however, production functions in business and economics realistically include fractional exponents. In addition, the inputs frequently are multiplied together rather than added as they are in the production function used in the previous example.

These two changes yield a production function with several characteristics that provide useful interpretations. Many of these are explained in textbooks on production economics and microeconomic theory. For this presentation, however, only the marginal physical product calculations for such functions are considered.

Example 11.13 demonstrates a production function in typical multiplicative form with fractional exponents.

Example 11.13
For a steel manufacturer using a particular process, output per day in tons of steel Y is expressed as a function of labor-hours X_1 and machine-hours X_2:

$$Y = X_1^{1/4} X_2^{3/4}$$

Find the expression for the marginal physical product of each input. Also, find the marginal physical product of each at an application of 16 labor-hours and 81 machine-hours.

Use of the product rule and the rule for the derivative of a constant yields the marginal physical product expression for each input:

MARGINAL PHYSICAL PRODUCT OF LABOR:

1. $\text{MPP}(X_1) = \dfrac{\partial Y}{\partial X_1} = X_1^{1/4} \left[\dfrac{\partial (X_2^{3/4})}{\partial X_1} \right] + X_2^{3/4} \left[\dfrac{\partial (X_1^{1/4})}{\partial X_1} \right]$

$\dfrac{\partial Y}{\partial X_1} = X_1^{1/4}(0) + X_2^{3/4} \left(\dfrac{1}{4} \right) X_1^{-3/4}$

$= \dfrac{1}{4} X_1^{-3/4} X_2^{3/4}$

MARGINAL PHYSICAL PRODUCT OF MACHINERY:

2. $\text{MPP}(X_2) = \dfrac{\partial Y}{\partial X_2} = X_1^{1/4} \left[\dfrac{\partial (X_2^{3/4})}{\partial X_2} \right] + X_2^{3/4} \left[\dfrac{\partial (X_1^{1/4})}{\partial X_2} \right]$

$\dfrac{\partial Y}{\partial X_2} = X_1^{1/4} \left(\dfrac{3}{4} \right) X_2^{-1/4} + X_2^{3/4} (0)$

$= \left(\dfrac{3}{4} \right) X_1^{1/4} X_2^{-1/4}$

Notice that the marginal physical product of each input is computed by assuming that the other input is a constant.

To find the output response of each input (marginal physical product) at the point of 16 labor-hours ($X_1 = 16$) and 81 machine-hours ($X_2 = 81$), the following calculations are completed:

1. MPP(X_1) at $X_1 = 16$ and $X_2 = 81$:

   $\text{MPP}(X_1) = \frac{1}{4} X_1^{-3/4} X_2^{3/4}$
   $= \frac{1}{4} (16)^{-3/4} (81)^{3/4}$
   $= \frac{1}{4} (\frac{1}{8}) (27) = \frac{27}{32}$ of a ton of steel

2. MPP(X_2) at $X_1 = 16$ and $X_2 = 81$:

   $\text{MPP}(X_2) = \frac{3}{4} X_1^{1/4} X_2^{-1/4}$
   $= \frac{3}{4} (16)^{1/4} (81)^{-1/4}$
   $= \frac{3}{4} (2) (\frac{1}{3}) = \frac{1}{2}$ of a ton of steel

Thus, for 16 labor-hours and 81 machine-hours, the marginal physical product of labor is $\frac{27}{32}$ ton of steel and the marginal physical product of machinery is $\frac{1}{2}$ ton of steel.

Each amount represents the incremental change in steel production in response to a 1-unit change in the respective input at the stated points. For example, if labor-hours are increased from 16 to 17 and machinery is held constant at 81 hours per day, steel production will increase by $\frac{27}{32}$ ton of steel per day.

The following exercises will provide practice in computing production return measurements and the shut-down price level.

EXERCISES

1. For each total cost function TC, find the average variable cost function and shut-down price.
   a. $TC = 0.6Q^3 - 24Q^2 + 410Q + 1500$
   b. $TC = 2Q^3 - 30Q^2 + 200Q + 100$
   c. $TC = 0.3Q^3 - 12Q^2 + 182Q + 700$
   d. $TC = 0.004Q^3 - Q^2 + 80Q + 1600$

2. For each marginal cost function MC, find the quantity Q corresponding to minimum marginal cost. Find marginal cost at this point and show that the point is a minimum. State the importance of this point to the analysis of a firm's production process.
   a. $MC = 0.1Q^2 - 6Q + 170$
   b. $MC = 3Q^2 - 54Q + 400$
   c. $MC = 0.05Q^2 - 5Q + 224$
   d. $MC = 3Q^2 - 180Q + 2900$

3. For each production function $Y = f(X_1, X_2)$, find the expression for the marginal physical product of X_1 and the expression for the marginal physical product of X_2. Interpret each result.
   a. $Y = 0.03X_1^3 - 0.4X_1X_2 + 0.6X_2^{1/2}$
   b. $Y = 0.4X_1^2 X_2 + 0.2X_2^3 - 0.3X_1^3 X_2^{-2} + 4X_1^2$

4. For your answers to part a of Question 3, find
   a. The marginal physical product of X_1 at $X_1 = 8$ and $X_2 = 4$.
   b. The marginal physical product of X_2 at $X_1 = 5$ and $X_2 = 4$.
   Interpret your results.
5. For each production function, find the expressions for the marginal physical product of X_1 and the marginal physical product of X_2.
   a. $Y = X_1^{4/3} X_2^{-1/3}$
   b. $Y = X_2^{3/7}$

11.6 Elasticity of Demand

In business and economics, "elasticity" is a term of general application used to express the change in one variable in response to a given change in a second variable. These changes are stated in percentage terms and therefore are not restricted by the particular unit measurements applied to each variable. This permits quantities and prices and other disparate data to be combined into a particular elasticity figure.

Some of the most common elasticity measurements refer to changes in the demand for a good or service caused by various other factors. This group is referred to as *elasticity of demand measurements*. Examples of elasticity of demand are the *income elasticity* of demand and the *cross-price elasticity* of demand. The first assesses the percentage change in the quantity demanded of a good in response to a percentage change in consumer income. The cross-price elasticity of demand measures the percentage change in the quantity demanded of one good in response to a percentage change in the price of a second good.

The particular focus of this section is the *price elasticity* of demand which evaluates the percentage change in the quantity demanded of a good in response to a percentage change in the price of the good.

$$\text{Price elasticity of demand for } X = \frac{\text{percentage change in the quantity demanded of } X}{\text{percentage change in the price of } X}$$

The price elasticity of demand can be computed at a single point on the demand function or over a range of the function, yielding the *point price elasticity of demand* and the *arc price elasticity of demand*, respectively. Each is concerned with the rate of change of the demand function. However, since differential calculus is used to determine the rate of change of a function at a point, point price elasticity of demand is the focus of this presentation.

In notation form, the percentage change ratio stated above can be expressed as follows:

$$\text{Price elasticity of demand for } X = \frac{\Delta Q_X / Q_X}{\Delta P_X / P_X}$$

where Q_X and P_X refer to the original quantity and price points, respectively. This expression can be restated as:

Price elasticity of demand for $X = \dfrac{\Delta Q_X}{\Delta P_X} \dfrac{P_X}{Q_Y}$

If this expression represents the change in Q_X in response to a change in P_X at a point (point elasticity of demand), then $\Delta Q_X/\Delta P_X$ can be stated dQ/dP because ΔP_X approaches the limit of zero at a point.

Therefore, the point price elasticity of demand where the quantity demanded of a good is a function of its price is expressed as:

Point price elasticity of demand $= \varepsilon_p = \dfrac{dQ}{dP} \dfrac{P}{Q}$

This expression will give the point price elasticity of demand at any point on the demand function. The point price elasticity of demand often is abbreviated ε_p.

In some cases, a practical computational problem exists as the demand function may be stated in the form $P = f(Q)$. However, dQ/dP—not dP/dQ—is required for determination of the point price elasticity of demand.

This situation is corrected by use of the *inverse function rule* as follows:

INVERSE FUNCTION RULE:
If $Y = f(X)$ is a monotonically increasing or monotonically decreasing function of X, then

$$\dfrac{dX}{dY} = \dfrac{1}{dY/dX}$$

A monotonically increasing function is one where, if $X_1 > X_2$, then $f(X_1) > f(X_2)$, so that, with increasing values of X, the value of $f(X)$ continually increases throughout the domain of the function. A monotonically decreasing function is one where, if $X_1 > X_2$, then $f(X_1) < f(X_2)$, so that, with increasing values of X, the value of $f(X)$ continually declines throughout the domain of the function. This also means that the slope of the function is always downward; i.e., the first derivative is negative for all values of X. Figure 11.10(a) shows a monotonically increasing function and Figure 11.10(b) shows a monotonically decreasing function.

Application of the inverse function rule is permitted in the case of the price elasticity of demand since any demand function has a downward slope throughout its domain. This characteristic reflects the law of demand, which states that there is an indirect relation between the price of a good and the quantity demanded of that good. Consequently, demand functions of the form $P = f(Q)$ pose no obstacle to computation of the point price elasticity of demand.

Differential Calculus: Applications

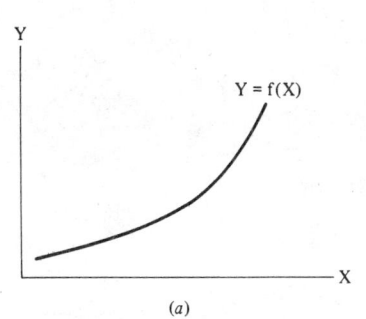

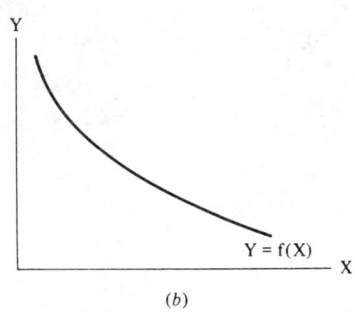

FIGURE 11.10 A monotonically increasing function (a) and a monotonically decreasing function (b).

The point price elasticity of demand can be determined by the expression below.

POINT PRICE ELASTICITY OF DEMAND ε_p:

$$P = f(Q)$$

$$\varepsilon_p = \frac{1}{dP/dQ} \frac{P}{Q}$$

Several examples will demonstrate computation of the point price elasticity of demand and introduce additional significant points.

Example 11.14

The demand, or average revenue, function for televisions is

$$P = 450 - 0.4Q$$

where P is expressed in dollars and Q represents the number of televisions demanded by consumers.

A firm wants to determine the point price elasticity of demand at a quantity of 120 televisions. Several steps are necessary to solve this problem.

First, the price corresponding to $Q = 120$ must be determined:

$$\begin{aligned} P &= 450 - 0.4Q \\ &= 450 - (0.4)(120) \\ &= 450 - 48 \\ &= \$402 \end{aligned}$$

Therefore, the coordinates of the relevant point on the demand curve are $Q = 120$, $P = \$402$.

Second, the rate of change at the above point must be determined by use of the inverse function rule:

$$P = 450 - 0.4Q$$

$$\frac{dP}{dQ} = -0.4$$

$$\frac{dQ}{dP} = \frac{1}{dP/dQ} = \frac{1}{-0.4} = -2.5$$

Finally, the point price elasticity of demand ε_p is computed:

$P = 450 - 0.4Q$

ε_p at $Q = 120$:

$$\varepsilon_p = \frac{dQ}{dP}\frac{P}{Q}$$

$$= (-2.5)\frac{402}{120} = -\frac{1005}{120}$$

$$= -8.375$$

Several points should be made about this result and its interpretation. At this point, the point price elasticity of demand indicates that a 1 percent change in price (either an increase or a decrease) from $402 will result in an 8.375 percent change in the quantity demanded in a direction opposite to the price change.

As a demand curve specifies an indirect relationship between price and quantity demanded, the sign on the point price elasticity of demand is always negative. Three categories of negative values have interpretative significance. By considering the absolute value of the point price elasticity of demand, $|\varepsilon_p|$, the categories can be described as shown below:

1. If $|\varepsilon_p| < 1$, demand at that point is inelastic with respect to price.
2. If $|\varepsilon_p| > 1$, demand at that point is elastic with respect to price.
3. If $|\varepsilon_p| = 1$, demand at that point is unitary with respect to price.

These classifications allow separation of three possible demand situations. If ε_p is inelastic, then the response in quantity demanded is smaller than the change—in the opposite direction—in price.

If ε_p is elastic, the response in quantity demanded is greater than the change in price—again, in the opposite direction.

Finally, if $\varepsilon_p = 1$ (unitary elasticity), the response in quantity demanded in one direction is offset exactly by the change in price in the other direction.

A second example will demonstrate computation and interpretation of point price elasticity of demand.

Example 11.15
A dairy products manufacturer has the following demand function for a brand of specialty cheese:

$P = 5.00 - 0.004Q$

where P represents price in dollars and Q denotes the quantity of cheese in pounds.

Find the point price elasticity of demand at a quantity of 500 pounds. Interpret this result.

At $Q = 500$, price is shown by the following:

$P = 5.00 - 0.004Q$
$ = 5.00 - (0.004)(500)$
$ = 5.00 - 2.00$
$ = \$3.00$

The derivative dQ/dP again is found by application of the inverse function rule:

$P = 5.00 - 0.004Q$

$$\frac{dP}{dQ} = -0.004$$

$$\frac{dQ}{dP} = \frac{1}{dP/dQ} = \frac{1}{-0.004} = -250$$

With these data, the point price elasticity of demand is determined as follows:

$$\varepsilon_p = \frac{dQ}{dP}\frac{P}{Q}$$

$$= (-250)\frac{3.00}{500} = -\frac{750}{500}$$

$$= -1.5$$

This result indicates that at a price of $3.00 per pound and quantity of 500 pounds, the price elasticity of demand is elastic. At this point, the quantity of the response will exceed the price change (as measured in percentages). Specifically, a 1 percent increase (decrease) in price from $3.00 per pound will cause a 1.5 percent decrease (increase) in the quantity of cheese demanded.

Knowledge of the price elasticity of demand is useful to a firm in computing the "sensitivity" of sales to price changes. Some product groups exhibit more price sensitivity than others. For example, necessities such as bread or household electricity exhibit inelastic demand; thus, their price sensitivity is low. On the other hand, luxury items such as personal yachts and jewelry tend to have a high price sensitivity (elastic demand). Therefore, it is important for firms to understand a product's elasticity of demand when developing pricing and marketing strategies.

Other Elasticity Measurements

The concept of elasticity as measured by percentage response can be extended to other factors which affect consumer demand or producer supply. Many elasticity figures are useful to a firm as it analyzes its operations. Differential calculus is used to determine each of these figures at a point of the function. Thus, for any dependent variable Y and independent variable X, a general statement of the elasticity of Y with respect to X at a point of Y is stated as follows. For $Y = f(X)$, the percentage change in Y in response to a percentage change in X at (x, y) is expressed as

$$\frac{dY}{dX} \frac{x}{y}$$

where x and y represent the coordinates of the point under consideration.

At times, it is necessary to find the elasticity associating the dependent variable with one independent variable in a function with several independent variables. In this case, the partial derivative with respect to the particular variable must be computed for the elasticity figure.

If Y is the dependent variable and X_i is the particular independent variable used in the elasticity figure, the elasticity of Y with respect to X_i at the point (x_i, y) is stated as follows: Percentage change in Y in response to a percentage change in X_i at (x_i, y) is:

$$\frac{\partial Y}{\partial X_i} \frac{x_i}{y}$$

where x_i represents the value of the variable X_i at the point under consideration. For this computation, all other X_i must be held constant at specific stated values. An example will demonstrate this technique.

Example 11.16

The weekly sales of home computers in a city is expressed by the following function:

$Q_c = 30 - 0.02P + 2.1I$

where Q_c = weekly sales of home computers
P = average retail price of home computers
I = average family income in thousands

A firm wants to determine the income elasticity of demand at an average family income of $20,000 ($I = 20$) and average retail price of $600 ($P = 600$).

In other words, the firm wants to determine the percentage change in computer sales in response to a percentage change in income at an income level of $20,000 holding price constant at $600. This problem requires the following steps:

1. $Q_c = 30 - 0.02P + 2.1I$

2. Find Q_c at $I = 20$ and $P = 600$:

$$Q_c = 30 - 0.02P + 2.1I$$
$$= 30 - (0.02)(600) + (2.1)(20)$$
$$= 30 - 12 + 42 = 60$$

3. Find $(\partial Q_c/\partial I)\, I/Q_c$:

$$\frac{\partial Q_c}{\partial I}\frac{I}{Q_c} = (2.1)\frac{20}{60} = \frac{42}{60}$$
$$= +0.7$$

4. Income elasticity of demand at an income of $20,000, holding price constant at $600, is equal to $+0.7$.

Therefore, a 1 percent increase in family income will increase home computer sales by 0.7 percent. Similarly, a 1 percent decline in family income will decrease home computer sales by 0.7 percent. This relation is valid if the average price is held constant at $600. Finally, this analysis shows that home computer sales are associated directly with family income and that the percentage sales response is somewhat less than a given percentage change in income.

The following example describes computation of price elasticity of demand for the same demand function. However, in this case, income is held constant at $20,000 ($I = 20$).

Example 11.17
Find the point price elasticity of demand at a price of $600 ($P = 600$) and an income level of $20,000 per year ($I = 20$) for the following demand function for home computers Q_c:

1. $Q_c = 30 - 0.02P + 2.1I$
$$= 30 - (0.02)(600) + (2.1)(20)$$
$$= 60$$

2. Point price elasticity of demand is $(\partial Q_c/\partial P)\, P/Q_c$

$$\frac{\partial Q_c}{\partial P}\frac{P}{Q_c} = (-0.02)\frac{600}{60}$$
$$= \frac{-12}{60} = -0.2$$

This analysis indicates that at a constant income level of $20,000 and constant price of $600, the demand is inelastic. Thus, the percentage change in sales will not be as great as the percentage change in price at this point of the function.

These two examples have shown that it is possible to compute the elasticity between the dependent variable and any independent variable in a function. For the interested reader, additional elasticity measurements and their determination are discussed in textbooks on microeconomics, managerial economics, and marketing.

The following exercise set will provide practice in solving and interpreting elasticity problems for functions both with one and with more than one independent variable.

EXERCISES

1. For each total revenue (TR) function, find the demand function, $P = f(Q)$. Find the expression for the first derivative dQ/dP or the change in quantity demanded in response to a change in price.
   a. $TR = -0.04Q^2 + 120Q$
   b. $TR = -3Q^2 + 450Q$
   c. $TR = -0.1Q^2 + 54Q$
   d. $TR = -Q^2 + 80Q$
   e. $TR = -\frac{1}{4}Q^2 + 50Q$
   f. $TR = -\frac{1}{10}Q^2 + 320Q$

2. Find the point price elasticity of demand at each specified point.
   a. $P = 32 - 0.004Q$ at $Q = 5000$
   b. $P = 360 - 5Q$ at $Q = 40$
   c. $P = 100 - Q$ at $Q = 30$
   d. $P = 70 - 0.02Q$ at $Q = 800$
   e. $P = 32$ at $Q = 400$

3. For the following demand function $f(Q)$, find the price elasticity of demand at $Q = 1000$ and at $Q = 2000$:

   $$P = 700 - 0.2Q$$

   Interpret each result with respect to the price sensitivity of demand at each specified output point.

4. The weekly demand for men's shirts at a retail store is expressed by the following function:

   $$Q_s = 150 - 4.3P_s + 3.4I$$

   where Q_s = number of shirts sold per week at the store
   P_s = price of shirts in dollars
   I = average annual household income in the region served by the store measured in thousands of dollars (e.g., $I = 18$ means $18,000 per household per year)

   a. Find the point price elasticity of demand for shirts at $P = \$20$ and $I = 15$.
   b. Find the point income elasticity of demand for shirts at $P = \$20$ and $I = 15$.
   c. If price increases to $25 and income remains at $I = 15$, what is the new point price elasticity of demand?
   d. What effect does the price increase in part c have on the price sensitivity of the demand for shirts holding income constant?
   Round all answers to two decimal places.

11.7 Identification of Stationary Points on Functions with Two Independent Variables

In this section, the procedures of Section 11.2 for finding and characterizing stationary points on functions are extended to the case of a function with two independent variables. The immediate goal of this extension is to prepare readers for the discussion of Lagrangian multipliers in the next section. However, the method is applicable to all problems involving functions of this type.

These methods can be expanded to functions with more than two independent variables. However, this extension requires a more detailed application of matrix algebra than is within the scope of this book. This presentation is developed without the use of matrix algebra.

The notation for a function with two independent variables X_1 and X_2 is as follows:

$$Y = f(X_1, X_2)$$

To find the stationary points of this function, the first partial derivative for each variable, $\partial Y/\partial X_1$ and $\partial Y/\partial X_2$, is determined and each is set equal to zero. These equations (two equations in the two-variable case) are solved simultaneously, revealing "candidate points" (possible stationary points) for X_1 and X_2.

Next, the second partial derivatives $\partial^2 Y/\partial X_1^2$ and $\partial^2 Y/\partial X_2^2$ and the cross partial derivative $\partial^2 Y/\partial X_1 \partial X_2$ are computed at the candidate points.

These three partial derivatives are used to develop a term D which is equal to the product of the second partial derivatives minus the square of the cross partial derivative.

$$D = \left(\frac{\partial^2 Y}{\partial X_1^2}\right)\left(\frac{\partial^2 Y}{\partial X_2^2}\right) - \left(\frac{\partial^2 Y}{\partial X_1 \partial X_2}\right)^2$$

D can be greater than 0, less than 0, or equal to 0.

If D is greater than 0, two possibilities exist for the candidate point:

1. If both $\partial^2 Y/\partial X_1^2$ and $\partial^2 Y/\partial X_2^2$ are negative, the candidate points represent a relative maximum point of the function.
2. If both $\partial^2 Y/\partial X_1^2$ and $\partial^2 Y/\partial X_2^2$ are positive, the candidate points represent a relative minimum point on the function.[1]

If the value of D is less than 0, the candidate points locate a *saddle point* of the function. This means that the candidate point on the function is one of the following:

1. The maximum value of X_1 holding X_2 constant but the minimum value of X_2 holding X_1 constant.
2. The maximum value of X_2 holding X_1 constant but the minimum value of X_1 holding X_2 constant.

If D is equal to 0, the test fails. In this case, points to the right and to the left of each candidate point must be substituted into the original function to determine if the point is a maximum, a minimum, or neither.

Since the situations where D is less than 0 and equal to 0 require a more extensive presentation than is necessary for this introduction, the discussion and applications will be limited to functions where the value of D is greater than 0. The following is an example of optimizing a function with two independent variables.

Example 11.18

An agricultural chemicals firm knows that yield in bushels per acre of soybeans Y is related to the application (in pounds) of nitrogen X_1 and phosphorus X_2 by the following function:

$$Y = 4X_1X_2 + 12X_1 + 16X_2 - 2X_1^2 - 3X_2^2$$

Find the number of pounds of nitrogen and phosphorus which will maximize soybean yield and show that these amounts represent a maximum point on the function.

First $\partial Y/\partial X_1$ and $\partial Y/\partial X_2$ must be determined.

$$Y = 4X_1X_2 + 12X_1 + 16X_2 - 2X_1^2 - 3X_2^2$$

$$\frac{\partial Y}{\partial X_1} = 4X_2 + 12 - 4X_1$$

$$\frac{\partial Y}{\partial X_2} = 4X_1 + 16 - 6X_2$$

Setting each of these partial derivatives equal to zero and solving the resulting system of equations leads to a value for X_2 of 14:

$$\begin{aligned}
\text{Eq. 1:} \quad & 4X_2 - 4X_1 + 12 = 0 \\
\text{Eq. 2:} \quad & \underline{-6X_2 + 4X_1 + 16 = 0} \\
\text{Eq. 1 + Eq. 2:} \quad & -2X_2 + 28 = 0
\end{aligned}$$

$$2X_2 = 28$$

$$X_2 = 14$$

Substitution of $X_2 = 14$ into either equation 1 or equation 2 yields an X_1 value of 17:

$4X_2 - 4X_1 + 12 = 0$
$4(14) - 4X_1 + 12 = 0$
$56 - 4X_1 + 12 = 0$

---

[1] Note that $\partial^2 Y/\partial X_1^2$ and $\partial^2 Y/\partial X_2^2$ cannot be of different signs (one positive, one negative) if D is to be greater than 0. Therefore, only the above two possibilities exist for this case.

$$4X_1 = 68$$
$$X_1 = 17$$

Consequently, candidate points for an extreme point on the function are $X_1 = 17$ and $X_2 = 14$.

The second partials are constants; thus, substitution of the candidate points is not necessary:

$$Y = 4X_1X_2 + 12X_1 + 16X_2 - 2X_1^2 - 3X_2^2$$

$$\frac{\partial^2 Y}{\partial X_1^2} = -4$$

$$\frac{\partial^2 Y}{\partial X_2^2} = -6$$

In addition, the cross partial $\partial^2 Y / \partial X_1 \, \partial X_2$ is equal to 4:

$$\frac{\partial^2 Y}{\partial X_1 \, \partial X_2} = \frac{\partial Y}{\partial X_2}(4X_2 - 4X_1 + 12) = 4$$

These three figures permit computation of D:

$$D = \left(\frac{\partial^2 Y}{\partial X_1^2}\right)\left(\frac{\partial^2 Y}{\partial X_2^2}\right) - \left(\frac{\partial^2 Y}{\partial X_1 \, \partial X_2}\right)^2$$
$$= (-4)(-6) - (4)^2$$
$$= 24 - 16$$
$$= 8$$

It has been shown that:

1. D is greater than 0.
2. Both $\partial^2 Y / \partial X_1^2$ and $\partial^2 Y / \partial X_2^2$ are negative.

By the rules stated previously, the point on the function where $X_1 = 17$ and $X_2 = 14$ represents a maximum point on the function.

Therefore, soybean yield per acre is maximized with the application of 17 pounds of nitrogen and 14 pounds of phosphorus per acre. The corresponding maximum yield (in bushels) is computed below.

$$Y = 4X_1X_2 + 12X_1 + 16X_2 - 2X_1^2 - 3X_2^2$$
$$= (4)(17)(14) + (12)(17) + (16)(14) - (2)(17)^2 - (3)(14)^2$$
$$= 952 + 204 + 224 - 578 - 588$$
$$= 214 \text{ bushels per acre}$$

This technique for identifying and characterizing stationary points on functions with two independent variables will be extended in the next section to the topic of Lagrangian multipliers.

11.8 Constrained Optimization Models and Lagrangian Multipliers

As mentioned in Chapter 7, a business often attempts to optimize an objective while operating within a particular constraint or set of constraints. This section extends this discussion to the optimization by means of calculus of constrained functions with two independent variables.

A common calculus technique used to determine the extreme points on constrained functions is the *method of Lagrangian multipliers*. Although these introductory remarks may make it appear that Lagrangian multipliers are merely an alternative to linear programming, there are two important differences between the techniques.

First, as stated in Chapter 7, linear programming is restricted to the analysis of linear objective functions subject to several linear constraints. The method of Lagrangian multipliers can be applied to both linear and nonlinear functions.

Secondly, in linear programming the constraints may be in the form of equalities or inequalities. Lagrangian multipliers are restricted to problems having equality constraints; i.e., the restrictions must be satisfied exactly. Thus, the two techniques are different and each has its particular restriction.

The specific steps in an application of Lagrangian multipliers follow closely the methodology of the previous section for finding and characterizing extreme points on functions. Consequently, the procedure will be described by means of an example.

Example 11.19

A manufacturer of freezer motors used by the food industry uses steel X_1 and aluminum X_2. Variable amounts of each material can be combined in producing a motor. However, each motor must have exactly 31 pounds of steel and aluminum to provide proper balance in the freezer.

Production cost in dollars C where $C = f(X_1, X_2)$ is expressed by the following function:

$$C = 2X_1^2 + X_2^2 - 4X_1 - 12X_2 + 30$$

where X_1 and X_2 represent pounds of steel and aluminum, respectively.

The input requirement of 31 pounds is stated as

$$X_1 + X_2 = 31$$

The object of the analysis is to determine the pounds of steel and aluminum which will minimize the total cost of a motor while exactly meeting the constraint.

To find the minimum cost combination given the constraint, a *La-*

grangian function Z is developed by combining the cost function and the constraint as follows:

$$Z = 2X_1^2 + X_2^2 - 4X_1 - 12X_2 + 30 - \lambda(X_1 + X_2 - 31)$$

In forming Z, a new term λ is introduced. The symbol λ (lambda) represents an undetermined number referred to as the *Lagrange multiplier*. Notice that if the constraint is satisfied (i.e., $X_1 + X_2 = 31$), λ can have any value and the expression $\lambda(X_1 + X_2 - 31)$ will equal zero. Thus, when the constraint is satisfied, the functions C and Z are identical since $X_1 + X_2 - 31 = 0$.

As Z incorporates the constraint into the objective function, the optimizing solution to the Lagrangian function Z will always be identical to the optimizing solution to the original function C subject to the constraint. Therefore, the problem is to optimize Z. To accomplish this, procedures from the previous section are applied.

In following the method for optimizing functions with more than one independent variable, λ is considered a third variable. Thus, for this Lagrangian problem, the set of *three* first partial derivatives form the system of equations which must be solved to determine the candidate points. This system of equations is developed below:

$$Z = 2X_1^2 + X_2^2 - 4X_1 - 12X_2 + 30 - \lambda(X_1 + X_2 - 31)$$

$$\frac{\partial Z}{\partial X_1} = 4X_1 - 4 - \lambda$$

$$\frac{\partial Z}{\partial X_2} = 2X_2 - 12 - \lambda$$

$$\frac{\partial Z}{\partial \lambda} = -X_1 - X_2 + 31$$

Notice that the partial derivative of the Lagrangian function with respect to the Lagrange multiplier λ yields the constraint. Thus, by setting the partial derivative $\partial Z/\partial \lambda$ equal to zero, it is assured that at the extreme point the constraint is satisfied exactly. Furthermore, if $-X_1 - X_2 + 31 = 0$, the Lagrangian function Z is the original objective function C, and the solution to Z will be the solution to C.

First, each partial derivative is set equal to zero. Then, the system of equations is solved for X_1, X_2, and λ.

STEP 1: Eq. 1: $4X_1 - \lambda - 4 = 0$
Eq. 2: $2X_2 - \lambda - 12 = 0$
Eq. 3: $-X_1 - X_2 + 31 = 0$

STEP 2: Eq. 2 − Eq. 1: $2X_2 - 4X_1 = 8$
Eq. 3: $X_2 + X_1 = 31$

STEP 3: Solving the equations of step 2 yields the following:

$$\begin{aligned}
\text{Eq. 2} - \text{Eq. 1:} \quad & 2X_2 - 4X_1 = 8 \\
+ \quad 4(\text{Eq. 3):} \quad & \underline{4X_2 + 4X_1 = 124} \\
& 6X_2 = 132 \\
& X_2 = 22
\end{aligned}$$

as $X_1 + X_2 = 31$, then

$$\begin{aligned}
X_1 &= 31 - X_2 \\
&= 31 - 22 \\
&= 9
\end{aligned}$$

Note that in going from step 1 to step 2 above, λ is the variable eliminated. Elimination of λ is the preferred step since the activity variables, X_1 and X_2 in this case, are of primary importance.

The solution shows that the candidate points for the extreme value on the constrained function are $X_1 = 9$ and $X_2 = 22$, or 9 pounds of steel and 22 pounds of aluminum. The value of λ can be established by substituting X_1 into Eq. 1 and solving for λ as follows:

$$\text{Eq. 1:} \quad 4X_1 - \lambda - 4 = 0$$

for $X_1 = 9$:
$$\begin{aligned}
4(9) - \lambda - 4 &= 0 \\
36 - 4 &= \lambda \\
32 &= \lambda
\end{aligned}$$

The value of λ (32 in this case) is a measure of the sensitivity of Z (and, therefore, of C) to changes in the constraint. Specifically, λ measures the change in the value of the objective function in response to a 1-unit change in the constraint. In this problem, if the weight constraint is decreased by 1 pound, total costs will decrease by \$32. Similarly, if the weight constraint is increased by 1 pound (to 32 pounds), the total cost of a motor will increase by \$32. Therefore, readers should note the similarity between the interpretation of λ in the present analysis and the interpretation of shadow prices in Chapter 7.

Thus far, the analysis has shown that the values $X_1 = 9$ and $X_2 = 22$ satisfy exactly the constraint. The next part of the problem is to determine whether this candidate point represents a relative maximum, a relative minimum, or neither. Again, procedures described above are applied.

First, the components of the expression for D are developed. As before, D is represented by the product of the two second partial derivatives for the activity variables (excluding $\partial^2 Z/\partial \lambda^2$) minus the square of their cross partial derivative:

$$D = \left(\frac{\partial^2 Z}{\partial X_1^2}\right)\left(\frac{\partial^2 Z}{\partial X_2^2}\right) - \left(\frac{\partial^2 Z}{\partial X_1 \, \partial X_2}\right)^2$$

For this function, the second partial derivatives and the cross partial derivative are as follows:

$$Z = 2X_1^2 + X_2^2 - 4X_1 - 12X_2 + 30 - \lambda(X_1 + X_2 - 31)$$

$$\frac{\partial^2 Z}{\partial X_1^2} = 4$$

$$\frac{\partial^2 Z}{\partial X_2^2} = 2$$

$$\frac{\partial^2 Z}{\partial X_1 \, \partial X_2} = 0$$

$$D = (4)(2) - (0)^2 = 8$$

As D is greater than 0, the test is conclusive if both second partial derivatives evaluated at the candidate points have the same sign. For this problem, both X_1 and X_2 ($X_1 = 4$ and $X_2 = 2$) are positive, indicating that the candidate point $X_1 = 9$, $X_2 = 22$ is a minimum point on the constrained function. Substitution of these values into the Lagrangian function Z gives the minimum cost of producing a motor while meeting the weight constraint. The following is the value for Z:

$$\begin{aligned} Z &= 2X_1^2 + X_2^2 - 4X_1 - 12X_2 + 30 - \lambda(X_1 + X_2 - 31) \\ &= (2)(9)^2 + (22)^2 - (4)(9) - (12)(22) + 30 - \lambda(9 + 22 - 31) \\ &= 162 + 484 - 36 - 264 + 30 - \lambda(0) \\ &= 376 \end{aligned}$$

The minimum cost of $376 also is the value of C at $X_1 = 9$ and $X_2 = 22$ as the coefficient $(X + Y - 31)$ equals 0 at the candidate point.

As this has been a lengthy description of the technique of Lagrangian multipliers applied to one problem, the next subsection is a restatement of the steps in the procedure.

The Method of Lagrangian Multipliers: a Restatement

To determine and characterize extreme points on a constrained function with two independent variables by means of Lagrangian multipliers, these steps are followed:

1. A Lagrangian function combining the original function and the constraint is formed by subtracting from the original function the product of the constraint and a Lagrange multiplier λ. In this product, the constraint is expressed as being equal to zero.
2. The first partial derivative of the Lagrangian function with respect to each independent variable and with respect to λ is determined. Each of

these first partial derivatives is set equal to zero. Together, they are considered a system of three equations and three unknowns.
3. The system of equations from 2 is solved simultaneously, to determine candidate values for the independent variables. At this point, a value for λ also may be computed.
4. The second partial derivative for each activity variable and the cross partial derivative between the two activity variables are determined and evaluated at the candidate points.
5. A term D representing the product of the two second partial derivatives minus the square of the cross partial derivative for the activity variables is computed.
6. If D is equal to 0, points near each value for the independent variable are evaluated in the original function to determine whether the candidate point represents a relative maximum, a relative minimum, or neither (not discussed in this chapter).
7. If D is less than 0, a "saddle point" has been found (not discussed in this presentation).
8. If D is greater than 0 and both second partial derivatives are negative, the candidate point represents a maximum point on the function. If D is greater than 0 and both second partial derivatives are positive, the candidate point represents a minimum point on the function.
9. The value of λ in the final solution is a measure of the sensitivity of Z to changes in the constraint.
10. The values of the activity variables at the candidate point are substituted into the constrained Lagrangian function to determine the extreme value for the function.
11. As the constraint has been satisfied exactly by this procedure, the optimum value of the Lagrangian function and the optimum value of the original function are the same.

EXERCISES

1. For each function, find and characterize any stationary points.
   a. $Y = 40X_1 + 20X_2 - 4X_1^2 - X_2^2$
   b. $Y = 395X_1 - 20X_1^2 - X_2^2 + X_1X_2$
   c. $Y = 2X_1^2 + 3X_2^2 - 10X_1 - 9X_2 - X_1X_2$
   d. $Y = 16X_1 + 30X_2 - X_1^2 - 3X_2^2 - X_1X_2$
2. For each function and constraint, express the Lagrangian function:
   a. $C = 3X_2^2 - 4X_1^2 - 3X_1 + 2X_2 + 60$
      Subject to: $X_1 + X_2 = 60$
   b. $C = 2X_1^2 + X_2^2 - 4X_1 - 2X_2 + 80$
      Subject to: $X_1 + X_2 = 5$
   c. $C = 6X_1 + 4X_2 - X_1^2 - 3X_2^2 + 120$
      Subject to: $X_1 + X_2 = 100$
3. For each function and constraint, set up the Lagrangian function and

solve for the optimum values of X_1 and X_2. Find the value of the original function and state whether it is a maximum or a minimum.
  a. $C = 3X_1^2 + 4X_2^2 + 2X_1X_2$
     Subject to: $X_1 + X_2 = 25$
  b. $C = 16X_1 + 14X_2 - X_1^2 X_2^2$
     Subject to: $X_1 + X_2 = 23$
  c. $C = 10X_1 + 20X_2 - X_1^2 - 2X_2^2$
     Subject to: $3X_1 + X_2 = 20$
  d. $C = 2X_1X_2 - X_1^2 - 2X_2^2 + 100$
     Subject to: $X_1 + 2X_2 = 20$
4. For parts a and b of Question 3, find the value of λ. Interpret the result for each problem.
5. A firm uses two groups of workers, machinists X_1 and electrical engineers X_2, to process components for computers. Machinists are paid $10 per hour and electrical engineers are paid $20 per hour.

   The production function P expressing processed components per hour as a function of the number of workers in the two groups is:

   $$P = -2X_1^2 - 3X_2^2 + 30X_1 + 40X_2$$

   The firm wants to spend exactly $410 per hour on labor costs related to production of these components. Within this constraint, the firm wants to use a mix of workers of the two categories which will maximize the number of components processed per hour.
   a. Set up the Lagrangian function Z for this problem of constrained maximization.
   b. How many employees of each group should be used to maximize hourly output within the constraint?
   c. What is the number of components manufactured per hour using the amounts of labor found in part b?
6. A firm uses two ingredients, X_1 and X_2, to make each batch of a new drug used by hospitals. In a batch of the drug, there must be exactly 32 grams of vitamin C. An ounce of ingredient X_1 contains 5 grams of vitamin C and an ounce of X_2 contains 4 grams of vitamin C. The cost function for a batch of this new drug is the following:

   $$C = 2X_1^2 + X_2^2 + 2X_1X_2 - 4X_1 - 3X_2$$

   Thus, C represents the cost of a batch of the drug as a function of the ounces of the two ingredients used. The firm wants to determine the least costly combination of the two ingredients which will satisfy the batch constraint of 32 grams of vitamin C.
   a. State the Lagrangian function Z for this problem of constrained cost minimization.
   b. How many ounces of each ingredient should be used to minimize (within the constraint) the cost of a batch of the drug?
   c. What is the constrained minimum cost of a batch of the drug?

11.9 A Note on Functional Form

Throughout this chapter (and, in fact, throughout the book), functions expressing business relations often have been stated without providing background as to why it is believed that a function depicts a given relation accurately. For example, why are total costs for a product stated by one particular function (such as a cubic function) and not better expressed by some other function?

The study of correct functional form is a combination of mathematics and statistical inference. The determination of correct functional form can be approached in three general ways.

First, theoretical considerations may dictate the functional form. For example, the inverse relationship between price and quantity in an average revenue function mandates a negative sign on the coefficient of the quantity term or terms. And the law of diminishing returns often necessitates use of a third-degree polynomial for total cost functions. As business and economic theories have substantial practical relevance, theoretical considerations may be very helpful in establishing proper functional form.

A second way to establish functional form is to plot data corresponding to the values of the variables. Once this *scatter diagram* of points is viewed, a particular functional relationship may be indicated. Although scatter diagrams are useful in some cases, functional form often cannot be identified visually.

A third method uses the techniques of experimental statistics. This topic is discussed only briefly in this book (Chapter 13). Experimental statistics includes the use of statistical procedures to ascertain which functional form best expresses the relation between a set of variables. One point of correct method restricts their use, since each statistical test for a functional form should use different data. Although this procedure reduces researcher bias, the data requirements associated with it are substantial. This third method of determining functional form is discussed more thoroughly in books on statistical inference.

The object of introducing the question of proper functional form in this chapter is to alert readers to the reality that functions found in this and other chapters are not found easily or assumed arbitrarily. The development of an appropriate functional relation is an exacting and often time-consuming part of mathematical analysis. Therefore, this section is an important disclaimer in a chapter which has stressed the analysis and interpretation of functional relations.

11.10 Chapter Summary

This chapter has introduced several additional techniques in differential calculus and extended these and the topics of Chapter 10 to business applications.

A fundamental part of the chapter has been discussion of the procedures for finding and characterizing stationary points on functions. Because the identification of relative maximum and minimum points is important to the use of many mathematical models, these procedures should be understood. A third type of stationary point, a stationary inflection point, also can be identified by the techniques introduced in this chapter. A stationary inflection point is associated with a point of changing concavity on a function (i.e., the point where the rate of change of the function switches from increasing to decreasing or from decreasing to increasing).

Stationary points also can be specified on functions with more than one independent variable. Procedures for the two-independent-variable case have been introduced and applied to the topic of Lagrangian multipliers. Lagrangian multipliers are used to find the optimum point on a constrained function, such as finding minimum cost or maximum profit subject to a constraint. Unlike linear programming, Lagrangian multipliers can be used to analyze both linear and nonlinear functions. However, the method of Lagrangian multipliers is applicable only to situations where the constraint is satisfied exactly. In this respect, the method is more restrictive than linear programming.

After studying this chapter, readers should be able to apply differential calculus to questions of profit maximization, cost minimization, resource productivity analysis, and specific topics such as the lowest operational price ("shut-down" price) and the elasticity of demand. It is hoped that exposure to these applications has helped make differential calculus less abstract and more practical.

11.11 Problem Set

Review Questions

1. Distinguish between marginal revenue and marginal cost. Why is each important to business analysis?
2. What is the slope of a line tangent to a function at a stationary point?
3. Relate the relative minimum point and the stationary inflection point of a function to the concavity of the function at each point.
4. Explain how the first-derivative test is used to determine that a stationary point is a minimum.
5. What outcome for the first-derivative test leads to the conclusion that a stationary point is a stationary inflection point?
6. If marginal revenue exceeds marginal cost at a production point, what should the firm do to increase profit? Why?
7. Briefly describe the relation between the slope of a linear average revenue function and the slope of the corresponding linear marginal revenue function.
8. How is differential calculus used to determine the lowest price which a firm should accept for continued production?
9. Why is knowledge of the point of minimum marginal cost useful to a firm in its production analysis?

10. What is expressed by a production function? How is the marginal product of a particular input determined from the production function?
11. Why can the inverse function rule be applied to the differentiation of most typical demand functions?
12. Contrast "point" price elasticity of demand and "arc" price elasticity of demand. Which measurement has more relevance to differential calculus? Why?
13. What is measured by point income elasticity of demand for a demand function with three independent variables (income, price of the good, and price of a substitute good)?
14. What is the relative advantage and the relative disadvantage of the Lagrangian optimization technique compared to linear programming?
15. How does the Lagrangian multiplier technique assure that the constraint is satisfied exactly at the candidate point?

Review Problems

1. Find and characterize any stationary points on the following functions.
   a. $Y = X^2 - 6X - 20$
   b. $Y = -X^2 + 15$
   c. $Y = \frac{1}{4} X^2 - 22X + 170$
   d. $Y = \frac{1}{3} X^3 - 7X^2 + 48X + 80$
   e. $Y = \frac{2}{3} X^3 - 24X^2 + 126X + 40$
   f. $Y = \frac{1}{3} X^3 - 36X + 75$

2. For each function, show that the second-derivative test fails to characterize the stationary point. Characterize each stationary point by means of either the original function test or first-derivative test.
   a. $Y = X^3 - 15X^2 + 75X$
   b. $Y = X^4$
   c. $Y = \frac{4}{3} X^3 - 20X^2 + 100X + 1500$
   d. $Y = 3X^4 + 150$
   e. $Y = \frac{1}{3} X^3 - 4X^2 + 16X - 36$
   f. $Y = -7 X^3$

3. A manufacturer of electric motors has established the following profit function (PR) for the firm. Quantity of motors is represented by Q.

   $PR = -Q^2 + 80Q - 500$

   a. Find the quantity corresponding to maximum profit.
   b. Compute profit at this quantity.
   c. Is profit increasing or decreasing at $Q = 50$? Defend your answer.

4. A firm produces window air conditioners. The total revenue (TR) and total cost (TC) functions for this firm are given below.

   $TR = -2Q^2 + 360Q$

   $TC = Q^2 - 60Q + 7000$

   where Q represents the number of air conditioners sold per week.
   a. Find the marginal revenue and marginal cost functions.
   b. Use the functions in part a to determine the quantity corresponding to maximum profit.
   c. What is the air conditioner price corresponding to this quantity?
   d. What is maximum profit?

5. A computer firm has established the following total revenue (TR) and total cost (TC) functions for computers:

   $TR = -0.2Q^2 + 900Q$

   $TC = 0.03Q^3 - 0.2Q^2 + 6000$

where Q represents the number of computers.
  a. Find the corresponding marginal revenue and marginal cost functions.
  b. Use the results of part a to find the quantity of computers corresponding to maximum profit.
  c. What is maximum profit?
6. A shirt manufacturer has the following total revenue (TR) and total cost (TC) functions:

$$TR = -0.003Q^2 + 20Q$$

$$TC = 0.002Q^2 - 1.5Q + 3000$$

where Q notates number of shirts.
The firm currently is producing 2000 shirts a month.
  a. Is 2000 shirts the profit-maximizing quantity of production? If so, why? If not, what should the firm do to increase profit?
  b. What is profit at $Q = 2000$?
  c. What is the maximum amount of profit that this firm could earn?
7. The following is the total cost (TC) function for a firm which sells office lighting fixtures. Total cost is a function of the quantity produced Q.

$$TC = Q^3 - 28Q^2 + 300Q + 1500$$

What is the lowest price that the firm should accept for lighting fixtures and continue to produce the fixtures? Why will the firm not accept a lower price than this for the fixtures?
8. A manufacturer of automatic transmissions for U.S. automobiles has the following total cost (TC) function:

$$TC = 2Q^3 - 60Q^2 + 800Q + 1800$$

where Q is the number of transmissions manufactured.
  a. Find the lowest price for transmissions which this firm will accept for continued production.
  b. At this price and quantity, what is the amount of total loss to the firm?
11. A production process for a consumer products firm has the following total cost (TC) function:

$$TC = 0.01Q^3 - 45Q^2 + 1100Q + 5000$$

where Q represents output units.
  a. Find the quantity point at which diminishing returns to the use of the variable factors (labor, machines, etc.) begin.
  b. What is represented by the figure 5000 in the total cost function? Is this number relevant to determining the answer to part a? Why, or why not?
10. The following production function expresses output of an agricultural process in tons in response to hours of labor time X_1 and hours of machine time X_2. The variable Y represents output of the process.

$$Y = X_1^{2/3} X_2^{1/3}$$

  a. Find the expressions for the marginal physical product of labor and the marginal physical product of machinery.
  b. At the point of 27 labor-hours and 64 machine-hours used, what is the marginal physical product of labor? Interpret this answer.

c. At the same resource use levels as part b, what is the marginal physical product of machinery? Interpret this answer.

11. Each function below is either a monotonically increasing or a monotonically decreasing function of X. For each, find the expression for dX/dY.
   a. $Y = X^{1/2} + 25$
   b. $Y = 78 - 0.02X$
   c. $Y = 2X^{1/3}$
   d. $Y = 8X + 300$
   e. $Y = 120 - X^{-2}$
   f. $Y = 2X^{-3}$

12. An automobile supply firm has the following total revenue (TR) function for the sale of tires:

$$TR = -0.4Q^2 + 76Q$$

where Q represents the number of tires.
   a. Find the average revenue function.
   b. Find the expression for the point price elasticity of demand.
   c. Find the point price elasticity of demand at $Q = 80$.
   d. Interpret your answer to part c.

13. For the total revenue (TR) function,

$$TR = -0.3Q^2 + 1200Q$$

find the point price elasticity of demand at the points specified in parts a, b, and c.
   a. $Q = 1000$
   b. $Q = 2000$
   c. $Q = 3000$
   d. Based on these results, what can you conclude about decreases in price and the degree of price sensitivity as measured by the responsiveness of sales of the product?

14. At a typical retail food store, the following function explains the sales of beef in pounds Q_B per week:

$$Q_B = 900 - 4P_B + 1.5P_C$$

where P_B = beef price in cents per pound
   P_C = chicken price in cents per pound

   a. If $P_B = 90$ and $P_C = 70$, find the point price elasticity of demand for beef.
   b. Interpret the negative coefficient of the P_B term and the positive coefficient of the P_C term.
   c. Determine the sensitivity of beef sales to a change in the price of chicken at the point $P_B = 90$ and $P_C = 70$. (This is referred to as the point cross-price elasticity of demand.)
   d. If $P_B = 100$ and $P_C = 60$, find the new point price elasticity of demand for beef. At this point, also find the point cross price elasticity of demand for beef with respect to a change in the price of chicken. Round all answers to two decimal places.

15. An industrial process uses two resources, labor-hours X_1 and machine-hours X_2. Each output unit must use exactly 30 hours of labor and machine time in any combination.
    Profit per unit of output is expressed by the following function, where PR represents profit (in dollars):

$$PR = 40X_1 + 16X_2 - 2X_1^2 - X_2^2$$

a. State in equation form the constraint on this profit function and the related Lagrangian function Z.
b. What are the optimum amounts of labor-hours and machine-hours to use in this process to maximize profit per unit of output?
c. What is maximum per unit profit?
d. Demonstrate that the amount in part c represents a maximum.

16. Two chemicals are used to produce an industrial compound. Pounds of chemical 1 are notated X_1 and pounds of chemical 2 are represented by X_2. There must be exactly 20 pounds of ingredients X_1 and X_2, in any combination, in a production lot. The total cost of manufacturing a production lot is expressed by the following function:

$$TC = 4X_1^2 + 2X_2^2 - 20X_1 - 16X_2$$

a. State the Lagrangian function Z.
b. How many pounds of each ingredient should be used to minimize the cost of a production lot?
c. Show that your answer to part b is a minimum.

12 Integral Calculus with Applications

12.1 Introduction

In Chapter 10, it was pointed out that the two operations of calculus, differentiation and integration, are reverse operations much like addition and subtraction. This chapter introduces integral calculus and its basic operation, integration.

The business and economic applications of integral calculus are somewhat different and, it should be noted, less numerous than the applications of differential calculus. However, there are many interesting business uses of integral calculus and the field also provides a theoretical foundation for the study of probability and inferential statistics. The basics of probability theory are introduced in Chapter 13.

The primary concept of differential calculus is the derivative, which measures the rate of change of a function at a point as the limiting form of the difference quotient. Integral calculus employs the concept of the integral, which represents the limiting form of a sequence (see Chapter 9 for a review of sequences). The relation of the integral to a sequence is developed as this chapter progresses.

Mathematics for Business and Economics

This chapter includes both an introduction to the principles of integral calculus and a discussion of some related business applications. Before presenting this material, several business situations where integral calculus may be employed are presented in order to give students an overall direction to the chapter.

12.2 Integral Calculus and Mathematical Models

In this section, several examples of integral calculus in a business environment are described. The applications concern the two primary uses of integral calculus. First, integral calculus can be used to find a function knowing only its first derivative, or rate of change. A second use of integral calculus is to investigate significant intervals within the original function. Geometrically, this can be viewed as a problem of calculating the area under a curve. Both aspects of integral calculus have value to business analysis as will be pointed out in the following examples:

1. Consider again the example from Chapter 11 concerning the marginal cost and marginal revenue relations for a typewriter manufacturer. Assume that, instead of the situation described there, the firm knows the functional relation between the additional cost per unit (marginal cost) and output. The firm also knows the total cost of producing 600 typewriters. The firm does not know the total cost function. Techniques of integral calculus can be employed to derive the total cost function from the marginal cost relation and the single total cost value. Therefore, in general, integration provides a means of determining total relations in business and economics based on knowledge of the corresponding marginal relations.
2. As a second example, consider capital formation, which many believe is an important determinant of the long-run economic stability and growth of a region or nation. Frequently, integral calculus is used in analyses in this field.

    For example, assume that a researcher knows the value of a region's net investment occurring during a given period (a month or a year). A significant question may be, "If this rate of net investment continues, what will be the total value of the region's capital stock at some future time?" In this case, integral calculus can be used to estimate a functional expression for the value of the capital stock at any time.
3. In finance, integral calculus can be employed to determine the present value of an asset knowing a particular cash flow from that asset. Integration allows one to calculate the present value of the cash flow either for a specified period or in perpetuity. Perpetual flow concepts can be applied to evaluation of the present value of an indestructible asset, such as an area of land, based on the cash flow from the asset and a constant discount factor.

4. The study of the regional consumption of a good such as electric power serves as a fourth application of integral calculus. A power company knows the current consumption and a function which expresses the current rate of growth in consumption. By using integral calculus, the firm can compute total electricity consumption over a specified future period such as the next 5 years or the next 20 years.
5. As a final descriptive example, consider the use of integral calculus in computing the probability of a particular event's occurrence. Probability is an important foundation of statistical testing. As an example of the connection between integral calculus and probability, assume that a firm knows the functional relationship expressing the probability of various sales levels for a consumer good. In this case, integral calculus can be used to determine the combined probability of sales at several different levels. This aspect of integral calculus is developed further in Chapter 13.

These descriptive examples should clarify the two aspects of integral calculus as applied to the modeling of real-world problems. First, integration is used to derive a function knowing the derivative of that function. Second, integration can be used to determine the area under a function over a specified interval (e.g., time period, distance, or outcomes of an event). These two aspects of integral calculus are explained in greater detail in the next two sections.

12.3 Indefinite Integrals and the Antiderivative

Depending on the object of the analysis, one or two types of *integrals* can be associated with a given relation. If one has knowledge of the derivative of a function and wants to find the function itself, one can do so by means of the *antiderivative* and the related *indefinite integral*. Alternatively, if upper and lower boundaries (e.g., two points in time) are placed on the indefinite integral and it is evaluated at these boundary points, the result is a *definite integral*. Indefinite integrals are introduced in this section, and the definite integral is presented in Section 12.4.

Finding an indefinite integral can be viewed as the process of determining the parent function $F(X)$ from the derivative function $f(X)$ (e.g., the total cost function from the marginal cost function). The function $F(X)$ also is referred to as the antiderivative.

The relation of the antiderivative $F(X)$ to the derivative $f(X)$, is expressed in the following way:

$\int f(X)\, dX = F(X) + c$

The left-hand side of this equality is read "the integral of $f(X)$ with respect to X." The elongated ess, or $\int$, refers to a summation (a more detailed explanation of the meaning of this summation is given below in the discussion of the definite integral). Other components of the expression are $f(X)$, referred to as the *integrand,* and dX, which indicates that the integration is performed with respect to X. The term $F(X)$ on the right-hand side of the equality is the particular integral and c is referred to as the constant of integration.

No boundaries on the variable are specified when developing the indefinite integral. This means, for example, that no limits are placed on the value of X. As a result, the constant of integration c is not specified and the original function $F(X)$ is not determined completely by the integration process. An interesting implication of this principle is that two functions with the same derivative can differ by, at most, the constant of integration. Specific techniques for finding the antiderivative are included in Section 12.5. At this point, consider the following example:

Example 12.1
For the derivative function

$$f(X) = 2X + 3$$

find the parent function $F(X)$.

Thus, a function with the derivative $2X + 3$ must be found. A process of trial and error leads to the parent function

$$F(X) = X^2 + 3X + c$$

as $\quad F'(X) = 2X + 3$

where c represents *any* constant. In other words, the parent function may be

1. $F(X) = X^2 + 3X + 10$
2. $F(X) = X^2 + 3X - 4$
3. The function $F(X)$ with any constant

Thus, $F(X)$ is not determined completely by the integration process and the correct notation for this process is

$$\int (2X + 3)\, dX = X^2 + 3X + c$$

Two of the situations mentioned in Section 12.2 can be evaluated by using indefinite integrals. First, indefinite integrals are used to express the total cost function for a product given the function for marginal cost. In this case, the constant of integration represents the fixed costs. Similarly, an indefinite integral can be used to represent the function for growth in a nation's capital stock given the function for the net investment flow per year. The value of the initial capital stock is the constant of integration.

Additional examples and applications of the indefinite integral are deferred until Section 12.5, which presents the rules and techniques of integration. At this point, readers should have a thorough understanding of the relation between an original function and its derivative and the definition of the indefinite integral.

12.4 The Definite Integral

To introduce the definite integral, consider Figure 12.1. Assume that one wants to determine the area bounded by a function, $Y = f(X)$, between two points on the X axis, $X = a$ and $X = b$. This is represented by the shaded area in Figure 12.1.

The bounded area can be determined by evaluating the definite integral of $f(X)$ between $X = a$ and $X = b$. As presented, this problem is geometric, but using the concept of the limit provides a good way to explain the definite integral.

If the base of the area, or (a, b), is divided into n subintervals where each subinterval has the length ΔX_i for i values from 1 to n, then n rectangles, each with area equal to $[f(X_i)](\Delta X_i)$, can be formed.

Area of a rectangle = length × width

Area of each rectangle = $[f(X_i)](\Delta X_i)$

The total of the n rectangles can be expressed as follows:

$$\sum_{i=1}^{n} [f(X_i)](\Delta X_i)$$

However, as shown in Figure 12.2, the sum of the areas of the rectangles may not be equal to the area under the curve.

The shaded areas of Figure 12.2 are under $f(X)$ but are not included in the summation $\sum_{i=1}^{n} [f(X_i)](\Delta X_i)$. However, if $f(X)$ is continuous, then as n approaches infinity (the number of rectangles increases without bound),

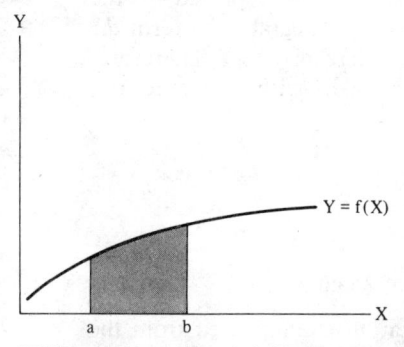

FIGURE 12.1 The definite integral as an area.

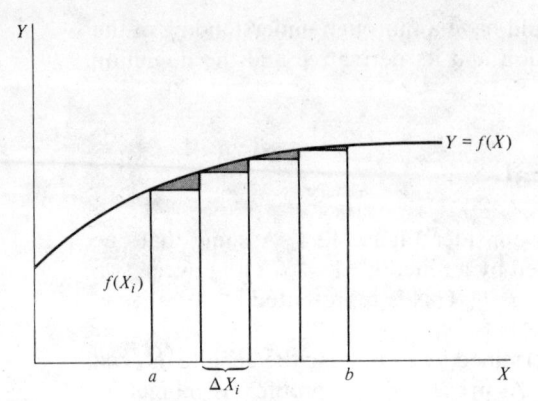

FIGURE 12.2 The definite integral and the sum of the areas of rectangles.

the base of each rectangle ΔX_i approaches 0. Under these conditions, the total of the shaded areas approaches zero and the sum of the areas of the rectangles equals the total area between a and b on $f(X)$.

As there are functional values corresponding to $X = a$ and $X = b$, this area can be stated as a number. Specifically, the area between a and b and $f(X)$ is the definite integral of $f(X)$ between a and b. This is expressed as follows:

THE DEFINITE INTEGRAL OF $f(X)$ BETWEEN $X = a$ AND $X = b$

$$\int_a^b f(X)\, dX$$

With this explanation, additional meaning can be attached to the integral symbol. The integral symbol $\int$ represents a type of summation sign expressing the sum of the areas of n rectangles as n approaches infinity over the interval a, b. Also, as ΔX_i approaches 0, it can be replaced by the differentiation symbol dX in the expression for the integral. The term dX indicates that the integration is to be carried out with respect to X. Therefore, this expression indicates that the integral of $f(X)$ taken with respect to X is to be evaluated between the points a and b.

This answer is computed by

1. Finding the antiderivative of $f(X)$
2. Substituting b for X in the antiderivative
3. Substituting a for X in the antiderivative
4. Finding the difference between the results of 2 and 3

Observe that in step 4 the constant of integration is eliminated from the expression since it appears in the evaluated term at both a and b.

Integral Calculus with Applications

The result of this process can be shown by the following notation:

$$\int_a^b f(X) \, dX = F(b) - F(a)$$

where $f(X)$ represents the derivative, $F(b)$ notates the antiderivative evaluated at b, and $F(a)$ is the antiderivative evaluated at a.

Example 12.2
Using the derivative function of Example 12.1,

$$f(X) = 2X + 3$$

find the area under this curve between $X = 5$ and $X = 3$. This is stated as

$$\int_3^5 (2X + 3) \, dX$$

Thus, this computation is expressed as:

$$\int_3^5 (2X + 3) \, dX = F(5) - F(3)$$

$$= (5)^2 + (3)(5) + c - [(3)^2 + (3)(3) + c]$$

$$= 40 - 18 = 22$$

This is the value of the definite integral between the stated boundaries $X = 5$ and $X = 3$.

This result can be summarized more formally as the *fundamental theorem of integral calculus*.

FUNDAMENTAL THEOREM OF INTEGRAL CALCULUS:
If $f(X)$ is the derivative of $F(X)$ and both functions are continuous and positive over the range $X = a$ to $X = b$, then:

$$\lim_{\substack{n \to \infty \\ \Delta X_i \to 0}} \sum_{i=1}^n [f(X_i)] (\Delta X_i) = \int_a^b f(X) \, dX = F(b) - F(a)$$

A common notation used in this book is:

$$\int_a^b f(X) \, dX = F(X) \Big|_a^b$$

In this form, $F(X)$ is the original function and a vertical line is used to show the upper limit b and lower limit a for the integration.

This fundamental theorem establishes a link between differential and integral calculus as it serves to connect the antiderivative to the definite integral.

12.5 The Rules of Integration

Before the basic rules of integration are stated, two points should be stressed. First, readers should be aware that there are many exceptions and special cases within the rules of integration. For this reason, a Table of Integrals is included at the end of the book (Table IX). This table includes all the rules presented in this chapter and many of the special cases. The use of this table is described in Section 12.8. Second, the following rules are described in terms of the indefinite integral. Section 12.6 applies several of these rules to definite integrals.

As these rules are presented, the concept of antidifferentiation and how each rule relates to the reverse operation of differentiation should be kept in mind; that is, each rule can be checked by determining the derivative of the given antiderivative. If the result is the integrand, the rule is shown to be valid. The rules are numbered so that each can be referred to as the chapter continues.

First, the integral of zero is a constant.

Rule 1: $\int 0 \, dX = K$

As stated in Chapter 10, the derivative of a constant is equal to zero. Thus, the concept of antidifferentiation confirms this rule.

The integral of a constant function, $f(X) = K$, is K times the variable (X, in this case).

Rule 2: $\int K \, dX = KX + c$

Note that c in this case is the constant of integration referred to several times previously.

Example 12.3

$\int 6 \, dX = 6X + c$

Again, antidifferentiation applies to this rule, as

$$\frac{d}{dX}(6X + c) = 6$$

As in differential calculus, integral calculus also has a simple power rule as follows.

Rule 3: Simple Power Rule

$$\int X^n \, dX = \frac{X^{n+1}}{n+1} + c \quad \text{if } n \neq -1$$

This means that to integrate a power of X, the exponent is increased by 1, the term is divided by the resultant new exponent, and the constant of integration is added.

Example 12.4

1. $\int X^6 \, dX = \dfrac{X^7}{7} + c$

2. $\int X^{1/3} \, dX = \dfrac{3X^{4/3}}{4} + c$

3. $\int X^{-1/2} \, dX = 2X^{1/2} + c$

If the exponent n is equal to -1, the divisor of the integral would be zero. Therefore, a different rule must be applied when $n = -1$. This exception is covered by Rule 4.

Rule 4: Power Rule for $n = -1$

$$\int X^{-1} \, dX = \int \frac{1}{X} \, dX = \ln X + c$$

Rule 4 is derived from Chapter 10 where it was shown that

$$\frac{d(\ln X)}{dX} = \frac{1}{X}$$

Example 12.5

$$\int Z^{-1} \, dZ = \int \frac{1}{Z} \, dZ = \ln Z + c$$

Rules 5 and 6 follow directly from the two corresponding rules for differentiation presented in Chapter 10.

Rule 5: The integral of a constant times a function is equal to the constant times the integral of the function. If K is any constant, then

$$\int K f(X) \, dX = K \int f(X) \, dX$$

Example 12.6

1. $\int 8X^{3/4} \, dX = 8 \int X^{3/4} \, dX$

    $= 8 \left(\dfrac{4}{7}\right) (X^{7/4}) + c$

    $= \dfrac{32}{7} X^{7/4} + c$

2. $\int 6X^2 \, dX = 6 \int X^2 \, dX$

    $= 6 \dfrac{X^3}{3} + c$

    $= 2X^3 + c$

Rule 6: Integration may be carried out term by term.

$$\int f(X) \pm g(X) \, dX = \int f(X) \, dX \pm \int g(X) \, dX$$

Example 12.7

$$\int (7X^2 - 3X + 8)\, dX = \int 7X^2\, dX - \int 3X\, dX + \int 8\, dX = \frac{7X^3}{3} - \frac{3X^2}{2} + 8X + c$$

To integrate the power of a linear function, Rule 7 is applied.

Rule 7: Integral of the power of a linear function.

$$\int (mX + b)^n\, dX = \frac{(mX + b)^{n+1}}{m(n + 1)} + c \quad \text{if } n \neq -1$$

The rule is the antidifferentiation operation of the chain rule of differentiation introduced in Chapter 10.

Example 12.8

1. $\int (4X + 7)^5\, dX = \dfrac{(4X + 7)^6}{(4)(6)} + c = \dfrac{(4X + 7)^6}{24} + c$

2. $\displaystyle\int \dfrac{dX}{(6X + 15)^4} = \int (6X + 15)^{-4}\, dX$

   $\qquad = \dfrac{(6X + 15)^{-3}}{(6)(-3)} + c$

   $\qquad = \dfrac{1}{-18(6X + 15)^3} + c$

If the exponent of the linear function is -1, Rule 8 must be applied.

Rule 8: Integration of a linear function raised to the power -1.

$$\int (mX + b)^{-1}\, dX = \int \frac{dX}{mX + b} = \frac{\ln(mX + b)}{m} + c$$

This rule demonstrates antidifferentiation as applied to the chain rule for differentiating a logarithmic function. To restate that rule from Chapter 10,

$$\frac{d}{dX} \ln(mX + b) = \left(\frac{1}{mX + b}\right) \left[\frac{d(mX + b)}{dX}\right]$$

Example 12.9

$$\int (7X - 12)^{-1}\, dX = \int \frac{dX}{7X - 12} = \frac{\ln(7X - 12)}{7} + c$$

Integrals of Exponential and Logarithmic Functions

An integral of an exponential function represents the antidifferentiation of the derivative of an exponential function. As stated in Chapter 10, e^X is its own derivative:

$$\frac{d(e^X)}{dX} = e^X$$

The integral is established in a similar way.

Rule 9: The integral of e^X.

$$\int e^X \, dX = e^X + c$$

Example 12.10

$$\int e^{4.6} \, dX = e^{4.6} + c$$

Rule 10: The integral of an exponential function with base e.

$$\int e^{mX+b} \, dX = \frac{e^{mX+b}}{m} + c$$

Example 12.11

$$\int e^{4X+17} \, dX = \frac{e^{4X+17}}{4} + c$$

The validity of Example 12.11 is shown by the reverse operation of differentiation applied to the result of the example.

$$\frac{d}{dX} \frac{e^{4X+17}}{4} + c = \frac{1}{4} \left[\frac{d}{dX} (e^{4X+17} + c) \right] = \frac{1}{4} (e^{4X+17})(4) = e^{4X+17}$$

Rule 11: Exponential rule for integration of any positive base (except $+1$).

$$\int a^X \, dX = \frac{a^X}{\ln a} + c \quad \text{for } a \neq +1$$

Example 12.12

$$\int 5^X \, dX = \frac{5^X}{\ln 5} + c = \frac{5^X}{1.60944} + c$$

Rule 12: Integration of an exponential function for any positive base except $+1$.

$$\int a^{mX+b} \, dX = \frac{a^{mX+b}}{m \ln a} + c \quad \text{for } a \neq +1$$

Example 12.13

$$\int 5^{3X+2} \, dX = \frac{5^{3X+2}}{3(\ln 5)} + c$$

$$= \frac{5^{3X+2}}{3(1.60944)} + c$$

$$= \frac{5^{3X+2}}{4.82832} + c$$

The rule for finding the integral of a logarithm also can be demonstrated by comparison to the corresponding rule of differentiation.

Rule 13: $\int \ln X \, dX = X(\ln X - 1) + c$.

This rule can be explained by using the product rule for differentiation as applied to the result of the integration, $X(\ln X - 1) + c$. This result is as follows:

Example 12.14

$$\frac{d}{dX}[X(\ln X - 1)] + c = X\left[\frac{d}{dX}(\ln X - 1)\right] + (\ln X - 1)\left(\frac{d}{dX}X\right) + \frac{d}{dX}c$$

$$= X\left(\frac{1}{X}\right) + (\ln X - 1) + 0$$

$$= 1 + \ln X - 1$$

$$\frac{d}{dX}[X(\ln X - 1)] = \ln X$$

Thus, Rule 13 also is demonstrated by means of antidifferentiation.

The final rule of integration presented in this section concerns integration of the logarithm of a linear function.

Rule 14: Integration of the logarithm of a linear function.

$$\int \ln(mX + b) \, dX = \frac{(mX + b)[\ln(mX + b) - 1]}{m} + c$$

Example 12.15

$$\int \ln(6X + 22) \, dX = \frac{(6X + 22)[\ln(6X + 22) - 1]}{6} + c$$

All the rules listed above can be applied to problems with either indefinite or definite integrals. If a rule is applied to a definite integral, upper and lower boundaries are placed on X and consequently c is eliminated when the difference is computed. Several examples of this technique are included in the next section.

The set of exercises after Section 12.6 includes problems directed toward the computation of both indefinite and definite integrals.

Section 12.8 discusses using the Table of Integrals (Table IX at the end of the book) and examines several integrals not presented above.

12.6 Definite Integrals and the Rules of Integration

The following examples apply the rules of the previous section to the determination of definite integrals. In each case, the format and notation for definite integrals presented in Section 12.4 is used. Readers should confirm each result by referring to the corresponding rule of integration.

Example 12.16

$$\int_4^7 8 \, dX = 8X \Big|_4^7 = 56 - 32 = 24$$

Example 12.17

$$\int_2^4 6X^3 \, dX = 6 \int_2^4 X^3 \, dX = 6 \frac{X^4}{4} \Big|_2^4 = 6 \left(\frac{256}{4} - \frac{16}{4} \right) = 6(60)$$
$$= 360$$

Example 12.18

$$\int_7^{10} X^{-1} \, dX = \ln X \Big|_7^{10} = \ln 10 - \ln 7$$
$$= 2.30259 - 1.94591 = 0.35668$$

Example 12.19

$$\int_3^6 (2X^2 - 4X + 8) \, dX = 2 \int_3^6 X^2 \, dX - 4 \int_3^6 X \, dX + \int_3^6 8 \, dX$$
$$= \frac{2X^3}{3} - \frac{4X^2}{2} + 8X \Big|_3^6$$
$$= \frac{432}{3} - \frac{144}{2} + 48 - \left(\frac{54}{3} - \frac{36}{2} + 24 \right)$$
$$= 144 - 72 + 48 - 18 + 18 - 24$$
$$= 96$$

Example 12.20

$$\int_2^4 (3X - 4)^2 \, dX = \frac{(3X - 4)^3}{(3)(3)} \Big|_2^4$$
$$= \frac{(12 - 4)^3}{9} - \left[\frac{(6 - 4)^3}{9} \right]$$

$$= \frac{512 - 8}{9}$$
$$= 56$$

Example 12.21

$$\int_0^3 e^X \, dX = e^X \Big|_0^3$$
$$= e^3 - e^0$$
$$= 20.0855 - 1$$
$$= 19.0855$$

Example 12.22

$$\int_5^{10} \ln X \, dX = X \cdot (\ln X - 1) \Big|_5^{10}$$
$$= [10(\ln 10 - 1)] - [5(\ln 5 - 1)]$$
$$= [10(1.30259)] - [5(0.60944)]$$
$$= 13.0259 - 3.0472 = 9.9787$$

The following exercises will give readers the opportunity to apply the rules of integration to problems requiring both indefinite and definite integrals.

EXERCISES

1. Find each indefinite integral.
   a. $\int 6 \, dX$
   b. $\int 3 \, dX$
   c. $\int 2X^2 \, dX$
   d. $\int \frac{1}{5} X^3 \, dX$
   e. $\int 4X^{-1/3} \, dX$
   f. $\int 3X^{-1} \, dX$
   g. $\int (6Y^2 + 4Y - 14) \, dY$
   h. $\int (3X^3 + 4X^{1/2} + 10) \, dX$
   i. $\int (5Y + 7)^3 \, dY$
   j. $\int (2X + 4)^{-2} \, dX$
   k. $\int (3W + 18)^{-1} \, dW$
   l. $\int 3(2X - 16)^3 \, dX$
   m. $\int 4Z^{-1/4} \, dZ$
   n. $\int \frac{1}{(3X - 4)^4} \, dX$
   o. $\int (14X - X^{-1/3}) \, dX$
   p. $\int \frac{Y^2 + 3}{8} \, dY$
   q. $\int \frac{1}{4} X^{2/3} \, dX$
   r. $\int \frac{X}{2} \, dX$
   s. $\int (5X^4 + 3X + 2X^{-2} - 4) \, dX$
   t. $\int (2X - 3)^{-1/3} \, dX$

2. Find the indefinite integral for each of the exponential and logarithmic functions below.
   a. $\int e^{-6X} \, dX$
   b. $\int 8^{4X-6} \, dX$
   c. $\int \ln(2Y - 3) \, dY$
   d. $\int e^{-2X+17} \, dX$
   e. $\int 2^{4Y+17} \, dY$
   f. $\int \ln(22X) \, dX$
   g. $\int \ln(3X) \, dX$
   h. $\int e^{-X} \, dX$
   i. $\int 2.4^Y \, dY$
   j. $\int \ln(6Y + 1) \, dY$

3. Evaluate each integral between the stated limits.
   a. $\int_6^8 3 \, dX$
   b. $\int_0^7 2X^3 \, dX$
   c. $\int_3^6 X^{-1} \, dX$
   d. $\int_0^4 (4X^2 + 3X^{1/2} + 7) \, dX$
   e. $\int_{20}^{25} (3X^2 + 10) \, dX$
   f. $\int_5^{10} (4X - 2)^3 \, dX$
   g. $\int_{-4}^8 (X + 2)^2 \, dX$
   h. $\int_4^6 (8X - 4)^{-1} \, dX$
   i. $\int_1^6 \frac{1}{(3X + 5)^2} \, dX$
   j. $\int_3^5 \frac{1}{4X + 5} \, dX$
   k. $\int_{-3}^0 (3Y - 2) \, dY$
   l. $\int_3^6 (4Y^2 - Y^{-2}) \, dY$

4. Evaluate each of the exponential and logarithmic functions below between the stated limits.
   a. $\int_{1.5}^2 e^X \, dX$
   b. $\int_{-1}^0 e^X \, dX$
   c. $\int_1^2 e^{2Y-2} \, dY$
   d. $\int_3^5 e^{-2Y+7} \, dY$
   e. $\int_3^6 2^X \, dX$
   f. $\int_1^2 14^{2X} \, dX$
   g. $\int_2^3 10^{3X-5} \, dX$
   h. $\int_{15}^{30} \ln Y \, dY$
   i. $\int_{40}^{50} \ln(X - 14) \, dX$
   j. $\int_3^7 \ln(3Y + 12) \, dY$

12.7 Integration by Parts

The technique of integration by parts employs the principle of the product rule of differentiation in deriving the integral in cases where the integrand is separated into two parts. Specifically, integration by parts is used when an expression involving products or logarithms cannot be integrated by any of the rules of Section 12.5 or the other general forms of integration.

To understand integration by parts, consider first the product rule of differential calculus. This rule, as stated in Chapter 10, is that if $f(X)$ and $g(X)$ are two differentiable functions, then

1. $\dfrac{d}{dX}[f(X)\,g(X)] = f(X)\,g'(X) + g(X)\,f'(X)$

For simplification in presenting this process, let $u = f(X)$ and $v = g(X)$ in the following steps. Thus,

2. $d(uv) = u\,dv + v\,du$

Integrating both sides of this result yields the following expression:

3. $\int d(uv) = \int u\,dv + \int v\,du$

As $\int d(uv) = uv$, this expression can be stated as:

4. $uv = \int u\,dv + \int v\,du$

A rearrangement of terms in step 4 gives the general notational form for integration by parts:

5. $\int u\,dv = uv - \int v\,du$

where $u = f(X)$ and $v = g(X)$.

Thus, the initial step in integration by parts is to form the integral in such a way that it is expressed as $\int u\,dv$. In other words, the integrand consisting of two functions of X is separated such that one is u or $f(X)$, and the other is the derivative of v, or $g'(X)$. Care in the selection of the respective parts $f(X)$ and $g'(X)$ minimizes the difficulty of a particular computation.

Three examples will illustrate integration by parts.

Example 12.23

Find $\int X^4\,dX$ by the method of integration by parts. (In this case, integration by parts is not as easy as application of the simple power rule. However, a solution using integration by parts will provide an understanding of this technique.)

For $\int X^4\,dX$, let $u = X^4$ and $dv = dX$. Consequently, $du = 4X^3$ and $v = \int dX = X$. At this point, the formula of step 4 is applied:

1. $\int u\,dv = uv - \int v\,du$
2. $\int X^4\,dX = (X^4)(X) - \int (X)(4X^3)\,dX$
3. $\int X^4\,dX = X^5 - \int 4X^4\,dX$
4. $\int 4X^4\,dX = \dfrac{4X^5}{5} + c$ by the simple power rule
5. $\int X^4\,dX = X^5 - \dfrac{4X^5}{5} + c$
6. $\int X^4\,dX = \dfrac{X^5}{5} + c$

Step 6 is the integral of $X^4\,dX$, as can be verified by the simple power rule.

Integral Calculus with Applications   **377**

Example 12.24
Find $\int \ln X \, dX$ using integration by parts. In this case, let $u = \ln X$ and $dv = dX$. Therefore, $du = 1/X$ and $v = X$. Substituting these four terms into the formula for integration by parts leads to the following result:

1. $\int u \, dv = uv - \int v \, du$
2. $\int \ln X \, dX = (\ln X)(X) - \int (X)\left(\frac{1}{X}\right) dX$
3. $ = X \ln X - \int 1 \, dX$
4. $ = X \ln X - X + c$
5. $ = X(\ln X - 1) + c$

Step 5 coincides with Rule 13 in Section 12.5 for finding the integral of a logarithm. In this example, notice that the selection of u and dv is extremely important since the choice dictates the form of $\int v \, du$ that must be integrated.

Example 12.25 is a third and more complex illustration of integration by parts.

Example 12.25
Find $\int X(5 + X)^3 \, dX$ using integration by parts. For this problem, let $u = X$ and $dv = (5 + X)^3$. Therefore, $du = 1$ and v is equal to the following:

$$v = \int (5 + X)^3 \, dX = \frac{(5 + X)^4}{(4)(1)} = \frac{(5 + X)^4}{4} + c$$

Thus, the formula for integration by parts is shown below:

$$\int u \, dv = uv - \int v \, du$$

$$\int X(5 + X)^3 \, dX = X\left[\frac{(5 + X)^4}{4}\right] - \int \frac{(5 + X)^4}{4} \, dX$$

and as $\int \frac{(5 + X)^4}{4} \, dX = \frac{(5 + X)^5}{20} + c$

$$\int X(5 + X)^3 \, dX = \frac{X(5 + X)^4}{4} - \frac{(5 + X)^5}{20} + c$$

$$= \left[\frac{(5 + X)^4}{4}\right]\left(X - \frac{5 + X}{5}\right) + c$$

$$= \left[\frac{(5 + X)^4}{4}\right]\left(\frac{4X - 5}{5}\right) + c$$

In this example, a rather complex product was integrated in a relatively straightforward way by means of integration by parts.

A useful technique to apply in the selection of u and dv is to choose the function that appears to be the most difficult to integrate for dv. This selection means that the integral $\int v\,du$ will be relatively less difficult to integrate. Thus, in Example 12.25, the term $(5 + X)^3$ is more difficult to integrate than X. By selecting $(5 + X)^3$ to be dv, difficulty is minimized when integrating the expression $\int v\,du = \int [(5 + X)^4/4]\,dX$.

This section has described integration by parts. When the integrand is in the form of a product or logarithm and the rules of integration cannot be applied, integration by parts may be a simplifying procedure. Admittedly, integration by parts is a trial-and-error method dependent on the adaptability of the integrand to this format and careful selection of the respective parts. However, where the technique can be applied, integration by parts is helpful in finding complex integrals.

EXERCISES

1. Integrate each of the following power functions by means of integration by parts:
   a. $\int X^3\,dX$ c. $\int X^{-2}\,dX$
   b. $\int 4X^2\,dX$ d. $\int y^5\,dy$
2. Integrate each logarithmic function by means of integration by parts.
   a. $\int \ln y\,dy$
   b. $\int \ln 3X\,dX$
   c. $\int 8 \ln X\,dX$
   d. $\int \dfrac{\ln X}{3}\,dX$
3. Integrate each by means of integration by parts.
   a. $\int X^2(2X^4)\,dX$ d. $\int y^2(y + 7)\,dy$
   b. $\int X(X^2 + 3)\,dX$ e. $\int y(y^5 + 5y)\,dy$
   c. $\int X^4(X + 7)\,dX$ f. $\int X^{1/2}(X + 3)\,dX$

12.8 Using Tables of Integrals

The 14 rules of integration presented in Section 12.5 and some other common forms of integrals not presented previously are listed in Table IX at the end of this book. In contrast to the rules for finding derivatives, there are no general rules applicable to computing many indefinite integrals. Thus, for many integration problems, one must be able to relate the particular functional form to one of the forms in Table IX.

Frequently, the use of integral tables eliminates the need to integrate a particular function by the technique of integration by parts.

Example 12.26

Find $\displaystyle\int \dfrac{e^x}{5}\,dX$

This exact form does not appear in Table IX. However, if the constant $\frac{1}{5}$ is taken outside the integral sign, integration can be performed by following Rule 9, as follows:

$$\int \frac{e^x}{5}\, dx = \frac{1}{5} \int e^x\, dx = \frac{1}{5}(e^x) + c$$

Example 12.27

Find $\int \ln 5X\, dX$

In this case, although a constant is not added to form the term $mX + b$, Rule 14 in Table IX applies. Thus,

$$\int \ln 5X\, dX = \frac{(5X)[\ln(5X) - 1]}{5} + c$$

Example 12.28

Find $\int \frac{5X}{X + 3}\, dX$

Here, Rule 20 is applicable. By moving the constant 5 outside the integral sign, the integral resembles

$$\int \frac{X}{mX + b}\, dX$$

For this integral, $m = 1$ and $b = 3$. Thus, following Rule 20 yields

$$\int \frac{5X}{X + 3}\, dX = 5 \int \frac{X}{X + 3}\, dX$$

$$= 5[X - 3 \ln(X + 3)] + c$$

Example 12.29

Find $\int \frac{1}{4X^2 + 3X}\, dX$

In this case, factoring X out of the denominator of the integrand leads to the following result:

$$\int \frac{1}{4X^2 + 3X}\, dX = \int \frac{1}{X(4X + 3)}\, dX$$

In this form, Rule 22 can be applied where $m = 4$ and $b = 3$. Thus, the integral is as follows:

$$\int \frac{1}{4X^2 + 3X}\, dX = \frac{1}{3}\left(\ln \frac{X}{4X + 3}\right) + c$$

The following exercise set will give practice in determining indefinite integrals with the help of Table IX.

EXERCISES

Determine the indefinite integral for each problem below by use of Table IX.

1. $\int (X + 3)^2 \, dX$
2. $\int (4X + 12) \, dX$
3. $\int \dfrac{e^{3x}}{5} \, dX$
4. $\int 7^{4X} \, dX$
5. $\int \dfrac{12}{X} \, dX$
6. $\int X e^{3X} \, dX$
7. $\int \dfrac{X}{3X - 2} \, dX$
8. $\int (5X)^4 \, dX$
9. $\int 2X^4 \ln X \, dX$
10. $\int \dfrac{-5}{2X} \, dX$
11. $\int \dfrac{1}{e^x} \, dX$
12. $\int \dfrac{\ln X}{6X} \, dX$
13. $\int (5X)(5)^x \, dX$
14. $\int (10X + 80)^2 \, dX$
15. $\int \dfrac{1}{2X(3X + 4)} \, dX$
16. $\int 6X e^{2X^2 - 4} \, dX$

12.9 Applications: Indefinite Integrals

The next two sections present business applications of integral calculus. In this section, problems with indefinite integrals are discussed, and in Section 12.10, applications of the definite integral are described. Thus, this section includes problems which require finding the original function knowing the derivative of the function. In Section 12.10, functions are evaluated over specific ranges.

Marginal Relationships and Total Relationships

At times, firms know the functional relation between the quantity produced and the cost of each additional unit made (marginal cost). Also, a firm may understand the relation between the quantity of sales and the revenue gained from each additional unit sold (marginal revenue).

The firm may desire to determine the functional relations for total cost and total revenue based on these marginal relations. For example, a producer may know that resource limitations act in a certain way to cause additional unit costs to follow a pattern as output expands. However, the firm needs to understand the functional relation which identifies total cost at any particular output.

The next two examples describe the computation of the total cost and total revenue functions from the corresponding marginal cost and marginal revenue relationships.

Example 12.30

A manufacturer of tool dies knows the marginal cost function for its production process. The firm wants to determine the functional relation between total production cost and the quantity produced. It is known that fixed costs for the tool-die operation are $12,000.

Marginal cost (MC) is the following function of the quantity produced Q:

$$MC = 0.01Q^2 - Q$$

This function must be integrated to yield the total cost function. Integration and addition of the fixed-cost component leads to the following total cost (TC) function:

$$TC = \int MC \, dQ = \int 0.01Q^2 - Q$$

$$= \frac{Q^3}{300} - \frac{Q^2}{2} + c$$

$$= \frac{Q^3}{300} - \frac{Q^2}{2} + 12,000$$

Observe that the fixed cost of $12,000 represents the constant of integration.

If the firm wants to determine the marginal cost (MC) of the 180th die and the total cost (TC) of producing 180 dies, the following results are found:

$$MC = 0.01Q^2 - Q$$
$$MC(180) = 0.01(180)^2 - 180$$
$$= (0.01)(32,400) - 180$$
$$= 324 - 180 = \$144$$

$$TC = \frac{Q^3}{300} - \frac{Q^2}{2} + 12,000$$

$$TC(180) = \frac{(180)^3}{300} - \frac{(180)^2}{2} + 12,000$$

$$= 19,440 - 16,200 + 12,000$$

$$= \$15,240$$

As the example demonstrates, any value can be substituted for Q yielding the marginal cost of that unit ($144) and the total cost of the stated number of units ($15,240).

At the point $Q = 180$, the average or per unit cost (AC) is determined by dividing total cost by 180. This leads to the following result:

$$AC = \frac{TC}{Q} = \frac{15,240}{180}$$

$$AC(180) = \$84.67$$

Thus, the integration process has enabled the firm to determine that at an output of 180 dies, the additional cost of a die is $144, total cost is $15,240, and cost per die is $84.67.

Example 12.31
A supplier of owner-installed automobile air conditioners knows the marginal revenue function for the sale of air conditioners. This means that the functional relation between the quantity sold Q and revenue received from the sale of an additional air conditioner MR is known. The marginal revenue function is as follows:

$$MR = 380 - 0.5Q - \frac{Q^2}{20}$$

The supplier wants to specify the functional relation for total revenue (TR) and per unit revenue (average revenue = AR). In deriving the total revenue function by integration of the marginal revenue function, it is known that the constant of integration c is equal to zero as no revenue is generated without sales.

The indefinite integral of marginal revenue (MR) where $c = 0$ yields the total revenue (TR) function as the following demonstrates:

$$TR = \int MR \, dQ = \int \left(380 - 0.5Q - \frac{Q^2}{20}\right) dQ$$

$$= 380Q - 0.25Q^2 - \frac{Q^3}{60}$$

The average revenue function $AR = f(Q)$ is found by dividing the total revenue function by the quantity sold Q. This average revenue function is related to a demand curve where price is a function of quantity sold. This function is as follows:

$$AR = price = \frac{TR}{Q}$$

$$= \frac{380Q}{Q} - \frac{0.25Q^2}{Q} - \frac{Q^3}{60Q}$$

$$= 380 - 0.25Q - \frac{Q^2}{60}$$

By knowing the three functions MR, TR, and AR, analyses can be conducted at particular quantity points. For example, at $Q = 30$ (30 air conditioners), marginal revenue, total revenue, and average revenue are the following amounts:

1. $MR = 380 - 0.5Q - \dfrac{Q^2}{20}$

$$MR(30) = 380 - (0.5)(30) - \frac{(30)^2}{20}$$
$$= 380 - 15 - 45$$
$$= \$320$$

2. $TR = 380Q - 0.25Q^2 - \dfrac{Q^3}{60}$

$$TR(30) = (380)(30) - (0.25)(30)^2 - \frac{(30)^3}{60}$$
$$= 11,400 - 225 - 450$$
$$= \$10,725$$

3. $AR = \text{price} = \dfrac{TR}{Q}$

$$AR(30) = \frac{10,725}{30}$$
$$= \$357.50$$

The computations have indicated that at a quantity of 30 air conditioners, the firm will

1. Receive $320 from the sale of an additional air conditioner (marginal revenue)
2. Receive total revenue of $10,725 from the sale of 30 air conditioners
3. Obtain a price of $357.50 per air conditioner (average revenue)

This analysis is facilitated by knowing that the total revenue function is the integral of the marginal revenue function and the resulting integration process.

The final example of indefinite integrals concerns specification of the functional relation for the accumulation of a stock of capital goods, or *capital formation*. Relations of this type are used frequently in the analysis of national or regional economies. If capital formation (new plants, equipment, machinery, etc.) is viewed as a continuous process over time, the value of capital stock at any point in time can be expressed as a function of time. The rate of capital formation (rate of net new investment) at any point in time must be known to determine the total capital stock.

Indefinite integrals can be employed to determine a function for capital formation given the rate of net new investment at any time. The common notation used for a problem of this type is that time is designated t (measured in years, months, days, etc.) and the value of capital stock at any time t is designated $K(t)$.

Example 12.32
A group of business leaders is interested in knowing the functional relation for capital formation in a rural region of a state. The executives want to know this relation as they believe that capital accumulation is a crucial component of the region's prosperity.

Two facts are known. First, the value of capital stock in the region at an initial time period is $17 billion. Second, the rate of net new investment as a function of time, $g(t)$, is

$$g(t) = 0.5t^{1/3}$$

where t is measured in years.

The goal of the study is to establish the function expressing the value of capital, in billions of dollars, as a function of time, $K(t)$. To determine this relationship, the net investment function $g(t) = 0.5t^{1/3}$ must be integrated with respect to t. In this case, the constant of integration is equal to the initial capital stock, or $17 billion ($c = 17$). The result is as follows:

$$\begin{aligned} K(t) &= \int g(t)\, dt \\ &= \int 0.5 t^{1/3}\, dt \\ &= 0.5 \int t^{1/3}\, dt \\ &= 0.5 \left(\tfrac{3}{4} t^{4/3}\right) + c \\ &= \tfrac{3}{8} t^{4/3} + c \\ &= \tfrac{3}{8} t^{4/3} + 17 \end{aligned}$$

This function gives the amount of capital stock at any time (measured in years) after the initial year.

For example, after 8 years ($t = 8$), the value of capital stock is the following:

$$\begin{aligned} K(t) &= \tfrac{3}{8} t^{4/3} + 17 \\ &= \tfrac{3}{8} (8)^{4/3} + 17 \\ &= \tfrac{3}{8} (16) + 17 \\ &= \$23 \text{ billion} \end{aligned}$$

Therefore, after 8 years, the value of capital stock in the region will be $23 billion.

In each of these examples the same basic procedure is followed. First, the known rate-of-change function is integrated to obtain the original function. Specific X values can be substituted into the original function to derive values as desired. It should be noted that, when working with indefinite integrals, the constant of integration is not always known, as in these examples. If this is the case, the integral is not completely specified and particular points on the original function cannot be evaluated.

12.10 Applications: Definite Integrals

Before presenting applications, the concept of the definite integral will be restated. When boundary limits are imposed on an integral expression such as

Integral Calculus with Applications   **385**

$$\int_a^b f(X)\,dX$$

it is an instruction that the indefinite integral of $f(X)$ is to be evaluated at point b and at point a and the difference computed. This subtraction process eliminates the constant of integration, and the result is the definite integral. This is written as follows:

$$\int_a^b f(X)\,dX = F_X \Big|_a^b = F(b) - F(a)$$

The numerical result represents the area under the curve $f(X)$ between $X = b$ and $X = a$.

Three applications of the definite integral are presented in this section. Each solution will follow the same computational process.

Example 12.33

A national firm knows the marginal revenue function for the sale of power lawn mowers in a sales region. The marginal revenue function (MR) relating marginal revenue and quantity of lawn mowers sold Q has the following form:

$$\text{MR} = f(Q)$$
$$= 400 - 0.3Q$$

This function appears in Figure 12.3. The firm wants to know the additional total revenue that will result by increasing weekly sales in the region from 160 to 200 lawn mowers.

To determine this amount, the marginal revenue curve must be integrated over the specified sales range. This integration process will account

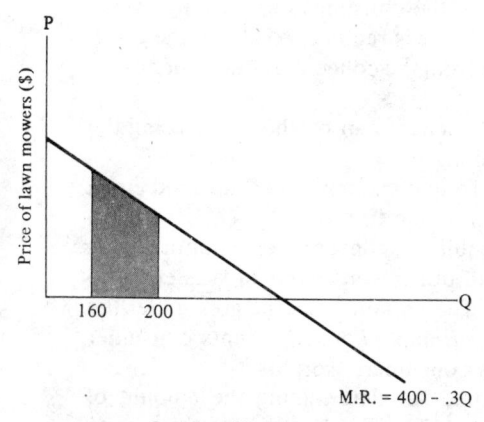

FIGURE 12.3   The area under a marginal revenue curve.

for all additional revenue between 160 and 200 lawn mowers. The sales range is shown as the shaded area in Figure 12.3.

Observe that the area under the marginal revenue function represents total revenue over the range 160 to 200 lawn mowers per week. Thus, integration of the marginal revenue function over a range yields the amount of total revenue over that range.

Integration of the marginal revenue function is shown below:

$$MR = f(Q)$$
$$= 400 - 0.3Q$$
$$\int_{160}^{200} MR\, dQ = \int_{160}^{200} 400 - 0.3Q\, dQ$$
$$= 400Q - 0.15Q^2 \Big|_{160}^{200}$$
$$= [(400)(200) - (0.15)(200)^2] - [(400)(160) - (0.15)(160)^2]$$
$$= 74{,}000 - 60{,}160 = \$13{,}840$$

The analysis indicates that the company will achieve $13,840 in additional weekly revenue if regional sales increase from 160 to 200 lawn mowers per week.

This computation is based on the principle that the integral of the marginal revenue function yields the total revenue function. Imposing limits on the integral allows determination of additional revenue over a specified sales range.

Consumers' surplus is a concept used in economic analysis. It is based on the indirect relation between the price of a good and the quantity demanded. Evaluation of consumers' surplus requires examination of the market demand for a good representing the sum of the amounts of the good bought by all consumers at various prices.

At any given market price, some of the consumers are willing to pay a higher price for the good if that higher price is required to obtain the good. In other words, some consumers benefit from the collective actions of buyers and sellers in setting a particular price.

The total amount of this consumer benefit can be shown by using the market demand curve, *DD* in Figure 12.4.

Consumers receive a total benefit from consumption of the good equal to the entire area under the demand curve and to the left of Q_1. However, of this total value received, only part requires a consumer expenditure. This is represented by the rectangle *bcde*. In other words, this area is equal to the price times the quantity consumed. The remainder of the area under the demand curve and to the left of Q_1, the triangle *abc*, represents consumer benefits in excess of price paid. This is consumers' surplus.

Integral calculus provides a method for determining the amount of consumers' surplus, the area *abc* in Figure 12.4. The data required to specify

Integral Calculus with Applications

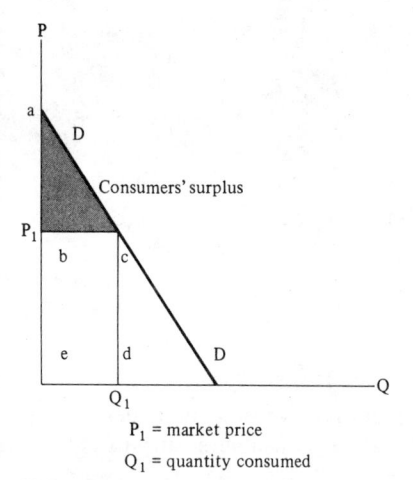

FIGURE 12.4 Market price and consumers' surplus.

P_1 = market price
Q_1 = quantity consumed

this include the functional relation of the demand curve $P = f(Q)$, the market price P_1, and the quantity consumed Q_1.

As price is a function of the quantity demanded, the dollar amount represented by abc is found by integrating the demand function with respect to Q between 0 and Q_1 and subtracting from this amount the product $P_1 Q_1$. In dollar terms, the resulting consumers' surplus is the difference between total benefit received and total amount paid by consumers.

Example 12.34

The demand function for a particular brand of pocket calculator is stated below.

$$P = 75 - 0.3Q - 0.05Q^2$$

It is desired to estimate the consumers' surplus at a quantity of 15 calculators.

Price corresponding to 15 calculators is $59.25 as the following demonstrates:

$P = 75 - (0.3)(15) - (0.05)(15)^2$
$= 75 - 4.5 - 11.25$
$= \$59.25$

The total amount paid for 15 calculators is equal to $P_1 Q_1$ or $(59.25)(15) = \$888.75$.

The total monetary value which consumers receive from the 15 calculators is found by integrating $P = f(Q)$ between $Q = 0$ and $Q = 15$. This is derived here:

$$P = 75 - 0.3Q - 0.05Q^2$$

$$\int_0^{15} P\, dQ = \int (75 - 0.3Q - 0.05Q^2)\, dQ$$

$$= 75Q - 0.15Q^2 - \frac{Q^3}{60}\bigg|_0^{15}$$

$$= (75)(15) - (0.15)(15)^2 - \frac{(15)^3}{60} - 0$$

$$= 1125 - 33.75 - 56.25$$

$$= \$1035$$

At this price-quantity combination, consumers receive benefits equal to $1035 and make total payments of $888.75. Therefore, consumers' surplus is equal to the difference, or $146.25.

$$\text{Consumers' surplus} = \int_0^{Q_1} P\, dQ - (P_1)(Q_1)$$

$$= \$1035 - \$888.75 = \$146.25$$

Consumers' surplus is a useful concept for the analysis of questions of public policy and other social questions in economics. As a mathematical technique, it is an excellent example of applied integral calculus.

Definite integrals can be used to analyze many financial questions involving interest rate and time calculations. The application presented here concerns the determination of interest earned with continuous compounding.

In Example 9.19, it was shown that a principal P of $2000 invested at an 8 percent continuously compounded interest rate i for 18 months ($t = 1.5$ years) is worth $2255. To compute this amount, the formula is

$$S_t = Pe^{it}$$

where S_t = value of the account after 1.5 years ($t = 1.5$). This result is derived as follows:

$$S_t = Pe^{it}$$
$$= (2000)\, e^{0.08(1.5)}$$
$$= 2000\, e^{0.12}$$
$$e^{0.12} = 1.1275 \quad \text{from Table III}$$
$$S_t = (2000)(1.1275)$$
$$= \$2255$$

Thus, the account earns $255 in interest during the 18-month period.

The definite integral can be applied to the computation of interest earned on accounts over stated time intervals. The next two examples demonstrate this procedure for an 18-month time period and for several years during a 5-year time period.

Example 12.35
Find the interest earned on a $2000 principal earning 8 percent annually, continuously compounded, for 1.5 years.

First, observe that the nominal simple (not compounded) interest payment on this principal is $160 per year [(0.08)(2000) = 160]. Thus, the problem can be viewed as one of determining the value of interest after 1.5 years when interest is earned at the continuous rate of 160 times the continuous compounding factor e^{it}. In this case, as $i = 0.08$, the continuous compounding factor is $e^{0.08t}$ where t represents the number of years.

To determine interest earned, the continuous rate $160e^{0.08t}$ must be integrated between $t = 0$ and $t = 1.5$. The basic rule of integration used to do this is Rule 10, which is restated here:

Rule 10: $\int e^{mX+b} \, dX = \dfrac{e^{mX+b}}{m} + c$

The steps in the computations are as follows:

$$\int_0^{1.5} 160e^{0.08t} \, dt = 160 \int_0^{1.5} e^{0.08t} \, dt$$

$$= 160 \left(\dfrac{e^{0.08t}}{0.08} \right) \Big|_0^{1.5}$$

$$= \dfrac{160}{0.08} (e^{0.08t}) \Big|_0^{1.5}$$

$$= 2000(e^{0.12} - e^0)$$

Table III yields $e^{0.12} = 1.1275$ and $e^0 = 1$.

$$\int_0^{1.5} 160e^{0.08t} \, dt = 2000(1.1275 - 1)$$

$$= 2000(0.1275) = \$255$$

Therefore, interest accumulating at the continuous annual rate of $160 \, e^{0.08t}$ has a value of $255 after 1.5 years. The result confirms the amount of interest found in Example 9.19.

A second application of this technique is presented in Example 12.36.

Example 12.36
Find the total interest accumulation between the end of year 3 and the end of year 5 for an account earning interest at the continuously compounded rate of $300e^{0.06t}$.

$$\int_3^5 300e^{0.06t} = 300 \int_3^5 e^{0.06t}$$

$$= 300 \left(\frac{e^{0.06t}}{0.06}\right)\Big|_3^5$$

$$= 5000[e^{(0.06)(5)} - e^{(0.06)(3)}]$$

Using e values in Table III.

$$\int_3^5 300\, e^{0.06t} = 5000(1.3499 - 1.1972)$$

$$= 5000(0.1527) = 763.50$$

Consequently, $763.50 in interest will be accumulated between the end of year 3 and the end of year 5.

These examples have illustrated several applications of the definite integral. The technique followed for each is that the indefinite integral is developed and evaluated between the stated boundaries. Thus, unlike the examples for the indefinite integral which lead to functions and specific points on functions, evaluation of the definite integral provides a measure of the integral over a stated range of values.

The following exercises provide practice in determining both indefinite and definite integrals in applied situations.

EXERCISES

1. The following represent marginal revenue (MR) and marginal cost (MC) functions for particular firms. Each marginal function is stated as a function of quantity Q.

   Find the total revenue function corresponding to each MR function and the total cost function corresponding to each MC function in parts a through f.
   a. $MR = 200 - 3.2Q$
   b. $MR = 600 - 0.5Q^2$
   c. $MC = Q^2 + 4Q$
   d. $MC = \dfrac{Q^2}{3} + 3Q^{1/2}$
   e. $MR = 2000 - 0.6Q^{1/2}$
   f. $MC = 4Q^2 - 0.7$
   g. For each total revenue function, what is the value of the constant of integration? Why?
   h. What cost component is represented by the constant of integration in each total cost function?
2. a. For the following, where marginal cost (MC in dollars) is a function of the quantity produced Q,

$$MC = 0.05Q^2 + 0.5Q$$

find the total cost function and the amount of fixed cost if it is known that total cost equals $5800 at $Q = 60$.

b. For the following, where marginal cost (MC in dollars) is a function of the quantity produced Q,

$$MC = Q^2 - 1.2Q$$

find the total cost function and the amount of fixed cost if it is known that total cost equals $500 at $Q = 12$.

3. A firm manufactures oil-operated furnaces used in homes. The fixed cost for the production of furnaces is $45,000. The function for the marginal cost (MC) of an additional furnace is shown below where Q represents the quantity of furnaces.

$$MC = \frac{Q^2}{3} - 10Q$$

a. Find the total cost function.
b. Find the marginal cost of producing the 60th furnace.
c. Find the total cost of producing 60 furnaces.
d. Find the cost per furnace at an output of 60 furnaces.
e. Interpret the relation between marginal cost and average cost at the output of 60 furnaces.

4. An electronics company sells tape players for home use. Marginal revenue (MR in dollars) as a function of the quantity of tape players Q is known by the firm.

$$MR = 300 - 0.4Q$$

a. Find the corresponding expression for total revenue.
b. Find the average revenue function.
c. Compare average revenue and marginal revenue functions with respect to slope.
d. At $Q = 500$, find marginal revenue, total revenue, and average revenue. Interpret these findings.

5. New capital (plants, equipment, etc.) is being added to "high-technology" industries at a continuous rate in a region of the southwestern United States. At the beginning of the period under consideration, $100 million of capital had been invested in such industries in the region.

The function expressing this continuous rate of growth is

$$c(t) = 5t^2 - 2t$$

where $c(t)$ represents capital at any point in time (t measured in years).
a. Find the expression for the amount of capital in high-technology industries in this region at any time t.

b. At this rate shown by $c(t)$, what will be the value of invested capital at the end of year 2? At the end of year 6?

6. An automobile tire manufacturer has established the following marginal revenue (MR) function for tires, where Q represents the quantity of tires sold per month:

   $MR = 80 - 0.004Q$

   a. Find the corresponding expression for total revenue.
   b. If monthly tire sales increase from 4000 tires to 5000 tires, what will be the additional monthly total revenue to the firm?

7. A manufacturer of men's shirts knows that the marginal cost (MC) function for shirt production Q is the following:

   $MC = 0.001Q^2 - 0.02Q$

   The firm also knows that the fixed cost of the production process is $1000.
   Find the additional total cost involved in increasing production from 150 to 180 shirts per day.

8. The demand or average revenue function for fresh whole milk is

   $P = 5.00 - 0.0004Q$

   where P represents dollars per gallon and Q is the number of gallons sold.
   a. At a sales quantity of 7000 gallons, what is the amount of consumers' surplus?
   b. What is measured by the answer to part a?
   c. At a sales quantity of 8000 gallons, what is the amount of consumers' surplus?
   d. What is demonstrated by comparison of the answers to parts a and c?

9. Use techniques of integration to answer the following:
   a. Find the interest earned during the first 8 years on a $6000 savings account at 9 percent interest, continuously compounded.
   b. How much interest will be earned on this account during the second year (i.e., between the end of year 1 and end of year 2)?
   c. If the interest rate on this account is increased to 11 percent continuously compounded, how much interest will be earned during the first 8 years?

10. A grain exporting firm knows that the rate of maintenance expenditure on one of its storage silos is expressed by the following function:

    $M(t) = 500 + t^2$

    where $M(t)$ measures dollar expenditures per year for maintenance and t represents time in years since construction of the silo.

How much will the company spend on maintenance expenditures between $t = 6$ and $t = 9$?

12.11 Improper Integrals

The final topic of this chapter is improper integrals. This is a subject which both uses the definite integral and provides a link to the elements of probability presented in Chapter 13.

Improper integrals often are used in the evaluation of functions which express asymptotic areas under curves. An *asymptotic area* is one where the function approaches but never touches the X axis, the Y axis, or both axes. Figure 12.5 shows functions which are asymptotic to the X axis (a) and asymptotic to the Y axis (b).

Two types of improper integrals are introduced in this discussion. The first includes situations when the integrand becomes infinite or undefined at some point in the interval of integration. An example of this type of improper integral is as follows.

Example 12.37

$$\int_0^1 \frac{1}{X} dX = \ln X \Big|_0^1$$
$$= 0 - \ln 0$$
$$= \text{undefined, as } \ln 0 \text{ is undefined}$$

Under certain conditions, integrals of this form can be evaluated. However, the evaluation requires use of the concept of the limit and can be explained in a more practical framework by introducing the second type of improper integral.

Asymptotic to the X axis   Asymptotic to the Y axis

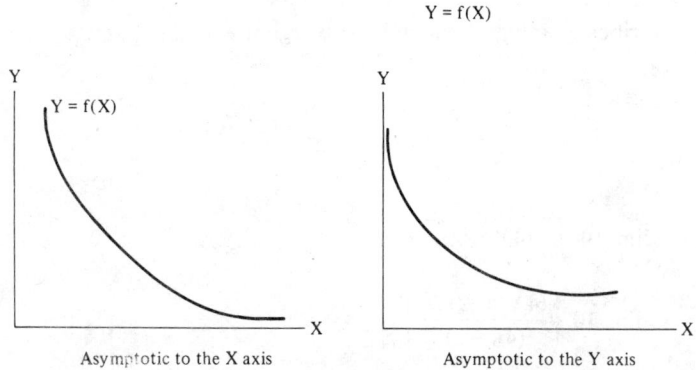

FIGURE 12.5 Functions asymptotic to the X and Y axes.

This other type of improper integral includes situations when one of the limits of integration is infinite. For example, the integrals $\int_2^\infty f(X)\, dX$ and $\int_{-\infty}^7 5f(X)\, dX$ have infinite limits. As infinity is not a defined boundary, integrals of this type cannot be evaluated by using techniques previously presented.

At times, this type of improper integral can be evaluated using the concept of the limit. This process is explained by first altering the notational form of the definite integral to be as shown below:

$$\int_2^\infty f(X)\, dX = \lim_{b \to \infty} \int_2^b f(X)\, dX$$

$$\int_{-\infty}^7 f(X)\, dX = \lim_{a \to -\infty} \int_a^7 f(X)\, dX$$

In this form, if the limit exists, the improper integral is *convergent* and can be evaluated. If the limit does not exist, the improper integral is *divergent* and cannot be evaluated.

As an example of the divergent case, consider again the integral $\int X^{-1}\, dX = \int (1/X)\, dX$. However, unlike Example 12.37, assume the limits of integration include ∞ as in the following example.

Example 12.38

Find $\int_1^\infty X^{-1}\, dX = \int_1^\infty \frac{1}{X}\, dX$

1. $\int_1^\infty \frac{1}{X}\, dX = \lim_{b \to \infty} \int_1^b \frac{1}{X}\, dX$

2. $\int_1^\infty \frac{1}{X}\, dX = \lim_{b \to \infty} (\ln X + c) \Big|_1^b$

At step 2 it is remembered that $\ln \infty$ is equal to infinity and, therefore, the integral does not have a limit. Evaluation cannot be carried out on this integral.

Example 12.39 describes an integral which is convergent with an upper boundary of infinity.

Example 12.39

Find $\int_0^\infty \frac{10}{(4X + 2)^3}\, dX$

1. $\int_0^\infty \frac{10}{(4X + 2)^3}\, dX = \lim_{a \to \infty} 10 \int_0^a (4X + 2)^{-3}\, dX$

2. $= \lim_{a \to \infty} 10 \left\{ \frac{(4X + 2)^{-2}}{(4)(-2)} \Big|_0^a \right\}$

3. $= \lim_{a \to \infty} \left\{ -\frac{10}{8} \left[\frac{1}{(4X + 2)^2} \right] \right\} \Big|_0^a$

At the upper limit of a,

4. $\lim\limits_{a \to \infty} \left\{ -\dfrac{10}{8} \left[\dfrac{1}{(4X + 2)^2} \right] \right\} = 0$

Since the upper boundary exists, the integral is convergent. The lower limit is evaluated in step 5.

5. $\dfrac{-10}{8} \left[\dfrac{1}{(4X + 2)^2} \right]$ at $X = 0$ yields

$\left(\dfrac{-10}{8} \right) \left(\dfrac{1}{2^2} \right) = \left(\dfrac{-10}{8} \right) \left(\dfrac{1}{4} \right) = \dfrac{-10}{32}$

Combining steps 4 and 5 yields the value of the definite integral:

6. $\int_0^\infty \dfrac{10}{(4X + 2)^3} \, dX = 0 - \left(\dfrac{-10}{32} \right) = \dfrac{10}{32}$

Improper integrals can be applied to questions in finance. The example discussed below concerns evaluation of the present value of a perpetual flow. This concept was presented in the context of an infinite geometric series in Section 9.8. Similar results can be obtained by evaluating an improper integral representing the perpetual flow.

The present value P of an income stream of S dollars per year with continuous compounding at r percent per year is expressed by the formula

$P = Se^{-rt}$

where $t = $ number of years.

If the continuously compounded flow is perpetual, as from a perpetual bond or an indestructible asset such as land, the present value is found by integrating $P = Se^{-rt}$:

1. $P = \int_0^\infty S e^{-rt} \, dt$

2. $= \lim\limits_{a \to \infty} S \int_0^a e^{-rt} \, dt$

3. $= \lim\limits_{a \to \infty} S \left(\dfrac{e^{-rt}}{-r} \right) \Big|_0^a$

4. $= \lim\limits_{a \to \infty} \left[-\dfrac{S}{r} (e^{-rt}) \right] \Big|_0^a$

5. $= \lim\limits_{a \to \infty} \left[-\dfrac{S}{r} (e^{-ra} - e^{-0}) \right]$

6. $= -\dfrac{S}{r} (0 - 1)$

7. $= \dfrac{S}{r} = \dfrac{\text{income stream}}{\text{annual interest rate}}$

Several points should be made about this derivation. Steps 1 and 2 state the problem and introduce the limit. Step 3 establishes the indefinite integral for e^{-rt} and step 4 simplifies the e term for evaluation at the limit of a.

As $\lim_{a \to \infty} e^{-ra} = 1/e^{ra}$, this term approaches zero in the limit. Thus, the upper limit exists as the term e^{-0} is equal to 1. The final result, step 7 shows that the present value of a perpetual stream of money is equal to the yearly income stream S divided by the annual interest rate r.

Example 12.40
Determine the present value of a perpetual yield of $500 per year from an acre of land with interest compounded continuously at 8 percent per year. Integration is used to derive this result.

$$P = \int_0^\infty 500\, e^{0.08t}\, dt$$

$$= \lim_{a \to \infty} 500 \int_0^a e^{-0.08t}\, dt$$

$$= \lim_{a \to \infty} 500 \left(-\frac{e^{-0.08t}}{0.08}\right)\Big|_0^a$$

$$= \lim_{a \to \infty} \left[-\frac{500}{0.08}(e^{-0.08t})\right]\Big|_0^a$$

$$= \lim_{a \to \infty} \left\{-\frac{500}{0.08}[e^{(-0.08)(a)} - e^{(-0.08)(0)}]\right\}$$

$$= -6250\,(0 - 1)$$

$$P = \$6250 \quad \text{or} \quad P = \frac{500}{0.08} = \$6250$$

It is demonstrated that a perpetual flow of $500 per year at a continuously compounded interest rate of 8 percent per year has a present value of $6250. This also is equal to the income stream ($500) divided by the annual rate of interest (0.08).

Another important application of improper integrals is in probability and statistics. In this field, improper integrals often are employed when evaluating the normal curve. The normal curve is asymptotic to the X axis as shown in Figure 12.6.

The normal curve has an upper boundary of $+\infty$ and a lower boundary of $-\infty$. Thus, it never touches the X axis in either direction. It is used frequently to determine the probability of a particular event or events.

The normal curve will be discussed in more detail in Chapter 13 and it will be encountered in statistics courses.

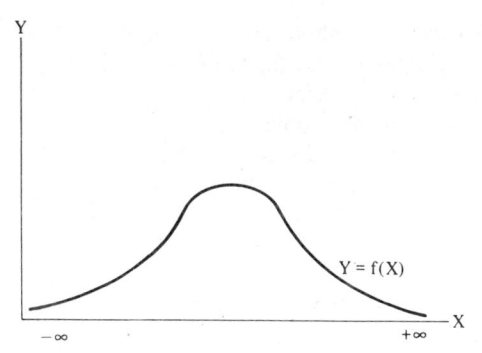

FIGURE 12.6 The normal curve.

EXERCISES

1. State whether each of the following improper integrals is convergent or divergent. Justify your answer in each case. For each convergent integral, find the value of the term of convergence.

   a. $\int_0^\infty X^{-2}\, dX$

   b. $\int_0^\infty 72(3X + 4)^{-4}\, dX$

   c. $\int_5^\infty (3X + 6)\, dX$

   d. $\int_2^\infty X^{-3}\, dX$

   e. $\int_5^\infty e^{0.3X}\, dX$

   f. $\int_0^\infty e^{-X}\, dX$

   g. $\int_4^\infty 10X^{-4}\, dX$

   h. $\int_9^\infty X^{-0.5}\, dX$

2. In parts a through d below, find the present value of the perpetuity for each annual yield S and continuously compounded annual interest rate r.
   a. $S = 1800$ $r = 0.12$
   b. $S = 600$ $r = 0.08$
   c. $S = 400$ $r = 0.02$
   d. $S = 9000$ $r = 0.04$
   e. From your answers to parts a through d, what can you conclude about the relation between r, S, and the present value of a perpetual stream? Give a brief explanation for this relation.

3. A pharmaceutical firm prints coupons for a nonprescription drug in a Sunday newspaper at time $t = 0$. The redemption rate in decimal form for the coupons compared to the number of coupons printed is described by the following function:

   $R(t) = 0.523e^{-t}$

   Thus, $R(t)$ is the fraction (in decimal form) of coupons redeemed at any time t measured in weeks from $t = 0$.

As time after the coupon was issued goes to infinity, does the percent of coupons redeemed converge to a single percentage figure? If not, why not? If so, what is the value of the convergence term?
Interpret your answer in the context of the problem.
4. A program of police and citizen involvement has reduced robberies in an urban area. The rate of robberies per month is declining at a continuous rate according to the following function:

$$C(t) = 4000(t + 5)^{-3}$$

In this function, $C(t)$ specifies the number of robberies as a function of months t after the start of the program, $t = 0$. As time continues indefinitely, will the number of robberies converge to a particular number? If not, why not? If so, what is the value of the convergence term?

12.12 Chapter Summary

This chapter has been limited in scope and directed toward the basic definitions and applications of integral calculus. Some of the more theoretical topics in integral calculus have been omitted so that readers may concentrate on the principles.

This chapter has stressed that the two broad uses of integral calculus are (1) to determine the original function knowing the expression for the rate of change of the function and (2) to evaluate the area under a curve, or function, between stated boundaries.

Rules for developing indefinite integrals have been presented and applied to both indefinite and definite integrals. In some cases, the rules presented in the chapter are inadequate for determining the indefinite integral. Table IX at the end of the book is a Table of Integrals, including both the rules introduced in this chapter and integrals applicable to other types of functional forms. In many instances, it is necessary to relate functional forms to particular forms listed in Table IX.

Several applications in the chapter have concerned developing total cost and total revenue functions from the corresponding marginal cost and marginal revenue functions. These total functions have been used to determine cost and revenue at particular quantity points. Other applications have extended these ideas to cost and revenue ranges and the concept of consumers' surplus.

Examples also have described capital accumulation and financial asset calculations. A final section has introduced improper integrals, which have particular application to the mathematics of finance and to probability.

Although the business uses of integral calculus are not as extensive as those of differential calculus, integral calculus is particularly useful in several analytical areas. It is hoped that this chapter has provided both an appreciation of these applications and the ability to carry out similar analyses.

12.13 Problem Set

Review Questions

1. Why is the original function often not specified completely by the indefinite integral?
2. What is measured by the bounded definite integral?
3. Is the constant of integration a component in the final evaluation of a definite integral? Why, or why not?
4. Explain why the integral instruction $\int$ is a type of summation instruction.
5. How does the antidifferentiation operation apply to demonstrating the rules of integration?
6. When integrating a marginal cost function, what cost component is represented by the constant of integration?
7. Why is the simple power rule of integration not valid when the exponent n is equal to -1?
8. Briefly describe why integration by parts is considered a "trial-and-error" procedure.
9. Relate integral calculus to the study of total and marginal relations in economics. Give one example.
10. Distinguish between the rate of capital formation and the stock of capital at any time.
11. What is measured by consumers' surplus? How is integral calculus used to determine this amount?
12. Relate asymptotic areas under curves to the application of improper integrals.
13. Distinguish between a convergent and a divergent improper integral.
14. What is meant by the nominal rate of interest on an asset? How is the nominal rate of interest used to determine the amount of interest earned by an asset earning interest at a continuously compounded annual rate?
15. How are the annual rate of interest and income stream from a perpetual asset used to determine the present value of the perpetual asset?

Review Problems

1. Find each indefinite integral.
   a. $\int 0 \, dX$
   b. $\int (6X^2 - 3X^{-2}) \, dX$
   c. $\int 5 \, dy$
   d. $\int e^{2y} \, dy$
   e. $\int (3Z^2 - 2Z + 7) \, dZ$
   f. $\int X^{-1/5} \, dX$
   g. $\int y^{-5/3} \, dy$
   h. $\int (6X + 3)^{-3} \, dX$
   i. $\int \ln 4X \, dX$
   j. $\int \ln(X - 14) \, dX$
   k. $\int e^X \, dX$
   l. $\int (y^2 - 2y + 16) \, dy$
   m. $\int (2y + 4)^{1/3} \, dy$
   n. $\int (3y + 6)^{-1} \, dy$
   o. $\int 3X^{-1/4} \, dX$
   p. $\int (y^3 - 0.02y^2 + 1.1y) \, dy$
   q. $\int \frac{3}{(y + 4)^2} \, dy$
   r. $\int (X^7 - 14X^{-2}) \, dX$

2. Evaluate each definite integral between the stated limits.
   a. $\int_1^3 0 \, dX$
   k. $\int_6^{15} y^{-1} \, dy$

b. $\int_{-2}^{2} 12 \, dy$

c. $\int_{20}^{30} (2X + 4) \, dX$

d. $\int_{-1.5}^{0} e^X \, dX$

e. $\int_{4}^{8} (0.02y^3 + 2Y^2 - 3y + 4) \, dy$

f. $\int_{3}^{5} (200 - 0.2X) \, dX$

g. $\int_{0}^{5} e^{0.4X} \, dX$

h. $\int_{4}^{16} X^{1/2} \, dX$

i. $\int_{-4}^{-1} (X + 3)^{-2} \, dX$

j. $\int_{0}^{1} \frac{1}{5} X^2 \, dX$

l. $\int_{3}^{8} \ln X \, dX$

m. $\int_{0}^{20} (120 - 2.1y) \, dy$

n. $\int_{0}^{\infty} \frac{1}{(3X + 2)^2} \, dX$

o. $\int_{4}^{\infty} \frac{3}{2X^3} \, dX$

p. $\int_{0}^{\infty} e^{-3X} \, dX$

q. $\int_{0}^{4} (3X + 1)^{-3} \, dX$

r. $\int_{2}^{6} e^{-0.4y} \, dy$

s. $\int_{5}^{8} \ln 4y \, dy$

t. $\int_{0}^{3} (4X + 2)^{-2} \, dX$

3. Integrate each of the following by the technique of integration by parts:
   a. $\int X^{1/3} \, dX$
   b. $\int -3X^{-4} \, dX$
   c. $\int \ln 4X \, dX$
   d. $\int y^3 (y^2 + 7) \, dy$
   e. $\int X^{-5} (X - 4) \, dX$
   f. $\int 2y^{-2} \, dy$
   g. $\int \ln X \, dX$
   h. $\int (X^3)(X - 2) \, dX$
   i. $\int (X^{1/3})(X^3 + 3) \, dX$
   j. $\int (y^{-3})(y^3 + 1) \, dy$

4. A firm has the following marginal cost (MC measured in dollars) function where Q represents the quantity of output.

   MC = $0.03Q^2 - 0.15Q$

   a. Find the total cost function.
   b. If the total cost at $Q = 50$ is equal to $1400, what is the fixed cost?
   c. Find total cost at $Q = 60$ and $Q = 70$ using the results of parts a and b.

5. For each marginal revenue (MR) function stated below, find the corresponding total revenue function. For each, find total revenue and average revenue at $Q = 120$, where Q represents the quantity of goods sold.
   a. MR = $60 - 0.4Q$
   b. MR = $9.3 - 0.05Q$
   c. MR = 30

6. A firm has the following marginal revenue (MR) function

   MR = $62.50 - 0.01Q$

   where Q represents the quantity sold per week. The firm is considering the effects of a sales expansion from 600 to 800 units per week.
   a. What effect will such an expansion have on the firm's total revenue?
   b. What is the marginal revenue at $Q = 8000$? Interpret this result.

7. A manufacturer of electric drills knows that the cost of an additional unit of output (MC) is explained by the following function:

   MC = $0.03Q^2 + 1.2Q$

where Q represents hourly output of drills at a particular factory.
a. Find the total cost function if total cost is $2200 at $Q = 40$.
b. Find the average cost per drill at $Q = 40$.
c. The firm is considering expansion to 50 drills per hour at this plant. What effect will this have on the average cost per drill?
d. What does your answer to part c indicate about the feasibility of this output expansion to $Q = 50$?

8. The rate of customer entry into a shopping mall between 10 a.m. and 3 p.m. on a typical day is given by the function

$$c(t) = 30t^2 + 16t$$

where $c(t)$ represents the number of customers entering at any time t during these hours and t is measured in hours after the mall opens at 10 a.m., so that 10 a.m. is represented by $t = 0$.
a. How many people enter the mall during this 5-hour span ($t = 0$ to $t = 5$)?
b. How many people enter the mall between 11 a.m. ($t = 1$) and 2 p.m. ($t = 4$)?
c. How would you characterize the pattern of customer entry during the period?

9. The total value of capital investment in oil exploration in a region of Canada at the end of 1980 ($t = 0$) was $3 billion. Since this time, capital investment in oil exploration in this region has expanded at the rate $g(t)$ measured in billions of dollars.

$$g(t) = t^{-1/2} + 0.3t$$

a. Find the expression for the value of capital stock in oil exploration at any point in time.
b. After 4 years, at the end of 1984, what is the value of capital investment in oil exploration in this region?
c. How much capital investment will be undertaken between the end of 1984 ($t = 4$) and the end of 1989 ($t = 9$)?

10. In a drought-stricken region of the world, cases of malnutrition are occurring at the following exponential rate

$$m(t) = 715e^{0.2t} + 50$$

where $m(t)$ measures the number of cases of malnutrition t months after the start of the severe food shortages ($t = 0$). If this problem persists, how many cases of malnutrition will there be starting at $t = 0$, during the next
a. 4 months?   b. 8 months?   c. 12 months?

11. The demand for a type of sweater is expressed by the function

$$p(q) = 50 - q^{1/2}$$

where q is the number of sweaters sold and $p(q)$ represents the corresponding price.
a. Find $p(q)$ corresponding to $q = 225$.
b. Determine consumers' surplus at the price-quantity combination found in part a.
c. At $q = 324$, what is the amount of consumers' surplus?
d. Interpret the difference in your answers to parts b and c.

12. Home computer sales in a particular city are growing at a continuously com-

pounded rate of 6 percent per year. The function for home computer sales during any year t is expressed as follows, where $h(t)$ represents number of computers:

$h(t) = 150e^{0.06t} + 110$

It is assumed that the current year is represented by $t = 0$.
a. What will home computer sales be over the next 5 years?
b. What will sales be between $t = 3$ and $t = 5$?
c. What are home computer sales during year 2?

13. A person has a $5000 savings account that may be invested in either a 5-year account earning interest at 9 percent per year continuously compounded, or a 7-year account paying 7 percent per year continuously compounded.

    Use techniques of integration to determine the amount of interest accumulated in each account for the time periods stated.

14. A parcel of land in an urban area earns a $300 per year perpetual rent payment. Interest is based on a 12 percent per year continuously compounded rate.

    Use techniques of integration to determine the present value of this parcel of land.

15. Because of improved diagnosis and treatment, the number of deaths from Legionnaires' disease in the United States is decreasing. The function of time t in years expressing the number of annual deaths from this disease $L(t)$ is the following.

    $L(t) = 1800(2t + 3)^{-3}$

    a. If this rate continues from $t = 0$ for an unlimited number of years ($t = \infty$), will the integral converge?
    b. If your answer to part a is "no," explain why. If your answer to part a is "yes," what is the value of the convergence term?

13 Probability: Principles and Applications

13.1 Introduction

To this point, this textbook has emphasized mathematical techniques for analyzing deterministic relationships; that is, relationships between the variables have been expressed in terms of mathematical equations or inequalities. No elements of chance or likelihood of error in either observations or results have been stated. In this chapter, concepts and methods directed toward uncertain situations are introduced. The theory of probability and its application to business is the specific subject of this chapter.

The study of probability serves three purposes in an introduction to mathematical analysis. First, probability is a field of study with many special business applications. A few of these are discussed in the next section in order to introduce this topic in an applied framework. Second, several concepts of probability are linked to the techniques of integral calculus presented in the previous chapter. Finally, probability theory is a foundation for the study of statistical inference. Thus, the study of probability serves as a bridge between mathematical analysis and statistical analysis. Although statistical inference is not a specific topic of this text, this chapter on probability will help prepare students for the future study of statistics.

Before introducing the theoretical and applied material, several business situations which are probabilistic in nature are described.

13.2 Business Analysis and Probability

In this section, three examples of business problems adaptable to analysis with the help of probabilistic models are presented.

1. A consumer products firm knows the percentage of the population of a city who are women and the percentage of the city population who earn over $20,000 per year. The firm, in developing its marketing strategy, would like to know the percentage of the city's population who are women earning over $20,000 per year.
2. A pharmaceutical firm conducts purity checks on a drug at three different stages in the production process. The firm knows the probability of finding an impurity at each of the three stages. The firm wants to determine the probability of finding an impurity in a particular drug at all three stages of production.
3. An automobile parts manufacturer produces emission control devices at three locations. The devices are sold to independent dealers. The firm knows the percentage of devices which are defective at each production facility. The firm wants to determine the probability that a device was made at a particular factory given that a dealer returns a defective device.

These examples are intended to illustrate some specific applications of probability theory and to demonstrate that probability is neither abstract nor limited to providing foundation material for statistical inference. The business-related aspects of probability theory are the subject matter of this chapter.

One additional characteristic of the study of probability may be inferred from these examples; that is, a central focus of probability problems is the enumeration of data, e.g., *percentage* of women, *number* of production stages at which impurities are found, and *number* of defective parts returned. Consequently, the next section begins the study of probability by examining techniques for enumerating data, a topic referred to as "counting techniques."

13.3 Counting Techniques

Frequently, a first step in probabilistic model development is determination of what is possible, i.e., the number of situations relevant to evaluation of the problem. Several basic counting principles apply to this question.

In general, there are two categories of counting techniques. One includes ways to determine the total number of situations that can occur for a particular problem. A second group of counting techniques provides methods for specifying the number of groups of various sizes relevant to a particular problem. For example, the first group allows one to determine that there are twelve possible outcomes if a product is tested at three different stages of production. The second type provides ways to specify the number of subgroups of six women executives that can be selected from a group of fourteen women executives for inclusion on a consumer panel.

This section discusses some of the concepts used in analyzing both types of enumeration, or counting, problems.

Tree Diagrams

Frequently, in probability studies, a "tree diagram" provides a pictorial method for specifying the number of different outcomes. An example will demonstrate the development and use of a tree diagram.

Example 13.1

A food processing firm periodically tests a brand of cereal for its protein, carbohydrate, and fat content to ascertain whether or not each factor meets a predetermined level in a serving of the cereal. Certification for each factor is a separate test; i.e., satisfying the protein standard does not necessarily mean that the cereal will satisfy the fat standard.

If the firm wants to know all the possible outcomes for a tested serving of cereal for the three factors and two possible results (meets standard and does not meet standard) for each, a tree diagram can be used. The following notation is used in the tree diagram:

SP = meets protein standard

NSP = does not meet protein standard

SC = meets carbohydrate standard

NSC = does not meet carbohydrate standard

SF = meets fat standard

NSF = does not meet fat standard

A tree diagram describing all possible results for the three factors and two outcomes is included in Figure 13.1.

Figure 13.1 shows that there are eight possible results for each test of the cereal product. Each "branch" of the tree diagram (such as the sequence SP, NSC, SF) represents one complete outcome of tests. In this problem, the order in which tests are performed (protein, carbohydrate, fat) has no bearing on the number of possible outcomes. Although this frequently is the case, there are problems where the order of the tests may affect the total number of outcomes.

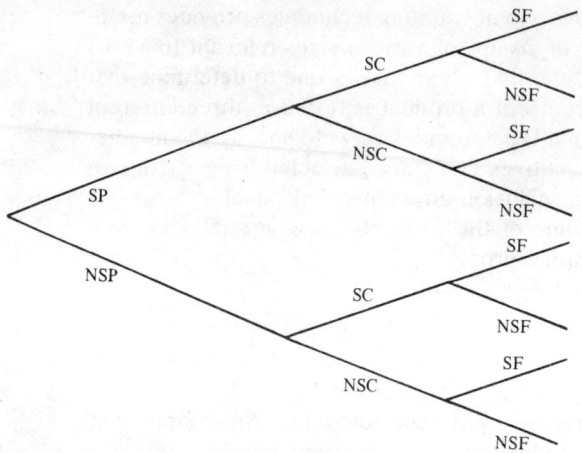

FIGURE 13.1 A tree diagram of the data in Example 13.1.

The example may be generalized into the following rule applicable to determination of the number of outcomes associated with a particular tree diagram.

Rule 1: If a process has K separate parts (three factors above) of which the first can be carried out in n_1 different ways, the second in n_2 different ways, . . ., and the Kth in n_K different ways, then the total number of possibilities is equal to the product $(n_1)(n_2) \cdots (n_K)$.

In this rule, the words "separate parts" are used as a general term to indicate the number of items, each of which is evaluated for a particular outcome. In Example 13.1, three items (protein, carbohydrate, and fat) are each evaluated for the outcome "meets the standard" or "does not meet the standard." Thus, $K = 3$, $n_1 = 2$, $n_2 = 2$, $n_3 = 2$, and the total possible outcomes is 8.

This example demonstrates that tree diagrams provide an excellent means for determining the total possible outcomes for a problem and the composition of each outcome. Each "branch" of the tree yields an outcome, and the components of this outcome are specified by reading out from the beginning of the diagram to the end of the branch.

Subsets

When examining a group of possible outcomes, a second consideration may be to determine the number of subgroups, or subsets, that can be formed from the total group.

This topic concerns the total number of subgroups that can be formed from a larger group without regard to the size of the subgroup. In other words, the question is how many groups can be constituted from a single group? For example, how many committees (of any size) can be selected from a group of 12 middle management employees?

To answer this and similar questions, note first that each individual or item either is or is not a member of a particular subset. Consequently, there are two possible outcomes (included or not included) associated with each item when constructing a subset. The following rule is used to determine the number of subsets:

Rule 2: If there are n elements in a group, and there is a choice between two categories (in the subset or not in the subset) for each, then the total number of subsets that can be formed from this group is 2^n.

Therefore, if there are 12 individuals in a group, $2^{12} = 4096$ subsets can be constructed from the people in this group. Example 13.2 may clarify this rather abstract concept.

Example 13.2

A firm has three brands in its household detergent product group. The firm wants to determine how many subgroups of brands can be developed from this set of brands. This information is to be used in the preliminary planning of a pricing strategy for the product group.

Assume that the brands are referred to as A, B, and C. The above rule states that there can be $2^3 = 8$ subsets composed of the elements of this group. The two outcomes for each brand are (1) in the subgroup and (2) not in the subgroup. Following this procedure, the following eight subsets result where each listed letter refers to an included brand:

1. A
2. B
3. C
4. AB
5. AC
6. BC
7. ABC
8. NONE $= \emptyset$

One subset representing "not included" for each brand must be considered a subset. In general, this subset is referred to as the empty set and is notated $\emptyset$. It is a subset of every group. Also, note that the total group (A, B, C) is a subset as it specifies an "included" designation for each element. Thus, there are eight subgroups of brands which can be developed from this group of three brands.

Permutations and Combinations

After using the above rule, a logical question of readers may be, how does one determine the number of subsets of a particular size from a group? But, before this question can be answered, the concept of a *factorial* must be discussed.

As used in quantitative analysis, a number followed by an exclamation mark, such as 5!, is read "five factorial." This is equal to the number 5 multiplied by all smaller positive integers, i.e., $5! = 5 \cdot 4 \cdot 3 \cdot 2 \cdot 1 = 120$. By definition, $0! = 1$. Factorials are used in the development of permutations and combinations.

Example 13.3

1. Find 3!

    $3! = 3 \cdot 2 \cdot 1 = 6$

2. Find 1!

    $1! = 1$

3. Find 0!

    $0! = 1$ (by definition)

4. Find 8!

    $8! = 8 \cdot 7 \cdot 6 \cdot 5 \cdot 4 \cdot 3 \cdot 2 \cdot 1 = 40,320$

If one is interested in specifying the number of subsets of a particular size in a set of elements, two computational methods may be used depending on the nature of the problem. If the order of the elements in each subset is important (e.g., *AB* has a different meaning than *BA*), the subsets are called *permutations*. Alternatively, if the order of elements in each subset is not important (e.g., *AB* is no different from *BA*), the subsets are referred to as *combinations*. It may be apparent to the astute reader that for any given set and subset size, often there will be more permutations than combinations. This difference is demonstrated in the formula for each.

The following formula is used to compute the number of permutations of size x from a set of n elements.

NUMBER OF PERMUTATIONS OF SIZE x FROM A SET OF n ELEMENTS:

$$_nP_x = \frac{n!}{(n-x)!}$$

This means that if n elements are to be grouped into subgroups of size x where the order of the x elements is important, then the number of subgroups is equal to $n!/(n-x)!$

The formula used to find the number of combinations of size x from a set of n elements is as follows.

NUMBER OF COMBINATIONS OF SIZE x FROM A SET OF n ELEMENTS:

$$_nC_x = \frac{n!}{x!(n-x)!}$$

Therefore, if n elements are to be grouped into subgroups of size x where the order of the x elements is not important, the number of subgroups is equal to $n!/x!(n-x)!$

Some examples may clarify these definitions and formulas.

Example 13.4

A firm has a central warehouse which serves 10 retail stores. The one delivery truck owned by the firm is capable of carrying enough goods for three stores in a single delivery; that is, the truck can go to three stores during one trip, or route.

How many different routes can be formed for the 10-store chain?

This is a problem of permutations as the order of delivery leads to different routes, i.e., going from store 3 to store 6 to store 9 is a different route than going from 6 to 9 to 3. Therefore, the number of routes is equal to the number of permutations of 10 items (stores) taken 3 at a time:

$$\text{Number of routes} = {_{10}P_3} = \frac{10!}{(10-3)!} = \frac{10 \cdot 9 \cdot 8 \cdot 7!}{7!} = 10 \cdot 9 \cdot 8 = 720$$

The conclusion is that there are 720 different three-store routes for this firm.

Example 13.5

The business editor of a newspaper wants to arrange interviews with 3 of the 10 members of the Board of Directors of the city's Chamber of Commerce.

From how many different three-member groups can the editor choose in forming the interview group?

In this case, the order of individuals within the group of three is not important. Therefore, the editor must determine the number of three-person combinations from the 10-member group:

$$\text{Number of interview groups} = {_{10}C_3} = \frac{10!}{3!(10-3)!} = \frac{10 \cdot 9 \cdot 8 \cdot 7!}{3 \cdot 2 \cdot 1 \cdot 7!} = \frac{10 \cdot 9 \cdot 8}{3 \cdot 2 \cdot 1} = 120$$

The result shows that there are 120 possible three-person groups from which the editor may choose.

These examples point out that for a set of a given size, the number of combinations many times is less than the number of permutations. This difference results from whether or not subgroup order is important to the analysis.

An extension of these ideas concerns determination of the number of permutations of n items taken all together. In this case, $n = x$ and the formula is the following:

NUMBER OF PERMUTATIONS WHERE $n = x$:

$$_nP_x = \frac{n!}{(n-x)!} = \frac{n!}{0!} = \frac{n!}{1} = n!$$

Example 13.6
How many ways can five stores be listed for identification purposes? The answer is found by evaluating $_5P_5$ as follows:

Number of store listings $= {_5P_5} = \dfrac{5!}{(5-5)!} = \dfrac{5 \cdot 4 \cdot 3 \cdot 2 \cdot 1}{1} = 120$

The following exercises will give practice applying these counting techniques. With this background knowledge of counting, the next section considers techniques for determining the likelihood, or probability, of particular events.

EXERCISES

1. Find each permutation $_nP_x$ and combination $_nC_x$ as instructed.
   a. $_nP_x$, $n = 4$, $x = 3$
   b. $_nP_x$, $n = 6$, $x = 3$
   c. $_nC_x$, $n = 12$, $x = 2$
   d. $_nC_x$, $n = 9$, $x = 4$
   e. $_nP_x$, $n = 5$, $x = 5$
   f. $_nC_x$, $n = 5$, $x = 5$
   g. $_nP_x$, $n = 8$, $x = 4$
   h. $_nC_x$, $n = 5$, $x = 4$
   i. $_nP_x$, $n = 6$, $x = 1$
   j. $_nC_x$, $n = 3$, $x = 2$
2. Find the number of subsets of any size which can be formed from each group of size n:
   a. $n = 6$
   b. $n = 2$
   c. $n = 4$
   d. $n = 9$
   e. $n = 1$
   f. $n = 3$
3. How many different groups of three retail stores can be set up from a group of eight if the order within each group is not important?
4. How many different groups of 10 employees can be selected from a group of 13 if order within each group is not important?
5. How many delivery routes can be developed for a set of six stores if all six stores are included on each route?
6. Three food nutrients out of a total of ten nutrients in a product are tested each day. The order of testing the three each day is important for analytical accuracy. How many different groups of three nutrients can be set up?
7. A salesman must call on four of seven customers during the next six hours. Each customer is located in a different part of the city. How many different groups of four customers does the salesman have to consider in

evaluating his schedule? Is this a permutation or a combination question? Why?

8. A group of twelve children is to be tested for motor skills, three at a time. How many groups of three can be formed? Is this a permutation or combination question? Why?

13.4 Basic Definitions of Probability

Sample Spaces and Events

In probability, the outcome of an experiment is called an *event*. In this context, the term *experiment* refers to any occurrence of interest such as finding an unemployed person in a survey or identifying a defective item turned out by a production line.

All possible outcomes of the experiment (that is, all events) make up the *sample space*.

The *probability of an event* represents the likelihood of the event's occurrence in the defined sample space. The probability of all events in the sample space together is 1, or 100 percent. The probability of an event or events may be expressed as a fraction, a decimal, or a percentage of the sample space.

Example 13.7

There are 200 purchasing agents from large companies listed in a certain registry. Of these, 50 subscribe to a publication forecasting business conditions.

What is the probability of selecting from this registry a purchasing agent who subscribes to the forecasting publication?

In this problem, the event of interest is purchasing agents who subscribe to the forecast publication. The sample space includes all purchasing agents listed in the registry. Thus, the probability of the event (referred to as "subscriber") is as follows:

$$P(\text{subscriber}) = \frac{\text{number of subscribers}}{\text{number in registry}} = \frac{50}{200} = .25$$

where P is a notation used to designate probability.

Thus, the probability of selecting a subscriber is 25 percent or .25. Alternatively, it can be stated that there is a 1 in 4 chance of selecting a subscriber from the group of purchasing agents.

Venn Diagrams

Venn diagrams have been introduced in the discussion of sets in Chapter 2 (Section 2.2). Venn diagrams also are used extensively to explain probabilities.

Mathematics for Business and Economics **412**

When applied to probability questions, Venn diagrams use a rectangle to represent the sample space, and events or groups of events are shown within the rectangle by circles, parts of circles, or smaller rectangles.

An example will describe construction of a Venn diagram.

Example 13.8
The work force of a city has 50,000 people and is considered the sample space for an analysis of unemployment. In the city's work force, 4,000 people currently are unemployed (designated by u).

This situation is described in the Venn diagram of Figure 13.2.

Venn diagrams will be used below to assist in showing some additional definitions and concepts of probability theory.

Mutually Exclusive Events

If the occurrence of one event precludes the possibility of another, the events are *mutually exclusive*. On a Venn diagram, there will be no common area shared by two (or more) mutually exclusive events.

Example 13.9
Construct a Venn diagram showing the events "male" and "female" if the sample space includes all residents of the state of Illinois. If 52 percent of the population of Illinois is female and 48 percent is male, a Venn diagram showing these two mutually exclusive events is as shown on Figure 13.3. As Figure 13.3 shows, no resident can be in both groups, and the events are mutually exclusive.

The following paragraphs will extend these preliminary concepts of probability.

Joint Events and Conditional Events

Table 13.1 provides data to explain the concepts of joint events and conditional events. These data are used in the next several examples.

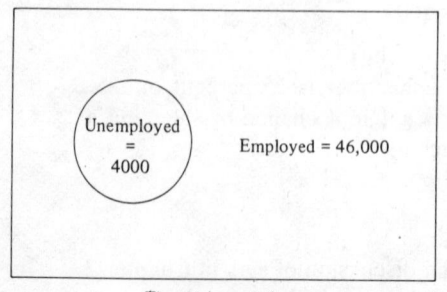

The city's work force

FIGURE 13.2   A venn diagram for Example 13.8.

```
┌──────────────┬──────────────────┐
│              │                  │
│   Female     │     Male         │
│    52%       │     48%          │
│              │                  │
│              │                  │
└──────────────┴──────────────────┘
          Illinois
```
FIGURE 13.3   A venn diagram for Example 13.9.

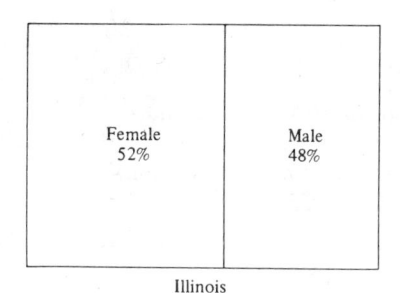

Data in Table 13.1 include the portion of residents (in decimal form) of a city based on two characteristics, age and sex. Thus, the table describes a set of known probabilities for the events age and sex in a sample space which includes all the residents of a city. In Table 13.1, abbreviations for each category are included to facilitate the subsequent discussion.

The data indicate that 40 percent of city residents are males and 60 percent are females. Also, 25 percent of city residents are 21 and under, 30 percent are between 22 and 45, and 45 percent are over 45 years old. These data provide the category totals for the sample space.

Table 13.1 also provides cross-category probabilities. For example, 10 percent of all city residents are males 21 years of age and under and 25 percent of residents are females over 45 years old.

If two or more events occur simultaneously in the sample space, the events are *joint events*. If one is measuring sex and age probabilities as above, some females are members of each age group. For example, the probability of being a female 21 years old and under in the city is 15 percent. This is a joint event and its probability is measured in relation to the sample space.

The probability of joint events is abbreviated by the symbol ∩. Thus, in the above table, if F represents female and T represents 21 years old and under, then the joint event is abbreviated as follows:

P(female; 21 years old and under) $= P(F \cap T) = .15$

TABLE 13.1   Age-Sex Probabilities for the Residents of a City

Age	Male (M)	Female (F)	Total
21 and under, T	.10	.15	.25
22 to 45, H	.10	.20	.30
Over 45, O	.20	.25	.45
Total	.40	.60	1.00

Example 13.10
Using the data of Table 13.1, find and interpret (1) $M \cap H$ and (2) $F \cap O$.

1. The joint event $M \cap H$ includes all males who are between 22 and 45 years old. Thus, $P(M \cap H) = .10$ or 10 percent of all city residents.
2. The joint event $F \cap O$ includes all females who are more than 45 years old. This probability is equal to .25, or $P(F \cap O) = .25$.

As a final point, observe that the joint probability of two or more mutually exclusive events is 0. Thus, in the data used above

$$P(F \cap M) = 0$$

Conditional events are appropriate when some limited but certain information exists about an event. The goal, however, is to assess the probability that the event may have other characteristics associated with it. An example will help explain conditional events.

Example 13.11
It is known that an individual in the sample space enumerated in Table 13.1 is a male, but his age is unknown. What is the probability that he is 21 years old or less?

In other words, what is the probability that a person in the city is 21 years old or less if it is known that he is a male? This conditional situation (often associated with use of the word "given") can be expressed by the abbreviation $P(T/M)$. This abbreviation is read as, the probability that one is 21 years old or less *given* that the individual is a male.

The way to compute the value for a conditional probability is to divide the joint probability of the two events, in this case $P(T \cap M)$, by the given, or known, probability. Using data in Table 13.1, the probability of a person being 21 years old or less given that the person is a male is

$$P(T/M) = \frac{P(T \cap M)}{P(M)} = \frac{.10}{.40} = .25$$

This indicates, for example, that if a male is selected in a marketing survey, the probability is .25 (one chance in four) that the male is 21 years old or less.

A helpful way to visualize conditional probability is to consider that the conditional statement, or the known information, reduces the size of the sample space by restricting it to only that part represented by the known factor (males or 40 percent of the original sample space in this example). The known factor's probability becomes the new sample space and, consequently, the denominator for any computation.

Example 13.12
Using the data in Table 13.1, what is the probability that, if a person over 45 is selected for a test survey, the person is a female?

In this problem, the known factor (over 45) restricts the sample space to the 45 percent of city residents who are over 45 years old. The answer is as follows:

Probability of selecting a female given that the person selected is over 45 years old $= P(F/O) = \dfrac{P(F \cap O)}{P(O)} = \dfrac{.25}{.45} = .556$

Thus, if an individual is over 45, there is a 55.6 percent chance that the individual is a female.

Dependent and Independent Events

Joint events and conditional events provide the basis of the determination of dependent and independent events. It must be stressed at the outset of this discussion that the terms dependent and independent events have strict probabilistic meanings and the distinction is not based on what one intuitively believes dependent and independent to be. Therefore, the events formally are referred to as being *statistically dependent* or *statistically independent*.

For events A and B, the notational form of each of these terms is as follows:

1. If $P(A/B) = P(A)$, and $P(B/A) = P(B)$ then A and B are statistically independent.
2. If $P(A/B) \neq P(A)$, or $P(B/A) \neq P(B)$ then A and B are statistically dependent.

Therefore, two events are statistically independent if the conditional probability is equal to the probability of the event which is not given in the conditional statement. If this is not the case, the events are statistically dependent.

A manipulation of the definition of independent events and the use of the formula for conditional probability leads to an alternative definition of statistically independent events:

If $P(A/B) = P(A)$

and

$P(A/B) = \dfrac{P(A \cap B)}{P(B)}$

then A and B are statistically independent if

$P(A \cap B) = P(A) \cdot P(B)$

This derivation shows that if A and B are independent, then the probability of the joint event $P(A \cap B)$ is equal to the product of the probabilities for each separate event. This is described further in the following examples.

Example 13.13

Using the data in Table 13.1 and the results of Example 13.12, can it be concluded that the events female and over 45 years old are statistically dependent or that they are statistically independent?

Mathematics for Business and Economics

In Example 13.12, it was shown that

$$P(F/O) = \frac{P(F \cap O)}{P(O)} = \frac{.25}{.45} = .556$$

Table 13.1 includes the probability of a female as

$P(F) = .6$

As

$P(F/O) \neq P(F)$

the events female and over 45 years old are not statistically independent.

Example 13.14
Based on the data of Table 13.1, are the events male and female *statistically independent?*

The events male and female are mutually exclusive, or $P(F \cap M) = 0$. Thus, the conditional probability $P(M/F)$ or $P(F/M)$ is equal to 0 as

$$P(M/F) = \frac{P(M \cap F)}{P(F)} = \frac{0}{.6} = 0$$

As $P(M/F) = 0$ and $P(M) = .4$, the events male and female are not statistically independent.

This example leads to the general rule that if two events have nonzero probabilities and are mutually exclusive, they are necessarily statistically dependent. On the other hand, if two events with nonzero probabilities are not mutually exclusive, they may be either statistically independent or statistically dependent.

Example 13.15 uses data from Table 13.1 to describe a situation of statistically independent events.

Example 13.15
For the city population enumerated in Table 13.1, are the events female and 21 years old and less statistically dependent or statistically independent?

Notational form is used to answer this question. First, the conditional probability of an individual being a female given that the person is 21 years old or less is

$$P(F/T) = \frac{P(F \cap T)}{P(T)} = \frac{.15}{.25} = .6$$

In Table 13.1, the probability of a female resident is listed as .6. Therefore, the events female and 21 years old and less are statistically independent as:

$P(F/T) = P(F)$

or

$.6 = .6$

Probability: Principles and Applications 417

This result can be confirmed by considering the reverse of the conditional statement, $P(T/F)$.

$$P(T/F) = \frac{P(T \cap F)}{P(F)} = \frac{.15}{.60} = .25$$

Thus, the probability of selecting a person 21 years old or less given that the person is a female is .25. This also is the probabiliity that a city resident is 21 years old or less. The two events again are proven to be statistically independent.

These definitions will be used in the subsequent parts of this chapter.

The Union of Events

In many applications, questions arise about the probability of combined events. For example, what is the probability of selecting someone from either the 21 and under or the over 45 age groups? To answer this and related questions, the concept of the *union of events* must be considered.

The notation for the union of two events A and B is as follows:

$P(A \cup B)$

Specifically, the union of two or more events measures the percentage of the sample space represented by both events. The general formula for computing the union of two events A and B is

$P(A \cup B) = P(A) + P(B) - P(A \cap B)$

The rationale for this formula is discussed by means of Example 13.16.

Example 13.16

Based on the data in Table 13.1, what is the probability that a city resident either is a man or is between 22 and 45 years old? In notation form, this is expressed by the following union notation:

Probability of either a male or between 22 and 45 years old = $P(M \cup H)$

where M = the probability of being male and H is the probability of being in the age group between 22 and 45.

Figure 13.4 is a Venn diagram describing this relationship.

Three probabilities are included in the Venn diagram: $P(M) = .4$, $P(H) = .3$ and $P(M \cap H) = .1$. Each is obtained from Table 13.1. Note that 10 percent of the sample space, representing the intersection of the events, has been counted both within the male event and within the 22- to 45-year-old group event.

To compute the combined probability of males and those between 22 and 45, this intersection must be subtracted from the sum of the individual probabilities to avoid double counting. In other words, 10 percent of the sample space representing males between 22 and 45 is included in the male

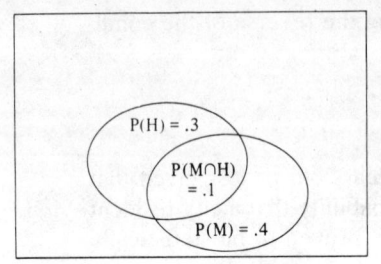

FIGURE 13.4 A venn diagram for Example 13.16.

event and should not be counted again in the 22- to 45-year-old event. The union of the two events is computed below.

PROBABILITY OF MALES OR BETWEEN 22 AND
45 YEARS OF AGE:

$P(M \cup H) = P(M) + P(H) - P(M \cap H)$
$= .4 + .3 - .1$
$= .6$

The solution indicates that 60 percent of the sample space (city residents) are either males of any age or females between 22 and 45 years of age.

The union of two or more mutually exclusive events is equal to the sum of the individual probabilities. That is, if X and Y are mutually exclusive events, then $P(X \cap Y) = 0$ and the formula for the union of X and Y simplifies to $P(X \cup Y) = P(X) + P(Y) - P(X \cap Y) = P(X) + P(Y)$. This result can be extended to any number of mutually exclusive events.

Example 13.17

Utilizing data in Table 13.1, find the union of the events 21 years old and less (T) and over 45 years old (O). This union is expressed as follows.

$P(T \cup O) = P(T) + P(O) - P(T \cap O)$

As $P(T \cap O) = 0$, the union is

$P(T \cup O) = P(T) + P(O) - P(T \cap O)$
$= .25 + .45 - 0$
$= .70$

Therefore, 70 percent of the sample space includes residents who are either 21 years old or less or over 45 years old.

Finally, this discussion of the union of events permits definition of the concept of *collectively exhaustive events*. Events are collectively exhaustive if the union of their probabilities comprises the entire sample space. Also, one event may be collectively exhaustive if the probability of the event is one.

For example, in the data in Table 13.1, the events male and female are collectively exhaustive since $P(M \cup F) = 1$. However, in Table 13.1 the events 21 and under (T) and 22 to 45 (H) are not collectively exhaustive, as $P(T \cup H) = P(T) + P(H) - P(T \cap H) = .25 + .30 - 0 = .55$. Although T and H are mutually exclusive, they are not collectively exhaustive events. Readers should be careful not to confuse the concepts of mutually exclusive and collectively exhaustive events.

13.5 The General Rules of Multiplication and Addition

In order to summarize the discussion of the previous section, the general rules for the multiplication and addition of probabilities are presented in this section. For this discussion, notational forms developed previously will be used to provide brevity.

The joint probability (also referred to as the *intersection*) of two events is computed by means of the general rule of multiplication. The general rule of multiplication is based on the formula for conditional probability and may be derived from the fact that

1. $P(A/B) = \dfrac{P(A \cap B)}{P(B)}$ and $P(B/A) = \dfrac{P(A \cap B)}{P(A)}$
2. Therefore, $P(A \cap B) = P(A/B) \cdot P(B)$ and $P(A \cap B) = P(B/A) \cdot P(A)$

Step 2 represents the general rule of multiplication.

GENERAL RULE OF MULTIPLICATION:
For the events A and B,

$P(A \cap B) = P(A/B) \cdot P(B) = P(B/A) \cdot P(A)$

But if A and B are independent events, then the special rule of multiplication applies.

SPECIAL RULE OF MULTIPLICATION:
For the independent events A and B,

$P(A \cap B) = P(A) \cdot P(B)$

Therefore, the probability that two events occur together is the product of the probability of one and the conditional probability of the second given that the first has occurred. When the two events are independent, the occurrence of one has no effect on the other; therefore, the joint probability is equal to the product of the individual events.

When considering the union of two events A and B, the probabilities are added and the general rule of addition is applied.

GENERAL RULE OF ADDITION:
For the events A and B,

$P(A \cup B) = P(A) + P(B) - P(A \cap B)$

If A and B are mutually exclusive, the intersection is zero and the special rule of addition results.

SPECIAL RULE OF ADDITION:
For $P(A \cup B) = P(A) + P(B) - P(A \cap B)$, where $P(A \cap B) = 0$,

$P(A \cup B) = P(A) + P(B)$

These rules of addition should be approached intuitively rather than as something to memorize and apply. The question one should ask when computing the union of events is, what part of the sample space is attributable to both events? Any such intersections must be counted only once in the final result.

These four rules are applicable to many business applications. Combining these rules with the computational techniques described in Section 13.4, readers should be able to analyze many related applications.

The following set of exercises will allow practice in dealing with problems related to the principles of these sections. Readers should be thoroughly familiar with all the basic definitions and notation used before attempting the exercises.

EXERCISES

1. For the probabilities $P(A) = .4$, $P(B) = .2$, $P(A/B) = .5$, find,
    a. $P(A \cap B)$
    b. $P(A \cup B)$
    c. $P(B/A)$
    d. Are A and B statistically independent? Why or why not?
2. For the probabilities $P(A \cap B) = 0$, $P(A) = .4$, $P(B) = .6$, find,
    a. $P(A \cup B)$
    b. $P(A/B)$
    c. $P(B/A)$
    d. Are A and B statistically independent? Why or why not?
3. For the probabilities $P(X) = .4$, $P(Y) = .4$, $P(X \cap Y) = .3$, find,
    a. $P(X/Y)$
    b. $P(Y/X)$
    c. $P(X \cup Y)$
    d. Are X and Y statistically independent? Why or why not?
4. For the probabilities $P(X \cup Y) = .4$, $P(X) = .3$, $P(X \cap Y) = .3$, find,
    a. $P(Y)$
    b. $P(X/Y)$
    c. $P(Y/X)$
    d. From the results, what can you conclude about the events X and Y?

5. A customer group is 50 percent female and 50 percent male. The group also is separated by income into those earning $20,000 a year or less, with a probability of .3, and those earning over $20,000 a year (probability = .7) In addition, it is known that 40 percent of all males earn over $20,000 per year.
   a. What percentage of customers are males earning over $20,000 per year?
   b. What percentage of customers are females earning over $20,000 per year?
   c. If a customer is a female, what is the probability that she earns over $20,000 a year?
6. Products are tested at two separate production points to determine whether each product is defective or not defective. Each test is statistically independent of any other test.
   The probability of finding a defective product at point 1 is .2, and at point 2 the probability of a defective product is .1.
   a. What is the probability of finding a defective product at both points?
   b. What is the probability of finding a defective product at point 2, given that a defective product was found at point 1?
   c. What is the probability of finding a nondefective product at both testing points?

13.6 Bayes' Rule

In the previous discussion, probabilities associated with events have been given and, subsequently, computations have been carried out using these probabilities. In the real world, what is the basis of these probabilities? Often, they come from data in government and industry documents, the past history of a company, the personal knowledge of the researcher, or they are experimentally established.

Probabilities obtained in these ways are referred to as *prior probabilities*; i.e., they are established either before or at a preliminary stage of the experiment. In some situations, additional information is collected as an experiment progresses or with the passage of time and events. This additional information can be used to revise prior probabilities. Such revised prior probabilities are called *posterior probabilities*.

Bayes' rule is a technique for changing prior probabilities into posterior probabilities based on additional information. This technique is described and generalized by means of the following examples.

Example 13.18
A firm sells a special type of minicomputer to banks, stock-brokerage firms, and insurance companies. Based on the firm's past records, sales to banks are 20 percent of sales, stock-brokerage firms account for 30 percent of sales, and 50 percent of total sales are to insurance companies.

In addition, the manufacturer knows that 60 percent of banks, 70 percent of stock brokerage firms, and 40 percent of insurance companies who buy a minicomputer from the firm also purchase a maintenance contract.

These prior probabilities are condensed on the tree diagram of Figure 13.5. The following notation is applicable to Figure 13.5 and the corresponding probabilities:

B = banks
S = stock brokerage firms
I = insurance companies
M = does buy maintenance contract
M' = does not buy maintenance contract

Probabilities for each event based on the data mentioned above are shown in parentheses. Conditional probabilities can be read from the tree diagram without computation. For example, $P(M/B)$, representing the probability of buying a maintenance contract given that the computer buyer is a bank, is equal to .6. This is taken from the appropriate branch associated with the successive events bank = B and maintenance contract = M.

Bayes' rule is used to examine these data from a different perspective. For example, assume that the manufacturer knows that a maintenance contract has been sold and wants to compute the probability that the maintenance contract was purchased by a bank. This result represents the revised probability of bank purchase based on the additional information that a maintenance contract has been purchased.

In other words, it is known that banks purchase 20 percent of all minicomputers and the firm wants to determine the percentage of maintenance contract buyers represented by banks.

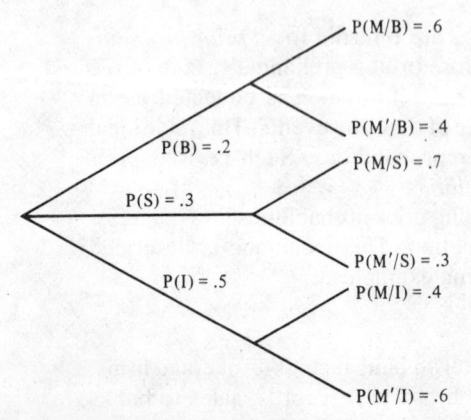

FIGURE 13.5 A tree diagram for Example 13.18.

To answer this, only a part of the original tree diagram is evaluated. The branches representing the probabilities of not buying a maintenance contract (M') are not needed in this analysis. Therefore, a different and smaller sample space is specified for the problem. In notation form, $P(M/B)$ is known and is equal to .6, but the problem concerns determination of $P(B/M)$. Because of this, the total probability of maintenance contract purchase $P(M)$ becomes the new sample space. However, $P(M)$ is not known.

In notational form, the problem requires the following computation:

$$P(B/M) = \frac{P(B \cap M)}{P(M)}$$

The denominator $P(M)$ must be computed from data in the original sample space. Therefore, the intersection between M and each buyer category must be determined. These are found by the general rule of multiplication as used to find $P(B \cap M)$ above.

$P(B \cap M) = (.2)(.6) = .12$

$P(S \cap M) = (.3)(.7) = .21$

$P(I \cap M) = (.5)(.4) = .20$

As these intersections add to .53, it is concluded that 53 percent of the original sample space represents maintenance contract buyers. This represents the denominator for

$$P(B/M) = \frac{P(B \cap M)}{P(M)}$$

Therefore, if a maintenance contract is purchased, the probability that it is purchased by a bank is equal to .2264, with rounding, as computed below:

$$P(B/M) = \frac{P(B \cap M)}{P(M)} = \frac{.12}{.53} = .2264$$

The analysis indicates that, although banks represent 20 percent of computer buyers, they make up 22.64 percent of all service contract buyers. This information may be used by the computer firm in product development, marketing, and personnel planning.

Example 13.18 yields the following generalization of Bayes' rule:

Bayes' Rule: If for the event B and the mutually exclusive events A_1, $A_2, \ldots, A_K$ leading to B, $P(A_i)$ and $P(B/A_i)$ are known for all A_i, then

$$P(A_i/B) = \frac{P(A_i) \cdot P(B/A_i)}{P(A_1)P(B/A_1) + P(A_2)P(B/A_2) + \cdots + P(A_K) \cdot P(B/A_K)}$$

This expression measures the conditional probability of A_i given B.

A second example will demonstrate further the application of Bayes' rule.

Example 13.19
A firm manufactures refrigerators at three plant locations A, B, and C. For each location, the firm maintains a record of the percentage of refrigerators made at that plant which require repair before expiration of the warranty.

Plant A produces 30 percent of all refrigerators and has a repair rate before warranty expiration R of 5 percent ($R = .05$). Consequently R' or the percent of refrigerators made at Plant A not requiring repair before warranty expiration is .95 ($R' = .95$). Plant B produces 45 percent of all refrigerators with $R = .03$ and $R' = .97$. Plant C produces 25 percent of the refrigerators with $R = .07$ and $R' = .93$. These data give the prior probabilities shown on the tree diagram of Figure 13.6.

If a refrigerator requires repair before warranty expiration, what is the probability that it was manufactured at Plant B?

In notation form, this question requires finding $P(B/R)$, where the known data include $P(R/B)$ and $P(B)$. Bayes' rule can be used to find this probability:

$$P(B/R) = \frac{P(B) \cdot P(R/B)}{P(A) \cdot P(R/A) + P(B) \cdot P(R/B) + P(C) \cdot P(R/C)}$$

$$= \frac{(.45)(.03)}{(.3)(.05) + (.45)(.03) + (.25)(.07)}$$

$$= \frac{.0135}{.015 + .0135 + .0175}$$

$$= \frac{.0135}{.0460} = .2935$$

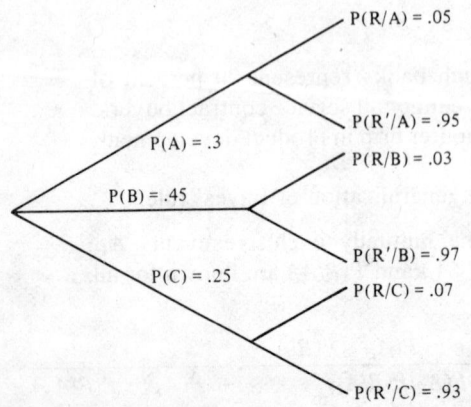

```
                        P(R/A) = .05
                    ╱
                   ╱
                  ╱ P(R'/A) = .95
          P(A) = .3
                    P(R/B) = .03
          P(B) = .45
                    P(R'/B) = .97
          P(C) = .25
                    P(R/C) = .07

                    P(R'/C) = .93
```

FIGURE 13.6 A tree diagram for Example 13.19.

It is concluded that the probability is .2935 that a refrigerator requiring repair before warranty expiration is manufactured in Plant B. This means that there is about a 29 percent chance of this event. Note that only 4.6 percent of the original sample space (the denominator above) represents refrigerators requiring repair before warranty expiration.

Two aspects of Bayes' rule should be emphasized. First, the additional information adjusts the sample space so that unnecessary prior probabilities (such as R' above) are eliminated. Second, with this revised sample space, the formula for conditional probability $P(A/B) = (P(A \cap B)/P(B)$, is utilized where $P(B)$ represents the adjusted sample space as a percentage of the original sample space.

These two examples have introduced the technique and some typical applications of Bayes' rule. The following exercises will give more practice in applying this technique.

EXERCISES

1. A factory tests motors at two points during the production process. At point 1, it is found that 10 percent are defective and 90 percent are not defective.

    Of those found defective at point one, 20 percent still are defective at point 2, but 80 percent are not defective due to changes that have been made. Also, at point 2, 15 percent of those found to be not defective at point 1 are now found to be defective and 85 percent still are not defective.
    a. Draw a tree diagram showing these prior probabilities.
    b. What percent of the sample space represents parts found defective at stage 2?
    c. What is the probability that a defective part found at stage 2 was not defective at stage 1?
    d. What is the probability that a nondefective part found at stage 2 was also defective at stage 1?
    Round answers to three decimal places.
2. A flight training program operated by a commercial airline includes two successive tests administered to potential pilots. Grades of "good," "fair," and "poor" are given on the first test, but only "pass" and "fail" grades are given on the second test.

    Of all potential pilots, 40 percent receive a grade of "good," 50 percent receive a "fair" grade, and 10 percent receive a "poor" grade on the first test.

    Of those receiving a grade of "good" on the first test, 90 percent "pass" the final test and 10 percent "fail." Of those receiving "fair" on the first test, the probability of passing the second test is .6. Those receiving "poor" on the first test have a 30 percent pass rate on the final test.

a. Draw a tree diagram of all the prior probabilities.
b. If someone fails the final test, what is the probability that the individual received a "good" grade on the first test?
c. If a pilot passes the final test, what is the probability that the person received a "poor" grade on the first test?
d. What percent of all pilots pass the final test?
Round answers to three decimal places.
3. In a consumer survey, it is found that 30 percent of consumers have seen an advertisement for a new shaving cream (70 percent have not seen it). If someone has seen the ad, the probability is 20 percent that the person bought the product during a subsequent 2-week period. If a consumer has not seen the ad, the probability of purchase during the 2-week period is 10 percent.
   a. What percent of consumers both have seen the ad and bought the product?
   b. If someone buys the shaving cream during the 2-week period, what is the probability that he or she has not seen the advertisement?
   c. What percent of all consumers did not buy the product during the 2-week period?
   Round answers to three decimal places.
4. Flu vaccines are given to some members of a group of elderly citizens before winter. Of the total group, 30 percent receive the vaccine and 70 percent do not receive it.
   Of those receiving the vaccine, 10 percent contract the flu, 30 percent contract another form of respiratory illness, and 60 percent do not have any problems of this type during the winter period.
   Among the group not receiving the vaccine, 20 percent contract the flu, 40 percent contract another form of respiratory illness, and 40 percent have no problems of this type.
   a. What percent of the group contract neither the flu nor respiratory illness during the winter period?
   b. If a member of the test group contracts another form of respiratory illness, what is the probability that he or she was not given the vaccine?
   c. If a member of the test group remains free of health problems of this type during the winter, what is the probability that the individual took the flu vaccine?
   Round answers to three decimal places.
5. Thirty percent of all long distance calls are made before 7 p.m. and 70 percent are made after this time. Forty percent of those made before 7 p.m. are for 5 minutes or less and 60 percent are for more than 5 minutes. Of the calls made after 7 p.m., 20 percent are for 5 minutes or less and 80 percent are for more than 5 minutes.
   a. What percent of all long distance calls are made after 7 p.m. for more than 5 minutes?
   b. What percent of all long distance calls made for more than 5 minutes are made after 7 p.m.?

c. If a long distance call is less than 5 minutes long, what is the probability that it was made before 7 p.m.?
Round answers to three decimal places.

13.7 Discrete Probability Distributions

This section and Section 13.8 introduce random variables and probability distributions.

A random variable is a numerically valued function which takes values in accordance with the outcome of an experiment. For example, random variables may be used to represent sales for a group of retail stores or incomes for the families in a city.

A probability distribution is a mathematical formula expressing the probability of each possible value for a random variable in an experiment. Knowledge of the probability distribution for a particular random variable allows certain facts to be known about that random variable. In addition, probability distributions provide the foundation for tests of statistical inference.

There are two types of probability distributions, discrete and continuous, corresponding to the type of random variable associated with each. *Discrete random variables* have values that can be counted within a range. For example, the number of refrigerators requiring repair before warranty expiration can be represented by a discrete random variable. *Continuous random variables* can have any value in a range. For example, the birth weight of infants at a hospital can be represented by a continuous random variable.

Formulas stating the probability of events for discrete and continuous random variables are referred to, respectively, as discrete probability distributions and continuous probability distributions. In this section a discrete probability distribution, the binomial probability distribution, is discussed. In Section 13.8 a continuous probability distribution, the normal distribution, is introduced.

The Binomial Probability Distribution

The binomial probability distribution is used to evaluate random variables having only two mutually exclusive forms (or outcomes of an experiment)— for example, man or woman, employed or unemployed, bought or did not buy a product. An experiment for which there are only two mutually exclusive outcomes is called a *Bernoulli experiment*.

The two outcomes of an experiment conventionally are referred to as *success* and *failure*. Therefore, in a particular problem "bought the product" or "unemployed" could be considered as the success outcomes. In other words, "success" is used to classify the factor of interest in a problem and not to imply a value judgment of good or bad.

There are three characteristics of the binomial probability distribution.

1. There are only two possible outcomes for each experiment.
2. The trials of the experiment are statistically independent.
3. The probabilities of success and failure remain the same for all trials of the experiment.

As the binomial probability distribution is discrete, the number of successes and failures can be counted.

The formula for the binomial probability distribution is

$$P(x) = {}_nC_x(p)^x(q)^{n-x}$$

This formula yields the probability of getting x successes in n experiments. The term ${}_nC_x$ indicates the number of combinations of n experiments taken x at a time (x = successes). Earlier in this chapter this was shown to be equal to

$${}_nC_x = \frac{n!}{x!(n-x)!}$$

The terms p and q correspond, respectively, to the constant probability of success and failure for each experiment. Each of these probabilities is raised to the power representing the number of successes x and the number of failures $n - x$.

Example 13.20 will show an application of the binomial probability distribution.

Example 13.20

Within the union membership of a local unit of the United Automobile Workers, 90 percent of workers are employed and 10 percent are unemployed. What is the probability that in a random sample[1] of five members, two unemployed workers will be included?

In this case, let p (success) be the category unemployed as that is the tested characteristic. The formula for the binomial probability distribution yields the following result for $x = 2$.

Probability of two unemployed workers in a sample of five:

$$P(x) = {}_nC_x(p)^x(q)^{n-x}$$

$$P(2) = {}_5C_2(.1)^2(.9)^3$$

$$= \frac{5!}{3!2!}(.1)^2(.9)^3$$

$$= 10(.01)(.729)$$

$$= .0729$$

Therefore, the analysis concludes that there is approximately a 7 per-

---

[1] A random sample is one where each member of the set (each union member in this case) has an equal probability of being selected in the survey.

cent (.0729) chance that a randomly selected group of five union members will include two who are unemployed.

A second example will demonstrate another use of the binomial formula.

Example 13.21
The U.S. Army has determined that 20 percent of all new recruits are classified as being overweight at the time of their entrance physical examination. What is the probability of finding three or more overweight recruits in a random sample of four new recruits?

In order to answer this problem, the individual probabilities of finding three and four recruits who are overweight must be added. This total will yield the probability of finding three or more who are overweight. The individual probabilities are found by the following application of the binomial probability formula:

1. Probability of three overweight recruits:

$$P(3) = {}_4C_3(.2)^3(.8)^1 = \frac{4!}{1!3!}(.008)(.8) = .0256$$

2. Probability of four overweight recruits:

$$P(4) = {}_4C_4(.2)^4(.8)^0 = \frac{4!}{4!0!}(.0016)(1) = .0016$$

Total probability = .0256 + .0016 = .0272

Thus, the probability of finding three or more overweight recruits from a sample of four is .0272 or 2.72 percent. This example demonstrates computation of a *cumulative binomial probability* since more than one individual probability (in this case three and four recruits) is included in the answer.

The binomial formula is applicable to problems of any sample size. However, as sample size increases, it becomes increasingly difficult to compute combinations and raise decimal probabilities to their indicated powers. As a consequence, mathematical tables exist showing binomial probabilities for various groupings of p, x, and n. These tables and their use are not discussed in this introductory presentation but can be found in many books on statistics.

This introduction to the binomial probability distribution has shown it to be a useful discrete distribution when considering problems with two mutually exclusive data categories.

13.8 Continuous Probability Distributions

It has been pointed out that a continuous random variable can have any value within a range and that a probability distribution specifies the probability of each and every event in the stated range.

As a continuous random variable can have any value in a range, there are an infinite number of values in the range. Therefore, the probability associated with any one value of the continuous random variable is zero. Because of this relation, probabilities can be stated only for intervals of a continuous random variable. Probability distributions for continuous random variables take note of this characteristic so that they are referred to as *probability density functions*.

The probability associated with an interval of a continuous random variable is found by integrating the probability density function between the interval limits.

Consider the probability of any single value of a continuous random variable in this context of integral calculus. The probability that $x = a$ on the probability density function $f(x)$ is equal to 0:

$$P(x = a) = \int_a^a f(x)\, dx = 0$$

The probability associated with the interval (a, b) of the random variable x of some positive length is the following:

$$P(a \le x \le b) = \int_a^b f(x)\, dx$$

where $P(a \le x \le b)$ indicates the probability that x will fall between $x = a$ and $x = b$.

Along with all probability distributions, the sum of all the probabilities for a probability density function is equal to one:

$$\int_{\text{all } x} f(x)\, dx = 1$$

The Mean and the Variance

Two measurements encountered in the application of random variables and probability density functions are the *expected value*, or *mean*, and the *variance*.

The expected value of a continuous random variable can be viewed as the center of gravity of the probability density function. In other words, the expected value represents the weighted center of the probability density function.

For a continuous random variable X, the expected value, $E(X)$, is found by performing the following integration:

EXPECTED VALUE OF A CONTINUOUS RANDOM VARIABLE:

$$E(X) = \int_{\text{all } x} x\, P(x)\, dx$$

In other words, the expected value is equal to the definite integral over the entire range of x or x times the probability density function. The expected value also is referred to as the mean, with the designation u.

EXPECTED VALUE, OR MEAN, OF A CONTINUOUS RANDOM VARIABLE:

$$E(X) = u = \int_{\text{all } x} x f(x)\, dx$$

Example 13.22

The birth weights of infants at a hospital is a continuous random variable with weights occurring at an equal frequency between 4 and 12 pounds. What is the expected value, or mean, of the birth weights?

For this problem, the probability density function is equal to $\int \frac{1}{8}\, dx$, representing the equal dispersion of weights between 4 and 12 pounds.[2]

Therefore, the expected value, or mean, of the birth weights is equal to the following:

EXPECTED VALUE OF BIRTH WEIGHTS:

$$E(X) = u = \int_{4}^{12} x \frac{1}{8}\, dx$$

$$= \frac{x^2}{16} \bigg|_{4}^{12}$$

$$= \frac{144}{16} - \frac{16}{16} = \frac{128}{16} = 8$$

The conclusion is that the mean birth weight, or the mean of the continuous random variable, is 8 pounds.

The variance of a continuous random variable, designated by the symbol σ^2, is a measure of the spread of the x values around the mean of the continuous random variable.

Because the mean is the center of gravity of the distribution, the weighted sum of the observations on each side of the mean are equal. Consequently, the sum of the differences between each observation and the mean will be zero when considering all observations.

As a result of this, the variance includes the squared differences between each observation x and the mean u. These squared differences are multiplied by the probability density function to yield the variance.

---

[2]This example of infant weights applies the uniform probability distribution, used to describe situations where all outcomes are equally likely over a given range. In this case, all infant weights between 4 and 12 pounds have an equal likelihood of occurrence.

VARIANCE OF A CONTINUOUS RANDOM VARIABLE:

$$\text{Variance } (X) = \sigma_X^2 = \int_{\text{all } x} (x - u)^2 f(x)\, dx$$

where $u = E(X)$.

The square root of the variance, or σ, is the *standard deviation* of the continuous random variable.

The mean and variance often are used to characterize the probability density function for a continuous random variable. The primary purpose of introducing them at this point in the chapter is to provide a definitional framework for the discussion of the normal distribution.

13.9 The Normal Distribution

The *normal distribution* is a continuous probability distribution which represents the limiting form of the discrete binomial distribution. Specifically, the normal distribution approximates the binomial distribution when n approaches infinity and the probability of success p approaches .5. Because it is a continuous distribution, the probability of a single x value is zero in the normal distribution.

Research has established that many data sets in the natural and social sciences, business, and economics are represented by the normal distribution. Thus, the normal distribution is an important concept for mathematical and statistical analysis in many disciplines.

The normal distribution is represented graphically by the bell-shaped curve of Figure 13.7. This curve also is referred to as the *normal curve*.

In addition to being a continuous distribution, the normal distribution has two other important characteristics: it is symmetric about its mean and it is asymptotic to the X axis.

The symmetry property means that exactly 50 percent of the total area under the probability density function lies on each side of the mean. Thus, the mean u in Figure 13.7 separates the distribution into two areas of equal

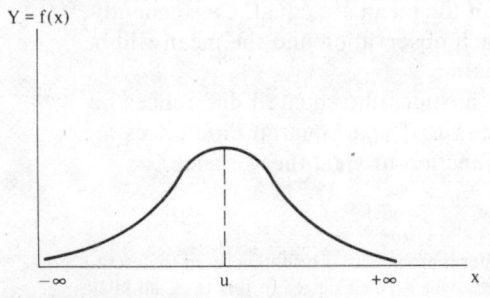

FIGURE 13.7 The normal curve.

size. The asymptotic property (see Chapter 10) means that values for $f(x)$ approach, but never equal, zero as the x values get infinitely large and as they get infinitely small. This property also can be seen on Figure 13.7.

The probability density function for the normal distribution is stated below.

PROBABILITY DENSITY FUNCTION FOR
THE NORMAL DISTRIBUTION:

$$f(x) = \frac{1}{\sigma \sqrt{2\pi}} e^{-1/2[(x-u)/\sigma]^2}$$

In this equation, u represents the mean or expected value of the distribution, σ^2 is the variance, σ is the standard deviation, π is the constant 3.14159..., and e is equal to 2.71828....

The distribution is dependent on the values for u and σ^2 (and its square root σ) as all other terms in the equation are constants. This fact leads to the result that a normal distribution can be developed for any mean and variance (or standard deviation).

Because of the asymptotic property, x values can be between $-\infty$ and $+\infty$. As a result, the development of the normal distribution for any mean and variance by means of integral calculus is extremely difficult and time consuming. Fortunately, a table has been developed which assists formation of a normal distribution for any mean and variance. The normal distribution table is included as Table X at the end of this book.

The normal distribution table uses numbers referred to as *standard normal deviates,* or z values. Consequently, the x values of concern to a particular problem (e.g., incomes, weights, and sales) must be transformed to z values before using Table X.

The conversion formula for changing x values into standard normal deviates (z values) is as follows:

$$z = \frac{x - u}{\sigma}$$

where u and σ are the mean and standard deviation, respectively, of the distribution of x values. This equation for z "standardizes" any particular x value so that it becomes a value in a normal distribution.

The mean of the standardized values z is always equal to 0 and the standard deviation is equal to 1. In keeping with the property of symmetry, 50 percent of all z values are above the mean of 0 and 50 percent are below the mean. Figure 13.8 describes the z distribution.

Using Figure 13.8, assume one is considering an x distribution with $u = 50$ and $\sigma = 3$. An x value of 56 is converted to a z value of 2 as follows:

$$z = \frac{x - u}{\sigma} = \frac{56 - 50}{3} = 2$$

f(x)

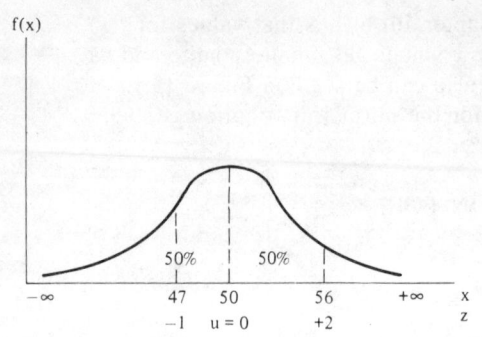

```
         50% | 50%
  -∞    47  50   56   +∞    x
        -1  u=0  +2         z
```

FIGURE 13.8 The Z distribution and the normal curve.

Similarly, an x value of 47 is comparable to a z value of -1:

$$z = \frac{x - u}{\sigma} = \frac{47 - 50}{3} = -1$$

Finally, observe that an x value of 50, the mean, corresponds to the z value of 0. This relation between x values and z values is shown by the x row and z row under the normal curve of Figure 13.8.

After conversion of an x value or set of x values, Table X can be used to provide information about the normal distribution as related to the variable of interest (x in this case).

In Table X, z values are read from the first column and first row. The body of the table yields the area under the curve between 0 (mean) and the specified z value. In other words, the numbers in the body of Table X represent the probability associated with the interval between 0 and the particular z value. These probabilities can be used to make statements about the probabilities associated with values of x.

Several examples will demonstrate use of the normal distribution table.

Applications of the Normal Distribution

The following five examples will show the use of the normal distribution table in applied situations. First, the background for the examples is described.

The checks drawn on a large bank during a day are normally distributed with a mean amount of $90 and a standard deviation of $10 ($u = 90, \sigma = 10$). Bank officials are interested in assessing the following probabilities for purposes of improved cash-management control. In these examples, each probability question is phrased in percentage terms.

Example 13.23
What percent of checks drawn are between $90 and $105?

This answer requires conversion of $105 to a standard normal deviate as follows:

$$z = \frac{x - u}{\sigma} = \frac{105 - 90}{10} = \frac{15}{10} = 1.5$$

The area between $90 and $105 is comparable to the area between $z = 0$ and $z = 1.5$. Table X yields the area under the normal curve between $z = 0$ and $z = 1.5$ as .4332.

Therefore, about 43 percent of all checks drawn will be between the amounts of $90 and $105. This probability is shown in the shaded area of Figure 13.9.

Example 13.24
Determine the percentage of checks drawn which are between $70 and $90.
The standardized value of 70 for x is equivalent to a z value of -2:

$$z = \frac{70 - 90}{10} = \frac{-20}{10} = -2.00$$

As the normal distribution is symmetric around a mean of zero, the z values in Table X can be considered absolute values. Therefore, the area between 0 and $+2$ is exactly equal to the area between 0 and -2.

The area between 0 and $+2$ is equal to .4772 and 47.72 percent. Thus, 47.72 percent of all checks drawn are for amounts between $70 and $90. Figure 13.10 indicates this probability in the shaded area.

Example 13.25
What percentage of all checks drawn are in excess of $115?
Answering this question requires computation of the area under the normal curve between $115 and positive infinity (as a result of the asymptotic property).

As the area between the mean of $z = 0$ ($u = 90$) and positive infinity is .5000, the solution is found by subtracting the area between $90 and $115 from .5000.

The z value for $x = 115$ is:

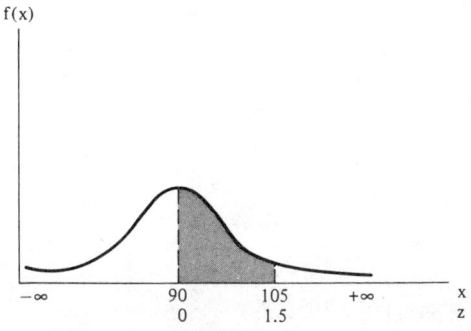

FIGURE 13.9 The normal curve and Example 13.23.

f(X)

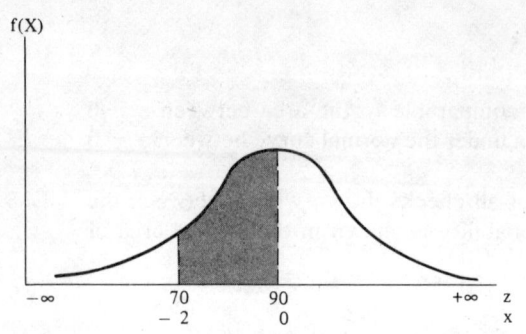

−∞	70	90	+∞	z
	−2	0		x

FIGURE 13.10 The normal curve and Example 13.24.

$$z = \frac{115 - 90}{10} = 2.5$$

Table X gives the area between $z = 0$ and $z = 2.5$ as .4938. Therefore, the percent of checks drawn which are in excess of $115 is computed as follows:

.5000 − .4938 = .0062 = .62 percent

Figure 13.11 shows this probability in the shaded area on the extreme right-hand side of the distribution.

Example 13.26

Find the percentage of checks drawn which are between $75 and $100.

For this problem, z values must be found for both $x = 75$ and $x = 100$. The area for each from Table X must be added as each is on a different side of the mean. These areas are computed in the following equations:

1. $z = \dfrac{75 - 90}{10} = \dfrac{-15}{10} = -1.5$

The area for $z = 1.5$ is equal to .4332 = 43.32 percent

f(x)

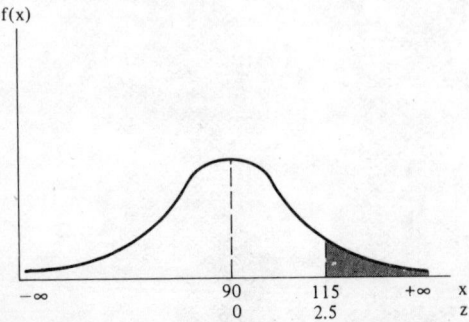

−∞	90	115	+∞	x
	0	2.5		z

FIGURE 13.11 The normal curve and Example 13.25.

2. $z = \dfrac{100 - 90}{10} = \dfrac{10}{10} = +1.0$

The area for $z = 1.0$ is equal to .3413 = 34.13 percent.

The percentage of checks drawn between these two amounts is equal to the sum of the areas or 77.45 percent:

Area 1 + area 2 = total area
.4332 + .3413 = .7745 = 77.45 percent

Figure 13.12 shows the mean, the area on each side of the mean, and the sum of the areas.

Example 13.27
Determine the percentage of checks drawn which are between $100 and $110.

To answer this, the z values corresponding to $x = 100$ and $x = 110$ must be found:

1. $z = \dfrac{100 - 90}{10} = +1.0$

The area for $z = 1.0$ is equal to .3413 = 34.13 percent.

2. $z = \dfrac{110 - 90}{10} = \dfrac{20}{10} = +2.0$

The area between $z = 2$ and $z = 0$ is .4772 = 47.72 percent.

In this case, the area between $x = 100$ and $x = 110$ must be established. Therefore, the difference between the areas in 1 and 2 yields the answer.

Area 2 − area 1 = area between 110 and 100
0.4772 − 0.3413 = 0.1359 = 13.59 percent

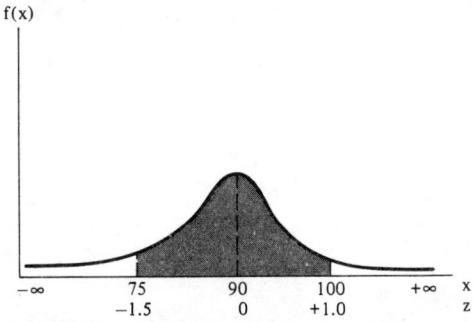

FIGURE 13.12 The normal curve and Example 13.26.

It is concluded that 13.59 percent of all checks drawn are for amounts between $100 and $110.

Figure 13.13 describes this area in the shaded portion of the normal curve.

This same technique can be used for evaluating an interval between two values which are less than the mean.

These five examples have presented typical applications of the normal distribution and corresponding table. In all cases, the technique involves standardizing the x value or values of interest and using the resulting z value or values to find the appropriate area. In addition to this conversion process, the symmetry and asymptotic properties of the normal distribution are employed in answering specific problems.

The following exercises include problems using the binomial and normal distributions.

EXERCISES

1. Using the formula for computing binomial probabilities,

   $$_nC_x(p)^x(q)^{n-x}$$

   answer the following questions.
   a. State the formula in words rather than mathematical notation.
   b. For the following sets of values, find the corresponding binomial probability:
      (1) $n = 5, x = 3, p = 0.3, q = 0.7$
      (2) $n = 8, x = 5, p = 0.4, q = 0.6$
      (3) $n = 7, x = 2, p = 0.2, q = 0.8$
      (4) $n = 10, x = 3, p = 0.5, q = 0.5$
      Round answers to three decimal places.
   c. Explain what you have measured in parts (2) and (4) above.

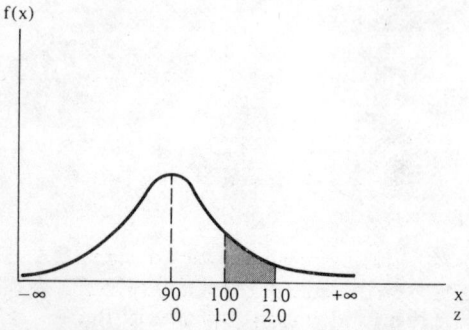

FIGURE 13.13 The normal curve and Example 13.27.

2. Find the standardized value for each of the following values from a normal probability distribution with $u = 60$ and $\sigma = 5$.
   a. $x = 64$ d. $x = 70$
   b. $x = 52$ e. $x = 45$
   c. $x = 68$ f. $x = 72$
3. Using the normal distribution table, find the area under the normal curve between 0 and each z value found in question 2.
4. For values of x with a mean of 200 and a standard deviation of 10 taken from the normal probability distribution, find
   a. The percentage of x values less than 200.
   b. The percentage of x values between 200 and 230.
   c. The percentage of x values between 180 and 200.
   d. The percentage of x values less than 190.
   e. The percentage of x values more than 215.
   f. The percentage of x values between 185 and 205.
5. Of all television viewers, 30 percent saw a special presentation on a recent Sunday night. From a sample of five television viewers, what is the probability that:
   a. Three viewed the special?
   b. Four viewed the special?
   c. Five viewed the special?
   d. None viewed the special?
   Round answers to three decimal places.
6. The age of all city residents is a continuous random variable which is normally distributed about a mean of 32 with a standard deviation of 20 years.
   a. What percentage of all residents are older than 45?
   b. What percentage of all residents are less than 10 years old?
   c. What percentage of all residents are younger than 16?
   d. What percentage of all residents are between 25 and 40 years old?
7. Scores on an armed services entrance examination are normally distributed with a mean of 70 points and a standard deviation of 8 points.
   a. What percentage of all scores are between 60 and 80?
   b. What percentage of all scores are greater than 86?
   c. What percentage of all scores are less than 80?
   d. What percentage of all scores are either greater than 90 or less than 50?

13.10 Chapter Summary

As this chapter has stressed, probabilistic models are applicable to many analytical questions in business and economics. In addition, probability theory is a topic which links mathematical analysis and statistical analysis, the two components of quantitative business analysis.

In this chapter, the basic concepts and definitions of probability theory have been introduced and related to business and economic situations. Probability theory provides the means to evaluate and better understand sets of data and can be applied to the analysis of past, present, or future possibilities.

Specific computational topics presented in the chapter have included the general rules of addition and multiplication of probabilities, Bayes' rule, the enumeration of binomial probabilities, and the evaluation of areas under the normal curve. In addition, the principles of "counting" and how these principles can be used to study groups of data have been discussed.

It is hoped that this chapter has provided a basic understanding of probability theory as this topic will be encountered by many readers in both future quantitative study and in the business professions.

13.11 Problem Set

Review Questions

1. What are the upper and lower limits on the probability of an event?
2. What is shown on a tree diagram of probabilities?
3. Define the empty set. Why is it a subset of all sets?
4. Distinguish between the number of permutations and the number of combinations of a certain size that can be formed from the elements of a set.
5. If A and B are statistically independent events, what is the expression for the probability of the conditional event $P(A/B)$? Why?
6. Why is it not possible for two mutually exclusive events with nonzero probabilities to be statistically independent?
7. When computing the probability of the union of two events which are not mutually exclusive, why must the probability of their intersection be subtracted from the sum of their individual probabilities?
8. What is the probability of
   a. The intersection of two mutually exclusive events?
   b. The union of two collectively exhaustive events?
9. Bayes' rule provides a technique for determination of posterior probabilities based on a smaller sample space than the sample space applicable to the prior probabilities. Explain.
10. What is described by a probability distribution?
11. Why is the binomial probability distribution referred to as a discrete probability distribution?
12. Name the three characteristics of the experiments providing the data for a binomial probability distribution.
13. Give an example of a business problem requiring use of the cumulative binomial probability formula.
14. What is the probability of any single value for a random variable in a continuous probability distribution? Why?
15. What is the mean of the distribution of the standardized or z values in the normal distribution? What is the variance of z?
16. Define "symmetrical" and "asymptotic" as applied to the normal probability distribution.

Review Problems

1. The following use the notation developed in the chapter. Give a numerical answer for each.
   a. $_6P_5$ f. $_{10}C_4$
   b. $_2P_1$ g. $_6C_6$
   c. $_5P_5$ h. $_6C_3$
   d. $_8P_3$ i. $_7C_6$
   e. $_{10}P_2$ j. $_8C_2$
2. How many subsets of any size can be developed from a set of four elements? List the subsets using the elements A, B, C, D.
3. Events A and B are collectively exhaustive with $P(A) = .4$ and $P(B/A) = .3$. Find:
   a. $P(B)$
   b. $P(A \cap B)$
   c. $P(A \cup B)$
   d. Are A and B statistically independent? Why, or why not?
4. Events A and B are statistically independent with $P(B) = .5$ and $P(A/B) = .2$. Find:
   a. $P(A)$ c. $P(A \cup B)$
   b. $P(A \cap B)$ d. $P(B/A)$
5. For the mutually exclusive events X and Y, $P(X) = .5$ and $P(Y) = .2$. Find:
   a. $P(X \cup Y)$ c. $P(X/Y)$
   b. $P(X \cap Y)$ d. $P(Y/X)$
6. Find the binomial probability for each situation described below:
   a. The probability of 6 successes out of 8 trials with P(success) $= .3$.
   b. The probability of 4 successes out of 5 trials with P(success) $= .6$.
   c. The probability of 3 successes out of 4 trials with P(success) $= .9$.
   d. The probability of 4 successes out of 4 trials with P(success) $= .5$.
   e. The probability of 0 successes out of 5 trials with P(success) $= .8$.
   Round answers to five decimal places.
7. The following x values are from a normal probability distribution with $u = 20$ and $\sigma = 3$. Find the standardized value (z value) corresponding to each x.
   a. $x = 25$ e. $x = 10$
   b. $x = 32$ f. $x = 0$
   c. $x = 20$ g. $x = 17$
   d. $x = 15$ h. $x = 23$
8. The following situations apply to a normal probability distribution for the random variable x with $u = 42$ and $\sigma = 5$. Use the normal distribution table to find the probability that
   a. x is between 42 and 47.
   b. x is greater than 50.
   c. x is between 40 and 45.
   d. x is less than 35.
   e. x is between 30 and 40.
   f. x is equal to 42.
   g. x may be either less than 38 or greater than 48.
   h. x is greater than 36.
9. A hospital has nine floors. Meals can be delivered to patients on only three floors during one cycle of the kitchen schedule. Within the three floors, the exact order

of delivery, such as floor 5, floor 4, floor 3 as opposed to 3, 4, 5 is used in staff planning. How many possible food delivery schedules exist for this hospital?

10. Eleven computer operators on each shift are responsible for monitoring a nuclear power facility. Safety requirements allow only four operators at one time to take a break. How many different groups of four individuals on break at any one time can be formed from this group of eleven?

11. A company uses ten chemicals to manufacture an industrial compound. Two chemicals can be added to the compound at any one time during processing. How many different groups of two exist for this process?

12. Police officials know that the probability of a crime occurring in District 7 is .4 (4 out of every 10 crimes in the city are committed in this district). If a crime is committed in district 7, the probability is .2 that it occurred between 12 midnight and 4 a.m.

    What is the percentage of all city crimes committed in district 7 between 12 midnight and 4 a.m.?

13. A grocery store chain in an urban area uses two advertising media, radio and newspapers. A consultant has estimated that 35 percent of all consumers have been exposed to the chain's radio advertising and 45 percent have been exposed to its newspaper advertising. Also, 30 percent of all consumers have been exposed to both types of advertising for the store.

    What percentage of all consumers in this urban area have been exposed to any of the chain's advertising?

14. A bank has 60 percent male employees and 40 percent female employees. Eighty percent of all positions at the bank are held by whites and 20 percent are held by nonwhites. It is known also that 30 percent of all employees are white women.

    The firm wants to determine the probability of selecting from the employee group a nonwhite, given that the selected individual is a male. Compute the probability.

15. Of a city's work force, 8 percent is unemployed and 92 percent is employed. Within the unemployed group, 40 percent are between 16 and 24 years old, 25 percent are between 25 and 54, and 35 percent are over 54 years of age. For the employed group, 25 percent are between 16 and 24, 45 percent are between 25 and 54, and 30 percent are more than 54 years old.

    A member of the work force between 25 and 54 years old is selected for an in-depth survey of social services in the city. What is the probability that the selected individual is unemployed? Round answer to three decimal places.

16. For an insurance company, 20 percent of all automobile insurance policies are held by drivers under 25 years old, 70 percent are held by drivers between 25 and 65 years old, and 10 percent are held by drivers over 65 years old.

    Of policy holders under 25 years old, 30 percent had traffic violations during the past 3 years and 70 percent have not had any violations. For the 25- to 65-year-old group, 10 percent have had violations and 90 percent have not had violations during the past 3 years. For the over-65 group, 20 percent have had violations and 80 percent have not had violations during the 3-year period.

    a. What percent of all policy holders have had traffic violations during the past 3 years?
    b. If a policy holder has not had a traffic violation during the past 3 years, what is the probability that the person is under 25 years old? Round answer to three decimal places.

17. A retail clothing firm operates four types of outlet: budget (B), self-service (S), full-service (F), and mail order (M). The percentage of the firm's total sales for each type of store are $B = 25$, $S = 5$, $F = 40$, and $M = 30$.

    The percentage of sales returned by customers after being bought in each type of store are 2 percent for budget stores, 6 percent at self-service stores, 9 percent at full-service outlets, and 10 percent for the mail-order business. All customer returns are processed at a central office.
    a. Construct a tree diagram showing all prior probabilities.
    b. What percent of all items sold are returned?
    c. If an item is returned to the central office, what is the probability that it was sold in a full-service store?
    Round answers to three decimal places.

18. In a small college, 70 percent of students are men and 30 percent are women. In selecting a group of five student records from all records, what is the probability that
    a. Three of the records will be of men?
    b. None of the records will be of men?
    c. Three or more of the records will be of women?
    Round answers to four decimal places.

19. A can manufacturing facility produces defective cans at a 10 percent rate (90 percent of production is in acceptable form). In a sample of eight cans, what is the probability that
    a. All eight will be in acceptable form?
    b. Two or less will be defective?
    Round answers to four decimal places.

20. Researchers for a consumer products company know that the per store sales of the firm's liquid detergent are normally distributed. The mean annual sales per store are 70 cases and the standard deviation is 20 cases.
    a. What percentage of all stores have annual sales of less than 30 cases per year?
    b. What percentage of all stores have annual sales between 60 and 80 cases?
    c. What percentage of all stores sell more than 100 cases per year?
    d. What percentage of all stores sell between 75 and 90 cases per year?
    Round answers to four decimal places.

Mathematical Models and Business Analysis: A Final Word

14.1 Introduction

It is a basic theme of this book that mathematical models are important to the overall methodology of business analysis. This final chapter discusses the relation between applied mathematics, mathematical models, and business and economics. These few pages will relate the topic-by-topic presentation of the first 13 chapters to the discussion of mathematical modeling introduced in Chapter 1.

In Chapter 1, it was pointed out that mathematical models provide a quantitative basis for the explanation of a phenomenon. With mathematical models, decision makers in an organization have the means to abstract and evaluate the most essential parts of the phenomenon. Thus, mathematical models need not be as complex as the real situation under investigation. This simplification allows decision makers to develop generalizations which may be valid for a wide range of options.

For example, mathematical models may be used to describe the following relations:

1. The pattern of per unit costs as a firm's output varies
2. The optimum allocation of resources for a firm, given its available resources and production demands

3. The amount of each ingredient used in a product which must be purchased to produce a stated amount of the product

Probabilistic models include elements of chance in the explanation of the situation and deterministic models yield information which is not subject to chance. The mathematical techniques presented in this book are applicable to one or the other or both of these types of models.

The next three sections will summarize the mathematical techniques of this text with respect to how each relates to the process of mathematical modeling. Specifically, in Section 14.2 the topic is linear models, Section 14.3 will summarize nonlinear models, and in Section 14.4 probabilistic models in business are discussed.

Although this chapter is not an exhaustive description of the techniques of mathematical modeling, it is an appropriate way to conclude the book in the context of one cohesive topic.

14.2 Linear Models

Chapters 4, 5, 6, and 7 have discussed mathematical techniques applicable to linear models in business.

Two basic linear models in business which use two equations and two unknowns are linear demand-and-supply analysis for one product and break-even analysis. Both are employed frequently as simplifications of more complex functions. Their advantage is that decision makers can comprehend easily the results of the analysis. Thus, the deviation from reality found in these models often is more than compensated for by their ease of understanding. These and other such simplified models serve a useful purpose in business analysis.

As the number of equations and variables increase, analysis requires solution of systems of equations. Such analyses are used, for example, in models describing ingredient mixes, investment strategies, and multiproduct demand-and-supply situations.

Some models, when formulated, have a structure which leads to the conclusion that the model does not have a unique solution. The Gauss-Jordan method of elimination for solving systems of equations can detect this possibility, thus indicating the need for model reformulation if possible. Reformulation may include alteration of the coefficients and/or constants in the equation. Such reformulation should not cause the model to deviate substantially from the actual situation being described.

An additional analysis technique often applied to linear models with many equations and variables is matrix algebra. To employ matrix algebra, the coefficients, variables, and constants of the system are manipulated as arrays of data. The solution methods which use matrix algebra are the Gauss-

Jordan method of elimination and the Gauss-Jordan method of matrix inversion.

Computerized linear analysis frequently employs matrix inversion as opposed to the Gauss-Jordan method of elimination. Matrix inversion as a solution technique provides flexibility to the model as the equation constants may be varied without causing undue difficulties in determining a new solution.

Matrix algebra also is used as the mathematical technique for many input-output models. Input-output models concern large interdependent demand-and-supply situations. These models increasingly are found helpful to planning in large corporations, other large institutions, and various levels of government.

Thus, Chapters 4, 5, and 6 include the mathematical techniques applicable to linear models with any number of equations and variables. These deterministic models often concern establishment of a single solution for the various equations and corresponding values for each variable at that solution point.

Linear programming (Chapter 7) permits evaluation of alternative solution points for linear models which may include equalities and inequalities. This technique is applicable particularly to resource allocation models where profits, sales, or costs may be constrained by considerations of resource availability, production quotas, or product quality. Linear programming techniques yield the "best" solution consistent with the conditions stated in the model. At the solution point, all the conditions (constraints) of the model may not be satisfied exactly. In general, linear programming has the flexibility to be applied to models used to assess alternatives available to an organization.

Two features of all the linear techniques presented in this book should be restated. First, all the linear models discussed in Chapters 4, 5, 6, and 7 are deterministic. That is, answers applicable to these models are not qualified by probabilities or the elements of chance. Second, the techniques are applied to models where all the variables are in linear form; i.e., none have powers greater than 1. As stated in Chapter 4, linear models are employed with such frequency in business because they both accurately mirror many real-world situations and provide an easily comprehended approximation to many other actual business situations.

14.3 Nonlinear Models

The chapters on the mathematics of finance (Chapter 9) and calculus (Chapters 10, 11, and 12) present techniques for analyzing deterministic models with variables of any power, including 0 and 1. Often, models incorporate nonlinear variables as use of the linear form may cause a substantial deviation from the actual situation.

The constant e has a special importance to many nonlinear models used in business. It is employed as a base for both natural logarithm functions and a large number of exponential functions. Growth models and decay models in finance, sales, population, and other fields often use the constant e to describe changes in a variable over time.

Functions applied to production and profit models often are nonlinear as they reflect the law of diminishing returns. As these functions and related models are used many times to determine optimum points (maximum or minimum), the techniques of differential calculus are employed.

Integral calculus also is applied frequently in the analysis of nonlinear models. Models concerned with questions such as revenue or cost over a range of output, capital investment over time, and accumulated interest during a specified interval often utilize integral calculus. Integral calculus also serves as the foundation for many probabilistic models. However, the material of Chapter 12 concerns applications of integral calculus in deterministic models only.

In conclusion, it should be pointed out that the techniques of both differential and integral calculus may be applied to the same linear or nonlinear models. For example, with a model relating a firm's production costs and output, differential calculus may be used to determine the least-cost level of production, and integral calculus may be employed to find the effect on total production cost caused by an expansion in output from, for example, 1000 to 1500 units per week.

14.4 Probabilistic (Stochastic) Models

The laws and principles of probability (Chapter 13) are applied to models which incorporate chance or randomness in the evaluation and interpretation of results.

Probabilistic models may be simple as when applying the definitions and basic operations of probability to sample spaces such as consumer groups and groups of products. Alternatively, more complex probabilistic models may incorporate the use of Bayes' rule or other aspects of conditional probabilities.

Another analytical aspect of probabilistic models includes the use of probability distributions such as the uniform, binomial, and normal probability distributions. These and other probability distributions assign a probability to each possible value for a random variable in an experiment. If the experimental results are expected to conform to a particular preestablished pattern of probabilities (e.g., the normal distribution), then statements can be made about the probability of an event or events. This pattern of probabilities represents the analytical model.

For example, if a model includes outcomes of an experiment which fall into two groups (e.g., male and female or employed and unemployed), the binomial probability distribution may be appropriate for the analysis. Or, if the number of outcomes is so large that the probability of any single outcome is infinitesimally small (e.g., birth weights), the normal probability distribution often should be applied. Probabilistic models and their related probability distributions form the foundation for tests of statistical inference, a topic not included in this text.

One important topic of applied probability in business is simulation. Although simulation and simulation models are not discussed in the first 13 chapters, a brief introduction at this point is valuable.

Simulation involves formulating and experimenting with numerical models of a real-world situation. Simulation models do not result in solution values but rather use probabilities to describe a real-world operation through time (such as the operation of a shipping facility or a retail store).

Examples of applied simulation models are customer arrival patterns, machine repair times, and sales patterns. Each model includes a pattern for the specified activity (arrival, sales, etc.) based on computed probabilities. Thus, simulation models are probabilistic and results are in the form of statistical estimates not optimal solutions. Simulation models are considered one of the most flexible of all mathematical models as changing organizational conditions through time can be evaluated and probabilities can be adjusted based on new conditions.

The presentation of this and the previous two sections has been a brief summary of mathematical models and modeling in the topical framework of the text's first 13 chapters. Mathematical techniques and applied mathematical models have been shown to be two related topics which permit sophisticated and more accurate analysis of business problems. As this discussion has established this correspondence between mathematical techniques and modeling, the next section includes a summary statement of the textbook and its overall objectives.

14.5 Mathematical Analysis in Business: The Future

The increasing use of mathematical models by business demonstrates, in part, the changing educational experiences of decision makers. As the skills of quantification and abstraction have increased among decision makers, these individuals have placed increased confidence in the applicability of models to their day-to-day business operations. And, as their understanding of mathematical models has expanded, decision makers have been more inclined to accept responsibility for the results of the particular models. Consequently, mathematical models are being employed by increasing numbers of small- and medium-sized firms in addition to the existing substantial number of large organizations using these techniques.

The increased application of mathematics to business will establish a new set of demands on future organizational decision makers. In general, future decision makers will face less computational demands but more demands related to the formulation of models and interpretation of model results. As stated in Chapter 1, the ability to create structured analytical models from primarily unstructured situations will be one of the most important skills required of future managers. Consequently, people entering the fields of business and economics must have a thorough foundation knowledge of mathematical concepts in order to develop, interpret, and communicate to others the results of mathematical models.

A firm understanding of how mathematics may be used to solve real-world problems and the ability to interpret quantitative results in the context of these real-world problems will be a skill crucial to successful future management. The need for individuals with such skills will exceed by far the demands for those able to carry out only the computational aspect of problem analysis.

This text has emphasized the relation between mathematical techniques, mathematical models, and business analysis. Although mathematical techniques necessarily must be stressed in an introductory text of this type, the overriding objective has been to give readers an appreciation of how mathematics may be used in the analysis of organizations. Hopefully, readers will benefit from this applied approach when career demands require the use of mathematical analysis.

APPENDIX: The Summation Operator

In many mathematical computations, groups of observations must be added in some stated order. Applications of this summation process are encountered throughout mathematical analysis and statistics. The following is a brief introduction to the summation process so that this method may be applied to quantitative business analysis.

In mathematics, the symbol Σ represents the summation sign. The summation sign is an instruction to add either a group of observations of a variable or a group of constants.

For example, to express the sum of four observations on the variable X, the summation sign is used as follows:

$$\sum_{i=1}^{4} X_i = X_1 + X_2 + X_3 + X_4$$

This expression is read, "the sum of X_i as i ranges from 1 to 4." The symbol i can take on only integer values and is called the *summation index*. The first observation number for the group to be added is identified below the summation sign and the last observation is stated above the symbol. The expression X_i represents the constant or variable that is to be added, referred to as the *summand*.

The notation

$$\sum_{j=5}^{11} Y_j$$

means that the fifth through eleventh observations on the variable Y are to be added:

$$\sum_{j=5}^{11} Y_j = Y_5 + Y_6 + Y_7 + Y_8 + Y_9 + Y_{10} + Y_{11}$$

Several other properties of the summation sign frequently encountered in mathematical analysis are discussed below in Rules 1 through 6.

Rule 1: For a constant C, the expression $\sum_{j=1}^{3} C_j$ means that C_1, C_2, and C_3 are to be added where all C_j are equal. Example A.1 shows this operation.

Example A.1

$$\sum_{j=1}^{3} 4 = 4 + 4 + 4 = 12$$

and

$$\sum_{i=1}^{4} 15 = 15 + 15 + 15 + 15 = 60$$

Therefore, in general, for a constant,

$$\sum_{i=1}^{n} C_i = nC_i$$

Rule 2: If a group of observations on a variable is multiplied by a constant, the expression can take either of the following forms:

$$\sum_{i=1}^{3} CX_i = C \sum_{i=1}^{3} X_i$$

Example A.2

If $C = 4$, $X_1 = 6$, $X_2 = 8$, $X_3 = 10$, and $X_4 = 12$, then

$$\sum_{i=1}^{4} CX_i = CX_1 + CX_2 + CX_3 + CX_4$$
$$= (4)(6) + (4)(8) + (4)(10) + (4)(12)$$
$$= 24 + 32 + 40 + 48 = 144$$

and, similarly,

$$C \sum_{i=1}^{4} X_i = 4(6 + 8 + 10 + 12) = 4(36) = 144$$

Rule 3: A third property of the summation operator is that it may be applied term by term to an expression. Therefore,

$$\sum_{i=1}^{n} (X_i + Y_i) = \sum_{i=1}^{n} X_i + \sum_{i=1}^{n} Y_i$$

and

$$\sum_{i=1}^{n} (X_i - Y_i) = \sum_{i=1}^{n} X_i - \sum_{i=1}^{n} Y_i$$

This property is valid regardless of the number of terms in an expression, e.g.,

$$\sum_{i=1}^{n} (X_i + Y_i - Z_i) = \sum_{i=1}^{n} X_i + \sum_{i=1}^{n} Y_i - \sum_{i=1}^{n} Z_i$$

Example A.3
If $X_1 = 5$, $X_2 = -2$, $X_3 = 6$, $X_4 = 3$ and $Y_1 = -3$, $Y_2 = 6$, $Y_3 = 11$, $Y_4 = 7$, then

$$\sum_{i=1}^{4} (X_i + Y_i) = (5 - 3) + (-2 + 6) + (6 + 11) + (3 + 7) = 33$$

and

$$\sum_{i=1}^{4} X_i + \sum_{i=1}^{4} Y_i = (5 - 2 + 6 + 3) + (-3 + 6 + 11 + 7) = 12 + 21 = 33$$

The summation of products and quotients are shown as Rules 4 and 5, respectively.

Rule 4: $\sum_{i=1}^{n} (X_i Y_i) = X_1 Y_1 + X_2 Y_2 + X_3 Y_3 + \cdots + X_n Y_n$

Example A.4
If, $X_1 = 5$, $X_2 = -2$, $X_3 = 1$ and $Y_1 = 2$, $Y_2 = 4$, $Y_3 = 6$, then

$$\sum_{i=1}^{3} (X_i Y_i) = (5)(2) + (-2)(4) + (1)(6) = 8$$

Rule 5: $\sum_{i=1}^{n} \dfrac{X_i}{Y_i} = \dfrac{X_1}{Y_1} + \dfrac{X_2}{Y_2} + \dfrac{X_3}{Y_3} + \cdots + \dfrac{X_n}{Y_n}$

Example A.5

If, $X_1 = 6$, $X_2 = 10$, $X_3 = 15$, and $Y_1 = 3$, $Y_2 = 2$, $Y_3 = 6$, then

$$\sum_{i=1}^{3} \frac{X_i}{Y_i} = \frac{6}{3} + \frac{10}{2} + \frac{15}{6} = 2 + 5 + 2.5 = 9.5$$

Observe particularly that

$$\sum \frac{X_i}{Y_i} \neq \frac{\Sigma X_i}{\Sigma Y_i}$$

For the data of Example A.5,

$$\sum \frac{X_i}{Y_i} = 9.5 \neq \frac{\Sigma X_i}{\Sigma Y_i} = \frac{31}{11} = 2.818$$

Rule 6: In certain situations, the number of observations on a variable or constant may be infinite. The summation of any infinite number of observations on X is expressed as

$$\sum_{i=1}^{\infty} X_i$$

The summation sign is used at various points in the text. It is particularly relevant to the discussions of sequences and series, the mathematics of finance (Chapter 9), and probability (Chapter 13). As this has been only a brief examination of the summation operator, additional principles and applications will be presented throughout the text where appropriate. The following problems will provide practice in applying these basic principles.

EXERCISES

1. Express in summation notation, where X and Y are variables and a represents a constant.
   a. $X_1 + X_2 + X_3$
   b. $a_1 X_1 + a_2 X_2 + a_3 X_3 + a_4 X_4 + a_5 Y_5$
   c. $X_6 + X_7 + X_8 + X_9$
   d. $X_2 + X_3 + X_4 + Y_2 + Y_3 + Y_4$
2. Write each of the following in expanded form where X, Y, and W are variables.
   a. $\sum_{i=1}^{5} W_i$ d. $\sum_{i=1}^{4} - 6 Y_i$
   b. $\sum_{i=4}^{10} X_i$ e. $\sum_{i=1}^{6} X_i Y_i$
   c. $\sum_{i=1}^{6} 7 X_i$ f. $\sum_{i=5}^{9} 8 X_i Y_i$

3. Evaluate the following, given that $X_1 = 4, X_2 = 6, X_3 = 7, X_4 = 13$, and $Y_1 = 5, Y_2 = 8, Y_3 = 11, Y_4 = 12$.

a. $\sum_{i=1}^{3} X_i$

b. $\sum_{i=1}^{4} 5X_i$

c. $\sum_{i=1}^{4} (X_i + Y_i)$

d. $\sum_{i=1}^{4} (X_i - Y_i)$

e. $\sum_{i=1}^{4} 4(X_i + Y_i)$

f. $\sum_{i=1}^{4} 7(X_i - Y_i)$

g. $\sum_{i=1}^{3} \frac{X_i}{Y_i}$

h. $\sum_{i=1}^{4} (X_i Y_i)$

TABLE I Common Logarithms

N	0	1	2	3	4	5	6	7	8	9
10	0000	0043	0086	0128	0170	0212	0253	0294	0334	0374
11	0414	0453	0492	0531	0569	0607	0645	0682	0719	0755
12	0792	0828	0864	0899	0934	0969	1004	1038	1072	1106
13	1139	1173	1206	1239	1271	1303	1335	1367	1399	1430
14	1461	1492	1523	1553	1584	1614	1644	1673	1703	1732
15	1761	1790	1818	1847	1875	1903	1931	1959	1987	2014
16	2041	2068	2095	2122	2148	2175	2201	2227	2253	2279
17	2304	2330	2355	2380	2405	2430	2455	2480	2504	2529
18	2553	2577	2601	2625	2648	2672	2695	2718	2742	2765
19	2788	2810	2833	2856	2878	2900	2923	2945	2967	2989
20	3010	3032	3054	3075	3096	3118	3139	3160	3181	3201
21	3222	3243	3263	3284	3304	3324	3345	3365	3385	3404
22	3424	3444	3464	3483	3502	3522	3541	3560	3579	3598
23	3617	3636	3655	3674	3692	3711	3729	3747	3766	3784
24	3802	3820	3838	3856	3874	3892	3909	3927	3945	3962
25	3979	3997	4014	4031	4048	4065	4082	4099	4116	4133
26	4150	4166	4183	4200	4216	4232	4249	4265	4281	4298
27	4314	4330	4346	4362	4378	4393	4409	4425	4440	4456
28	4472	4487	4502	4518	4533	4548	4564	4579	4594	4609
29	4624	4639	4654	4669	4683	4698	4713	4728	4742	4757
30	4771	4786	4800	4814	4829	4843	4857	4871	4886	4900
31	4914	4928	4942	4955	4969	4983	4997	5011	5024	5038
32	5051	5065	5079	5092	5105	5119	5132	5145	5159	5172
33	5185	5198	5211	5224	5237	5250	5263	5276	5289	5302
34	5315	5328	5340	5353	5366	5378	5391	5403	5416	5428
35	5441	5453	5465	5478	5490	5502	5514	5527	5539	5551
36	5563	5575	5587	5599	5611	5623	5635	5647	5658	5670
37	5682	5694	5705	5717	5729	5740	5752	5763	5775	5786
38	5798	5809	5821	5832	5843	5855	5866	5877	5888	5899
39	5911	5922	5933	5944	5955	5966	5977	5988	5999	6010
40	6021	6031	6042	6053	6064	6075	6085	6096	6107	6117
41	6128	6138	6149	6160	6170	6180	6191	6201	6212	6222
42	6232	6243	6253	6263	6274	6284	6294	6304	6314	6325
43	6335	6345	6355	6365	6375	6385	6395	6405	6415	6425
44	6435	6444	6454	6464	6474	6484	6493	6503	6513	6522
45	6532	6542	6551	6561	6571	6580	6590	6599	6609	6618
46	6628	6637	6646	6656	6665	6675	6684	6693	6702	6712
47	6721	6730	6739	6749	6758	6767	6776	6785	6794	6803
48	6812	6821	6830	6839	6848	6857	6866	6875	6884	6893
49	6902	6911	6920	6928	6937	6946	6955	6964	6972	6981
50	6990	6998	7007	7016	7024	7033	7042	7050	7059	7067
51	7076	7084	7093	7101	7110	7118	7126	7135	7143	7152
52	7160	7168	7177	7185	7193	7202	7210	7218	7226	7235
53	7243	7251	7259	7267	7275	7284	7292	7300	7308	7316
54	7324	7332	7340	7348	7356	7364	7372	7380	7388	7396
55	7404	7412	7419	7427	7435	7443	7451	7459	7466	7474
56	7482	7490	7497	7505	7513	7520	7528	7536	7543	7551
57	7559	7566	7574	7582	7589	7597	7604	7612	7619	7627

TABLE I Common Logarithms (*Continued*)

N	0	1	2	3	4	5	6	7	8	9
58	7634	7642	7649	7657	7664	7672	7679	7686	7694	7701
59	7709	7716	7723	7731	7738	7745	7752	7760	7767	7774
60	7782	7789	7796	7803	7810	7818	7825	7832	7839	7846
61	7853	7860	7868	7875	7882	7889	7896	7903	7910	7917
62	7924	7931	7938	7945	7952	7959	7966	7973	7980	7987
63	7993	8000	8007	8014	8021	8028	8035	8041	8048	8055
64	8062	8069	8075	8082	8089	8096	8102	8109	8116	8122
65	8129	8136	8142	8149	8156	8162	8169	8176	8182	8189
66	8195	8202	8209	8215	8222	8228	8235	8241	8248	8254
67	8261	8267	8274	8280	8287	8293	8299	8306	8312	8319
68	8325	8331	8338	8344	8351	8357	8363	8370	8376	8382
69	8388	8395	8401	8407	8414	8420	8426	8432	8439	8445
70	8451	8457	8463	8470	8476	8482	8488	8494	8500	8506
71	8513	8519	8525	8531	8537	8543	8549	8555	8561	8567
72	8573	8579	8585	8591	8597	8603	8609	8615	8621	8627
73	8633	8639	8645	8651	8657	8663	8669	8675	8681	8686
74	8692	8698	8704	8710	8716	8722	8727	8733	8739	8745
75	8751	8756	8762	8768	8774	8779	8785	8791	8797	8802
76	8808	8814	8820	8825	8831	8837	8842	8848	8854	8859
77	8865	8871	8876	8882	8887	8893	8899	8904	8910	8915
78	8921	8927	8932	8938	8943	8949	8954	8960	8965	8971
79	8976	8982	8987	8993	8998	9004	9009	9015	9020	9025
80	9031	9036	9042	9047	9053	9058	9063	9069	9074	9079
81	9085	9090	9096	9101	9106	9112	9117	9122	9128	9133
82	9138	9143	9149	9154	9159	9165	9170	9175	9180	9186
83	9191	9196	9201	9206	9212	9217	9222	9227	9232	9238
84	9243	9248	9253	9258	9263	9269	9274	9279	9284	9289
85	9294	9299	9304	9309	9315	9320	9325	9330	9335	9340
86	9345	9350	9355	9360	9365	9370	9375	9380	9385	9390
87	9395	9400	9405	9410	9415	9420	9425	9430	9435	9440
88	9445	9450	9455	9460	9465	9469	9474	9479	9484	9489
89	9494	9499	9504	9509	9513	9518	9523	9528	9533	9538
90	9542	9547	9552	9557	9562	9566	9571	9576	9581	9586
91	9590	9595	9600	9605	9609	9614	9619	9624	9628	9633
92	9638	9643	9647	9652	9657	9661	9666	9671	9675	9680
93	9685	9689	9694	9699	9703	9708	9713	9717	9722	9727
94	9731	9736	9741	9745	9750	9754	9759	9763	9768	9773
95	9777	9782	9786	9791	9795	9800	9805	9809	9814	9818
96	9823	9827	9832	9836	9841	9845	9850	9854	9859	9863
97	9868	9872	9877	9881	9886	9890	9894	9899	9903	9908
98	9912	9917	9921	9926	9930	9934	9939	9943	9948	9952
99	9956	9961	9965	9969	9974	9978	9983	9987	9991	9996

Taken by permission from Ernest Kurnow, Gerald J. Glasser, and Frederick R. Ottman, *Statistics for Business Decisions*, (Homewood, Ill., Richard D. Irwin, Inc., 1959), pp. 507–508.

TABLE II Natural Logarithms

N	0	1	2	3	4	5	6	7	8	9
				Natural Logarithms, 0 to 4.49						
0.0		4.60517	3.91202	3.50656	3.21888	2.99573	2.81341	2.65926	2.52573	2.40795
0.1	2.30259	2.20727	2.12026	2.04022	1.96611	1.89712	1.83258	1.77196	1.71480	1.66073
0.2	1.60944	1.56065	1.51413	1.46968	1.42712	1.38629	1.34707	1.30933	1.27297	1.23787
0.3	1.20397	1.17118	1.13943	1.10866	1.07881	1.04982	1.02165	.99425	.96758	.94161
0.4	0.91629	.89160	.86750	.84397	.82098	.79851	.77653	.75502	.73397	.71335
0.5	0.69315	.67334	.65393	.63488	.61619	.59784	.57982	.56212	.54473	.52763
0.6	0.51083	.49430	.47804	.46204	.44629	.43078	.41552	.40048	.38566	.37106
0.7	0.35667	.34249	.32850	.31471	.30111	.28768	.27444	.26136	.24846	.23572
0.8	0.22314	.21072	.19845	.18633	.17435	.16252	.15082	.13926	.12783	.11653
0.9	0.10563	.09431	.08338	.07257	.06188	.05129	.04082	.03046	.02020	.01005
1.0	0.0 0000	0995	1980	2956	3922	4879	5827	6766	7696	8618
1.1	9531	*0436	*1333	*2222	*3103	*3976	*4842	*5700	*6551	*7395
1.2	0.1 8232	9062	9885	*0701	*1511	*2314	*3111	*3902	*4686	*5464
1.3	0.2 6236	7003	7763	8518	9267	*0010	*0748	*1481	*2208	*2930
1.4	0.3 3647	4359	5066	5767	6464	7156	7844	8526	9204	9878
1.5	0.4 0547	1211	1871	2527	3178	3825	4469	5108	5742	6373
1.6	7000	7623	8243	8858	9470	*0078	*0682	*1282	*1879	*2473
1.7	0.5 3063	3649	4232	4812	5389	5962	6531	7098	7661	8222
1.8	8779	9333	9884	*0432	*0977	*1519	*2058	*2594	*3127	*3658
1.9	0.6 4185	4710	5233	5752	6269	6783	7294	7803	8310	8813
2.0	9315	9813	*0310	*0804	*1295	*1784	*2271	*2755	*3237	*3716
2.1	0.7 4194	4669	5142	5612	6081	6547	7011	7473	7932	8390
2.2	8846	9299	9751	*0200	*0648	*1093	*1536	*1978	*2418	*2855
2.3	0.8 3291	3725	4157	4587	5015	5442	5866	6289	6710	7129
2.4	7547	7963	8377	8789	9200	9609	*0016	*0422	*0826	*1228
2.5	0.9 1629	2028	2426	2822	3216	3609	4001	4391	4779	5166
2.6	5551	5935	6317	6698	7078	7456	7833	8208	8582	8954
2.7	9325	9695	*0063	*0430	*0796	*1160	*1523	*1885	*2245	*2604
2.8	1.0 2962	3318	3674	4028	4380	4732	5082	5431	5779	6126
2.9	6471	6815	7158	7500	7841	8181	8519	8856	9192	9527
3.0	9861	*0194	*0526	*0856	*1186	*1514	*1841	*2168	*2493	*2817
3.1	1.1 3140	3462	3783	4103	4422	4740	5057	5373	5688	6002
3.2	.6315	6627	6938	7248	7557	7865	8173	8479	8784	9089
3.3	9392	9695	9996	*0297	*0597	*0896	*1194	*1491	*1788	*2083
3.4	1.2 2378	2671	2964	3256	3547	3837	.4127	4415	4703	4990
3.5	5276	5562	5846	6130	6413	6695	6976	7257	7536	7815
3.6	8093	8371	8647	8923	9198	9473	9746	*0019	*0291	*0563
3.7	1.3 0833	1103	1372	1641	1909	2176	2442	2708	2972	3237
3.8	3500	3763	4025	4286	4547	4807	5067	5325	5584	5841
3.9	6098	6354	6609	6864	7118	7372	7624	7877	8128	8379
4.0	8629	8879	9128	9377	9624	9872	*0118	*0364	*0610	*0854
4.1	1.4 1099	1342	1585	1828	2070	2311	2552	2792	3031	3270

Appendix **459**

TABLE II Natural Logarithms (*Continued*)

N	0	1	2	3	4	5	6	7	8	9
4.2	3508	3746	3984	4220	4456	4692	4927	5161	5395	5629
4.3	5862	6094	6326	6557	6787	7018	7247	7476	7705	7933
4.4	8160	8387	8614	8840	9065	9290	9515	9739	9962	*0185

Natural Logarithms, 4.50 to 8.99

N	0	1	2	3	4	5	6	7	8	9
4.5	1.5 0408	0630	0851	1072	1293	1513	1732	1951	2170	2388
4.6	2606	2823	3039	3256	3471	3687	3902	4116	4330	4543
4.7	4756	4969	5181	5393	5604	5814	6025	6235	6444	6653
4.8	6862	7070	7277	7485	7691	7898	8104	8309	8515	8719
4.9	8924	9127	9331	9534	9737	9939	*0141	*0342	*0543	*0744
5.0	1.6 0944	1144	1343	1542	1741	1939	2137	2334	2531	2728
5.1	2924	3120	3315	3511	3705	3900	4094	4287	4481	4673
5.2	4866	5058	5250	5441	5632	5823	6013	6203	6393	6582
5.3	6771	6959	7147	7335	7523	7710	7896	8083	8269	8455
5.4	8640	8825	9010	9194	9378	9562	9745	9928	*0111	*0293
5.5	1.7 0475	0656	0838	1019	1199	1380	1560	1740	1919	2098
5.6	2277	2455	2633	2811	2988	3166	3342	3519	3695	3871
5.7	4047	4222	4397	4572	4746	4920	5094	5267	5440	5613
5.8	5786	5958	6130	6302	6473	6644	6815	6985	7156	7326
5.9	7495	7665	7834	8002	8171	8339	8507	8675	8842	9009
6.0	9176	9342	9509	9675	9840	*0006	*0171	*0336	*0500	*0665
6.1	1.8 0829	0993	1156	1319	1482	1645	1808	1970	2132	2294
6.2	2455	2616	2777	2938	3098	3258	3418	3578	3737	3896
6.3	4055	4214	4372	4530	4688	4845	5003	5160	5317	5473
6.4	5630	5786	5942	6097	6253	6408	6563	6718	6872	7026
6.5	7180	7334	7487	7641	7794	7947	8099	8251	8403	8555
6.6	8707	8858	9010	9160	9311	9462	9612	9762	9912	*0061
6.7	1.9 0211	0360	0509	0658	0806	0954	1102	1250	1398	1545
6.8	1692	1839	1986	2132	2279	2425	2571	2716	2862	3007
6.9	3152	3297	3442	3586	3730	3874	4018	4162	4305	4448
7.0	4591	4734	4876	5019	5161	5303	5445	5586	5727	5869
7.1	6009	6150	6291	6431	6571	6711	6851	6991	7130	7269
7.2	7408	7547	7685	7824	7962	8100	8238	8376	8513	8650
7.3	8787	8924	9061	9198	9334	9470	9606	9742	9877	*0013
7.4	2.0 0148	0283	0418	0553	0687	0821	0956	1089	1223	1357
7.5	1490	1624	1757	1890	2022	2155	2287	2419	2551	2683
7.6	2815	2946	3078	3209	3340	3471	3601	3732	3862	3992
7.7	4122	4252	4381	4511	4640	4769	4898	5027	5156	5284
7.8	5412	5540	5668	5796	5924	6051	6179	6306	6433	6560
7.9	6686	6813	6939	7065	7191	7317	7443	7568	7694	7819
8.0	7944	8069	8194	8318	8443	8567	8691	8815	8939	9063
8.1	9186	9310	9433	9556	9679	9802	9924	*0047	*0169	*0291
8.2	2.1 0413	0535	0657	0779	0900	1021	1142	1263	1384	1505
8.3	1626	1746	1866	1986	2106	2226	2346	2465	2585	2704
8.4	2823	2942	3061	3180	3298	3417	3535	3653	3771	3889

TABLE II Natural Logarithms (Continued)

N	0	1	2	3	4	5	6	7	8	9
8.5	4007	4124	4242	4359	4476	4593	4710	4827	4943	5060
8.6	5176	5292	5409	5524	5640	5756	5871	5987	6102	6217
8.7	6332	6447	6562	6677	6791	6905	7020	7134	7248	7361
8.8	7475	7589	7702	7816	7929	8042	8155	8267	8380	8493
8.9	8605	8717	8830	8942	9054	9165	9277	9389	9500	9611
9.0	9722	9834	9944	*0055	*0166	*0276	*0387	*0497	*0607	*0717
9.1	2.2 0827	0937	1047	1157	1266	1375	1485	1594	1703	1812
9.2	1920	2029	2138	2246	2354	2462	2570	2678	2786	2894
9.3	3001	3109	3216	3324	3431	3538	3645	3751	3858	3965
9.4	4071	4177	4284	4390	4496	4601	4707	4813	4918	5024
9.5	5129	5234	5339	5444	5549	5654	5759	5863	5968	6072
9.6	6176	6280	6384	6488	6592	6696	6799	6903	7006	7109
9.7	7213	7316	7419	7521	7624	7727	7829	7932	8034	8136
9.8	8238	8340	8442	8544	8646	8747	8849	8950	9051	9152
9.9	9253	9354	9455	9556	9657	9757	9858	9958	*0058	*0158
				Natural Logarithms, 10 to 99						
1	2.30259	39790	48491	56495	63906	70805	77259	83321	89037	94444
2	99573	*04452	*09104	*13549	*17805	*21888	*25810	*29584	*33220	*36730
3	3.40120	43399	46574	49651	52636	55535	58352	61092	63759	66356
4	68888	71357	73767	76120	78419	80666	82864	85015	87120	89182
5	91202	93183	95124	97029	98898	*00733	*02535	*04305	*06044	*07754
6	4.09434	11087	12713	14313	15888	17439	18965	20469	21951	23411
7	24850	26268	27667	29046	30407	31749	33073	34381	35671	36945
8	38203	39445	40672	41884	43082	44265	45435	46591	47734	48864
9	49981	51086	52179	53260	54329	55388	56435	57471	58497	59512
				Natural Logarithms, 100 to 349						
10	4.6 0517	1512	2497	3473	4439	5396	6344	7283	8213	9135
11	4.7 0048	0953	1850	2739	3620	4493	5359	6217	7068	7912
12	8749	9579	*0402	*1218	*2028	*2831	*3628	*4419	*5203	*5981
13	4.8 6753	7520	8280	9035	9784	*0527	*1265	*1998	*2725	*3447
14	4.9 4164	4876	5583	6284	6981	7673	8361	9043	9721	*0395
15	5.0 1064	1728	2388	3044	3695	4343	4986	5625	6260	6890
16	7517	8140	8760	9375	9987	*0595	*1199	*1799	*2396	*2990
17	5.1 3580	4166	4749	5329	5906	6479	7048	7615	8178	8739
18	9296	9850	*0401	*0949	*1494	*2036	*2575	*3111	*3644	*4175
19	5.2 4702	5227	5750	6269	6786	7300	7811	8320	8827	9330
20	9832	*0330	*0827	*1321	*1812	*2301	*2788	*3272	*3754	*4233
21	5.3 4711	5186	5659	6129	6598	7064	7528	7990	8450	8907
22	9363	9816	*0268	*0717	*1165	*1610	*2053	*2495	*2935	*3372
23	5.4 3808	4242	4674	5104	5532	5959	6383	6806	7227	7646
24	8064	8480	8894	9306	9717	*0126	*0533	*0939	*1343	*1745
25	5.5 2146	2545	2943	3339	3733	4126	4518	4908	5296	5683
26	6068	6452	6834	7215	7595	7973	8350	8725	9099	9471

Appendix **461**

TABLE II Natural Logarithms (*Continued*)

N	0	1	2	3	4	5	6	7	8	9
27	9842	*0212	*0580	*0947	*1313	*1677	*2040	*2402	*2762	*3121
28	5.6 3479	3835	4191	4545	4897	5249	5599	5948	6296	6643
29	6988	7332	7675	8017	8358	8698	9036	9373	9709	*0044
30	5.7 0378	0711	1043	1373	1703	2031	2359	2685	3010	3334
31	3657	3979	4300	4620	4939	5257	5574	5890	6205	6519
32	6832	7144	7455	7765	8074	8383	8690	8996	9301	9606
33	9909	*0212	*0513	*0814	*1114	*1413	*1711	*2008	*2305	*2600
34	5.8 2895	3188	3481	3773	4064	4354	4644	4932	5220	5507
				Natural logarithms, 350 to 79						
35	5793	6079	6363	6647	6930	7212	7493	7774	8053	8332
36	8610	8888	9164	9440	9715	9990	*0263	*0536	*0808	*1080
37	5.9 1350	1620	1889	2158	2426	2693	2959	3225	3489	3754
38	4017	4280	4542	4803	5064	5324	5584	5842	6101	6358
39	6615	6871	7126	7381	7635	7889	8141	8394	8645	8896
40	9146	9396	9645	9894	*0141	*0389	*0635	*0881	*1127	*1372
41	6.0 1616	1859	2102	2345	2587	2828	3069	3309	3548	3787
42	4025	4263	4501	4737	4973	5209	5444	5678	5912	6146
43	6379	6611	6843	7074	7304	7535	7764	7993	8222	8450
44	8677	8904	9131	9357	9582	9807	*0032	*0256	*0479	*0702
45	6.1 0925	1147	1368	1589	1810	2030	2249	2468	2687	2905
46	3123	3340	3556	3773	3988	4204	4419	4633	4847	5060
47	5273	5486	5698	5910	6121	6331	6542	6752	6961	7170
48	7379	7587	7794	8002	8208	8415	8621	8826	9032	9236
49	9441	9644	9848	*0051	*0254	*0456	*0658	*0859	*1060	*1261
50	6.2 1461	1661	1860	2059	2258	2456	2654	2851	3048	3245
51	3441	3637	3832	4028	4222	4417	4611	4804	4998	5190
52	5383	5575	5767	5958	6149	6340	6530	6720	6910	7099
53	7288	7476	7664	7852	8040	8227	8413	8600	8786	8972
54	9157	9342	9527	9711	9895	*0079	*0262	*0445	*0628	*0810
55	6.3 0992	1173	1355	1536	1716	1897	2077	2257	2436	2615
56	2794	2972	3150	3328	3505	3683	3859	4036	4212	4388
57	4564	4739	4914	5089	5263	5437	5611	5784	5957	6130
58	6303	6475	6647	6819	6990	7161	7332	7502	7673	7843
59	8012	8182	8351	8519	8688	8856	9024	9192	9359	9526
60	9693	9859	*0026	*0192	*0357	*0523	*0688	*0853	*1017	*1182
61	6.4 1346	1510	1673	1836	1999	2162	2325	2487	?	2811
62	2972	3133	3294	3455	3615	3775	3935	4095	?	4413
63	4572	4731	4889	5047	5205	5362	5520	5677	?	5990
64	6147	6303	6459	6614	6770	6925	7080	7235	7.	7543
65	7697	7851	8004	8158	8311	8464	8616	8768	8920	9072
66	9224	9375	9527	9677	9828	9979	*0129	*0279	*0429	*0578
67	6.5 0728	0877	1026	1175	1323	1471	1619	1767	1915	2062
68	2209	2356	2503	2649	2796	2942	3088	3233	3379	3524
69	3669	3814	3959	4103	4247	4391	4535	4679	4822	4965

TABLE II Natural Logarithms (*Continued*)

N	0	1	2	3	4	5	6	7	8	9
70	5108	5251	5393	5536	5678	5820	5962	6103	6244	6386
71	6526	6667	6808	6948	7088	7228	7368	7508	7627	7786
72	7925	8064	8203	8341	8479	8617	8755	8893	9030	9167
73	9304	9441	9578	9715	9851	9987	*0123	*0259	*0394	*0530
74	6.6 0665	0800	0935	1070	1204	1338	1473	1607	1740	1874
75	2007	2141	2274	2407	2539	2672	2804	2936	3068	3200
76	3332	3463	3595	3726	3857	3988	4118	4249	4379	4509
77	4639	4769	4898	5028	5157	5286	5415	5544	5673	5801
78	5929	6058	6185	6313	6441	6568	6696	6823	6950	7077
79	7203	7330	7456	7582	7708	7834	7960	8085	8211	8336
Natural logarithms, 800 to 1209										
80	8461	8586	8711	8835	8960	9084	9208	9332	9456	9580
81	9703	9827	9950	*0073	*0196	*0319	*0441	*0564	*0686	*0808
82	6.7 0930	1052	1174	1296	1417	1538	1659	1780	1901	2022
83	2143	2263	2383	2503	2623	2743	2863	2982	3102	3221
84	3340	3459	3578	3697	3815	3934	4052	4170	4288	4406
85	4524	4641	4759	4876	4993	5110	5227	5344	5460	5577
86	5693	5809	5926	6041	6157	6273	6388	6504	6619	6734
87	6849	6964	7079	7194	7308	7422	7537	7651	7765	7878
88	7992	8106	8219	8333	8446	8559	8672	8784	8897	9010
89	9122	9234	9347	9459	9571	9682	9794	9906	*0017	*0128
90	6.8 0239	0351	0461	0572	0683	0793	0904	1014	1124	1235
91	1344	1454	1564	1674	1783	1892	2002	2111	2220	2329
92	2437	2546	2655	2763	2871	2979	3087	3195	3303	3411
93	3518	3626	3733	3841	3948	4055	4162	4268	4375	4482
94	4588	4694	4801	4907	5013	5118	5224	5330	5435	5541
95	5646	5751	5857	5961	6066	6171	6276	6380	6485	6589
96	6693	6797	6901	7005	7109	7213	7316	7420	7523	7626
97	7730	7833	7936	8038	8141	8244	8346	8449	8551	8653
98	8755	8857	8959	9061	9163	9264	9366	9467	9568	9669
99	9770	9871	9972	*0073	*0174	*0274	*0375	*0475	*0575	*0675
100	6.9 0776	0875	0975	1075	1175	1274	1374	1473	1572	1672
101	1771	1870	1968	2067	2166	2264	2363	2461	2560	2658
102	2756	2854	2952	3049	3147	3245	3342	3440	3537	3634
103	3731	3828	3925	4022	4119	4216	4312	4409	4505	4601
104	4698	4794	4890	4986	5081	5177	5273	5368	5464	5559
105	5655	5750	5845	5940	6035	6130	6224	6319	6414	6508
106	6602	6697	6791	6885	6979	7073	7167	7261	7354	7448
107	7541	7635	7728	7821	7915	8008	8101	8193	8286	8379
108	8472	8564	8657	8749	8841	8934	9026	9118	9210	9302
109	9393	9485	9577	9668	9760	9851	9942	*0033	*0125	*0216

TABLE II Natural Logarithms (*Continued*)

N	0	1	2	3	4	5	6	7	8	9
110	7.0 0307	0397	0488	0579	0670	0760	0851	0941	1031	1121
111	1212	1302	1392	1481	1571	1661	1751	1840	1930	2019
112	2108	2198	2287	2376	2465	2554	2643	2731	2820	2909
113	2997	3086	3174	3262	3351	3439	3527	3615	3703	3791
114	3878	3966	4054	4141	4229	4316	4403	4491	4578	4665
115	4752	4839	4925	5012	5099	5186	5272	5359	5445	5531
116	5618	5704	5790	5876	5962	6048	6133	6219	6305	6390
117	6476	6561	6647	6732	6817	6902	6987	7072	7157	7242
118	7327	7412	7496	7581	7665	7750	7834	7918	8003	8087
119	8171	8255	8339	8423	8506	8590	8674	8757	8841	8924
120	9008	9091	9174	9257	9340	9423	9506	9589	9672	9755

Notes for Table II:

1. For N between 0.01 and 0.99, insert a minus sign before all table entries.
2. The * notation before a table entry indicates that the natural logarithm includes the *next* listed first two digits.

Taken by permission from Earl K. Bowen, *Mathematics with Applications in Management and Economics*, 5th ed. (Homewood, Ill., Richard D. Irwin, Inc., 1980), pp. 945–949.

TABLE III Values of e^x and e^{-x}

x	e^x	e^{-x}	x	e^x	e^{-x}	x	e^x	e^{-x}
0.00	1.0000	1.0000	0.49	1.6323	0.6126	0.98	2.6645	0.3753
0.01	1.0101	0.9900	0.50	1.6487	0.6065	0.99	2.6912	0.3715
0.02	1.0202	0.9801	0.51	1.6653	0.6004	1.00	2.7183	0.3678
0.03	1.0305	0.9704	0.52	1.6820	0.5945	1.1	3.0042	0.3329
0.04	1.0408	0.9607	0.53	1.6989	0.5886	1.2	3.3201	0.3012
0.05	1.0513	0.9512	0.54	1.7160	0.5827	1.3	3.6693	0.2725
0.06	1.0618	0.9417	0.55	1.7333	0.5769	1.4	4.0552	0.2466
0.07	1.0725	0.9323	0.56	1.7507	0.5712	1.5	4.4817	0.2231
0.08	1.0833	0.9231	0.57	1.7683	0.5655	1.6	4.9530	0.2019
0.09	1.0942	0.9139	0.58	1.7860	0.5598	1.7	5.4739	0.1827
0.10	1.1052	0.9048	0.59	1.8040	0.5543	1.8	6.0496	0.1653
0.11	1.1163	0.8958	0.60	1.8221	0.5488	1.9	6.6859	0.1496
0.12	1.1275	0.8869	0.61	1.8404	0.5433	2.0	7.3891	0.1353
0.13	1.1388	0.8780	0.62	1.8589	0.5379	2.1	8.1662	0.1225
0.14	1.1503	0.8693	0.63	1.8776	0.5325	2.2	9.0250	0.1108
0.15	1.1618	0.8607	0.64	1.8965	0.5272	2.3	9.9742	0.1003
0.16	1.1735	0.8521	0.65	1.9155	0.5220	2.4	11.023	0.0907
0.17	1.1853	0.8436	0.66	1.9348	0.5168	2.5	12.182	0.0821
0.18	1.1972	0.8352	0.67	1.9542	0.5117	2.6	13.464	0.0743
0.19	1.2092	0.8269	0.68	1.9739	0.5066	2.7	14.880	0.0672
0.20	1.2214	0.8187	0.69	1.9937	0.5015	2.8	16.445	0.0608
0.21	1.2337	0.8105	0.70	2.0138	0.4965	2.9	18.174	0.0550
0.22	1.2461	0.8025	0.71	2.0340	0.4916	3.0	20.086	0.0498
0.23	1.2586	0.7945	0.72	2.0544	0.4867	3.1	22.198	0.0450
0.24	1.2712	0.7866	0.73	2.0751	0.4819	3.2	24.533	0.0408
0.25	1.2840	0.7788	0.74	2.0959	0.4771	3.3	27.113	0.0369
0.26	1.2969	0.7710	0.75	2.1170	0.4723	3.4	29.964	0.0334
0.27	1.3100	0.7633	0.76	2.1383	0.4676	3.5	33.115	0.0302
0.28	1.3231	0.7557	0.77	2.1598	0.4630	3.6	36.598	0.0273
0.29	1.3364	0.7482	0.78	2.1815	0.4584	3.7	40.447	0.0247
0.30	1.3499	0.7408	0.79	2.2034	0.4538	3.8	44.701	0.0224
0.31	1.3634	0.7334	0.80	2.2255	0.4493	3.9	49.402	0.0202
0.32	1.3771	0.7261	0.81	2.2479	0.4448	4.0	54.598	0.0183
0.33	1.3910	0.7189	0.82	2.2705	0.4404	4.1	60.340	0.0166
0.34	1.4049	0.7117	0.83	2.2933	0.4360	4.2	66.686	0.0150
0.35	1.4191	0.7046	0.84	2.3164	0.4317	4.3	73.700	0.0136
0.36	1.4333	0.6976	0.85	2.3396	0.4274	4.4	81.451	0.0123
0.37	1.4477	0.6907	0.86	2.3632	0.4231	4.5	90.017	0.0111
0.38	1.4623	0.6838	0.87	2.3869	0.4189	4.6	99.484	0.0101
0.39	1.4770	0.6770	0.88	2.4109	0.4147	4.7	109.55	0.0091
0.40	1.4918	0.6703	0.89	2.4351	0.4106	4.8	121.51	0.0082
0.41	1.5068	0.6636	0.90	2.4596	0.4065	4.9	134.29	0.0074
0.42	1.5220	0.6570	0.91	2.4843	0.4025	5	148.41	0.0067
0.43	1.5373	0.6505	0.92	2.5093	0.3985	6	403.43	0.0025
0.44	1.5527	0.6440	0.93	2.5345	0.3945	7	1096.6	0.0009
0.45	1.5683	0.6376	0.94	2.5600	0.3906	8	2981.0	0.0003
0.46	1.5841	0.6312	0.95	2.5857	0.3867	9	8103.1	0.0001
0.47	1.6000	0.6250	0.96	2.6117	0.3828	10	22026.0	0.00005
0.48	1.6161	0.6187	0.97	2.6379	0.3790			

Appendix **465**

TABLE IV   Future Value of $1, $(1 + i)^n$ Compound int $S_n = P \cdot (1+i)^n$

n	1%	2%	3%	4%
1	1.01000	1.02000	1.03000	1.04000
2	1.02010	1.04040	1.06090	1.08160
3	1.03030	1.06121	1.09273	1.12486
4	1.04060	1.08243	1.12551	1.16986
5	1.05101	1.10408	1.15927	1.21665
6	1.06152	1.12616	1.19405	1.26532
7	1.07214	1.14869	1.22987	1.31593
8	1.08286	1.17166	1.26677	1.36857
9	1.09369	1.19509	1.30477	1.42331
10	1.10462	1.21899	1.34392	1.48024
11	1.11567	1.24337	1.38423	1.53945
12	1.12683	1.26824	1.42576	1.60103
13	1.13809	1.29361	1.46853	1.66507
14	1.14947	1.31948	1.51259	1.73168
15	1.16097	1.34587	1.55797	1.80094
16	1.17258	1.37279	1.60471	1.87298
17	1.18430	1.40024	1.65285	1.94790
18	1.19615	1.42825	1.70243	2.02582
19	1.20811	1.45681	1.75351	2.10685
20	1.22019	1.48595	1.80611	2.19112
21	1.23239	1.51567	1.86029	2.27877
22	1.24472	1.54598	1.91610	2.36992
23	1.25716	1.57690	1.97359	2.46472
24	1.26973	1.60844	2.03279	2.56330
25	1.28243	1.64061	2.09378	2.66584
26	1.29526	1.67342	2.15659	2.77247
27	1.30821	1.70689	2.22129	2.88337
28	1.32129	1.74102	2.28793	2.99870
29	1.33450	1.77584	2.35657	3.11865
30	1.34785	1.81136	2.42726	3.24340
31	1.36133	1.84759	2.50008	3.37313
32	1.37494	1.88454	2.57508	3.50806
33	1.38869	1.92223	2.65234	3.64838
34	1.40258	1.96068	2.73191	3.79432
35	1.41660	1.99989	2.81386	3.94609
36	1.43077	2.03989	2.89828	4.10393
37	1.44508	2.08069	2.98523	4.26809
38	1.45953	2.12230	3.07478	4.43881
39	1.47412	2.16474	3.16703	4.61637
40	1.48886	2.20804	3.26204	4.80102

TABLE IV Future Value of $1, $(1 + i)^n$ (Continued)

n	5%	6%	7%	8%
1	1.05000	1.06000	1.07000	1.08000
2	1.10250	1.12360	1.14490	1.16640
3	1.15762	1.19102	1.22504	1.25971
4	1.21551	1.26248	1.31080	1.36049
5	1.27628	1.33823	1.40255	1.46933
6	1.34010	1.41852	1.50073	1.58687
7	1.40710	1.50363	1.60578	1.71382
8	1.47746	1.59385	1.71819	1.85093
9	1.55133	1.68975	1.83846	1.99900
10	1.62889	1.79085	1.96715	2.15892
11	1.71034	1.89830	2.10485	2.33164
12	1.79586	2.01220	2.25219	2.51817
13	1.88565	2.13293	2.40985	2.71962
14	1.97993	2.26090	2.57853	2.93719
15	2.07893	2.39656	2.75903	3.17217
16	2.18287	2.54035	2.95216	3.42594
17	2.29202	2.69277	3.15882	3.70002
18	2.40662	2.85434	3.37993	3.99602
19	2.52695	3.02560	3.61653	4.31570
20	2.65330	3.20714	3.86968	4.66096
21	2.78596	3.39956	4.14056	5.03383
22	2.92526	3.60354	4.43040	5.43654
23	3.07152	3.81975	4.74053	5.87146
24	3.22510	4.04893	5.07237	6.34118
25	3.38635	4.29187	5.42743	6.84848
26	3.55567	4.54938	5.80735	7.39635
27	3.73346	4.82235	6.21387	7.98806
28	3.92013	5.11169	6.64884	8.62711
29	4.11614	5.41839	7.11426	9.31727
30	4.32194	5.74349	7.61226	10.06266
31	4.53804	6.08810	8.14511	10.86767
32	4.76494	6.45339	8.71527	11.73708
33	5.00319	6.84059	9.32534	12.67605
34	5.25335	7.25103	9.97811	13.69013
35	5.51602	7.68609	10.67658	14.78534
36	5.79182	8.14725	11.42394	15.96817
37	6.08141	8.63608	12.22362	17.24563
38	6.38548	9.15425	13.07927	18.62528
39	6.70475	9.70351	13.99482	20.11530
40	7.03999	10.28572	14.97446	21.72452

Taken by permission from Earl K. Bowen, *Mathematics with Applications in Management and Economics*, 5th ed. (Homewood, Ill., Richard D. Irwin, Inc., 1980), pp. 931–932.

Appendix **467**

TABLE V Present Value of $1, $(1 + i)^{-n}$ Compound amt $P = S_n(1+i)^{-n}$

n	1%	2%	3%	4%
1	0.990099	0.980392	0.970874	0.961538
2	0.980296	0.961169	0.942596	0.924556
3	0.970590	0.942322	0.915142	0.888996
4	0.960980	0.923845	0.888487	0.854804
5	0.951466	0.905731	0.862609	0.821927
6	0.942045	0.887971	0.837484	0.790315
7	0.932718	0.870560	0.831092	0.759918
8	0.923483	0.853490	0.789409	0.730690
9	0.914340	0.836755	0.766417	0.702587
10	0.905287	0.820348	0.744094	0.675564
11	0.896324	0.804263	0.722421	0.649581
12	0.887449	0.788493	0.701380	0.624597
13	0.878663	0.773033	0.680951	0.600574
14	0.869963	0.757875	0.661118	0.577475
15	0.861349	0.743015	0.641862	0.555265
16	0.852821	0.728446	0.623167	0.533908
17	0.844377	0.714163	0.605016	0.513373
18	0.836017	0.700159	0.587395	0.493628
19	0.827740	0.686431	0.570286	0.474642
20	0.819544	0.672971	0.553676	0.456387
21	0.811430	0.659776	0.537549	0.438834
22	0.803396	0.646839	0.521893	0.421955
23	0.795442	0.634156	0.506692	0.405726
24	0.787566	0.621721	0.491934	0.390121
25	0.779768	0.609531	0.477606	0.375117
26	0.772048	0.597579	0.463695	0.360689
27	0.764404	0.585862	0.450189	0.346817
28	0.756836	0.574375	0.437077	0.333477
29	0.749342	0.563112	0.424346	0.320651
30	0.741923	0.552071	0.411987	0.308319
31	0.734577	0.541246	0.399987	0.296460
32	0.727304	0.530633	0.388337	0.285058
33	0.720103	0.520229	0.377026	0.274094
34	0.712973	0.510028	0.366045	0.263552
35	0.705914	0.500028	0.355383	0.253415
36	0.698925	0.490223	0.345032	0.243669
37	0.692005	0.480611	0.334983	0.234297
38	0.685153	0.471187	0.325226	0.225285
39	0.678370	0.461948	0.315754	0.216621
40	0.671653	0.452890	0.306557	0.208289

TABLE V Present Value of $1, $(1 + i)^{-n}$ *(Continued)*

n	1%	2%	3%	4%
1	0.952381	0.943396	0.934579	0.925926
2	0.907029	0.889996	0.873439	0.857339
3	0.863838	0.839619	0.816298	0.793832
4	0.822702	0.792094	0.762895	0.735030
5	0.783526	0.747258	0.712986	0.680583
6	0.746215	0.704961	0.666342	0.630170
7	0.710681	0.665057	0.622750	0.583490
8	0.676839	0.627412	0.582009	0.540269
9	0.644609	0.591898	0.543934	0.500249
10	0.613913	0.558395	0.508349	0.463193
11	0.584679	0.526788	0.475093	0.428883
12	0.556837	0.496969	0.444012	0.397114
13	0.530321	0.468839	0.414964	0.367698
14	0.505068	0.442301	0.387817	0.340461
15	0.481017	0.417265	0.362446	0.315242
16	0.458112	0.393646	0.338735	0.291890
17	0.436297	0.371364	0.316574	0.270269
18	0.415521	0.350344	0.295864	0.250249
19	0.395734	0.330513	0.276508	0.231712
20	0.376889	0.311805	0.258419	0.214548
21	0.358942	0.294155	0.241513	0.198656
22	0.341850	0.277505	0.225713	0.183941
23	0.325571	0.261797	0.210947	0.170315
24	0.310068	0.246979	0.197147	0.157699
25	0.295303	0.232999	0.184249	0.146018
26	0.281241	0.219810	0.172195	0.135202
27	0.267848	0.207368	0.160930	0.125187
28	0.255094	0.195630	0.150402	0.115914
29	0.242946	0.184557	0.140563	0.107328
30	0.231377	0.174110	0.131367	0.099377
31	0.220359	0.164255	0.122773	0.092016
32	0.209866	0.154957	0.114741	0.085200
33	0.199873	0.146186	0.107235	0.078889
34	0.190355	0.137912	0.100219	0.073045
35	0.181290	0.130105	0.093663	0.067635
36	0.172657	0.122741	0.087535	0.062625
37	0.164436	0.115793	0.081809	0.057986
38	0.156605	0.109239	0.076457	0.053690
39	0.149148	0.103056	0.071455	0.049713
40	0.142046	0.097222	0.066780	0.046031

Taken by permission from Earl K. Bowen, *Mathematics with Applications in Management and Economics*, 5th ed. (Homewood, Ill., Richard D. Irwin, Inc., 1980), pp. 933–934.

TABLE VI Future Value of $1 per Period Payment, $[(1 + i)^n - 1]/i$

n	1%	2%	3%	4%
1	1.00000	1.00000	1.00000	1.00000
2	2.01000	2.02000	2.03000	2.04000
3	3.03010	3.06040	3.09090	3.12160
4	4.06040	4.12161	4.18363	4.24646
5	5.10101	5.20404	5.30914	5.41632
6	6.15202	6.30812	6.46841	6.63298
7	7.21354	7.43428	7.66246	7.89829
8	8.28567	8.58297	8.89234	9.21423
9	9.36853	9.75463	10.15911	10.58280
10	10.46221	10.94972	11.46388	12.00611
11	11.56683	12.16872	12.80780	13.48635
12	12.68250	13.41209	14.19203	15.02581
13	13.80933	14.68033	15.61779	16.62684
14	14.94742	15.97394	17.08632	18.29191
15	16.09690	17.29342	18.59891	20.02359
16	17.25786	18.63929	20.15688	21.82453
17	18.43044	20.01207	21.76159	23.69751
18	19.61475	21.41231	23.41444	25.64541
19	20.81090	22.84056	25.11687	27.67123
20	22.01900	24.29737	26.87037	29.77808
21	23.23919	25.78332	28.67649	31.96920
22	24.47159	27.29898	30.53678	34.24797
23	25.71630	28.84496	32.45288	36.61789
24	26.97346	30.42186	34.42647	39.08260
25	28.24320	32.03030	36.45926	41.64591
26	29.52563	33.67091	38.55304	44.31174
27	30.82089	35.34432	40.70963	47.08421
28	32.12910	37.05121	42.93092	49.96758
29	33.45039	38.79223	45.21885	52.96629
30	34.78489	40.56808	47.57542	56.08494
31	36.13274	42.37944	50.00268	59.32834
32	37.49407	44.22703	52.50276	62.70147
33	38.86901	46.11157	55.07784	66.20953
34	40.25770	48.03380	57.73018	69.85791
35	41.66028	49.99448	60.46208	73.65222
36	43.07688	51.99437	63.27594	77.59831
37	44.50765	54.03425	66.17422	81.70225
38	45.95272	56.11494	69.15945	85.97034
39	47.41225	58.23724	72.23423	90.40915
40	48.88637	60.40198	75.40126	95.02552

TABLE VI Future Value of $1 per Period Payment, $[(1 + i)^n - 1]/i$ (Continued)

n	1%	2%	3%	4%
1	1.00000	1.00000	1.00000	1.00000
2	2.05000	2.06000	2.07000	2.08000
3	3.15250	3.18360	3.21490	3.24640
4	4.31012	4.37462	4.43994	4.50611
5	5.52563	5.63709	5.75074	5.86660
6	6.80191	6.97532	7.15329	7.33593
7	8.14201	8.39384	8.65402	8.92280
8	9.54911	9.89747	10.25980	10.63663
9	11.02656	11.49132	11.97799	12.48756
10	12.57789	13.18079	13.81645	14.48656
11	14.20679	14.97164	15.78360	16.64549
12	15.91713	16.86994	17.88845	18.97713
13	17.71298	18.88214	20.14064	21.49530
14	19.59863	21.01507	22.55049	24.21492
15	21.57856	23.27597	25.12902	27.15211
16	23.65749	25.67253	27.88805	30.32428
17	25.84037	28.21288	30.84022	33.75023
18	28.13238	30.90565	33.99903	37.45024
19	30.53900	33.75999	37.37896	41.44626
20	33.06595	36.78559	40.99549	45.76196
21	35.71925	39.99273	44.86518	50.42292
22	38.50521	43.39229	49.00574	55.45676
23	41.43048	46.99583	53.43614	60.89330
24	44.50200	50.81558	58.17667	66.76476
25	47.72710	54.86451	63.24904	73.10594
26	51.11345	59.15638	68.67647	79.95442
27	54.66913	63.70577	74.48382	87.35077
28	58.40258	68.52811	80.69769	95.33883
29	62.32271	73.63980	87.34653	103.96594
30	66.43885	79.05819	94.46079	113.28321
31	70.76079	84.80168	102.07304	123.34587
32	75.29883	90.88978	110.21815	134.21354
33	80.06377	97.34316	118.93343	145.95062
34	85.06696	104.18375	128.25876	158.62667
35	90.32031	111.43478	138.23688	172.31680
36	95.83632	119.12087	148.91346	187.10215
37	101.62814	127.26812	160.33740	203.07032
38	107.70955	135.90421	172.56102	220.31595
39	114.09502	145.05846	185.64029	238.94122
40	120.79977	154.76197	199.63511	259.05652

Taken by permission from Earl K. Bowen, *Mathematics with Applications in Management and Economics*, 5th ed. (Homewood, Ill., Richard D. Irwin, Inc., 1980), pp. 935–936.

TABLE VII Present Value of $1 per Period, $[1 - (1 + i)^{-n}]/i$

n	1%	2%	3%	4%
1	0.99010	0.98039	0.97087	0.96154
2	1.97040	1.94156	1.91347	1.88609
3	2.94099	2.88388	2.82861	2.77509
4	3.90197	3.80773	3.71710	3.62990
5	4.85343	4.71346	4.57971	4.45182
6	5.79548	5.60143	5.41719	5.24214
7	6.72819	6.47199	6.23028	6.00205
8	7.65168	7.32548	7.01969	6.73274
9	8.56602	8.16224	7.78611	7.43533
10	9.47130	8.98259	8.53020	8.11090
11	10.36763	9.78685	9.25262	8.76048
12	11.25508	10.57534	9.95400	9.38507
13	12.13374	11.34837	10.63496	9.98565
14	13.00370	12.10625	11.29607	10.56312
15	13.86505	12.84926	11.93794	11.11839
16	14.71787	13.57771	12.56110	11.65230
17	15.56225	14.29187	13.16612	12.16567
18	16.39827	14.99203	13.75351	12.65930
19	17.22601	15.67846	14.32380	13.13394
20	18.04555	16.35143	14.87747	13.59033
21	18.85698	17.01121	15.41502	14.02916
22	19.66038	17.65805	15.93692	14.45112
23	20.45582	18.29220	16.44361	14.85684
24	21.24339	18.91393	16.93554	15.24696
25	22.02316	19.52346	17.41315	15.62208
26	22.79520	20.12104	17.87684	15.98277
27	23.55961	20.70690	18.32703	16.32959
28	24.31644	21.28127	18.76411	16.66306
29	25.06579	21.84438	19.18845	16.98371
30	25.80771	22.39646	19.60044	17.29203
31	26.54229	22.93770	20.00043	17.58849
32	27.26959	23.46833	20.38877	17.87355
33	27.98969	23.98856	20.76579	18.14765
34	28.70267	24.49859	21.13184	18.41120
35	29.40858	24.99862	21.48722	18.66461
36	30.10751	25.48884	21.83225	18.90828
37	30.79951	25.96945	22.16724	19.14258
38	31.48466	26.44064	22.49246	19.36786
39	32.16303	26.90259	22.80822	19.58448
40	32.83469	27.35548	23.11477	19.79277

TABLE VII Present Value of $1 per Period,
$[1 - (1 + i)^{-n}]/i$ *(Continued)*

n	1%	2%	3%	4%
1	0.95238	0.94340	0.93458	0.92593
2	1.85941	1.83339	1.80802	1.78326
3	2.72325	2.67301	2.62432	2.57710
4	3.54595	3.46511	3.38721	3.31213
5	4.32948	4.21236	4.10020	3.99271
6	5.07569	4.91732	4.76654	4.62288
7	5.78637	5.58238	5.38929	5.20637
8	6.46321	6.20979	5.97130	5.74664
9	7.10782	6.80169	6.51523	6.24689
10	7.72173	7.36009	7.02358	6.71008
11	8.30641	7.88687	7.49867	7.13896
12	8.86325	7.38384	7.94269	7.53608
13	9.39357	8.85268	8.35765	7.90378
14	9.89864	9.29498	8.74547	8.24424
15	10.37966	9.71225	9.10791	8.55948
16	10.83777	10.10590	9.44665	8.85137
17	11.27407	10.47726	9.76322	9.12164
18	11.68959	10.82760	10.05909	9.37189
19	12.08532	11.15812	10.33560	9.60360
20	12.46221	11.46992	10.59401	9.81815
21	12.82115	11.76408	10.83553	10.01680
22	13.16300	12.04158	11.06124	10.20074
23	13.48857	12.30338	11.27219	10.37106
24	13.79864	12.55036	11.46933	10.52876
25	14.09394	12.78336	11.65358	10.67478
26	14.37519	13.00317	11.82578	10.80998
27	14.64303	13.21053	11.98671	10.93516
28	14.89813	13.40616	12.13711	11.05108
29	15.14107	13.59072	12.27767	11.15841
30	15.37245	13.76483	12.40904	11.25778
31	15.59281	13.92909	12.53181	11.34980
32	15.80268	14.08404	12.64656	11.43500
33	16.00255	14.23023	12.75379	11.51389
34	16.19290	14.36814	12.85401	11.58693
35	16.37419	14.49825	12.94767	11.65457
36	16.54685	14.62099	13.03521	11.71719
37	16.71129	14.73678	13.11702	11.77518
38	16.86789	14.84602	13.19347	11.82887
39	17.01704	14.94907	13.26593	11.87858
40	17.15909	15.04630	13.33171	11.92461

Taken by permission from Earl K. Bowen, *Mathematics with Applications in Management and Economics*, 5th ed. (Homewood, Ill., Richard D. Irwin, Inc., 1980), pp. 937–938.

TABLE VIII Per Period Equivalent of $1 Present Value, $i/[1 - (1 + i)^{-n}]$

n	1%	2%	3%	4%
1	1.010000	1.020000	1.030000	1.040000
2	0.507512	0.515050	0.522611	0.530196
3	0.340022	0.346755	0.353530	0.360349
4	0.256281	0.262624	0.269027	0.275490
5	0.206040	0.212158	0.218355	0.224627
6	0.172548	0.178526	0.184598	0.190762
7	0.148628	0.154512	0.160506	0.166610
8	0.130690	0.136510	0.142456	0.148528
9	0.116740	0.122515	0.128434	0.134493
10	0.105582	0.111327	0.117231	0.123291
11	0.096454	0.102178	0.108077	0.114149
12	0.088848	0.094560	0.100462	0.106522
13	0.082415	0.088118	0.094030	0.100144
14	0.076901	0.082602	0.088526	0.094669
15	0.072124	0.077825	0.083767	0.089941
16	0.067945	0.073650	0.079611	0.085820
17	0.064258	0.069970	0.075953	0.082199
18	0.060982	0.066702	0.072709	0.078993
19	0.058052	0.063782	0.069814	0.076139
20	0.055415	0.061157	0.067216	0.073582
21	0.053031	0.058785	0.064872	0.071280
22	0.050864	0.056631	0.062747	0.069199
23	0.048886	0.054668	0.060814	0.067309
24	0.047073	0.052871	0.059047	0.065587
25	0.045407	0.051220	0.057428	0.064012
26	0.043869	0.049699	0.055938	0.062567
27	0.042446	0.048293	0.054564	0.061239
28	0.041124	0.046990	0.053293	0.060013
29	0.039895	0.045778	0.052115	0.058880
30	0.038748	0.044650	0.051019	0.057830
31	0.037676	0.043596	0.049999	0.056855
32	0.036671	0.042611	0.049047	0.055949
33	0.035727	0.041687	0.048156	0.055104
34	0.034840	0.040819	0.047322	0.054315
35	0.034004	0.040002	0.046539	0.053577
36	0.033214	0.039233	0.045804	0.052887
37	0.032468	0.038507	0.045112	0.052240
38	0.031761	0.037821	0.044459	0.051632
39	0.031092	0.037171	0.043844	0.051061
40	0.030456	0.036556	0.043262	0.050523

TABLE VIII Per Period Equivalent of $1 Present Value, $i/[1 - (1 + i)^{-n}]$ (Continued)

n	5%	6%	7%	8%
1	1.050000	1.060000	1.070000	1.080000
2	0.537805	0.545437	0.553092	0.560769
3	0.367209	0.374110	0.381052	0.388034
4	0.282012	0.288591	0.295228	0.301921
5	0.230975	0.237396	0.243891	0.250456
6	0.197017	0.203363	0.209796	0.216315
7	0.172820	0.179135	0.185553	0.192072
8	0.154722	0.161036	0.167468	0.174015
9	0.140690	0.147022	0.153486	0.161080
10	0.129505	0.135868	0.142378	0.149029
11	0.120389	0.126793	0.133357	0.140076
12	0.112825	0.119277	0.125902	0.132695
13	0.106456	0.112960	0.119651	0.126522
14	0.101024	0.107585	0.114345	0.121297
15	0.096342	0.102963	0.109795	0.116830
16	0.092270	0.098952	0.105858	0.112977
17	0.088699	0.095445	0.102425	0.109629
18	0.085546	0.092357	0.099412	0.106702
19	0.082745	0.089621	0.096753	0.104128
20	0.080243	0.087185	0.094393	0.101852
21	0.077996	0.085005	0.092289	0.099832
22	0.075971	0.083046	0.090406	0.098032
23	0.074137	0.081278	0.088714	0.096422
24	0.072471	0.079679	0.087189	0.094978
25	0.070952	0.078227	0.085811	0.093679
26	0.069564	0.076904	0.084561	0.092507
27	0.068292	0.075697	0.083426	0.091448
28	0.067123	0.074593	0.082392	0.090489
29	0.066046	0.073580	0.081449	0.089619
30	0.065051	0.072649	0.080586	0.088827
31	0.064132	0.071792	0.079797	0.088107
32	0.063280	0.071002	0.079073	0.087451
33	0.062490	0.070273	0.078408	0.086852
34	0.061755	0.069598	0.077797	0.086304
35	0.061072	0.068974	0.077234	0.085803
36	0.060434	0.068395	0.076715	0.085345
37	0.059840	0.067857	0.076237	0.084924
38	0.059284	0.067358	0.075795	0.084539
39	0.058765	0.066894	0.075387	0.084185
40	0.058278	0.066462	0.075009	0.083860

Taken by permission from Earl K. Bowen, *Mathematics with Applications in Management and Economics*, 5th ed. (Homewood, Ill., Richard D. Irwin, Inc., 1980), pp. 939–940.

Appendix **475**

TABLE IX Table of Integrals

1. $\int 0 \, dX = K$
2. $\int K \, dX = KX + c$
3. $\int X^n \, dX = \dfrac{X^{n+1}}{n+1} + c \quad \text{if } n \neq -1$
4. $\int X^{-1} \, dX = \ln X + c$
5. $\int K f(X) \, dX = K \int f(X) \, dX$
6. $\int [f(X) \pm g(X)] \, dX = \int f(X) \, dX \pm \int g(X) \, dX$
7. $\int (mX + b)^n \, dX = \dfrac{(mX + b)^{n+1}}{m(n+1)} + c \quad \text{if } n \neq -1$
8. $\int (mX + b)^{-1} \, dX = \dfrac{\ln(mX + b)}{m} + c$
9. $\int e^X \, dX = e^X + c$
10. $\int e^{mX+b} \, dX = \dfrac{e^{mX+b}}{m} + c$
11. $\int a^X \, dX = \dfrac{a^X}{\ln a} + c \quad \text{for } a \neq +1$
12. $\int a^{mX+b} \, dX = \dfrac{a^{mX+b}}{m \ln a} + c \quad \text{for } a \neq +1$
13. $\int \ln X \, dX = X(\ln X - 1) + c$
14. $\int \ln(mX + b) \, dX = \dfrac{(mX + b)[\ln(mX + b) - 1]}{m} + c$
15. $\int \dfrac{a}{X} \, dX = a \ln|X| + c \quad \text{for } a \neq 0$
16. $\int X^n \ln X \, dX = X^{n+1} \left[\dfrac{\ln X}{n+1} - \dfrac{1}{(n+1)^2} \right] + c \quad \text{for } n \neq -1$
17. $\int X e^{mX+b} \, dX = \dfrac{e^{mX+b}(mX - 1) + c}{m^2}$
18. $\int X a^{mX+b} \, dX = \dfrac{X a^{mX+b}}{m(\ln a)} - \dfrac{a^{mX+b}}{(m \ln a)^2} + c$
19. $\int X e^{mX^2+b} \, dX = \dfrac{e^{mX^2+b}}{2m} + c$
20. $\int \dfrac{X \, dX}{mX + b} = \dfrac{X}{m} - \dfrac{b}{m^2} \ln(mX + b) + c$
21. $\int \dfrac{X \, dX}{(mX + b)^2} = \dfrac{b}{m^2(mX + b)} + \dfrac{\ln(mX + b)}{m^2} + c$
22. $\int \dfrac{dX}{X(mX + b)} = \dfrac{1}{b} \ln \left(\dfrac{X}{mX + b} \right) + c$
23. $\int \dfrac{(\ln X)^n}{X} \, dX = \dfrac{1}{n+1} (\ln X)^{n+1} + c$
24. $\int e^{-X} \, dX = -e^{-X} + c$

TABLE X Standard Normal Distribution Areas

z	.00	.01	.02	.03	.04	.05	.06	.07	.08	.09
0.0	.0000	.0040	.0080	.0120	.0160	.0199	.0239	.0279	.0319	.0359
0.1	.0398	.0438	.0478	.0517	.0557	.0596	.0636	.0675	.0714	.0753
0.2	.0793	.0832	.0871	.0910	.0948	.0987	.1026	.1064	.1103	.1141
0.3	.1179	.1217	.1255	.1293	.1331	.1368	.1406	.1443	.1480	.1517
0.4	.1554	.1591	.1628	.1664	.1700	.1736	.1772	.1808	.1844	.1879
0.5	.1915	.1950	.1985	.2019	.2054	.2088	.2123	.2157	.2190	.2224
0.6	.2257	.2291	.2324	.2357	.2389	.2422	.2454	.2486	.2518	.2549
0.7	.2580	.2612	.2642	.2673	.2704	.2734	.2764	.2794	.2823	.2852
0.8	.2881	.2910	.2939	.2967	.2995	.3023	.3051	.3078	.3106	.3133
0.9	.3159	.3186	.3212	.3238	.3264	.3289	.3315	.3340	.3365	.3389
1.0	.3413	.3438	.3461	.3485	.3508	.3531	.3554	.3577	.3599	.3621
1.1	.3643	.3665	.3686	.3708	.3729	.3749	.3770	.3790	.3810	.3830
1.2	.3849	.3869	.3888	.3907	.3925	.3944	.3962	.3980	.3997	.4015
1.3	.4032	.4049	.4066	.4082	.4099	.4115	.4131	.4147	.4162	.4177
1.4	.4192	.4207	.4222	.4236	.4251	.4265	.4279	.4292	.4306	.4319
1.5	.4332	.4345	.4357	.4370	.4382	.4394	.4406	.4418	.4429	.4441
1.6	.4452	.4463	.4474	.4484	.4495	.4505	.4515	.4525	.4535	.4545
1.7	.4554	.4564	.4573	.4582	.4591	.4599	.4608	.4616	.4625	.4633
1.8	.4641	.4649	.4656	.4664	.4671	.4678	.4686	.4693	.4699	.4706
1.9	.4713	.4719	.4726	.4732	.4738	.4744	.4750	.4756	.4761	.4767
2.0	.4772	.4778	.4783	.4788	.4793	.4798	.4803	.4808	.4812	.4817
2.1	.4821	.4826	.4830	.4834	.4838	.4842	.4846	.4850	.4854	.4857
2.2	.4861	.4864	.4868	.4871	.4875	.4878	.4881	.4884	.4887	.4890
2.3	.4893	.4896	.4898	.4901	.4904	.4906	.4909	.4911	.4913	.4916
2.4	.4918	.4920	.4922	.4925	.4927	.4929	.4931	.4932	.4934	.4936
2.5	.4938	.4940	.4941	.4943	.4945	.4946	.4948	.4949	.4951	.4952
2.6	.4953	.4955	.4956	.4957	.4959	.4960	.4961	.4962	.4963	.4964
2.7	.4965	.4966	.4967	.4968	.4969	.4970	.4971	.4972	.4973	.4974
2.8	.4974	.4975	.4976	.4977	.4977	.4978	.4979	.4979	.4980	.4981
2.9	.4981	.4982	.4982	.4983	.4984	.4984	.4985	.4985	.4986	.4986
3.0	.4986	.4987	.4987	.4988	.4988	.4989	.4989	.4989	.4990	.4990

Glossary

activity variables the unknowns of a linear programming problem, representing the primary topic of the analysis (e.g., the products sold or the ingredients used in a product).

asymptote a point or a line approached but not touched by a function.

augmented matrix a matrix which is increased in size from its orginal dimension by adding rows or columns.

basic feasible solution a solution to a linear programming problem which represents a point on the boundary of the solution space.

basic variable a variable which is in the solution to a linear programming problem.

basis the group of basic variables in a linear programming problem.

Bayes' rule a technique for adjusting prior probabilities based on the occurrence of a subsequent event or events.

binomial factoring the process of finding two products from one polynomial expression.

binomial probability distribution a discrete distribution representing only two possible outcomes of an experiment whose repetitions are independent of each other.

break-even point that sales level corresponding to equality between total revenue and total cost, or zero profit.

Cartesian coordinate system a plane formed by two perpendicular crossed number lines intersecting at the origin with a unique ordered pair of numbers corresponding to each point in the plane.

coefficient matrix a rectangular array which includes the coefficients of a system of equations.

combination the number of ways a group of x objects can be selected from a group of n objects without regard for the order of the x objects.

common logarithm a logarithm to the base 10.

complement of a set all the elements of the universal set which are not included in the particular set.

compound interest interest which is paid on the principal and all accrued interest.

conditional event an event whose occurrence is subject to the occurrence of some other event.

477

consistent system of equations a system of equations having a unique solution.
constant a symbol designating a single real number for a given problem.
constant function a functional relationship having the dependent variable equal to a single real number.
constraint a restriction used in a linear programming problem. (This terminology may also be used in reference to any equation or inequality.)
consumers' surplus the benefit to consumers in excess of the price paid for a given quantity of a good as measured by the demand function for that good.
continuous compounding the process of compounding interest every instant.
continuous function a function which is graphed without lifting the pencil from the paper.
continuous probability distribution a probability distribution having a probability for every value over a range.
convergent improper integral an improper integral having a definite limit to its area.
convex set a set in which the line segment connecting any two points in the set also is in the set.
corner point any intersection of two or more lines or a line and an axis in a solution space.
cross-price · elasticity of demand a number expressing the quotient of the percentage change in the quantity demanded of one good divided by the percentage change in the price of the second good.
cubic function a polynomial function of the general form $f(X) = b_0 + b_1X + b_2X^2 + b_3X^3$, where $b_3 \neq 0$

definite integral an integral having both a specified lower limit of integration and a specified upper limit of integration.
dpendent system of equations a system of equations with the solution of one equation identical to the solution of the other equations
dependent variable a variable having a value determined by the value(s) of the independent variable or independent variables.
derivative a function found from an original function representing the instantaneous rate of change at any point on the original function.
deterministic model a mathematical model which does not incorporate elements of chance or probability.

diagonal matrix a matrix having zeroes in all off-diagonal positions.
difference quotient a quotient formed by dividing the verticle change between two points on a function by the horizontal change between those same two points.
dimension of a matrix the number of rows and and number of columns in a matrix.
discrete probability distribution a probability distribution having probabilities only for certain fixed values.
divergent improper integral an improper integral having an unlimited area.
dual problem a counterpart of the primal linear programming problem formulated from information in the primal problem.

e a nonrepeating constant equal to 2.71828...
effective rate of interest the actual percentage interest earned, based on the compounding characteristics of the asset.
elasticity a term of general usage in business and economics which measures the percentage change in one variable divided by the percentage change in another variable.
element of a matrix one real number in the array forming a matrix.
equation a statement that two expressions are equal.
event the outcome of an experiment.
expected value of an event the average outcome of an experiment over many repetitions of the experiment.
exponent a real number representing the power to which a variable or constant is raised.
exponential decay a process which declines at a continuous rate over time.
exponential function a function having an independent variable which is an exponent.
exponential growth a process which increases at a continuous rate over time.

factor one of the separate multipliers in a product.
factorial the product of all positive integers from one to the number under consideration. Thus, $n! = n \cdot (n-1) \cdot (n-2) \cdots 3 \cdot 2 \cdot 1$.
factoring the process of converting a sum or difference of terms to a single term with two or more factors.
final demand vector a column of numbers used in input-output analysis to represent the value of consumer demand for various industries.
finite series a series representing a sequence with a countable group of numbers.

finite set a set with a countable number of elements.

first-derivative test a technique which uses the value of the first derivative on either side of a stationary point to determine whether the stationary point is a relative maximum, relative minimum, or stationary inflection point.

fundamental theorem of integral calculus a theorem which states that the limit of a definite integral can be determined by evaluating the antiderivative of $f(X)$, if it exists, at the end points of the interval. In notation form, the theorem is the following:

$$\int_a^b f(X)\,dX = F(b) - F(a)$$

where $F'(X) = f(X)$.

Gauss-Jordan method of elimination a solution technique for systems of equations which applies row operations to an augmented matrix consisting of the coefficients and constants of the system of equations.

Gauss-Jordan method of inversion a solution technique for systems of equations which applies row operations to the matrix of coefficients to form its inverse.

geometric series the sum of a sequence of terms with the first term being the constant a, and each successive term equal to r (the common ratio) times the previous term.

identity matrix a matrix with an equal number of rows and columns having the number one in each position on the main diagonal and zeroes elsewhere

implicit differentiation a method for differentiating with respect to one variable a function which does not explicitly state that the variables are identifiable as to independent and dependent variable(s).

improper integral an integral which has an infinite limit(s) of integration.

income elasticity of demand the quotient formed by dividing the percentage change in the quantity demanded of a good by a corresponding percentage change in group (or individual) income.

inconsistent system of equations a system of equations which does not have a solution.

indefinite integral a symbol used to represent all the antiderivatives of a particular function.

independent variable a designation for the set of domain values or those values assigned in accordance with the purpose of the study.

inequality an expression indicating that two or more terms are unequal.

infinite geometric series the sum of a geometric progression with an unlimited number of terms.

infinite series a series with an unlimited number of terms.

infinite set a set with an unlimited number of elements.

inner product a scalar developed by multiplying each element of a row vector by the corresponding element in a column vector and algebraically summing these products for the entire row.

input-output analysis a technique for determining economic equilibrium conditions which will assure that each industry's output will satisfy exactly both final demand and the demands of all other industries.

integer the set of whole positive and whole negative numbers including zero.

integral symbol a notation indicating computation of the antiderivative of the expression which follows.

integrand the function to be integrated.

integration the process of finding the antiderivative of a function.

intersection of sets those elements that are common to two or more sets.

inverse function rule a rule which states that the derivative of the inverse function is the reciprocal of the derivative of the original function for all monotonically increasing and monotonically decreasing functions.

inverse matrix a square matrix $\mathbf{A}^{-1}$ formed from another square matrix of the same dimension $\mathbf{A}$ such that $\mathbf{A}\mathbf{A}^{-1} = \mathbf{I} = \mathbf{A}^{-1}\mathbf{A}$, where $\mathbf{I}$ is the identity matrix.

irrational number a number that cannot be expressed as the ratio of two integers.

isocost line a line used in linear programming to describe various resource-use combinations which result in the same total cost.

isoprofit line a line used in linear programming to describe various product-sale combinations which result in the same profit.

joint event an event which includes the common elements of two or more sets.

Lagrangian multipliers a technique for solving problems of constrained optimization by means of differential calculus.

linear combination of equations an equation formed by adding the respective sides of a pair of equations.

linear function a function having a Y intercept, constant slope, and variables raised to the first power. Linear functions have the general form $Y = b_0 + b_1 X$.

linear model a mathematical model including relations and functions with all variables raised to the first power.

linear programming an iterative optimization technique with equation or inequality constraints and an objective function, all in linear form.

loan amortization the process of repaying a loan over a stated period of time.

logarithmic function a function with one or more of the variables in logarithmic form.

mathematical function a correspondence between data sets with each element of the domain corresponding to one and only one element of the range.

mathematical model the abstraction of a real-world situation which utilizes symbols and numbers.

mathematical modeling the process of developing, verifying, implementing, and updating mathematical models.

mathematical relation a correspondence between the elements of two or more sets which are grouped in ordered pairs (ordered triples, etc.)

matrix a rectangular array of numbers.

model auditing the process of adjusting, assessing and finding additional applications for a mathematical model.

model implementation the incorporation of the mathematical model into the decision-making processes of the organization.

model verification assessment of a mathematical model as to its ability to predict and its relevance to the operation of the organization.

monotonically decreasing function a function characterized by successively larger values of the independent variable being associated with successively smaller values of the dependent variable.

monotonically increasing function a function characterized by successively larger values of the independent variable being associated with successively larger values of the dependent variable.

multiplier a numerical measure of the full economic impact resulting from a change in some spending component in the economy.

multivariate function a function having more than one independent variable.

mutually exclusive events two or more events with no common elements.

natural logarithm a logarithm to the base e.

nominal interest rate the stated annual interest rate.

nonbasic variable a variable which is not part of the solution set of variables for a linear programming problem.

nonlinear model a mathematical model employing functions having variables of any degree.

nonnegativity constraint an inequality stating that a vriable may not have negative values.

normal curve a bell-shaped symmetrical cuve which is asymptotic to the X axis.

normal distribution a continuous probability distribution which is bell-shaped, asymptomic to the X axis, and symmetric around its central value.

objective function the function which expresses the goal (e.g., maximum profit or minimum cost) of the linear programming problem.

optimal tableau the linear programming tableau which identifies the optimal point and yields information about that point.

origin of the coordinate axis the point representing a value of zero for both the horizontally measured variable X and the vertically measured variable Y.

original function test a method for determining the characteirstics (i.e., relative maximum, relative minimum, or stationary inflection point) of a stationary point wheh no conclusion can be reached by using the second-derivative test.

overconstrained system of equations a system of equations with a number of equations greater than the number of variables.

partial derivative the derivative with respect to one independent variable of a multivariate function.

permutation the number of ways which a group of x objects can be selected from a group of n objects taking into consideration the order of the x objects.

perpetuity an annuity including paymetns from a principal which begin on a given date and continue forever.

pivot column the nonbasic variable in a tableau which will be included in the set of basic variables in the next iteration of the linear programming problem.

pivot element the element of a linear programming tableau which is at the inter-section of the pivot row and pivot column.

pivot row the basic variable in tableau which will be included in the set of nonbasic variables in the next iteration of the linear programming problem.

polynomial function (one independent variable) a function with the general form $Y = b_0 + b_1X + b_2X^2 + \cdots + b_kX^k$, where Y is the dependent variable, X is the independent variable, and b_k is a nonzero constant specifying the degree of the polynomial.

posterior probability the probability of an event which has been altered because of additional information.

present value the amount of money which, deposited today, will yield a future specified amount.

price elasticity of demand a number representing the quotient of the percentage change in the quantity demanded of a good divided by the corresponding change in the price of the good.

primal problem the original linear programming problem which states the goal of the study.

prior probability the probability of an event as determined by existing data or previous experience.

probabilistic (stochastic) model a mathematical model which yields an outcome with values subject to an element of uncertainty.

probability density function a function used to describe the probabilities corresponding to the values of a continuous random variable.

quadratic formula a formula used to determine the solution set to a quadratic equation. The quadratic formula is

$$X = \frac{-b \pm \sqrt{b^2 - 4ac}}{2a}$$

quadratic function a function of the general form $Y = b_0 + b_1X + b_2X^2$, where b_0, b_1, and b_2 are constants and b_2 is not equal to zero.

random variable a numerically valued function which takes values in accordance with the outcome of an experiment.

rational number a number which can be stated as the ratio of two integers.

real number the set including all rational and irrational numbers.

region of feasible solutions the set of points which satisfies simultaneously all the constraints, including nonnegativity constraints of, a linear programming problem.

relative maximum the highest point for a function within the immediate neighborhood of the point.

relative minimum the lowest point for a function within the immediate neighborhood of the point.

sample space the totality of possible outcomes of an experiment.

scalar a single real number used in matrix algebra.

scatter diagram the graphical description of two data sets.

secant slope the slope of a line connecting two points on a graph.

second derivative the derivative of the function representing the first derivative.

second-derivative test a technique used to determine whether a stationary point is a relative maximum or relative minimum. The second-derivative test also is used to determine whether further tests must be carried out in order to classify the point.

sequence a succession of numbers formed according to some order.

series the sum of the numbers in a sequence.

set any collection of objects.

shadow price the value imputed to a resource based on the results of a linear programming problem.

simple discount the present value of an asset without compounded interest.

simple interest the return on an asset without compounded interest.

simplex method an iterative technique for solving problems of constrained optimization by testing corners of the solution space until the optimum point is determined.

simulation model a numerical model of a real-world situation which uses probabilities to describe the organization's operation through time.

sinking fund an account established to hold money committed to future debt repayment.

slack variable a variable used in linear programming to convert less-than-or-equal-to inequalities to equations.

slope-intercept form of linear equation an equation of the form $Y = b_0 + b_1 X$, where b_1 is the slope of the line and b_0 represents the Y intercept.

slope of a line a ratio of the vertical change along a line divided by the horizontal change along the line.

solution space the area of the coordinate plane which satisfies simultaneously all the inequalities and equations of a system.

standard form of linear equation a linear equation of the form $cX + dY = e$, where X and Y are variables and c, d, and e are constants.

standard normal deviation observations from a normal distribution which have been converted to z values by the equation $z = (x - u)/\sigma$, where x is the particular observation, u is the mean of the normal distribution, and σ is its standard deviation.

stationary inflection point a point of changing concavity having a slope of zero.

statistically dependent events two or more events with the probability of each affected by the occurrence of the others.

statistically independent events two or more events with the probability of each not affected by the occurrence of the others.

subset a set of elements contained within another set.

substitution rate a number representing the trade-off between two variables which may be interchanged.

surplus variable a variable used in linear programming to convert greater-than-or-equal-to inequalities to equations.

tangent slope the slope of a line touching a function at one and only one point.

technological matrix an array used in input-output analysis to describe interindustry demands for goods and services.

transpose of a matrix a matrix formed from an original matrix by interchanging the rows and columns.

tree diagram a pictorial representation of the events in a sample space and their corresponding probabilities.

unbounded solution a linear programming solution which indicates that the constraints do not limit the objective function.

underconstrained system of equations a system of equations with a number of equations less than the number of variables.

union of events the set of elements which are members of any set or group of sets under consideration.

universal set the set of all elements relevant to a particular problem.

variable a symbol used to designate a group of real numbers.

variance of a random variable a measure of the spread of the observations around the mean value of a random variable.

vector an array of one row (row vector) or one column (column vector).

vector of constants the column of constants for a system of equations in matrix form.

vector of unknowns the column of unknowns for a system of equations in matrix form.

Venn diagram a pictorial representation of set relationships.

vertex of a vertical parabola the highest point or lowest point on a vertical parabola.

X coordinate the X or horizontal observation of a coordinate in the Cartesian coordinate system.

X intercept the X value corresponding to a Y value of zero in the Cartesian coordinate system.

Y coordinate the Y or vertical observation of a coordinate in the Cartesian coordinate system.

Y intercept the Y value corresponding to an X value of zero in the Cartesian coordinate system.

Answers to Even-Numbered Exercises

Chapter 2

Page 16

2. a. All males between 25 and 44 who are not unemployed and all unemployed people between 16 and 64.
   b. Unemployed males between 25 and 44.
   c. All females between 16 and 64 and males between 45 and 64 and between 16 and 24.
   d. All people between 16 and 64 who are not unemployed.
   e. Everyone in the city between 16 and 64, except males between 25 and 44 who are not unemployed.
   f. All males between 16 and 24 and 45 and 64 and females between 16 and 64 who are not unemployed.
4. $(A \cup B) \cup C = A \cup (B \cup C)$

   The union of all females and the union between family heads and people earning under $25,000 per year is equal to the union of family heads with the union between people earning under $25,000 per year and all females. Both sets include all females, all males earning under $25,000 per year, and male family heads earning more than $25,000 per year.

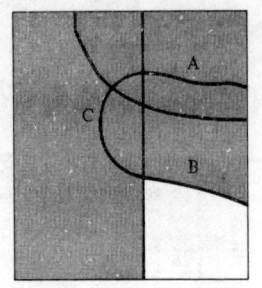

6. a. $A' = 3500$
   b. $A \cap B = 300$, $(A \cap B)' = 4700$
   c. $B \cup C = 600 + 700 - 50 = 1250$
      $(B \cup C)' = 3750$
   d. 2750
   e. $A' \cap B' \cap C' = 2750$
8. a.

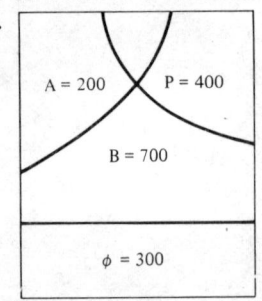

   $A = 200$, $P = 400$, $B = 700$, $\phi = 300$

   b. Let P = the set of pneumonia vaccine recipients.
      $(A \cap P) = 150$
   c. $A \cup (B \cup P) = (A \cup B) \cup P$
      $700 = 700$

Page 25

2. a. $\frac{1}{3}$ k. 125
   b. 4   l. 4
   c. $\frac{1}{18}$ m. 27
   d. 750   n. $\frac{1}{3}$
   e. 1   o. 1
   f. $\frac{1}{5}$ p. 81
   g. $\frac{1}{12}$ q. $\frac{1}{64}$
   h. $\frac{1}{32}$ r. 10,000
   i. $\frac{16}{9}$ s. 100
   j. 3   t. 8

Page 29

2. a. $2X(3X^2 - 2X + 6Y)$
   b. $2X^2Y(2XY - 1 + 8X^2Y^2 - X^2)$
   c. $W(3XY - 2Z + 7WZ^2Y)$
   d. $3ab(-2ab + 3a^2b^2 + 1)$
   e. $6X^2(2X^2 + 1)$
   f. $Y^2(1 - 4Y + 8Y^2 - Y^3)$
4. a. $(X + 6)(X - 6)$ d. $(X^2 + 5)(X^2 - 5)$
   b. $(X + 15)(X - 15)$ e. $(5X - 13)(5X + 13)$
   c. $4(X + 2)(X - 2)$ f. $(4X^2 - 7)(4X^2 + 7)$

Review Problems

2. a. $(A \cap B) = \{4, 11\}$
   b. $(A \cup B) = \{1, 2, 3, 4, 7, 11, 13, 15\}$
   c. $(A \cup B \cup C) = \{1, 2, 3, 4, 7, 11, 13, 15, 16, 18\}$
   d. $(B \cup C) = \{1, 2, 3, 4, 7, 11, 15, 16, 18\}$
   e. $(A \cap B \cap C) = \{\emptyset\}$
   f. $A \cup (B \cap C) = \{1, 4, 7, 11, 13, 15\}$
4. a. $(X \cup Y) \cup Z = \{2, 3, 4, 5, 6, 7, 8, 9, 10, 11\}$
   b. $(X \cap Y) \cap Z = \{\emptyset\}$
   c. $X \cup (Y \cap Z) = \{2, 3, 4, 5, 6, 7, 8, 9, 10, 11\}$
   $(X \cup Y) \cap (X \cup Z) = \{2, 3, 4, 5, 6, 7, 8, 9, 10, 11\}$
   d. $X \cap (Y \cup Z) = \{2, 4, 6, 8, 10\}$
   $(X \cap Y) \cup (X \cap Z) = \{\emptyset \cup (2, 4, 6, 8, 10)\} = \{2, 4, 6, 8, 10\}$
6. a. $\frac{16}{9}$ f. 36
   b. $\frac{1}{729}$ g. 2
   c. 16   h. 1
   d. $\frac{4}{9}$ i. 1
   e. 256   j. 8
8. a. $5 \cdot 20 = 100 = 20 \cdot 5$ and $(5 \cdot 20)c = 100c = 5(20 \cdot c)$
   b. $5 - 20 \neq 20 - 5$ and $(5 - 20) - c \neq 5 - (20 - c)$
   c. $5/20 \neq 20/5$
10. a. $(X + 3)(X - 3)$ e. $(a^2 + 5)(a^2 - 5)$
    b. $(X + 6)(X - 3)$ f. $(X^2 - 8)(X^2 + 1)$
    c. $4(X + 2)(X - 2)$ g. $2(2X + 3)(X + 8)$
    d. $(a - 8)(a + 2)$ h. $(3X + 1)(-X + 2)$
12. a. $\sqrt{(14^3)}$ e. $\dfrac{1}{\sqrt[5]{52^3}}$
    b. $\dfrac{1}{\sqrt[5]{21^4}}$ f. $\sqrt[3]{60^4}$
    c. $\sqrt[4]{16}$ g. $\sqrt{25^5}$
    d. $\dfrac{1}{\sqrt[3]{20}}$ h. $\dfrac{1}{\sqrt{36^7}}$

14. a. $X' = 2500$ d. $S \cap Y' = 1500$
    b. $X \cap Y' = 1500$ e. $S \cap (Y \cup Z) = 500$
    c. $Y' = 4000$ f. $S' \cup X' = 3500$

Chapter 3

Review Problems

2. a. Function
   b. Not a function, more than one Y value for a given X
   c. Function
   d. Not a function, more than one Y value for a given X
   e. Function
   f. Function

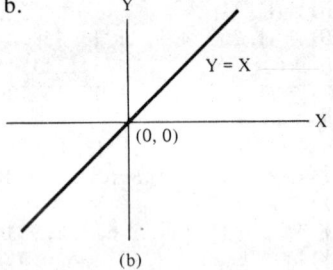

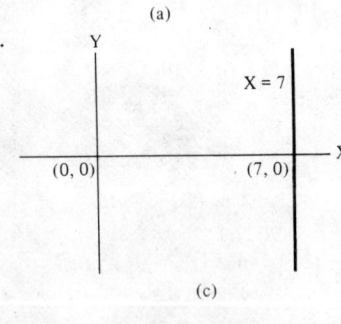

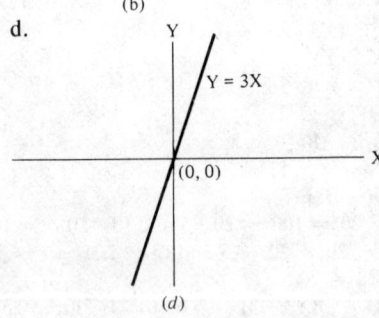

4. a. $Y = -2$, passing through $(0, 0)$ and $(0, -2)$
   b. $Y = X$, passing through $(0, 0)$
   c. $X = 7$, passing through $(0, 0)$ and $(7, 0)$
   d. $Y = 3X$, passing through $(0, 0)$

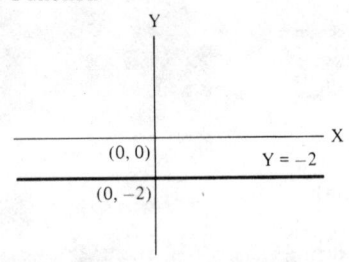

6.

X	$2^X = Y$
2	$2^2 = 4$
4	$2^4 = 16$
6	$2^6 = 64$

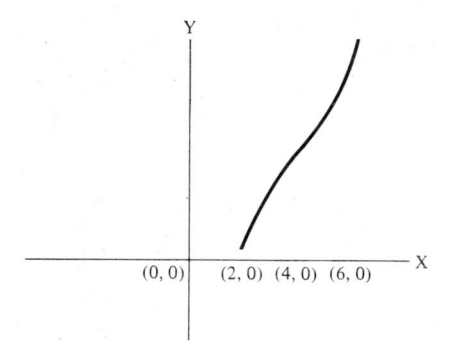

8. a. Degree 3   d. Degree 1
   b. Degree 2   e. Degree 6
   c. Degree 4
10. a. Total cost $Y = 850{,}000 + 16.75$ (Number produced $= X$.)
    b. Each X corresponds to one and only one Y value.
    c. Degree 1 as X is raised to the first power.

Chapter 4

Page 54

2. a. $X = 10, Y = 92$ d. $X = 14, Y = 62 + (3)(14) = 104$
      $X = 34, Y = 164$ $X = 12, Y = 75 + (3)(12) = 111$
   b. $X = 15, Y = 107$ e. $X = 20, Y = 62 + (3)(20) = 122$
      $X = 6, Y = 80$ $X = 30, Y = 50 + (3)(30) = 140$
   c. $X = 5, Y = 62 + (3)(5) = 77$
      $X = 5, Y = 70 + (3)(5) = 85$
4. a. $Y = 0, X = 26.67$ d. $Y = 0, X = 2.5$
   b. $Y = 0, X = 9$ e. $Y = 0, X = 0$
   c. $Y = 0, X = 1.5$
   Each point represents the X intercept of the function, or the point of intersection between the function and the X axis. The point in part e is the origin.
6. Total cost $Y = 7000 + 0.12$ ($X =$ number of copies printed) at $X = 25{,}000$, $Y = 7000 + (0.12)(25{,}000) = \$10{,}000$.
8. a. At each income level, a constant $60 is subtracted from 0.06 of the corresponding income.
   b. Each additional dollar of family income leads to $0.06 additional spending on clothing.
   c. At $X = \$15{,}000, Y = -60 + (0.06)(15{,}000) = \$840$.
   d. At $Y = 0, X = 1000$. This indicates that families with incomes under $1000 do not make, on average, any clothing purchases during the year.

Page 62

2. a. $b_1 = 0.5$
$$\frac{Y - 0}{X - 0} = 0.5$$
$Y = 0.5X$
b. $b_1 = -0.43$
$$\frac{Y - 5}{X - 3} = -0.43$$
$Y = 6.29 - 0.43X$
c. $b_1 = \frac{3}{4}$
$$\frac{Y - 8}{X - 10} = \frac{3}{4}$$
$Y = 0.5 + 0.75X$

d. $b_1 = -2$
$$\frac{Y - 6}{X - 0} = -2$$
$Y = 6 - 2X$
e. $b_1 = 1.25$
$$\frac{Y - 2}{X - 2} = 1.25$$
$Y = -0.5 + 1.25X$
f. $b_1 = -1.5$
$$\frac{Y - 0}{X - 12} = -1.5$$
$Y = 18 - 1.5X$

4. $Y = 298 - 0.02X$
6. $Y = -700 + 0.45X$
8. $Y = 1500 + 0.6X$
   Fixed cost = $1500
   at $X = 10,000$
   $Y = \$7500$

Review Problems

2. a. $X = 20, Y = 7.8$
   $X = 30, Y = 8.8$
   Y increases by 1
   b. $X = 55, Y = 11.3$
   $X = 40, Y = 9.8$
   Y decreases by 1.5
   c. $Y = 10, X = 42$
   $Y = 12, X = 62$
   X increases by 20
   d. $Y = 16, X = 102$
   $Y = 9, X = 32$
   X decreases by 70
   e. Y increases from 8.3 to 10.7, or by 2.4
   f. Y decreases from 10.6 to 5.96, or by 4.64
4. a. Y intercept $(0, -16)$
   X intercept $(-5.33, 0)$
   b. Y intercept $(0, 11)$
   X intercept $(4.4, 0)$
   c. Y intercept $(0, 4.5)$
   X intercept $(-45, 0)$
   d. Y intercept $(0, 4.8)$
   X intercept $(8, 0)$
   e. Y intercept $(0, -2)$
   X intercept $(.286, 0)$
6. a. $Y = 3.33 + 0.33X$
   b. $Y = 8.8 - 0.4X$
   c. $Y = -6 + 2X$
   d. $Y = -2.625 + 1.375X$
   e. $Y = 0.25X$
   f. $Y = 3$
8. Function: $Y = -.5X + 17$
   $X = 0, Y = 17 =$ maximum Y value
   $X = 34, Y = 0 =$ maximum X value
10. a. Total cost $= 450 + 1.50$ quantity produced

b.

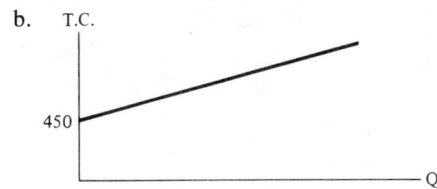

```
T.C.
    |        _____
    |       /
450 |_____/
    |
    |_____ Q
```

12. a. At $Q = 3000$, TC = $22,500
    b. If $V = 2.50$, TC = $40,000
       If $V = 3.00$, TC = $45,000
    c. $Q = 18,000$
    d. If $F = 15,000$ and $V = 2.50$, TC = $20,500
       If $F = 18,000$ and $V = 2.25$, TC = $22,950
14. a. Each change of 1 percent in the consumer loan rate results in a change of the car sales of 30 in the opposite direction.
    b. Car sales respond by a multiple of 0.05 cars to each $1 change in average family income from the $15,000 level.
    c. $Y = 636$
    d. At $X_1 = 9$, $Y = 780$
       At $X_1 = 12.4$, $Y = 678$
16. a. The Y intercept indicates that at a (hypothetical) interest rate of 0, housing sales will be 4500. The slope indicates that for each 1 percent change in the mortgage interest rate, housing sales change by 90 in the opposite direction.
    b. $Y = 3240$
    c. At $X = 15$, $Y = 3150$
       At $X = 12.5$, $Y = 3375$

Chapter 5

Page 78

2. a. Price = 19, quantity = 31.25
   b. Price = 148.75, quantity = 55.625
   c. Price = 42, quantity = 625
4. First functions: price = $0.31, quantity = 130
   Second functions: price = $0.46, quantity = 90
6. a. Break-even quantity:
      Firm A, $Q = 4000$
      Firm B, $Q = 4000$
   b. For firm A, $Q = 6000$
   c. For firm A, $Q = 6000$
      For firm B, $Q = 6000$
8. Original break-even point, $Q = 125,000$
   New break-even point, $Q = 250,000$

Page 89

2. a. $Y = 4 - 1.5X$
   $Y = 1.33 - 0.33X$
   Intersect at a point
   b. $Y = -3 + 0.5X$
   $Y = -3 + 0.5X$
   Same line
   c. $Y = 18 - 3X$
   $Y = 13 - 3X$
   Never intersect
   d. $Y = 10 - 4X$
   $Y = -10 + 4X$
   Intersect at a point

4. a. $X = 4.67$ b. Infinite number of solutions as Equation
   $Y = 5.33$ $2 = 3$ (Equation 3).
   $Z = 3.33$
   c. $X = 0.386$ d. No solutions as a contradiction is encoun-
   $Y = 3.318$ tered during the elimination process.
   $Z = 1.886$

6. $X = 125$ pounds
   $Y = 1125$ pounds

8. $X = 10.8$ ounces
   $Y = 7.2$ ounces
   $Z = 1.2$ ounces

Page 101

2. a. At $X = 16$, $Y \leq 40$ d. At $X = 30$, $Y \leq -33$
   b. At $X = 4$, $Y \leq 18$ e. At $X = 21$, $Y \geq 24.25$
   c. At $X = 150$, $Y \leq 22.5$

4.

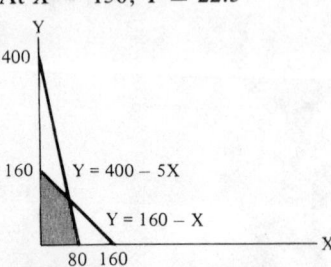

Intersection points: (X, Y)
(0, 160)
(80, 0)
(60, 100)
(0, 0)

6.

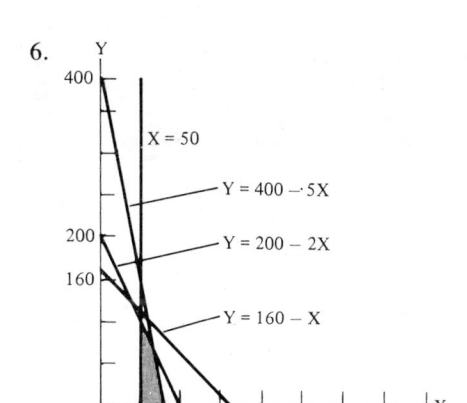

[Graph showing:
- X = 50
- Y = 400 − 5X
- Y = 200 − 2X
- Y = 160 − X
Axis marks: Y at 400, 200, 160; X at 50, 80, 100]

Intersection points: (X, Y)
$(50, 100)$
$(50, 0)$
$(66.67, 66.67)$
$(80, 0)$

8.

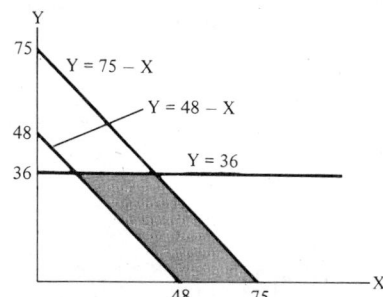

[Graph showing:
- Y = 75 − X
- Y = 48 − X
- Y = 36
Axis marks: Y at 75, 48, 36; X at 48, 75]

Intersection points: (X, Y)
$(12, 36)$
$(39, 36)$
$(48, 0)$
$(75, 0)$

Review Problems

2. a. Price = 260
    Quantity = 100
  b. Price = 180
    Quantity = 54.375
  c. Price = 281.25
    Quantity = 1750
  d. Price = 18
    Quantity = 175

4. a. Break-even quantity = 280. At $Q = 250$, TR = 4000 and TC = 4300.
  b. Break-even quantity = 750. At $Q = 700$, TR = 1750 and TC = 1870.
  c. Break-even quantity = 2450. At $Q = 2400$, TR = 57,600 and TC = 57,800.
  d. Break-even quantity = 6500. At $Q = 6400$, TR = 8832 and TC = 8952.

6. a. Infinite number of solutions as Equation 1 = 2 (Equation 2).
   b. No solution, as a contradiction occurs during the solution process. The lines are parallel.
   c. No solution, as a contradiction occurs during the solution process. The lines are parallel.
   d. Infinite number of solutions, as Equation 2 = 3.5 (Equation 1).
8. a. $Y \leq -5.33 + 1.33X$. Solution space is on and below this line.
   b. $Y \leq 5.67 - 0.167X$. Solution space is on and below this line.
   c. $Y \geq -4(1 - X)$. Solution space is on and above this line.
   d. $Y \geq 2.4 + 0.6X$. Solution space is on and above this line.
   e. $Y \geq -2 - 1.5X$. Solution space is on and above this line.
   f. $Y \leq 2X$. Solution space is on and below this line.

10.

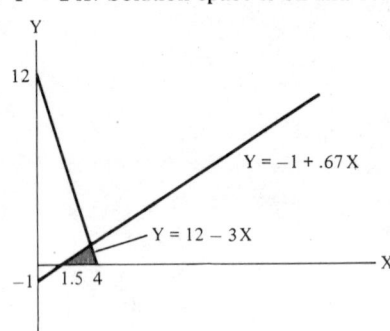

a.

Intersection points:
(X, Y)
(1.5, 0)
(4, 0)
(3.55, 1.36)

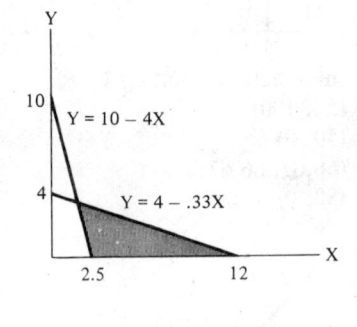

b.

Intersection points:
(X, Y)
(2.5, 0)
(12, 0)
(1.64, 3.45)

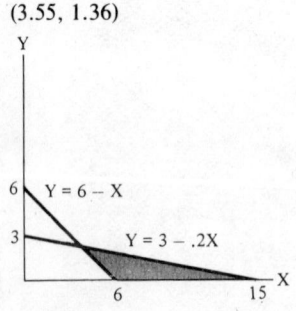

c.

Intersection points:
(X, Y)
(6, 0)
(15, 0)
(3.75, 2.25)

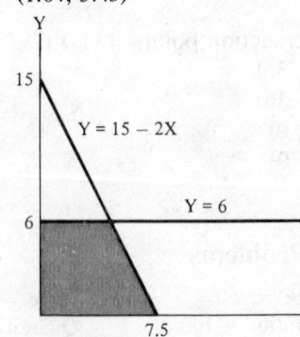

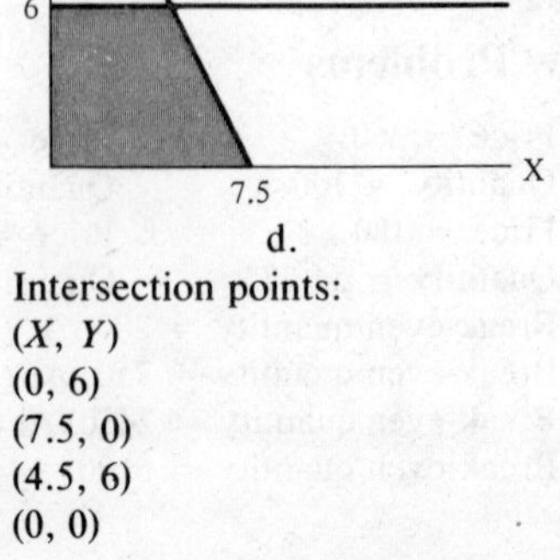

d.

Intersection points:
(X, Y)
(0, 6)
(7.5, 0)
(4.5, 6)
(0, 0)

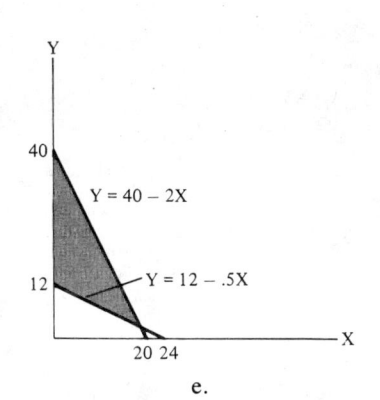

Answers to Even-Numbered Exercises

e.
Intersection points:
(X, Y)
$(0, 12)$
$(0, 40)$
$(18.67, 2.67)$

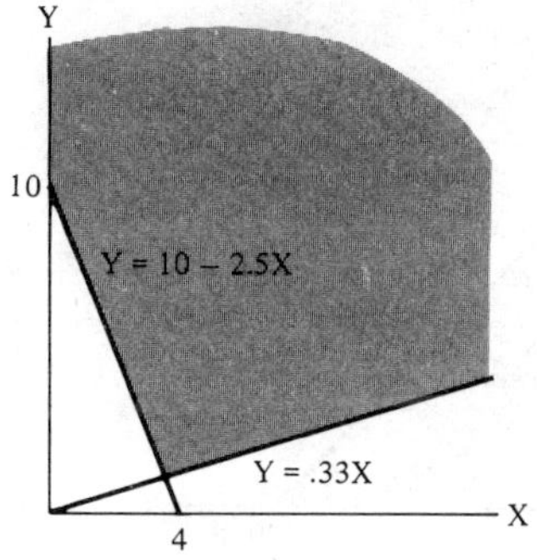

f.
Intersection points:
(X, Y)
$(0, 10)$
$(3.53, 1.18)$

12. The change represents a greater quantity purchased at all prices.
    New equilibrium:
    Price = $1.35
    Quantity = 7500
14. Break-even quantity = 67,500 bushels
16. $X = 15$ hours, $Y = 75$ hours
18.

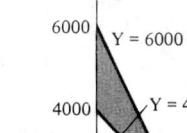

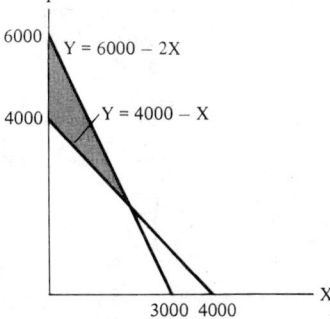

Intersection points:
(X, Y)
$(0, 4000)$
$(0, 6000)$
$(2000, 2000)$

20.

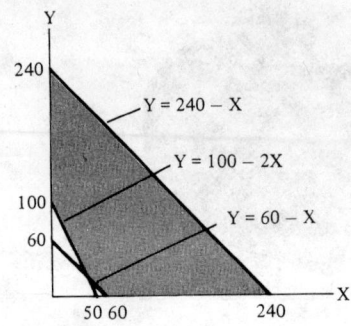

$Y = 240 - X$
$Y = 100 - 2X$
$Y = 60 - X$

Intersection points:
(X, Y)
$(0, 240)$
$(0, 100)$
$(60, 0)$
$(240, 0)$
$(40, 20)$

Chapter 6

Page 117

2. a. (46)

b. $\begin{pmatrix} 24 & 0 & 28 \\ -12 & 0 & -14 \\ 18 & 0 & 21 \end{pmatrix}$

c. $\begin{pmatrix} 32 & 10 \\ 34 & 21 \end{pmatrix}$

d. $\begin{pmatrix} 16 & 10 & -4 \\ 8 & 8 & -3 \\ -5 & 0 & 15 \end{pmatrix}$

e. $\begin{pmatrix} 20 & 2 & -3 \\ 32 & 8 & 0 \end{pmatrix}$

f. $(31 \quad 49 \quad 45 \quad -9)$

g. $\begin{pmatrix} -5 & 0.5 & 4 \\ -7 & 2.5 & 8 \\ 6 & 2 & -0.5 \end{pmatrix}$

h. $\begin{pmatrix} 5 & 15 & 20 & -5 \\ -10 & 0 & 30 & 5 \\ -15 & -20 & 25 & 45 \end{pmatrix}$

4. a. $\mathbf{A}^T = \begin{pmatrix} 2 & 3 & 1 & 1 \\ 0 & 6 & 3 & -1 \\ 2 & 4 & 0 & -3 \\ -5 & 2 & 2 & 6 \end{pmatrix}$

b. $\mathbf{XA} = (20 \quad 10 \quad 1 \quad 16)$

c. $\mathbf{AX}^T = \begin{pmatrix} -15 \\ 38 \\ 20 \\ 29 \end{pmatrix}$

d. $\mathbf{XA}^T = (-15 \quad 38 \quad 20 \quad 29)$

e. $XX^T = (46)$

f. $AA^T = \begin{pmatrix} 33 & 4 & -8 & -34 \\ 4 & 65 & 25 & -3 \\ -8 & 25 & 14 & 10 \\ -34 & -3 & 10 & 47 \end{pmatrix}$

6. a. $A = \$205.50$
$B = \$94.25$
$C = \$107.50$

b. $(6 \; 9 \; 20) \begin{pmatrix} 30 & 10 & 20 & 30 & 40 \\ 10 & 5 & 20 & 10 & 15 \\ 8 & 30 & 8 & 5 & 20 \end{pmatrix} = (430 \; 705 \; 460 \; 370 \; 775)$

8. a. $\begin{pmatrix} 93{,}000 & 0 & 0 \\ 0 & 98{,}500 & 0 \\ 0 & 0 & 111{,}000 \end{pmatrix}$

b. $\begin{pmatrix} 50{,}000 & 0 & 0 & 0 & 0 \\ 0 & 54{,}000 & 0 & 0 & 0 \\ 0 & 0 & 95{,}000 & 0 & 0 \\ 0 & 0 & 0 & 47{,}000 & 0 \\ 0 & 0 & 0 & 0 & 56{,}500 \end{pmatrix}$

Page 129
2. a. $X = 4, Y = 4$
   b. $X = -\frac{28}{9}, Y = \frac{49}{9}$
   c. $X = 6, Y = 0$
   d. $X = 7, Y = 1$
4. a. No solutions
   b. Unlimited solutions
   c. No solutions
   d. Unlimited solutions
   e. Unlimited solutions
   f. No solutions
   g. Unlimited solutions
   h. No solutions

Page 135

2. a. Inverse $= \begin{pmatrix} \frac{23}{8} & \frac{3}{8} & \frac{19}{8} \\ \frac{10}{8} & \frac{2}{8} & \frac{10}{8} \\ \frac{8}{8} & 0 & \frac{8}{8} \end{pmatrix} = \begin{pmatrix} \frac{23}{8} & \frac{3}{8} & \frac{19}{8} \\ \frac{5}{4} & \frac{1}{4} & \frac{5}{4} \\ 1 & 0 & 1 \end{pmatrix}$

b. Inverse $= \begin{pmatrix} -2 & -3 & 13 \\ \frac{3}{2} & 2 & -\frac{17}{2} \\ -1 & -1 & 5 \end{pmatrix}$

c. Inverse $= \begin{pmatrix} -\frac{2}{14} & \frac{6}{14} & -\frac{1}{14} \\ \frac{8}{14} & -\frac{10}{14} & -\frac{3}{14} \\ 0 & 0 & \frac{7}{14} \end{pmatrix} = \begin{pmatrix} -\frac{1}{7} & \frac{3}{7} & -\frac{1}{14} \\ \frac{4}{7} & -\frac{5}{7} & -\frac{3}{14} \\ 0 & 0 & \frac{1}{2} \end{pmatrix}$

4. a. $4X + 2Y + 5Z = 17$
$Y + 3Z = 38$
$-4X + 6Y - Z = 20$
b. $4X_1 + 6X_2 - 2X_3 + 4X_4 = 78$
c. $2X_1 + X_2 + 4X_3 = 44$
$6X_1 - 2X_2 + 3X_3 = 29$
d. $11X_1 + 8X_2 + 6X_3 + 14Y_1 - 6Y_2 = 121$
$4X_1 - 6X_2 + 10X_3 + 2Y_1 + 12Y_2 = 87$
6. a. $X = 3, Y = 2, Z = 5$
b. $X = 4, Y = 3, Z = 0$
c. $X = 5, Y = 5, Z = 4$
8. First set of constraints:
$2X + 6Y = 48$
$X - Y = 12$
Answers: $X = 15$ ounces
$Y = 3$ ounces
Second set of constraints:
$2X + 6Y = 48$
$X - Y = 8$
Answers: $X = 12$ ounces
$Y = 4$ ounces
10. $X = 800$ pounds
$Y = 600$ pounds
$Z = 500$ pounds

Review Problems

2. a. $\begin{pmatrix} 24 & 8 & 4 \\ 28 & 28 & 32 \\ -8 & 12 & 4 \end{pmatrix}$

b. $\begin{pmatrix} 12 & 18 & 0 & -36 & 42 \\ 4 & 6 & 0 & -12 & 14 \\ 14 & 21 & 0 & -42 & 49 \\ 2 & 3 & 0 & -6 & 7 \end{pmatrix}$

c. Cannot be multiplied as first matrix has three columns and second matrix has four rows.

d. $\begin{pmatrix} 16 & -12 & 38 \\ 30 & 9 & 33 \\ 68 & 82 & 0 \\ 10 & 17 & -6 \end{pmatrix}$

e. $\begin{pmatrix} 36 & 28 & 32 \\ 84 & 36 & 12 \\ 9 & 9 & -9 \end{pmatrix}$

f. $\begin{pmatrix} -12 & 18 & 0 \\ 0 & 6 & 30 \\ 24 & 12 & -18 \end{pmatrix}$

4. $X^T = \begin{pmatrix} 3 & 0 & 4 \\ 2 & 3 & 8 \\ 7 & 0 & 2 \end{pmatrix}$

   $XX^T = \begin{pmatrix} 62 & 6 & 42 \\ 6 & 9 & 24 \\ 42 & 24 & 84 \end{pmatrix}$

6. Taxes owed:
   Store 1 = $1533.44
   Store 2 = $991.91
   Store 3 = $949.80

8. a. $X = -1, Y = 4$ d. $X = 5, Y = 0$
   b. $X = 1, Y = 4, Z = 2$ e. $X = 3, Y = -2, Z = 4$
   c. $X = 0, Y = 4, Z = 1$ f. $X = 8, Y = 12, Z = 12$

10. a. Inverse = $\begin{pmatrix} \frac{1}{2} & 0 \\ \frac{3}{8} & \frac{1}{4} \end{pmatrix}$ c. Inverse = $\begin{pmatrix} \frac{5}{2} & -3 \\ -2 & \frac{5}{2} \end{pmatrix}$

    b. Inverse = $\begin{pmatrix} -\frac{3}{10} & \frac{1}{5} \\ \frac{1}{10} & -\frac{2}{5} \end{pmatrix}$ d. Inverse = $\begin{pmatrix} -1 & \frac{5}{2} \\ 1 & -2 \end{pmatrix}$

12. a. $AA^{-1} = A^{-1}A = \begin{pmatrix} 1 & 0 & 0 \\ 0 & 1 & 0 \\ 0 & 0 & 1 \end{pmatrix}$

    b. $X = 1, Y = 2, Z = 0$
    c. $X = 2, Y = 4, Z = 0$
    d. Doubling of the constants will double each value of the unknowns.

14. $X = \frac{8}{3}, Y = \frac{16}{3}$

16. a. $A^T = \begin{pmatrix} 3 & 2 & 5 \\ 2 & 1 & 1 \\ 4 & 2 & 1 \end{pmatrix}$

    b. $AA^T = \begin{pmatrix} 29 & 16 & 21 \\ 16 & 9 & 13 \\ 21 & 13 & 27 \end{pmatrix}$

    c. $(I - A) = \begin{pmatrix} -2 & -2 & -4 \\ -2 & 0 & -2 \\ -5 & -1 & 0 \end{pmatrix}$

18. a. Row 1 = 2 (row 3)
    b. Row 3 = 3 (row 1)
    c. Row 3 = $\frac{4}{3}$ (row 2)
    d. Row 3 = $\frac{-2}{3}$ (row 1)

20. $5X + 6Y + 2Z = 20{,}000$
    $4X + 3Y + 4Z = 22{,}000$
    $6X + 4Y + 5Z = 30{,}000$
    Solution: $X = 2400, Y = 400, Z = 2800$

22. Steel = $820 million
    Chemicals = $1740 million

Chapter 7

Page 166

2. Minimize: $Z = 20X_1 + 15X_2 + 24X_3$
   Subject to: $3X_1 + 2X_2 + 3X_3 \geq 200$
   $X_1 + 2X_2 + 4X_3 \geq 300$
   $X_1 \geq 0$
   $X_2 \geq 0$
   $X_3 \geq 0$

   Minimize: $Z = \begin{pmatrix} 20 & 15 & 24 \end{pmatrix} \begin{pmatrix} X_1 \\ X_2 \\ X_3 \end{pmatrix}$

   Subject to: $\begin{pmatrix} 3 & 2 & 3 \\ 1 & 2 & 4 \end{pmatrix} \begin{pmatrix} X_1 \\ X_2 \\ X_3 \end{pmatrix} \geq \begin{pmatrix} 200 \\ 300 \end{pmatrix}$

   $X_1 \geq 0$
   $X_2 \geq 0$
   $X_3 \geq 0$

4. Feasible corners:

(X_1, X_2)	Z
(0, 24)	72
(16, 0)	48
(4, 12)	48

   Two minimum points are (16, 0) and (4, 12).

6. Feasible corners:

(X_1, X_2)	Z
(15, 0)	60
(0, 10)	20
(7.5, 2.5)	35

   Minimum occurs at (0, 10).

8. Feasible corners:

(X_1, X_2)	Z
(0, 24)	72
(10, 0)	20
(5, 5)	25
(2.25, 10.5)	36

   Minimum occurs at (10, 0).

10. Feasible corners:

(X_1, X_2)	Z
(0, 16)	32
(24, 0)	48
(4, 8)	24
(18.67, .67)	38.67

Minimum occurs at (4, 8).

Page 178

2. a. Two basic variables, representing the number of resource constraints in the problem statement.
   b. No, negative numbers under X_1 and X_2 in the Z row indicate that profit can be increased by changing the basis.
   c. New pivot element is the two at the intersection of the X_1 column and S_1 row. This is because X_1 has the largest negative number in the Z row and (40 ÷ 2) yields the smallest positive quotient between the X_1 column entries and the right-hand side entries.
   d. S_1 has 40 hours of slack time at this point.
4. a. No, X_1 should not be produced as its production would decrease total profit.
   b. The shadow price of S_1 is $10 indicating the additional profit associated with one more unit of S_1. The shadow price of S_2 is $3 indicating the additional profit associated with one more unit of S_2.
   c. There are three nonbasic variables in the solution as this represents the number of activity variables in the original problem statement.

Page 192

2.

	Y_1	Y_2	D_1	D_2	D_3	RHS
Z	−300	−200	0	0	0	0
D	2	1	1	0	0	10
D_2	4	5	0	1	0	7
D_3	5	3	0	0	1	4

4. a.

	Y_1	Y_2	Y_3	D_1	D_2	RHS
Z	−450	−520	−610	0	0	0
D_1	2	1	5	1	0	45
D_2	4	3	2	0	1	65

   b. The value imputed to hourly output cannot exceed the hourly cost of operation of the machine.

c. In the dual objective function, the imputed value of the machine output is maximized.
d. In the primal problem, there are two activity variables and three surplus variables, one for each production requirement. In the dual problem, there are three activity variables representing the imputed value for each product and two slack variables, representing the opportunity costs of the machines.

6. a.

	Y_1	Y_2	Y_3	D_1	D_2	D_3	RHS
Z	-50	-60	-90	0	0	0	0
D_1	1	2	6	1	0	0	0.5
D_2	3	1	4	0	1	0	0.2
D_3	5	5	4	0	0	1	0.25

Right-hand side values represent the max.mum imputed value for each corresponding vitamin (D_1, D_2, and D_3).
b. Minimum cost = \$4.969.
c. X_2, X_3, and P_1 are basic in the primal solution.
d. Ingredient X_1 should not be used.
e. P_1 has a surplus of 36.25 units.
f. The value 0.047 in the right-hand side of the Y_2 row of the optimal dual tableau indicates that a one unit reduction in the P_2 requirement will reduce total cost by \$0.047. Similarly, the value 0.012 in the right-hand side of the Y_3 row of the optimal dual tableau indicates that a one unit reduction in the P_3 requirement will reduce total cost by \$0.012.

Review Problems

2. a. Feasible corners:

(X_1, X_2)	Z
(0, 0)	0
(30, 0)	60
(0, 47.5)	190
(10, 40)	180

Maximum value occurs at the point (0, 47.5).

b. Feasible corners:

(X_1, X_2)	Z
(0, 80)	240
(40, 40)	200
(160, 0)	320

Minimum value occurs at the point (40, 40).

Answers to Even-Numbered Exercises **501**

c. Feasible corners:

(X_1, X_2)	Z
(0, 60)	90
(75, 0)	225
(66, 3)	202.5
(30, 30)	135

Minimum value occurs at the point (0, 60).

d. Feasible corners:

(X_1, X_2)	Z
(0, 0)	0
(50, 0)	150
(0, 80)	160
(12.5, 75)	187.5

Maximum value occurs at the point (12.5, 75).

4. a. Optimal point as no changes into or out of the basis can add to profit.
   b. Not optimal as the -6 in the X_1 column and the -4 in the X_2 column indicate that profit can be increased by altering the basis. Pivot element for the next iteration is at the intersection of the X_1 column and S_1 row (4).
   c. Not optimal as the -3 in the X_1 column indicates that profit can be increased by altering the basis.
      Pivot element for the next iteration is at the intersection of the X_1 column and S_2 row (4).
6. a. One more hour of S_1 is associated with two less units of X_1 (-2) and 5 more units of X_2 (5).
   b. For S_1, the $40 shadow price is valid between 170 and 400 hours of labor availability per week.
      For S_3, the $28 shadow price is valid between 80 and 190 hours of packaging time available per week.
8. a.

	Y_1	Y_2	Y_3	D_1	D_2	RHS
Z	-800	-900	-950	0	0	0
D_1	6	5	6	1	0	25
D_2	3	7	8	0	1	31

   b. There are two basic variables corresponding to an opportunity cost for each activity variable (X_1 and X_2) in the primal problem.
   c. To maximize the values imputed to the machines by the products produced.
   $$Z = 800Y_1 + 900Y_2 + 950Y_3$$
   d. For D_1, the values imputed to the products must be no greater than the cost of operation of the machine used for these products ($25).
      For D_2, the values imputed to the products from 1 hour of machine operation must be no greater than the cost per hour of operation of the machine ($31).
10. a. $X_1 = 170$ pounds, $X_2 = 60$ pounds.
    b. $Z = (9)(170) + (10)(60) = \$2130$.

Mathematics for Business and Economics **502**

  c. There is a surplus of 90 ounces of P_2. In the primal solution, there will be 690 ounces of P_2.
  d. $P_1 = (2)(170) + (1)(60) = 400.$
     $P_3 = (3)(170) + (4)(60) = 750.$
  e. For Y_1, the range is from 250 to 500. Thus, the shadow price of $1.20 for P_1 is valid between 250 and 500 ounces.
     For Y_3, the range is from 600 to 1600. Thus, the shadow price of $2.20 for P_3 is valid between 600 and 1600 ounces.

Chapter 8

Page 208

2. a. No solutions as the term $b^2 - 4ac$ has a negative value.
   b. One solution as the term $b^2 - 4ac$ equals zero.
   c. Two solutions as $b^2 - 4ac$ equals a nonzero positive number.
   d. Two solutions as $b^2 - 4ac$ equals a nonzero positive number.
   e. Two solutions as $b^2 - 4ac$ equals a nonzero positive number.
   f. No solutions as $b^2 - 4ac$ has a negative value.
4. a. Total revenue $= 36Q - 0.06Q^2$
   b. Vertex occurs where $Q = 300$ and TR $= 5400$
   c. $b_2 = -0.06$
   d. $P = \$18$

Page 218

2. a. $X = 2, Y = 1$
      $X = 4, Y = 9$
   b. $X = 2, Y = 0.2$
      $X = 4, Y = \frac{1}{125} = 0.008$
   c. $X = 2, Y = 0.001$
      $X = 4, Y = 0.00001$
   d. $X = 2, Y = 2$
      $X = 4, Y = 0.5$
   e. $X = 2, Y = \frac{1}{9} = 0.11$
      $X = 4, Y = 81$
   f. $X = 2, Y = 1$
      $X = 4, Y = 100$
4. a. $P = 15e^{0.12} = 16{,}912{,}500$
      A population of 15 million growing at 3 percent per year for 4 years will be equal to 16,912,500 people at the end of the four years.
   b. $P = 180e^{0.12} = 202{,}950{,}000$
   c. $P = 45e^{0.25} = 57{,}780{,}000$
   d. $P = 20e^1 = 54{,}366{,}000$
   e. $P = 56e^{1.6} = 277{,}368{,}000$
6. a. 25.94 percent
   b. 28.51 percent
   c. The percentage of customers approaches but does not equal 30 percent.

Review Problems

2. a. Vertex is a minimum as b_2 is greater than zero.
   b. Average cost is 75 at the vertex.

c. No solution, therefore average cost is never equal to zero because of the fixed-cost component.
4. Three conclusions:
   a. If the base is a positive number greater than 1, Y is monotonically increasing with increasing values of X.
   b. If the base is a positive number less than 1, Y is monotonically decreasing with increasing values of X.
   c. If the exponent is negative, Y is monotonically decreasing with increasing values of X.
6. a. Value = $1.6e^{-0.08t}$
   b. At $t = 4$, value = \$1,161,760
      At $t = 6$, value = \$989,920
8. a. Number of cases = 28.15
   b. Decline in cases = $37.25 - 33.04 = 4.21$
10. a. $Y = 0.69315$ d. $Y = 2.07944$
    b. $Y = 1.38629$ e. $Y = 2.30259$
    c. $Y = 1.79176$ f. $Y = 2.48491$
12. a. $S_n = \$767.32$ d. $S_n = \$680.59$
    b. $S_n = \$915.92$ e. $S_n = \$349.88$
    c. $S_n = \$310.59$

Appendix

2. a. $X = 13.743$ d. $X = 2.9645$
   b. $X = 4.4062$ e. $X = 1$
   c. $X = 0.53764$ f. $X = 54.6005$
4. a. $Y = 0.64$ d. $Y = 2.10$
      $e^Y = 1.8965$ $e^Y = 8.1662$
   b. $Y = 0.92$ e. $Y = 1.30$
      $e^Y = 2.5093$ $e^Y = 3.6693$
   c. $Y = -0.46$ f. $Y = 0.34$
      $e^Y = 0.6313$ $e^Y = 0.7118$

Chapter 9

Page 235

2. a. $4 + 1 + \dfrac{1}{4} + \dfrac{1}{16} = \dfrac{85}{16} = 5.31$

   b. $4 - 1 + \dfrac{1}{4} - \dfrac{1}{16} = \dfrac{51}{16} = 3.19$

   c. $8 + 12 + 18 + 27 = 65$

   d. $10 - 20 + 40 - 80 = -50$

   e. $15 + 5 + \dfrac{15}{9} + \dfrac{15}{27} = \dfrac{600}{27} = 22.22$

4. a. 4   d. 2
   b. 10   e. 1.43
   c. 20

Page 240

2. a. $0.388337   d. $0.613913
   b. $0.452890   e. $0.942596
   c. $0.925926
4. ($10,000)(1.60844) = $16,084.40
6. ($3000)(0.553676) = $1661.03
8. Additional amount that must be deposited = $235.84
10. ($3000)(0.698925) = $2096.78

Page 245

2. a. $2697.35   c. $66,438.85
   b. $12,148.68   d. $10,435.47
4. $980.74
6. $92,142.30
8. $35,271.53
10. $140,924.16

Page 251

2. a. $0.101852   c. $0.061157
   b. $0.063280   d. $0.052871
4. a. $1748.34   c. $235.40
   b. $20,235.05   d. $69,748.00
6. Yes, they have deposited more than enough, as these withdrawals require an initial deposit of $1996.36
8. The payments will be $132.86, thus they will exceed the limit.
10. $345.10

Page 254

2. The greater the per period interest rate i, the greater the value of the term $1 - [1/(1 + i)]$.
4. a. $11,000.00   c. $130,000.00
   b. $15,600.00   d. $10,100.00
6. $30,277.74

Page 257

2. a. $0.7046   d. $0.9512
   b. $0.9704   e. $0.0907
   c. $0.9231

Answers to Even-Numbered Exercises   **505**

4. a. $5164.20 c. $2331.00
   b. $6376.00 d. $5984.00
6. a. $7686.40
   b. $5808.80
   c. $1615.20
8. $335,150.00

Review Problems

2. a. $5845.52 c. $8583.60
   b. $7300.90 d. $2309.61
4. $4262.26
6. a. $3979.28 c. $5385.69
   b. $62,701.47 d. $3450.44
8. $23,717.46
10. $208.69
12. a. $6540.57 c. $6021.50
    b. $40,144.72 d. $19,175.04
14. $44,966.43
16. $37,757.20
18. 1. Payments for 6-year loan = $532.76 every 6 months
    2. Payments for 5-year loan = $647.52 every 6 months
20. $52,500
22. Account value after 5 years:
    Bank A = $2377.52
    Bank B = $2159.84

Chapter 10

Page 275

2. a. 6
   b. Limit does not exist, as the denominator limit is zero.
   c. 0
   d. -4
   e. Limit does not exist, as the denominator limit is zero.
   f. 0

Page 287

2. a. $6(6x^2 + 1)$
   b. $30X^{3/2} - 36X + 7X^{-1/2}$
   c. $\dfrac{1}{2}\left[\dfrac{4X^2 + 32X - 13}{(X + 4)^2}\right]$
   d. $\dfrac{3(X^2 - 4X + 2)}{(X - 2)^2}$
   e. $\dfrac{1}{X^{5/6}} = X^{-5/6}$
   f. $-\dfrac{1}{2X^2}$
   g. $\dfrac{3X^4 - 8X^3 + 3X^2 - 12X - 14}{(X - 2)^2}$
   h. $8X$
   i. $\dfrac{2(2 - 3X^{-2})}{9X^{1/3}}$
   j. 7

4. a. $18X + 36 = 18(X + 2)$
   b. $2(4X - 2)^{1/2} [1 + 2X(4X - 2)^{-1}]$
   c. $3(8X + 1)(4X^2 + X - 14)^2$
   d. $-2X^{-3}(4 + 24X^{-2} + 27X^{-4})$
   e. $98X(4 - 6X^{-2/3} - 14X^{-4/3} + 21X^{-2})$
   f. $5(18X^2 - 6X + 17)(6X^3 - 3X^2 + 17X - 20)^4$

Page 291

2. a. $2X^{-1} = \dfrac{2}{X}$ d. $X^{-1} = \dfrac{1}{X}$

   b. $\dfrac{4X - 5}{2X^2 - 5X + 16}$ e. $\dfrac{-6 - X}{X(3 + X)}$

   c. $-3X^{-1} = \dfrac{-3}{X}$ f. $-3X - 1 = \dfrac{-3}{X}$

Page 293

2. a. $f''(X) = 32$ at $X = 2$ d. $f''(X) = \tfrac{3}{128} = 0.023$ at $X = 4$
   b. $f''(X) = 20$ at $X = 3$ e. $f''(X) = 0$ at $X = 7$
   c. $f''(X) = -\tfrac{2}{2187} = -0.0009$ at $X = 27$ f. $f''(X) = \tfrac{45}{4} = 11.25$ at $X = 9$

4. a. $f'(X) = 6$, a constant
      $f''(X) = 0$, no rate of change in a constant
   b. $f'(-3) = -14$
      $f''(-3) = 6$
      $f'(3) = 22$
      $f''(3) = 6$
      The rate of change of the slope at each point is the same, but the slopes are different at each point.
   c. $f'(3) = 52$
      $f''(3) = 6$
      $f'(6) = 43$
      $f''(6) = -12$
      Slopes are similar but the rate of change of the slope changes from positive to negative between $X = 3$ and $X = 6$.

Page 302

2. a. $\dfrac{dy}{dx} = \dfrac{X^2(10X^2 - 9)}{4Y(Y^2 - 2)}$ c. $\dfrac{dy}{dx} = \dfrac{9X^2 - 4Y + 4XY^2}{4X(1 - XY)}$

   b. $\dfrac{dy}{dx} = \dfrac{4X - 7Y}{7X - 6Y}$ d. $\dfrac{dY}{dX} = \dfrac{X^{-\frac{1}{2}} - 6X^2Y}{2Y(2X^3 - 1)}$

4. All partial derivatives measure the change in Y in response to a change in the specified X variable or variables.

   a. $\dfrac{\partial Y}{\partial X_1} = 3(X_2 + X_1^2 - 1)$

at $X_1 = 2$ and $X_2 = 3$, $\dfrac{\partial Y}{\partial X_1} = 18$

b. $\dfrac{\partial Y}{\partial X_2} = 2X_1^2 X_2(X_1^{-\frac{1}{3}} X_2^{-\frac{1}{3}} + 1)$

at $X_1 = 4$ and $X_2 = 16$, $\dfrac{\partial Y}{\partial X_2} = 513$

c. $\dfrac{\partial Y}{\partial X_3} = 2X_2^{\frac{1}{3}} X_1 X_3 + 6X_1 - 8X_2 X_3 = 2(X_2^{\frac{1}{3}} X_1 X_3 + 3X_1 - 4X_2 X_3)$

at $X_1 = 4$, $X_2 = 8$ and $X_3 = -3$, $\dfrac{\partial Y}{\partial X_3} = 120$

d. $\dfrac{\partial^2 Y}{\partial X_2 \partial X_1} = 4X_1$

at $X_1 = 8$ and $X_2 = 4$, $\dfrac{\partial^2 Y}{\partial X_2 \partial X_1} = 32$

e. $\dfrac{\partial^2 Y}{\partial X_1 \partial X_2} = 2(6X_2 - X_1)$

at $X_1 = 8$ and $X_2 = 5$, $\dfrac{\partial^2 Y}{\partial X_1 \partial X_2} = 44$

Review Problems

2. a. $\Delta f(X) = 32$
   b. $\Delta f(X) = 33$
   c. $\Delta f(X) = -15$
   d. $\Delta f(X) = -1.5$

4. a. At $X = 4$, $\dfrac{dY}{dX} = 6$

   At $X = 6$, $\dfrac{dY}{dX} = 14$

   Slope increases between $X = 4$ and $X = 6$.

   b. At $X = 8$, $\dfrac{dY}{dX} = 9$

   At $X = 16$, $\dfrac{dY}{dX} = -7$

   Slope changes from positive to negative between $X = 8$ and $X = 16$.

   c. At $X = 5$, $\dfrac{dY}{dX} = -4$

   At $X = 7$, $\dfrac{dY}{dX} = 0$

   At $X = 9$, $\dfrac{dY}{dX} = +4$

   Slope decreases, becomes stationary, and then increases in the interval containing the three points.

d. At $X = -3$, $\dfrac{dY}{dX} = -6$

At $X = 0$, $\dfrac{dY}{dX} = 0$

At $X = 3$, $\dfrac{dY}{dX} = +6$

Slope decreases, becomes stationary, and increases in the interval containing the three points.

6. a. $\dfrac{dY}{dX} = 18(6X - 3)^2$, at $X = 2$, $\dfrac{dY}{dX} = 1458$

 b. $\dfrac{dY}{dX} = \dfrac{4(4X - 5)}{3}(2X^2 - 5X + 5)^{1/3}$

 At $X = 3$, $\dfrac{dY}{dX} = \dfrac{56}{3} = 18.67$

 c. $\dfrac{dY}{dX} = 3(3X^2 - 4X + 6)(X^3 - 2X^2 + 6X)^2$

 At $X = 2$, $\dfrac{dY}{dX} = 4320$

 d. $\dfrac{dY}{dX} = \dfrac{1}{8}X^{-7/8} = \dfrac{1}{8X^{7/8}}$

 At $X = 1$, $\dfrac{dY}{dX} = \dfrac{1}{8} = 0.125$

8. a. $f''(X) = 6$, $f''(10) = 6$
 b. $f''(X) = 6X - 4$, $f''(5) = 26$
 c. $f''(X) = 12X + 34$, $f''(4) = 82$
 d. $f''(X) = e^X$, $f''(1.2) = 3.3201$
 e. $f''(X) = 6X^{-4}$, $f''(2) = \dfrac{3}{8} = 0.375$
 f. $f''(X) = 8X^2$, $f''(6) = 288$
 g. $f''(X) = 12(9X^2 - 7)$, $f''(2) = 348$
 h. $f''(X) = 0$, $f''(8) = 0$

10. a. $\dfrac{\partial Y}{\partial X_1} = 12X_1 + X_2 - 2X_1X_2$

 $\dfrac{\partial Y}{\partial X_2} = -12X_2^2 + X_1 - X_1^2$

 b. $\dfrac{\partial Y}{\partial X_3} = X_1 + 4X_2 - 9X_1^2 X_3^2$

 $\dfrac{\partial^2 Y}{\partial X_3^2} = -18X_1^2 X_3$

 c. $\dfrac{\partial^2 Y}{\partial X_1 \partial X_2} = -12X_1X_2$

 d. $\dfrac{\partial Y}{\partial X_2} = 3X_1X_2^2 - 2X_1^3X_2 + 3X_1^2 - 6X_2$

 e. $\dfrac{\partial Y}{\partial X_1} = 2(X_1 - 6X_1X_2 + X_2^2 + 9X_1X_2^2 - 3X_2^3)$

 $\dfrac{\partial Y}{\partial X_2} = 2(-3X_1^2 + 9X_1^2 X_2 - 9X_1X_2^2 + 2X_1X_2 + 2X_2^3)$

f. $\dfrac{\partial Y}{\partial X_2} = X_3(10 - 4X_1 + 3X_1X_3)$

$\dfrac{\partial^2 Y}{\partial X_2 \partial X_3} = 10 + 6X_1X_3 - 4X_1$

12. a. $f'(Q) = 0.04Q - 60$
    $f'(1200) = -12$
    $f'(1500) = 0$
    $f'(1800) = 12$
    b. Costs decrease, reach a minimum, then increase. The firm may be interested in determining the quantity point of lowest average cost ($Q = 1500$).

14. a. $\dfrac{\partial Y}{\partial X_1} = 0.06X_1 + X_2 + 0.04X_2^3$

    This measures the change in sales in response to a change in average family income.

    b. $\dfrac{\partial Y}{\partial X_2} = X_1 + 0.12X_1X_2^2$

    c. At $X_1 = 18$ and $X_2 = 4$, $\dfrac{\partial Y}{\partial X_2} = 52.56$

    At these income and population levels, sales will change at this rate in response to any change in area population.

Chapter 11

Page 318

2. a. Stationary point: $X = 10$, $Y = -48$, minimum
   b. Stationary point: $X = 5$, $Y = 90$, maximum
   c. Stationary point: $X = 4$, $Y = -24$, minimum
   d. No stationary point as the function is a monotonically increasing function of X.
   e. Stationary points: $X = 0$, $Y = 81$, maximum
      $X = 3$, $Y = 0$, minimum
   f. Stationary points: $X = 4$, $Y = -256$, minimum
      $X = -4$, $Y = 256$, maximum.
   g. Stationary points: $X = 1$, $Y = -10$, minimum
      $X = -4.5$, $Y = 322.75$, maximum
   h. Stationary points: $X = 6$, $Y = 15$, minimum
      $X = 2$, $Y = 25.67$, maximum
   i. Stationary points: $X = 4$, $Y = -75$, minimum
      $X = -2$, $Y = 33$, maximum
   j. Stationary points: $X = 3$, $Y = 51$, maximum
      $X = 7$, $Y = 29.67$, minimum

4. a. For all parts, the second derivative equals zero.
   b. Testing by the first derivative is applied to each part of the problem.

(1) $f'(-1) = -6, f'(1) = 6$, minimum
(2) $f'(5) = 2, f'(7) = 2$, stationary inflection point
(3) $f'(3) = 1, f'(5) = 1$, stationary inflection point
(4) $f'(-1) = -2, f'(1) = 2$, minimum
(5) $f'(9) = -0.5, f'(11) = -5$, stationary inflection point
(6) $f'(-1) = 1.25, f'(1) = 1.25$, stationary inflection point

Page 327

2. a. $MC = 0.09Q^2 + 10Q - 12$
   b. $MR = -0.0032Q + 0.04$
   c. $MC = 0.12Q^2 + 0.25Q^{-\frac{1}{2}}$
   d. $MC = \dfrac{Q^{-2/3}}{3} - 1.2Q + 40$
   e. $MC = 6Q$
   f. $MR = 3Q^2 + 0.4Q + 6$
   g. $MR = -0.06Q^2 + 18$
   h. $MR = 65$
4. a. Profit $= -0.08Q^3 + 96Q - 200$
   b. Maximum profit at $Q = 20$
   c. Profit $= -0.08(20)^3 + (96)(20) - 200 = 1080$
      $TR = (-3)(20)^2 + (216)(20) = 3120$
      $TC = (.08)(20)^3 - (3)(20)^2 + (120)(20) + 200 = 2040$
      $TR - TC = 3120 - 2040 = 1080$
6. a. $MR = -0.1Q + 150$
      $MC = 0.4Q + 10$
   b. $Q = 280$
   c. Profit $= \$18,800$
8. a. $Q = 52$
   b. Price $= \$172$
   c. Profit $= \$5360$

Page 336

2. a. $Q = 30, MC = 80, f''(Q) = 0.2$
   b. $Q = 9, MC = 157, f''(Q) = 6$
   c. $Q = 50, MC = 99, f''(Q) = 0.1$
   d. $Q = 30, MC = 200, f''(Q) = 6$
4. a. MPP of X_1 at $X_1 = 8$ and $X_2 = 4$ is equal to 4.16. This means that Y will change by 4.16 units in response to a one unit change in X_1 in the same direction at $X_1 = 8$ and $X_2 = 4$.
   b. MPP of X_2 at $X_1 = 5$ and $X_2 = 4$ is equal to -1.85. This means that Y will change by 1.85 units in response to a one unit change in X_2 in the opposite direction at $X_1 = 5$ and $X_2 = 4$.

Page 344

2. a. $\varepsilon_p = -0.6$ d. $\varepsilon_p = -3.375$
   b. $\varepsilon_p = -0.8$ e. $\varepsilon_p = $ undefined
   c. $\varepsilon_p = -2.33$
4. a. $\varepsilon_p = -0.75$
   b. Point income elasticity of demand $= +0.44$.
   c. $\varepsilon_p = -1.15$
   d. The price increase increases the price elasticity of demand.

Page 352

2. a. $Z = 3X_2^2 - 4X_1^2 - 3X_1 + 2X_2 + 60 - \lambda(X_1 + X_2 - 60)$
   b. $Z = 2X_1^2 + X_2^2 - 4X_1 - 2X_2 + 80 - \lambda(X_1 + X_2 - 5)$
   c. $Z = 6X_1 + 4X_2 - X_1^2 - 3X_2^2 + 120 - \lambda(X_1 + X_2 - 100)$
4. a. $\lambda = 110$; c will change by 110 for each change of 1 in the same direction in the constraint.
   b. $\lambda = -8$; c will change by 8 for each change of 1 in the opposite direction in the constraint.
6. a. $Z = 2X_1^2 + X_2^2 + 2X_1X_2 - 4X_1 - 3X_2 - \lambda(5X_1 + 4X_2 - 32)$
   b. $X_1 = 2$ ounces
      $X_2 = 5.5$ ounces
   c. $Z = \$35.75$

Review Problems

2. Testing by the first derivative test is applied to each part of the problem.
   a. Stationary point: $X = 5$, $Y = 125$
      $f'(4) = 3, f'(6) = 3$, stationary inflection point
   b. Stationary point: $X = 0$, $Y = 0$
      $f'(-1) = -1, f'(+1) = 1$, minimum point
   c. Stationary point: $X = 5$, $Y = 1666.67$
      $f'(4) = 4, f'(6) = 4$, stationary inflection point
   d. Stationary point: $X = 0$, $Y = 150$
      $f'(-1) = -12, f'(1) = 12$, minimum point
   e. Stationary point: $X = 4$, $Y = -14.67$
      $f'(3) = 1, f'(5) = 1$, stationary inflection point
   f. Stationary point: $X = 0$, $Y = 0$
      $f'(-1) = -21, f'(1) = -21$, stationary inflection point
4. a. $MR = -4Q + 360$
      $MC = 2Q - 60$
   b. Profit maximizing quantity $= 70$ air conditioners
   c. Price $= \$220$
   d. Profit $= \$7700$
6. a. Production should be 2150 shirts per month
   b. Profit at $Q = 2000$ is $\$20,000$
   c. Maximum profit $= \$20,112.50$

8. a. Lowest price = $350, quantity = 15 transmissions
   b. Loss = $1800
10. a. MPP labor = $\dfrac{2X_1^{-1/3} X_2^{1/3}}{3}$

   MPP machinery = $\dfrac{X_1^{2/3} X_2^{-2/3}}{3}$
   b. MPP labor = $\tfrac{8}{9}$ = 0.89
   At the point $X_1 = 27$ and $X_2 = 64$, a 1-hour change in labor usage will result in 0.89 ton output change in the same direction.
   c. MPP machinery = $\tfrac{9}{48}$ = 0.1875
   At the point $X_1 = 27$ and $X_2 = 64$, a 1-hour change in machinery usage will result in a 0.1875 ton output change in the same direction.
12. a. Average revenue = $-0.4Q + 76$
   b. $\varepsilon_p = -2.5 \dfrac{P}{Q}$
   c. ε_p at $Q = 80$ is equal to -1.375.
   d. At $Q = 80$, a 1 percent change in price will result in a 1.375 percent quantity demand change in the opposite direction.
14. a. $\varepsilon_p = -0.56$
   b. Beef price and beef sales are negatively related and the price of chicken and beef sales are positively related.
   c. Cross-price elasticity of demand = $+0.16$
   d. $\varepsilon_p = -0.68$, cross-price elasticity of demand equals 0.15.
16. a. $Z = 4X_1^2 + 2X_2^2 - 20X_1 - 16X_2 - \lambda(X_1 + X_2 - 20)$
   b. $X_1 = 7$ pounds
   $X_2 = 13$ pounds
   c. $D > 0$
   $\dfrac{\partial^2 Z}{\partial X_1^2} = 8$
   $\dfrac{\partial^2 Z}{\partial X_2^2} = 4$

Chapter 12

Page 374

2. a. $-\dfrac{e^{-6X}}{6} + c$
   b. $\dfrac{8^{4X+6}}{8.31776} + c$
   c. $\dfrac{(2Y - 3)[\ln(2Y - 3) - 1]}{2} + c$
   d. $-\dfrac{e^{-2X+17}}{2} + c$

e. $\dfrac{2^{4Y+17}}{2.7726} + c$

f. $X(\ln 22X - 1) + c$

g. $X(\ln 3X - 1) + c$

h. $-e^{-X} + c$

i. $\dfrac{2.4^Y}{0.87547} + c$

j. $\dfrac{(6Y + 1)[\ln(6Y + 1) - 1]}{6} + c$

4. a. 2.9074   f. 7241.215
   b. 0.6321   g. 1446.20
   c. 3.19455   h. 46.42
   d. 1.33425   i. 34.30
   e. 80.79   j. 13.15

Page 378

2. a. $Y(\ln Y - 1) + c$ c. $8X(\ln X - 1) + c$

   b. $X(\ln 3X - 1) + c$ d. $\dfrac{X(\ln X - 1)}{3} + c$

Page 380

2. $\dfrac{(4X + 12)^2}{8} + c$ 10. $-\dfrac{5 \ln|X|}{2} + c$

4. $\dfrac{7^{4X}}{7.78364} + c$ 12. $\dfrac{(\ln X)^2}{12} + c$

6. $\dfrac{e^{3X}(3X - 1)}{9} + c$ 14. $\dfrac{(10X + 80)^2}{20} + c$

8. $125X^5 + c$ 16. $\dfrac{3(e^{2X^2 - 4})}{2} + c$

Page 390

2. a. Total cost $= \dfrac{Q^3}{60} + \dfrac{Q^2}{4} + 1300$

   Fixed cost $= \$1300$

   b. Total cost $= \dfrac{Q^3}{3} = 0.6Q^2 + 10.40$

   Fixed cost $= \$10.40$

4. a. Total revenue $= 300Q - 0.2Q^2$

   b. Average revenue $= 300 - 0.2Q$

Mathematics for Business and Economics **514**

    c. Marginal revenue function has a slope equal to twice the slope of the average revenue function.

    d. At $Q = 500$
       Total revenue = \$100,000
       Marginal revenue = \$100
       Average revenue = \$200

6. a. Total revenue $- 80Q - 0.002Q^2$
   b. Additional revenue = \$62,000
8. a. Consumers' surplus = \$9800
   b. This measures the benefits received in excess of total amount paid for milk.
   c. Consumers' surplus = \$12,800
   d. As price decreases (as from a to c), the amount of consumers' surplus increases.
10. Amount spent = \$1671

Page 397

2. a. Present value = \$15,000
   b. Present value = \$7500
   c. Present value = \$20,000
   d. Present value = \$225,000
   e. Higher interest rates imply smaller present values for the same annual yield.
4. Yes, the number of robberies will converge to 80 as time continues indefinitely.

Review Problems

2. a. 2   k. 0.91629
   b. 48   l. 8.33969
   c. 540   m. 1980
   d. 0.7769   n. $\frac{1}{6} = 0.167$
   e. 261.86   o. $\frac{3}{64} = 0.047$
   f. 398.4   p. $\frac{1}{3} = 0.333$
   g. 15.97   q. 0.166
   h. 37.33   r. 0.8965
   i. $-\frac{3}{2} = -1.5$ s. 9.75
   j. $\frac{1}{15} = 0.067$ t. 0.1071
4. a. Total cost = $0.01Q^3 - 0.075Q^2 + c$
   b. Fixed cost = \$337.50
   c. At $Q = 60$, total cost = \$2227.50
      At $Q = 70$, total cost = \$3400
6. a. Revenue will increase by \$11,100.
   b. At $Q = 8000$, MR $= -17.50$
      At this level, there is a loss in revenue from selling additional units. A quantity of 8000 exceeds the point of maximum total revenue.

8. a. 1450 people
   b. 750 people
   c. Rapidly increasing numbers through the period.
10. a. 4581.16
    b. 14,531.975
    c. 36,432.225
12. a. 1424.75
    b. 601.75
    c. 274.25
14. $2500

Chapter 13

Page 410

2. a. 64   d. 512
   b. 4   e. 2
   c. 16   f. 8
4. 286
6. 720
8. 220

Combination, as the order within each subgroup is not important.

Page 420

2. a. 1.0   c. 0
   b. 0   d. No, as $P(B/A) \neq P(A)$ and $P(A/B) \neq P(B)$
4. a. .4
   b. .75
   c. 1
   d. X is a subset of Y
6. a. .02
   b. .1
   c. .72

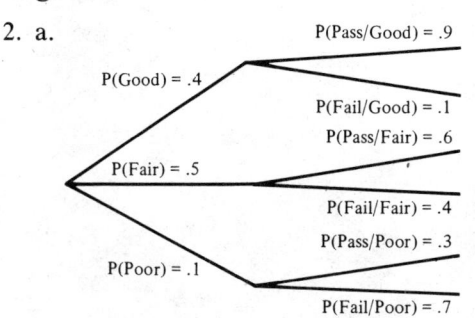

Page 425

2. a.

$P(\text{Good}) = .4$
$P(\text{Pass/Good}) = .9$
$P(\text{Fail/Good}) = .1$
$P(\text{Fair}) = .5$
$P(\text{Pass/Fair}) = .6$
$P(\text{Fail/Fair}) = .4$
$P(\text{Poor}) = .1$
$P(\text{Pass/Poor}) = .3$
$P(\text{Fail/Poor}) = .7$

b. .129
   c. .043
   d. .69, or 69 percent
4. a. .460 or 46 percent
   b. .757
   c. .391

Page 438

2. a. .8   d. 2.0
   b. −1.6 e. −3.0
   c. 1.6   f. 2.4
4. a. 50 percent
   b. 49.87 percent
   c. 47.72 percent
   d. 15.87 percent
   e. 6.68 percent
   f. 62.47 percent
6. a. 25.78 percent
   b. 13.57 percent
   c. 21.19 percent
   d. 29.22 percent

Review Problems

2. 16 subsets
   $A, B, C, D, AB, AD, AC, BC, BD, CD, ABC, BCD, ACD, ABD, ABCD, \emptyset$
4. a. $P(A) = 0.2$
   b. $P(A \cap B) = 0.1$
   c. $P(A \cup B) = 0.6$
   d. $P(B/A) = 0.5$
6. a. .0100
   b. .2592
   c. .2916
   d. .0625
   e. .00032
8. a. .3413   e. .3364
   b. .0548   f. 0
   c. .3811   g. .3270
   d. .0808   h. .8849
10. 330 groups
12. .08, or 8 percent
14. .1667, or 16.67 percent
16. a. .15, or 15 percent
    b. .165, or 16.5 percent

18. a. .3087
 b. .00243
 c. .1631
20. a. .0228, or 2.28 percent
 b. .3830, or 38.30 percent
 c. .0668, or 6.68 percent
 d. .2426 or 24.26 percent

Index

Abscissa, 38
Absolute maximum, 311
Absolute minimum, 311
Activity (choice) variables, 153
Algebra of sets, 14–16
Annuities:
   defined, 241
   future value of, 241–242
   and loan amortization, 249–251
   present value of, 246–248
   and sinking funds, 244–245
Antiderivative, 363–364, 368
Antilogarithm, 228–229
Associative law of sets, 14
Associative property of real numbers, 20–21
Asymptotic property, 212
Auditing of the model, 5–6
Augmented matrix, 123
Average revenue, 322–323
Average variable cost, 329–330

Basic feasible solution, 170
Basic variables, 170
Basis, 170

Bayes' rule, 423
Bernoulli experiment, 427
Binomial factoring, 27–28
Binomial probability distribution, 427–429
Break-even analysis, 76–78

Capital formation, 383–384
Cartesian coordinate system, 38
Chain rule of differentiation, 285–286, 304
Closure property of real numbers, 20
Collectively exhaustive events, 418–419
Combinations, 409–410
Common logarithms, 220
Common ratio, 233
Commutative law of sets, 14
Commutative property of real numbers, 20
Complement of a set, 12
Compound interest, 237–239
Concavity, 205
Conditional events, 414–415
Consistent system of equations, 73

Constant, 18
   differentiation of, 283, 304
   of integration, 368
Constant function, 47, 53
Consumers' surplus, 386–388
Continuity, 272–274, 278–280
Continuous compounding, 254–257, 388–390
Continuous probability distribution, 429–432
Convergent improper integral, 394
Convex set, 160
Corner point, 159–160
Counting techniques, 404–410
Cross-price elasticity of demand, 337
Cubic functions, 41, 209–211
Cumulative binomial probability, 429

Data, 2
Definite integral, 363, 365–367, 373–374
Degeneracy, 194
Delta notation, 276
Demand-and-supply analysis, 74–76
Dependent events, 415–417

519

Index

Dependent system of equations, 73, 87–89
Dependent variables, 37–38
Derivative, 278–283
   continuity and, 278–280
   defined, 278
   partial, 298–302
   second, 292–293
   and slope, 282–283
Deterministic model, 3, 446
Development of the model, 5
Diagonal matrix, 111
Difference of two squares, 28
Difference quotient, 276
Differentiation:
   chain rule of, 285–286, 304
   of constants, 283, 304
   of exponential functions, 288–289, 305
   higher partial, 300–302
   implicit, 294–298
   of logarithmic functions, 290–291, 305
   partial, 298–302
   power function rule of, 286–287, 304
   product rule of, 284, 304
   quotient rule of, 284–285, 304
   simple power rule of, 280–282, 304
Dimension of a matrix, 110
Diminishing marginal returns, 331–332
Discrete probability distribution, 427–429
Discriminant, 207
Disjoint sets, 13
Distributive law of sets, 15–16
Distributive property of real numbers, 21
Divergent improper integral, 394
Dual problem, 180–182

e, 213–214
Effective interest rate, 258
Elastic demand, 340
Elasticity of demand, 337–344
   arc price, 337
   cross-price, 337
   income, 337–343
   point price, 337, 339–341
Element:
   of a matrix, 110
   of a set, 12
Elimination method, 80–87
   Gauss-Jordan, 123–128

Empty (null) sets, 12
Equations, 19–20
   (*See also* System of equations)
Events, 411
   collectively exhaustive, 418–419
   conditional, 414–415
   dependent, 415–417
   independent, 415–417
   intersection of, 412–414
   joint, 412–414
   mutually exclusive, 412
   union of, 417–419
Exactly constrained system of equations, 73
Expected value, 431
Experiment, 411
Explicit form of a linear equation, 55
Exponential decay, 214–216
Exponential functions, 41, 211–218
   differentiation of, 288–289, 305
   integration of, 371
   modified, 216–218
Exponential growth, 214–216
Exponents, 23
   computational rules of, 24–25
Expressions, 19

Factor, 19
Factoring, 26–29
   of two cubes, 28–29
Finite series, 232–233
Finite sets, 12
First-derivative test, 315–316
Functional form, 354
Functions, 36–37
Fundamental theorem of integral calculus, 367
Future value of an annuity, 241–242

Gauss-Jordan method of elimination, 123–128
Gauss-Jordan method of inversion, 131–135
General rule of addition, 420
General rule of multiplication, 419
Geometric series, 233–235
   unit, 233–234

Identity matrix, 111
Implementation of the model, 5
Implicit differentiation, 294–298
Implicit form of a linear equation, 55–56

Improper integral, 393–396
   convergent, 394
   divergent, 394
Inconsistent system of equations, 73, 87–89
Indefinite integral, 363–365
Independent events, 415–417
Independent variables, 37–38
Index of the radical sign, 23
Inelastic demand, 340
Inequalities:
   defined, 19, 92
   double, 93
   inconsistent, 94
   solution of, 94–97
   strong, 92
   systems of, 97–101
   weak, 92
Infinite series, 232–233
Infinite sets, 12
Information, 2
Initial tableau, 171
Inner product, 116
Input-output analysis, 140–144
Integral, 363
Integrand, 364
Integration:
   concept of, 363
   constant of, 368
   of exponential functions, 371
   of logarithmic functions, 372
   by parts, 375–378
   of the power of a linear function, 370
   simple power rule of, 368–369
Interpolation (natural logarithms), 227–229
Intersection of events, 412–414
Intersection of sets, 13
Inverse of a matrix, 129–131, 138–140
Inverse function rule, 338
Irrational numbers, 18
Isocost lines, 164
Isoprofit lines, 159

Joint events, 412–414

Lagrange multiplier, 349
Lagrangian function, 348–349
Lagrangian multiplier technique, 348–352
Law of diminishing returns, 210
Leontief, Wassily W., 140

Index

imit, 267–270
  of a function, 267–268
imit theorems, 270–272
inear functions, 47–69
  implicit form of, 55–56
  through the origin, 54
  point-slope method for finding, 61–62
  slope of, 49
  slope-intercept form of, 55
  two-point method for finding, 58–61
  Y intercept of, 49
inear models, 446–447
inear programming, 151–201
oan amortization, 249–251
ogarithmic functions:
  business use of, 220–223
  defined, 41
  differentiation of, 290–291, 305
  integration of, 372

arginal cost, 266, 310, 321–322, 380–382
arginal product, 310, 333–334
arginal propensity to consume, 234–235
arginal revenue, 310, 322–323, 380–383, 385–386
athematical model, 1, 445
  deterministic, 3, 446
  linear, 446–447
  nonlinear, 447–448
  probabilistic, 2, 446, 448–449
athematical modeling, 2–6, 450
  auditing, 5–6
  development of, 5
  implementation of, 5
  problem specification as a part of, 4
  verification of, 5
atrix, 109–150
  addition of, 112–113
  augmented, 123
  defined, 110
  diagonal, 111
  dimension of, 110
  elements of, 110
  identity, 111
  inverse of, 129–131, 138–140
  linear dependence of equations and, 138–140
  multiplication of, 113–117
  nonsingular, 131
  null, 111

Matrix (Cont.):
  singular, 131, 138
  subtraction of, 112–113
  and system of linear equations, 120–122
  technological, 140–142
  transpose of, 111
  unit, 111
Mean of a continuous random variable, 430–431
Modified exponential function, 216–218
Monomial factoring, 26
Monotonically decreasing function, 213
Monotonically increasing function, 212
Multiplier, 233–235
Multivariate functions, 42, 63–64
Mutually exclusive events, 412

Natural logarithm:
  antilogarithm of, 228–229
  defined, 220
  interpolation, 227–229
Nonalgebraic functions, 41–42
Nonbasic variables, 170
Nonlinear models, 447–448
Nonnegativity restriction, 153
Nonsingular matrix, 131
Normal curve, 396–397
Normal probability distribution, 432–438
  standard normal deviates (z values), 433
Null matrix, 111
Null (empty) sets, 12

Objective function, 153
Ordered pairs, 36
Ordinate, 38
Origin, 38
Original function test, 315–316
Overconstrained system of equations, 73, 91–92

Partial derivative, 298–302
Permutations, 407–410
Perpetuity, 252–253
Pivot column, 172
Pivot element, 172
Pivot row, 172
Point-slope method of finding a linear equation, 61–62
Polynomial function:
  defined, 40–41
  degree of, 42–43

Polynomial function (Cont.):
  with more than one independent variable, 42–43
  with one independent variable, 40–42
Power function, differentiation of, 286–287, 304
Present value:
  of an annuity, 246–248
  compounded, 239–240
  concept of, 236–237
Primal problem, 180
Priority of mathematical operations, 21–22
Probabilistic (stochastic) models, 2, 446, 448–449
Probability:
  of an event, 411
  normal probability distribution, 432–433
  posterior, 421
  prior, 421
Probability density function, 430
Problem specification, 4
Product rule of differentiation, 284, 304
Production function, 210–211
Profit contribution (profit margin), 77
Profit maximization, 319–327

Quadrants of graph, 38
Quadratic formula, 207–208
Quadratic functions, 41
Quotient rule of differentiation, 284–285, 304

Radical sign, 23
Radicand, 23
Rational numbers, 18
Real numbers, 18
Region of feasible solutions, 157
Relations, 36–37
Relative maximum, 311
Relative minimum, 311
Right-hand side (RHS) values, 171, 174

Saddle point, 345
Sample space, 411
Scalar, 110
Scaling, 4
Scatter diagram, 58, 354
Secant line, 276–277
Second-derivative test, 314–315
Sequence, 232

Series, 232–235
  finite, 232–233
  geometric, 233–235
  infinite, 232–233
  unit geometric, 233–234
Sets:
  algebra of, 14–16
  complement of, 12
  defined, 12
  disjoint, 13
  element of, 12
  finite, 12
  infinite, 12
  intersection of, 13
  null, 12
  subset of, 12
  universal, 12
Shadow price, 175
Shadow price ranges, 175–178
Shut-down price, 329–331
Simple discount, 235–237
Simple interest, 235–237
Simple power rule of differentiation, 282, 304
Simplex method, 168–174
Simulation, 449
Singular matrix, 131, 138
Sinking fund, 244–245
Slack variable, 169
Slope:
  and the derivative, 282–283
  of a linear function, 49–54

Slope-intercept form of a linear equation, 55
Special rule of addition, 420
Special rule of multiplication, 419
Standard form of a linear equation, 55–56
Standard normal deviate (z value), 433
Stationary inflection point, 311
Stationary point:
  defined, 311
  saddle point, 345
  with two independent variables, 345–347
Subset, 12, 406–407
Substitution rate, 176–178
Summation operator, 451–455
  properties of, 452–454
  summand, 451
  summation index, 451
  summation sign, 451
Surplus variable, 183
System of equations:
  consistent, 73
  dependent, 73, 87–89
  exactly constrained, 73
  inconsistent, 73, 87–89
  matrix algebra and, 120–122
  overconstrained, 73, 91–92
  underconstrained, 73, 91–92

Tangent line, 276–277
Technological matrix, 140–142

Terms, 19
Total cost function, 210–211
Transpose of a matrix, 111
Tree diagram, 405–406
Two-point method of finding a linear equation, 58–61

Unbounded solution, 166
Underconstrained system of equations, 73, 91–92
Union of events, 417–419
Union of sets, 13
Unit geometric series, 233–234
Unit matrix, 111
Unitary elasticity of demand, 340
Universal sets, 12

Variables, 18
Variance of a continuous random variable, 432
Vector, 110
Venn diagrams, 14, 411–412
Verification of the model, 5
Vertex, 205
Vertical parabola, 205

X intercept, 207

Y intercept, 49

Zeroes-first method, 124

[145]

Tapes 5
Book 18
Brushes 10